Innovative Practices for Higher Education Assessment and Measurement

Elena Cano
University of Barcelona, Spain

Georgeta Ion
Universitat Autònoma de Barcelona, Spain

A volume in the Advances in Higher Education and Professional Development (AHEPD) Book Series

www.igi-global.com

Published in the United States of America by
    IGI Global
    Information Science Reference (an imprint of IGI Global)
    701 E. Chocolate Avenue
    Hershey PA, USA 17033
    Tel: 717-533-8845
    Fax: 717-533-8661
    E-mail: cust@igi-global.com
    Web site: http://www.igi-global.com

Library of Congress Cataloging-in-Publication Data

Names: Cano, Elena.
Title: Innovative practices for higher education assessment and measurement /
  Elena Cano and Georgeta Ion, editors.
Description: Hershey PA : Information Science Reference, 2016. | Includes
  bibliographical references and index.
Identifiers: LCCN 2016017820| ISBN 9781522505310 (hardcover) | ISBN
  9781522505327 (ebook)
Subjects: LCSH: Educational evaluation. | Education, Higher.
Classification: LCC LB2822.75 .I537 2016 | DDC 378.1/662--dc23 LC record available at https://lccn.loc.gov/2016017820

This book is published in the IGI Global book series Advances in Higher Education and Professional Development (AHEPD) (ISSN: 2327-6983; eISSN: 2327-6991)

British Cataloguing in Publication Data
A Cataloguing in Publication record for this book is available from the British Library.

For electronic access to this publication, please contact: eresources@igi-global.com.

Advances in Higher Education and Professional Development (AHEPD) Book Series

Jared Keengwe
University of North Dakota, USA

ISSN: 2327-6983
EISSN: 2327-6991

MISSION

As world economies continue to shift and change in response to global financial situations, job markets have begun to demand a more highly-skilled workforce. In many industries a college degree is the minimum requirement and further educational development is expected to advance. With these current trends in mind, the **Advances in Higher Education & Professional Development (AHEPD) Book Series** provides an outlet for researchers and academics to publish their research in these areas and to distribute these works to practitioners and other researchers.

AHEPD encompasses all research dealing with higher education pedagogy, development, and curriculum design, as well as all areas of professional development, regardless of focus.

COVERAGE

- Adult Education
- Assessment in Higher Education
- Career Training
- Coaching and Mentoring
- Continuing Professional Development
- Governance in Higher Education
- Higher Education Policy
- Pedagogy of Teaching Higher Education
- Vocational Education

IGI Global is currently accepting manuscripts for publication within this series. To submit a proposal for a volume in this series, please contact our Acquisition Editors at Acquisitions@igi-global.com or visit: http://www.igi-global.com/publish/.

Titles in this Series

For a list of additional titles in this series, please visit: www.igi-global.com

Handbook of Research on Study Abroad Programs and Outbound Mobility
Donna M. Velliaris (Eynesbury Institute of Business & Technology, Australia) and Deb Coleman-George (University of Adelaide, Australia)
Information Science Reference • copyright 2016 • 754pp • H/C (ISBN: 9781522501695) • US $335.00 (our price)

Setting a New Agenda for Student Engagement and Retention in Historically Black Colleges and Universities
Charles B. W. Prince (Howard University, USA) and Rochelle L. Ford (Syracuse University, USA)
Information Science Reference • copyright 2016 • 343pp • H/C (ISBN: 9781522503088) • US $185.00 (our price)

Handbook of Research on Professional Development for Quality Teaching and Learning
Teresa Petty (University of North Carolina at Charlotte, USA) Amy Good (University of North Carolina at Charlotte, USA) and S. Michael Putman (University of North Carolina at Charlotte, USA)
Information Science Reference • copyright 2016 • 824pp • H/C (ISBN: 9781522502043) • US $310.00 (our price)

Administrative Challenges and Organizational Leadership in Historically Black Colleges and Universities
Charles B. W. Prince (Howard University, USA) and Rochelle L. Ford (Syracuse University, USA)
Information Science Reference • copyright 2016 • 301pp • H/C (ISBN: 9781522503118) • US $170.00 (our price)

Developing Workforce Diversity Programs, Curriculum, and Degrees in Higher Education
Chaunda L. Scott (Oakland University, USA) and Jeanetta D. Sims (University of Central Oklahoma, USA)
Information Science Reference • copyright 2016 • 398pp • H/C (ISBN: 9781522502098) • US $185.00 (our price)

Handbook of Research on Transforming Mathematics Teacher Education in the Digital Age
Margaret Niess (Oregon State University, USA) Shannon Driskell (University of Dayton, USA) and Karen Hollebrands (North Carolina State University, USA)
Information Science Reference • copyright 2016 • 679pp • H/C (ISBN: 9781522501206) • US $235.00 (our price)

Handbook of Research on Engaging Digital Natives in Higher Education Settings
Margarida M. Pinheiro (University of Aveiro, Portugal) and Dora Simões (University of Aveiro, Portugal)
Information Science Reference • copyright 2016 • 500pp • H/C (ISBN: 9781522500391) • US $300.00 (our price)

Exploring the Social and Academic Experiences of International Students in Higher Education Institutions
Krishna Bista (University of Louisiana at Monroe, USA) and Charlotte Foster (Missouri Western State University, USA)
Information Science Reference • copyright 2016 • 363pp • H/C (ISBN: 9781466697492) • US $185.00 (our price)

www.igi-global.com

701 E. Chocolate Ave., Hershey, PA 17033
Order online at www.igi-global.com or call 717-533-8845 x100
To place a standing order for titles released in this series, contact: cust@igi-global.com
Mon-Fri 8:00 am - 5:00 pm (est) or fax 24 hours a day 717-533-8661

Editorial Advisory Board

Table of Contents

Section 1
Theoretical Approaches on Students' Assessment

Section 2
Research- Based Evidences on Assessment

Section 3
Innovative Practices in Students' Assessment

Detailed Table of Contents

Section 1
Theoretical Approaches on Students' Assessment

Better feedback is commonly demanded by students and institutions as a way of improving student satisfaction, encouraging more scholarly approaches to assessment, and building students' capacity for self-regulated learning. Student responses to surveys are very clear on what they think makes good feedback: it is prompt, regular, specific, and accurate. Institutional efforts therefore typically try to improve feedback by improving in these four areas. However, some have questioned if the customer is always right. This chapter looks at the main models of feedback from the research literature and etymology, in particular how these relate to concepts of self-regulated learning and sustainable assessment. It is argued that dialogic feedback and feedforward are wrongly currently conceptualised in a purely positive way, which serves to limit effective critique of these models. The chapter ends by describing principles of any type of feedback, providing a working definition which is more compatible with self-regulated learning.

To support students, make effective use of feedback to improve their learning, this chapter provides practical tips and strategies for teachers to stimulate their students' interest in feedback, assimilate its significant role and get involved in interpreting, reflecting and acting upon feedback comments. The author focuses on both summative and formative feedback. For summative feedback, one's concern is to encourage students to interpret grades/marks, reflect upon them and transform them into plans and actions. This is through using reflective worksheets and other post-exam tasks in class which are designed by the author. Feedback within self, peer and group assessment approaches is also concerned in this chapter. Other kinds of reflective worksheets are suggested to be used to reflect on the student learning process as part of the student portfolio, journal or set separately, in addition to the use of technology, i.e., class blogs to enhance such reflection.

Chapter 3

This chapter provides an overview of current e-assessment activity in Higher Education (HE) for those interested in improving their assessment practices. Despite substantial changes in HE teaching and learning strategies with the introduction of Information and Communication Technologies (ICT), little effort has been made in the area of assessment, where traditional methods are still commonly used. ICT and computers are seen as a medium for supporting and guiding the whole learning process, but these options have not yet been fully explored. In view of this, we would like to review the trends and challenges of e-assessment to enhance student learning in future scenarios, taking into consideration several publications, cases and contributions from both the practice and research perspective.

Chapter 4

Competency-based Assessment (CBA) is the measurement of student's competency against a standard of performance. It is a process of collecting evidences to analyze student's progress and achievement. In higher education, Competency-based Assessment puts the focus on learning outcomes to constantly improve academic programs and meet labor market demands. As of to date, competencies are described using natural language but rarely used in e-learning systems, and the common sense idea is that: the way competency is defined shapes the way it is conceptualized, implemented and assessed. The main objective of this chapter is to introduce and discuss Competency-based Assessment from a methodological and technical perspectives. More specifically, the objective is to highlight ongoing issues regarding competency assessment in higher education in the 21st century, to emphasis the benefits of its implementation and finally to discuss some competency modeling and assessment techniques.

Chapter 5

Neuroscience has disclosed important information about the brain and how it learns. Brain-Based Learning is student centered learning that utilizes the whole brain and recognizes that not all students learn in the same way. Assessment and evaluation are necessary and important elements of the instructional cycle. Feedback also motivates students and allows students to apply what they have learned to real-life situations. This chapter presents attempts to explain brain-compatible assessment and alternative or authentic assessment and its different forms that can be used in providing brain-based education.

Chapter 6

Students engaging in the assessment and evaluation process is becoming increasingly popular because it helps students become active participants in their own learning. In this chapter we discuss ways to involve students in the assessment and evaluation process in the classroom. It brings together multiple perspectives on critical thinking, metacognition, interteaching and student evaluations of teaching (SETs). The commonality between these four key elements is the importance of engaging students to become active participants in their own learning because they can help improve student learning outcomes. This chapter goes on to examine how these assessments and evaluations play a role in developing critical thinking skills and metacognition in students.

Marije Lesterhuis, University of Antwerp, Belgium
San Verhavert, University of Antwerp, Belgium
Liesje Coertjens, University of Antwerp, Belgium
Vincent Donche, University of Antwerp, Belgium
Sven De Maeyer, University of Antwerp, Belgium

To adequately assess students' competences, students are asked to provide proof of a performance. Ideally, open and real-life tasks are used for such performance assessment. However, to augment the reliability of the scores resulting from performance assessment, assessments are mostly standardised. This hampers the validity of the performance assessment. Comparative judgement (CJ) is introduced as an alternative judging method that does not require standardisation of tasks. The CJ method is based on the assumption that people are able to compare two performances more easily and reliable than assigning a score to a single one. This chapter provides insight in the method and elaborates on why this method is promising to generate valid, reliable measures in an efficient way, especially for large-scale summative assessments. Thereby, this chapter brings together the research already conducted in this new assessment domain.

Section 2
Research- Based Evidences on Assessment

Rebecca Hamer, International Baccalaureate, The Netherlands
Erik Jan van Rossum, University of Twente, The Netherlands

Understanding means different things to different people, influencing what and how students learn and teachers teach. Mainstream understanding of understanding has not progressed beyond the first level of constructivist learning and thinking, ie academic understanding. This study, based on 167 student narratives, presents two hitherto unknown conceptions of understanding matching more complex ways of knowing, understanding-in-relativism and understanding-in-supercomplexity requiring the development of more complex versions of constructive alignment. Students comment that multiple choice testing encourages learning focused on recall and recognition, while academic understanding is not assessed often and more complex forms of understanding are hardly assessed at all in higher education. However, if study success depends on assessments-of-learning that credit them for meaning oriented learning and deeper understanding, students will put in effort to succeed.

Unlike studies of teacher feedback on student writing, research into teacher self-assessment of their own feedback practices is quite rare in the assessment literature. In this reflective case study, the researcher/ teacher systematically analyzed feedback practices to clearly determine the form and kind of formative feedback being provided on student essays, and also to compare these feedback practices to recommended practice from the feedback literature. The research took place in an academic English writing course for third-year students at a Japanese university. A close examination of the teacher feedback on the first draft of 21 student essays was undertaken, and more than 800 feedback interventions were identified and coded. Results of this investigation show a number of patterns of practice in giving feedback, including; extensive use of questions in teacher commentary, very limited use of praise comments, and varying amounts of feedback provided on individual essays. Results also show that the feedback practices discovered through this investigation align well with recommended best practice. The case study positions the teacher as 'learner' in this feedback process, and calls for similar published research describing in detail what teachers do when providing feedback to students on their work.

Chapter 10

In higher education context, it is important to stimulate feedback and students' self-regulation. Shute (2007) ensures that giving a formative feedback means to communicate information to the students to change their thinking or behavior in order to improve their learning. This improvement through constant feedback has been the basis of the experience presented below. The work presented here is part of the project "Design, implementation and evaluation of proposals for sustainable feedforward" (reference REDICE2014-966), funded by the Institute of Education Sciences at the University of Barcelona, which aims to design and implement feedforward practices in different degrees at the Spanish universities participating in the project. The analysis of this research highlights what kind of feedback is being implemented in higher education and which the perceptions of students and teachers relating to the implemented practices and the obtained results are.

Chapter 11

As higher education teachers, the authors are committed to supporting students in their epistemological development, specifically in their transition towards self-direction. In this chapter, they share their experience of using self-assessment in a Teacher Training Degree course as a way to both enhance self-direction and assess its development. A thematic analysis of the self-assessments of a sample of 30 students is carried out, and four themes are identified: 1) the degree of authorship, 2) the degree of elaboration, 3) "taking notice of" subtle levels of analysis, and 4) the identification of temporal milestones throughout the course. These themes enable a different pattern of mental complexity to be identified, a complexity which is understood as evidence of students' different degrees of self-direction. The findings are discussed in the light of developmental constructivist theories. In addition, some implications for education regarding the current debates on self-assessment literature are presented.

Chapter 12

The participation of students in higher education assessment processes has been proven to have many benefits. However, there is a diverse range of techniques and options when implementing participative assessment, with each offering new possibilities. This chapter focuses on the topic of student participation in assessment processes, and it explores the main stages when it can be developed: participation in design, during implementation, and in grading. This chapter also considers the different modalities that can be used, especially self-assessment, peer assessment, and co-assessment and the three stages that characterise them. Finally, it analyses three experiences of student participation in higher education assessment, highlighting their strengths and weaknesses. These experiences show how participative assessment can be developed in everyday classes, in groups, or individually and how participative assessment can occur in different class settings. They also demonstrate the importance of design, assessment literacy, and some difficulties that might appear during the process.

Chapter 13

In this work, making use of Tinoca, Oliveira and Pereira framework for assessment quality ion digital contexts, we discuss the students' perspective about self and peer assessment practices in online environments. This research is based in the analysis of the students' perceptions in a fully online master's course being offered in a distance education university since 2007. We discuss the students' representations since that date until the present, reflecting on their roles as assessors, the challenges they faced, and the strategies they developed to overcome them. The results illustrate the participants' perceptions of self and peer assessment as innovative practices. There is a strong tendency throughout this period towards greater confidence with these practices, and increased trust in their peers' feedback and competence to share the assessment responsibility. Moreover, the transparency promoted by the sharing during the process and of the final products is recognized as crucial to support participants' reflection process and competence development.

Chapter 14

In this chapter it will present partial results from the DevalS Project (Developing Sustainable Assessment – Improving Students' Assessment Competence through Virtual Simulations), financed by the Spanish Ministry of Economy and Competitiveness (Ref. EDU2012-31804). The results will be focused on the use and usefulness of serious games for e-assessment literacy from a students' point of view. Firstly, it will introduce the project. Secondly, it will review the serious games that have been developed and implemented in different undergraduate courses. Finally, it will present the results and conclusions of surveys undertaken by students.

Section 3
Innovative Practices in Students' Assessment

Chapter 15

Stefanie Panke, University of North Carolina at Chapel Hill, USA

Assessment plays a vital role in delivering, evaluating, monitoring, improving and shaping learning experiences on the Web, at the desk and in the classroom. In the process of orchestrating educational technologies instructional designers are often confronted with the challenge of designing or deploying creative and authentic assessment techniques. For an instructional designer, the focus of assessment can be on individual learning, organizational improvement or the evaluation of educational technologies. A common question across these domains is how to translate pedagogical concepts such as authenticity and creativity into concrete practical applications and metrics. Educational technologies can support creative processes and offer connections to authentic contexts, just as well as they can curtail creativity and foster standardized testing routines. The chapter discusses theoretical frameworks and provides examples of the conceptual development and implementation of assessment approaches in three different areas: Needs assessment, impact assessment and classroom assessment.

Chapter 16

Esperanza Mejías, Universitat Autònoma de Barcelona, Spain
Carles Monereo, Universitat Autònoma de Barcelona, Spain

The authors present an innovative practice of authentic evaluation of competences carried out in the "teaching and learning strategies" course of the psychology degree. The evaluation proposal central to this course is based on a real, relevant and socializing practice context in which students have to act as counsellors to respond to a high-school teacher's request: to improve a teaching sequence or unit. In order for this authentic project to work and generate a gradual construction of learning, course teachers used a series of evaluation strategies directed at the assessment of both the result and the learning process and aimed at facilitating students' learning self-regulation and teachers' provision of educational help. Results show that students value the processes of formative assessment because they allow them to act in an authentic context. In turn, teachers are highly satisfied with the involvement and quality of the projects.

Chapter 17

The purpose of this chapter is to examine the role that professional development programmes for higher education lecturers and teachers can play in promoting positive, learner-centred assessment practice. Whilst they vary in their coverage, these programmes address a broad range of teaching, learning and other pedagogical issues, and almost all include assessment and good assessment practice as a key component of their curriculum. Therefore, this chapter is used to explain and argue that professional development programmes can and should have a key and distinctive role in developing and sharing innovative assessment practice. The argument is supported by drawing on series of seven principles and ideas, as well as a single-institution case study. Points and arguments are also supported with a range of theory, literature and examples, as well as the experience of the author in working on one programme of this type.

Chapter 18

Good assessment assures attainment and drives learning. In vocational and practical programmes, the important learning outcomes are non-cognitive skills and attitudes - for example, dexterity, situational awareness, professionalism, compassion, or resilience. Unfortunately, these domains are much more difficult to assess. There are three main reasons. First, the constructs themselves are tacit - making them difficult to define. Second, performance is highly variable and situation-specific. Third, significant assessor judgement is required to differentiate between good and poor performance, and this brings subjectivity. The chapter reviews seven existing strategies for addressing these problems: delineating the constructs, using cognitive assessments as a proxy, making the subjective objective, sampling across performances and opinions, using outcome measures as a proxy, using meta-cognition as a proxy, and abandoning the existing measurement paradigm. Given the limitations of these strategies, the author finishes by offering three promising ways forward.

Chapter 19

The purpose of this chapter is to analyze and discuss the concept of authentic assessment at Master's degree level. Firstly, this chapter attempts to provide a better understanding of the Master's program within the context of the Bologna system by providing a short historical perspective on the evolution of the Bologna process, as well as trying to identify the true beneficiaries. The chapter also addresses some of the challenges of the assessment process with two main themes: types and aim of the assessment process. Furthermore, the authors focus on the role of the authentic assessment, at a Master's degree level – as reflected by students' perception and correlated with its intended purpose. Drawing on the findings, the authors attempt to shape a description of what authentic assessment is and what it should be at Master's degree level.

Chapter 20

Catalina Ulrich, University of Bucharest, Romania
Lucian Ciolan, University of Bucharest, Romania

Main goal of the chapter is to focus on project based learning (PjBL) as an effective learning and assessment method effectively used in higher education. Chapter provides an understanding of Romanian higher education contextual challenges, current pedagogy trends and specific examples to support the idea that PjBL leads to the type of authentic learning needed for nowadays students. Theoretical framework and examples are enriched by reflections on undergraduate and master degree students' perceptions on learning process and learning outcomes.

Preface

The field of assessment is a complex aspect of teaching and learning process in higher education. Academics and students are both involved in the assessment process and they are expected to perform high level assessment in the face of multiple and varied competing conditions.

In the last years there are an ample variety of studies focused on innovations developed in order to enhance the participation of different agents in the assessment activities, especially enhancing the role of students in their own assessment through self-assessment and peer- feedback and the introduction of new technologies in the assessment process. Despite the wide interest in these topics, the consequences of such innovations and processes measured in terms of satisfaction and perceived learning, and especially in terms of performance improvements remain still under-investigated.

This book will focus on educational assessment especially in the field of innovations carried out at international level, from a triple perspective: theoretical, practical and research-based. The aim is to provide the latest research based on first-hand practice, experience, observation and knowledge of scholars and researchers in the field, in order to provide an international framework for those interested in improving their assessment practices.

Regarding to this topic fits in the world today, international and local perspectives on Educational Assessment are very much in demand nowadays, especially in the present moment when the both professionals in the educational field and stakeholders are interested in measure and improve students learning in order to form them to the challenges of the current society. In the recent years, concepts as change, reform and innovation appear with a greater frequency in the researchers' studies and interest. All these are referring from micro- individuals' level, mezzo-organizational and macro- policy making level and are justified by the preoccupation to ensure better prepared students. The book approaches all these levels and its justify its importance can be articulated around several arguments: the adequacy of the temporary time; the relationship between theory and practice and the desirability of contributing to the enrichment of a very relevant sub-area of knowledge.

First, the book topic is justified by the opportunity of this historic moment. In 1999 the Bologna Declaration marked the starting point for the creation of the European Higher Education Area, setting 2010 as the horizon to be launched leading to the harmonization of qualifications, to the implementation of necessary reforms, Credit System European curricula and competency-based approaches. There is still a very recent experience, with a few classes or cohorts of graduates trained under the new competency-based designs. While changes are reflected in the policy and strategic documents, the teaching practice is still traditional and the changes in the academics' ways to do are changing very slowly. The process of European Convergence is complex and requires time as any innovation process involves. We expect this book will bring new insights at innovative strategies already implemented and successful and it could stimulate the implementation of new ones in the field of higher education.

Secondly, in recent years an extensive literature about assessment processes in higher education has been published. However, a gap between the political discourses, theoretical approaches on effective assessment processes and teaching practices implemented in both to-face and online classes, still exists. Academics often referred to difficulties in design and implement formative assessment practices viable and coherent to the contextual conditions and applicable to different scenarios at European universities. For all this, we consider that this book justify its opportunity arguing in favor of necessity collecting not only the state of the art regarding the assessment but to offer a set of successful innovative practices that can be useful to all readers.

Thirdly, the book aims to make a contribution to the field of educational knowledge and more specifically to the subarea of learning process and assessment based on students' competences. The fact of assessment is a key element in the learning process, while guiding these processes and determines the type of cognitive skills that students develop, is something well known. Therefore, the book is not intended to justify the importance of assessment but to enhance a different conception on the topic, in the direction indicated by the current pedagogical knowledge centred on constructive approaches and connectivist models; reviewing the agents involved; looking for a truly formative purpose through implementation of dialogic feedback experiences and incorporating possibilities of technology. The book indeed must to offer a framework on the current situation and to open new perspective on assessment practices.

For all these reasons mentioned above, the book includes both theoretical contributions as research on assessment processes in higher education as concrete experiences of innovation in the universities classrooms around the world.

Regarding to people that might be interested in this book, the audience for the book consists in the following categories:

1. Academics working in higher education field who will find valuable theoretical and practical knowledge for teaching and assessment improvement;
2. Professionals working in training for teachers and researchers who will use the book in their professional development activities;
3. Practitioners who serve in secondary and high school for their continuous professional development;
4. Academic coordinators and leaders in higher education. They will find interesting information which orients their managerial activities, designing and implementing teaching and assessment plans and programs;
5. Policymakers involved in educational field in general and in higher educational in particular. They will be able to analyze the impact of the assessment strategies implemented by academics and propose new strategic lines for improvement and
6. Graduate and postgraduate students carrying out their research projects in the field of educational assessment. They will discover new methodological strategies to approach students' assessment issue.

All these collectives will find theoretical, practical and research-based contributions from a deep approach and under an international framework. In this way, the book is organized in three different sections: theoretical contributions, research –based evidences and teaching innovative experiences.

In the first section, the various chapters tackle with issues of assessment theories in the local and international contexts.

More specifically, the chapter by Mark Claver titled: 'Feedback, Feedforward, or Dialogue?: Defining a Model for Self-regulated Learning', following Sadler's theories, discusses about feedback, feedforward or dialogue. The author offers arguments that dialogic feedback and feedforward are currently conceptualized in a purely positive way, which serves to limit effective critique of these models. The chapter's main contribution consists in describing principles of any type of feedback which have clear links to self-regulated learning, offering these as a reframing of feedback preferable to current etymological models.

In the same line, the chapter authored by Zineb Djoub and titled: 'Assessment for learning: Feeding back and feeding forward' also addresses the issue of feedback and feedforward and the quality of these processes. This chapter aims first to clarify for teachers what quality feedback means. Then, it provides practical tips and strategies for teachers to stimulate their students' interest in feedback, assimilate its significant role and get involved in interpreting, reflecting and acting upon feedback comments. The author focuses on both summative and formative feedback. The author also discusses strategies and instruments as reflective worksheets and other post-exam tasks in class useful to improve students' learning. Feedback within self, peer and group assessment approaches is also concerned in this chapter.

Guardia, Crisp and Alsina, in their chapter 'Trends and challenges of e-assessment to enhance student learning in Higher Education' make a reflection on the online assessment, including a brief catalogue of both traditional and innovative formats relevant to this type of training. The main purpose of this chapter is precisely to highlight the necessity for teachers to be aware of the new opportunities for enhancing the quality of assessment tasks through the use of computers and the Internet and offers strategies in order to achieve it. Some of these strategies discussed by authors are: reviewing the literature, exploring what is already done basically in online and blended environments and what are the trends and challenges of eAssessment to enhance student learning in Higher Education.

The next chapter, 'Competency-based Assessment: From conceptual model to operational tool', written by Mohammed Khalidi Idrissi, Meriem Hnida and Samir Bennani, shows the characteristics of CBA (Competency-Based Assessment) model. The main purpose of the chapter is to present an online placement test for assessing student competencies, describing a developed competence model using domain ontology and Instructional Management System (IMS) Global standards. Also, it tends to demonstrate how to use a psychometric model that belongs to the Item Response Theory, to effectively analyze student level of competence and classify learners into homogeneous groups.

Walaa M. El-Henawy in the chapter 'Assessment Techniques in EFL Brain-Compatible Classroom' offers approached the topic of brain-supported classroom and the main challenges of this practice. The information provided by this chapter is related about the brain and how it learns. Brain-Based Learning is student centered learning that utilizes the whole brain and recognizes that not all students learn in the same way. Feedback also motivates students and allows students to apply what they have learned to real-life situations.

In the chapter 'Formative Evaluations of Teaching: Involving Students in the Assessment Process', Gina Mariano reviews current research on Students Evaluation of teaching, while highlighting ways to effectively use the information given in Students Evauation of Teaching (SETs) to help students become active participants in their learning by better understanding student perceptions of courses. This chapter presents interest for any to faculty in higher education looking to improve teaching quality and assessment related to teaching improvement.

The section 1 of the book ends with the contribution of Marije Lesterhuis, San Verhavert, Liesje Coertjens, Vincent Donche, and Sven De Maeyer on the validity and reliability of comparative judgment and focuses on the advantages of the method in order to achieve reliable and valid scores, especially for large-scale (summative) performance assessments.

The second section of the book is dedicated to the research based evidences on assessment and presents in seven chapters interesting contributions on different topics from students' perspectives to academics views in face to face and online environments.

The first chapter on this section is titled 'Students' Conceptions of Understanding and Its Assessment' and it's authored by Rebecca Hamer, and Erik Jan van Rossum. The chapter provides a revision of the historical conceptions (reproduction vs meaning) of assessment. This is an empirical study with 170 Dutch and German psychology students who were asked to elaborate their understanding of the concept of 'understanding' and to describe their views on how to best assess understanding. The data consisted of written essays that were analyzed using the phenomenographic method. This study introduces two new conceptions of understanding beyond the interpretation of flexible performance.

In the chapter 'Teacher Self-Assessment of Feedback Practices in an EFL Academic Writing Class: A Reflective Case Study', Eddy White explains a research about Classroom-based assessment, showing how essays could be assessed and how the feedback interventions scaffold the second version of the essays. The purpose of the study presented is to systematically analyze his written feedback practices, in a writing course at a Japanese university, to determine the form and kind of feedback provided on student essays, and, to see how these feedback practices would measure up against recommended practice in the feedback on writing literature. A close examination of the teacher feedback on the first draft of 21 student essays was undertaken and more than 800 feedback interventions were identified and coded.

Maite Fernández-Ferrer and Laura Pons-Seguí show in the chapter number ten, entitled 'Feedforward. The key to improve learning in higher education', data derived from a inter-university experience about feedforward in terms of motivation and achievement of students. The purpose of this study is to detect an improvement in students' learning linked to an improvement in their results (assessed in the second version of each assignment) and in the final achievement of the course.

The next chapter titled 'Teaching for Epistemological Change: Self-direction by Self-Assessment', written by Gloria Nogueiras, David Herrero, and Alejandro Iborra, shares an experience regarding innovative assessment practices as Higher Education teachers in a Teacher Training Degree. Authors approached the use of self-assessment as a way to promote and supervise the competence of self-direction in freshmen students. Data have been collected in a course on Developmental Psychology that was taught to 149 students.

Victoria Quesada, Eduardo Garcia-Jimenez, and Miguel Angel Gomez-Ruiz, in their chapter about 'Student Participation in Assessment Processes: way forward 'presents an investigation that aims to explore students' participation in the assessment processes and to analyze different approaches to promote it, both at course and module level. The chapter answers the following questions: what is understood as 'student participation in assessment processes'? To what extend can we enhance student participation in assessment? At the end of the chapter authors provide recommendations on how to develop student's participation in assessment.

'Peer assessment in an online context: What do students say?' is the chapter thirteen. It is written by Alda Pereira, Luis Tinoca, and Isolina Oliveira, who presents a longitudinal research on a process of peer assessment on line in Portugal. They show the lack of confidence of students in assessments of their peers but also show the benefits of increasing reflective practice and responsibility. The results illustrate the students' perceptions of self and peer assessment as innovative practices and show the necessity to include the students in the definition of the competences to be assessed and on the development of the assessment criteria.

The last chapter of this section is entitled 'Serious Games for Students' E-assessment Literacy in Higher Education' and it's authored by Gregorio Rodriguez-Gomez and María Soledad Ibarra-Sáiz. They explain the results of the use of simulations and alternative assessment formats in ad hoc platforms. Data is derived from a survey administrated to students in the framework of DevalS Project (Developing Sustainable Assessment – Improving Student's Assessment Competence through Virtual Simulations).

The third section of the book is dedicated to present innovative practices in students' assessment and is organized in six chapters.

The first chapter of this section is proposed by Stefanie Panke and it is titled 'Designing Assessment, Assessing Instructional Design: From Pedagogical Concepts to Practical Applications'. This chapter shows a teaching innovation focusing on authentic assessment. The chapter provides examples of the conceptual development and implementation of assessment approaches in three different areas: "Needs Assessment" (for designing projects with stakeholders through focus groups, interviews and surveys), "Impact Assessment" (using learning analytics, and interviews) and "Classroom Assessment" (for supporting students' critical thinking abilities with portfolios, rubrics or peer-to-peer assessment).

The chapter number sixteen is dedicated to show an innovative experience of competence-based assessment. The title is 'As Life Itself. Authentic teaching and evaluation of professional consulting competences in a Psychology course' and its author are Esperanza Mejías, and Carles Monereo. The study analyze the influences on what and how students learn and also on the representation they construct about the future professional role they will play in a real context, when they start working.

The chapter 'Demonstrating Positive, Learner-Centred Assessment Practice in Professional Development Programmes', proposed by Patrick Baughan, shows a teaching innovation based on student-centered programs evaluation, incorporating the elements that makes a good evaluation practice. The chapter contributes to explain and argue that professional development programmes can and should have a key and distinctive role in developing and sharing innovative assessment practice.

In the same topic, James G M Crossley, shows 8 dimensions to study at an OSCE experience, from the health sciences field. The chapter eighteen reviews seven existing strategies for addressing these problems: delineating the constructs, using cognitive assessments as a proxy, making the subjective objective, sampling across performances and opinions, using outcome measures as a proxy, using meta-cognition as a proxy, and abandoning the existing measurement paradigm. Given the limitations of these strategies, the author finishes by offering three promising ways forward.

Simona Iftimescu, Romita Iucu, Elena Marin, and Mihaela Monica Stingu in the chapter entitled 'Authentic Assessment: An Inquiry into the Assessment Process at Master's Degree Level', propose a study showing the student's perception after an authentic assessment process carried out in the field of education in Romania. This chapter contributes to a better understanding of the Master's program within the context of the Bologna system by providing a short historical perspective on the evolution of the Bologna process, as well as trying to identify the true beneficiaries. In addition challenges of the assessment process are identified.

The chapter number twenty, 'Beyond the walls: project-based learning and assessment in higher education', proposed by Catalina Ulrich and Lucian Ciolan provides an useful perspective on the current pedagogy trends and specific examples to support the idea that Project Based Learning leads to the type of authentic learning needed for nowadays students. Theoretical framework and examples are enriched by reflections on undergraduate and master degree students' perceptions on learning process and learning outcomes.

All these 20 chapters contribute to outline an overview of educational assessment and its current challenges and to provide examples of innovative practices that have been implemented in different scenarios and which effects have been proved by research. In addition, this book provides a scholar account of the many facets of assessment, with particular focus on evidence and practice-based approaches. Assessment for self-regulated learning is a powerful academic tools and this book will constitute a comprehensive guide to the methods and issues involved. The relevance of the book is for both scholars, students and academic leaders in higher education context, all of them will find in this book valuable examples and guidelines in order to experiment new ways of assessment and to improve their practices.

Acknowledgments

The editors of this book would like to acknowledge the contribution of all the authors involved in this proposal and the reviewers who took part to the peer- review process. Without their support, this book would not have become a reality.

The editors also thank to the valuable support offered by the IGI Publishing team who offered all their help during the edition process.

Elena Cano
Universitat de Barcelona, Spain

Georgeta Ion
Universitat Autònoma de Barcelona, Spain

Section 1
Theoretical Approaches on Students' Assessment

Chapter 1
Feedback, Feedforward, or Dialogue?
Defining a Model for Self–Regulated Learning

Mark Carver
Edinburgh Napier University, UK

ABSTRACT

Better feedback is commonly demanded by students and institutions as a way of improving student satisfaction, encouraging more scholarly approaches to assessment, and building students' capacity for self-regulated learning. Student responses to surveys are very clear on what they think makes good feedback: it is prompt, regular, specific, and accurate (e.g. Bols & Wicklow, 2013). Institutional efforts therefore typically try to improve feedback by improving in these four areas. However, Price (2013) has questioned if the customer is always right. This chapter looks at the main models of feedback from the research literature and etymology, in particular how these relate to concepts of self-regulated learning and sustainable assessment (Boud & Molloy, 2013). It is argued that dialogic feedback and feedforward are wrongly currently conceptualised in a purely positive way, which serves to limit effective critique of these models. The chapter ends by describing principles of any type of feedback, providing a working definition which is more compatible with self-regulated learning.

INTRODUCTION

From its origins as a straightforward method of error detection and correction, feedback is now recognised as playing a crucial and increasingly nuanced role in learning in higher education. However, there remains great variety in how feedback is experienced to the extent that "when we refer to feedback, we need to be aware that it means different things to different people" (Carless, 2015, p. 192). Whilst it seems contradictory, students both have a seemingly insatiable appetite for feedback and a nonchalance towards it: for example, some tutors complain that students often fail to even collect their written feedback (Bailey & Garner, 2010; Carless, 2006), while considerable written comments by tutors, even if read,

DOI: 10.4018/978-1-5225-0531-0.ch001

can still be poorly used by students (Dysthe, 2011). It is therefore "not inevitable that students will read and pay attention to feedback even when that feedback is lovingly crafted and provided promptly" (Gibbs & Simpson, 2004, p. 20). This means that engaging students with feedback does not just require giving good feedback, but challenging students to have a different understanding of feedback which challenges an often passive conceptualisation from secondary education (Sambell et al., 2012).

One of the key barriers to changing students' conceptualisation of feedback is students' increasingly strategic approaches to assessment (Entwistle, 2000; Marton et al., 1984). If feedback is seen as only helping to improve grades in a few particular assessment tasks, it follows that students have little incentive to collect feedback on an assignment that has already been graded. A student's understanding of the purpose of assessment will therefore also influence their understanding of feedback. If an assessment is seen as a learning opportunity with long term value, it is more likely that feedback will be seen as flowing back to improving a student's general understanding as well as flowing forwards into helping the student perform the assessed task. However, assessment can also be seen as to measure learning or ensure accountability (Stobart, 2008), with multiple intended functions typically forcing compromises in the design of any assessed task (Bloxham & Boyd, 2007). One of the first challenges in engaging students in their feedback is therefore convincing them that feedback supports an assessment which is truly formative in its intention, that is assessment which primarily seeks to improve teaching and learning (Wiliam, 2011).

In addition to needing to know the intent of an assessment, students also need to be confident that they will be fairly evaluated. The perception that assessment is a game which needs to be played emphasises the value of learning those "rules of the game" (Carless, 2006, p. 230), where feedback becomes part of the game as it is mined for clues or the student tries to please their tutor by how they respond to feedback. Becker et al. (1968, p. 95) first wrote of this as students seeing value in "getting next to" their tutor if they were otherwise unable to get the grade they felt they deserved, concluding that if students "can do the job, they do it, putting their major efforts into academic work. If they cannot, they try to influence their grade in some other way".

Other explanations for students strategically diverting their effort away from learning have focused on social class, making strategic behaviour a limited choice rather than a rational choice. In the US, Horowitz (1988) saw it as a result of increased competitiveness by first-generation university students who aligned themselves with faculty and demonstrated their determination to work hard as a way to set themselves apart from a lazy, well-networked upper class who wanted to have fun before the pressure of real life. In the UK, Stuart et al. (2012) explained it more as related to taste or even a product of social capital (Bourdieu, 1990), that hard work and strategically maximising grades came to be a dominant paradigm, often at the expense of valuable extra-curricular learning. Whatever the reason, if students see themselves as competing for grades, and particularly if their competitors are thought of as leveraging strategic advantages, the fairness of assessment will be doubted. Consequently, feedback cannot be taken at face value because it is bound up in the 'game' of assessment where rewards can not only be gained by actions other than learning, but learning also fails to guarantee those some rewards.

Understanding how students see feedback therefore requires understanding how feedback has changed in meaning through its adoption by the academic literature, but also more generally by how current understanding of feedback fits in with the complementary literature on student approaches to learning. This chapter outlines the major changes in how feedback has been used as a term, including adaptations such as feedforward, feedback for learning, and formative feedback. Discussing these changes offers insight into how the way that feedback is understood in the academic literature has started to branch away from how students seem to conceptualise feedback. The chapter ends by recommended that the literature on self-regulated learning offers the clearest bridge between these two areas, which marks an important first step in reconciling the differing conceptions of feedback held by academics and students.

Background

Information given to students and how they respond to it has long been researched, but it is only since Sadler's (1989) seminal work that this was commonly referred to as feedback. For example, Becker et al. (1968) was one of the first major studies to explore how students took deliberate approaches towards assessed tasks, but the study does not refer to feedback at all - instead students engage in 'information seeking' and tutors offer 'information' or 'comments'. In this way, information given to students on work that they had produced was not conceptualised any differently from information given to students as routine parts of the course. This seems to be the first step in deciding whether or not something is just information or if it is feedback: it must come from something the student has done.

The idea that the source of the input is part of the definition of feedback can be seen in the first recorded usage of the term in the Oxford English Dictionary (Simpson & Weiner, 1989). Dating from 1920, feedback described the "return of a fraction of the output signal from one stage…to the input of the same or a preceding stage" (Simpson & Weiner, 1989). This also includes the idea that feedback should have a direction, returning back to make a change in how something occurs. This is still an important aspect of modern usage of the term. For example, Boud and Molloy make powerful use of Sadler's phrase "dangling data" to criticise information intended as feedback but which should not be called feedback because no resulting action is taken (Boud & Molloy, 2013, p. 699; Sadler, 1989, p.121).

A later example of usage suggests that taking action as a result of feedback became an important part of the definition. The OED quotes *The Times* in 1955, in which "constant" feedback is argued as the only way that "one can ascertain how far a message has been understood rightly" (Simpson & Weiner, 1989). This shows a subtle shift from feedback defined as information which improves a learner's performance to feedback which improves the tutor's performance, in this case by frequently checking understanding. The constant nature of feedback is also an important element in ensuring that small changes happen quickly rather than waiting to make big changes once the 'output' is complete. Thinking of feedback as occuring constantly also moves the definition on from information feeding back to earlier stages, as feedback can be sought to make changes in the moment. In an educational context, it therefore seems important to distinguish between feedback which is primarily for the learner to reflect upon and feedback which affects learning indirectly by giving the tutor information with which to improve their teaching.

The first example from the OED corpus of feedback being used in an educational context comes from an early teaching guide (Quirk & Smith, 1959), that in a lecture "the live speaker has a reaction, a 'feed-back' from the listeners" (Simpson & Weiner, 1989). This further highlights a shift from the idea of feedback being a gift from the teacher to feedback being something that is sought by the person using that feedback, in this case a speaker looking for reactions to their lecture. This also shows a subtle return to the root definition of feedback as a return of a fraction of the output, that is something naturally occurring during the natural performance of a task - the listeners will be reacting regardless of whether those reactions are acted upon by the speaker. In turn, this emphasises that the person intending to benefit from feedback is active in engaging with it. Feedback is no longer a gift from an expert, but something to be sought out by a learner.

At this point, it becomes difficult to find further developments the etymology of feedback. This does not, however, mean that the definition stabilised and became widely accepted but that writers took to distinguishing their own particular use of the term. Wiener (1954) described two different uses of feedback. First was feedback used "as numerical data for the criticism of the system and its regulation" (Wiener, 1954, p. 61). Here a performance is altered and feedback sought until actual performance satisfactorily closes the gap with desired performance. However, Weiner notes an alternative use if feedback "proceeds backward from the performance [and] is able to change the general method and pattern of performance" (Wiener, 1954, p. 61). Both of these definitions of feedback could still conceptualise the learner as passive, being told how to improve or change by an expert, although there is also the suggestion that self-reflection could be used for the same outcome.

Weiner's definition offers insight into the intent of feedback, whether it is to improve a particular performance or to make general improvements. Quirk and Smith (1959) likewise suggest that feedback should be actively sought. However, these definitions are still vague about the source of feedback: it is either from an expert or is drawn from naturally occurring data, with the only check on accurate understanding of feedback being another iteration of the feedback cycle. It would be another 30 years before discussion of feedback explicitly mentioned the role of the learner, with Sadler (1989) introducing conditions that the learner understand for themselves the required standard, make a comparison between that and their performance, and engage in action to close the gap. Even here, however, Sadler retained the onus on the teacher to ensure that this happened.

Sadler also expanded the definition of feedback to consider the difficulty teachers faced making their knowledge explicit and easy enough for their learners to understand. He argued that teachers' "conceptions of quality are typically held, largely in unarticulated form, inside their heads as tacit knowledge" (Sadler, 1989, p. 126). From this, it followed that frequent feedback exchanges - what might today be called dialogic feedback - would be required to gradually transfer this knowledge. Assessing the impact of feedback on the learner would also be less straightforward, since the learner would also hold this knowledge tacitly. In this way, feedback became even more closely related to assessment, since reliable feedback could now be seen to rely on reliable assessment whilst at the same time acknowledging that 'reliable' would be necessarily complex.

Bodman (2007) explains the contribution of Sadler's (1989) seminal paper as moving attention from the information provided in feedback to a focus instead on the effect of that feedback. The effect of Sadler's work was to emphasise the responsibility of both the tutor and the learner in ensuring that feedback happened - if either party was not engaged in active meaning-making, then what they were doing should not be called feedback. As well as helping to create a distinct definition of feedback in definition by rejecting encroachments on its use, Sadler later explicitly located his discussion in a constructivist framework by emphasising how feedback must develop new understanding or critical reflection in the learner (Sadler, 1998). This constructivist definition of feedback for learning, however, has clear connections with what Wiener simply called learning - feedback which "is able to change the general method and pattern of performance" (Wiener, 1954, p. 61).

Sadler's work effectively shifted feedback from being a by-product of expert judgement into something which should be co-created. It also started to differentiate improved task performance from learning. More recently, Sadler (2009) has linked this to requiring the learner to develop their own understanding of tacit knowledge, a development of his earlier argument that the teacher relied on tacit knowledge during assessment. This further stresses the central role of the learner in developing their own understanding by reducing emphasis on the teacher's responsibility to make their knowledge explicit. It also re-asserts the importance of self-assessment, as the purpose of the learner developing tacit knowledge is so that they can modify their own performance by understanding the complexity of what is required rather than simply being told what to do or how to do it.

Over the last 10 years, the meaning of feedback in the academic literature has become increasingly bound up with assessment. In the same way that Sadler prompted a distinction between feedback for learning and feedback for task performance, Stobart (2008) distinguishes between different intentions of assessment. Assessment primarily intended to measure learning would emphasise the importance of feedback which aimed to improve task performance, whereas assessment which saw its primary aim as supporting learning would require feedback which took a more in-depth approach to a student's tacit understanding of quality and their general ways of thinking. Whereas assessment for measuring learning might place the onus on the student to prepare for an assessment, assessment for learning requires teachers to think about how they prepare students for assessment. For example, Bloxham and Boyd (2007) recommend a limited repertoire of assessment types so that students can acclimatise to the tacit requirements of different types of assessment. This suggests that feedback needs to be generalisable and transferable, so avoiding too many different types of task helps to prevent feedback which is too task-specific.

A similar argument is made for "authentic assessment" (Wiggins, 1989, p. 703), where improving the relevancy of the test improves its contribution to learning. Rather than limiting assessment variety so that students waste less time figuring out the tacit demands of a particular assessment, an authentic assessment would be designed to directly improve learning rather than just measuring. Feedback on authentic assessments can therefore avoid the distractions of an artificial assessment task, meaning that feedback on authentic assessments is, by its nature, feedback in support of learning since the assessment relates far more closely to the context within knowledge is expected to be used (Boud, 2007).

In terms of assessment, feedback can be seen as either helping students to avoid the distractions of an artificial assessment task or as working in tandem with authentically designed assessment. Either way, the student is not left alone to figure it out. This marks an important but subtle shift in how feedback is discussed in the literature, since it is no longer seen as information which is generated in the normal order of performing a task. Rather, feedback is specifically created for the purpose of improving task performance. The timing has similarly shifted so that feedback might try to pre-empt problems, becoming more proactive where before it seemed, by definition, to be a reactive process. With the introduction of tacit knowledge as a concept, feedback has also taken on some dialogic qualities, emphasising its iterative nature rather than being a simple transmission of information. The relationship between the creator and user of feedback also seems to have changed, with the teacher now at least partly responsible for ensuring not only that their feedback is understandable and usable, but that the learner actually uses it to improve their learning and performance.

More recently, the discussion of feedback has implied a more important role for the learner. In many cases, however, the teacher is still seen as responsible for encouraging learners to take up this role. For example, Bodman (2007) argues argument that effective feedback attends to motivation - hence, the onus remains with the person giving feedback. Bodman relates the possible effects of feedback on a learner to the literature on change processes, distinguishing between feedback which forms a collision, acts as a catalyst, or stimulates transformative change, although in all these cases feedback is still something done to the learner. Similarly, despite Sadler (1998) moving the academic discussion of feedback towards a more constructivist perspective, "feedback practices enacted on the ground still tend to pull heavily on behaviourist views of feedback" (Boud & Molloy, 2013, p. 52). For example, the feedback activities recommended in Nicol and Macfarlane-Dick (2006) present students reading and thinking about their feedback as the starting point for student engagement, so even within their broader aim of promoting self-regulated learning the students are reacting to feedback rather than being involved in creating it.

An alternative argument is that students should be the starting point for generating feedback, and take some responsibility for maintaining dialogue. Yang and Carless (2012) describe a highly labour-intensive experience for tutors as they need to be in constant contact to keep students engaged in dialogue. The extent of the tutor's responsibility for maintaining feedback as a dialogue might even be seen to violate the basic assumptions of cooperative dialogue (Grice, 1975), raising doubts as to whether dialogic feedback is even possible given the power differences that exist between teachers and students. One suggested solution is to allow students to specify the feedback they would like, so that they at least set the topic of conversation and tutors do not waste time giving feedback which is either poorly valued or which students are not yet ready to engage with (Nicol, 2010). Sadler (2010) similarly points out that providing feedback to large groups of students can be a waste of time if students do not act upon that feedback. Indeed, students being receptive is so crucial that Jones and Gorra (2013) successfully trialed only giving feedback to students who actively sought it, thereby reducing waste from creating feedback which would not be collected or acted upon whilst also giving more time to those who would engage with feedback. These arguments reject the idea that the tutor is responsible for engaging the learner, making a student's willingness to engage a prerequisite.

Less assertive approaches have worked on a similar principle, where students engaging with the construction of feedback receive more or better feedback, but the student is still expected to make the first move. A simple suggestion from Bloxham and Campbell (2010) required students to specify on assignment cover sheets what they wanted feedback to focus on, meaning that the tacit nature of the tutor's judgement was less problematic and their feedback far more tailored. A similar approach was recommended in Brannon and Knoblauch (1982), with students required to give a running commentary alongside their assignment to indicate what they were thinking or trying to do. Both recommendations give the learner more agency whilst also trying to make feedback more relevant by supporting "the student in what they are trying to achieve, rather than as a transmission of feedback given by an 'expert' on what the student *should* have done" (McGinty, 2007, p. 149).

As the pedagogy of feedback has become a more popular topic, the meaning of feedback seems to have taken another shift. In particular, resolving the roles and responsibilities of tutors and learners has exposed the underlying, and largely unresolved, tension between constructivist and behaviourist assumptions. As a result, feedback has become bound up with the idea that the student must act - feedback without action is simply information or, less kindly, "dangling data" (Boud & Molloy, 2013, p. 699). This now seems to be such a strong component of feedback that students being open to acting on feedback can be argued to be a prerequisite, that nothing the tutor does can make feedback happen unless the student is first willing to engage. With increased pressures on faculty time, this has led to suggestions that feedback is only worth the time and effort for those students who take the lead. Forcing students to reflect on their needs and open the dialogue might also help to redress some of the power imbalance between students and tutors, or even generate a kind of internal feedback for themselves.

Alternatively, feedback can be seen to extend beyond the information and action stage, so that anything the tutor does to prompt a student's engagement might also be seen as feedback. Similarly, feedback from the learner's perspective should be about moving from thinking together with their tutor as part of a structured dialogue (Gravett & Petersen, 2002) to being able to create their own internal feedback independently. The most recent working definition of feedback offered in Carless (2015, p. 192) seems to take account of this development by seeing feedback more as a process than a product, emphasising that feedback is "a dialogic process in which learners make sense of information from varied sources and use it to enhance the quality of their work or learning strategies". Within this, he includes "internal feedback" (Carless, 2015, p. 190) in recognition of the importance of multiple sources of feedback which learners need to draw on, utilising not just teachers but peers and technology.

Running alongside the redefining work led by Boud, Molloy, and Carless is an attempt to create new terms rather than fighting to change what is understood by feedback. The most notable of these efforts is the concept of feedforward, emphasising the vital requirement that feedback must lead to specific future actions (Duncan, 2007). Irons (2010) uses feedforward to explain the difference in expectations between tutors and students because tutors expected that students would have the skills to take their feedback forwards, highlighting the need to support students through this crucial stage. Price et al. (2010) specifically include this in their meaning of feedforward by including the requirement for developing slowly learnt literacies (Knight & Yorke, 2004).

Agreeing on a contemporary definition of feedback can therefore be problematic as it can vary based on the assumed roles and responsibilities of tutors and students, the nature of their relationship, and the intended outcomes of feedback. Carless (2015) has argued that feedback can currently be seen as following a continuum from conventional feedback to sustainable feedback. This has been accompanied by efforts to assert the value of feedback, moving it from the periphery. The most significant change seems to be that the learner is now regarded as playing a crucial role in both generating and using feedback, although this seems to be in tension with teachers being held responsible for what their learners do.

The contemporary understanding of feedback also depends heavily on the assessment environment, hence feedback can be vulnerable to being misused if students take overly-strategic approaches to their interactions with their tutors. This effect can be seen in recent efforts to distance feedback from the term 'formative assessment', since students seem to regard this as less important than summative assessment. The recently coined "learning-oriented assessment" (Carless, 2015, p. 1) tries to assert the importance of intent, matching well with the most recent definitions of sustainable feedback. The academic literature seems to already be moving away from focusing on feedforward and the action learners take to a more careful look at the intention behind feedback, so as well as ensuring that the learner acts upon feedback it is now also important that the way they act contributes to their learning rather than just helping with a specific task or being of short-term value.

ISSUES, CONTROVERSIES, PROBLEMS

Innovative practice in feedback in higher education can be limited by the over-simplified way feedback is commonly understood and evaluated. For example, if speed and detail are the main ways a tutor is evaluated, they do not have an incentive for personalising their feedback. The effect of this can be seen in the arguments made by Stevens and Levi (2011) for more widespread use of rubrics as a way to give feedback more efficiently, even though this strategy would be largely incompatible with more dialogic approaches to feedback and may not even be reliable for assessment judgements (Bloxham et al., 2011). In this way, the controversies and problems related to feedback can be seen to relate more broadly to the controversies and problems related to assessment: if too much attention is placed on performance rather than learning, then teaching and learning becomes too focused on efficiency. Dialogic feedback is particularly vulnerable to this as, like most dialogue, it takes time to develop its full effectiveness.

Tutors hoping to innovate in their feedback practices may simply have to accept that their performance management scores will suffer, and console themselves that their students will see the long-term benefits. However, students' perceptions of high quality feedback tend not to be so sophisticated either. The UK's National Union of Students conducted a large-scale survey and "great feedback amnesty", in which students were asked to share examples of good and bad feedback, summarised what students wanted as feedback needing to be prompt, early in the course, in a range of formats, easily understandable, with clear advice on how to improve (Bols & Wicklow, 2013). This list of criteria strongly implies that students have a transmission model of feedback, emphasising the tutor's responsibility for making feedback easy for the student to access and understand. Other recommendations in the same report, for example that feedback be given anonymously, further emphasise how feedback can be caught up in the controversies related to assessment, since dialogic feedback requires that the tutor get to know the student.

In addition to understanding what students want from feedback, tutors also have to wary of what students consider to be feedback. For example, some students and tutors might only regard feedback as comments given on assessed written work, whereas a broader definition would include any information the tutor gives students which was based on input from the students - for example, answering a student's question during class could be seen as a simple type of feedback. Students might also regard tutorials as something separate from feedback, not seeing those discussions as feedback unless they also receive something in writing, or even seeing such a tutorial not as a type of feedback but rather as discussion about their written feedback. Again, advice to tutors can be too simplistic, so instead of engaging students in a discussion of what feedback is they are told to clearly state when they are giving feedback.

When giving feedback, therefore, there is a tension between giving the best feedback for learning and the best feedback for the assessment. If tutors are judged on how understandable their feedback is, there might also be an incentive to over-simplify and avoid engaging in more complex or tacit knowledge. An example of this is assignment feedback which emphasises referencing, grammar or other technical elements rather than engaging more critically with a student's writing (Wilson, 2015).

It is also increasingly common for courses to be organised into modules, which can also cause problems for changing feedback practice. If assessment demands and types are not seen as consistent across a course, students and tutors may have to spend more feedback time on the specific requirements of each module rather than giving feedback which can carry forwards into later modules (Bloxham & Boyd, 2007). Similarly, modularisation can increase the risk of students seeing feedback as arriving too late to act upon as they do not see learning as occurring across modules (Weaver, 2006). The frequent summative assessment that occurs in a modular course therefore encourages traditional models of feedback, although this need not necessarily be the case if courses are planned and conceived of as coherent (Fraser & Bosanquet, 2006).

Assessment can have a particularly detrimental effect on how feedback on drafts is used. Court (2012) notes that students can see acting on draft feedback as too demanding or time-consuming, so are only interested in very specific feedback and corrections which can be made quickly and easily. An attempt to provide extra feedback to students before assessment also found this problem, with nearly half of the students producing poorer quality work and only improving it if threatened with failure (Covic & Jones, 2008). In contrast, Bland and Gallagher (2009) found that making assessment higher-stakes by removing the chance to repeat an assignment actually increased student engagement with informal feedback. In these examples, feedback seems to rely on the threat of failure, even though failing a higher education course in the UK is very rare (Floud, 2002). Whilst this threat increases student engagement, the risk is that this is an instrumental engagement where the student is only seeking reassurance that they will pass or are looking for quick fixes. The author's own research found some support for this view among students, but also rather surprisingly in feedback from faculty which seemed to reinforce the idea that students just had to add enough polish to "get over the line" (Author, 2015a).

This highly strategic use of feedback reinforces the idea that feedback is simply information from an expert. Just as critical reading requires finding the key information quickly, the effective student must mine their feedback for those key tips. This perspective can be seen to underpin students' demands for more and clearer feedback. Becker et al. (1968) saw this as completely unsustainable, since students would continue to demand more detailed feedback until it reached the point that their learning became entirely directed by their tutor, only requiring the student to memorise what they have been told. Today's students seem every bit as insatiable, but they may well have been made this way by their assessment regime. If feedback were seen as something more time-consuming which had to be co-constructed by engaged students, then there would be little incentive for students to demand more feedback other than to improve their learning. One of the key challenges to overcome for feedback therefore is the idea that tutors should be working harder than their students to give detailed, clear, understandable feedback which all but guarantees a successful grade.

In summary, it seems that many of the problems for feedback are caused by limited conceptions of, and attitudes to, assessment. Where assessment is seen as an end in itself, there is little incentive for feedback to take a long-term view. Likewise, if tasks are seen as terminal rather than as part of an overall learning strategy there is little motivation to reflect on performance or how those tasks could be improved. More expansive models of feedback seem to cover almost all aspects of learning (Askew & Lodge, 2000), but the everyday reality of feedback as something measurable and auditable remains firmly in a straightforward transmission paradigm. Feedback also risks being abused by students who are looking for an advantage, demanding more feedback and more specificity in the feedback to ensure that they gain the most marks for the least effort. This also seems to be a result of seeing feedback from a limited perspective, particularly when feedback is seen as the tutor's responsibility. Overcoming these challenges requires not just a better understanding of feedback, but a better understanding of assessment.

SOLUTIONS AND RECOMMENDATIONS

Recommendations for improving feedback practice in higher education typically take one of two approaches. The first is to imply that improving the quality of feedback will improve its use by students, so the feedback produced by tutors should be improved so that students will engage more. This implication can be seen most clearly in advice which has been reduced to tips, such as Hounsell's feedback wheel (The University of Edinburgh, 2015). The same idea can also be seen in advice which tries to give a more detailed explanation of the principles staff should work to, particularly when the focus is on making feedforward which students can easily act upon (Nicol, 2010).

An alternative implication in recommendations for improvements is that it is not necessarily the feedback information or provision that needs to change, but students' engagement with that feedback. For example, Price et al. (2010) and Bailey and Garner (2010) show how well-crafted feedback can fail to have an impact on student learning. This in turn leads to the recommendation that efforts should focus on building students' understanding of the value of feedback and their skills in using feedback effectively (Duncan, 2007), for example by helping students to understand the concept of slowly learnt literacies as an alternative to a simple transmission approach to knowledge (Knight & Yorke, 2004).

All of these recommendations will of course focus on both the production of feedback and its use, varying by how much emphasis they place on each aspect. Recommendations which fully explore the interrelation between the two will inevitably be more complex, and so cannot be easily reduced to tips and require staff to invest time in building their own understanding of the principles of sustainable feedback practice. An interesting attempt is made in Carless (2015) to look at what can be learnt from award-winning staff, helping to tease out the subtleties between feedback practices which are easily transferable or imitable in other contexts and those which seem bound up in the individual, although again this can still be seen to focus too much on what staff do.

Attempting to give recommendations based on what students do is significantly limited by the dominance of a deficit model of students (Biggs & Tang, 2011), where the typical description is of students failing to make good use of feedback, although there are notable exceptions such as Nicol (2013). How students use feedback is also typically associated with their approaches to assessment, so feedback is something to be mined it for clues about forthcoming assessments, attempting to "determine the implicit rules of the assessment game" (Entwistle et al., 1979, p. 366). Recommendations for improving feedback practice therefore focus on shifting students towards deeper approaches to learning (Marton & Saljo, 2005) and away from this surface or strategic approach to feedback. Making a tutor responsible for how their students engage with feedback at least emphasises the importance of feedback being used, but this fails to appreciate the time pressure created by good feedback practice - hence compromises such as using rubrics or only giving feedback to students who first show a willingness to engage.

A rather curious, but nevertheless appealing, recommendation suggests a more laissez-faire approach to engaging students in learning dialogue. Attempting to use assessment to engage students in more productive use of feedback is seen as counter-productive since any intervention can be seen as interfering "with whatever tendency students might have to engage in academic activities", hence "instead of trying to get students to do what we want, we look only for ways of not encouraging them to do what we do not want" (Becker et al., 1968, p. 138). The recommendation therefore is to avoid assessment design which rewards overly-simplistic uses of feedback, rather than explicitly attempting to reward desired behaviours. This recommendation to trust students to do the right thing is perhaps telling of a time before mass higher education, where it was enough to simply encourage those rare students who came with positive attitudes towards learning. Today's system may require more explicit attempts to redress the dominance of transmission models of learning. However, Becker et al.'s recommendation is included here as a final thought to simply pose the question of whether or not it is appropriate for recommendations to improve feedback to take as their premise that students might actually use feedback well if only it was detached from coercive assessment practices.

Whether assessment is seen as getting in the way of students using feedback or as being a lever tutors can use to encourage students to engage, there is general consensus that current assessment practice is a poor match for the type of feedback practice which is desired. Similarly, there are differences in the role of the tutor in feedback, from doing no harm through to satisfying a consumer or scaffolding tacit knowledge, but the consensus is that the tutor does play an important role: feedback can no longer be understood as information given to a student, feedback as a definition must now consider the environment in which the information is shared and the resultant actions students take. These changes provide an important opportunity to refocus higher education on learning (Falchikov & Boud, 2007), so any recommendation must have a clear focus on how it seeks to improve learning rather than performance or satisfaction.

A MODEL FOR SELF-REGULATED LEARNING

Any categorisation of feedback will miss some of the subtleties and overlaps of categories, but with so many similar terms it is important to try make these distinctions. It would therefore be preferable to think of feedback as describing a category of learner interactions. Rather than thinking about good feedback, prompt feedback or poor feedback, thinking of feedback as a category of learner interaction enables a more nuanced evaluation. This also draws out any implicit assumptions about what is meant by 'learning'. Self-regulated learning was the assumption in this chapter since this matches with more ambitious intentions of Higher Education. This has been used to create the table below, in which different types of feedback are positioned according to their implied learner role and the likely outcome of that interaction as seen from a self-regulated learning perspective. Other tables could be created for other learning assumptions. For example, a learning environment such as a production line would reject the self-regulation goals since consistency to an external standard would be much more important. In this way, it can be seen that evaluating feedback as good or bad must draw out the learning assumptions behind such judgements. A 'good' appraisal might be 'poor' dialogue, so knowing the likely outcome of feedback for a particular goal is useful when judging feedback.

An everyday definition of feedback emphasises the transmission of knowledge from tutor to learner, with the learner being a relatively passive recipient. Using the more precise vocabulary outlined in this chapter, such feedback could be described either as transmissive feedback or dangling data. Such feedback is very unlikely to lead to anything that a constructivist might call learning, nor will it help a learner to develop independence from their tutor. This is because the transmitted information is only used in a limited context, with the learner not understanding for themselves how to improve. In more everyday language, this type of feedback might be more usefully thought of as 'correction'.

When a learner takes this correction and uses it to make improvements beyond the context of that immediate correction, the outcome is closer to what might be called learning. In the vocabulary introduced in this chapter, this type of feedback would best be described as feedforward. The learner is still a recipient of transmitted knowledge or correction, but has either been helped to generalise from this or has done so for themselves. Using feedback in this way shows at least some understanding on the part of the learner, and that they are willing to act upon the feedback. In the majority of cases, this will enable the learner to improve their short-term performance and might even inform reflection on more general approaches.

Other types of feedback require that the learner take a more active role. This requires not just understanding feedback which is given by their tutor, but learners proactively seeking specific feedback. Tied into this is a notion of judgement, that the learner will be able to consider the relevance and quality of the feedback as they decide on their next steps. This may well simply lead to short-term improvements as many learners might only want feedback which helps them to pass an assessment. However, students taking an active role involves them in understanding for themselves the quality of their work and the desired standard. This would therefore suggest that improving longer-term approaches is the more likely outcome since the learner is starting to regulate their own learning, making them less dependent on their tutor.

This same outcome of improving long-term approaches might also be achieved by learners taking a co-creator role, either being scaffolded through the process by a tutor or taking the lead in the feedback conversation. This is what distinguishes dialogic feedback from sustainable feedback, and the different likely outcomes. Whereas dialogic feedback has a long-term benefit and demands a more engaged learner in the feedback process, the intention of that feedback is still on helping the learner to understand

Table 1. Feedback

		Likely Outcome of Feedback			
		Little Effect	**Improves Short-Term Performance**	**Improves Long-Term Approaches**	**Improves Self-Evaluation Skills**
Learner's Relationship to Knowledge	**Recipient**	Transmissive feedback Dangling data	Feedforward	Feedforward	
	Initiator			Dialogic feedback	Sustainable feedback
	(Co) Producer			Dialogic feedback Sustainable feedback	Sustainable feedback

the concept of quality held by their tutor or their professional community. The intention to take a more critical approach to these concepts of quality distinguishes sustainable feedback from dialogic feedback, since the eventual aim is that the learner will be independent and have their own personal understanding of quality and how to achieve it. Sustainable feedback is therefore far more likely to focus on developing learners' self-evaluation skills, so the tutor becomes just one of the sources a learner uses to inform and calibrate their own self-evaluation as they come to regulate their own learning (Table 1).

An example from the author's own practice, teaching academic writing, may be helpful. Much of the feedback given to learners in this subject is correction or transmission of a tutor's knowledge. The immediate risk is therefore that this will become dangling data, that corrections will be ignored and the same mistakes occur. There is also a risk of this only informing short-term improvements as a limited form of feedforward in which corrections are only used on that particular assignment. Very similar, or even the same, errors may reappear in future assignments or even future drafts of the same assignment.

Other learners will infer strategies from this feedback, changing their overall approach. This might initially lead to other errors, such as awkward phrasing as a learner emphatically avoids pronouns, but will typically inform some change in the learner's overall approach which effectively addresses a particular issue in their academic writing. Multiple feedback loops might reinforce the success of a learner's new approach, so that in time it becomes habit. This would still be classed as feedforward, since the change comes from the tutor both diagnosing a problem and recommending a solution.

Some learners take up the invitation to request specific feedback, or are prompted to do so by mis-understanding the corrections offered by their tutor. For example, a learner might question feedback which seems to contradict feedback from another tutor or want to know the reasons behind corrections. Learners might also come with the knowledge that they have certain areas which they need to improve and regard this as important, so request feedback in these areas.

In this example, these learners would be engaging with dialogic feedback or sustainable feedback. If their objective was to improve their understanding of their faults and remedy them, then this would be dialogic feedback since the purpose of the dialogue is still mostly remedial. However, students might also take a more genuine interest in understanding the ideas behind the feedback: why do some tutors recommend active voice and others passive? As students discuss the concept of academic writing, the dialogue opens up flaws and contradictions not just in their own understanding but in that of their tutor. Learners come to understand that even if there are clear wrong answers, this does not mean there is a single right answer. This would be an example of sustainable feedback, which must be the ultimate intention of any feedback which seeks to develop self-regulated learning. The learner has come to understand the values of their tutors and peers, but has gone beyond this by integrating these with their own personal values.

FUTURE RESEARCH DIRECTIONS

Considerably more is written about what students think about or want from feedback than what they actually do with feedback, presumably because students typically do so little with feedback. Evaluating how feedback is used also raises methodological problems, since the use of feedback is most readily observed in assessment but using assessment as a data source takes for granted a narrow conception of feedback as the servant of assessment, whereas the central argument of this chapter has been that feedback needs to be reconceptualised as the servant of learning. Recommendations for what students should do with feedback therefore have a much narrower evidence base to draw upon, since it becomes difficult to identify excellent students without relying on their performance in assessments. Carless (2015) had access to excellent tutors through their winning of awards, but there is no comparable award for students other than the achievement of excellent grades. One important future direction for research on feedback might simply therefore be to find ways of identifying and rewarding students who make excellent use of feedback for their learning, thereby giving a new subject of research and helping to move the literature beyond simply looking at how feedback is used in assessed tasks or what students think about their feedback.

Survey-based research into feedback will also need to be sensitive to the different models of feedback which their participants might hold, and which models could be implied by their choice of survey item. The author's own research found, for example, that questions related to student satisfaction with feedback were excellent quick proxies to judge whether or not feedback was effectively supporting learning, but that these questions did not help to explain what type of feedback was helpful to different students (Author, 2015b). It is therefore important that survey-based research differentiates between survey items which are useful proxies and those which are useful outcomes. Hence, whilst it might be quick, cheap and easy to measure the promptness of feedback, it is far more important to understand what students see as the intent behind feedback.

Finally, future research needs to carefully consider the terminology used to describe different models of feedback. Over the last ten years, terms such as sustainable feedback, feedback for learning and feedforward have sought to challenge over-simplified understandings of feedback, emphasising that it is not just about giving information and challenging the everyday definition of feedback. However, the phrasing of these has strong positive connotations which can limit critique since no academic would reject the idea of their feedback being 'for learning', 'sustainable' or taking their students 'forwards'. Even attempts to describe feedback models starting from good practice, such as in Carless (2015), are drawn into implied value judgements by summarising some of these practices as 'traditional' whilst others are labelled as 'sustainable'. The research literature would benefit from agreeing terms for different models of feedback, but more importantly needs to be able to find the language to critique these models so that they can be challenged, amended and delineated. Currently, it is difficult to even discuss the differences between sustainable feedback, learning-oriented feedback, dialogic feedback, self-regulating feedback and feedback for learning, so it is even more difficult to explain which model is most appropriate for a particular setting.

CONCLUSION

Changing feedback requires changing assessment, or at least attitudes to assessment. As Sambell et al. (2012) point out, even those students most focused on learning for the long-term will recognise opportunity costs in how they devote their efforts. Although there will be students who appreciate the importance of sustainable feedback, they will therefore be incentivised to change approaches if they feel that it is necessary for their assessment. Ramsden (1992) argued that assessment formed a de facto curriculum for students, that what they learnt was driven not by learning goals but by what was assessed and how it was assessed. This influence can be seen to underpin students' use of feedback, that whatever broader learning goals students might have, the assessment will by necessity become the most important consideration. As Falchikov and Boud (2007) put it, assessment needs to be rethought as if learning were important. So too must feedback be rethought to drive learning, rather than student engagement, performance or satisfaction.

Alternatively, this chapter has argued that there is still significant work to do in defining clearly delineated models of feedback. Academic staff who are unable to influence assessment practice might therefore usefully invest some time in thinking about which of these models will be most supportive of learning in their context, even if they are constrained by assessment practices or an instrumentalist culture. Tips for practitioners are undoubtedly helpful, but the discussion of different feedback models in this chapter has emphasised that it is the intent of feedback that most determines its effectiveness. It is therefore crucial for practitioners to find a model of feedback where they feel comfortable with the spirit of the approach, since changing feedback practices should be the start of a fundamental change in their approach to learning and teaching.

REFERENCES

Askew, S., & Lodge, C. (2000). Gifts, ping-pong and loops – linking feedback and learning. In S. Askew (Ed.), *Feedback for learning* (pp. 1–18). London: Routledge Falmer.

Bailey, R., & Garner, M. (2010). Is the feedback in higher education assessment worth the paper it is written on? Teachers' reflections on their practices. *Teaching in Higher Education, 15*(2), 187–198. doi:10.1080/13562511003620019

Becker, H. S., Geer, B. S., & Hughes, E. C. (1968). *Making the grade: The academic side of college life.* New Jersey: Transaction publishers.

Biggs, J., & Tang, C. (2011). *Teaching for quality learning at university: What the student does* (4th ed.). Maidenhead: Open University Press.

Bland, M., & Gallagher, P. (2009). The impact of a change to assessment policy on students from a New Zealand School of Nursing. *Nurse Education Today, 29*(7), 722–730. PMID:19327874

Bloxham, S., & Boyd, P. (2007). *Developing assessment in higher education: A practical guide.* Maidenhead: Open University Press.

Bloxham, S., Boyd, P., & Orr, S. (2011). Mark my words: The role of assessment criteria in UK higher education grading practices. *Studies in Higher Education, 36*(6), 655–670. doi:10.1080/03075071003777716

Bloxham, S., & Campbell, L. (2010). Generating dialogue in assessment feedback: Exploring the use of interactive cover sheets. *Assessment & Evaluation in Higher Education, 35*(3), 291–300. doi:10.1080/02602931003650045

Bodman, S. (2007). *The power of feedback in professional learning. (EdD)*. London: University of London.

Bols, A., & Wicklow, K. (2013). Feedback - what students want. In S. Merry, M. Price, D. Carless, & M. Taras (Eds.), *Reconceptualising Feedback in Higher Education: Developing dialogue with students* (pp. 19–29). London: Routledge.

Boud, D. (2007). Reframing assessment as if learning were important. In N. Falchikov & D. Boud (Eds.), *Rethinking assessment in higher education: Learning for the longer term* (pp. 14–25). London: Routledge.

Boud, D., & Molloy, E. (2013). Rethinking models of feedback for learning: The challenge of design. *Assessment & Evaluation in Higher Education, 38*(6), 698–712. doi:10.1080/02602938.2012.691462

Bourdieu, P. (1990). *In other words: Essays towards a reflexive sociology*. Stanford, CA: Stanford University Press.

Brannon, L., & Knoblauch, C. H. (1982). On students' rights to their own texts: A model of teacher response. *College Composition and Communication, 33*(2), 157–166. doi:10.2307/357623

Carless, D. (2006). Differing perceptions in the feedback process. *Studies in Higher Education, 31*(2), 219–233. doi:10.1080/03075070600572132

Carless, D. (2015). *Excellence in University Assessment: Learning from Award-winning Practice*. London: Routledge.

Court, K. (2012). Tutor feedback on draft essays: Developing students' academic writing and subject knowledge. *Journal of Further and Higher Education, 38*(3), 327–345. doi:10.1080/0309877X.2012.706806

Covic, T., & Jones, M. K. (2008). Is the essay resubmission option a formative or a summative assessment and does it matter as long as the grades improve? *Assessment & Evaluation in Higher Education, 33*(1), 75–85. doi:10.1080/02602930601122928

Duncan, N. (2007). 'Feed-forward': Improving students' use of tutors' comments. *Assessment & Evaluation in Higher Education, 32*(3), 271–283. doi:10.1080/02602930600896498

Dysthe, O. (2011). 'What is the Purpose of Feedback when Revision is not Expected?' A Case Study of Feedback Quality and Study Design in a First Year Master's Programme. *Journal of Academic Writing, 1*(1), 135–142. doi:10.18552/joaw.v1i1.26

Entwistle, N. (2000). Approaches to studying and levels of understanding: the influences of teaching and assessment. In J. C. Smart (Ed.), *Higher Education: Handbook of Theory and Research* (Vol. XV, pp. 156–218). New York: Agathon.

Entwistle, N., Hanley, M., & Hounsell, D. (1979). Identifying distinctive approaches to studying. *Higher Education, 8*(4), 365–380. doi:10.1007/BF01680525

Falchikov, N., & Boud, D. (2007). *Rethinking assessment in higher education: learning for the longer term*. London: Routledge.

Floud, R. (2002). Policy implications of student non-completion: government, funding councils and universities. In M. Peelo & T. Wareham (Eds.), *Failing students in higher education* (pp. 56–69). Buckingham: Open University Press.

Fraser, S. P., & Bosanquet, A. M. (2006). The curriculum? That's just a unit outline, isn't it? *Studies in Higher Education, 31*(3), 269–284. doi:10.1080/03075070600680521

Gibbs, G., & Simpson, C. (2004). Conditions under which assessment supports students' learning. *Learning and teaching in higher education, 1*(1), 3-31.

Gravett, S., & Petersen, N. (2002). Structuring dialogue with students via learning tasks. *Innovative Higher Education, 26*(4), 281–291. doi:10.1023/A:1015833114292

Grice, H. (1975). In P. Cole & J. Morgan (Eds.), *Logic and Conversation* (Vol. 3, pp. 41–58). Syntax and semanticsNew York: Academic Press.

Horowitz, H. (1988). Campus life: Understanding cultural from the end of the eighteenth century to the present (2dfdc ed.). Chicago: University of Chicago Press.

Irons, A. (2010). An Investigation into the Impact of Formative Feedback on the Student Learning Experience [PhD]. Durham: Durham University. Retrieved from http://etheses.dur.ac.uk/890/

Jones, O., & Gorra, A. (2013). Assessment feedback only on demand: Supporting the few not supplying the many. *Active Learning in Higher Education, 14*(2), 149–161. doi:10.1177/1469787413481131

Knight, P., & Yorke, M. (2004). *Learning, curriculum and employability in higher education*. London: Routledge.

Marton, F., Hounsell, D., & Entwistle, N. (1984). *The Experience of learning*. Edinburgh: Scottish Academic Press.

Marton, F., & Saljo, R. (2005). Approaches to learning. In D. Hounsell (Ed.), The Experience of Learning: Implications for teaching and studying in higher education (3rd ed., pp. 39-58). Edinburgh: University of Edinburgh.

McGinty, S. (2007). First year Humanities and Social Science students' experiences of engaging with written feedback in a post-1992 university. (PhD). Wolverhampton: University of Wolverhampton. Retrieved from http://wlv.openrepository.com/wlv/bitstream/2436/210189/1/Mcginty%20Phd%20Thesis.docx

Nicol, D. (2010). From monologue to dialogue: Improving written feedback processes in mass higher education. *Assessment & Evaluation in Higher Education, 35*(5), 501–517. doi:10.1080/02602931003786559

Nicol, D. (2013). Resituating feedback from the reactive to the proactive. In D. Boud & E. Molloy (Eds.), *Feedback in higher and professional education: understanding it and doing it well* (pp. 34–49). London: Routledge.

Nicol, D., & Macfarlane-Dick, D. (2006). Formative assessment and self-regulated learning: A model and seven principles of good feedback practice. *Studies in Higher Education, 31*(2), 199–218. doi:10.1080/03075070600572090

Price, M. (2013). Student views on assessment: critical friend commentary. In L. Clouder, C. Broughan, S. Jewell, & G. Steventon (Eds.), *Improving Student Engagement and Development through Assessment: Theory and practice in higher education* (pp. 16–18). London: Routledge.

Price, M., Handley, K., Millar, J., & O'Donovan, B. (2010). Feedback: All that effort, but what is the effect? *Assessment & Evaluation in Higher Education, 35*(3), 277–289. doi:10.1080/02602930903541007

Quirk, R., & Smith, A. (1959). *The teaching of English*. London: Martin Secker & Warburg Ltd.

Ramsden, P. (1992). *Learning to teach in higher education*. London: Routledge. doi:10.4324/9780203413937

Sadler, D. R. (1989). Formative assessment and the design of instructional systems. *Instructional Science, 18*(2), 119–144. doi:10.1007/BF00117714

Sadler, D. R. (1998). Formative assessment: Revisiting the territory. *Assessment in Education: Principles, Policy & Practice, 5*(1), 77–84. doi:10.1080/0969595980050104

Sadler, D. R. (2010). Beyond feedback: Developing student capability in complex appraisal. *Assessment & Evaluation in Higher Education, 35*(5), 535–550. doi:10.1080/02602930903541015

Sambell, K., McDowell, L., & Montgomery, C. (2012). *Assessment for Learning in Higher Education*. London: Routledge.

Simpson, J., & Weiner, E. (Eds.). (1989). *The Oxford English Dictionary* (2nd ed.). Oxford: Clarendon Press.

Stevens, D. D., & Levi, A. J. (2011). *Introduction to rubrics: An assessment tool to save grading time, convey effective feedback, and promote student learning*. Sterling, Virginia: Stylus.

Stobart, G. (2008). *Testing times: the uses and abuses of assessment*. London: Routledge.

Stuart, M., Lido, C., & Morgan, J. (2012). Choosing a Student Lifestyle? Questions of Taste, Cultural Capital and Gaining a Graduate Job. In T. Hinton-Smith (Ed.), *Widening participation in higher education: casting the net wide?* (pp. 129–145). Basingstoke: Palgrave Macmillan. doi:10.1057/9781137283412.0015

The University of Edinburgh. (2015). Enhancing feedback. Retrieved from www.tla.ed.ac.uk/feedback/index.html

Weaver, M. R. (2006). Do students value feedback? Student perceptions of tutors' written responses. *Assessment & Evaluation in Higher Education, 31*(3), 379–394. doi:10.1080/02602930500353061

Wiener, N. (1954). *The human use of human beings: Cybernetics and society*. Boston: Houghton Mifflin.

Wiggins, G. (1989). A true test: Towards more authentic and equitable forms of assessment. *Phi Delta Kappan, 70*(9), 703–713.

Wiliam, D. (2011). *Embedded formative assessment*. Bloomington, IN: Solution Tree Press.

Wilson, A. (2015). An Exploration of Tutor Feedback on Essays and the Development of a Feedback Guide. *European Journal of Open, Distance and E-Learning*.

Yang, M., & Carless, D. (2012). The feedback triangle and the enhancement of dialogic feedback processes. *Teaching in Higher Education*, 2012, 1–13.

KEY TERMS AND DEFINITIONS

Dangling Data: Coined by Sadler, a term which emphasises information given which is intended by the giver to be feedback. However, this information is not used effectively by the recipient, so rather than feeding on it is left 'dangling'.

Dialogic Feedback: Feedback which significantly involves the learner in its production, attempting to be responsive to their needs and desires and giving the learner agency in directing the feedback.

Feedforward: A contested term, but generally used to mean feedback which has had an influence on the performance of a future task, contrasted against feeding 'back' into a learner's more general ways of operating.

Learning-Oriented Feedback/Feedback for Learning: Feedback which aims to have a direct, far-reaching and longer-term impact on learning, rather than specific and shorter-term (as in *feedforward*) or influencing other learner behaviours, such as managerial feedback or appraisal which might focus more on effort than learning.

Prompt/Timely Feedback: A measure of how quickly feedback is given to learners after the completion of a task. Prompt is usually taken to mean within two weeks, whereas timely emphasises the return of feedback in time for the student to use it before a graded assessment.

Student Satisfaction: A measure used to evaluate courses and institutions, in terms of feedback it emphasises the importance of the learner seeing their feedback as useful and usable. The measure is typically either taken from a direct statement about satisfaction with feedback or is a composite of statements related to whether or not the feedback was timely enough, gave enough information, or was clear enough to understand.

Sustainable Feedback: Practices which tutors can use consistently through the year might be described as sustainable in that their demands on time do not make them too onerous, but more than this is an emphasis on feedback helping students in developing their own self-regulation skills so that they can generate a kind of internal feedback or reflection, thereby ensuring that the benefits of feedback are sustained beyond formal education.

Tacit: Knowledge which cannot easily be explained or articulated, or by its very nature might be impossible to articulate. Tacit might relate to subject knowledge or expert judgement, for example in helping to explain that assessment involves an element of connoisseurship and cannot be made fully transparent or routine. Feedback aiming to develop tacit knowledge will therefore be obliged to take a slower, more dialogic approach.

Chapter 2
Assessment for Learning:
Feeding Back and Feeding Forward

Zineb Djoub
Abdelhamid Ibn Badis University of Mostaganem, Algeria

ABSTRACT

To support students, make effective use of feedback to improve their learning, this chapter provides practical tips and strategies for teachers to stimulate their students' interest in feedback, assimilate its significant role and get involved in interpreting, reflecting and acting upon feedback comments. The author focuses on both summative and formative feedback. For summative feedback, one's concern is to encourage students to interpret grades/marks, reflect upon them and transform them into plans and actions. This is through using reflective worksheets and other post-exam tasks in class which are designed by the author. Feedback within self, peer and group assessment approaches is also concerned in this chapter. Other kinds of reflective worksheets are suggested to be used to reflect on the student learning process as part of the student portfolio, journal or set separately, in addition to the use of technology, i.e., class blogs to enhance such reflection.

INTRODUCTION

Assessment as an educational practice plays an important role in shaping students' future. Its washback may contribute to building up their beliefs and attitudes towards learning thereby acting either as a driving engine that pushes students towards success, or as a demotivating source which impedes their progress. Yet, within pedagogy for autonomy assessment is considered not only as a tool for measuring learners' achievement, but also improving the quality of their learning. Within such culture, students are active agents in the assessment process who make judgments about their own work and that of others, monitor their progress and make decisions to improve.

Feedback is an important component of the assessment process upon which students learning can be enhanced. It reflects how much learning has been achieved thus indicating the effectiveness and efficiency of the teaching process. Nevertheless, within traditional assessment contexts where the focus is on testing knowledge and comprehension at the end of a given course, feedback remains limited to marks

DOI: 10.4018/978-1-5225-0531-0.ch002

or grades which might not mirror students' process and progress in learning. Yet, with the increasing need to promote an assessment for learning culture in higher education feedback's goals and processes need to go beyond grading practices to support the development of student autonomy. In such contexts, both self-assessment (internal feedback) and teacher feedback (external feedback) should help achieve this objective.

In fact, it is necessary for students to process their teacher feedback to understand their mistakes, reflect on their learning needs and take actions to improve it. Whether it is reflecting negative or positive comments, feedback need not be viewed as an end in itself referring to passing or failing. Rather, it should be considered a source of learning and making progress. Therefore, to help students get that potential, this chapter suggests teaching ideas and strategies that aim to encourage students interpret their teacher's feedback and act to close the learning gap. But, before introducing them there is a need to clarify for teachers what feedback and quality feedback mean to make from assessment practices more effective.

A DEFINITION OF FEEDBACK

In fact, feedback can be defined from various perspectives. For Hattie and Timperley (2007), it refers to "information provided by an agent with respect to one's performance or understanding" (p.81). However, feedback can include the consequences of performance since "a teacher or parent can provide corrective information, a peer can provide an alternative strategy, a book can provide information to clarify ideas, a parent can provide encouragement, and a learner can look up the answer to evaluate the correctness of a response (Hattie & Timperley, 2007, p.81). Moreover, feedback needs to serve other purposes as Philpott (2009) explains:

Feedback is the information communicated to a student in regard to their understanding of shared learning objectives of a given task against an agreed set of criteria. This information will include guidance on how to improve. Feedback is the information that is relayed to the student about their progress and can be based upon a variety of forms of evidence including: marked work, un-graded teacher checked worked, oral contribution, practical displays, draft work and re-drafted work. (Philpott, 2009, pp. 73-74)

It follows from this definition that, providing feedback does not mean only telling students about their learning performance, thereby revealing their progress on the basis of collected evidence, but it also includes communicating and clarifying assessment criteria and learning objectives of a given task. In this respect, Brown and Knight (1994) claim that "worthwhile feedback is related to the clarity of assessment criteria" (p. 114). Besides, feedback needs to show to students what is required from them to improve their actual performance as Ramaprasad (1983) definition of feedback indicates: "Feedback is information about the gap between the actual level and the reference level of a system parameter to alter the gap in some way" (p.04).

It is worth noting, however, that feedback does not only concern students' performance. Teachers as well need to obtain feedback from their colleagues and students about their teaching, in order to improve it and enhance students' learning. This is through engaging in what Stanley (1999) labels 'reflective dialogue' as he states: "a reflective and investigative dialogue with another person who listened well and asked important questions helped teachers to re-shape the quality of their own inner dialogue" (p.119).

In addition to that, feedback can concern teachers/test-developers in order to evaluate their assessment practices as Bachman and Palmer (2010) put forward:

Feedback is information from administering the assessment that the test developer can use to confirm or revise the original Design Statement and Blueprint and to make changes in the assessment tasks themselves. Some of this information will be about how the assessment achieves the purpose for which it was intended, and some will be about real world considerations, especially in the use of resources. (Bachman & Palmer, 2010, p. 394)

Thus, feedback in this case is likely to reveal the problems with the assessment environment, assessment procedures, the clarity of the instruction and language input of the test's task(s), besides test-takers beliefs and attitudes towards assessment (i.e., washback). This kind of feedback can be obtained through observations, self-reporting of test-takers, interviews with test administrators, etc. (Bachman & Palmer, 2010).

It can be concluded that, feedback's objective determines its content, the persons concerned as well as the means through which it can be obtained. Therefore, there is no clear cut definition for this concept. Still, one accepts that feedback refers to collected information on the basis of certain evidence (exams, observations, interviews, etc.) about the actual state of learning progress and rate of achievement; teaching and assessment practices, their effectiveness and impact on students' learning process and outcome. This is through referring to internal goals or standards, reference level; norms of teaching as well as assessment practices. Yet, the kind of feedback that is of more interest for the present chapter is the one communicated to students in regard to their learning process, outcome within a given course, or what is referred here as teacher feedback.

TEACHER FEEDBACK

Teacher feedback has been regarded as a vital concept in language teaching and learning and a source of learners' motivation within (Weiner, 1990). Indeed, there has been a common consensus upon its benefit on learners (Bitchener, 2008; Leki, 1991). In this respect, Falchikov (1995) suggests that "positive feedback reinforces positive action while negative feedback can cause self-devaluative responses and interfere the information of feedback" (p. 158). She also added that negative feedback may also cause anxiety in students. It follows from this, that receiving feedback is related to the affective aspect of learning or as Higgins (2000) states: "receiving feedback is also an emotional business" (p. 4).

In fact, teacher's feedback can have a negative washback effect on students' learning beliefs and attitudes. In this respect, Djoub's (2013) research has shown that students who received a negative feedback believed that the educational system is hard and that their teachers are severe, besides maintaining that studying at university is boring and achievement is far from their reach. Holding such beliefs, students are unlikely to take the initiative to learn by themselves and make further efforts to improve their performance. Thus, teacher's feedback plays an important role in shaping students' learning beliefs and attitudes. It can act either as a motivating engine that drives students towards success or a de-motivating source that impedes their progress.

Moreover, teacher's feedback helps students "check their internal construction of goals, criteria and standards" (Nicol & Milligan, 2006, p. 68). In doing so, it can guide their self-regulation and assessment of learning. This can contribute to the development of their autonomy in learning. Therefore, providing positive feedback which can enhance learning and improvement is among the primary goal of teachers as well as researchers in the field of ELT.

Quality Feedback

Within both summative and formative assessment, good quality feedback contributes to students' learning, rather than dampening it down. To this end, it needs to be both directive, telling the student what needs to be fixed or revised as well as facilitative, providing comments and suggestions to help guide them in their own revision and conceptualization (Shut, 2007). It should be the teacher's source for providing guidance and support along with students' learning. This is through raising their awareness of their strengths and weaknesses, indicating meanwhile their progress and the deficiencies in their own learning. Good quality feedback is thus "information that helps students trouble-shoot their own performance and self-correct; that is, it helps the students take action to reduce the discrepancy between their intentions and the resulting effects" (Nicol & Macfarlane-Dick, in press).

Moreover, good quality feedback needs to communicate explicitly to students the goals, criteria and expected standards of a given task. This can include information about errors, the missing information, neatness or format of that task (Brookhart, 2008). Indeed, students cannot reflect on their learning progress, identify the learning gap and take decisions to improve unless they understand what the required performance entails. Therefore, to help them learn from their mistakes and become better processors of information, teachers need to give them clear, structured feedback according to the assignment's goals, criteria and standards (Gibbs, 2006). Also, Gipps (1994) suggests in order for students to improve, they must have a notion of the desired standards and compare actual performance with the desired performance. For instance, providing students with exemplars of performance with attached feedback has proved to be a powerful approach since it involves students in comparing their performance with the task standards and goals (Orsmond et al., 2002). It has been also claimed that students need to receive feedback at the beginning of their studies because delaying its provision might be detrimental as Mauranen's (1994) study shows.

Understanding the tasks goals, criteria and standards is a prerequisite for engaging in reflection and self-assessment. Yet, feedback does not only concern the task, but also the processing of the task and self-regulation (Hattie & Timperley, 2007). Using portfolios, for instance, requires students' reflection on their learning and collection of work that meets the defined standards. To accomplish such a process teacher's need to provide feedback that clarifies such standards and show clearly the process of completing them, thereby allowing students to hold control on what materials to select, how to present them and reflect regularly on them. Meanwhile, giving students information regarding how they monitor and control their learning (self-regulation) is likely to encourage them to engage in this process and develop their self-confidence, thus getting more willing to expends efforts to deal with feedback (Brookhart, 2008).

Furthermore, since "the purpose of feedback is to help a person to improve what he or she is doing" (Brown et al., 1997, p.04), it has to be useful and acceptable to the receiver. To meet these criteria, "feedback has to be timely, clear, focused upon the attainable and expressed in a way which will encourage a person to think and, if he or she thinks that is necessary to change" (Brown et al.,

1997, p.04). Thus, it needs to prompt students' reflection over their learning process and results in decision making and taking for the sake of improving it. In short, it needs to lead to actions as Boud (2000) notes: "Unless students are able to use the feedback to produce improved work through for example, re-doing the same assignment, neither they nor those giving the feedback will know that it has been effective" (p.158).

Hence, supporting students' learning also entails considering affective factors. Therefore, good quality feedback needs to have a positive effect on students' motivational beliefs and self-esteem. A positive feedback, however, does not entail describing the work as good when it is not. It is rather describing how the strengths in a student's work match the criteria for good work and how those strengths show what h/she is learning, besides pointing out where improvement is needed and suggesting what could be done about it (Brookhart, 2008). It follows from this, that feedback needs to focus on the process of learning including efforts and strategic behaviors instead of being concerned with the person's ability or intelligence as Black and Wiliam (1998) maintain: "feedback which draws attention away from the task and towards self-esteem can have a negative effect on attitudes and performance" (p. 23). This is because providing feedback about the person (e., g, you are an intelligent student) can lead the student to think that intelligence is fixed and so achievement is beyond his/her control while giving information about the process is likely to instill beliefs that achievement depends on specific efforts and strategies which lie under the student's control (Brookhart, 2008).

Additionally, to generate a motivational effect from feedback its language should be handled with care by teachers. Even in case of good performance, if the student is expecting a positive word like 'excellent' and h/she receives 'very good' this may lead to questioning. So, quality feedback needs to be descriptive rather than evaluative which means showing the gap between the student actual performance and the goals, criteria and standards which define the academic competence (Wiggins, 2001). This is through providing more details in feedback rather than limiting it to adjectives. Still, feedback needs to be focused and reflect the learning intentions or objectives for a particular piece of work.

In fact, there is now a common consensus that "feedback without marks leads to better learning than marks only, or even than marks with feedback" (Gibbs, 2006, p. 27). Indeed, research has shown that grading student performance has less effect than feedback comments because it leads students to compare themselves against others (ego involvement) rather than to focus on the difficulties in the task and on making efforts to improve (task-involvement (Butler, 1987). Feedback given as grades has also been shown to have especially negative effects on the self-esteem of low ability students (Craven, et al., 1991). Thus, since the focus of formative assessment is on the learning process rather than the outcome, teachers' use of feedback comments is advocated. Students can be invited to guess the scores or grades out of those comments.

Nevertheless, an effective feedback must be understood and internalized by the student before it can be used productively. Thus, in addition to making their hand writings clear and so legible teachers need to ensure that students can construct meaning from the provided feedback. To this end, feedback needs to involve students in dialogue with their teacher about that feedback so that they can get an immediate response about their difficulties, develop their understanding and expectations to standards and so decide what to do to close the learning gap. When providing one-to-one feedback, it is necessary that students have the opportunity to ask, inquire and seek for more clarification. Also, teachers can sometimes give feedback to groups of students and discuss it so that each student can learn from the other's mistakes and realize that s/he is not the only one who makes mistakes.

In effect, encouraging peer feedback is prerequisite to promote student's autonomy since the teacher here is not the 'all-knowing ideal type of a teacher' (Aviram, 2000), but rather s/he is the facilitator who promotes students' discussion, exchange of opinions, construction of new meaning and shows them how to make use of such interaction to improve their learning. There is a need to provide opportunities for students to review their peer's work and provide feedback in a form of dialogue. This is because the process of reviewing someone else's work can help learners reflect on and articulate their own views and ideas, ultimately improving their own work (Dunlap & Grabinger, 2003)

This implies that good feedback practice is a stimulus for dialogue interaction and reflection on the process of learning, generating thus a response on the part of students to close the learning gap and improve their performance as Boud (2000) notes:

The only way to tell if learning results from feedback is for students to make some kind of response to complete the feedback loop (Sadler, 1989). This is one of the most forgotten aspects of formative assessment. Unless students are able to use the feedback to produce improved work, through for example, re-doing the same assignment, neither they nor those giving the feedback will know that it has been effective. (Boud, 2000, p.158)

Accordingly, feedback needs to help students understand their mistakes, reflect on their needs, make plans and decisions to improve, thus preparing them for the next assignment. Hill and Hawk (2000) identify this as 'feed forward' and argue that it should be "directly related to and should build on the feedback that has been given" (p.07). To help students make effective use of feedback, there is a need for:

- Providing feedback on work on progress and involving them in planning strategies for improvement (Nicol & Milligan, 2006). This means that there are cases where feedback should be provided while the students' work is being undertaken.
- Teachers can also send their feedback via emails so that students can read it again as well as file it.
- Giving students time to absorb and act upon or consolidate the feedback comments.
- Resubmission of the students' work. Providing students with the chance to revise their work, re-do it and resubmit it allows them to work out the meaning of the teacher's feedback and learn from their mistakes.
- Giving students reflective worksheets on their teacher feedback asking them about their own interpretation of and opinions about that feedback, how they need to improve their performance, thereby prompting them to think about what strategies to select.
- Supporting them with a checklist which relates to the task at hand, so that they can revise their work before their submission.
- Discussing their work in groups before submitting them and providing oral feedback.

In addition to that, an effective feedback does not only entail providing information to students about their learning and encouraging them to reflect over it and improve, but it also guides teacher's practices and helps them to understand how students proceed along this process. Indeed, teachers need to obtain regular feedback about students' learning through using different assessment tools, e.g., diagnostic tests, portfolios, etc. "The act of assessing has an effect on the assessor as well as the student. Assessors learn about the extent to which they [students] have developed expertise and can tailor their teaching accordingly" (Yorke, 2003, p.482). Thus, an effective feedback also needs to communicate to teachers relevant information that can help them track their students' learning progress and refine their teaching and assessment practices accordingly.

To achieve this objective, teachers need to talk to students about the quality of feedback to get valuable information about its effectiveness. They can also ask them about the feedback they would like when they make an assignment submission. Observation and questionnaire can be used to elicit such data. Besides, continuous evaluation of the feedback is necessary to find out whether it contributes to students' learning, improvement, motivation, autonomy and makes the classroom a place where feedback, including constructive criticism, is valued and viewed as productive (Brookhart,2008).

SUPPORTING STUDENTS TO MAKE EFFECTIVE USE OF FEEDBACK

"A response to feedback should be expected as long as the teacher's comments are brief, clearly written and easy for the learner to understand" (Suffolk County Council, 2001, p.24). As teachers give feedback on students' work, it is crucial that students' responses to the feedback are fed back to teachers as a heuristic to help them develop reflective and effective feedback practices. But, even in cases where constructive feedback is provided students may not use it to improve their learning owing to their lack of awareness, willingness or skills to articulate that feedback. Thus, to make from assessment more effective whether it is summative or formative there is a need to support students make effective use of feedback to improve their learning.

In effect, feedback needs to be conceived by students as a gate leading to their improvement and self-confidence instead of viewing it as an end in itself, reflecting either their success or failure. To increase students' interest in feedback, teachers need to raise their awareness of the importance of processing feedback to learn more about their strengths and weaknesses in relation to a specific course, then plan and take decisions to improve their performance. So, it needs to be considered as a stimulus for evaluating their learning process and outcome. In cases where it is conveying a criticism, feedback remains a source of learning which does not intend to demotivate or lower students' self-esteem but rather to motivate and prompt them to learn from their mistakes, their teachers' and peers' comments. In case it is congratulating students, further efforts are always required to make from success an intrinsic experience which goes beyond just passing. Teachers also need to encourage them to process feedback through rewarding those who transformed it into effective plan and actions, thus having improved their performance.

To help students assimilate the significant role of feedback, teachers need to provide them with opportunities to learn from its comments. Still, there is a need to teach them from the outset how to use effectively these comments. Indeed, as Sadler's (1989) observation show for students to be able to compare actual performance with a standard and take action to close the gap, then they must already possess some of the same evaluative skills as their teacher. To help students develop these skills one is suggesting the following strategies and teaching tips to use with students within both summative and formative assessment.

Summative Assessment

To stimulate students' interest in working out their teacher's feedback of exams, there is a need as well to clarify what this process entails. To illustrate, teachers can provide their students with the following figure which indicates its stages (figure 1).

Figure 1. The Stages of Processing Feedback

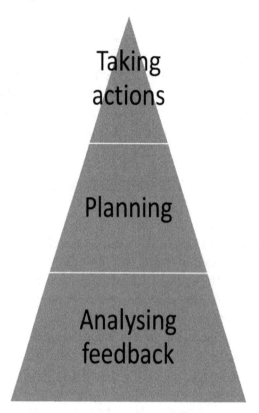

Analyzing teachers' feedback involves interpreting the mark/grade and its corresponding comment. To help them achieve this stage, teachers can provide them with questions that help prompt such interpretation. These can, for instance, include:

- What are the key words in the feedback comments?
- What mistakes or deficiencies these comments are addressing?
- What piece of advice is advocated?
- How does the grade/mark relate to the grading scale?
- How do these comments relate to my performance?
- What kind of knowledge/skills are reflected by the feedback comments?

To support students, answer those questions, teachers can use the following worksheet which can be handed to students immediately after obtaining their mark and attending the exam correction in class. Still, it needs to be noted that prior to engaging them in such a task, teachers should clarify the assessment criteria and the required performance of that exam (Figure 2).

After understanding their teacher's feedback, students need to act to close the learning gap. To this end, they can be asked to:

Figure 2. Reflective worksheet for interpreting teacher's summative feedback

> - According to my teacher's feedback :
>   - The Do's ✓ are:
>
>   ....
>
>   - The Don'ts ✪ are:
>
>   ....
>
> - I would not have had this grade/mark and comments if I did not...
>
> - I did not do well at/when......................................
>
> - I was quite good at/when.......................................
>
> - I will do better next time if I................................

- Indicate their needs to improve their performance;
- State what mark and comments they want to get;
- Tell their teacher about the kind of support they need to improve;
- Plan for their actions through setting a schedule and the deadline to achieve their learning goals.

Students can evaluate their own learning progress through assessing their achievement of their own plans. Besides, they can compare their last received feedback with the previous one. Table.1 below can be used for this sake. In comparing their teacher's feedback of semester one and semester two, for instance, students indicate if there is any improvement in the second exam by crossing either yes or no. Those who have improved are asked to indicate how much improvement they have made through calculating the difference between the two marks: (mark2− mark1) x 100÷20. For example, if the student obtains in the first exam 10/20 while in the second exam of the same course s/he got 14/20, the rate of improvement is 20% (Table 1).

Hence, it is important for students to recognize the difference between their performance of the first exam and that of the second exam. They can, therefore, indicate here that difference through pointing out to the type of mistakes and errors they did in the first exam. Then, they can state the reason why they have improved, i.e., what plans and actions were more effective. In case there is no improvement or rather drawbacks, students can describe their performance referring to their weaknesses and stating why they have not achieved their learning goals.

Table 1. Comparing teacher's summative feedback

Any improvement	Yes No
Rate of improvement	%
Difference between performance 1 and performance 2	
Reason(s) behind that difference	

Formative Assessment

Teachers need to give students opportunities to hold control over their learning through the use of self-assessment approach. This is because it "teaches them where feedback comes from. They will learn the strategy at the same time as they learn how to improve their project, writing assignment, math problem solving, or whatever they are working on" (Brookhart,2008, p.60). Involving students, for instance, in writing portfolios allows them to reflect on their performance and the provided feedback, thereby relating them to the task goals and criteria and setting plans to improve their performance.

Within self-assessment, students can be involved in interpreting, reflecting and acting upon feedback comments. To interpret the latter, students need time in class to compare their performance with the required performance. They can be provided with the above questions to interpret formative assessment feedback. In addition to that, since this feedback may consist only of the teacher's comments, students can be asked about the kind of grade or mark which corresponds to that feedback. It needs to be noted that, in formative assessment more opportunities are to be provided for students to work out their teacher's feedback. This should be done on a regular basis to help students gain insight into their learning strengths and weaknesses in a given course. Conferences can be scheduled for this purpose where teachers need to listen to each student's interpretation and provide response, i.e., explanation, etc. Holding such dialogue enables them to clarify and justify more their feedback, thereby identifying the learning gap.

Furthermore, encouraging students to reflect on the received feedback comments is crucial to help them close the learning gap. This includes the student's description of his/her opinions and feelings towards teacher's feedback comments and indication as well of the learning needs and plans to achieve them. To do so, reflective worksheets can be provided to students to complete them after class. These worksheets can be kept as part of the student portfolio, journal or set separately. An illustration is provided below (Figure 3).

Acting upon feedback comments implies involving in actions in attempt to close the learning gap. Indeed, after interpreting and reflecting on these comments, students need to be encouraged to initiate and take an active role to improve their performance. For example, a student receiving a feedback comment indicating a deficiency in the use of punctuation and capitalization, s/he needs to practice more exercises on this topic and attach them to those reflective worksheets so that the teacher can relate her/his plans to that practice (there must be a connection between the two). To encourage them to submit their reflection along with their initiative for correction, teachers can reward students for their efforts.

Moreover, students can get trained into how to process formative feedback. This is by introducing them to examples of feedback comments which relate to the course and ask them to interpret and reflect on them, besides guessing how it needs to be worked out more effectively. Another alternative would be giving students examples of feedback's interpretations, reflection, decisions and plans intended to

Figure 3. Reflective worksheet for teachers' formative feedback

1) How was your performance?
   Very Good ☐ *Good* ☐ *Ok* ☐ *Poor* ☐
   Very Poor☐

2) Explain why ?...

3) Did you expect to get such feedback comments? *Yes* ☐ *No* ☐

4) Explain why? ....

5) How did you feel after getting them?

   ▪ Happy because I expected to get less.
   ▪ Satisfied because they reflect my performance.
   ▪ Disappointed; I was expecting a better performance.

6) What do you need to do to improve your performance?

7) Indicate how you think it needs to be done.

learn from them then asking them to guess the kind of feedback comments relative to them. This can be done in class (e.g., as a warm-up task) or assigned in groups as homework.

Hence, the reader can address the need to give grades in addition to teacher's comments. It should be stated, that providing grades or marks is not just limited to summative assessment forms, but teachers' need to provide them with formative assessment is also common to measure students' progress over time. Yet, grades may distract students from learning from feedback. Thus, since the objective of formative feedback is to contribute to students' learning, it is worth returning students' work with feedback comments without grades. But, the marks are written down in teacher's records and students can get them after submitting their feedback reflection and initiative. It is up to the teacher to decide whether s/he deserves extra points to improve the obtained mark.

Peer-feedback can also help achieve the above objective since it is likely to support students learn about what kind of feedback needs to be provided, in which cases, its way of delivery and articulation. To do so, peer-assessment needs to be integrated. Yet, training students into the process is required. Teachers need first to explain the benefit and purpose of reviewing another student's work and providing her/him with feedback. Then, they need to clarify the task objective, how to use the scoring rubrics, which errors to point out and how in the student's work. They can also give students the ground rules for peer editing to guide more their practices (see the example below). In pairs, students can peer edit each other, then engage in discussion to justify their feedback in relation to those rules (Figure 4).

Figure 4. Ground rules for peer editing, source: Brookhart, 2008, p. 70)

- Read your peer's work carefully.

- Compare the work with the rubric.

- Talk about the work, not the person.

- Don't judge (e.g., don't say, "That's bad");

  rather, describe what you think is good about

  the work and what's missing and could be

  done better.

- Make specific suggestions.

- Tell what you think, and then ask what the

  author thinks.

In the same concern, teachers can use peer-assessment of class presentations which is likely to stimulate students' interest and feeling of self-confidence. Students can record their views, comments and suggestions regarding the quality of their peers' presentations and discuss them later in groups. Time can be devoted to indicating what kind of feedback they found more constructive and how it can be used to improve future class presentations. Still, to structure their feedback and focus more their observation there is a need to familiarize students with the criteria or rubrics set for such presentations. This can be achieved by having them as a guide which they can refer to as they work on those presentations (Brookhart,2008) or using assignment return sheets. Students can also rely on the above ground rules to achieve this task.

Class blogs can also be used for peer-feedback. Students can post their feedback comments regarding their classmates' performance of projects' presentations in class. In turn, their classmates respond to their feedback through addressing questions to their teacher in relation to it. For instance, in case a student/ group of students got a feedback comments indicating that they had a problem in managing time and making their ideas coherent, their question can cover how to write a project outline for presentation and use efficiently the allotted time for performing. However, students need teachers' guidance regarding the kind of feedback comments to be provided. It is important that those comments need to be explicit (clear: using a simple language), relevant (constructive: supporting students to improve), besides students should be objective, i.e., honest and respectful in expressing them. Teachers can guide them with a set of questions such as:

- How did you find the project/its presentation?
- What have you learned from them?
- What remarks, advice or recommendations would you put forward for your classmates?

In addition to peer and self-assessment approach, teachers can help students learn to use feedback through providing them with opportunities to use it fairly as soon as they receive it. According to Brookhart (2008) this can be achieved by designing lessons which involve students in using feedback on previous work to produce better work. This is by using, for instance, a series of homework, quizzes and projects which provide them with feedback on how to work and prepare for the next assignment (Brookhart, 2008). Seminars can also support this aim as they provide opportunities for teachers to interact with students and discuss their feedback in case of large classes. Besides, teachers can use blogs to post their feedback on students' projects where they can post in turn their comments and views regarding the tasks.

Teachers need to understand how their students feel about and respond to their feedback, in addition to what they want as feedback in order to avoid using strategies that are counter-productive. There are those who seek for how to improve their work and get a better grade. Others react indifferently to detailed comments concerning their work, whereas there are students who consider feedback comments as crucial. Therefore, teachers need to get an idea about their students' learning styles and try to tailor their feedback accordingly (Brown & Knight, 1994).

CONCLUSION

Teacher's feedback can act as a powerful tool for students' reflection, plan and initiation to improve. To contribute to such effect, teachers need to be aware of what quality feedback means in order to know what, how and when it should be provided. Still, feedback quality does matter, but supporting students learn from it remains the key issue. Therefore, it is important that students process their teacher's feedback of both summative and formative assessment through interpreting its meaning and working towards closing the learning gap. To this end, teachers need to raise their awareness of the importance of engaging in that process and support them to do it more effectively. Teachers can refer to and use the worksheets and teaching ideas suggested in this chapter to involve their students in interpreting and reflecting on the feedback comments besides planning and taking actions to improve their future performance within summative and formative assessment approaches. Yet, maintaining dialogue with students is essential to decode and discuss feedback comments. Besides, assessment criteria, the goals and purposes of feedback should be explicit to students so that they can participate actively in the feedback process.

REFERENCES

Aviram, A. (2000). Beyond constructivism: Autonomy-oriented education. *Studies in Philosophy and Education, 19* (5-6), 465-489. Doi: :100526711174110.1023/A

Bachman, L., & Palmer, A. (2010). *Language assessment in practice*. Oxford: Oxford University Press.

Bitchener, J. (2008). Evidence in support of written corrective feedback. *Journal of Second Language Writing, 17*(2), 69–124. doi:10.1016/j.jslw.2007.11.004

Black, P., & William, D. (1998). Assessment and classroom learning. *Assessment in Education: Principles, Policy & Practice, 5*(1), 7–74. doi:10.1080/0969595980050102

Brookhart, S. M. (2008). *How to give effective feedback to your students*. USA: ASCD publications.

Brown, G., Bull, J., & Pendlebury, M. (1997). *Assessing students learning in higher education*. New York: Routledge.

Brown, S., & Knight, P. (1994). *Assessing learners in higher education*. London: Kogan.

Butler, R. (1987). Task-involving and ego-involving properties of evaluation: Effects of different feedback conditions on motivational perceptions, interest and performance. *Journal of Educational Psychology*, *78*(4), 210–216.

Craven, R. G., Marsh, H. W., & Debus, R. L. (1991). Effects of internally focused feedback on the enhancement of academic self-concept. *Journal of Educational Psychology*, *83*(1), 17–27. doi:10.1037/0022-0663.83.1.17

Djoub, Z. (2013). Assessment and students' autonomy in language learning. In Z. Arezki, H. Amziane & A. Guendouzi (Eds.), Studies in the teaching and learning of foreign languages in Algeria (pp.197-208). Tizi-Ouzou, Algeria: University of Mouloud Mammeri of Tizi-Ouzou.

Dunlap, J. C., & Grabinger, S. (2003). Preparing students for lifelong learning: A review of instructional features and teaching methodologies. *Performance Improvement Quarterly*, *1*(2), 6–25.

Falchikov, N. (1995). Improving feedback to and from students. In P. Knight (Ed.), *Assessment for learning in higher education. Staff and Educational Development Series* (pp. 157–166). London: Kogan Page.

Gibbs, G. (2006). How assessment frames student learning. In C. Bryan & K. Clegg (Eds.), *Innovative assessment in higher education* (pp. 23–36). New York: Routledge.

Gipps, C. (1994). *Beyond testing*. Washington, DC: Falmer Press.

Hattie, J., & Timperley, H. (2007). The power of feedback. *Review of Educational Research*, *77*(1), 181–112. doi:10.3102/003465430298487

Higgins, R. (2000, September 7-10). Be More Critical!: Rethinking assessment feedback. *Paper presented at the British Educational Research Association Conference*, Cardiff University.

Hill, J., & Hawk, K. (2000, November). Four Conceptual Clues to Motivating Students: learning from the practice of effective teachers in low-decile, multi-cultural schools. *Paper presented to the NZARE Conference*, Waikato.

Leki, I. (1991). The preferences of ESL students for error correction in college-level writing classes. *Foreign Language Annals*, *24*(3), 203–218. doi:10.1111/j.1944-9720.1991.tb00464.x

Mauranen, A. (1994). Two discourse worlds: Study genres in Britain and Finland. *FINLANCE. A Finnish Journal of Applied Linguistics*, 13, 1-40.

Nicol, D., & Milligan, C. (2006). Rethinking technology-supported assessment practices in relation to the seven principles of good feedback practice. In C. Bryan & K. Clegg (Eds.), *Innovative assessment in higher education* (pp. 64–77). New York: Routledge.

Nicol, D. J., & Macfarlane-Dick, D. (2004). *Rethinking formative assessment in HE: a theoretical model and seven principles of good feedback practice*. Higher Education Academy. Retrieved from: http://www-new1.heacademy.ac.uk/assets/documents/assessment/web0015_rethinking_formative_assessment_in_he.pdf

Orsmond, P., Merry, S., & Reiling, K. (2002). The use of formative feedback when using student derived marking criteria in peer and self-assessment. *Assessment & Evaluation in Higher Education, 27*(4), 309–323. doi:10.1080/0260293022000001337

Philpott, J. (2009). *Captivating your class: Effective Teaching skills*. UK: Antony Rowe.

Ramaprasad, A. (1983). On the definition of feedback. *Behavioral Science, 28*(1), 4–13. doi:10.1002/bs.3830280103

Sadler, D. R. (1989). Formative assessment and the design of instructional systems. *Instructional Science, 18*(2), 145–165. doi:10.1007/BF00117714

Shut, V. J. (2007). Focus on formative feedback. *Review of Educational Research, 78*(1), 153–189. doi:10.3102/0034654307313795

Stanley, C. (1999). Learning to think, feel and teach reflectively. In J. Arnold (Ed.), *Affect in language learning* (pp. 109–124). Cambridge: Cambridge University Press.

Suffolk County Council. (2001). *How am I doing? Assessment and feedback to learners*. Ipswich: Suffolk Advisory Service. Retrieved from: http://www.slamnet.org.uk/assessment/edp_booklet.htm

Weiner, B. (1990). History of motivational research in education. *Journal of Education & Psychology, 82*(4), 616–622. doi:10.1037/0022-0663.82.4.616

Wiggins, G. (2001). *Educative assessment*. San Francisco: Jossey-Bass.

Yorke, M. (2003). Formative assessment in higher education: Moves towards theory and the enhancement of pedagogic practice. *The Journal of Higher Education, 45*(4), 471–501.

ADDITIONAL READING

Bennett, R. E. (2011). Formative assessment: A critical review. *Assessment in Education: Principles, Policy & Practice, 18*(1), 5–25http://www.skolverket.se/polopoly_fs/1.126607!Menu/article/attachment/formative_assassement.pdf. RetrievedJanuary252011. doi:10.1080/0969594X.2010.513678

Bitchener, J. (2008). Evidence in support of written corrective feedback. *Journal of Second Language Writing, 17*(2), 69–124. doi:10.1016/j.jslw.2007.11.004

Boud, D. (2000). Sustainable assessment: Rethinking assessment for the learning society. *Studies in Continuing Education, 22*(2), 151–167. doi:10.1080/713695728

Briggs, J. (1998). Assessment and classroom learning: A role for summative assessment? *Assessment in Education: Principles, Policy & Practice, 5*(1), 103–110. doi:10.1080/0969595980050106

Cambra- Fierro, J., & Cambra-Berdún, J. (2007). Students' self-evaluation and reflection (Part 2): An Empirical Study. *Education +Training*, 49(2),103-111.

Harris, M., & McCann, P. (1994). *Assessment*. Oxford: Heinemann.

Lam, R., & Lee, I. (2010). Balancing the dual functions of portfolio assessment. *ELT Journal*, *64*(1), 54–64. doi:10.1093/elt/ccp024

McDonald, B., & Boud, D. (2003). The impact of self-assessment on achievement: The effects of self-assessment training on performance in external examinations. *Assessment in Education: Principles, Policy & Practice*, *10*(2), 209–220. doi:10.1080/0969594032000121289

Morrison, K. (1996). Developing reflective practice in higher degree students through learning journal. *Studies in Higher Education*, *21*(3), 317–332. doi:10.1080/03075079612331381241

Murphy, R. (2006). Evaluating new priorities for assessment in higher education. In C. Bryan & K. Clegg (Eds.), *Innovative assessment in higher education* (pp. 37–47). New York: Routledge.

OECD. (2005). *Formative assessment: Improving learning in secondary classrooms*. Paris: OECD.

Patri, M. (2002). The influence of peer feedback on self- and peer-assessment of oral skills. *Language Testing*, *19*(2), 109–131. doi:10.1191/0265532202lt224oa

Poehner, M. E., & Lantolf, J. (2005). Dynamic assessment in the language classroom. *Language Teaching Research*, *9*(3), 1–33. doi:10.1191/1362168805lr166oa

Stiggins, R. J. (1996). *Student centered classroom assessment*. Columbus, OH: Merrill Publishing.

Stiggins, R. J. (2001). *Student involved classroom assessment*. Columbus, OH: Merrill Publishing.

Stiggins, R. J. (2008). *An introduction to student-involved assessment for learning*. Upper Saddle River, New Jersey: Pearson-Merrill Prentice Hall.

KEY TERMS AND DEFINITIONS

Assessment: The process of collecting information about student learning. Throughout the learning process, assessment is used to inform teaching and student learning. As a result of assessment, teachers can adjust their teaching. Students also benefit from assessment. They need to receive a considerable amount of descriptive feedback to enable them to continue or adjust what they are doing to be effective learners.

Blog: Regularly updated journal or newsletter in the form of a web page, usually kept by one individual and intended for public consumption.

Formative Assessment: Refers to a wide variety of methods that teachers use to conduct in-process evaluations of student comprehension, learning needs, and academic progress during a lesson, unit, or course. Formative assessments help teachers identify concepts that students are struggling to understand, skills they are having difficulty acquiring, or learning standards they have not yet achieved so that adjustments can be made to lessons, instructional techniques, and academic support.

Learning Goals: Specific statements of intended student attainment of essential concepts and skills.

Peer-Assessment: A process whereby students or their peers grade assignments or tests based on a teacher's benchmarks. The practice is employed to save teachers time and improve students' understanding of course materials as well as improve their metacognitive skills.

Planning: (also called *forethought*): The process of thinking about and organizing the activities required to achieve a desired goal. It involves preparing a sequence of action steps to achieve some specific goal. If a person does it effectively, he can reduce much the necessary time and effort of achieving the goal. A plan is like a map. When following a plan, he can always see how much he have progressed towards his project goal and how far he is from his destination.

Portfolio: A compilation of student work assembled for the purpose of (1) evaluating coursework quality and academic achievement, (2) creating a lasting archive of academic work products, and (3) determining whether students have met learning standards or academic requirements for courses, grade-level promotion, and graduation.

Reflective Practice: The capacity to reflect on action so as to engage in a process of continuous learning. A critical attention to the practical values and theories which inform everyday actions, by examining practice reflectively and reflexively. A key rationale for reflective practice is that experience alone does not necessarily lead to learning; deliberate reflection on experience is essential.

Self-Assessment: The process of looking at oneself in order to assess aspects that are important to one's identity. It is one of the motives that drive self-evaluation, along with self-verification and self-enhancement.

Summative Assessment: Used to evaluate student learning, skill acquisition, and academic achievement at the conclusion of a defined instructional period—typically at the end of a project, unit, course, semester, program, or school year.

Chapter 3
Trends and Challenges of E-Assessment to Enhance Student Learning in Higher Education

Lourdes Guàrdia
Open University of Catalonia (UOC), Spain

Geoffrey Crisp
University of New South Wales, Australia

Ivan Alsina
Open University of Catalonia (UOC), Spain

ABSTRACT

This chapter provides an overview of current e-assessment activity in Higher Education (HE) for those interested in improving their assessment practices. Despite substantial changes in HE teaching and learning strategies with the introduction of Information and Communication Technologies (ICT), little effort has been made in the area of assessment, where traditional methods are still commonly used. ICT and computers are seen as a medium for supporting and guiding the whole learning process, but these options have not yet been fully explored. In view of this, we would like to review the trends and challenges of e-assessment to enhance student learning in future scenarios, taking into consideration several publications, cases and contributions from both the practice and research perspective.

INTRODUCTION

According to the Quality Assurance Agency for Higher Education (HE) (2010), assessment is an essential part of the instructional process as a whole, not just a matter of marking. Assessment should promote the enhancement of teaching and learning outcomes for both formative and summative processes (Clements & Cord, 2013). In this regard, approaches like "dynamic assessment" recommend assessing students'

DOI: 10.4018/978-1-5225-0531-0.ch003

potential to learn rather than measure what they have just done (Sharples, Adams, Ferguson, Gaved, McAndrew, Rienties, Weller, & Whitelock, 2014:23).

In spite of substantial changes in HE teaching and learning strategies with the introduction of Information and Communication Technologies (ICT), little effort has been made in the area of assessment, where traditional methods are still commonly used.

The evolution of ICT is providing new opportunities for strategies that can be used for assessment. For this reason, e-assessment is playing an increasingly important role in the transformation of HE (Whitelock, 2010), but new assessment paradigms and methodologies are still needed. In fact, most of the existing e-assessment experiments do not consider the adoption of user-centred approaches with the potential to engage students in authentic assessment tasks, a form of assessment in which students are asked to perform real-world tasks that demonstrate meaningful application of essential knowledge and skills (Mueller, 2014; Mora, Sancho-Bru, Iserte & Sánchez, 2012) or aimed at testing higher order capabilities (Crisp, 2010).

Traditional assessment methods are often based on the student being treated as an isolated individual with limited access to resources and other people. This approach is inconsistent with the new learning environments in HE that are open, collaborative and distributed in nature with access to almost unlimited digital resources. New generation learning spaces facilitate the integration of physical and virtual learning activities, yet we have not seen the extension of this approach to assessment. The widespread availability of MOOCs, the gamification of learning and the adoption of more evidence-centred design approaches to learning activities call for a review of the alignment between these new approaches to learning and the assessments designed to test that learning (Crisp, 2014a).

Predominant e-assessment tasks are still based on traditional forced-choice measures of multiple-choice tests, short answer, fill-in-the-blanks, true-false and matching. Students typically select an answer or recall information to complete the assessment (Marriott, 2009; Pachler, Daly, Mor & Mellar, 2010; Stödberg, 2012). Furthermore, current studies still claim that the power of e-assessment lies in the way in which automated computer-marked questions ease the teachers' workload. However, we would like to highlight that the feedback provided through computer-marked assessment is most effective when it is understood by the student, tailored to any misconceptions they may have and when it prompts students to reflect and refine their responses rather than just giving the answer (Jordan, 2012).

Some of the recent reviews of e-assessment literature (e.g. Hepplestone, Holden, Irwin, Parkin & Thorpe, 2011; Jisc 2009; Kay & LeSage 2009; Stödberg 2012) have focused on a subset of technology-enhanced assessment or feedback.

Reasons for the rising interest in reimagining assessment and e-assessment include accreditation and recognition of the need for more convincing evidence of student accomplishment in areas related to higher level cognitive and affective skills (Kuh, Jankowski, Ikenberry, & Kinzie, 2014). A greater emphasis on authentic assessment also facilitates the portability of credentials across national borders; the report developed by the High Level Group on the Modernisation of Higher Education (European Commission, 2014) recommends that the European Commission and national authorities encourage and incentivise the awarding and recognition of credits under the European Credit Transfer System (ECTS) for all forms of online courses.

Therefore, more research is needed to provide an understanding of how to use the full potential of e-assessment procedures to transform students' learning and teachers' work in this new personalised environment that promotes authentic learning and assessment (Whitelock, 2009).

ICT provides a unique medium for supporting and guiding the whole learning process (Daly, Pachler, Mor & Mellar, 2010), but this tool has not yet been fully explored. ICT tools are discussed at specialized conferences and tested in relatively isolated research projects, but are not yet integrated into a coherent policy or implemented on a large scale.

1. DEFINITION, TERMINOLOGY AND EMERGING TRENDS

In a broader sense, e-assessment (also called technology-enhanced assessment or online assessment) could be conceptualized as the use of ICT to facilitate the entire assessment process, from designing and delivering assignments to marking (by computers, or humans assisted by digital tools), reporting, storing the results and/or conducting the statistical analysis (Jisc, 2007; Osuji, 2009). This includes an end-to-end assessment process from the perspective of learners, tutors, learning establishments or institutions; awarding bodies such as regulators and the general public (Hettiarachchi, Huertas & Mor, 2013).

E-assessment also refers to the process of appraising knowledge, skills and competences against predefined criteria, such as expectations or measurement of learning outcomes. Assessment-related activities and the range of tools used for e-assessment purposes (e.g., plagiarism detectors and online marking) have increased (Dunn, Morgan, O'Reilly & Parry, 2004; Dahl, 2007). In particular, electronic assessment, e-assessment or ICT-based assessment, is considered a priority (Hawksey, 2015), although it is rarely clear how it should be applied (European Commission, 2012).

Crisp (2010) used the term e-assessment to refer to all the assessment tasks using a computer or the web. This definition embraces a wide range of tools and methodologies ranging from simple computer-marked multiple-choice questions, to more sophisticated e-assessment tasks (Boyle & Hutchison, 2009) and complex embedded assessment systems based on immersive environments, simulations, games (Redecker & Johannessen, 2013) or learning analytics (Williams, 2014).

Recently, e-assessment has attracted increased interest due to the awareness of the education community of the need to adequately assess 21st-century skills, competences and abilities. High-order skills such as problem-solving, reflection, creativity, critical thinking, learning to learn, risk-taking, collaboration and entrepreneurship are recognized in the European Recommendations on Key Competences for Lifelong Learning (Eur-Lex, 2006). Boyle and Hutchison (2009) stressed the great potential of ICT to allow a meaningful assessment of these higher-order skills but also to test new skills and abilities (for example ICT literacy). However, e-assessments are still commonly used for tasks focused on testing the acquisition of declarative knowledge (Bull & McKenna, 2003). As pointed out by several authors (Crisp, 2014b; Redecker & Johannessen, 2013; Williams, 2014) e-assessment tasks should go beyond testing superficial learning to capture more sophisticated skills, knowledge and competences. For instance, new technologies are especially well suited to engaging students in authentic activities and allowing for the assessment of competences required to function in the information society (Pellegrino, 2010).

This view was supported by the "Tomlinson Report" (Working Group on 14–19 Reform, 2004), which stated:

E-assessment should not be construed as limited to quick multiple-choice testing; it has the potential to test learners in both structured and unstructured environments, with both short and long answer questions, as well as the ability to use techniques such as video clips to test a wider range of knowledge, skills and understanding than is possible at present. (Working Group on 14–19 Reform 2004, 63)

To understand both the mainstream and the incoming trends in e-assessment, it is useful to distinguish between four essential types of technology-enhanced assessment (Crisp, 2014b).

- **Diagnostic Assessment**: Usually carried out before the beginning of a learning process, it provides an opportunity for identifying and updating students' prior knowledge and skills. Makes it possible to match the activities to the students' level.
- **Formative Assessment**: Carried out during the learning process, providing the learner with developmental feedback on his/her current understanding and skills. Formative assessment allows for the provision of strategic and timely feedback to be given to individuals at critical points of their learning process. The tutor or the teacher has the opportunity to modify the learning experience in order to achieve the desired outcomes. As mentioned by Whitelock (2007), formative e-assessment is a means of promoting reflection and encouraging students to take control of their own learning. Formative assessment can be also referred as *assessment for learning*.
- **Summative Assessment**: This is referred to as the final assessment, used after the learning has been completed. It usually leads to progression, a formal qualification or the certification of a specific skill. Summative assessment is also referred as *assessment of learning*.
- **Integrative Assessment**: The primary purpose of this type of assessment is to influence students' approaches to future learning goals by tracking the strategies that are used to respond to specific tasks. This type of assessment involves the use of complex tasks, may have multiple stakeholders and would not depend on simple or convergent responses (Crisp, 2012).

Nowadays, HE institutions commonly use digital technologies to provide summative assessment using closed formats such as multiple choice questions (MCQ), matching, hot spots or short answer questions (Marriott, 2009; Pachler et al., 2010; Stödberg, 2012). However, cognitive skills where students should apply their analytical, creative and constructive abilities cannot be assessed with these tasks. Therefore, the field needs to move forward to take a full advantage of ICT when designing formative and integrative e-assessment tasks focused on testing complex cognitive skills. In addition, several authors (Ashford-Rowe, Herrington & Brown, 2013; Crisp, 2010; Redecker & Johannessen, 2013) highlight the need to develop new approaches capable of engaging students in more authentic e-assessment activities (Brown, Collins, & Duguid, 1989). These tasks would allow students to examine issues and problems from different perspectives, to develop a set of new skills and capabilities, to collaborate with other agents and to integrate learning into new perspectives. This could be achieved by using more dynamic, immersive and interactive learning environments, allowing students to explore and describe the consequences associated with their responses (Crisp, 2014b).

Other initiatives like FREMA (Framework Reference Model for Assessment) (Wills *et al.* 2009) developed a reference model for systems linking e-assessment and e-learning; this model was built on top of Service-Oriented Architectures, such as Web Services and the Grid, and in particular the Jisc (Joint Information Systems Committee) e-Learning Framework (ELF). The Assessment Reference Model described how the assessment domain maps to this framework and thus acts as a driver for implementation and evaluation. The goals of the model were to define the scope of the assessment domain in terms of existing practice, to define common assessment solution patterns in terms of use case studies and scenarios and to relate them explicitly to the ELF in the form of a service profile and service descriptions. FREMA outlined prototype services that fulfil the profile of the assessment domain, validated the Assessment Reference Model and allowed the reference model to be evaluated. The model was

Figure 1. Current and future e-Assessment strategies
Adapted from Redecker (2013:11) and based on the source elaborated by Bunderson, Inouye & Olsen, (1989)

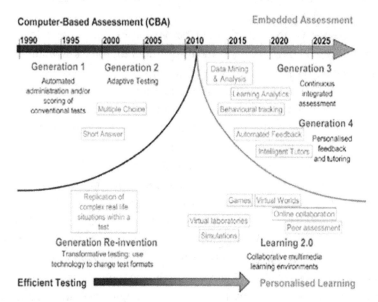

particularly useful for focussing attention on the various elements of the assessment process and how these could be facilitated by technology.

It is also important to highlight the report *The Use of ICT for the Assessment of Key Competences*, in which Redecker (2013) describes the four generations of computerized educational measurements already identified more than two decades ago by Bunderson, Inouye and Olsen (1989), thus providing a useful framework for e-assessment (see Figure 1):

- **Generation 1. Computerized Testing**: This refers to the translation of existing paper-and-pencil tests into a computerized format, allowing for the automation of some assessment-related processes (e.g., delivering, marking, etc.).
- **Generation 2. Computerized Adaptive Testing:** The system adapts the difficulty of the contents of the next task to be presented or an aspect of the timing of the next item, depending on examinees' responses.
- **Generation 3. Continuous Measurement:** This uses calibrated measures embedded in a curriculum to continuously and unobtrusively estimate dynamic changes in the student's achievement trajectory and profile as a learner.
- **Generation 4. Intelligent Measurement:** Tasks are oriented to producing intelligent scoring, interpretation of individual profiles and advice to learners and teachers using knowledge bases and inferencing procedures.

To date, the first two generations have become the most common e-assessment practices (Crisp, 2010; Redecker & Johannessen, 2013; Stödberg, 2012). These practices usually include multiple-choice questions, extended-matched questions, free text responses and essays and closed exercises, among others tasks (Crisp, 2014b). One of the main purposes of these tasks is to simplify and reduce the cost of learning assessment, but in many cases the range of learning objectives covered is very sparse, belonging to low levels of cognitive capabilities (e.g., information that needs to be memorized and reproduced during the assessment).

Recently, e-assessment tools have been enriched to include more sophisticated tasks that can be used to assess new constructs and also used to provide summative and formative processes. Boyle and Hutchinson (2009) have described sophisticated these as:

- Tasks that contain multimedia stimulus material.
- The test taker is required to interact with the stimulus material in a variety of ways.
- The work that the student produces a more complex responses compared to a simple-item test.
- They tend to be expensive and slow to develop and are not easily written by a non-specialist teacher.

The present generation of e-assessment technologies includes the possibility of documenting learning achievements through easy-to-use multimedia devices; analysing learners' behaviour in tackling process-related challenges; involving a learning community in witnessing and appreciating a peer's learning results; empowering learners to continuously assess and document their learning progress or involving high-level specialist assessors without moving them in space (Hounsel, 2009). Current practices also include the use of formative assessment for learning where timely feedback from the teacher, peers or the computer enhances the student experience (Handley & Williams, 2011; Hepplestone et al, 2011; Jordan, 2012). Intelligent tools capable of providing adaptive testing are also being used (Ortigosa, Paredes & Rodriguez, 2010; Xanthou, 2013).

In the coming years, the main challenge will be to make the transition from traditional computer-based testing (generation 1 and 2) to the latter two (generation 3 and 4) (see figure 1), a new era called "embedded assessment" (Redecker & Johannessen, 2013) or Assessment 2.0 (Elliott, 2008). In this near future, questions and tasks will be quite different to current practices. Forthcoming trends will include innovative formats such as learning analytics (Williams, 2014), data mining and analysis (Redecker & Johannessen, 2013), intelligent tutors (Crisp, 2014b), immersive environments, virtual worlds, games and simulations (Boyle & Hutchinson, 2009). The new e-assessment era will probably be based on the integrating holistic and personalized assessment into learning processes. Learners could be continuously tracked and guided by digital environments, merging formative and summative assessment within the learning process (Redecker & Johannessen, 2013). Although currently at the developmental stage, these emerging trends could become a reality during the next few years (Johnson, Smith, Willis, Levine, & Haywood, 2011) providing a sound alternative for assessing skills, competences and abilities crucial for life in the 21st century.

It is interesting to mention the work recently developed by Tinoca, Pereira and Oliveira (2014) in which they present a new conceptual framework for digital assessment in HE supported by a set of four quality dimensions—authenticity, consistency, transparency and practicability—each one composed of a set of fifteen criteria for developing and using of e-assessment in HE virtual environments and also aimed at promoting the quality of the assessment strategies being used. This framework was developed based on the expansion of the concept of validity supported by edumetric qualities.

2. ADVANTAGES AND DISADVANTAGES FROM E-ASSESSMENT TOOLS AND SYSTEMS

Adopting e-assessment has more radical implications than just changing the mode of assessment –it can challenge assumptions about the way the education system is structured and change patterns of work for staff and students. The significant drivers for change in e-assessment in HE include the increased requirements for evidence and the use of external benchmarks, standards and auditing procedures, the global international marketplace for educational services, the ubiquitous spread of mobile devices with Internet access and students' changing expectations about their learning environments (Crisp, 2014b). In this section, the main advantages and limitations for implementing technology-enhanced assessment for HE are outlined.

The use of e-assessment to evaluate students' outcomes in HE has gained ground all over the world because of the wide range of benefits deriving from its use. As suggested by several authors (Crisp, 2014b; Dermo, 2009: Evans & Sabry, 2003; Jisc, 2007; Jisc, 2010; Mora et al., 2012; Osuji, 2009; PingSoft, 2007; Redecker & Johannenssen, 2013; Whitelock & Watt, 2008), the main advantages for adopting e-assessment tasks are:

- Paperless distribution and data collection: e-assessment can be accessed at a wider range of locations than paper-based assessment.
- New strategies to cope with large student/candidate numbers. It can be used for all kinds of different scaled examinations.
- Automatic marking. In some situations (especially when using closed questions and essays), the e-assessment system can record and analyse responses automatically and provide appropriate feedback. The time saved in marking can be used in more productive ways (e.g., supporting learners with difficulties) and the system ensures greater accuracy and objectivity than is achieved by humans.
- E-assessment can increase the range of what is assessed (e.g., high order or novel skills) and encourage deeper learning. In this regard, is important to note that assessment can provide evidence of both cognitive and skills-based achievements.
- Enhanced quality of the feedback. E-assessment tools make it easier to provide timely and constructive feedback, motivating students to learn more effectively. Adequate feedback helps students to improve their learning process.
- Immediate expert feedback could be given to students, helping them to monitor their own progress. The ability to give feedback quickly means that the student's next problem-solving iteration can begin sooner.
- There is considerable potential for multimedia resources and emerging technologies to make the feedback richer and more personal.
- Online assessment tools support and encourage peer and self-assessment. These e-assessment tasks play a significant role in developing students' ability to regulate their own learning.
- The tools facilitate interactivity between the students and the contents. The questions can incorporate multimedia materials where the students have some control over using the digital resources. More immersive materials, such virtual worlds or augmented reality environments, can also be used.

- Opportunities for learners to personalize their learning by taking online assessments when ready.
- Positive effects of the provided feedback on students' motivation, concentration and performance (Garrett, Thoms, Alrushiedat & Ryan, 2009).

There are also some drawbacks to introducing digital technologies in assessment processes (Crisp, 2014a; Mora et al., 2012; Osuji, 2009; Whitelock & Brasher, 2006), although these are thought to be surmountable. These obstacles need to be overcome in order to successfully implement e-assessment tasks in HE institutions and can be summarized as follows:

- The principal barrier to developing of e-assessment tasks is commonly associated with academic staff training (Whitelock & Brasher, 2006). Crisp (2014b) also highlights the cost of lecturer training.
- Low level of computer literacy. This is a crucial issue, especially in developing countries, where there is a need for both intensive and extensive manpower development in the area of ICT training and usage. Along similar lines, the cost of acquiring a computer can also be a challenge.
- Practitioners' concerns about plagiarism detection, invigilation issues and identity issues.
- The reliability and validity of high-stakes assessments, mainly in their "non-psychometric" senses.
- Issues related to the accessibility of e-assessment systems and tools.
- Lack of studies on the suitability of e-assessment for evaluating different kinds of skills and learning outcomes.
- Some drawbacks are also associated with e-assessment software and systems (Bull & McKenna, 2003). These difficulties are usually associated with interoperability, reusability, manageability scalability, performance level, limitations of upgrading procedures, support and maintenance, security and confidentiality.

Much of the innovative work in e-assessment in HE has been carried out in institutions where systems and tools has been developed and seeded by project funding. Even then, use is often limited to a few departments. Scaling up the use of e-assessment requires financial commitment and senior management support. In addition, with the implementation of an e-assessment system, a number of existing roles will be changed. These roles may include invigilation, internal and external verifications, examination administration and statistical analysis (Osuji, 2009). Where these exist, many experiences show that there is greater confidence in the capability of e-assessment to deliver a return on investment and wider acceptance among staff of the benefits of change (Jisc, 2007). Effective e-assessment for summative, formative or integrative purposes can be set up relatively simply by using the assessment tool within the institution's VLE, but a sustainable programme of technical and teaching support for academic staff is still needed. In most cases, wider-scale use has only been achieved when a central support unit has been established. Medium- to high-stakes e-assessments demand a dedicated team, whose role is to ensure the reliability of systems, provide technical support for academic staff and facilitate interoperability with other systems in the institution. The next stage of development is to create e-assessment tasks that can be shared between departments, or even between institutions. However, mutually compatible interfaces adhering to universal technical standards must be in place to make systems fully interoperable. To date, these complex and costly issues have been barriers to vigorous growth in e-assessment practices (Jisc, 2007).

Table 1. General criteria to guide the design and development of e-assessment task or activity

1	E-assessment tasks should be open-ended.
2	Tasks should have a clear purpose and learning outcome.
3	Tasks should be authentic.
4	There should be an emphasis on the process over the product.
5	Collaboration and communication should be incorporated into tasks.
6	Students should have varying degrees of choice in their assessment tasks.
7	Tasks should enable students to present multiple perspectives.
8	Tasks should be linked to stated outcomes.
9	Tasks should encourage the appropriate, discriminating use of online resources.
10	Tasks should enable students to examine and present many viewpoints.

Beyond specific e-assessment formats we will see in the next section, Kendle and Northcote (2000) proposed ten general criteria to guide the design and development of any kind of e-assessment task or activity that we adapted after the last decade. The criteria can be used as a checklist for engaging in successful e-assessment practices and combine qualitative and quantitative measures of performance (table 1):

The next section outlines the current types of e-assessment tasks and activities are outlined.

3. CURRENT E-ASSESSMENT FORMATS

Nowadays, it is not feasible to offer an exhaustive list of e-assessment systems, tools, methodologies and activities. Any assessment task can be converted into a digital format that would allow the examinee to respond in a way that indicates the development of a specific skill or competence. In addition, a significant number of assessment functionalities are integrated as a component of current Learning Management Systems (LMS) and/or Virtual Learning Systems (VLE), such as ATutor, BlackBoard, Claroline, Desire2Learn, Moodle, Canvas or Sakai (Amelung, Krieger & Rösner, 2011; Gutiérrez, Trenas, Ramos, Corbera, & Romero, 2010).

To shed some light on the subject, after a systematic revision of the literature, Stödberg (2012), classified higher education e-assessment tasks into five main categories: closed questions (multiple-choice questions, extended matching questions and image hotspots); open-ended questions (including questions without fixed-answer alternatives, such as free text responses and essays); ePortfolio (includes all the approaches in which ePortfolios are used for assessment purposes); products (including prototypes, computer programs and similar approaches), and discussion (including e-assessments based on discussion among peers). Beyond Stödbergs' classification, the purpose of this section is to provide a brief outline of the most common e-assessment formats/tasks and provide insights into the emerging trends (Table 2).

Multiple-Choice Questions (MCQ)

MCQ are very popular because they are easy to write, deliver and implement within common LMS. Teachers do not need a significant amount of training or time to use them satisfactorily. In this type of

Table 2. E-assessment formats/tasks

1	Multiple-choice questions (MCQ)
2	Visual identification/Hot spot
3	Matching, ordering or sequencing
4	Short answer
5	Judged mathematical expression
6	Free text responses and essays
7	ePortfolio assessment
8	Blogs
9	Online discussion
10	Concept maps
11	Clickers or Personal Response Systems (PRCS)
12	MOOCs and e-assessment
13	Badging and microcredentialling
14	Online role-plays and scenario-based activities

task, students usually respond by selecting an option from a list of possible alternatives. The alternatives may include multimedia files, such as audio, images or movie sequences or a numerical slider. MCQ have been shown to be valid and reliable (Considine, Botti, & Thomas, 2005; Crisp, 2014a; Johnstone, 2003). Some variations on traditional MCQ are sorting questions, true/false or multiple response questions (in which the user can choose one or more correct responses) (Crisp, 2014a). A good alternative to MCQ is EMQ (Extended Matching Questions). EMQ retain the main characteristics of MCQ but allow the solution of cohesive problems (not individual and isolated questions) (Wood, 2003).

Although MCQ are widely used, they have been criticized for encouraging a superficial approach to learning. However, some authors (e.g. Draper, 2009; Jordan, 2012) suggest several ways in which MCQ can be used for deep learning in the sense of focusing on relationships between items rather than simply recalling disconnected items. Thus, for example, MCQ could incorporate student commentary, decision-making, interactive tools or functions that facilitate the writing of specific feedback on students' responses (Crisp, 2014a, Jordan, 2013).

Visual Identification/Hot Spot

Task in which the student clicks on the computer screen to identify a specific part of a visual representation. Hot Spot questions are useful when the test-taker should be able to detect, interpret or identify components of a picture or a diagram.

Matching, Ordering or Sequencing

Question type used where the students are required to select or arrange choices in an ordered sequence based on a predetermined criterion. Students are normally required to drag the responses into the correct order.

Short Answer

Task where the student enters a short text or just one word to answer to specific questions. Tasks such as fill-in-the-blanks (a passage of text or images with keywords/images missing), gap fill and word match are standard varieties of traditional short answer questions (Scottish Qualifications Authority, 2005).

Judged Mathematical Expression

Students must enter a number or an algebraic expression in a text entry field. Usually these are responses to mathematical or statistical questions. This task could be conceptualized as a form of short answer question where only one response is correct, or in the case of algebraic expressions, where equivalent expressions are judged to be correct.

Free Text Responses and Essays

One of the main advances in the area of e-assessment has been the improvement of automatic feedback (Whitelock, 2014) and scoring techniques for essays and other types of written text assignments (Dikli, 2006; He, Hui & Quan, 2009; Noorbehbahani & Kardan, 2011). These systems are especially valuable for diagnostic and formative assessments, as feedback is a core part of the learning process. Beyond that, automated scoring could reduce time and costs when evaluating complex skills such as writing or programming languages. A great variety of software applications are now available making it possible to automatically assess free text responses and essays. Among these, we could highlight the OpenEssayist, the Mathematics Statistics and Operational Research, Maple T.A., NUMBAS and the Design Science's WebEQ.

The tasks mentioned above are among the most commonly used e-assessment formats (Marriott, 2009; Pachler et al., 2010; Stödberg, 2012). These tasks are good for assessing students' knowledge levels but they have serious limitations when it comes to assessing skills and competences that involve complex or multiple solutions (Millard et al., 2005). Traditional e-assessment tasks often fail to illuminate the existence of critical thinking, effective decision-making, collaborative skills, or the ability to apply what is learnt in the real world, and can only be used effectively to measure abilities at the lower levels of Bloom or SOLO taxonomies.

To overcome these deficiencies, new e-assessments formats have been used. These include:

ePortfolio Assessment

An ePortfolio offers an opportunity to create and manage an online space of digital artefacts (including documents, graphics, audio files, videos, reflections, feedback, ideas, etc.) that provide evidence of students' knowledge, skills, competences, experiences and achievements. Students can present extended pieces of work that have been refined through reflection. In HE, ePortfolios are usually used as a tool/strategy for making student learning and assessment more user-centred, thus allowing them to manage their own educational journey over time (Guàrdia, Maina, Barberà, & Alsina, 2014, 2015). In addition, ePortfolios help teachers to observe students' work and processes over a specific period of time, allowing them to provide timely and constructive feedback. ePortfolios could also be used to foster feedback among peers. The European Network of ePortfolio Experts and Practitioners (EPNET) http://www.eportfolio. eu/ presents examples and guidance to implement ePortfolio as an assessment strategy.

Blogs

Using blogs, students can reflect on their learning journey and provide written evidence of their educational experiences. Blogs also offer a shared online environment that facilitates reflections concerning other learners' comments on the blog post. The entries, displayed in reverse chronological order, usually consist of reflections, information and/or commentary on a particular topic (Crisp, 2014a). Blogs can be produced in different forms, such as written postings, video-blogs (vlogs) or audio recordings (podcasts).

There is now evidence of the effectiveness of blogging in online HE environments for providing formative feedback (Olofsson, Lindberg & Stödberg, 2011).

Online Discussion

Students can engage in asynchronous discussion through the use of forums. Online discussion supports both individual and group work, providing a space for social reflection and critiquing. Online discussion can build a sense of community of practice in participants.

Concept Maps

Concept maps require students to name concepts/constructs in a specific domain and to create associations between them. Computer-based concept maps with automatic scoring have been used by some authors to provide an assessment of critical and creative thinking and complex relationships (Harlen & Deakin Crick, 2003).

Clickers or Personal Response Systems (PRCS)

An area that has seen extensive growth in recent years is the use of handheld student response devices (clickers). Clickers are well situated to engage in synchronous e-assessment activities and are designed to promote classroom participation (Crisp, 2014b). Students' responses are usually accumulated during face-to-face sessions so that everyone can view the statistics of the responses. Some software examples are: Turning Point and ResponseWare from Turning Technologies (http://www.turningtechnologies. com/) and the IML audience response system (http://lumiinsight.com/). Clickers can also be combined with interactive whiteboards.

MOOCs and E-Assessment

Another challenge for e-assessment comes when talking about MOOCs. Here the assessment design should explicitly mention the value of peer feedback; building trust and capacity in self and peer assessment can be addressed by defining the objectives using precise criteria and providing students with examples. The design of rubrics, scales and explanatory automatic answers are supportive tools for the learner. Furthermore, the MOOC can provide embedded assistance for learners on how to collect evidence of meaningful learning and organize it to provide validity for their learning trajectories. Using blogs or ePortfolios to gather evidence, annotate and share learning outcomes and reflections would allow the successful completion of MOOCs to be authenticated in a more rigorous manner (Guàrdia, Maina & Sangrà, 2013).

Badging and Microcredentialling

Badging and microcredentialling are recent variations of a structured learning and assessment approach that is gaining interest with educational and training organizations (Devedžić & Jovanović, 2015). Badging is designed to recognize that assessment takes place in many locations and that learners can provide evidence of achieving learning outcomes in informal as well as formal settings. Often informal learning spaces provide opportunities for authentic assessment, such as those encountered in the work place or on field trips, but the educational institution requires a formal process for validating the assessment outcomes. So badges need to be aligned with a robust assessment process that can use many of the features we have described so far, including self and peer assessment, e-portfolios, blogs and online discussions.

Online Role-Plays and Scenario-Based Activities

Online role-plays and scenario-based activities allow for assessments requiring divergent responses from learners as the tasks involve complex situations, multiple participants and branching in terms of progression through the assessment (Crisp, 2014b). The outcomes from a role-play may vary with different groups of learners and involve recording the reflections of learners on the consequences of their decisions and actions within the assessment.

Although e-assessment tasks have strong potential to improve assessment and provide formative feedback between peers and teacher-student, more sophisticated tasks are still needed to assess complex skills within scenarios capable of replicating the real world. Over the coming years, e-assessments will become more dynamic, interactive, immersive, intelligent, authentic and ubiquitous. Future e-assessment tasks should not mimic traditional paper-and-pencil tests, so teachers and instructional designers will need to redesign assessment tasks to make use of the new capabilities offered by technology. As stressed by Crisp (2014b), in the near future e-assessments will replicate real world experiences and the tasks to be performed will be like sophisticated games involving role-playing and scenario-based environments. By posing authentic problems using emerging technologies (such as online virtual worlds, virtual reality or augmented reality), students will be more meaningfully engaged in their learning journey. Incorporating automatic, precise and constructivist feedback should become a normal part of the assessment process. Social networking and collaborative group opportunities will be also incorporated to the entire learning process. Redecker and Johannessen (2013) and Williams (2014) highlighted the relevance of learning analytics in using the data produced by students during the learning process as the main basis for providing feedback and guidance for teachers and students. In this regard, emerging learning environment data-mining techniques will be used to provide formative and integrative assessment and facilitate individual tutoring. Virtual worlds, virtual laboratories, games and simulations will also be used for tracking individual learners' activity and will make learning behaviour more assessable. Although these options are still in an experimental phase, over the next few years' integrated assessment formats capable of capturing 21st-century skills and competences will arise (Johnson et al., 2011).

4. CONCLUSION

To enhance e-assessment and implement it successfully, it is necessary to explore its institutional and pedagogic dimensions, addressing sustainability and cultural issues, as well as technological barriers. We need to understand in greater depth how technology can be used to enhance assessment practices, rather than simply making them more efficient, and how to deploy e-assessment alongside other strategies.

The use of e-assessment tasks has gradually been changing. Instead of the traditional use of closed questions, assessment is being complemented and developed by more sophisticated tasks and competence-based assessment that allow cognitive skills to be evaluated within more authentic and significant settings.

Emerging trends in e-assessment cover a wide range of activities, from simple computer-marked multiple-choice questions to elaborate role-plays, interactive simulations and online scenarios. The adoption of virtual worlds, simulations, virtual reality, augmented reality, intelligent tutors, learning analytics, behavioural tracking and data mining and analysis are included in these new views.

We therefore need to review not only the new opportunities, but also the ability of e-assessment to provide appropriate evidence of higher-level learning. This evidence could come from learning analytics that may allow assessment to be embedded in immersive environments, multiplayer games and computer simulations reproducing learning situations. Learning analytics is emerging from the realm of the specialist to be seen as a critical component of learning, teaching and assessment and a resource with which all teachers must engage (Knight, Shum & Littlejohn, 2014). As we move to change our assessments so they replicate or integrate authentic contexts requiring complex thinking, problem-solving and collaboration strategies we will facilitate the development and reporting of more sophisticated learning outcomes.

Two of the key elements of e-assessment are the ability to provide timely and rich e-feedback and to collect data on how students have engaged with the assessment task. Learners need substantial, regular and meaningful feedback (OECD, 2010) and e-assessment provides a systematic format for the provision of personalised feedback. The provision of data to teachers on how students have engaged with the assessment task is invaluable to improving assessment itself and the learning environment. More research is urgently needed on how to convert the vast array of data available from e-assessments into a meaningful format that discipline teachers can use to improve their teaching and the curriculum itself.

Furthermore, there is an urgent need to convince learning and teaching stakeholders of the effectiveness and appropriateness of using computers for assessment purposes. Educational strategies based on ICT assessment should choose e-assessment methods that promote alternative solutions and encourage experimentation through peer-assessment and self-regulated learning using different media and communication formats.

Another relevant aspect is the relationship between instructional design and the results of e-assessment. Through learning analytics strategy teaching staff can align learning design applied in their courses with the outcomes in order to improve the students' learning assessment experience. In this regard, Miller and Mork (2013) propose a chain for discovery, Integration, and exploitation of large-scale data. This strategy can guide teaching staff in deciding when to offer assistance to their students and can help course designers to improve the learning resources, assessment strategies and activities of their courses.

Many good, innovative examples of e-assessment practices have been found in the literature. However, more research must be done on e-assessment's impact on learning and teaching in Higher Education.

There is evidence that current cultural and administrative practices in HE are often barriers to the propagation of successful e-assessment initiatives. For this reason, it is important to highlight that research on e-assessment has been dominated by a focus on investigating benefits of use and adoption rather than building an understanding of development and implementation (Tomas, Borg & McNeil, 2015).

The Bologna accords set out to align academic degree standards across Europe. This will have an impact on the whole degree accreditation process. Aspects of e-assessment will be critical to this process due to its potential for assessing skills, abilities and competences for the knowledge-based society. This means that in the near future more resources should be devoted to e-assessment to promote the European alignment of qualifications.

REFERENCES

Amelung, M., Krieger, K., & Rösner, D. (2011). E-assessment as a service. *IEEE Transactions on Learning Technologies, 4*(2), 162–174. doi:10.1109/TLT.2010.24

Ashford-Rowe, K., Herrington, J., & Brown, C. (2013). Establishing the critical elements that determine authentic assessment. *Assessment & Evaluation in Higher Education, 39*(2), 205–222. doi:10.1080/02 602938.2013.819566

Boyle, A., & Hutchison, D. (2009). Sophisticated tasks in e-assessment: What are they and what are their benefits? *Assessment & Evaluation in Higher Education, 34*(3), 305–319. doi:10.1080/02602930801956034

Brown, J. S., Collins, A., & Duguid, P. (1989). Situated Cognition and the culture of learning. *Educational Researcher, 18*(1), 32–42. doi:10.3102/0013189X018001032

Bull, J., & McKenna, C. (2003). *Blueprint for computer-assisted assessment*. London: Routledge Falmer.

Bunderson, V. C., Inouye, D. K., & Olsen, J. B. (1989). The four generations of computerized educational measurement. In R. L. Lynn (Ed.), *Educational Measurement* (pp. 367–407). New York: Macmillan.

Clements, M. D., & Cord, B. A. (2013). Assessment guiding learning: Developing graduate qualities in an experiential learning programme. *Assessment & Evaluation in Higher Education, 38*(1), 114–124. doi:10.1080/02602938.2011.609314

Considine, J., Botti, M., & Thomas, S. (2005). Design, format, validity and reliability of multiple- choice questions for use in nursing research and education. *Collegian: Journal of the Royal College of Nursing Australia, 12*(1), 19–24. doi:10.1016/S1322-7696(08)60478-3 PMID:16619900

Crisp, G. T. (2010). Interactive e-Assessment – Practical approaches to constructing more sophisticated online tasks. *Journal of Learning Design, 3*(3), 1–10. doi:10.5204/jld.v3i3.57

Crisp, G. T. (2012). Integrative assessment: Reframing assessment practice for current and future learning. *Assessment & Evaluation in Higher Education, 37*(1), 33–43. doi:10.1080/02602938.2010.494234

Crisp, G. T. (2014a). *Designing and using e-Assessments*. Milperra, NSW, Australia: HERDSA Guide, Higher Education Research and Development Society of Australasia.

Crisp, G. T. (2014b). Assessment in Next Generation Learning Spaces. In K. Fraser (Ed.), *The Future of Learning and Teaching in Next Generation Learning Spaces. International Perspectives on Higher Education Research* (Vol. 12, pp. 85–100). Emerald Group Publishing Limited.

Dahl, S. (2007). The student perspective on using plagiarism detection software. *Active Learning in Higher Education, 8*(2), 173–191. doi:10.1177/1469787407074110

Daly, C., Pachler, N., Mor, Y., & Mellar, H. (2010). Exploring formative e-Assessment using case stories and design patterns. *Assessment & Evaluation in Higher Education, 35*(5), 619–636. doi:10.1080/02602931003650052

Dermo, J. (2009). e-Assessment and the student learning experience: A survey of student perceptions of e-assessment. *British Journal of Educational Technology, 40*(2), 203–214. doi:10.1111/j.1467-8535.2008.00915.x

Devedžić, V., & Jovanović, J. (2015). Developing Open Badges: a comprehensive approach. *Educational Technology Research and Development, 63*(4), 603–620.

Dikli, S. (2006). An overview of automated scoring essays. *The Journal of Technology, Learning, and Assessment, 5*(1), 4–35.

Draper, S. W. (2009). Catalytic assessment: Understanding how MCQs and EVS can foster deep learning. *British Journal of Educational Technology, 40*(2), 285–293. doi:10.1111/j.1467-8535.2008.00920.x

Dunn, L., Morgan, C., O'Reilly, M., & Parry, S. (2004). *The Student Assessment Handbook. New Directions in Traditional & Online Assessment*. London: RoutledgeFalmer.

Elliott, R. J. (2008). Assessment 2.0. *International Journal of Emerging Technologies in Learning, 3*, 66–70.

Eur-Lex (2006). Recommendation of the European Parliament and of the Council of 18 December 2006 on key competences for lifelong learning (2006/962/EC). *Official Journal of the European Union*. Retrieved from http://eur-lex.europa.eu/legal-content/EN/TXT/?uri=celex:32006H0962

European Commission. (2012). *Assessment of Key Competences in Initial Education and Training: Policy Guidance*. Commission staff working document. Retrieved from http://eose.org/wp-content/uploads/2014/03/Assessment-of-Key-Competences-in-initial-education-and-training.pdf

European Commission. (2014). *New modes of learning and teaching in higher education*. Retrieved from http://ec.europa.eu/education/library/reports/modernisation-universities_en.pdf

Evans, C., & Sabry, K. (2003). Evaluation of the interactivity of web-based learning systems: Principles and process. *Innovations in Education and Teaching International, 40*(1), 89–99. doi:10.1080/1355800032000038787

Garrett, N., Thoms, B., Alrushiedat, N., & Ryan, T. (2009). Social ePortfolios as the new course management system. *On the Horizon, 17*(3), 197–207. doi:10.1108/10748120910993222

Guàrdia, L., Maina, M., Barberà, L., & Alsina, I. (2014, November 13). Open resources for implementing ePortfolios in Higher Education. *Paper presented at the 1st International Workshop on Technology-Enhanced Assessment, Analytics and Feedback (TEAAF2014)*, Barcelona.

Guàrdia, L., Maina, M., Barberà, L., & Alsina, I. (2015, July 2-4). Matriz conceptual sobre usos y propósitos de los eportfolios. *Procedia - Social and Behavioral Sciences, 196*, 106 – 112.

Guàrdia, L., Maina, M., & Sangrà, A. (2013) MOOC Design Principles. A Pedagogical Approach from the Learner's Perspective. *eLearning Papers, 33.* Retrieved from http://www.openeducationeuropa.eu/en/article/MOOC-Design-Principles.-A-Pedagogical-Approach-from-the-Learner%E2%80%99s-Perspective

Gutiérrez, E., Trenas, M. A., Ramos, J., Corbera, F., & Romero, S. (2010). A new Moodle module supporting automatic verification of VHDL-based assignments. *Computers & Education, 54*(2), 562–577. doi:10.1016/j.compedu.2009.09.006

Handley, K., & Williams, L. (2011). From copying to learning: Using exemplars to engage students with assessment criteria and feedback. *Assessment & Evaluation in Higher Education, 36*(1), 95–108. doi:10.1080/02602930903201669

Harlen, W., & Deakin Crick, R. (2003). *A systematic review of the impact on students and teachers of the use of ICT for assessment of creative and critical thinking skills.* Retrieved from http://eppi.ioe.ac.uk/cms/Default.aspx?tabid=109

Hawksey, M. (2015). *Association for Learning Technology Annual Survey 2014 Data and Report.* Retrieved from http://repository.alt.ac.uk/2358/

He, Y., Hui, S. C., & Quan, T. T. (2009). Automatic summary assessment for intelligent tutoring systems. *Computers & Education, 53*(3), 890–899. doi:10.1016/j.compedu.2009.05.008

Hepplestone, S., Holden, G., Irwin, B., Parkin, H. J., & Thorpe, L. (2011). Using technology to encourage student engagement with feedback: A literature review. *Research in Learning Technology, 19*(2), 117–127. doi:10.1080/21567069.2011.586677

Hettiarachchi, E., Huertas, M. A., & Mor, E. (2013). Skill and Knowledge E-Assessment: A Review of the State of the Art. *IN3 Working Paper Series.* Retrieved from http://journals.uoc.edu/index.php/in3-working-paper-series/article/view/n13-hettiarachchi-huertas-mor/n13-hettiarachchi-huertas-mor-en

Hounsel, D. (2009). Evaluating courses and teaching. In H. Fry, S. Ketteridge, & S. Marshall (Eds.), *A Handbook for teaching and learning in Higher Education. Enhancing academic practice* (pp. 198–231). New York, London: Routledge.

Jisc. (2007). *Effective practice with e-Assessment. An overview of technologies, policies and practice in further and higher education.* Retrieved from http://www.webarchive.org.uk/wayback/archive/20140615085433/http://www.jisc.ac.uk/media/documents/themes/elearning/effpraceassess.pdf

Jisc. (2009). *Effective Assessment in a Digital Age.* Retrieved from http://www.webarchive.org.uk/wayback/archive/20140614115719/http://www.jisc.ac.uk/media/documents/programmes/elearning/digiassass_eada.pdf

Johnson, L., Smith, R., Willis, H., Levine, A., & Haywood, K. (2011). *The 2011 Horizon Report.* Austin, Texas: The New Media Consortium.

Johnstone, A. (2003). *LTSN physical sciences practice guide effective practice in objective assessment: The skills of fixed response testing. LTSN Physical Sciences* Centre. Retrieved from https://www.heacademy.ac.uk/sites/default/files/ps0072_effective_practice_in_objective_assessment_mar_2004.pdf

Jordan, S. (2012). Student engagement with assessment and feedback: Some lessons from short-answer free-text e-assessment questions. *Computers & Education, 58*(2), 818–834. doi:10.1016/j.compedu.2011.10.007

Jordan, S. (2013, July 9-10). Using e-assessment to learn about learning. *Presented at the 2013 International Computer Assisted Assessment Conference*, Southampton.

Kay, R. H., & LeSage, A. (2009). A strategic assessment of audience response systems used in higher education. *Australasian Journal of Educational Technology, 25*(2), 235–249. doi:10.14742/ajet.1152

Kendle, A., & Northcote, M. (2000). The struggle for balance in the use of quantitative and qualitative online assessment tasks. *Proceedings of ASCILITE 2000*. Retrieved from http://www.ascilite.org/conferences/coffs00/papers/amanda_kendle.pdf

Knight, S., Shum, S. B., & Littlejohn, K. (2014). Epistemology, Assessment, Pedagogy: Where Learning Meets Analytics in the Middle Space. *Journal of Learning Analytics, 1*(2), 23–47.

Kuh, G. D., Jankowski, N., Ikenberry, S. O., & Kinzie, J. (2014*). Knowing What Students Know and Can Do: The Current State of Student Learning Outcomes Assessment in US Colleges and Universities*. Urbana, IL: University of Illinois and Indiana University, National Institute for Learning Outcomes Assessment (NILOA). Retrieved from http://www.learningoutcomesassessment.org/documents/2013%20Survey%20Report%20Final.pdf

Marriott, P. (2009). Students' Evaluation of the use of Online Summative Assessment on an Undergraduate Financial Accounting Module. *British Journal of Educational Technology, 40*(2), 237–254. doi:10.1111/j.1467-8535.2008.00924.x

Millard, D., Howard, Y., Bailey, C., Davis, H., Gilbert, L., Jeyes, S., et al. (2005). Mapping the e-learning assessment domain: Concept maps for orientation and navigation. *Proceedings of e-Learn 2005*. Retrieved November 20, 2015, from http://eprints.soton.ac.uk/261553/

Miller, H. G., & Mork, P. (2013). From data to decisions: A value chain for big data. *IT Professional, 15*(1), 57–59. doi:10.1109/MITP.2013.11

Mora, M. C., Sancho-Bru, J. L., Iserte, J. L., & Sánchez, F. T. (2012). An e-assessment approach for evaluation in engineering overcrowded groups. *Computers & Education, 59*(2), 732–740. doi:10.1016/j.compedu.2012.03.011

Mueller, J. (2014). *Authentic Assessment Toolbox*. Retrieved from http://jfmueller.faculty.noctrl.edu/toolbox/whatisit.htm#authentic

Noorbehbahani, F., & Kardan, A. A. (2011). The automatic assessment of free text answers using a modified BLEU algorithm. *Computers & Education, 56*(2), 337–345. doi:10.1016/j.compedu.2010.07.013

OECD. (2010) *The Nature of Learning: using research to inspire practice*. Retrieved from http://www.oecd.org/edu/ceri/thenatureoflearningusingresearchtoinspirepractice.htm

Olofsson, A. D., Lindberg, J. O., & Stödberg, U. (2011). Shared video media and blogging online. Educational technologies for enhancing formative e-assessment? *Campus-Wide Information Systems, 28*(1), 41–55. doi:10.1108/10650741111097287

Ortigosa, A., Paredes, P., & Rodriguez, P. (2010). AH-questionnaire: An adaptive hierarchical questionnaire for learning styles. *Computers & Education, 54*(4), 999–1005. doi:10.1016/j.compedu.2009.10.003

Osuji, U. S. A. (2009). The use of e-Assessments in the Nigerian higher education system. *Turkish Online Journal of Distance Education, 13*(4), 140–152.

Pachler, N., Daly, C., Mor, Y., & Mellar, H. (2010). Formative E-Assessment: Practitioner Cases. *Computers & Education, 54*(3), 715–721. doi:10.1016/j.compedu.2009.09.032

Pellegrino, J. W. (2010). Technology and Formative Assessment. In P. Peterson, E. Baker, & B. McGaw (Eds.), *International Encyclopaedia of Education* (3rd ed., Vol. 8, pp. 42–47). Oxford: Elsevier. doi:10.1016/B978-0-08-044894-7.00700-4

PingSoft. (2007). *HyperAuthor e-Examination System.* Retrieved from http://www.pingsoft.net/english/product/haes.asp

Quality Assurance Agency for Higher Education. (2010). *Code of practice for the assurance of academic quality and standards in higher education.* Retrieved from https://www.brookes.ac.uk/Documents/Students/QAACode/

Redecker, C. (2013). *The use of ICT for the assessment of key competences* (JRC scientific and policy reports). European Commission, Joint Research Centre. Institute for prospective Technological Studies. Retrieved from http://ftp.jrc.es/EURdoc/JRC76971.pdf

Redecker, C., & Johannessen, Ø. (2013). Changing Assessment — Towards a New Assessment Paradigm Using ICT. *European Journal of Education, 48*(1), 79–96. doi:10.1111/ejed.12018

Scottish Qualifications Authority. (2005). *SQA Guidelines on e-assessment for Schools.* Glasgow: Hanover House. Retrieved from http://www.sqa.org.uk/files_ccc/SQA_Guidelines_on_e-assessment_Schools_June05.pdf

Sharples, M., Adams, A., Ferguson, R., Gaved, M., McAndrew, P., Rienties, B., et al. (2014). Exploring new forms of teaching, learning and assessment, to guide educators and policy makers. Innovating Pedagogy 2014: Open University Innovation Report 3. Milton Keynes: The Open University. Retrieved from http://www.openuniversity.edu/sites/www.openuniversity.edu/files/The_Open_University_Innovating_Pedagogy_2014_0.pdf

Stödberg, U. (2012). A research review of e-assessment. *Assessment & Evaluation in Higher Education, 37*(5), 591–604. doi:10.1080/02602938.2011.557496

Tinoca, L., Oliveira, I., & Pereira, A. (2014). A Conceptual Framework for E-Assessment in Higher Education: Authenticity, Consistency, Transparency and Practicability. In S. Mukerji & P. Tripathi (Eds.), Handbook of Research on Transnational Higher Education Management. IGI Global (pp. 652–673). Hershey, PA, USA: IGI Global. doi:doi:10.4018/978-1-4666-4458-8.ch033 doi:10.4018/978-1-4666-4458-8.ch033

Tomas, C., Borg, M., & McNeil, J. (2015). E-assessment: Institutional development strategies and the assessment life cycle. *British Journal of Educational Technology, 46*(3), 588–596. doi:10.1111/bjet.12153

Whitelock, D. (2007). Computer Assisted Formative Assessment: Supporting Students to Become More Reflective Learners. In C.P. Constantinou, Z.C. Zacharia & M. Papaevripidou, (Eds). *Proceedings of 8th International Conference on ComputerBased Learning in Science*, (CBLIS'07) (pp. 492-503).

Whitelock, D. (2009). Editorial: e-assessment: Developing new dialogues for the digital age. *British Journal of Educational Technology*, *40*(2), 199–202. doi:10.1111/j.1467-8535.2008.00932.x

Whitelock, D. (2010). Activating assessment for learning: Are we on the way with Web 2.0? In M. J. Lee & C. McLoughin (Eds.), Web 2.0-Based-E-Learning: Applying Social Informatics for Tertiary Teaching (pp. 319–342). Hershey, PA, USA: IGI Global. doi:doi:10.4018/978-1-60566-294-7.ch017 doi:10.4018/978-1-60566-294-7.ch017

Whitelock, D. (2014, November 13). Empirical Investigations that supported the development of OpenEssayist: A tool for drafting academic essays. *Paper presented at1st International Workshop on Technology-Enhanced Assessment, Analytics and Feedback (TEAAF2014)*, Barcelona.

Whitelock, D., & Brasher, A. (2006). Developing a Roadmap for E-Assessment: Which Way Now? In M. Danson (ed.). *Proceedings of the 10th CAA International Computer Assisted Assessment Conference* (pp. 487–501). Loughborough, UK: Loughborough University.

Whitelock, D., & Watt, S. (2008). Reframing E-Assessment: Adopting New Media and Adapting Old Frameworks. *Learning, Media and Technology*, *33*(3), 151–154. doi:10.1080/17439880802447391

Williams, P. (2014). Squaring the circle: A new alternative to alternative-assessment. *Teaching in Higher Education*, *19*(5), 565–577. doi:10.1080/13562517.2014.882894

Wills, G. B., Bailey, C. P., Davis, H. C., Gilbert, L., Howard, Y., & Steve Jeyes, S. et al. (2009). An e-learning framework for assessment (FREMA). *Assessment & Evaluation in Higher Education*, *34*(3), 273–292. doi:10.1080/02602930802068839

Wood, E.J. (2003). What are extended matching sets questions? *Bioscience Educational eJournal*, 1(1). DOI:10.3108/beej.2003.01010002

Working Group on 14–19 Reform. (2004). *14–19 Curriculum and qualifications reform: Final report of the Working Group on 14–19 Reform*. Nottinghamshire: DfES.

Xanthou, M. (2013). An Intelligent Personalized e-Assessment Tool Developed and Implemented for a Greek Lyric Poetry Undergraduate Course. *The Electronic Journal of e-Learning, 11*(2), 101-114.

KEY TERMS AND DEFINITIONS

Authentic Assessment: Refers to assessment tasks that resemble the activities and the complexity of the real-world. These tasks can demonstrate meaningful application of essential knowledge and skills and are focused on testing higher order capabilities.

Dynamic Assessment: This approach is focused on students' progress and is strictly related to intervention. Teachers usually interact with students with difficulties or disabilities, identifying ways to overcome each leaner's current learning difficulties.

Diagnostic Assessment: A measurement approach that is usually carried out before starting the learning activities. Its purpose is to identify, prior to instruction, each student's knowledge, skills, strengths and weaknesses. This type of assessment allows the teacher to adjust the curriculum to meet each student's needs.

eAssessment: Includes all the assessment tasks using a computer or the web. eAssessment includes the use of ICTs in the whole assessment process, from designing and delivering assignments to marking, reporting, storing the results and/or conducting the statistical analysis.

Formative Assessment: Type of assessment that is carried out during the learning process, providing the learner with personalized feedback on his/her current knowledge and skills. Formative assessment allows strategic and timely feedback to be provided to learners at critical points of their learning process.

Summative Assessment: Summative assessment is carried out when the learning activities have finished. It is usually used for judgements or decisions about the individual grades or the verification of learners' achievements. Summative assessment leads to a formal qualification or to the certification of specific skills.

Integrative Assessment: Its primary purpose is to influence students' approaches to future learning goals by tracking the strategies that are used to respond to specific tasks. Integrative assessment involves the use of complex tasks, can have multiple stakeholders and may not depend on simple or convergent responses.

Learning Analytics: An educational application of web analytics that is commonly used for measuring, collecting, analysing and reporting learners' data and their educational contexts. The main purpose is to understand and enhance learning and the contexts in which it occurs.

Chapter 4
Competency-Based Assessment:
From Conceptual Model to Operational Tool

Mohammed Khalidi Idrissi
Mohammed V University in Rabat, Morocco

Meriem Hnida
Mohammed V University in Rabat, Morocco

Samir Bennani
Mohammed V University in Rabat, Morocco

ABSTRACT

Competency-based Assessment (CBA) is the measurement of student's competency against a standard of performance. It is a process of collecting evidences to analyze student's progress and achievement. In higher education, Competency-based Assessment puts the focus on learning outcomes to constantly improve academic programs and meet labor market demands. As of to date, competencies are described using natural language but rarely used in e-learning systems, and the common sense idea is that: the way competency is defined shapes the way it is conceptualized, implemented and assessed. The main objective of this chapter is to introduce and discuss Competency-based Assessment from a methodological and technical perspectives. More specifically, the objective is to highlight ongoing issues regarding competency assessment in higher education in the 21st century, to emphasis the benefits of its implementation and finally to discuss some competency modeling and assessment techniques.

DOI: 10.4018/978-1-5225-0531-0.ch004

INTRODUCTION

Educational systems have always benefited from technological advances to explore new research areas and improve the teaching-learning process. Over recent years, there has been an increased interest in incorporating competencies into educational curriculum to insure the teaching meets industry-required needs. A Competency-based Education (CBE) focuses on the outcomes of learning by defining goals and processes to achieve them (El Falaki et al.,2011). It contributes to student's career readiness since the main goal is to let students progress at their own pace and measure their achievement against a standard of performance. Educational programs based on CBE describe skills and capacities that one needs to achieve and should be align with both industry and academic standards (Johnstone & Leasure, 2015). CBE involves a methodology to describe, model and assess competencies. However, developing educational programs with a focus on competency as student's characteristic is challenging and needs further attention when it comes to learners' cognitive skills which are considered as unobservable traits, hard to conceive and objectively measure (Hnida, Idrissi, & Bennani, 2014). The research question addressed in this chapter is: how competencies are modeled and assessed within an e-learning platform.

The starting point of developing a competency assessment model is defining and modeling students' attributes to be measured. Based on our literature review, it seems that competencies still subject to different modeling and scales, and have suffered from a variety of interpretations and implementations within e-learning systems: (1) different conceptions of learner profile (2) various approaches promoting either knowledge, skills or attitudes, (3) different assessment strategies to meet specific needs. The variety in competency modeling and assessment techniques could be explained, then, by the fact that existing models and standardized tests don't follow the extremely rapid change.

In the above situation and in order to assess competencies in an online educational system, we need to clearly set a competency assessment model. This category of assessment is viewed as putting students on a competency scale in order to compare them, more specifically, it tends to pinpoint where their understanding is strong and where their understanding is less strong. For tutors, assessing student competencies help them generating concept maps, with understood concepts and misunderstood ones, that need further explanations or more practices in real contexts. This highlights the need to develop a guideline explaining how to effectively implement Competency-based Assessment.

Competency-based Assessment is an important research topic which might be divided into two open problems: (1) Assessment design, which includes competency modeling by test designers, it is about formulating a competency structure to assess and clearly link each competency to an appropriate situation, problem and material. (1) Assessment implementation by test developers, it includes means and tools used to capture measurable attributes of competency. However, assessing competencies involves a complex range of learners' characteristics such us: knowledge level, style, abilities, cognitive skills, background, etc.

The purpose of this chapter is to discuss and highlight open problems of Competency-based Assessment and issues regarding its implementation in online educational systems. It tends to find a common understanding of competency, reports and discusses competency modeling and assessment techniques and concludes with a set of best practices. The rest of this chapter is organized as follows:

In Section II, we report and analyze competency definition, trying to, first, understand what the term "competency" means and which of the students' attributes are involved in, and then, to find a form of consensus about how competencies could be defined and what criterion might be used to effectively measure a shown performance. In Section III, we discuss ongoing issues and challenges regarding competency assessment in higher education in the 21st century, then we highlight its benefits for teachers, students, administrators and e-learning systems. Finally, we report some approaches used for assessing competencies in e-learning systems. In section IV, we review related works. Then, we describe the methodology we have adopted to create a competency model. We emphasize the importance of ontology-based competency modeling and show useful steps to follow. An example of implementation of the proposed model within e-learning systems is briefly described. Finally, section V outlines the main conclusion and draws research perspectives.

COMPETENCY DEFINITION

The term competence was first proposed by David C.McCelelland, a professor of psychology at Harvard University. In his paper "Testing for Competence Rather than for Intelligence" (McClelland, 1973), he defines competency as "The knowledge, skills, traits, attitudes, self-concepts, values, or motives directly related to job performance or important life outcomes and shown to differentiate between superior and average performers" (McClelland, 1973). In this definition, the competence is considered as a personal characteristic which helps an individual effectively perform a task, a mean to distinguish between good and poor performance. It is task-specific, related to a shown performance and can be used as a scale of performance. According to Boyatzis, a colleague of David C.McCelelland, a competency is a feature of an individual (combined with other personal characteristics) which helps a person reach a good level of performance (Boyatzis, 1982). The word 'competency' is usually linked to underlying qualities, it refers to a latent trait that may not be easily observable and needs specific contexts and conditions. However, for Boyatzis and McCelelland competency remains job-specific. These two definitions presuppose grades are not predictors of competency and that one could demonstrate mastery only by processing a task in a concrete work situation. However, competency is the proven capability related to knowledge, skills and attitudes provided by any actors in any context: in school, organization or any situation involving a capability. Furthermore, competency should be transferable and portable from one context to another.

Gilbert Paquette defines competency as a combination of knowledge, ability and performance (Paquette, 2007). Knowledge might be divided into three categories: conceptual, procedural and strategic knowledge. Ability is the capacity to use acquired skills and knowledge in new contexts and situations. The performance refers to the level of mastery of competency. It is also described as meta-knowledge that one apply to knowledge or a knowledge about a preselected knowledge (Paquette, 2007). This definition tends to better define competency, the term competency is then not job-specific and it distinguishes between the knowledge as 'input', capability as "processing knowledge" and performance as a "tangible result".

According to (Sanghi 2007), there is a difference between the word "Competence" and the word "Competency". Competence is "skill-based" while competency is "behavior-based". The first one shows what a person is able to do while the second one is related to human factors which helps an individual reach a standard of performance. However, even though a person is competent in a subject there is no guarantee of good performance because it depends on other extremely personal or environmental factors. So, the performance is not a good predictor of having or not a competence. The same author defines competence as a set of visible (knowledge and skills) and hidden (Self-concept, traits, motive) components. For (Carlton & Levy, 2015) skills refers to interactions of a person with his/her environment and the performance is a result. Skills are developed by the practice, which is called "Learning by Doing", a step by step process to achieve a high-level of performance. It is worth highlighting that competency is a multidimensional construct, best described by McClelland as an iceberg: the visible part of the iceberg refers to knowledge and capabilities and the hidden one is underlying personal characteristics (McClelland, 1973). This leads to an open issue regarding modeling and assessing competencies in e-learning systems which is: what would best describe one's competency? How underlying and personal characteristics could be modeled and captured in an online environment?

Another relevant definition of competency was proposed by Guy Le Boterf (Le Boterf 2015). According to the author, the term competency cannot be defined without a link to a person. It shows a capacity of: "Know how to act. Want to act. Be able to act". To know how to act is to be able to choose relevant resources, to want to act refers to willing to do something (motivation) and to be able to act is to choose the right situation and moment to perform (Le Boterf, 2015). According to (Bissonnette & Richard, 2001),there is two kinds of competencies, the ones related to a domain knowledge and cross-disciplinary ones like attitudes that one needs in order to acquire autonomy.(Le Boterf, 2015) recognizes a difference between individual and collective competencies, and (Sellenet, 2010) between imitation, portable and innovation competencies, imitation to automatically reproduce learned actions, portable competencies refers to the capacity to reuse acquired knowledge and skills in new contexts and situations and innovation to develop skills associated with creativity (Sellenet, 2010)(Cuenca et al., 2015).

For (Bremgartner & de Magalhaes Netto, 2011) there is a difference between the term «Skill» and «Competency», a skill is a set of tasks that a learner can do with a level of proficiency using several equipment and learning materials while competency is a group of skills that one uses to reach a specific standard under specific conditions. (Nitchot, Gilbert, & Wills, 2010) notices two different states of competence whether it's an existing competency or desired one. The first one describes prerequisite skills/abilities and the second one refers to learning outcomes. For (Marques, Zacarias, & Tribolet, 2010), competencies are capabilities which take the shape of human actions and resources, and a capability is linked to a subject in order to reach a goal.

In the most recent works, the definition of competency has not yet been unified. Competency is defined as a combination of (knowledge, skill, strategy, experience, method, organization) which form a structure under specific conditions. It's a psychological character influenced by educational systems, cultures, the labor markets, etc. (Zhao, 2014). A competency can be used, in e-learning systems, as characteristic to personalize the learning experience, because individuals are able to learn at different pace and a competency-based program should provide what a learner should acquire and should pass what he/she already knows.

To sum up, several researchers have defined competency as a cluster of knowledge, attitudes and abilities which become apparent by showing a performance in doing tasks under specific conditions. A competency can be developed using a training program, and is portable from one context to another (Hnida, Idrissi, & Bennani, 2014). It is worth highlighting that all definitions of competency refer to a personal trait which depends on many human factors and environment. Also, the term "competency" in the literature usually goes with the term "action" that one performs to reach an objective. The terms "Experience" and "Practice" are also used in competency definition and development. Finally, the word "Performance" usually used to refer to conditions and contexts in which competency could be captured.

COMPETENCY-BASED ASSESSMENT

This section starts with discussing some ongoing issues regarding competency assessment in higher education in the 21st century. Then, it highlights some of its challenges and benefits. Finally, this section reports some approaches used for assessing competencies in e-learning systems.

Ongoing Issues and Challenges Regarding Competency Assessment in Higher Education in the 21st Century

One of the ongoing issues regarding assessment in higher education in the 21st century is supporting learners in the way they learn, helping them recognize their weakness and strength and providing them with specific guidance to achieve a standard of performance. Assessment should give students opportunities to learn and help them think at a high level. The focus should be on meaningful assessment activities supporting skills such us critical thinking, problem solving, decision making, communication, collaboration, etc. A good competency assessment needs to challenge students to make effective use of existing knowledge and skills to solve an open-ended problem, perform a task or create a new product individually or in a group project.

For the past decade, assessment has focused on putting students on a scale in order to narrow the gap between the lowest and the highest student's level. However, nowadays the emphasis is on linking students to their international peers and to the industry required needs. This leads to new assessment techniques moving from assessing for knowledge to assessing for competencies, where the emphasis is on learning outcomes rather than learning objectives. The challenge is to ensure every student attains the skills in a global race skills.

The term Competency-based Assessment is generic, it includes all types of measurement used in different areas such as education, health, psychology, sociology, etc. It usually refers to a process of gathering evidences in order to make decision. When based on competency, an assessment offers much to education, it analyzes student's progress and helps effectively improve curriculum and educational programs to be align with both industry and academic needs (Kaslow et al., 2009). It improves the student's overall learning. It is a self-driven process in which each student assesses himself against a set of required competencies, then he/she progresses based on his own pace in order to reduce the gap between the current level and the desired one. So, it could enhance the student's motivation since the purpose is to compare student's level against a standard of performance rather than comparing students between them.

For example, AHELO (Assessment of Higher Education Learning Outcomes) (Tremblay, Lalancette, & Roseveare, 2012) is an international attempt at assessing students' outcomes, it aims to create an international performance scale across cultures, languages and institutions. The purpose of the AHELO project is to come up with a standardize performance assessment tool, to be able to assess students in multiple countries and put them on the same global scale. However, some questions remain to be considered like how does it come to assess a range of learning outcomes trough the same standardize assessment tool? What does the term "standard" means across multiples countries and educational reforms? Interpreting students' competencies is context-dependent and could be different from one country to another.

Another example of Competency-based Assessment project is ALEKS available at (https://www.aleks.com/), an online assessment tool which assesses student's competency in mathematics. The term "ALEKS" stands for "Assessment and Learning in Knowledge Spaces". An online placement test which uses artificial-intelligence and knowledge Space Theory to effectively capture student's mastery level in mathematics. It uses adaptive testing techniques; this means each student answers his/her own set of specific questions. A reasonable assumption is that providing student with tailored questions would be more challenging and the fact of answering too easy or too difficult questions wouldn't capture much information about student's current level. It is clear that Competency-based Assessment seeks for a demonstration of skills. Still, one issue needs to be addressed: what is the difference between assessing for knowledge and assessing for competencies?

The difference between assessing for knowledge and assessing for competencies, or the difference between assessment of learning and assessment for learning derives from the idea of engaging students in the teaching-learning process. It tends to capture both student's level of knowledge and what he/she is able to do with it. It's a self-regulated process in which each student has to demonstrate a mastery. The paragraph bellow illustrates some benefits of Competency-based Assessment for teachers, students, administrators and e-learning systems.

For Teachers:

- Ensure the training is relevant to student's level of mastery: Competency-based Assessment provides teachers with information about the quality of their teaching plan and strategy.
- Analyzing student's progress toward a competency and provide feedback and guidance.
- Identify students with learning difficulties. Since competency is considered as individual assessment, the emphasis is on assessing the progress of each student toward a certain competency.

For Students:

- Identify existing knowledge and intended learning outcomes: students are more motivated when they realize the benefits of improving their level, they have an idea about what they will learn and how they can achieve a proficiency level.
- Interpret, synthetize and use acquired knowledge in real contexts.
- Promote problem solving, lifelong learning, critical thinking, communication, self-direction, decision-making and collaborating skills.
- Provide students with authentic and meaningful assessment activities.
- Student could succeed in a competitive environment at his/her own pace.

For Administrators:

- Provide information about curricular strength and weakness, this information is about the "value added" of colleges and universities.
- Reduce the gap between educational setting and labor market.
- Constantly improve educational programs to conform the ongoing rapid change.
- Compare students with their international peers.

For E-Learning Systems:

- Automatically generate concept maps, with understood concepts and misunderstood ones. Competency-based Assessment is used in online placement tests to pinpoint where student's understanding is strong and where their understanding is less strong.
- Automatically generate an individualized learning path with suitable learning activities.

In short, it could be effective to use different approaches of assessment so to cover different aspects of competency. Some Competency-based Assessment approaches are more beneficial for students than teachers, some of them could be used in the ongoing process of teaching and learning so to guide both learners and teacher while other assessment approaches tends to measure student's mastery across a standard of performance. The paragraph bellow discusses some Competency-based Assessment approaches used in e-learning systems.

Competency-Based Assessment Approaches in E-Learning Systems

A variety of learning outcomes leads to different assessment approaches. In an e-learning system Competency-based Assessment might be implemented using different approaches: individual or group project, simulations, problem solving, video recording, e-Portfolios, journals, students' logs. It usually encourages the student to use Information and Communication Technology to demonstrate a mastery level.

One of the approaches used to assess students' competencies is e-Portfolio which could be defined as: "Personalized, Web-based collections of work, responses to work, and reflections that are used to demonstrate key skills and accomplishment for a variety of contexts and time periods" (Lorenzo & Ittleson, 2005). In this definition, e-Portfolio is considered as a digital collection of evidences, used by students to demonstrate a mastery and by teachers to analyze students' progress. This assessment approach challenges students by giving them a mean to demonstrate a mastery by their own. It enhances student's productive learning by presenting and exchanging ideas, responses, results and reflections. Students share materials and get feedbacks from teachers and peers. It's a learner-centered approach which promotes student's autonomy. The benefits of using e-Portfolio remains in its potential to capture evidences about student's mastery but also to capture other skills such as communicating, collaborating, argumentative reasoning, knowledge management, social responsibility skills (Rhodes, 2011)(Yastibas & Yastibas, 2015).

Simulation-based approach is also used to capture information about student's competency. It refers to assessing student's mastery in a simulated environment. It's an evidence-centered (Cook, Zendejas, Hamstra, Hatala, & Brydges, 2013) approach typically used in some cases when the assessment could be dangerous in real context such us healthcare or when it requires expensive materials or products. Online simulations use technology to create assessment activities that mimic the real context. It puts the examinee in a virtual reality with a situation provoking his/her knowledge and skills.

Another approach for measuring competency is project-based assessment (Bennani, Idrissi, Fadouli, Yassine, & Ouguengay, 2012). The basic assumption behind using projects is to enable a group of learners to work together, in order to accomplish a task or demonstrate achievement of competencies. This approach encourages learners to put into practice their knowledge and skills. It is also a learner-centered approach which emphasis the importance of creating homogenous groups with complementary skills, each student brings a set of skills and contributes to a common goal. The assessment covers the results but also the processes, track each student's contribution and performance in relation to the common goal of a group. However, there are varying ways of using project-based assessment, whether the focus is on assessing one competency at a time or using a single project that covers multiple competencies. It might vary from self-assessment, peer-assessment or team-assessment depending on the purpose. Self-assessment gives each member the opportunity to describe his own contribution. Peer-assessment enables each member to assess his/her teammates' contribution and finally team-assessment each student to describe and assess the whole team performance and achievement.

There is also a growing interest into incorporating the potential of video recording. Still, videos do not capture a student's performance, but it could be a mean for teachers to assess communication and arguing skills. Using a self-made video recording gives student the opportunity to present and share the material to the world. Going over a video many times provide students with a great feedback on how he/she could improve his/her level.

One question that needs to be asked, however, is: the performance shown by the student is observable but the competencies that underlie the performance are not easily observable. Assessing competence involves a complex range of learners' characteristics such us his/her knowledge level, style, abilities, cognitive skills, background, etc. Another issue regarding assessment of competencies is that a student uses several acquired key competencies in a single assessment situation. Therefore, another common asked question is that the competence should be assessed in terms of key competencies or as one level of performance? This leads to another approach of Competency-based Assessment in e-learning systems which is called "Cognitive assessment". In this assessment approach competency is related to abilities called also latent trait. There is a growing interest in exploring psychometric approach for assessing competencies (Baker, 2001; Csapó, Ainley, Bennett, Latour, & Law, 2012; Ferrão, Costa, & Oliveira, 2015; Merrouch, Hnida, Idrissi, & Bennani, 2014; Rust & Golombok, 2014; Sharkness & DeAngelo, 2010; Sluijsmans, Prins, & Martens, 2006).

One solution to the above problem could be to use Item Response Theory (IRT) for an educational purpose. Item Response Theory is a set of psychometric models which assume that it is possible to estimate an individual latent trait (like ability, capability or attitude) based on his/her answers to a set of tailored questions. The logic of IRT scoring is as following:

- In a test, each student has a probability to answer correctly a question (or not) according to his/her level. The learner responses during an assessment are considered as a stochastic process in which the probability of giving a correct answer or not, depends on previous asked questions and answers and relies on the exact examinee ability.
- In a test, each question has 3 important parameters. The first parameter is called "difficulty parameter", it represents the difficulty degree of the item. The second parameter is the "discrimination parameter" used to distinguish group of individual according to their responses to a set of asked question. Giving a question a discriminative weight allows the question to classify learners who succeed from those who fail answering. (3) The pseudo guessing parameter shows the probability of an examinee of a very low ability level to get, by chance, a correct answer to a question.

In a test, each question test refers to a characteristic, or facet, of the competency to be measured. While answering an item the learner is showing an underlying ability that the test is trying to capture. A test based on IRT doesn't measure the competency as the sum of answers obtained at the end but by considering the student behavior toward each question. One of the important advantage of this mathematical assessment model is "objective measure": the questions or items are independent from individuals. It means that the competency measured by an IRT test must be independent of which questions were asked and may vary from one test to another. One thing worth highlighting is that, in a class students may have the same score and it doesn't mean they possess the same level of ability.

A significant conclusion is that nowadays Information and Communication Technology offers much to assessment in higher education, it provides students with tools and means to demonstrate a mastery, it also encourages students to share their work and review peer's work. For teachers, it is about tracking student's progress, giving feedbacks and guidance through the learning process and collecting evidences about students' achievement. As mentioned above, many approach could be used to assess one's competency.

Each assessment approach brings with it different challenges, benefits and drawbacks. Yet, the basic challenge is to clearly define competencies to assess as measurable attributes and link those competencies to relevant material and approaches.

COMPETENCY ASSESSMENT: DEFINING A COMPETENCY MODEL

In this section, we discuss some modeling techniques, namely:

- A Graphical Knowledge Modeling (Paquette, Mariño, Rogozan, & Léonard, 2015).
- Competency Based Knowledge Space Theory (Heller, Stefanutti, Anselmi, & Robusto, 2015).
- COMBA Model: Competence Based Learner Knowledge For Personalized Assessment (Onjira Sitthisak, Gilbert, & Davis, 2007).
- Semantic Approach (Marques et al., 2010).
- Universally Competency Definition using standards.
- Ontology-based modeling for modeling competencies.

The purpose is to identify best practices and techniques to define competencies in an online assessment environment.

A Graphical Knowledge Modeling for Defining and Assessing Competencies

Paquette Gilbert defines competency as a set of knowledge, abilities and performance that a learner is assumed to process in particular context and situation (Paquette, 2007; Paquette, Mariño, Rogozan, & Léonard, 2015). An ability is an action applied to knowledge with a level of performance. Paquette proposed an object-oriented modeling tool named MOT for competency self-management which represents competency using 3 components: knowledge, skill and performance.

1. The term "knowledge" means a cluster of concept, procedure or principles.
    a. Concept refers to a class of objects, it's known as conceptual knowledge and aims to describe learning content properties, and it's an answer for "what question"
    b. Procedure refers to a class of actions applied to knowledge, it gives an answer to how knowledge will be processed (Operations, Tasks, Activities, Learning Scenarios, etc.)
    c. Principles are a class of statement or conditions. It represents a set of rules and conditions to be satisfied. It takes the form of "if condition – then action"
2. The term "skill" (also called Meta-process) is a characteristic that can be described and evaluated using a taxonomy. It's a set of knowledge enabling a person to process a task, it's "a meta-knowledge applied to knowledge" like receiving, reproducing, creating or reinvesting, it usually take the form of "Verb".
3. The term "Performance" describes the context (for example: familiar or new) in which skills are applied. Also, it defines if a guidance is required or not, the type of coverage (Total or Partial).

Table 1. competency modeling concepts using MOT framework

Ability	Knowledge	Performance
Receive: pay attention, remember, identify, locate	Concept	Frequency: On occasion, steadily
Reproduce: Apply (Simulate, use), transpose, translate, instantiate, specify.	Procedure	Cover: partial total individual, collaborative
Produce: analyze (deduct, classify, predict, diagnose), repair, synthesize (induce, plan, design)	Principle	Autonomy: with assistance /without help
Self-management: assess, self-discipline, (influence, initiate, adapt, control)	Fact	Complexity: low, medium, high
Example of competence: Synthesize - the concept of communication - without help.		Context: familiar, new

To summarize, according to Paquette Gilbert, Competency is a combination of (Knowledge, Skill, and Performance). A competency is a set of skills applied to knowledge with a level of performance. The taxonomy of skills can be reduced to 10-levels scale: (0) Pay Attention (1) Memorize (2) Explicitate (3) Transpose, (4) Apply, (5) Analyze, (6) Repair, (7) Synthetize, (8) Evaluate, (9) Self Control. And the performance scale includes 5-levels scale: (1) Aware, (2) Familiar, (3) Productive, (4) Expert. The following table synthetizes competency modeling concepts using MOT framework (table 1).

An example of implementation of MOT framework for measuring competencies is reported by (Brisebois et al., 2005). It is a self-assessment tool in an online learning environment. The self-assessment competency tool works as follows: first, the student should describe his/her current level of mastery. Then, the system helps student self-diagnose his/her state of mastery. After that, it guides him/her reduce the gap by recommending a list of activities. However, one problem arises: how could student assess his/her own level objectively? Furthermore, how could a student choose between a set of activities the most relevant ones. The focus is on engaging students in the assessment process but we assume that teacher's feedbacks is highly recommended in this case.

Competency Based Knowledge Space Theory

The Competency Based Knowledge Space Theory (CbKST) (Albert, Hockemeyer, Kickmeier-Rust, Nussbaumer, & Steiner, 2012; El-Kechaï, Melero, & Labat, 2015; Heller et al., 2015) is a theory which is developed to support adaptive testing in e-learning systems (Heller, Mayer, Hockemeyer, & Albert, 2006). It represents an extended version of the Knowledge Space Theory (KST) but dealing with competencies. The main idea behind CbKST is that a domain knowledge can be structured based on prerequisite relationships, orders and constraints among competencies. The CbKST model links problems to competencies in order to assess latent skills (competencies) based on what kind of problems the student is capable of solving. Using a competence structure associated with a set of problems helps define a learning path taking into account the missing competencies and prerequisites ones.

The CbKST model is based on three fundamentals: precedence relations, competence state and competence structure. Precedence relations refers to a structure of competencies using prerequisites relations. For example, in the CbKST framework, CompetenceA <= CompetenceB means that competence A is a prerequisite to develop competence B, it also means that if a student masters the competence B, he/she definitely masters competence A. These prerequisite relations can be modeled using Hasse Diagram

Figure 1. CBST structure using Hasse diagram (Heller et al. 2006)

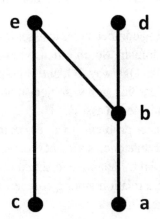

(Heller et al., 2006) as shown in the Figure 1 below. A prerequisite relation also means that one competence should be acquired before another.

In this exemple illustrated in Figure 2, a set of problems is modeled using a domain knowledge Q ={a, b, c, d, e}, each problem is linked to an underlying competency. In one hand, if a learnner is capable of solving the problem a and b then he has the potential to solve problem d. In the other hand, competency a, b and c are required to solve problem e. vice versa, if a learner is able to solve problem e then he could easily solve the problems a, b and c.

A competence state is the resulat of connection of singles competencies. {a}, {c}, {a,b}, {a,b,c}, {a,b,d}, {a,b,c,e},{a,b,c,e} are examples of competence states. A comeptence structure is the collection of all competence states of a given domain. If the competence structure is set empty ϕ (called also native state), it means that the learner doesn't master yet any competence. Its is considered as the lowest level. The competence structure shows the current level but also what a learner has to learn next. Q= { ϕ, {a} ,{c},{a,b},{a,b,c},{a,b,d},{a,b,c,e},{a,b,c,e}, Q}. Q refers to all domain competencies.

Figure 2. CBST framework competency assessment (Heller et al. 2015)

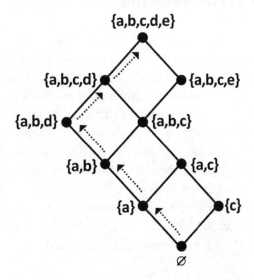

The CbKST theorical framework is used to structure a domain competencies using 4 steps:

1. Identifying competencies: choosing competencies to asses is a difficult task. It requires both experience and expertize in the target domain. So, in order to define a structure to assess competencies one has to call a domain specialist. One way to identify competencies, in education, is to analyze the curriculum which contains learning goals, subject matter and learning materials: this could help formulating a set of competencies to assess.
2. Creation of appropriate situations or problems to assess competencies.
3. Deriving prerequiste relations: competencies are not independent one from antoher and establishing prerequiste relations is essential for adaptive testing and also for personlized learning. Several methods can be used to describre relation among competencies, semantic approach to provide a textual description or mathematical approach.

The framework CbKST is used to model but also to assess competencies (Heller et al., 2015), For example, in the Hasse Diagram shown in (Figure 2) the assessment starts by giving the learner a problem associated with competence A. If he/she could answer the problem correctly, then the next step is to give the student another problem which is C. After that, the assessment will present to him/her a set of problems including 2 competencies A and C.

So based on the learner previously given answers and the prerequisite relations between competencies the next problem will be selected. By collecting the set of problems one can answer the system can assess learner competencies.

One exemple of integrating Knowledge Space Theory and competency model to assess student's mastery level is ALEKS system described above in section III. It's an online assessment tool which assesses student competency in mathematics using adaptive testing technique. Another example which implements Knowledge Space Theory in assessment is Iclass project see (http://kti.tugraz.at/css/projects/iclass/), it is an intelligent skill-based e-learning platform which includes a skill-based planner, an adaptive assessment and a self-evaluation tool.

The COMBA Model (Competence Based Learner Knowledge for Personlized Assessment)

(Onjira Sitthisak et al., 2007) defined competency as a capability associated with a subject matter and is usually linked to a situation or context. The COMBA Model illustrated in Figure bellow (Figure 3) is built upon the following components: "Capability", "Subject Matter Content", "Attitude", "Evidence", "Proficiency Level", "Tools" And "Situations". However, the most important ones are "Capability", "Subject Matter Content" and "Attitude", which are sufficient to assess learner's competencies using taxonomy, authors use Bloom Taxonomy for cognitive domain capabilities to represent a capability, Merrill's analysis for Subject Matter Content and Krathwohl's taxonomy for Attitude (Onjira Sitthisak et al., 2007). The basic Assumption behind the COMBA Model is to model learner's knowledge as multidimensional space of capabilities, each capability is linked to a specific context. The context includes situations and tools that justify the use of competency. In order to be measured, competency needs evidence which demonstrates the level of learner's competency in a subject content matter. Situation includes conditions under which a competency is performed.

Figure 3. COMBA Model (Sitthisak et al. 2007)

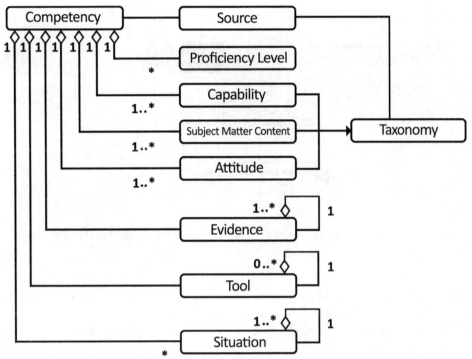

The COMBA assessment model is used to generate automated adaptive test questions. It uses ontology to describe a competency structure and IMS-QTI specification to define each test question in order to enable interoperability among systems. The COMBA Model is a mean to identify and structure domain competencies. Still, it's hard to transform the model to a practical assessment solution. Authors described in a later work in 2013 (O. Sitthisak, Gilbert, & Albert, 2013) that a combination of COMBA modeling technique and Knowledge Space Theory (Heller et al., 2006) is more likely to solve adaptive assessment of competencies. They proposed to use COMBA Model to explicitly define a competency structure and KST to assign assessment activities or problems. As a result, a COSMOS conceptual model is proposed and aims to define a practical solution for competency assessment. COSMOS model is based on three components: (1) COMBA Structure which contains relevant competencies of a domain. (2) KST structure which is a hierarchy of problems or assessments items. Each item should be linked to another one in order to ensure adaptive testing. (3) Merge which associate to each competency a relevant KST problem. COSMOS model is illustrated in Figure 4.

Modeling Competencies using Semantic Units

(Marques et al., 2010) proposed a "bottom-up approach" for modeling competencies. Authors used a multi-dimensional competency structure and defined competencies as a set of capabilities related to a subject matter which are represented by actions and resources (Onjira Sitthisak et al., 2007). The proposed model is based on two fundamental constructs: Entities and Relationships. The term "Entity" refers to things that have physical existence and the term "Relationship" is used to capture links between entities.

Figure 4. COSMOS Model (Sitthisak et al. 2013)

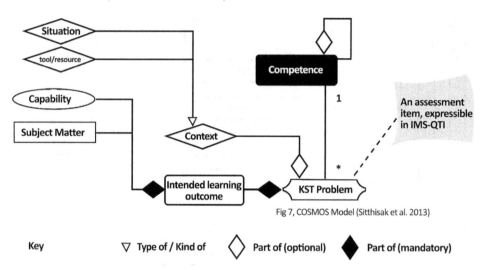

Fig 7, COSMOS Model (Sitthisak et al. 2013)

A relationship is described using (subject - predicate – object). Subjects and objects are entities while the predicate describes relation between them using a verb.

The model uses five components in order to define competencies: Competency, Task, Goal, Action, and Resource. Competency refers to a collection of "knowledge, Skills and Attitude" called KSA that an Actor processes in a given role. It is modeled using "Actions - Resources" Associated to "Task - Goal". "Actions-Resources" expresses an association entity between Action and Resource. A task is an action or group of actions performed by an Actor to reach an objective. A goal defines conditions and states of a task. An action refers to an atomic operation, a set of KSA processed by an actor to carry out a task which can be physical or mental. And resources are things or object on which actions are carried out. The competency model has been visualized and manipulated using an ontology language in Protégé (Marques et al., 2010).

Universally Competency Definition using Standards

This paragraph reports main international specifications dealing with competency definition:

1. IMS-RDCEO (Reusable Definition of Competency or Educational Objective (RDCEO)("IMS GLC: RDCEO Specification," n. d.).
2. HR-XML Competencies ("HR Open Standards Consortium, Inc," n. d.).
3. IEEE Reusable Competency Definitions (RCD) ("IEEE Xplore: IEEE Standard for Learning Technology - Data Model for Reusable Competency Definitions," n. d.).

IMS-RDECO specification defines competency as: *"the word competency is used in a very general sense that includes skills, knowledge, tasks, and learning outcomes"*. *IMS-RDCEO* competency definition includes (1) Competency Identifier: A unique label to the competency (2) Title: a human readable name of competency (3) Description: a human readable description of competency and educational objectives (4) Definition: to complete competency description with more complete definition of competency using statements, at least one statement should be used. (5) Additional Metadata can be used to fulfill competency model with author information or date of creation for example. The RDCEO data model is used for describing, referencing and exchanging information about competencies among e-learning systems.

The HR-XML Consortium HR-XML defines competency as: "*a specific, identifiable, definable, and measurable knowledge, skill, ability and/or other deployment-related characteristic (e.g. attitude, behavior, physical ability) which a human resource may possess and which is necessary for, or material to, the performance of an activity within a specific business context*". HR-XML attempts to extend similar tags as IMS-RDCEO but it adds elements for competency assessment like evidence and weight in order to substantiate a competence with a numeric value. Evidence includes test results, certificates, etc. And weight which make ranking, comparing and evaluation of competency possible.

IEEE Reusable Competency Definitions (RDC) provides a data model for describing, referencing and exchanging competency definitions in the context of e-learning systems. It uses a general definition that may be reused for more contexts and with various metrics and doesn't specify how competency elements should be captured. IEEE RDC Model definition includes: (1) Identifier: to uniquely identify competency, (2) Title: a textual label of competency, (3) Description: a human readable description of competency, (4) Metadata to capture more details about competency.

These specifications aim to define competency using XML (eXtensible Markup Language) making use of it in e-learning systems, to ensure interoperability and exchange of competency definitions. HR-XML is a model primarily developed for business but it's widely used in e-learning systems because it tends to capture measurable attributes of competency. However, in IMS-RDCEO, the information is intended directly for e-learning systems and is unstructured. All these specifications use a narrative format to promote a common human understanding and describe competency which make processing or automating this information difficult. Another issue is that none of the standards defined dimensions of competency like "personal characteristics" or "proficiency level", also they didn't address the aggregation or sequencing of competencies. It remains data models for describing, referencing and exchanging definitions.

Ontology-Based Competency Model

The following section provides a method to build a domain ontology, we illustrate the steps that we followed to construct a competency assessment model. The present work has followed several works using ontology to model competencies (Idrissi, Bennani, & Hachmoud, 2009; Lundqvist, Baker, & Williams, 2011; Ng & Hatala, 2006; Paquette et al., 2015; Põldoja, Väljataga, Laanpere, & Tammets, 2012; Schmidt & Kunzmann, 2007; Wang, Vogel, & Ran, 2011).

The purpose is to promote a common understanding of the concept or in some cases is used for specific implementation of competency in online assessment tools.

Methodology of Construction of Competency Assessment Model

In 1993, Gruber defined ontology as an "explicit specification of a conceptualization" (T. Gruber, 2009; T. R. Gruber, 1993). In 1997, Borst added one more detail "Formal specification of a shared conceptualization" (Borst, 1997) the term "shared" refers to a consensus rather than an individual point of view. An ontology structures a domain knowledge using concepts and relationships. It's a shared conceptualization, refers to a common understanding and should not be restricted to one individual. The ontology facilitates the communication between human and computer agents. Several ontology construction method has been proposed but there is no common guide. However, an ontology-based competency model can be constructed following 3 steps: (1) Conceptualization, (2) Ontoligization and (3) Operationalization (T. Gruber, 2009; T. R. Gruber, 1993).

1. The conceptualization or abstraction is a simplified view of a domain in order to construct a model of it. It's an enumeration of terms. The purpose is to capture concepts and relations among these concepts, then to classify retained ones into groups using a hierarchy. The level of details could vary depending on the domain. The end-result of this step is a conceptual model which should be independent from any particular symbol or encoding.
2. The ontoligization (Called also formalization) is to translate the lexical structure of a domain into conceptual model, which is readable by both human and machine actors. The ontology should be formal which means machine readable.
3. The operationalization is to transform the conceptual model to a formal language that can be processed by computers such us Owl, XML or RDF.

To construct a competency model we prepared a simplified view of Competency-based Education, the following description of competency could be customized and implemented in varying situation:

- A situation is the kernel of Competency-based Assessment. It's a situation in which a learner uses a set of acquired knowledge, tools and resources, in a particular context and coverage, and needs an assessment. A learning situation could be a problem to solve, a group activity, test, etc.
- A learning situation is also an accomplishment of activities in a context (new, familiar, real, simulation), the context is a required in order to define competence structure.
- Learners should demonstrate the mastery of competency in different contexts. The term context refers to conditions under which competency evidences are collected. Any conditions must be clarified because competency and the shown performance are always related to the context.
- An assessment activity involves content and have goals, content is knowledge which belongs to one subject or multiple subjects.
- An assessment activity generates a set of logs which might be used to update the learner profile or for recommending suitable learning resources. Analyzing these logs is also gathering evidences about a student performance.
- A situation overlay refers to assessment method: individual or collaborative work, it can also be partial or total, with or without assistance.
- A performance requires the mobilization of multiple resources which might be:(1) External resources like human, material or temporal (2) Contextual resources which depend on the context (3) Educational resources that can be, for example, courses, exercises, demonstrations or problems to solve. (4) Internal resources to represent learners' abilities, preferences, experiences and intelligence degree.
- In a situation, a mobilization has performance and frequency which measure learner's ability of reproduction, transposition or innovation. Reproduction to reproduce or repeat actions in an automatic way, transposing to mobilize an acquired skill in an appropriate context, and innovation to propose a new solution by using the knowledge and skills developed.

- A mobilization requires a set of knowledge related to a domain: general knowledge, expertise, skills.
- Knowledge can take 4 forms: General knowledge, learn to know, learn to do, and learn to be.
- Knowledge must have a structure for better interpretation, storage, handling and interoperability in e-Learning system.
- The trajectory of a learner is a series of learning activities. It can be static or dynamic.
- A competency may require the acquisition of other competencies.
- Ability is the capacity to reproduce, transpose or innovate.
- A log is used to feed the learner profile; it is also the result of a learner assessment.
- Competency is considered as a student internal resource. The terms competency and experience are different. A student uses competency in addition to accumulated experience to solve an assessment item.
- A competency assessment needs a situation, by situation we mean conditions and contexts to effectively capture student behavior.

Figure 5. Ontology-based representation of CBA

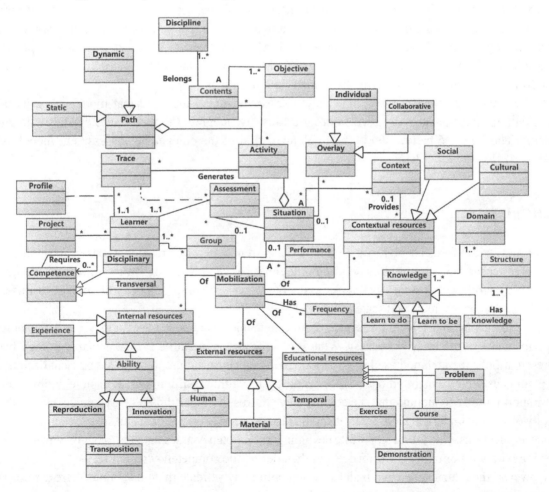

Figure 6. Transforming competency model to operational tool

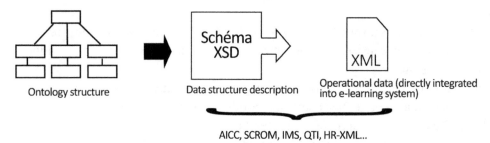

The ontology illustrated in Figure 5 can be used as the core of any production; in fact this ontology should reduce or even eliminate the conceptual and terminological confusion and ensure a shared understanding to adopt this approach effectively.

Implementing the Competency Assessment Model in E-Learning System

A formal language is highly recommended in order to implement the competency assessment model. The purpose is to translate the conceptual model into a machine readable format and enable interoperability among systems. The formal language XML associated with XSD schema tends to represent a good solution for e-learning platforms. However, XML is formal language to structure data, it uses an open format in order to be interpreted by humans and machines.

XML is used to translate the competency assessment model into a formal model. (2) e-learning specifications and standards are used in order to directly integrate the model into existing e-learning systems. The Figure 6 bellow shows the implementation of the competency assessment model using XML and e-learning standards.

CONCLUSION

The primary aim of this chapter, was to report the current state of Competency-based Assessment. A number of researchers proposed models and guidelines to help institutions in the process of designing and implementing Competency-based Assessment. However, competencies still subject to different modeling approaches, tools and scales.

Assessment of competencies takes into account student level of knowledge but most of all his/her level of performance as evidence of mastery. What is clear from the literature to date is that Ontology-based representation is the common used way to model competency structure, it helps assessment designer to adopt and customize existing models since ontology structure is particularly extensible and reducible. It is important to keep in mind that the competency end-result model should be dynamic so to cover the totality of student underlying attributes, it should also be directly operational and simple to implement in online applications. One useful step while designing a competency assessment is to begin with analyzing learning outcomes or target performance and then define the competency structure.

However, the main challenge remains how to continually validate the model since there are no common strategy for validating assessment models.

REFERENCES

Albert, D., Hockemeyer, C., Kickmeier-Rust, M. D., Nussbaumer, A., & Steiner, C. M. (2012). E-Learning Based on Metadata, Ontologies and Competence-Based Knowledge Space Theory. In D. Lukose, A. R. Ahmad, & A. Suliman (Eds.), Knowledge Technology (pp. 24–36). Springer Berlin Heidelberg; Retrieved from http://link.springer.com/chapter/10.1007/978-3-642-32826-8_3 doi:doi:10.1007/978-3-642-32826-8_3 doi:10.1007/978-3-642-32826-8_3

Bennani, S., Idrissi, M. K., Fadouli, N., Yassine, B. T., & Ouguengay, Y. A. (2012). Online Project based learning driven by competencies: A systematic strategy proposal for assessment. *Proceedings of the 2012 International Conference on Interactive Mobile and Computer Aided Learning (IMCL)* (pp. 92–97). IEEE. Retrieved from http://ieeexplore.ieee.org/xpls/abs_all.jsp?arnumber=6396457

Bissonnette, S., & Richard, M. (2001). *Comment construire des compétences en classe: Des outils pour la réforme*. Chenelière/McGraw-Hill.

Borst, W. N. (1997). *Construction of engineering ontologies for knowledge sharing and reuse*. Universiteit Twente. Retrieved from http://doc.utwente.nl/17864

Boyatzis, R. E. (1982). *The Competent Manager: A Model for Effective Performance*. John Wiley & Sons.

Bremgartner, V., & de Magalhaes Netto, J. F. (2011). An adaptive strategy to help students in e-Learning systems using competency-based ontology and agents. *Proceedings of the 2011 11th International Conference on Intelligent Systems Design and Applications (ISDA)* (pp. 978–983). http://doi.org/ doi:doi:10.1109/ISDA.2011.6121785 doi:10.1109/ISDA.2011.6121785

Brisebois, A., Ruelland, D., Paquette, G., Brisebois, A., Ruelland, D., & Paquette, G. (2005). Supporting self-assessment in a competency approach to learning (Vol. 2005, pp. 2828–2835*). Presented at the E-Learn: World Conference on E-Learning in Corporate, Government, Healthcare, and Higher Education*.

Carlton, M., & Levy, Y. (2015). *Expert assessment of the top platform independent cybersecurity skills for non-IT professionals* (pp. 1–6). SoutheastCon; doi:10.1109/SECON.2015.7132932

Cook, D. A., Zendejas, B., Hamstra, S. J., Hatala, R., & Brydges, R. (2013). What counts as validity evidence? Examples and prevalence in a systematic review of simulation-based assessment. *Advances in Health Sciences Education: Theory and Practice, 19*(2), 233–250. doi:10.1007/s10459-013-9458-4 PMID:23636643

Cuenca, L., Fernández-Diego, M., Gordo, M., Ruiz, L., Alemany, M. M. E., & Ortiz, A. (2015). Measuring Competencies in Higher Education. The Case of Innovation Competence. In M. Peris-Ortiz & J. M. M. Lindahl (Eds.), Sustainable Learning in Higher Education (pp. 131–142). Springer International Publishing; Retrieved from http://link.springer.com/chapter/10.1007/978-3-319-10804-9_10 doi:doi:10.1007/978-3-319-10804-9_10 doi:10.1007/978-3-319-10804-9_10

El Falaki, B., Idrissi, M. K., Bennani, S., & Associates. (2011). Design an Adaptive Competency-Based Learning Web Service According to IMS-LD Standard. In Innovative Computing Technology (pp. 37–47). Springer; Retrieved from http://link.springer.com/chapter/10.1007/978-3-642-27337-7_5

El-Kechaï, N., Melero, J., & Labat, J.-M. (2015). Quelques enseignements tirés de l'application de la Competence-based Knowledge Space Theory aux Serious Games. *Presented at the IC2015*. Retrieved from https://hal.archives-ouvertes.fr/hal-01170079/document

Gruber, T. (2009). Ontology. Encyclopedia of Database Systems, 1963–1965.

Gruber, T. R. (1993). A translation approach to portable ontology specifications. *Knowledge Acquisition*, *5*(2), 199–220. doi:10.1006/knac.1993.1008

Heller, J., Mayer, B., Hockemeyer, C., & Albert, D. (2006). Competence–based knowledge structures for personalised learning. *International Journal on E-Learning*, *5*, 75–88.

Heller, J., Stefanutti, L., Anselmi, P., & Robusto, E. (2015). On the Link between Cognitive Diagnostic Models and Knowledge Space Theory. *Psychometrika*, 2015, 1–25. doi:10.1007/s11336-015-9457-x PMID:25838246

Hnida, M., Idrissi, M.K., & Bennani, S. (2014). A formalism of the competency-based approach in adaptive learning systems. *WSEAS Transactions on Information Science and Applications*, 11, 83–93.

Hnida, M., Idrissi, M. K., & Bennani, S. (2014). Towards an adaptive e-learning system based on individualized paths in a competency-based approach. *Recent advances in educational technologies and education*, 73.

HR Open Standards Consortium, Inc. (n. d.). Retrieved from http://www.hropenstandards.org/?

Idrissi, M. K., Bennani, S., & Hachmoud, A. (2009). An ontology for the formalization of the competences-based approach. *Proceedings of theV International conference on multimedia and ICT in Education (m-ICTE2009), Lisbon (Portugal)* (pp. 22–24).

IMS GLC. RDCEO Specification. (n. d.). Retrieved from http://www.imsglobal.org/competencies/

Johnstone, S. M., & Leasure, D. E. (2015). How Competency-Based Education Can Fulfill the Promise of Educational Technology. In M. Antona & C. Stephanidis (Eds.), Universal Access in Human-Computer Interaction. Access to Learning, Health and Well-Being (pp. 127–136). Springer International Publishing. Retrieved from http://link.springer.com/chapter/10.1007/978-3-319-20684-4_13 doi :doi:10.1007/978-3-319-20684-4_13 doi:10.1007/978-3-319-20684-4_13

Le Boterf, G. (2015). *Construire les compétences individuelles et collectives: Agir et réussir avec compétence, les réponses à 100 questions*. Editions Eyrolles.

Lorenzo, G., & Ittleson, J. (2005). *An overview of e-portfolios*.

Lundqvist, K. Ø., Baker, K., & Williams, S. (2011). Ontology supported competency system. *International Journal of Knowledge and Learning*, *7*(3-4), 197–219. doi:10.1504/IJKL.2011.044539

Marques, J., Zacarias, M., & Tribolet, J. (2010). A Bottom-Up Competency Modeling Approach. In A. Albani & J. L. G. Dietz (Eds.), Advances in Enterprise Engineering IV (pp. 50–64). Springer Berlin Heidelberg. Retrieved from http://link.springer.com/chapter/10.1007/978-3-642-13048-9_4 doi:doi:10.1007/978-3-642-13048-9_4 doi:10.1007/978-3-642-13048-9_4

McClelland, D. C. (1973). Testing for competence rather than for "intelligence". *The American Psychologist*, *28*(1), 1–14. doi:10.1037/h0034092 PMID:4684069

Ng, A., & Hatala, M. (2006). Ontology-based approach to formalization of competencies. Retrieved from http://eprints.iat.sfu.ca/620/

Nitchot, A., Gilbert, L., & Wills, G. B. (2010). Towards a Competence Based System for Recommending Study Materials (CBSR). *Proceedings of the 2010 IEEE 10th International Conference on Advanced Learning Technologies (ICALT)* (pp. 629–631). Doi:10.1109/ICALT.2010.179

Paquette, G. (2007). An ontology and a software framework for competency modeling and management. *Journal of Educational Technology & Society*, *10*(3), 1–21.

Paquette, G., Mariño, O., Rogozan, D., & Léonard, M. (2015). Competency-based personalization for massive online learning. *Smart Learning Environments*, *2*(1), 1–19. doi:10.1186/s40561-015-0013-z

Põldoja, H., Väljataga, T., Laanpere, M., & Tammets, K. (2012). Web-based self- and peer-assessment of teachers' digital competencies. *World Wide Web (Bussum)*, *17*(2), 255–269. doi:10.1007/s11280-012-0176-2

Rhodes, T. L. (2011). Making Learning Visible and Meaningful through Electronic Portfolios. *Change: The Magazine of Higher Learning*, *43*(1), 6–13. doi:10.1080/00091383.2011.538636

Sanghi, S. (2007). *The Handbook of Competency Mapping: Understanding, Designing and Implementing Competency Models in Organizations*. SAGE Publications India.

Schmidt, A., & Kunzmann, C. (2007). Sustainable competency-oriented human resource development with ontology-based competency catalogs. In *eChallenges* (Vol. 2007). Retrieved from http://www.researchgate.net/profile/Andreas_Schmidt6/publication/228616563_Sustainable_competency-oriented_human_resource_development_with_ontology-based_competency_catalogs/links/0912f50a27d0b65d31000000.pdf

Sellenet, C. (2010). Approche critique de la notion de «compétences parentales». *La Revue Internationale de L'éducation Familiale*, *26*(2), 95–116. doi:10.3917/rief.026.0095

Sitthisak, O., Gilbert, L., & Albert, D. (2013). Adaptive Learning Using an Integration of Competence Model with Knowledge Space Theory. *Proceedings of the2013 IIAI International Conference on Advanced Applied Informatics (IIAIAAI)* (pp. 199–202). http://doi.org/ doi:doi:10.1109/IIAI-AAI.2013.15 doi:10.1109/IIAI-AAI.2013.15

Sitthisak, O., Gilbert, L., & Davis, H. C. (2007). Transforming a competency model to assessment items. *Presented at the PROLIX Workshop 2007 in conjunction with EC-TEL07*. Retrieved from http://eprints.soton.ac.uk/264541/

Tremblay, K., Lalancette, D., & Roseveare, D. (2012). Assessment of higher education learning outcomes. *Feasibility Study Report, 1*. Retrieved from http://citeseerx.ist.psu.edu/viewdoc/download?doi=10.1.1.269.7308&rep=rep1&type=pdf

Wang, M., Vogel, D., & Ran, W. (2011). Creating a performance-oriented e-learning environment: A design science approach. *Information & Management*, *48*(7), 260–269. doi:10.1016/j.im.2011.06.003

Xplore, I. E. E. E. IEEE Standard for Learning Technology - Data Model for Reusable Competency Definitions. (n. d.). Retrieved from http://ieeexplore.ieee.org/xpl/mostRecentIssue.jsp?punumber=4445690

Yastibas, A. E., & Yastibas, G. C. (2015). The Use of E-portfolio-based Assessment to Develop Students' Self-regulated Learning in English Language Teaching. *Procedia: Social and Behavioral Sciences, 176,* 3–13. doi:10.1016/j.sbspro.2015.01.437

Zhao, Z. (2014). Competence Research. In Z. Zhao & F. Rauner (Eds.), Areas of Vocational Education Research (pp. 167–188). Springer Berlin Heidelberg. Retrieved from http://link.springer.com/chapter/10.1007/978-3-642-54224-4_9 doi:doi:10.1007/978-3-642-54224-4_9 doi:10.1007/978-3-642-54224-4_9

Chapter 5
Assessment Techniques in EFL Brain–Compatible Classroom

Walaa M. El-Henawy
Port Said University, Egypt

ABSTRACT

Neuroscience has disclosed important information about the brain and how it learns. Brain-Based Learning is student centered learning that utilizes the whole brain and recognizes that not all students learn in the same way. Assessment and evaluation are necessary and important elements of the instructional cycle. Feedback also motivates students and allows students to apply what they have learned to real-life situations. This chapter presents attempts to explain brain-compatible assessment and alternative or authentic assessment and its different forms that can be used in providing brain-based education.

BRAIN-COMPATIBLE CLASSROOM

Education initiatives that link current practice with promising new research in neurological and cognitive science offer real possibilities for improving teaching and learning, especially for students with diverse learning needs (Hardiman, 2001). Neuroscience has disclosed important information about the brain and how it learns. Brain-Based Learning (BBL) involves acknowledging the brain's rules for meaningful learning and organizing teaching with those rules in mind (Caine & Caine, 1991). Brain-based education refers to learning in accordance with the way the brain is biologically designed to learn. Brain-based teaching encourages educators to consider the nature of the brain in their decision-making in an effort to reach more learners(Morris, 2010). Brain-compatible education introduces an orientation for ensuring that no child is left behind that is focused specifically on sustained achievement for all students (Ronis, 2007a).

Brain-based learning theory focuses on concepts that create an opportunity to maximize, the transfer of knowledge, attainment and retention of information. The principles of brain-based learning provide a theoretical framework for the effective learning and teaching process, seeking the optimal conditions in which the brain's infinite capacity to make connections and understand are maximized. Caine and Caine (1991) list these principles as follows:

DOI: 10.4018/978-1-5225-0531-0.ch005

1. Brain is a parallel processor,
2. Learning engages the entire physiology,
3. The search for meaning is innate,
4. The search for meaning occurs through patterning,
5. Emotions are critical to patterning,
6. Every brain simultaneously perceives and creates parts and wholes,
7. Learning involves both focused attention and peripheral attention,
8. Learning always involves conscious and unconscious processes,
9. We have at least two types of memory systems: spatial and rote learning,
10. The brain understands and remembers best when facts and skills are embedded in natural spatial memory,
11. Learning is enhanced by challenge and inhibited by threat,
12. Every brain is unique.

The principles of brain-based learning propose that effective learning could occur only through practicing real life experiences. Learning becomes more expressive when the brain supports the processes in search of meaning and patterning. Accordingly, it enables the learners to internalize and individualize learning experiences. Therefore, it is essential that learners be encouraged to participate in the learning and teaching process actively and that teaching materials be chosen according to their learning preferences (Ozden & Gultekin, 2008). It is the teacher's job to create enriched environments that help students learn (Caine, Caine, McClintic & Klimek, 2005).

According to Jensen (2008; cited in Morris, 2010), school administrators and teachers considering transforming schools into brain-based teaching environments must reflect on how schools influence the brain by addressing the following aspects:

1. **Curriculum (What We Teach):** The curriculum should incorporate real problems, organize simulation activities, and supply plenty of novelty and feedback.
2. **Instruction (How We Teach):** Teaching is the art of changing the brain. There are many ways to learn, so students should receive instruction in many styles, including visual, auditory, and kinesthetic. Every classroom should target the strengthening of some specific brain functions, such as attention controls, higher thinking abilities, or problem-solving skills.
3. **Environment (Where We Teach):** Classrooms should offer stimulating, collaborative atmospheres. These students need to be in an environment where students are known and where sharing and dealing with emotional issues are possible.
4. **Assessment (How We Measure Teaching):** Students should be informed of basic brain facts and ways to keep the brain in top condition for high test success. Teachers should plan test preparation activities for the student's developmental stage and unique ways of learning. Students should be evaluated in more than one way. For instance, students could choose to construct models or projects to demonstrate their learning.
5. **Staff Development (The Change Process):** Teachers should critically evaluate what is and is not working in order to improve student performance results. Teachers should always consider implementing current practices, such as brain-based education to enhance their instructional methods.

Current brain research offers general suggestions for educators to utilize in their classrooms. Several principles of brain research include creating a comfortable learning environment, immersing students in content, facilitating student learning rather than expecting rote memorization, making learning concrete and hands-on, and building connections to students' prior knowledge. In a classroom that provides for these skills, a student's ability to develop critical-thinking skills can be enhanced. Teaching with the brain in mind can require students and educators to make a change from simple rote memorization or test preparation practices to students being actively involved in the curriculum. As a result, teachers and students can go deeper into the concepts and gain a more meaningful understanding of the standards (McNamee, 2011).

Advocates of brain-based education (Erlauer, 2003; Slavkin, 2004; Caine, Caine, McClintic & Klimek, 2005; Jensen, 2005; Jack, 2010; McNamee, 2011; Hassan, 2013) offered suggestions for classroom practices including (a) hands-on discovery, (b) cooperative learning, (c) integrating curriculum to build connections, (d) creating a safe, comfortable learning environment, (e) encouraging students to construct knowledge rather than memorize facts, and (f) using more personalized assessment to improve learning, not to select or exclude.

Williams and Dunn (2008) state that teachers should use a new brain-compatible and authentic means of measuring student achievement as they promote the instructional process. Authentic assessment are those evaluative tools that are relevant and connected to real-life situations. In addition, they recognize the myriad of different student learning styles and provide repeated and various opportunities for students to demonstrate what they have learned. Thus, brain-compatible assessment is highly connected to using authentic assessment and other alternatives to traditional assessment that does not consider the principles of brain-based education.

ALTERNATIVE ASSESSMENT

North Carolina State Department of Public Instruction(NCSD) (1999) and Ronis (2007) agree that alternative assessment is a blanket term that covers any number of alternatives to standardized tests. Several terms are used of assessments other than traditional assessments. Alternative assessment, authentic assessment, and performance-based assessment are sometimes used "to mean variants of alternative assessments that require students to generate rather than choose a response. A broad definition of alternative assessment includes any type of assessment in which a student creates a response to a question rather than choosing a response from a given list (as with multiple choice, true/false, or matching). Some of the different alternative assessments include short-answer questions, essays, products, performances, oral presentations, demonstrations, exhibitions, and portfolios. However, Frey (2014) defines performance-based assessment as assessment that requires examinees to perform or produce something for evaluation that is intended to assess skill or ability and authentic assessment as assessment that aligns with real-world tasks and expectations. So the two approaches are not the same as some performance-based assessment are not authentic.

Hamayan (1995) refers to alternative assessment as alternatives to standardized assessment which has been referred to in literature in many ways such as informal assessment, authentic assessment, performance assessment, and direct assessment. Alternative assessment refers to procedures and techniques which can be used within the context of instruction and can be easily incorporated into daily activities of the school or classroom. Moreover, advocates of 21st century skills such as Partnership for 21st Century

Skills (2009) argues that traditional assessments measure knowledge of discrete facts, not the ability to apply knowledge in complex situations. High stakes assessments alone do not generate evidence of the skill sets that the business and education communities believe will ensure success in the 21st century.

Following are some reasons for incorporating alternative assessment in the foreign language classroom (North Carolina State Department of Public Instruction, 1999).

- To capture complex outcomes. Alternative assessment goes beyond the assessment of knowledge and facts to the more complex goals of assessing and developing life-long skills of creative thinking, problem solving, summarizing, synthesizing, and reflecting. With authentic assessment, products and processes are equally valued.
- To address realistic tasks. With authentic and performance-based assessments, students are involved in tasks, performances, demonstrations, and interviews reflecting everyday situations within realistic and meaningful contexts.
- To include good instructional tools. Assessment and instruction interact on a continuous basis. Assessment can be used to adapt instruction and to provide feedback for monitoring students' learning. Alternative assessment focuses on the students' strengths, therefore enabling the teacher to get a more accurate view of students' achievement, of what they can do, and of what they are trying to do.
- To communicate what we value. Assessment and instruction need to be aligned. If we value oral proficiency but only assess through written tests, students infer that only the written language matters.
- To meet the students' different learning styles. Alternative assessment offers a broad spectrum of assessment possibilities to address the different learning styles. Some students might choose to demonstrate understanding by writing about something while others might prefer to perform, to display visually, or to create a time-line.
- To collaborate and interact with students.

Herman, Aschbacher and Winters (1992) state that assessment is changing from paper-pencil to authentic assessment, from single occasion assessment to samples over time (portfolios), from single attribute to multi-dimensional assessment, from near exclusive emphasis on individual assessment to group assessment. Also, they present the common characteristics in alternative assessments as follows:

- Ask students to perform, create, produce, or do something.
- Tap higher-level thinking and problem-solving skills.
- Use tasks that represent meaningful instructional activities.
- Invoke real-world applications.
- People, not machines, do the scoring, using human judgment.
- Require new instructional and assessment roles for teachers.

Furthermore, Hamayan (1995) specifies some of the characteristics of alternative assessments as follows:

1. **Proximity to Actual Language Use and Performance:** Alternative assessment procedures are based on activities that have authentic communicative function.
2. **A Holistic View of Language:** Alternative assessment procedures are based on the interrelationships among the various aspects of language and the integration of the four skills of language. Also, alternative assessment considers the whole learner in various natural settings.
3. **An Integrative View of Learning:** Alternative assessment attempts to capture the total array of skills and abilities, the various dimensions of learning, and the various aspects of a learner's life.
4. **Developmental Appropriateness:** Alternative assessment procedures set expectations that are appropriate within the cognitive, social, and academic development of the learner.
5. **Multiple Referencing:** Alternative assessment usually entails obtaining information about the learner from numerous sources and through various means.

AUTHENTIC ASSESSMENT

The main goals of learning are to understand the concepts well, to remember them always, and to use them readily. It is the acquisition and application of useful knowledge and skills, rather than memorization of facts, that defines a true act of learning. Facts alone constitute very little knowledge without deeper understanding of their meaning and how we use them. As the paradigm shifts in education toward teaching more meaningful concepts and skills, assessment practices must change as well. Assessment must be an ongoing part of the learning process and, as often as possible, should be as authentic as the learning. The main assessment goals are to determine what students have learned, to ensure they can apply the new knowledge, and to guide teachers in planning future instruction (Erlauer, 2003).

Real learning is about the learner's ability to apply learned skills to real-life, contextual settings. True understanding is best represented by the learner's ability to solve unfamiliar problems that have no clear-cut, neat answers, problems that are unpredictable and that entail an ability to extrapolate from existing knowledge to create novel and unique solutions. Measurement of the development of real learning cannot be ascertained through traditional assessment methods alone (Ronis, 2007a). The Partnership for 21st Century Skills (2009) suggests that 21st century learning is about using knowledge, not just the acquisition of facts. Thus, educators need to build assessments for learning rather than assessment only of learning.

On the contrary, standardized tests tend to reveal what information students have or have not memorized rather than how well they can apply knowledge, think through situations, problem-solving, compare and contrast, draw conclusions, create models, and so on. Only alternative assessments reveal the more meaningful information—information that shows where a student stands in relation to specific learning goals for the instruction and learning occurring in the classroom (Erlauer, 2003).

Actually, assessment is the gathering of information about what students know and can do in order to make decisions that will improve teaching and learning. While the purpose of traditional assessment, and marking and grading practices has been to sort, select and justify, current thought about assessment and current research on the relationship between assessment and learning now point to a different purpose—assessment for learning. The focus on assessment for learning recognizes that effective assessment is not removed from the learning experience, but is embedded in authentic learning activities based on higher-order thinking skills, such as problem solving and analysis. Assessment for learning recognizes that students can be motivated to take increased responsibility for their own learning when they experience assessment as an integral part of the learning process. Assessment for learning is authentic and based on brain-based research. It also requires a high degree of assessment literacy, meaning that teachers need to understand how to use multiple types of assessment strategies (Alberta Education, 2005).

Authentic instruction and assessment, Gulikers (2006) mentions, reflect a correspondence between what is learned and assessed and what students are expected to do in the workplace. The idea of authentic learning became popular in learning theories such as situated learning and cognitive apprenticeship that focus on learning in meaningful contexts. These theories argue that meaningful, authentic learning requires learning in the working context or at least in the context of everyday life outside of school.

Similarly, Gielen, Dochy and Dierick (2003) indicate that current perspectives on learning are largely influenced by constructivism according to which learning is conceived as influenced by motivation, affect and cognitive styles. A central aspect of the assessment approach that is aligned with constructivist-based learning environments is the perception of assessment as a tool for learning. Assessment is supposed to supports students in active construction of knowledge in context-rich environments, in using knowledge to analyze and solve authentic problems, in reflection. Learning, as defined in this way, is facilitated when students are participating in the process of learning and assessment as self-regulated, self-responsible learners.

Authentic assessments are brain compatible. When correctly designed, they emphasize learning and thinking, especially those higher-order thinking skills involved in problem solving. Authentic assessments comprise meaningful tasks that reflect real-life, interdisciplinary challenges; they present students with complex, ambiguous, open-ended problems and tasks that integrate their knowledge and skills. Such assessments usually culminate in student products. or performances that recognize and value each student's multiple abilities, varied learning styles, and individual background (Ronis, 2007a).

Moreover, Winograd and Perkins (1995) define authentic assessment as assessment that occurs continually in the context of a meaningful learning environment and reflects actual and worthwhile learning experiences that can be documented through observation, anecdotal records, journals, logs, work samples, conferences, portfolios, writing, discussions, experiments, presentations, exhibits, projects, and other methods. Authentic assessments may include individual as well as group tasks. Authentic assessments emphasizes on self-reflection, understanding, and growth rather than on responses based only on the recall of isolated facts.

Gulikers, Bastiaens and Kirschner (2004) mention that to define authentic assessment, Five dimensions of authentic assessment were distinguished: (a) the assessment task, (b) the physical context, (c) the social context, (d) the assessment result or form, and (e) the assessment criteria.

The five dimensions were characterized as follows:

1. **Task:** What do you have to do?
2. **Physical Context:** Where do you have to do it?
3. **Social Context:** With whom do you have to do it?
4. **Result or Form:** What has to come out of it? What is the result of your efforts?
5. **Criteria:** How does what you have done have to be evaluated or judged?

Furthermore, Frey (2014) presents the dimensions that define authenticity of assessment including nine characteristics as follows:

1. The Context of the Assessment
    a. Realistic activity or context.
    b. The task is performance-based.
    c. The task is cognitively complex.
2. The Role of the Student
    d. A defense of the answer or product is required.
    e. The assessment is formative.
    f. Students collaborate with each other or with the teacher.
3. The Scoring
    g. The scoring criteria are known or student developed.
    h. Multiple indicators or portfolios are used for scoring.
    i. The performance expectation is mastery.

Also, Gielen, Dochy and Dierick (2003) explain the characteristics of authentic assessment as follows:

1. **A First Characteristic of Assessment Is the Kind of Tasks That Are Used:** New modes of assessment focus in the first place on assessing students' competences, such as their ability to use their knowledge in a creative way to solve problems. Tasks that are appropriate within new modes of assessment are characterized as being real problems or authentic representations of problems in reality, whereby different solutions can be correct.
2. **A Second Characteristic of New Assessment Forms Is Their Formative Function:** The term 'formative assessment' is interpreted here as encompassing all those activities explicitly undertaken by teachers, and/or students, to provide feedback to students to modify their learning behavior in which they are engaged. The term 'formative assessment' is only used for assessment that is directed at giving information to students with and after completing an assignment, and that is explicitly directed at supporting, guiding and monitoring their learning process.
3. **A Third Important Characteristic of Assessment, Is the Transparency of the Assessment Process and Student Involvement in the Assessment Process:** An effective way to make assessment transparent to students is to involve or engage them in the process of formulating criteria. As a consequence, students get a better insight in the criteria- and procedures of assessment. Clearly stated academic expectations and feedback to students are more likely to encourage students to adopt a deep approach to learning.
4. **The Last Characteristic of New Forms of Assessment Is the Norm That Is Applied:** In classical testing relative standard setting has been widely used, whereby the achievement of the students is interpreted in relation to his/her fellow students. This is considered as an unfair approach within the new assessment paradigm. . Within the new assessment paradigm, there is a tendency towards an absolute and / or self-referenced norm. When a self-referenced norm is applied, learning and assessment tasks can be used in a flexible way. Allowing a degree of student autonomy in choice of learning activities is a key factor in fostering intrinsic motivation, that leads to deeper and more self-regulated learning.

TYPES OF AUTHENTIC ASSESSMENTS

Hamayan (1995) and NCSD (1999) provides a list of activities that could serve as a source of alternative assessment information including writing samples, learning logs or journals, classroom projects, interviews, and think-alouds. Also, Alberta Education (2005) presents Examples of opportunities for multiple authentic assessment include learning tasks such as:

- Venn diagrams
- Mathematical word problems
- Scripts for radio shows
- Reactions to guest speakers, films or videos
- Storyboards
- Artwork/photographs
- Presentations
- Raps and poems
- Reflective learning logs

In addition, O'Malley and Pierce (1996) categorize types of authentic assessment as follows:

1. **Oral Interviews:** Teacher asks student questions about personal background, activities, readings, and other interests.
2. **Story or Text Retelling:** Student retells main ideas or selected details of text experienced through listening or reading.
3. **Writing Samples:** Student generates narrative, expository, persuasive, or reference paper.
4. **Projects/Exhibitions:** Student works with other students as a team to create a project that often involves multimedia production, oral and written presentations, and a display.
5. **Experiments/Demonstrations:** Student documents a series of experiments, illustrates a procedure, performs the necessary steps to complete a task, and documents the results of the actions.
6. **Constructed-Response Items:** Student responds in writing to open-ended questions.
7. **Teacher Observations:** Teacher observes and documents the students attention and interaction in class, response to instructional materials, and cooperative work with other students.
8. **Portfolios:** A focused collection of student work to show progress over time.

Furthermore, Scott (2000) and Lund in her "Overview of Authentic Assessment" agree that types of authentic assessments used to measure student learning include the following techniques:

1. **Projects:** Require students to create something to demonstrate learning. Some projects may reflect individual work as well as group work. Instead of requiring students to write a report on a topic, an authentic assessment might require students to create a pamphlet or brochure, prepare a multimedia presentation, design a piece of equipment could also demonstrate student knowledge. Projects allow students to demonstrate a variety of skills including communication, technical, interpersonal, organizational, problem-solving, and decision making skills. Projects usually require out of class time to prepare, which extends the amount of learning time in physical education.

2. **Role-Plays:** Provide students with a challenging, real-world problem and then ask students to demonstrate what they would do or how they would react. Role-plays can be an effective tool for measuring the affective domain of learning by translating feelings and attitudes into observable behavior.
3. **Interviews:** Assess student knowledge of many topics. Sometimes students make decisions that teachers question. By having the student give a rationale for the decision, teachers can detect instances of incomplete learning or even misinformation. Conversely, sometimes having students explain their actions will reveal new levels of understanding that teachers were unaware that they possessed. Interviews can be especially valuable for assessing learning for young children or students who do not have good writing skills. Students with English as the second language may also benefit from being assessed with interviews.
4. **Open Response Questions:** Assess cognitive knowledge by providing students with a real world problem and give them an opportunity to solve it. Students are expected to respond to the question by applying knowledge and information to address the situation presented. Open response questions are often interdisciplinary and typically require higher order thinking skills to answer.
5. **Journals:** Are excellent ways to assess students' dispositions by giving students an opportunity to reflect on some aspect of the lesson. Journals are often used to respond to situations, describe events, reflect on personal experiences and feelings, connect what is being learned with past learning, and predict how what is being learned can be used in real life. Journal writing can be done as classes conclude or at times when the whole class is not active. The fundamental purpose of learning logs and journals is to "allow students to communicate directly with the teacher regarding individual progress, particular concerns, and reflections on the learning process.

Hamayan (1995) and Lopes (2015) agree that the information obtained from such activities can be recorded and analyzed using various ways including anecdotal records of observation, checklists, rating scales, rubrics, and inventories.

1. **Anecdotal Records:** Notes written throughout the day or the class representing the teacher's observations on various students.
2. **Inventories:** This type of assessment can be used to list students' interests, language habits, or their learning activities.
3. **Checklists** *:* Checklists outline criteria for specific performance tasks or identify specific behaviours related to a skill or skill area. Generally, checklists have only two points—yes and not yet. Checklists are a written list of performance criteria. As a student's performance is observed or a product is judged, the scorer determines whether the performance or the product meets each performance criterion included in the checklist. Checklists are diagnostic, reusable and capable of charting students' progress (see table 1).
4. **Rating Scales:** Rating scales are checklists that require teachers to make a more detailed judgment, as teachers have to score students' performance on a scale from high to low. Teachers can use rating scales to record observations and students can use scales as self-assessment tools. Teaching students to use descriptive words, such as *always, usually, sometimes* and *never* helps them pinpoint specific strengths and needs. Rating scales also give students information for setting goals and improving performance.

Table 1. Argumentative Essay Parts Checklist (El-Henawy, 2012)

Name:	
Topic:	Date:

Directions:
Place a check by each section that you did while writing this argumentative essay
Introduction
—— I got the readers' attention or give some background information.
—— I stated a thesis or focus statement.
—— I mentioned three reasons supporting the thesis
Body
—— *I provided a first argument or reason to support my position*
—— I stated a topic sentence explaining my point and reason
—— I added elaborations to back my point.
—— *I provided a second argument or reason to support my position*
—— I stated a topic sentence explaining my point and reason
—— I added elaborations to back my point.
—— *I provided a third argument or reason to support my position*
—— I stated a topic sentence explaining my point and reason
—— I added elaborations to back my point.
—— *I provided an opposing viewpoint*
—— I stated opposing points to my argument.
—— I mentioned my rebuttal to the opposing point.
—— I added elaborations to back my rebuttal.
Conclusion:
—— I gave a summary of main points or reasons
—— I restated thesis statement.
—— I ended with a personal comment or a call to action.

5. **Rubrics:** A rubric is a chart of criteria, of "what counts," arranged according to a measure of quality. The criteria describe what a successfully completed piece of work looks like. In essence, it is a scoring guide. Depending on the contexts for which they are used, rubrics can be detailed and content-specific or generic and holistic. Rubrics are an advanced form of a rating scale. Rubrics are a set of clear expectations or criteria used to help teachers and students focus on what is valued in a subject, topic, or activity. Unlike a checklist that simply lists the criteria, a rubric provides a description of the expected level of performance for each criterion (see table 2).

STUDENTS INVOLVEMENT IN ASSESSMENT

For optimum learning to occur, Davies and Le Mahieu (2003) argue, students need to be involved in the classroom assessment process. When students are involved in the assessment process they are motivated to learn. This appears to be connected to choice and the resulting ownership. When students are involved in the assessment process they learn how to think about their learning and how to self-assess – key aspects of metacognition. Learners construct their own understandings therefore, learning how to learn – becoming an independent, self-directed, lifelong learner - involves learning how to assess and learning to use assessment information and insights to adjust learning behaviors and improve performance.

Zacharis (2010) indicates that students can be involved in the assessment process at three levels; self assessment, peer assessment, and group assessment. *Self assessment* refers to learners being involved in identifying standards and/or criteria to apply to their work and making judgments about the extent to

Table 2. Analytic Scoring Rubric for Argumentative Writing (El-Henawy, 2012)

Argumentation Domain
   Components
    • Stating position
    • Supporting reasons
    • Elaborations Opposing point of view
    • Refutation
    • Concluding statement with a call for action
   Score Level Description

26-30 Excellent An excellent persuasive argument. The paper takes a clear position and supports it consistently with well-chosen reasons. Reasons are explained clearly and elaborated using examples and convincing information. It mentions opposing opinions with reasons supporting it. Counterarguments presented are strong and elaborated or multiple counterarguments are presented. It deals with the opposing opinions either with refutation or alternative solutions. It includes a concluding statement or a call for action. It is free of inconsistencies and irrelevancies that would weaken the argument. Overall, the essay is persuasive and completely convincing.

21-25 Very Good A skillful persuasive argument. The paper states a clear point of view. It gives good and sufficient reasons to support it. The reasons are clearly explained and well-elaborated by using convincing information/examples. It may present reasonable opposing view(s) and also refute the opposing view(s) appropriately. It may include a concluding statement. Overall, the essay is very convincing.

16-20 Good A reasonably good and persuasive argument. The paper states a reasonably clear point of view. It gives generally plausible reasons to support it. Reasons are explained and elaborated to some extent, though not enough. There may be one or two inconsistencies or pieces of irrelevant information. It may present some opposing point of view(s), but may fail to refute them or the refutation may be ineffective. Overall, the essay is convincing.

11-15 Average A clearly recognizable argument but limited in effectiveness. The paper states a point of view. It gives one or two good reasons to support it. The reasons are not explained or supported in a fully coherent way. The reasons may be of limited plausibility and some inconsistencies exist. Overall, the essay is moderately convincing.

6-10 Poor A minimally acceptable argument paper, though not persuasive. The paper states a point of view. Only one good reason is provided to support the point of view; or the reasons given are unrelated to or inconsistent with the point of view; or the reasons are incoherent. Overall, the essay is little convincing.

1-5 Inadequate An ineffective argument with major gaps in reasoning. The paper attempts to take a position, but position is very unclear OR may only paraphrase the prompt. It may state some sort of a point of view, but it is vague or general. No reasons are provided for the point of view; or the reasons given are unrelated to or inconsistent with the point of view. Most of the content of the paper is not relevant to the task. Overall, the essay is not convincing at all.

Table 3. Student Self-Assessment & Reflections Sheet (original)

Name:		Subject:
Class:	Date:	Topic:
Things I did to complete the activity		
Things I like about this activity	Thing I do not like about this activity	
Things I did well	Things I could do better	
Things i learned from completing the activity		

Table 4. Peer Assessment Sheet (original)

Class:	Name of student:
Subject:	Name of peer- assessor:
Topic:	Date:
Things you have done well:	Criteria for assessment: ....
Recommendations for next time:	Things that need improvements: ....

which they have met these criteria. *Peer assessment* involves students making assessment decisions on other student's work and can be summative or formative. Getting students to participate in peer-assessment can help them to understand the assessment criteria operationally, internalize the characteristics of quality work and deepen their learning experience by applying them to other student's evidence such as essays, reports, presentations, performances, practical work and so on. *Group assessment* can refer to the assessment by a tutor of the products of student group work, or to the assessment of the product by students from other groups (inter-peer assessment), or the assessment of the product of group work by students within a group (intra-peer assessment), and can include self-assessment by individuals or by the group as a whole of the product they have generated, and/or their respective contributions towards the product. Therefore, it is usual for group assessment to involve at least some elements of peer-assessment and self-assessment. The following sheets (table 3 and table 4) are samples for self-assessment and peer-assessment sheets that can be used to involve students in the assessment process.

In addition, Politano and Paquin (2000) state that including students in self-assessment and peer-assessment reduces teachers' workload and teaches students to be reflective and responsive. Students learn to think about their own efforts and learn to be constructives in responding to the work of their peers. Peer feedback is another way students can be meaningfully involved in the assessment process. In "Brain-based Learning with Class", Politano and Paquin (2000) provide two frameworks students can use to give others constructive feedback including "two Hurrahs and a Hint" and "two Stars and a Wish" that encourage students to identify two strengths in a performance or assignment and offer one piece of constructive criticism.

Case (2008) asserts that involving students directly in the assessment process is another way to support learning. Case refers to such involvement as "Building Student Ownership of Assessment" that can be achieved through the following areas:

1.   **Setting Criteria and Standards:** Joint teacher and student negotiation of the criteria upon which students are to be judged increases student understanding of what is expected and ultimately of their performance in light of these expectations. Students can also be involved in deciding upon

standards—by articulating what might be required in order for the work to be regarded as excellent, good, and so on.

2. **Creating Assessment Tasks:** Another way to involve students is by inviting them to assist in developing the tasks upon which they will be assessed.

3. **Self and Peer Assessment** Involving students in self and peer assessment can greatly enhance their learning. The very exercise of assessing their peers on the specific criteria related to the lesson would likely reinforce the students' own understandings of what is expected of them. Furthermore, involving students in assessment encourages students to take greater ownership of their learning. An important dimension of self-assessment is communicating the results to others—either to the teacher, their peers, or parents.

BRAIN-COMPATIBILE ASSESSMENT

If learning is what we value, then we ought to value the process of learning as much as we value the result of it. Limiting education to the search for the right answer—as we do when we focus on standardized testing—violates the law of the adaptability of the developing brain. Quality education encourages a wide-open, creative problem-solving approach, thereby exploring alternative thinking options, multiple right answers, and creative insights (Jensen, 2005). Ronis (2007b) argues that teachers primarily use assessment to assign grades and to differentiate the successful students from the unsuccessful ones though assessment should be the classroom practice that links curriculum, teaching, and learning. Traditional assessment formats measure facts and skills in isolation. As the curriculum evolves to better reflect the skills that todays's students will need to function effectively in the twenty-first century - skills such as critical thinking, problem solving, and teamwork – the methods of assessing learning must also change. If such assessment is not in alignment with the curriculum, then there is no validity to the results achieved and students get a conflicting message as to what is valued.

Classroom assessment should be closely aligned to instruction and therefore reveals more significant data for determining what a student has learned and for driving instruction than any test imposed from outside the classroom. New understandings about the brain and learning necessitate a fresh look at assessment practices being used in our schools. Brain-compatible instruction is based on active learning and emotional engagement, consideration of students' attention spans, use of hands-on experiences with attention to multiple intelligences, promotion of physical movement, high-level thinking, and application of knowledge and skills. Brain-compatible assessment must be of the same nature. Assessment must match the instructional strategies as well as provide the data to drive the future instructional decisions (Erlauer, 2003).

Also, Ronis (2007b) mentions that traditional assessment formats break content down into unconnected bits and pieces taken out of context as fragmented information, both irrelevant and unconnected. These unrelated units of information are difficult for the brain to process for future use or store in long-term memory since they seem unrelated to any prior knowledge that the brain might use to make connections. On the other hand, performance assessments that employ rubric evaluations enhance the brain's ability to find connections and encourage the development of personal meaning for the learner.

Kaufeldt (2010) mentions that humans consistently seek new experiences and are curious so the brain begins to produce pleasurable feelings when accomplishing a task, enjoying an activity, succeeding, sharing affection, laughing, or being entertained. The brain self-satisfies by seeking out novelty and challenge. On the contrary, threatening environment and anxiety make the brain releases chemicals like adrenaline which generate a survival response, anger and aggression. In brain-compatible classrooms, learners have opportunities for the brain to generate intrinsic motivation and celebrate learning by setting reasonable goals, being encouraged to self-assess their own work and provide feedback for their peers. In addition, Politano and Paquin (2000) point out that evidence of authentic learning is embedded in the learning activities that happen in the classroom. The closer the assessment activity is to the everyday routines students are familiar with, the more authentic and dynamic assessment it is. Such authentic assessment activities are less threatening. In a brain-compatible classroom, teachers can help alleviate assessment stress and anxiety by

1. Giving students practice opportunities, and by teaching them relaxation techniques and test-wise strategies.
2. Providing various ways and choices by which students show what they know and represent their learning like talking, movement, drama, dance, songs, gestures, projects, drawings, paintings, mind maps, graphs, collages, charts, models, and different forms of writing.
3. Establishing criteria with students before assessment activities reduces anxiety and makes students have a clearer vision of what they are aiming toward, have a feeling of control.

Furthermore, Alberta Education (2005) states that assessment for learning is authentic and based on brain-based research. Such brain-compatible or brain-based assessment pays attention to the following elements:

1. **Trust and Belonging:** Familiar environments, practice assessments and second chances all provide the comfort that students need during assessment activities.
2. **Meaningful Content and Enriched Environment:** Assessment activities are chosen because they promote learning, not because they are easy to score.
3. **Intelligent Choices:** Students have some choice about how they are assessed and all students are not required to show their achievement in the same way.
4. **Adequate Time:** Students need time to become familiar with assessment activities. They also need sufficient time to demonstrate their learning. Time-limited assessment is only valid when time is a critical element in the learning.

Also, Ronis (2007a) presents some characteristics of brain-compatible assessment as follows

1. Establishes an environment where each child has the opportunity to succeed.
2. Allows teachers to develop meaningful curricula.
3. Assessment is ongoing throughout the unit of study, and provides an accurate picture of student achievement.
4. Puts the emphasis on student strengths rather than weaknesses.
5. Provides multiple sources of evaluation that give an in depth view of student progress
6. Treats each student as a unique human being.
7. Provides the opportunity to eliminate cultural bias and gives everyone an equal chance to succeed.
8. Regards instruction and assessment as being a single, integrated activity.

9. Engages the student in a continual process of self-reflection, learning, and feedback, as well as revision.
10. Deals with comprehension and the learning process as much as the final product.
11. More difficult to achieve consistent, objective scoring results.
12. Data cannot easily be simplified as a single number.
13. Difficult to compare different student populations.

Erlauer (2003) presents some suggestions for implementing brain-compatible assessment as follows:

1. Keep in mind that tests are just one form of assessment. Use product-based assessments such as models or presentations in addition to or instead of all written tests.
2. Keep in mind that assessment is not the end of learning but should guide continued learning.
3. Implement a wide range of assessment practices, both formal and informal.
4. Match assessments to the instruction and vice versa.
5. Consider students' differing multiple intelligences when designing assessment methods.
6. Infuse assessment into daily practices.
7. Make assessments as authentic or real-world as possible.
8. Try to reserve less than 50 percent of your assessment for proving foundation-level knowledge. Have the larger, more important half be dedicated to the student synthesizing, evaluating, or applying the new knowledge.
9. Promote emotional wellness and safe environment principles in assessment situations.

BRAIN-COMPATIBLE FEEDBACK

The results or feedback received from any form of assessment and what is done with the results are the crucial elements in making assessment meaningful. Assessment and feedback are integral parts of the learning process, not the end of the learning event (Erlauer, 2003). In the brain-based classroom, the other half of assessment is effective feedback. Jensen (2005) mentions that getting enough good-quality, accurate feedback may be the single greatest variable for improving learning. The feedback must be corrective and positive enough to tell the student what the desired change must be.

Giving constructive feedback and Learning from mistakes might be the most important aspect of cognitive development. Giving students regular feedback that is based on a level of assessment that goes deeper than grades or right/wrong answers. Duffy (2013) illustrates that constructive feedback aims to promote improvement or development of the person receiving feedback. Regular constructive feedback has many benefits. It can help students maintain and increase their motivation, increase their confidence and self-esteem, improve interpersonal relationships, promote personal development, develop teamwork and increase competence.

Teachers should focus on constructive feedback that is objective, specific and is directed towards the observed behaviour. Gielen, Dochy and Dierick (2003) point out that by giving descriptive feedback- not just a grade- and organizing different types of follow-up activities, a teacher creates a powerful learning environment. Powerful learning environments provoke and maintain a deep level approach and intrinsic motivation. Moreover, Dean, Hubbell, Pitler and Stone (2012) declare that by providing students with feedback that is corrective, timely, and focused on criteria, and by involving them in the feedback process, teachers can create a classroom environment that fosters and supports learning. The goal of providing feedback is to give students information about their performance relative to a particular learning objective so they can improve their performance and understand themselves better as learners.

Furthermore, Case (2008) affirms that teachers can enhance learning by helping students see how they might improve. Providing students with useful feedback must go beyond assigning a mark or offering a brief summative comment. If teachers want students to improve, their feedback must clearly communicate what has been successfully done, where improvement is needed, and how to do this. A carefully prepared rubric can go a long way in providing this feedback, both in terms of indicating how students have done and what might be done to improve their performance. Students benefit most from the use of rubrics when marks are not indicated. The lack of a summative judgment requires them to read the descriptors more carefully and encourages them to believe that it is not too late to improve. Other methods of providing effective feedback include:

1. Very specific written teacher comments;
2. Teacher conferences;
3. Comments by fellow students explaining areas for improvement;
4. Large and small group discussion of answers; and
5. Exemplars—samples of high-quality performance—of student work.

Because our brain is self-referencing (that is, decisions are made based upon what has happened previously), feedback is an essential part of optimal learning. Brain-compatible feedback is timely, corrective, regular and non-judgmental. Erlauer (2003) presents some suggestions for giving brain-compatible feedback as follows:

1. Remember, effective feedback can be either planned or spontaneous in nature.
2. Ensure that feedback to students is prompt and specific, and that it comes from several different sources.
3. Allow for logical, natural feedback to occur for students, from the crash of a paper airplane model to the applause from peers.
4. Make immediate, interactive feedback part of the learning process so students can avoid learning and practicing something incorrect.

In addition, Jensen (2004) claims that increasing the quantity and quality of feedback is the best way to increase the number of dendrites in the brain and accelerate learning. The brain is a complex organ that thrives on information; corrections allow it to improve its learning and survival behaviors. Teachers need to use various techniques to provide students with constructive feedback. Jensen (2004) provides some suggestions brain-compatible feedback as follows:

1. Provide ways that students can find answers to their work through self-correction.
2. Have students use checklists and timelines to set dialy or weekly goals. Then, have them to check their own progress.
3. Have students to write three quiz questions and test a colleague's knowledge of the previous day's class content.
4. Help stuents create a performance or grading rubric to assess themselves against this rubric.

Table 5. Suggestions for Providing Feedback (original)

Feedback Should Be Specific and Related to Learning Objectives.
✓ Feedback should elaborate on what students need to do next.
✓ Feedback should use self-referenced norm.
✓ Feedback should be given while it is still clearly relevant soon after a task is completed.
✓ Student should be given opportunities to demonstrate learning from feedback.
✓ Engage students in the feedback process (self- and peer-feedback).
✓ Constant feedback against the expected goals is preferable to competitive feedback against other students.
✓ Consider using technology to increase the rate of feedback, help organize it, and document it for further reflection.

5. Use a variety of tools to provide feedback to students, including audio and video recordings.
6. Establish rituals to deliver peer-feedback. For example, have student pairs assess each other after each assignment and conclude with a high five or sincere verbal thanks.

Scott (2000) concludes that mastery of complex learning activities extends beyond responding to probing questions following performance. Rather, it involves continuous feedback throughout the process of solving complex problems. Successful performance requires concurrent feedback inherent in the task itself or in the context in which the task is performed that enables learners to self-assess and self-correct. Feedback is best when it becomes an integral part of student's own mental processes, when they learn how to assess themselves. Similar to other real-life situations, feedback is comprised of a complex set of external (family members, friends, co-workers, and supervisors) and internal messages (reflective and metacognitive thinking). Supporting this view, the current researcher presents the following suggestion for providing students with brain-compatible feedback as shown in table 5.

CHALLENGES OF AUTHENTIC BRAIN-COMPATIBLE ASSESSMENT

Authentic assessment, Valencia, Hiebert and Afflerbach (2014) argue, presents many opportunities to literacy educators: the opportunity to assess many different dimensions of literacy, the potential to use classroom-based information, the capacity to involve students in their own evaluation, and the use of multiple measures of students' abilities. At the same time, authentic assessment presents a number of critical challenges. A first challenge involves the tension between assessments that support instruction and those that inform policymakers. Using parallel systems of gathering information for instruction and for policy creates a dilemma. Another challenge is about the issue of collaboration versus individual performance. In the typical testing context, children work by themselves. Collaboration among children is regarded as contaminating the results-or, as it is conveyed to children, cheating.

Furthermore, Frey (2014) states that applying authentic assessment procedures in the real classroom can be challenging. Though the community of classroom assessment scholars agrees that authentic assessments are potentially a powerful, transformative tool, there is not yet agreement on which aspects of authenticity are most important. Similarly, Zacharis (2010) affirms that though formative assessment has long been recognized as an indispensable part of an effective active learning environment, formative assessment is rarely used to its fullest advance, being very demanding of teacher time. In larger classes, assessment costs overtake teaching costs as lecturers spend more time each week marking assignments than lecturing in the classroom. To confront this assessment overload, teachers are forced to reduce the volume of assessment and, in particular, the volume of feedback that individual students receive. Also, Stefanou and Parkes (2003) point out that students are often uncomfortable with the change from traditional pencil and paper tests. This can be attributed to the comfort level and familiarity that students have with traditional testing formats.

In addition, Gulikers, Bastiaens and Kirschner (2004) proposed some considerations teachers or instructional designers need to consider to develop authentic assessments. The first consideration deals with the educational level of the learners. Lower-level learners may not be able to deal with the authenticity of a real, complex, professional situation. If they are forced to do this, it may result in cognitive overload and, in turn, have a negative impact on learning. Another consideration also sheds a light on the subjectivity of authenticity. The perception of what authenticity is may change as a result of educational level, personal interest, age, or amount of practical experience with professional practice. It is possible that assessing professional competence of students in their final year of study, when they have often served internships and have a better idea of professional practice, requires more authenticity of the physical context than when assessing first year students, who usually or often have little practical experience. Designers must take changing student perspectives into account when designing authentic assessment.

IMPLICATIONS FOR EDUCATORS AND CONCLUSION

Brain-based learning is based on the structure and function of the brain. It stresses that learning occurs through the active processing of information using authentic learning situations which increase the brain's ability to make connections and retain new information. Brain-compatibile assessment supports a balance of assessments, including high-quality standardized testing along with effective classroom formative and summative assessments. Also, it emphasizes constructive feedback on student performance that is embedded into everyday learning. Using authentic assessment techniques such as surveys, checklists, questionnaires, assignments, graphic organizers, portfolio work samples, rubrics helps in establishing a positive environment for assessment and helps students take ownership of their own learning.

Authentic assessment, Kurri Kurri High School (2009) asserts, encourages students to reflect on their learning. This gives students the opportunity to show what they know and can do as a result of their learning experience. It helps students to develop decision making and problem solving skills, planning and self-discipline, time management and resource management skills and substantive communication skills. Also, personal reflection is an important part of the authentic assessment. It assists students to understand how they learn and how best to overcome problems and challenges. By evaluating their tasks, students are able to identify the employment related skills involved and appreciate how they are transferable to learning in other subjects and their preparation to join the workforce.

Because of the previously mentioned importance of authentic and brain-compatible assessment, educators such as Lilly, Peacock, Shoveller and Struthers (2014) provide some recommendations for both the department for education and schools to consider as alternatives to assessment levels implemented within schools.

1. A culture shift regarding the nature, range and purposes of assessment needs to take place, in recognition of the new opportunities provided both by the new curriculum.
2. Conferences and seminars should be offered nationally, to enable all schools to confidently develop their assessment expertise and learn from each other.

3. New tracking software should be developed to provide school leaders with data that will enable monitoring of progress across year groups and over time.
4. Further opportunities for grant funding would greatly assist communities of schools to be 'research active' in the field of assessment.

Furthermore, Alberta Education, Aboriginal Services Branch (2005) supports developing assessment literacy which includes: (a) understanding and using multiple assessment methods, to ensure that the information gathered about student learning is complete and accurate, and that individual students have the opportunity to demonstrate their learning in a variety of ways, (b) communicating assessment criteria and results effectively, (c) involving students as partners in the assessment process.

In order to achieve assessment literacy, the following recommendations can be considered

1. Teachers need to be trained and encouraged differentiate assessment tools for assessing all students, informing instruction, and accommodating learners' individual needs.
2. Teachers need to use alternative assessment methods that are compatible with the way the brain learns and not to rely entirely on a 'one-size-fits-all' assessment method.
3. Teachers need to develop and utilize some alternative assessment techniques improve students' motivation to learn in order to overcome some of the negative effects of large-scale assessment.
4. Also, it is necessary to provide coaching and immediate feedback to promote effective teaching or learning. Immediate feedback is necessary for pattern seeking and knowledge building.
5. Students should be involved in the assessment process itself as it gives students the opportunity to take control of their own learning.
6. Student perceptions should be considered in designing effective authentic assessments.
7. The use of technology in the assessment process should support.

REFERENCES

Alberta Education, Aboriginal Services Branch. (2005). *Our words, our ways: teaching First Nations, Métis and Inuit learners.* Alberta, Canada: Minister of Education. Retrieved from https://education. alberta.ca/media/307199/words.pdf

Caine, R., & Caine, G. (1991). *Making connections: Teaching and the human brain.* Alexandria, Virginia: Association for Supervision and Curriculum Development.

Caine, R., Caine, G., McClintic, C., & Klimek, K. (2005). *12 Brain/Mind Learning Principles in Action: The Field book for Making Connections, Teaching, and the Human Brain.* Thousand Oaks, California: Corwin Press.

Case, R. (2008). Four principles of authentic assessment. In R. Case & P. Clark (Eds.), *The anthology of social studies: issues and strategies for secondary teachers* (Vol. 2, pp. 359–368). Vancouver, CA: Pacific Educational Press.

Scott, J. (2000). Authentic Assessment Tools. In Custer, R., Schell J. McAlister, B., Scott, J., Hoepfl, M. (Eds.) *Using Authentic Assessment in Vocational Education* (ERIC Clearinghouse on Adult, Career, and Vocational Education, Information Series No. 381) (pp. 33-48). Retrieved from http://calpro-online. org/eric/docs/custer/custer1.pdf

Davies, A., & Le Mahieu, P. (2003). Assessment for learning: reconsidering portfolios and research evidence. In M. Segers, F. Dochy, & E. Cascallar (Eds.), *Innovation and Change in Professional Education: Optimising New Modes of Assessment: In Search of Qualities and Standards* (pp. 141–169). Dordrecht: Kluwer Academic Publishers. doi:10.1007/0-306-48125-1_7

Dean, C., Hubbell, E., Pitler, H., & Stone, B. (2012). *Classroom instruction that works: Research-based strategies for increasing student achievement* (2nd ed.). Alexandria, VA: ASCD.

Duffy, K. (2013). Providing constructive feedback to students during mentoring. *Nursing Standard*, *27*(31), 50–56. doi:10.7748/ns2013.04.27.31.50.e7334 PMID:23641638

El-Henawy, W. (2012). *The Effectiveness of a Program Based on Self-Regulated Learning Strategies in Treating Written Expression Difficulties among English Department Students at Faculties of Education* [Doctoral dissertation]. Port-Said University, Egypt.

Erlauer, L. (2003). *The Brain-compatible classroom: Using what we know about learning to improve teaching*. Alexandria, Virginia: Association for Supervision and Curriculum Development.

Frey, B. (2014). *Modern Classroom Assessment*. California: Sage Publications.

Gielen, S., Dochy, F., & Dierick, S. (2003). Evaluating the consequential validity of new modes of assessment: The influence of assessment on learning. In M. Segers, F. Dochy, & E. Cascallar (Eds.), *Optimising new modes of assessment: In search of quality and standards* (pp. 37–54). Dordrecht, The Netherlands: Kluwer Academic Publishers. doi:10.1007/0-306-48125-1_3

Gulikers, J., Bastiaens, T., & Kirschner, P. (2004). A Five-Dimensional Framework for Authentic Assessment. *ETR&D*, *52*(3), 67–86. doi:10.1007/BF02504676

Gulikers, J. (2006). Authenticity is in the eye of the beholder. Beliefs and perceptions of authentic assessment and the influence on student learning [Doctoral dissertation]. Open University of the Netherlands, The Netherlands.

Hamayan, E. (1995). Approaches to alternative assessment. *Annual Review of Applied Linguistics*, *15*, 212–226. doi:10.1017/S0267190500002695

Hardiman, M. (2001). Connecting brain research with dimensions of learning. *Educational Leadership*, *59*(3), 52–55.

Hassan, W. (2013). Brain-compatible classroom: An investigation into Malaysia's secondary school science teachers' pedagogical beliefs and practices [Doctoral dissertation]. La Trobe University: Australia.

Herman, J., Aschbacher, P., & Winters, L. (1992). *A Practical Guide to Alternative Assessment*. Alexandria, VA: Association for Supervision and Curriculum Development.

Jack, C. (2010). Exploring Brain-Based Instructional Practices in Secondary Education Classes [Doctoral dissertation]. Boise State University.

Jensen, E. (2005). *Teaching with the brain in mind* (2nd ed.). Alexandria, VA: Association for Supervision and Curriculum Development.

Jensen, E. (2004). *Brain-compatible strategies* (2nd ed.). California: Crowin Press.

Kaufeldt, M. (2010). *Begin with the brain: Orchestrating the learner-centered classroom* (2nd ed.). Thousand Oaks, CA: Corwin Press. doi:10.4135/9781483350448

Kurri Kurri High School. (2009). Authentic Assessment. Retrieved from https://www.det.nsw.edu.au/vetinschools/schooltowork/teachers/kklc/Documents/Authentic%20Assessment%20for%20Toolkit.pdf

Lilly, J., Peacock, A., Shoveller, S., & Struthers, D. (2014). Beyond Levels: alternative assessment approaches developed by teaching schools (Research Report). National College for Teaching and Leadership. Retrieved from https://www.gov.uk/government/uploads/system/uploads/attachment_data/file/349266/beyond-levels-alternative-assessment-approaches-developed-by-teaching-schools.pdf

Lopes, L. (2015). *Alternative Assessment of Writing in Learning English as a Foreign Language: Analytical Scoring and Self-assessment. Master's Theses.* Bridgewater State University.

Lund, J. (n. d.). Overview of Authentic Assessment. Retrieved from http://www.pesta.moe.edu.sg/pesta/slot/u3057/PD/Overview%20of%20Authentic%20Assessment%20by%20Dr%20J%20Lund.pdf

McNamee, M. (2011). *The impact of brain-based instruction on reading achievement in a second-grade classroom* [Doctoral dissertation]. Walden University.

Morris, L. (2010). *Brain-based learning and classroom practice: A study investigating instructional methodologies of urban school teachers* [Doctoral dissertation]. Arkansas State University.

North Carolina State Department of Public Instruction. (1999). Assessment, articulation, and accountability: a foreign language project. Retrieved from http://files.eric.ed.gov/fulltext/ED436978.pdf

O'Malley, J., & Pierce, L. (1996). *Authentic Assessment for English Language Learning: Practical Approaches for Teachers.* New York: Addison-Wesley Publishing.

Ozden, M., & Gultekin, M. (2008). The Effects of Brain-Based Learning on Academic Achievement and Retention of Knowledge in Science Course. *Electronic Journal of Science Education*, *12*(1), 1–17.

Partnership for 21st Century Skills. (2009). Assessment: A 21st Century Skills Implementation Guide. Retrieved from http://www.p21.org/storage/documents/p21-stateimp_assessment.pdf

Politano, C., & Paquin, J. (2000). *Brain-based Learning with Class.* Winnipeg, Manitoba: Portage and Main Press.

Ronis, D. (2007a). *Brain-Compatible Assessments* (2nd ed.). California: Sage Publications.

Ronis, D. (2007b). *Brain-compatible mathematics.* Thousand Oaks, Calif: Corwin Press.

Slavkin, M. (2004). *Authentic learning: how learning about the brain can shape the development of students.* Lanham, Maryland: Scarecrow Education.

Stefanou, C., & Parkes, J. (2003). Effects of classroom assessment on student motivation in fifth-grade science. *The Journal of Educational Research*, *96*(3), 152–162. doi:10.1080/00220670309598803

Valencia, S., Hiebert, E., & Afflerbach, P. (2014). *Authentic Reading Assessment: Practices and Possibilities*. California: TextProject, Inc.

Williams, R., & Dunn, E. (2008). *Brain-compatible learning for the block* (2nd ed.). California: Sage Publications.

Winograd, P., & Perkins, F. (1995). Authentic assessment in the classroom: Principles and practices. In R. Blum & J. Arter (Eds.), *A handbook for student performance assessment in an era of restructuring* (pp. 1–11). Alexandria, VA: Association for Supervision and Curriculum Development.

Wolfe, P. (2001). *Brain matters: Translating research into classroom practice*. Alexandria, Virginia: Association for Supervision and Curriculum Development.

Zacharis, N. (2010). Innovative Assessment for Learning Enhancement: Issues and Practices. *Contemporary Issues In Education Research*, *3*(1), 61-70.

Chapter 6
Formative Evaluations of Teaching:
Involving Students in the Assessment Process

Gina Mariano
Troy University, USA

Frank Hammonds
Troy University, USA

Sheridan Chambers
Auburn University, USA

Gracie Spear
Troy University, USA

ABSTRACT

Students engaging in the assessment and evaluation process is becoming increasingly popular because it helps students become active participants in their own learning. In this chapter we discuss ways to involve students in the assessment and evaluation process in the classroom. It brings together multiple perspectives on critical thinking, metacognition, interteaching and student evaluations of teaching (SETs). The commonality between these four key elements is the importance of engaging students to become active participants in their own learning because they can help improve student learning outcomes. This chapter goes on to examine how these assessments and evaluations play a role in developing critical thinking skills and metacognition in students.

DOI: 10.4018/978-1-5225-0531-0.ch006

INTRODUCTION

Tell me and I forget, teach me and I may remember, involve me and I learn. This often-used quote is the backbone for the use of student evaluations of teaching (SET) because students become active participants in their own learning. They become *involved* in classroom assessment. In this chapter we discuss ways to involve college students in the assessment and evaluation process in the classroom. It brings together multiple perspectives on critical thinking, metacognition, interteaching and student evaluations of teaching (SETs). The commonality between these four key elements is the importance of engaging students to become active participants in their own learning because they can help improve student-learning outcomes.

This chapter begins with a discussion of critical thinking skills and metacognition and their importance to student assessments. The chapter then evolves into a discussion of the use of interteaching as a daily student self-assessment and how it can build skills. It then examines relevant and often controversial areas of SETs, which include lack of student participation, quality of student feedback, student perceptions of how instructors use SETs, instructors' perceptions and use of SETs, bias within SETs, and the relationship between SETs and student learning outcomes. Each of these areas are unique and important because they involve students in the assessment and evaluation process.

The use of formative evaluations (mid-semester evaluations) throughout the semester/term has been an area of increased research in the past few years. Research has found that more frequent SETs can be more useful to improving teaching quality (Brown, 2008; Diamond, 2004). They have also been found to improve student attitudes and alter students' perceptions of instructors (Brown, 2008). Effective formative assessments include instructional processes that are ongoing (Hudesman et al., 2013). By assessing students through this process, the information gained from the assessments not only betters the content of the courses, but also aids students in learning how to learn (Hudesman et al., 2013). These assessments differ from typical assessments by having professors expand and transform their teaching techniques while also offering students constructive comments as well suggestions to aid students in improving their learning strategies (Hudesman et al., 2013).

This chapter concludes with a discussion regarding how critical skill building, metacognitive skill building, interteaching and SETs can be useful for both teachers and students. While end-of-semester evaluations are used frequently and can provide valuable information, frequent evaluations along with in-class assessment such as through the use of interteaching assignments have several advantages. First, they provide an opportunity to improve a class in progress and assess student learning through involving students in the process. Second, students may become more involved and experience greater satisfaction with the course when they are given the opportunity to provide mid-semester feedback. The information gathered from student evaluations can be useful for all teachers and students because they actively *involve* students in shaping the courses. Third, and perhaps most importantly, students may learn more from classes that are improved through the use of mid-semester evaluations. Instructors can use student feedback to help shape the course because they will have a better understanding of how the students perceive the course content because students are directly *involved*.

Interteaching and SETs can be used to modify and shape a course, thereby encouraging students to become part of the assessment process. This chapter reviews current research on critical thinking, metacognition, interteaching, and SETs while highlighting ways to effectively use the information gained to help students become active participants in their learning by better understanding student perceptions of courses. This chapter should be of interest to faculty teaching in higher education looking to improve teaching quality and assessment related to teaching improvement.

BACKGROUND

Students use critical thinking skills for decision-making and analyzing information they learn in class. They also use these skills to evaluate and assess their own learning of this information. Critical thinking skills go hand-in-hand with metacognitive skills. The idea of metacognition has gained considerable attention in recent years. Metacognition put into the simplest of terms is "thinking about thinking" (K. Downing, Kwong, Chan, Lam, & W. K. Downing, 2008). The application of metacognitive processes is important in student assessments because they help student understand elements of information that they do not understand – meaning, they help students understand their confusion. If students are able to pinpoint where they are lost or confused, instructors can better help them, leading to improved student outcomes.

In order to ensure and promote quality teaching, many institutions of higher education utilize student evaluations of teaching (SET) at the end of each semester or term. Good teaching has a positive impact on student learning outcomes, therefore teaching, assessment, and evaluation are important. This is one of the reasons that many accreditation agencies such as the National Council for Accreditation of Teacher Education (NCATE) and the Southern Association of Colleges and Schools (SACS) include student evaluations as a part of the faculty review process (Onwuegbuzie, Daniel, & Collins, 2009). SETs are used as part of the evaluation process to help instructors understand how the courses are viewed through the eyes of the students. This is part of a system of continuous improvement, where programs are continually looking to improve student-learning outcomes.

Previous research on the use of SETs indicates that, when properly designed, these evaluations can provide valuable information about the quality of teaching (Ory & Ryan, 2001; Theall & Franklin, 2001). Wright and Jenkins-Guarnieri (2012) found that SETs could provide constructive feedback, which instructors could use to improve the quality of teaching. Hoefer, Yurkiewicz, and Byrne (2012) found positive correlations between grades and students' ratings of teachers. Another study tested a new course evaluation survey and reported that students who felt they had learned a lot rated the course more highly and reported higher grades. That paper also pointed out "The fact remains that numerous methodologically sound studies have shown positive and significant correlations between student global ratings of courses and student learning achievement" (Frick, Chadha, Watson, Wang, & Green, 2009).

STUDENT EVALUATIONS AND ASSESSMENTS AND SKILL BUILDING

Issues, Controversies, Problems

Critical Thinking

Critical thinking can be defined as increasing the potential of a desired outcome by using cognitive skills and strategies, while being logical and deliberate (Halpern, 1999). However, in the literature, the definition of critical thinking also includes "argument analysis, problem-solving, decision-making, and cognitive process" (Kim, Sharma, & Land, 2013). Critical thinking skills are important to the student assessment process because students need these skills to evaluate a class. Critical thinking skills are often used in analyzing situations and experiences, decision-making, cognitive processes, and problem-solving (Halpern, 1999). Student assessments utilize these skills in multiple ways. One way for students to learn critical thinking skills is through self-reflection by writing their viewpoints of their responses and actions to different situations (Crosier, 2011). Another way for students to develop critical thinking skills would be when they complete SETs or an interteaching assignment. Distinguishable critical thinking skills can be learned by students and when used appropriately can foster improved thinking skills (Halpern, 1999).

Based on evidence found in the literature, people who are able to logically reason based on relevant information and come to reliable conclusions are implementing critical thinking (Rezaee, Farahian, & Morad Ahmadi, 2012). One aspect that can be underdeveloped is the capability to incorporate multiple facts along with various perspectives to decide on the most logical and well-suited decision (Flores, Matkin, Burbach, Quinn, & Harding, 2012). If students are not able to learn critical thinking in their courses, it is likely they will have few additional opportunities to learn these skills (Rezaee et al., 2012). Incorporating assessments that help build critical thinking skills is important to student development. The use of interteaching assessments and SETs are examples of ways to implement assessment in class that can help build critical thinking skills among students by involving them in the assessment process. Critical thinking skills can be learned as well as transferred from one situation to another (Reid & Anderson, 2012). By developing these skills on one assignment, students can learn to transfer these skills to other assignments and courses. Helping students develop critical thinking skills has been found to improve learning outcomes (MacKnight, 2000; Gokhale, 1995).

The learning and implementation of critical thinking skills is useful both in school and once students have graduated (Rezaee et al., 2012). For example, students at one southwestern university often ask "Why do we need statistics?" (Pinkney & Shaughnessy, 2013). This question is primarily asked due to the thought that statistics will not benefit them in their decided major. In response to this question, many professors respond with the thought that statistics is an essential part of the scientific method (Pinkney & Shaughnessy, 2013). In addition to critical thinking skills being a major component of the scientific methods, they may also be an essential element in creating algorithm design skills (Korkmaz, 2012). This study looked at algorithms in terms of a step-by-step process for problem-solving. It found that when students worked individually instead of in groups it negatively impacted critical thinking skills. Students benefited from talking with each other and talking through the process of how they were solving problems. Korkmaz (2012) reported that critical thinking is a significant factor in the level of students' algorithm design skills in the sub-dimensions of analyticity, self-confidence, truth-seeking, and systematicity, although not in the open-mindedness and inquisitiveness sub-dimensions. There will be consequences once students enter the workforce if the educational system does not implement strategies to improve critical thinking skills among their students (Flores et al., 2012).

Gaining critical thinking skills can increase students' participation in the assessment process. Students will be better able to analyze the information in courses and through the use of self-reflection, better understand their own need areas in terms of misunderstandings, misconceptions, learning styles. Through this process they can more fully engage and more thoughtfully participate in the SETs process.

Metacognition

Metacognition is often defined as thinking about thinking. Understanding what one knows and how he or she has learned the information he or she knows is considered metacognitive knowledge (Schleifer & Dull, 2009). Metacognition also contains the categories of metacognitive knowledge and metacognitive skills (Pennequin, Sorel, Nanty, & Fontaine, 2010). Metacognition is related to student learning because students who understand their own confusion are better able to evaluate their own learning. Metacognitive skills involve being conscious of and examining one's own cognitive functions (Pennequin et al., 2010). Examining one's own cognitive functions are an integral part of the interteaching and SETs process. For a person to become a successful learner, he or she must be able to incorporate these aspects and components into becoming self-regulated, intrinsically motivated, and able to control one's behaviors to achieve his or her goals (Schleifer & Dull, 2009). Insufficient metacognitive skills can lead to students using inadequate study activities, which are likely to result in substandard learning (Tullis et al., 2013). Without the appropriate metacognitive skills, students' development and success in their professional life, their academic life, and as thinkers is hindered (Persky, Alford, & Kyle, 2013). Therefore, increasing student success by aiding students in developing metacognitive skills should become more common and more vital (Persky et al., 2013). Developing metacognitive skills through self-assessment and evaluation is important to improving student learning outcomes. If students are not aware of how they are thinking about the course material, then it becomes difficult for instructors to help students identify misconceptions.

Increasing critical thinking and metacognitive skills in students encourages students to truly understand their own thinking and become more fully aware of their own learning process. This will allow them to better communicate with instructors about their own confusion as well as how they are making sense of the course material. This also has the potential to improve the quality of student feedback in the SET process. These areas will be further discussed later in this chapter.

Interteaching

Boyce and Hineline (2002) introduced interteaching, a system of instruction that differs in several ways from traditional classroom lectures. Students are given reading assignments and questions to answer prior to that material being covered in class. Class meetings begin with a brief lecture over the material from the previous class meeting. Then, students work in pairs to discuss and review the day's assignment. During this discussion, the instructor answers any questions the students have. The key element to this being that students must identify their own confusion and misconceptions. At the end of the class meeting, instructors can have students complete an interteaching record sheet where they rate the quality of that day's discussion and identify any remaining questions so that these can be discussed during the review lecture in the next class (Arntzen & Hoium, 2010; Saville, Cox, O'Brien, & Vanderveldt, 2011; Saville & Zinn, 2011). Students must be able to identify where they are having confusion so that these questions are discussed in class. This has been found to improve student learning in the classroom (Arntzen; Saville, Cox, O'Brien, & Vanderveldt, 2011; Saville & Zinn, 2011). By including students in the assessment process, it can increase critical thinking and metacognitive skills, which can improve student outcomes.

One advantage of interteaching is that it provides frequent opportunities to assess student learning. Since students bring completed assignments to most class meetings, these assignments can be reviewed by the instructor while the students are working in pairs. While instructors could read the completed assignments, they are probably more likely to have brief discussions with the student pairs while answering questions. During this time, instructors have the opportunity to ask questions to see how well students understand the material. While researchers are still investigating which components of interteaching are most effective, the data have repeatedly demonstrated that interteaching results in increased critical thinking (Scoboria & Pascual-Leone, 2009) and learning when compared to traditional lectures and helps students become more involved in the class (Mason, 2012; Kienhuis & Chester, 2014; Saville & Zinn, 2011; Saville, Zinn, & Elliott, 2005).

Another advantage of interteaching is that it includes a formative evaluation following most class meetings. With the interteaching record sheets, students are given an opportunity to indicate how much they learned from and enjoyed the day's activities. Instructors are able to use information from the record sheets and from discussion with students during interteaching to improve the class and ensure the lectures focus on topics that will benefit the students (Saville, Lambert, & Robertson, 2011; Scoboria & Pascual-Leone, 2009).

Student Evaluations

SETs are an important aspect of the teaching and learning process in higher education. This type of assessment has been getting increased attention in recent years because it is an innovative way to not only encourage critical thinking skills among students, but also engage students in the assessment process and encourage them to be active participants in this process. Students are driving these assessments, meaning students' feedback can affect how courses are taught. When students engage in SETs, they have the potential to improve not only teaching practice, but also the assessment process. As students learn how to participate in SETs, teachers can better understand how the assessments can inform their teaching and use them as a tool to not only inform their pedagogy, but also better understand how the students' cognition is developing in relation to the course.

Student evaluations involve assessing student learning and cognition. While the definition of cognition is learning or thinking, adding the prefix "meta" incorporates the idea of learning and thinking in a more mature stage of development (Chick, Karis, & Kernahan, 2009). Metacognition is the manipulation of learning and thinking process by evaluating, self-regulating, and monitoring these processes (Chick et al., 2009). A major way for learning to be enhanced is through testing the information being learned (Karpicke, Butler, & Roedlger, 2009). This information should aid in determining if students are being taught thinking skills in their college courses (Smith, 2004). While formative assessments and metacognitive exercises can be useful in improving courses and in increasing student learning, they have not often been used together. Most formative assessments used in college classrooms have not made use of metacognitive and self-regulation strategies (Hudesman et al., 2013). This is unfortunate since formative evaluations involve data, which can be used to reflect on a course in progress. Instructors can make use of these data, but formative evaluations could also easily incorporate metacognitive components that would aid students in better understand both the course material and how they themselves are interacting with it. It is not clear why most formative evaluations do not include metacognitive strategies. It is possible that instructors and designers of formative evaluations simply do not know about metacognitive techniques. Alternatively, effective contingencies for instructors to put in the extra effort to deal with metacognitive items may not be in place. Finally, instructors and/or designers of formative evaluations may not feel that metacognitive components are useful or may feel that they are not relevant to the evaluation process.

Mid-Semester Teaching Evaluations

Mid-semester evaluations differ from student evaluation in that they are evaluating the instructor. They are focused on how the course is taught through the eyes of the student, essentially the students' perspective of how the course is going. While surveys conducted at the end of the term can certainly be useful in obtaining students' perspectives and suggestions, these evaluations are summative rather than formative. Many researchers (Brown, 2008; Diamond, 2004) point out that mid-semester evaluations can be more useful because these evaluations are obtained while discussions and changes to the course can still take place. Frick et al. (2009) recommend giving evaluations both at the beginning and at the end of courses and that instructors use the obtained information to revise their courses.

Research suggests that students favor mid-semester evaluations (MSE). Students indicated a preference for MSE due to the opportunity to witness the benefits of any positive changes in the course or teaching style that may result (McGowan, 2009). Brown (2008) found the majority of students like mid-semester evaluations (MSE). The students believed MSEs improved everyone's performance in the class (both instructors and students) and attitudes about the class itself (Brown, 2008). Frequently, the MSE altered the students' perception of the professor. They saw the professor as more caring about the students' success, more committed to teaching the material, and more likely to have clear goals for teaching the class (Brown, 2008).

Teachers who give mid-semester evaluations may receive higher ratings than their colleagues who only gave end-of-semester evaluations (e. g. Wilson and Ryan n. d.). One reason for this is that instructors are able to evaluate their effectiveness from the students' perspective and make improvements to their methods of teaching within the current semester (Diamond, 2004). Aultman (2006) suggests that these formative evaluations conducted early in the semester improve faculty-student communication, pointing out that these types of evaluations appear to encourage students to begin asking more questions and assuming more responsibility in the learning process. Wright and Jenkins-Guarnieri (2012) proposed adding SETs as a supplement to midterm and final examinations as a practical way to integrate them into courses, so instructors can make improvements before the end of the course.

As a result of receiving mid-term feedback, faculty members may feel that they are better able to understand student perspectives about their classes. Accordingly, many make modifications to their teaching techniques and grading criteria (Diamond, 2004). According to a study by Winchester and Winchester (2012) during exposure to weekly formative SETs, students indicated that their evaluations seemed to have an effect on future lectures, and were therefore more motivated to continue providing feedback on a regular basis. However, conducting an evaluation every week was seen as excessive, and students perceived such frequent evaluations as a chore. Winchester and Winchester (2011, 2014) suggest that evaluations should have the least amount of work possible for both teachers and students while still being informative and promoting reflection. In another study (Brown, 2008), students reported that instructors who conducted mid-semester evaluations appeared to be more committed to teaching and seeing students do well. Macdonald (2006) found that when evaluations were conducted regularly, more time was spent considering the evaluations and making an effort to implement changes.

Lack of Student Participation in Teaching Evaluations

Surratt and Desselle (2007) report that, when given the opportunity, students indicate willingness to complete evaluations. McGowan (2009) found that most students were willing to participate in evaluations because they genuinely wanted to provide their instructor with feedback. They may also be motivated by the belief that any beneficial feedback they provide will improve the class or teaching style (Slocombe, Miller, & Hite, 2011). Others are simply motivated by the opportunity to earn extra credit points. Offering points to students can act as an incentive for students to complete the exam. This can help encourage students to participate in the evaluation process initially. As time goes on, students may begin to feel more comfortable with the process, and as their critical thinking and metacognitive skills develop, their participation may become less based on a point system and more based on improving their own learning and course improvement. This could also help with the other primary reason student did not complete evaluations, which was the majority of students stated they had just forgotten (McGowan, 2009).

However, instructors frequently report that students do not participate in opportunities to give feedback. Svincki (2001) points out one possible explanation for this lack of participation that is based on a well-known and often-demonstrated effect in behavioral research. Experiences with inescapable aversive stimuli can produce an unfortunate pattern of behavior referred to as "learned helplessness" (Seligman & Maier, 1967). These experiences reveal that the individual's actions are not causally connected with certain following events. It may be that students have participated in evaluations, but did not experience substantive changes to the course. Thus, while the student has engaged in some effort that might have resulted in positive changes, they continued to experience aversive stimuli associated with ineffective teaching. This could very well lead students to be less likely to participate in subsequent evaluations. Mid-semester evaluations may be helpful in increasing student feedback for two reasons. First, students have greater incentive to provide feedback during the semester rather than at the end because mid-semester feedback has the potential to impact them directly and relatively quickly. End-of-semester feedback can't help a student who will not take another class with that particular instructor. Even if the student does have another class with that instructor, there may be considerable time between the classes. Further, feedback in one class may be less likely to result in changes in a different class. Second, mid-semester evaluations could combat the learned helplessness effect by allowing students to quickly see the changes resulting from their feedback. This could potentially encourage them to give more feedback on other mid-semester evaluations and even end-of-semester evaluations.

To encourage student feedback, it is important for the teacher and students to have a relationship. Teaching is not a one-sided event. It requires both students and teachers to be involved. Students who have a better relationship and communication with their instructors are going to feel more invested in the class. When a student feels more invested they are more motivated to learn and earn good grades, and they will give the instructors higher ratings at the end of the term (Wilson and Ryan n. d.). Mid-semester evaluations can be one way to build rapport between the professors and the students.

Seeking solutions to generate increased student participation, researchers have also attempted to evaluate student preferences pertaining to the format and distribution of SET. Schiekirka et al. (2012) found that students preferred evaluations that asked open-ended questions, with many students reporting that scaled questions do not provide a teacher with useful information or feedback about specific aspects on which to improve.

Quality of Student Feedback

Student written comments are generally more helpful than ratings alone (Svinicki, 2001). Lewis (2001) suggests using specific questions as prompts as a way to further increase the value of written responses. For example, several questions like "What helped your learning the most in this class?" may result in more informative feedback then a general request for written comments. However, students may still have trouble providing effective written comments. Writing, including writing comments on evaluations, is a skill that needs to be practiced; therefore, teachers should ask students for feedback early on and frequently during the semester and should model how to give constructive feedback (Svinicki, 2001). Under the instructional system known as interteaching (Boyce & Hineline, 2002), students are asked to give feedback about each class meeting and receive points for doing so. Instructors use the feedback to determine which topics to address in the next class meeting. Thus, students are encouraged to provide useful feedback. Gehringer (2010) notes that, after sending out post-class surveys to his students twice a week, the survey item that had the most useful responses was, "Name one thing that is still not clear from today's class."

It is worth noting that there are several other factors that have been examined in relation to how students respond to evaluations. For instance, it is a common belief among faculty members that students have a tendency to give more negative course/teaching evaluations to those courses with high workloads. Dee (2007) investigated student perceptions of course workloads, but results from this study did not demonstrate a correlation between perceptions of workloads and instructor performance. However, consistent with previous findings, the results suggested a strong association between the overall course/instructor ratings and the perceived organization and accessibility of the teacher.

Ahmadi, Helms, and Raieszadeh (2001) developed a questionnaire in which business students could report their perceptions of, and satisfaction with, the SET process. Their findings suggest that students believe the opportunity to complete evaluations is important and necessary. These findings have been consistently supported (Surratt & Desselle, 2007; Schiekirka, et al., 2012). Their results also suggest that most students take the SET process seriously.

Recent research on the evaluation process has attempted to uncover potential methods to improve student perceptions of and satisfaction with SET. Over half of students taking part in a survey reported that they are more likely to give honest ratings on online sites such as RateMyProfessor.com than on an SET. There is reason to believe that students are more likely to be honest because these ratings are accessible to other students. The authors point out that providing students with access to the results of official SET could elicit more honest ratings (Brown, Baillie, & Fraser, 2009). However, Nasser and Fresko (2002) imply that faculty members tend to oppose the distribution of official SET results. Surratt and Desselle (2007) suggest that in order to improve participation in evaluations, institutions should do more to educate the students on the process and inform them of how the scores are used in making administrative decisions. In particular, the authors point out that some students may be discouraged to participate in SET due to misconceptions of the process, believing that the professor has access to the feedback before administration of the final examination, when this is not the case. Darwin (2012) and Johnson, Narayanan, and Sawaya (2013) discuss several additional variables that may affect SET such as, timing of the evaluations, students' satisfaction with their grades, class size, whether the course was required, grades, and the gender of the instructor.

There is also concern that students do not always respond honestly on evaluations. Clayson and Haley (2011) found that a majority of students reported knowledge of respondents who had provided dishonest evaluation responses and almost one-third of respondents reported giving a dishonest evaluation themselves. The authors point out that these findings could potentially dispute the use of student evaluations in making helpful modifications to course instruction.

In one study conducted at a business school (Slocombe, Miller, & Hite, 2011), 100% of the students reported that they were honest in their evaluations of professors. However, some of these students reported that they did not believe other students were honest in their ratings. Al-Issa and Sulieman (2007) also explored business and engineering students' beliefs about the attitudes of other students, and found that students with a GPA of 3.5 and higher were those most likely to perceive that other students were dishonest during the SET process.

Student Perception of How Instructors Use SETs

Many of these questionnaires exploring student perceptions of SET ask students about their perceptions of how faculty members make use of evaluation feedback. In some cases, students have reported that they felt instructors value the evaluation feedback (Ahmadi, Helms, & Raieszadeh, 2001). Still, other findings suggest that first-year students are more likely than upperclassmen to feel that faculty take the evaluations seriously (Al-Issa & Sulieman, 2007; Heine & Maddox, 2009), while findings from Al-Issa and Sulieman (2007) show only a small number of students (39%) agreed that faculty members cared about the students' opinions. The authors propose this could explain the finding that students did not feel that their classmates were sincere in their responses to SET. Hann, Britt, McClellan, and Parks (2010) found there was not a significant difference in opinion about the SETs among students from on-campus classes or online classes. However, there was a significant difference in how traditional and non-traditional students perceived the SETs (Hann et al., 2010). Non-traditional students are those who did not come to college straight from high school, but instead entered the work force first. Many of these students believed that their professors would change the courses based on the responses on the SETs.

The reported perceptions of students toward evaluations also call into question the supposition that a faculty member's teaching will improve as a result of evaluation feedback. While students believe that their feedback *should* result in improved teaching performance, they do not necessarily feel that it will actually happen (Ahmadi, Helms, & Raiszadeh, 2001). Still, faculty members reported that, after receiving student feedback, they were likely to make changes to aspects of their classes such as assignments, workload, and teaching styles (Nasser & Fresko, 2002).

Among many colleges and institutions, these evaluations are considered when making decisions about salary increases, faculty advancement, promotion, and tenure. Students seem to agree that SET responses should be used in determining these decisions (Surratt & Desselle, 2007), but did not feel that their responses were actually being used for these purposes (Ahmadi, Helms, & Raiszadeh, 2001). This can lead many students to feel indifferent to SETs even though they realize they are often used for awarding promotions or deciding on hiring (Brown, 2008). Students do believe that SETs are an accurate measure of faculty teaching ability, but they are not sure whether or not anyone takes the SETs seriously, either the students doing the evaluations or the faculty reading the results (Brown, 2008). Surrat and Desselle (2007) also report that students felt that all faculty members should be evaluated, and that senior or tenured faculty should not be evaluated less frequently or be exempt from evaluations.

Certain factors that influence student responses may call into question the validity of the feedback obtained through SET. For instance, previous studies refer to both a *leniency* and a *reciprocity* effect, as students' perceptions of their grades appear to impact their evaluations (Clayson, 2009). The *leniency effect* suggests that students will give more positive evaluations to instructors who grade leniently; while the *reciprocity effect* suggests students who receive better grades will give more positive evaluations. In a meta-analysis of the literature, Clayson (2009) points out several studies that provide strong support for both of these effects (Johnson, 2003; Weinberg, Fleisher, & Hashimoto 2007), but the *reciprocity effect* is the only one supported by all data. Findings from combined data also suggest positive associations between learning and the SET, with stronger relationships amongst education and liberal arts disciplines. However, with more objective learning measures there were weaker associations (Clayson, 2009). Another factor that may influence student responses is class status. First-year students were found to give lower ratings (Liu, 2012). This may be due to a lack of experience with expectations for college-level courses.

Instructor Perceptions of and Use of SETs

Instructors' perceptions of the quality and efficacy of student evaluations of teaching are not always positive. Darwin (2012) points out that even though student evaluations have become an important part of higher education, they are often seen by professors as being "inherently narrow" and "potentially superficial". In a study that examined perceptions of students from one university, students did not perceive that their feedback was improving teaching at all (Kember, Leung, & Kwan, 2002). Data from this study indicated no evidence of improvement in teaching over the course of four years. However, the study included data collected from only one university, so the generalizability of the results might be questioned. Additionally, the authors suggest that instructors may not have been using the feedback effectively, or may have ignored it entirely. To address such issues, others have attempted to determine how instructors can most effectively interpret feedback.

Data from SETs are often misinterpreted because the instructors simply do not know how to make the best of the student feedback (Theall & Franklin, 2001). Lewis (2011) discussed how to better make sense of students' ratings by creating a matrix with overall course ratings (e.g. excellent, average, poor, etc.) as rows and teacher evaluation categories (e.g. subject matter, organization/clarity, interaction, dynamism/enthusiasm, etc.) as columns. Each cell of the matrix contains students' written comments from the evaluations. Thus, the comments are arranged by category and the instructor can easily see whether the comment was written by a student who rated the course as excellent, above average, average, below average, or poor (or whatever the rating scale may be). This organization results in a better opportunity to identify areas for improvement. The instructor can see whether students who rate the class highly have similar concerns to those who rate the class less favorably. For example, a comment like "The assignments were very challenging" might be written by a student who was very satisfied as well as by one who was very dissatisfied. The comment might be interpreted differently depending on which student it was. Further, if the instructor could determine that satisfied students' written comments generally fall into some categories and dissatisfied students' comments fall into other categories, this could make appropriate changes to the course much easier to identify.

It is also important for the instructor to be prepared to receive the feedback. It will only be harmful if the instructor gets defensive. Some teachers can develop "professorial melancholia," when they take the low rating personally, which alienates them from the students and does not motivate them to change their teaching styles (Svinicki, 2001). Some researchers believe schools should provide help in interpreting the student evaluations, so that instructors can interpret them correctly without getting defensive (Theall & Franklin, 2001). Darwin (2012) suggests that student evaluations may actually be counterproductive in that they may make instructors reluctant to try new techniques and instead stay with teaching methods the students have come to expect and that the use of student evaluations may result in a general trend to try to keep students happy rather than designing courses to improve learning outcomes.

Winchester and Winchester (2011) sought to determine if having teachers reflect on weekly student evaluations would improve student evaluation scores. How the instructors responded to the evaluations depended on the type of reflection (surface or pedagogical) that they employed. Surface reflection occurs when instructors look at specific episodes or isolated events, in other words, what they are doing. Whereas, pedagogical reflection occurs when instructors consider theories and a rationale for how they taught, essentially why they are doing what they do in the classroom. In a later paper, Winchester and Winchester (2014) reexamined the data from the 2011 study. On average there was an increase in student evaluation scores from year one, which was before the weekly evaluations, to year two during which the weekly evaluations took place. This study showed that even surface reflection improved student evaluations. However, teachers who had deeper reflective practices improved more than those who practiced surface level reflection. Previous studies showed that in order for the teachers to be able to use the student evaluations they would need counseling to learn how to best use the information; however, this research found that teachers were able to improve their evaluations even without counseling (Winchester & Winchester, 2014).

In order to provide useful feedback about the quality of teaching, student evaluations must be designed properly. Finelli, Wright, and Pinder-Grover (2010) discuss a Two Survey Method (TSM) as a potential solution to the problem many instructors have with interpreting student responses to open-ended questions. In this method, students complete a course survey six weeks into the term. Then, a faculty consultant observes a normal class period and uses the data from the first survey and the information obtained from observation to determine course strengths and weaknesses and potential strategies to improve the course and to develop a second survey. Faculty members reported high satisfaction with this method, and many indicated that the feedback seemed more valid, providing a more accurate sense of student responses.

Hodges and Stanton (2007) suggest that instructors should more carefully consider the questions included within evaluations, examining data from past evaluations and ensuring that the questions in future evaluations address those complaints that appear to be especially common. It was also recommended that evaluations should be utilized not only to assess teaching effectiveness, but also to better understand student learning and intellectual development. This method for interpreting evaluations may allow instructors to better grasp student insight, as the focus is not solely on judgments of instructor performance (Hodges & Stanton, 2007). The Frick et al. (2009) study mentioned previously offers a new set of course evaluation questions based on nine principles from the literature relevant to teaching and learning. Emery, Kramer, and Tian (2003) suggest that wording on SETs should be "more 'achievement' oriented rather than 'satisfaction' oriented" in order to focus more on student perceptions of how much they have learned in the course. Researchers have found that there are nine common areas that should be addressed in a student evaluation: organization, breadth of coverage, grading, assignments, workload, learning value, enthusiasm, rapport, and group interaction (McCarthy n.d.).

SOLUTIONS AND RECOMMENDATIONS

Clearly, improving critical thinking and metacognitive skills, and the use of interteaching and SETs can be useful for both teachers and students. Critical thinking skills and metacognitive skills are crucial for students to understand their own learning. If students are asked to evaluate instructors, then they must develop these skills in order to more fully participate in this process. While end-of-semester evaluations are used frequently and can provide valuable information, frequent assessments and evaluations throughout the semester have several advantages. First, they provide an opportunity to improve a class in progress and identify student perceptions of the course; end-of-semester evaluations are only useful for the instructor's future classes. Second, students may become more involved and experience greater satisfaction with the course when they are given the opportunity to provide mid-semester feedback. Students want to know they are being heard and truly are partners in their own learning. Third, students may be more inclined to explain confusion or misconceptions during the semester rather than at the end. If their feedback results in changes to the class, these students may then provide more feedback at the end of the semester than they would have otherwise. Forth, and perhaps most importantly, students may learn more from classes that are improved through the use of more frequent assessments and evaluations. Instructors can use student feedback to help shape the course because they will have a better understanding of how the students perceive the course content.

FUTURE RESEARCH DIRECTIONS

More research is needed to determine how best to utilize frequent student assessments and SETs. How often and exactly when these evaluations should take place is not yet clear. Further research is also needed to investigate how to develop critical thinking and metacognitive skills to help students give effective feedback. Also professional development focusing on how to help instructors interpret student feedback, as well as how to make maximum use of the feedback is needed. Involving students in the development of a course encourages students to ask, reflect and discuss. These are important areas when viewing students as partners in their own learning. It seems likely that greatly improving mid-semester evaluations is a reasonable goal. Given the potential benefit of incorporating critical thinking and metacognitive skill activities and interteaching assessments along with properly designed and implemented SETs for improving instruction at all levels of education, continued research should be a high priority for those interested in improving academic outcomes.

CONCLUSION

Involving students in the assessment process should be a priority in higher education. Increasing transferable critical thinking skills and metacognitive skills for students can be done using innovative assessments such as those used in interteaching and SETs. These have been shown to improve student-learning outcomes. By involving students more in the assessment process teachers can modify classes still in progress and tailor them to better meet the needs of all students.

REFERENCES

Ahmadi, M., Helms, M., & Raiszadeh, F. (2001). Business students' perceptions of faculty evaluations. *International Journal of Educational Management*, *15*(1), 12–22. doi:10.1108/09513540110366097

Al-Issa, A., & Sulieman, H. (2007). Student evaluations of teaching: Perceptions and biasing factors. *Quality Assurance in Education*, *15*(3), 302–317. doi:10.1108/09684880710773183

Arntzen, E., & Hoium, K. (2010). On the effectiveness of interteaching. *Behavior Analyst Today*, *11*(3), 155–160. doi:10.1037/h0100698

Aultman, L. P. (2006). An unexpected benefit of formative student evaluations. *College Teaching, 54*(3), 251–285. doi:10.3200/CTCH.54.3.251-285

Boyce, T. E., & Hineline, P. N. (2002). Interteaching: A strategy for enhancing the user-friendliness of behavioral arrangements in the college classroom. *The Behavior Analyst, 25*(2), 215–225. PMID:22478388

Brown, M. J. (2008). Student perceptions of teaching evaluations. *Journal of Instructional Psychology, 35*(2), 177–181.

Brown, M. J., Baillie, M., & Fraser, S. (2009). Rating ratemyprofessors.com: A comparison of online and official student evaluations of teaching. *College Teaching, 57*(2), 89–92. doi:10.3200/CTCH.57.2.89-92

Chick, N., Karis, T., & Kernahan, C. (2009). Learning from their own learning: How metacognitive and meta-affective reflections enhance learning in race-related courses. *International Journal for the Scholarship of Teaching & Learning, 3*(1). doi:10.20429/ijsotl.2009.030116

Clayson, D. E. (2009). Student evaluations of teaching: Are they related to what students learn? *Journal of Marketing Education, 31*(1), 16–30. doi:10.1177/0273475308324086

Clayson, D. E., & Haley, D. A. (2011). Are students telling us the truth? A critical look at the student evaluation of teaching. *Marketing Education Review, 21*(2), 101–112. doi:10.2753/MER1052-8008210201

Comm, C. L., & Manthaisel, D. F. X. (1998). Evaluating teaching effectiveness in America's business schools: Implications for service marketers. *Journal of Professional Services Marketing, 16*(2), 163–170. doi:10.1300/J090v16n02_09

Crosier, J. (2011). Please tell me what you are thinking: Workshop in analytical writing for college freshmen. *International Journal of the Humanities, 9*(6), 17–22.

Darwin, S. (2012). Moving beyond face value: Re-envisioning higher education evaluation as a generator of professional knowledge. *Assessment & Evaluation in Higher Education, 37*(6), 733–745. doi:10.1080/02602938.2011.565114

Dee, K. C. (2007). Student perceptions of high course workloads are not associated with poor student evaluations of instructor performance. *The Journal of Engineering Education, 96*(1), 69–78. doi:10.1002/j.2168-9830.2007.tb00916.x

Diamond, M. (2004). The usefulness of structured mid-term feedback as a catalyst for change in higher education classes. *Active Learning In Higher Education The Journal Of The Institute For Learning And Teaching, 5*(3), 217–231. doi:10.1177/1469787404046845

Downing, K., Kwong, T., Chan, S., Lam, T., & Downing, W. (2009). Problem-based Learning and the development of metacognition. *Higher Education, 57*(5), 609–621. doi:10.1007/s10734-008-9165-x

Efklides, A., & Vlachopoulos, S. P. (2012). Measurement of metacognitive knowledge of self, task, and strategies in mathematics. *European Journal of Psychological Assessment, 28*(3), 227–239. doi:10.1027/1015-5759/a000145

Emery, C. R., Kramer, T. R., & Tian, R. G. (2003). Return to academic standards: A critique of student evaluations of teaching effectiveness. *Quality Assurance in Education*, *11*(1), 37–46. doi:10.1108/09684880310462074

Finelli, C. J., Wright, M. C., & Pinder-Grover, T. (2010). Consulting the delphi: A new idea for collecting student feedback through the two survey method (TSM). *Journal of Faculty Development*, *24*(2), 25–33. Retrieved from http://search.proquest.com/ docview/868918564? accountid=38769

Flores, K. L., Matkin, G. S., Burbach, M. E., Quinn, C. E., & Harding, H. (2012). Deficient critical thinking skills among college graduates: Implications for leadership. *Educational Philosophy and Theory*, *44*(2), 212–230. doi:10.1111/j.1469-5812.2010.00672.x

Frick, T. W., Chadha, R., Watson, C., Wang, Y., & Green, P. (2009). College student perceptions of teaching and learning quality. *Educational Technology Research and Development*, *57*(5), 705–720. doi:10.1007/s11423-007-9079-9

Gehringer, E. F. (2010). *Daily course evaluation with Google forms.* Paper presented at the American Society for Engineering Educational Annual Conference, Louisville, KY. Retrieved from http://search.asee.org/search/fetch;jsessionid=23t2t08kfrlin?url=file://localhost/E:/search/conference/32/AC%25202010Full1151.pdf&index=conference_papers&space=129746797203605791716676178&type=application/pdf&charset

Gokhale, A. (1995). Collaborative learning enhances critical thinking. *Journal of Technology Education*, *7*(1), 22–30.

Haan, P., Britt, M., McClellan, S., & Parks, T. H. (2010). Business students' perceptions of course evaluations. *College Student Journal*, *44*(4), 878–887.

Halpern, D. F. (1999). Teaching for critical thinking: Helping college students develop the skills and dispositions of a critical thinker. *New Directions for Teaching and Learning*, *80*(80), 69–74. doi:10.1002/tl.8005

Haskell, R. E. (1997). Academic freedom, tenure, and student evaluation of faculty: Galloping polls in the 21st century. *Education Policy Analysis Archives*, *5*(6), 2.

Heine, P., & Maddox, N. (2009). Student perceptions of the faculty course evaluation process: An exploratory study of gender and class differences. *Research in Higher Education Journal*, *3*, 1–10.

Hodges, L. C., & Stanton, K. (2007). Translating comments on student evaluations into the language of learning. *Innovative Higher Education*, *31*(5), 279–286. doi:10.1007/s10755-006-9027-3

Hoefer, P., Yurkiewicz, J., & Byrne, J. C. (2012). The association between students' evaluation of teaching and grades. *Decision Sciences Journal of Innovative Education*, *10*(3), 447–459. doi:10.1111/j.1540-4609.2012.00345.x

Hudesman, J., & Crosby, S., Flugman, b., Issac, S., Everson, H., & Clay, D. B. (2013). Using formative assessment and metacognition to improve student achievement. *Journal of Developmental Education*, *37*(1), 2–13.

Johnson, M. D., Narayanan, A., & Sawaya, W. J. (2013). Effects of course and instructor characteristics on student evaluation of teaching across a college of engineering. *The Journal of Engineering Education*, *102*(2), 289–318. doi:10.1002/jee.20013

Johnson, V. E. (2003). *Grade inflation: A crisis in college education*. New York: Springer.

Karpicke, J. D., Butler, A. C., & Roedlger, H. L. (2009). Metacognitive strategies in learning: Do students practice retrieval when they study on their own? *Memory (Hove, England)*, *17*(4), 471–479. doi:10.1080/09658210802647009 PMID:19358016

Kember, D., Leung, D., & Kwan, K. (2002). Does the use of student feedback questionnaires improve the overall quality of teaching? *Assessment & Evaluation in Higher Education*, *27*(5), 411–425. doi:10.1080/0260293022000009294

Kienhuis, M., & Chester, A. (2014). Interteaching: A model to enhance student engagement. In M. Gosper, D. Ifenthaler (Eds.), Curriculum models for the 21st century: Using learning technologies in higher education (pp. 135-153). New York, NY, US: Springer Science + Business Media. doi:doi:10.1007/978-1-4614-7366-4_8 doi:10.1007/978-1-4614-7366-4_8

Kim, K., Sharma, P., Land, S. M., & Furlong, K. P. (2013). Effects of active learning on enhancing student critical thinking in an undergraduate general science course. *Innovative Higher Education*, *38*(3), 223–235. doi:10.1007/s10755-012-9236-x

Korkmaz, O. (2012). The impact of critical thinking and logico-mathematical intelligence on algorithmic design skills. *Journal of Educational Computing Research*, *46*(2), 173–193. doi:10.2190/EC.46.2.d

Lewis, K. G. (2001). Making sense of student written comments. *New Directions for Teaching and Learning*, *87*(87), 25–32. doi:10.1002/tl.25

Liu, O. L. (2012). Student evaluation of instruction: In the new paradigm of distance education. *Research in Higher Education*, *53*(4), 471–486. doi:10.1007/s11162-011-9236-1

Macdonald, R. (2006). The use of evaluation to improve practice in learning and teaching. *Innovations in Education and Teaching International*, *43*(1), 3–13. doi:10.1080/14703290500472087

Macknight, C. B. (2000). Teaching critical thinking through online discussions. *EDUCAUSE Quarterly*, *23*(4), 38–41.

Mason, L. L. (2012). Interteaching to increase active student responding and differentiate instruction. *Behavioral Technology Today*, *7*, 1–15.

McCarthy, M. A. M. E. Kite (Ed.), *(n. d.) Effective Evaluation of Teaching: A Guide for Faculty and Administration. Using Student Feedback as One Measure of Faculty Teaching Effectiveness* (pp. 30–39).

McGowan, W. R. (2009). *Faculty and student perceptions of the effects of mid-course evaluations on learning and teaching* [Unpublished doctoral dissertation]. Brigham-Young University, Provo, Utah.

Nasser, F., & Fresko, B. (2002). Faculty views of student evaluation of college teaching. *Assessment & Evaluation in Higher Education*, *2*(2), 187–198. doi:10.1080/02602930220128751

Onwuegbuzie, A. J., Daniel, L. G., & Collins, K. T. (2009). A meta-validation model for assessing the score-validity of student teaching evaluations. *Quality & Quantity: International Journal Of Methodology, 43*(2), 197–209. doi:10.1007/s11135-007-9112-4

Ory, J. C., & Ryan, K. (2001). How do student ratings measure up to a new validity framework? In M. Theall, P.C. Abrami, & L.A. Mets (Eds.), The student ratings debate: Are they valid? How can we best use them? New Directions for Teaching and Learning [Special issue], 87, 3-15. doi:doi:10.1002/ir.2 doi:10.1002/ir.2

Pennequin, V., Sorel, O., Nanty, I., & Fontaine, R. (2010). Metacognition and low achievement in mathematics: The effect of training in the use of metacognitive skills to solve mathematical word problems. *Thinking & Reasoning, 16*(3), 198–220. doi:10.1080/13546783.2010.509052

Persky, A. M., Alford, E. L., & Kyle, J. (2013). Not all hard work leads to learning. *American Journal of Pharmaceutical Education, 77*(5), 89. doi:10.5688/ajpe77589 PMID:23788801

Pinkney, J., & Shaughnessy, M. F. (2013). Teaching critical thinking skills: A modern mandate. *International Journal of Academic Research, 5*(3), 346–352. doi:10.7813/2075-4124.2013/5-3/B.52

Reid, J. R., & Andesron, P. R. (2012). Critical thinking in the business classroom. *Journal of Education for Business, 87*(1), 52–59. doi:10.1080/08832323.2011.557103

Rezaee, M., Farahian, M., & Morad Ahmadi, A. (2012). Critical thinking in higher education: Unfulfilled expectations. *BRAIN: Broad Research in Artificial Intelligence & Neuroscience, 3*(2), 64–73.

Saville, B. K., Cox, T., O'Brien, S., & Vanderveldt, A. (2011). Interteaching: The impact of lectures on student performance. *Journal of Applied Behavior Analysis, 44*(4), 937–941. doi:10.1901/jaba.2011.44-937 PMID:22219544

Saville, B. K., Lambert, T., & Robertson, S. (2011). Interteaching: Bringing behavioral education into the 21st century. *The Psychological Record, 61*(1), 153–165.

Saville, B. K., & Zinn, T. E. (2011). Interteaching. *New Directions For Teaching & Learning, 2011*(128), 53-61. doi:10.1002/tl.468

Saville, B. K., Zinn, T. E., & Elliot, M. P. (2005). Interteaching versus traditional methods of instruction: A preliminary analysis. *Teaching of Psychology, 32*(3), 161–163. doi:10.1207/s15328023top3203_6

Schiekirka, S., Reinhardt, D., Heim, S., Fabry, G., Pukrop, T., Anders, S., & Raupach, T. (2012). Student perceptions of evaluation in undergraduate medical education: A qualitative study from one medical school. *BMC Medical Education, 12*, 45-51.

Schleifer, L. F., & Dull, R. B. (2009). Metacognition and performance in the accounting classroom. *Issues in Accounting Education, 24*(3), 339–367. doi:10.2308/iace.2009.24.3.339

Scoboria, A., & Pascual-Leone, A. (2009). An 'interteaching' informed approach to instructing large undergraduate classes. *Journal of the Scholarship of Teaching and Learning., 9*, 29–37.

Seligman, M. E., & Maier, S. F. (1967). Failure to escape traumatic shock. *Journal of Experimental Psychology, 74*(1), 1–9. doi:10.1037/h0024514 PMID:6032570

Slocombe, T., Miller, D., & Hite, N. (2011). A survey of student perspectives toward faculty evaluations. *American Journal of Business Education*, *4*(7), 51–57.

Smith, G. S. (2004). Assessment strategies: What is being measured in student course evaluations? *Accounting Education*, *13*(1), 3–28. doi:10.1080/0963928032000168977

Surratt, C. K. & Desselle, S.P. (2007). Pharmacy students' perceptions of a teaching evaluation process. *American Journal of Pharmaceutical Education*, 71(1), 06.

Svinicki, M. D. (2001). Encouraging your students to give feedback. *New Directions for Teaching and Learning*, *87*(87), 17–24. doi:10.1002/tl.24

Theall, M., & Franklin, J. (2001). Looking for bias in all the wrong places: A search for truth or a witch hunt in student ratings of instruction? *New Directions for Institutional Research*, *109*(109), 45–56. doi:10.1002/ir.3

Tullis, J., Finley, J., & Benjamin, A. (2013). Metacognition of the testing effect: Guiding learners to predict the benefits of retrieval. *Memory & Cognition*, *41*(3), 429–442. doi:10.3758/s13421-012-0274-5 PMID:23242770

Weinberg, B. A., Fleisher, B. M., & Hashimoto, M. (2007). Evaluating Methods for Evaluating Instruction: The Case of Higher Education (NBER Working Paper No. 12844). Retrieved from http://www.nber.org/papers/w12844

Wilson, J. H., & Ryan, R. G. M. E. Kite (Ed.), *(n. d.). Effective Evaluation of Teaching: A Guide for Faculty and Administration. Formative teaching evaluations: Is student input useful?* (pp. 22–29).

Winchester, M. K., & Winchester, T. M. (2012). If you build it will they come? Exploring the student perspective of weekly student evaluations of teaching. *Assessment & Evaluation in Higher Education*, *37*(6), 671–682. doi:10.1080/02602938.2011.563278

Winchester, T. M., & Winchester, M. (2011). Exploring the impact of faculty reflection on weekly student evaluations of teaching. *The International Journal for Academic Development*, *16*(2), 119–131. doi:10.1080/1360144X.2011.568679

Winchester, T. M., & Winchester, M. K. (2014). A longitudinal investigation of the impact of faculty reflective practices on student evaluations of teaching. *British Journal of Educational Technology*, *4*(1), 112–124. doi:10.1111/bjet.12019

Wright, S. L., & Jenkins-Guarnieri, M. A. (2012). Student evaluations of teaching: Combining the meta-analyses and demonstrating further evidence for effective use. *Assessment & Evaluation in Higher Education*, *37*(6), 683–699. doi:10.1080/02602938.2011.563279

Chapter 7
Comparative Judgement as a Promising Alternative to Score Competences

Marije Lesterhuis
University of Antwerp, Belgium

San Verhavert
University of Antwerp, Belgium

Liesje Coertjens
University of Antwerp, Belgium

Vincent Donche
University of Antwerp, Belgium

Sven De Maeyer
University of Antwerp, Belgium

ABSTRACT

To adequately assess students' competences, students are asked to provide proof of a performance. Ideally, open and real-life tasks are used for such performance assessment. However, to augment the reliability of the scores resulting from performance assessment, assessments are mostly standardised. This hampers the validity of the performance assessment. Comparative judgement (CJ) is introduced as an alternative judging method that does not require standardisation of tasks. The CJ method is based on the assumption that people are able to compare two performances more easily and reliable than assigning a score to a single one. This chapter provides insight in the method and elaborates on why this method is promising to generate valid, reliable measures in an efficient way, especially for large-scale summative assessments. Thereby, this chapter brings together the research already conducted in this new assessment domain.

DOI: 10.4018/978-1-5225-0531-0.ch007

INTRODUCTION

Competence based education has an important share in the curricula in current higher education studies (Heldsinger & Humphry, 2010). As performances are the most direct manifestation of competences, most scholars agree that performance assessments are most suitable to evaluate these competences (Darling-Hammond & Snyder, 2000; Pollitt, 2004). This obviously brings along some challenges (Baker, O'Neil, & Linn, 1993). For a performance assessment to be valid, there needs to be close similarity between the type of performance the student has to execute for the test and the performance that is of interest (Kane, Crooks, & Cohen, 1999). Close-ended tasks and multiple choice exams, for example, are often very much focussed on knowledge reproduction and are quite limited in scope and complexity (Pollitt, 2004). In other words, there is a big difference between asking someone to describe how to do something and actually asking that person to do so. Furthermore, not every competence can be tested via knowledge reproduction alone. Therefore, close-ended tasks and multiple choice exams are less suitable for some types of performance assessment.

Open-ended tasks are more suited for performance assessment. But in open-ended tasks there possibly lies a big challenge, because answers on open-ended tasks are less predictable than those on close-ended tasks. Thus, students' answers will vary to a greater extent, as they have more freedom in the interpretation of the task and how they execute the task. Because there is more variation and unexpected responses of students, human scorers are needed who are able to interpret students' work (Brooks, 2012).

To guide the human scorers, rubrics are mostly used to score performance assessments. Rubrics consist of several criteria or categories concerning aspects or sub dimensions of the competence. Criteria are introduced because they are believed to assure that all assessors look at the same, predefined aspects (Jonsson & Svingby, 2007). However, problems with validity arise as it is almost impossible to formulate all relevant criteria in advance (Sadler, 2009a). In other words, criteria are too reductionist in nature (Pollitt, 2004). In addition to validity, reliability may also be at stake. It is often shown that people differ in how they score tasks, due to differences in severity or leniency (Andrich, 1978; Bloxham & Price, 2015). Also, it has been shown that assessors attribute different scores to the same tasks, dependent on their mood, the moment they assess the task, or the order in which the tasks are being evaluated (Albanese, 2000). Consequently, the use of rubrics does not guarantee high inter-rater reliabilities (Jonsson & Svingby, 2007). Although extensive effort in training assessors upfront can help, this is still not always sufficient in order to gain high reliabilities especially for performance assessments.

To summarize, a lot of different factors influence the validity and reliability of assessments. Unfortunately, rubrics, as an attempt to increase assessment reliability, do not necessarily lead to more reliable assessments and can impede validity. This chapter will introduce an alternative method for scoring in performance assessments, namely Comparative Judgement (CJ). CJ is based on the assumption that people are more reliable in comparing than in assigning scores to single performances (Thurstone, 1927). In CJ, various assessors independently compare several performances of students and decide each time which of them is best with regard to the competence. Based on this, the performances can be ranked from worst to best on a scale. Because the rank-order is based on decisions of several assessors, the scale represents the shared consensus of what a good performance comprises (Pollitt, 2012a). This method seems to be very promising. However, because it has only recently been introduced, many questions regarding its application, advantages and disadvantages remain unanswered. Based on previous research insights, this chapter will firstly provide some background by describing how CJ works, followed by a step-by-step description of how a CJ assessment can be set up in practice. Subsequent sections will further discuss the method with regard to its validity, quality measures and efficiency.

BACKGROUND

The method of CJ is derived from the work of Thurstone at the beginning of the last century. Thurstone, a psychometrician, was concerned with how objects could be scaled, especially when there was no clear definition of the construct that had to be measured, such as attitudes, for example. In his work he explained that every object is a stimulus, which elicits a specific response from its observer. However, this response varies over time and between observers. In his work, Thurstone (1927) showed that humans are better at comparing two stimuli than at assigning scores to a single stimulus. This claim was later amplified by Laming (2003), who concluded that every judgement made by humans is relative. Put differently, humans need something to compare with in order to express the quality of a stimulus.

In addition to to this conclusion, Thurstone (1925) worked on a method to scale stimuli. This method uses the judgement of assessors regarding their decision as to which stimulus contains more of a certain attribute. For example, which stimulus isbetter, longer, more beautiful than another stimulus. The number of times a certain stimulus wins or loses informs the rank-order. The calculation of the position in this rank-order is based on the normal distribution. In 1978, Andrich mathematically proved that the application of the Bradley-Terry-Luce model (BTL-model, Bradley & Terry, 1952; Luce, 1959) and the Rasch-model (Rasch, 1960) are equivalent. Using the BTL-model results in a logit score per stimulus which reflects how much more likely it is that a stimulus will win compared to a reference stimulus. In the earlier stage it was assumed that all assessors needed to make all possible comparisons. Fortunately, Kendall (1955) has shown that not every assessor needs to make all comparisons. Moreover, not all comparisons have to be made, as long as every representation is compared an equal number of times.

Thurstone introduced CJ in a series of articles between 1925 and 1935 (Bramley, 2007), in which its merits were proven. However, it has only recently been introduced in the educational domain. One of the foremost reasons for this delay is that the method is too time demanding when no tools or internet are available for support. The introduction to the assessment domain was carried out by Alastair Pollitt. Together with colleagues, he developed a tool and conducted research on the assessment of competences (Kimbell, 2007; Pollitt, 2004, 2012a). Additionally, he introduced methods to enhance efficiency by making the selection of pairs adaptive (Adaptive Comparative Judgement, ACJ). In this method earlier information gathered about the quality of the performance is used to inform the selection of pairs.

An Application of CJ

An example of a CJ application in the educational context will show how the procedures can be set. CJ is especially suitable in the case of summative assessments, wherein multiple assessors are available and the aim is to achieve reliable and valid scores in an efficient manner. The next section provides a step-by-step approach.

Step 1: Definition of the competence and task.

In order to assess students, it is crucial that the competence description and task are closely related to the intended measured competence. This means that the task must be as authentic as possible (Baartman, 2008; Moss, 1994). The execution of these tasks lead to the representation of the competence. This representation "represents" the performance. This is true for every type of performance assessment regardless of the scoring method. Studies in CJ show that these representations can vary from written text (Pollitt, 2012b) through audio-files (Newhouse & Cooper, 2013) to portfolios (Kimbell, Wheeler, Miller, & Pollitt, 2007).

Step 2: Choice of a tool.

Several tools are available to support CJ. The first developed tool was E-Scape, introduced and developed by a team of TAG Assessment in cooperation with Pollitt (http://www.tagdevelopments.com/acj) (Derrick, 2012; Kimbell et al., 2007). Other tools are NoMoreMarking (http://nomoremarking.com) (Jones, Swan, & Pollitt, 2014), D-PAC (http://d-pac.be), Edsteps (http://www.ccsso.org/Resources/Programs/EdSteps.html) and Brightpath (http://brightpath.com.au/) (Heldsinger & Humphry, 2010). All these tools use CJ to estimate the scores of students, and are similar in their approach. However, they show differences as well. Firstly, the tools differ in their license, from open-source (NoMoreMarking.com and D-PAC.be) to paid use (E-Scape and Brightpath). Secondly, the tools differ in the possibilities of using adaptive algorithms. For example, E-Scape uses an adaptive algorithm and Brightpath and D-PAC offer opportunities for higher efficiency after an initial (calibrated) set is created. Thirdly, the tools have different and extended features to provide students with feedback on their performance (e.g. E-Scape). Lastly, the tools vary in the types of representations that can be uploaded. However, most tools are still under development and new features will probably be introduced in the near future. When it comes to choosing one, it is recommended to take a look at the websites and contact the administrators.

Step 3: Selection of assessors.

In the current studies, the number of assessors involved ranged from four (Pollitt & Crisp, 2004) to 54 (Pollitt, 2012b). Besides that, different studies use different types of assessors. For example, in the study of Whitehouse and Pollitt (2012), 23 teachers and examiners, who were highly trained to assess students' work in the specific content domain, participated, and it was shown that the current teaching-level was of influence on the consistency of their judgements. Similar results were found by Heldsinger and Humphry (2010), who also selected 15 teachers for the comparisons. The example of Jones and Alcock (2013) shows that assessors do not necessary have to be trained in making evaluations, since peers and novices (possessing content knowledge, but no assessment experience) are also able to achieve reliable and similar rank-orders. However, experts were more confident in making the judgements. The study of Attili (2014) even took an additional step and recruited assessors via Amazon Mechanical Turk. These assessors, however, did receive some training.

Step 4: Preparation of assessment.

How an assessment needs to be set up depends on the specific tool. For example, decisions need to be made based on how many comparisons assessors need to make and/or how often a representation needs to be compared (Bramley, 2015). The latter can vary between nine (Pollitt, 2012b) and 69 (Heldsinger & Humphry, 2010). This decision can be informed by the time assessors are available or by the desired reliability level. However the studies of Pollitt (2012b) and Heldsinger and Humphry (2010) show similar reliabilities. Assessors can be prepared with a short introduction to the competence that needs to be assessed, the tool that is used and what is expected. Depending on the competence, there is no need for training (Whitehouse, 2012). However, when there is a lack of understanding of the competence, it can be fruitful to let assessors make a small number of comparisons together in order to get grip on the definition, as was done by Kimbell et al. (2007). This can also enhance their confidence, since making holistic comparisons is probably different from their current practice (Pollitt & Crisp, 2004). Moreover, as Bramley (2007) argues, a certain share of understanding is necessary in order to generate reliable rank-orders. The less shared understanding there is, the more comparisons need to be made.

Step 5: Assessment process.

Every assessor receives a pair of representations. The assessor is asked to point out the best one with regard to the assessed competence (i.e. which one has the highest perceived overall quality or shows most evidence of the competence). There is some debate on whether assessors need an importance statement or a more thorough full explanation of the competence that is being assessed. The comparison itself is called a judgement, referring to making a comparison between two representations. It can happen that an assessor thinks two representations are of equal quality. In this case, the assessor can choose one by "flipping the coin" since these two representations will probably end-up very close to each other in the final rank-order (Pollitt, 2012b). After choosing a representation, the assessor receives a new pair to compare. Several assessors need to make multiple comparisons. Some tools (e.g. E-Scape and D-PAC) offer a feature wherein assessors can write down comments to the students.

Step 6: Calculations.

Applying the BTL-model (Bradley & Terry, 1952; Luce, 1959), the judgements of assessors lead to a rank-order. The eventual rank-order can be graphically visualized, as in Figure 1. The y-axis represents the scores expressed in logits. The estimated scores of representations are indicated with the dots. The lines represent the confidence intervals of these estimated scores.

However, the final rank-order does not lead directly to interpretable marks that express the quality of the representations, or to a pass-fail boundary. It requires a standard setting exercise to determine this pass-fail boundary or any other boundary relevant for the assessment (e.g. boundary between levels of language proficiency). After this boundary is assigned, it is possible to send the representations which cross the pass/fail line with their confidence intervals several more times to the assessors (Pollitt, 2012b). This way, the certainty with which a representation has failed or passed increases.

This step-by-step approach shows that there is not yet a clear answer for every decision. However, since academic interest is growing, we can expect a better insight in the impact of some of these decisions.

Figure 1. Example of a rank-order

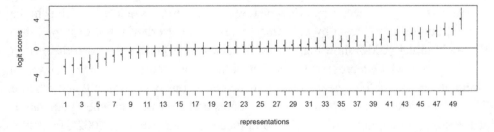

MAIN FOCUS OF THE CHAPTER

The willingness to give students authentic tasks seems to be in imbalance with the requirements of quality measures as reliability. This is especially the case in large-scale, summative assessments. CJ seems a promising alternative to score complex competences on a large scale. This chapter aims to bring together the research already executed in this new domain. Thereby, it attempts to provide insights on the advantages of this method. At the same time, the chapter will reveal the need for more scientific and practice-orientated research in this new assessment domain.

The following topics will be addressed: 1) validity arguments for CJ, 2) reliability and other quality measures which can be applied for CJ, and 3) efficiency.

VALIDITY

This section elaborates how CJ possibly enhances the validity of tests. The first section describes how scoring with CJ may have a positive influence on the design process of tasks and rubrics. The second section states why CJ results can lead to more valid conclusions or decisions, since the comparison process of judges is more natural to them than the judgement process wherein they use rubrics. The third section will describe why using several assessors enhances validity.

No Need for Standardisation

The requirement for reliable assessments have spiked the standardisation of assessments (Moss, 1994). However, the trend towards standardisation can impair validity. Assessing highly complex competences such as problem-solving requires evaluation of complex performances (Kane et al., 1999). Most ideally, students have to fulfill open-ended tasks in real-life. As these tasks are harder to score, the validity of assessment is already impaired during the development phase of the task. As Jones and Inglis (2015) show in their article on mathematical problem-solving, test-designers develop less standardized and more problem-based tasks if they do not have to reckon the scoring phase. Thus, it is not necessary to divide the question into sub-questions, so cognitive complexity is enhanced.

Standardisation of tasks not only impairs their validity, but also the development of rubrics. These are designed to ensure that all assessors look at the same aspects (Azarfam, 2012). However, the criteria can never represent the whole construct, with all its dimensions. For example, Sadler (1989) listed all published criteria for assessing the quality of a written composition. He came up with more than 50 criteria. Not only is assessing essays with 50 criteria impossible, problems arise as the level of abstraction differs and many criteria will show overlap. In order to make the scoring process more manageable, the number of criteria needs to be decreased. However, when a criterion is deleted which is highly relevant for the assessor, he or she will react by adjusting scores on other criteria. For example, the studies of Crisp (2013) and Lumley (2002) show that assessors' raise (or lower) the mark on other criteria in order to come to a final score which represents the quality of the essay according to their own vision (Brooks, 2012). Thirdly, it is impossible to create a rubric which also considers criteria that are harder to make explicit. Those criteria do, however, influence the scores and are essential when you want to define a score which is doing justice to the real quality of a piece of work (Lumley, 2002). Fourthly, concerns are raised if micro-judgement on criteria can be summed in order to decide a final mark which reflects the competence of the student (Pollitt & Crisp, 2004; Sadler, 2009a).

For these reasons, CJ seems especially fruitful in cases wherein the competence or task that needs to be assessed is less well delimited and wherein it is difficult to specify marking schemes (Pollitt, 2012a). This counts for domains where a less well-defined historically-developed body of knowledge is extant, so it becomes harder to define the right answers upfront. Thus, this applies for domains or tasks wherein experience from everyday life provides knowledge that overlaps the subject knowledge, which makes the boundaries of the subject knowledge more fuzzy. The report of Kimbell et al. (2007) shows how this is the case for the domain of design and technology. In this domain, the aim is to teach and assess students' abilities to be creative, innovative problem-solvers. In this case the students were asked to re-design a light-bulb packaging box, so the box could be transformed into a lighting feature once the bulb is taken out. Students worked on a digital portfolio, wherein they had to upload drawings and pictures and reflect on their design process. These portfolios were judged using ACJ. This example shows that CJ has an advantage in cases wherein standardisation of tasks would not do justice to the competence, and the development of rubrics is problematic due to difficulties with predicting how students will approach the task. Thereby, open-ended tasks provide insight into the abilities of students to be creative and innovative.

A More Natural Way of Assessing, Using the Strengths of Assessors

This section will describe why the use of CJ may enhance validity, due to the match with how humans assess naturally. CJ is based upon "The Law of Comparative Judgement" (Thurstone, 1927). Thurstone states that people are better at comparing than at assigning scores to single objects. Laming (2003) amplified this law by stating that every judgement is a comparison. Laming shows that although someone is asked to make an absolute judgement (the opposite of a comparison), humans need a reference point. As a consequence, humans choose their own reference point and/or their internal standard when a reference point is lacking. Studies in educational contexts show that the use of internal standards, however, lead to biases in the judgement. For example, Crisp (2013) points out that assessors need to compare the work of students, in order to get a grip on the quality. In CJ the assessors are offered something to compare with. Therefore, their decision will be less dependent on what they have assessed before. Moreover, severity or leniency will not influence the final scores (Greatorex, 2007), because assessors only have to point out the best representation.

Also, this method is presumably less cognitively demanding for the assessors, which is also an important aspect in favour of CJ (Bejar, 2012). This can be underpinned by the surveys published in the research of Pollitt (2012b) that show that most experienced assessors prefer CJ over using marking schemes. Among other things they refer to the easiness of making a judgement compared to constantly referring to increasingly complex mark schemes, and to the fact that they could use their experience and that comparing helped them to see more easily how well students were able to express themselves (this concerned a CJ writing assessment).

In CJ, assessors base their decision on their own conceptualisations, because they do not receive rubrics. This can enhance the validity, because they can take into consideration implicit and explicit quality aspects (Whitehouse, 2012). It is, however, important that assessors have relevant knowledge. For example, when they judge essays and are not able to discriminate between two essays based on argumentation structure, the validity of the assessment is impaired (Bramley, 2007). Whitehouse (2012) analyses the relevance of the reasons why assessors had chosen a paper and concludes that assessors were all able to base their decision on relevant aspects of the paper. She explains this by pointing out that all assessors were teachers with experience and training in the assessment of geography. However, further research should be conducted in other contexts and focusing on other competences.

Multiple Assessors

Inter-rater reliability seems to be the most crucial aspect in the studies on the quality of assessments. Using rubrics, a high inter-rater reliability can be achieved, when all assessors have exactly the same way of interpreting the rubrics and the same way of interpreting the tasks of students. In CJ the reliability can be obtained with subjective judgements (Jones & Inglis, 2015; Thurstone, 1925).

In CJ multiple assessors evaluate representations, and the final score is based on all the comparisons made. That means that the final rank-order and the final scores are an expression of the shared consensus of the assessors. Although a certain agreement among assessors about what the competence comprises is necessary, small differences between the focus of assessors or the aspects they weigh as more important do not cause problems (Bramley & Gill, 2010). At the same time that means that the final scores represent the score of all these different perspectives together, and not the sole interpretation of one assessor. The score is thereby more informed (Martin, 1997) and an outcome of these multiple perspectives (Shay, 2005). In other words, this method is doing justice to the incongruent nature of what quality comprises. Whereas in most scoring methods subjectivity is seen as a threat, this method acknowledges and uses the importance of different conceptualisations of what quality can comprise.

This section has focused on how CJ can enhance validity in the design phase, the scoring process and by using several assessors. The next section will provide insight into the possible quality measures CJ incorporates, which can be applied after the comparisons have been finished.

QUALITY MEASURES

Especially in cases where the assessment is high-stakes, it is important to have insight into the quality of the assessment (Pollitt, 2012b). Since CJ uses the BTL-model (Bradley & Terry, 1952; Luce, 1959), which is comparable to the Rasch model, a number of quality measures can be calculated. Reliability is the measure most reported on in the CJ literature. Additionally, it can be calculated whether one assessor deviates from the others (named assessor *Infit*) and whether there is disagreement on certain representations (named representation *Infit*). The next paragraphs will provide further detail on these quality measures as well as on the results obtained for them in CJ literature.

The Reliability of CJ Assessments

As mentioned previously, when using the CJ-method, reliability is fostered due to its collective nature, which rules out varying standards. Moreover, given that assessors only have to pick the better one, the difference in severeness between assessors is annulled (Bramley, 2007; Whitehouse, 2012; Whitehouse & Pollitt, 2012). These elements allow for high reliabilities, as evidenced in CJ-literature.

Of the CJ-studies published, one showed a reliability above .70 (Jones & Alcock, 2012), three report reliabilities above .80 (Jones & Alcock, 2013; Jones et al., 2014; McMahon & Jones, 2014), with most studies indicating reliabilities above .90 (for an overview, see Bramley, 2015). Certainly when comparing these reliabilities to those achieved using analytical scoring (Bloxham & Price, 2015), these estimates are viewed as a major appeal of the CJ method.

On the fact that CJ can provide adequate reliabilities, the field agrees. Remarkably, there is however less agreement on how reliability should be labelled. Ideally, reliability would be estimated by using CJ twice on the same set of representations and examining how the results correlate (Bramley, 2007). To our knowledge, only one study has provided evidence on this. Jones and Inglis (2015) put two groups of assessors to work in assessing mathematical problem solving. Subsequently, the rank-orders produced by both groups were correlated. Results indicated a high inter-rater reliability between the groups (*Pearson product-moment correlation coefficient* of .84). More evidence on this would certainly advance the CJ field and, given that research interest in CJ is on the rise, is likely to be forthcoming in the years ahead. However, for day-to-day practice, assessing inter-rater reliability between groups is difficult. Therefore, other measures are usually relied on.

Because CJ data can be analysed using the Rasch model (Andrich, 1978), the *Rasch separation reliability* can be calculated. This index of reliability is sometimes referred to as (*Rasch*) *alpha* or *Scale Separation Reliability*[1] (SSR; Bramley, 2015). Though both terms can be used interchangeably, we opt for the latter, given it represents more clearly what the measure signifies. The *SSR* indicates to what degree the spread in the results is not due to measurement error (Andrich, 1982; McMahon & Jones, 2014). This can then be interpreted as an indication of how well the scale separates the representations (Anshel, Kang, & Jubenville, 2013; Mack & Ragan, 2008). Furthermore, a high *SSR* indicates a minimal measurement error, which implies that the relative position of the items on the scale is quite fixed (Andrich, 1982).

Given that CJ data can be analysed using the Rasch model (Andrich, 1978), other quality measures from Rasch analysis can be used as well (Pollitt, 2012b). The next section will detail on assessor and representation *Infit*.

Assessor and Representation *Infit*

By using *chi-squared* (χ^2) *goodness of fit* statistics, Rasch (1960) evaluated the fit of the data to the model. These statistics, based on the residuals, make it possible to quantify how far judgements are different to what the model, or the eventual rank-order, predicts. This can then be aggregated to provide an estimate of how much assessors deviate from the group consensus on the one hand or how ambiguous a representation is for the group on the other hand. There are two types of fit statistics, namely *Infit* and *Outfit*.

Both misfit statistics are based on the standardized squared residuals, a measure signifying how much a decision deviates from what is expected from the model. The model expectation is actually the probability that the representation A will win over representation B. The decision can take the value 1, A is preferred to B, or 0, B is preferred to A. The measure thus quantifies how unexpected a response is, expressed in the same unit (standardized) and in the same direction (positive; squared).

Generally, the misfit statistics are calculated by summing these standardized squared residuals over assessors or over representations, dependent on who/what we want to know the misfit of. More specific, the *Outfit* is the mean of the standardized squared residual, signifying the mean *unexpectedness*. The *Infit* is the information weighted squared residual. It is calculated by attributing a weight to the standardized squared residuals that is proportional to the distance between the estimated logit scores of representations A and B and summing this. This summed value is then corrected or put on the same scale by the summed distance between representation pairs A and B, which actually comes down to a sum of the raw residuals squared (the squared deviation between what is expected and what was observed) and the summed distance between all representation pairs A and B. This weighting is done because it is worse to prefer A over B when A is of much poorer quality than B than when A and B are of comparable quality. But because to err is human, a correction is applied. This correction ensures that a larger weight is attributed to deviations with intermediate distance between A and B compared to large deviations. Therefore it is stated that the *Infit* is less prone to occasional mistakes and is therefore preferred (Linacre & Wright, 1994).

From these individual numbers it has to be determined which number is large. There are two approaches. The first comes directly from the Rasch literature and says that *Infit* statistics have a mean of 1 and follow a χ^2 distribution (Wright & Linacre, 1994). From a simulation and analysis experience, Linacre (2002) formulated the following standard: an *Infit* of 1.5 or higher can be considered a small deviance, and from 2 onwards it can be considered a big deviance. The second approach comes from general statistics where it is observed that mean square values do not have a fixed mean every time. Therefore, it is opted to calculate the mean and standard deviation of that assessment. An *Infit* that lies two standard deviations from the mean is considered large (Kimbell et al., 2009; Pollitt, 2012b). From their own observations, Pollitt (2012a) and also Kimbell et al. (2009) opted for the second alternative.

According to Pollitt (2012a) a large *Infit* for assessors means that they consistently judge away from the consensus. This could be because the assessors have other conceptualisations of what makes a representation better or worse (Bramley, 2007). Assessors might define the competence under judgement differently (Bramley, 2007) or they may attribute more weight to specific aspects of the competence. Representations with a large *Infit* are the ones that lead to more inconsistent judgements (Pollitt, 2004). A representation with a high *Infit* could contain something unusual in terms of the performance (Bramley, 2007), therefore assessors might find them difficult to judge (Pollitt, 2004). For example, the representation might contain a creative and correct solution to a problem, although that solution does not completely fit the competence description.

In the light of the respective causes of misfit there are some suggested solutions, if the misfit is diagnosed in time. With assessor misfit it is possible to give the assessors more training (Pollitt & Elliott, 2003) or to just remove the assessor. Representations that are misfitting can also be removed or they can be sent out for more comparisons (Pollitt, 2004). Sometimes it is only necessary to rephrase or redefine the assignment of assessors or the description for the assessed competence (Bramley, 2007; Pollitt, 2004).

It needs to be remarked that there has not been much research done on the meaning of *Infit* in the context of CJ. Pollitt (2004) states that there is a need for better statistics because in the current statistics the possibility exists that the misfitting assessor is the only good assessor due to the relative nature of the statistics. Furthermore, awareness is on the rise that the interpretations of the *Infit* from Rasch literature cannot easily be generalized to the context of CJ. More specifically, in Rasch literature changes in *Infit* and *Outfit* are interpreted in the light of patterns of correct and wrong answers, whereas in CJ we only have series of "A is better than B" judgements, of which some are the other way around than what the model predicts.

The first evidences on the CJ method are in favour of the validity and reliability of the results. The other quality measures are certainly considered to be an advantage as well. What is put into question when discussing the CJ method with practitioners is efficiency. The next section will detail on this efficiency and on pathways to increase it.

EFFICIENCY

Regarding the efficiency of the CJ-method, i.e. the time investment required to achieve adequate reliability, the existing research evidence is up to the present inconclusive. CJ has been claimed to be quite efficient, given that it requires assessors to make fast and intuitive decisions about which representation is the better one in light of a certain competence. It is believed that assessors can make adequate decisions fast: those assessors requiring more decision time were not found to make better judgements (Pollitt, 2012b). Moreover, if a mistake were to happen, with CJ this is diluted: a final score is always based on multiple comparisons by multiple assessors.

Nevertheless, given that multiple judgements per representation are required to generate a reliable rank-order, claiming CJ to be efficient appears counter-intuitive. Even at first sight, this is more time-consuming than rating by one assessor or even two. To counter the inefficiency of CJ, Pollitt (2004) was one of the first to introduce an adaptive procedure to construct pairs. With ACJ, in a first round, n/2 random pairs are formed and judged. From the second judgement round on, a Swiss tournament system is used. Thereby, student's' work is matched based on its win/loss ratio. After a number of Swiss rounds, the BTL-model (Bradley & Terry, 1952; Luce, 1959) is used to generate rough ability estimates (estimated logit scores) for each representation. Subsequently, these ability estimates are used to match papers with similar quality. Pollitt (2012b) reports that using these adaptive procedures, the same levels of reliability can be obtained with 40 to 50% fewer judgements. Applying such ACJ has been found to give quite high reliabilities in terms of *SSR*, ranging from .89 (Jones & Alcock, 2012) to .97 (Jones & Alcock, 2013; Whitehouse & Pollitt, 2012) for a reasonable number of comparisons ranging from 9 to 17 (Pollitt, 2012b).

However, ACJ is not without problems. Recently, Bramley (2015) has effectively demonstrated that when using Swiss tournament, reliability is artificially inflated. The estimated reliability is higher than it should be. He concludes that the same is likely for other adaptive procedures such as logit based matching. An implication of this is that the reliabilities provided in the previous paragraph are likely to be overestimating the true reliability. Furhter research might look for ways to correct for this inflation of the reliability measure.

There are however a set of studies - though limited in number - having examined the reliability of CJ instead of ACJ. By the fact that pairs are randomly generated in these studies, the bias of inflating the reliability is prevented. A downside of the CJ method is believed to be that, to reach acceptable levels of reliability, a large amount of comparisons need to be done (Bramley, Bell, & Pollitt, 1998). This is partially confirmed. In the study by Heldsinger and Humphry (2010), a - surreal - 69 comparisons per representation yielded a reliability of .98. However, three other samples in which CJ was used (one in McMahon and Jones, 2014, and in Jones et al. 2014) evidence that acceptable reliabilities can be reached, ranging from .80 (Jones et al., 2014) to .87 (McMahon & Jones, 2014). In these studies, the number of comparisons ranged from 16.7 (Jones et al., 2014) to 20 (McMahon & Jones, 2014), which was not much higher than using ACJ.

Efficiency-Reliability Trade-Off

For CJ to be convincingly promoted as a new method for evaluation in day-to-day educational practice, what is overlooked, in our view, is the time investment needed to achieve this reliability. Admittedly, a substantial time investment for a small gain in reliability will be unlikely to be invested in practice. Up to the present, only Pollitt (2012b) has reported on how the reliability increased per rounds of comparisons. To allow assessment practitioners to make informed choices on the time investment required for a desired reliability, it would be helpful if CJ-researchers presented how reliability increased during the judgement process.

Next to the question on how many comparisons are needed for a certain reliability, a "potential barrier to the use of CJ for summative teacher assessment is the relative inefficiency of the method compared to the marking procedure" (McMahon & Jones, 2014, p. 381). In the study by McMahon and Jones (2015) it was estimated that even compared to double marking, the time investment using CJ was double. Though this study is the first to compare this in such straightforward way, a critical note would be that the marking scheme used is very concise. A teacher was able to read responses to four questions and mark them within less than a minute. This is possibly due to the fact that - as acknowledged by the authors - factual recall was at stake in three of the four questions. Nevertheless, some of the marking schemes published in language education, for example, are much more elaborate (Van Weijen, 2007). For difficult to mark skills such as creativity, writing or conceptual understanding, the question whether CJ or marking shows a more favourable efficiency-reliability trade-off is clearly still open.

In evaluating this trade-off correctly, we believe that the entire effort to achieve final scores should be taken into account. In marking, time is devoted as well to develop, pilot and adjust the marking scheme. Moreover, a substantial amount of time is subsequently invested in providing training for assessors, so as to enhance reliability. Neither effort is required when using CJ. Thus, though at first sight CJ appears tedious in respect to marking, a comprehensive evaluation of the invested time should be investigated.

To allow for extensive use in educational practice, the relative efficiency of CJ is of importance. There are two exceptions to this. First, for very high stakes assessments such as entrance assessments or final assessments leading to certification, currently already a large number of markers may be included. Given that time investment here is already substantial, these practices could benefit from increased reliability using CJ. Second, CJ can be used for peer-assessment (e.g., Jones et al., 2014; McMahon & Jones, 2014; Seery, Canty, & Phelan, 2012). With peer-assessment there is inherently a large number of assessors among whom the work can be divided. Fortunately, for other assessments besides high stakes and peer-assessment, there are a number of views on how to increase the efficiency of CJ.

Pathways to Increase Efficiency

A number of pathways to increase the efficiency of CJ have been described in the literature. Four are worth mentioning, given that first evidence has been provided or that they will likely be looked into over the next year. First, as Bramley (2015) describes, an - albeit substantial - investment in constructing a calibration set of representations can give a large efficiency gain later. Such calibration set of representations is generated by making all possible comparisons among a limited number of comparisons. Subsequently, the remaining or new representations can be compared to an average representation of this calibration set and - depending on having won or lost this comparison - to representations in the calibration set showing more or less indication of quality. With this, representations could be placed on the scale from the calibration set in an efficient manner. This pathway seems most fruitful for recurring assessments in which new representations are placed on the initial scale, thereby also safeguarding standards over time and between assessors.

First evidence on the effectiveness and efficiency of this pathway has been provided by Heldsinger and Humphry (2013), regarding students' writing at the start of primary education. First, CJ was used to generate a calibration set. Second, teachers judged new representations using calibrated exemplars from this first phase. (Note that, in contrast to Bramley's suggestion (2015), CJ is abandoned in this second phase.) Evidence suggests that, when calibrated exemplars can be used in assessing writing, teachers can reliably judge which exemplar is most alike. Over the different representations, inter-rater reliability ranged from .87 to .95 with a mean of .92. Moreover, teachers were able to make these judgements with only a short time investment (i.e. three minutes per representation). Moreover, no time-consuming meetings to debate the common standard were required (Heldsinger & Humphry, 2013). In sum, the initial investment of the rank-order safeguarded reliability while improving efficiency. Further research may look at whether using CJ in this second phase as well would additionally improve reliability.

Second, an initial scale and benchmarks could be used to more swiftly categorise representations into predefined categories. By comparing representations to the benchmarks (Verhavert, 2015) for some representations it may be clear quite fast in which category they belong. For others, for which there is more uncertainty, more comparisons could be included until a level of certainty is achieved. This is in line with Pollitt's (2012a) view of focusing the comparisons on those representations that require more comparisons.

A third suggestion lies in the fact that until now the CJ methodology has been conceptualised as a *pairwise* comparison methodology. Bramley and Black (2008) point at the possibilities of asking assessors to rank-order three (or more) representations to further increase the efficiency of CJ. It can be hypothesized that this rank-order methodology is more efficient than the pairwise judgement process. On the other hand, rank-ordering of three representations may impose a tougher cognitive task on the assessors (Black, 2008), questioning the extent to which it leads to valid measures of competences (Attali, 2014). In examining this, not only the number of representations but also the length of the representation appears relevant. With short response questions for example, Attali (2014) asked assessors to rank-order five representations. Clearly, given the limited set of studies examining the possibilities of rank-ordering by asking assessors to order three (Black, 2008; Raikes, Scorey, & Shiell, 2008), five (Attali, 2014) or ten representations (Bramley, 2005), further research on this is required. Moreover, indications of the efficiency gains provided by such rank ordering are up to present lacking.

A fourth pathway is relying on information to speed up the rank-order. Two thoughts have been advanced on this. First, students' prior scores could be used to generate an initial rank-order (Pollitt, 2012a). Such first rank-order can be used in an adaptive algorithm to more efficiently compose the initial pairs. Second, indices stemming from prior automated evaluation which are known to correlate with the competence under study could be relied on as a starting point. The study by Attali (2014) is the sole study reporting on this to our knowledge and used response length of short answer responses. Evidence as to which degree the final rank-order with and without using information are correlated is absent up to the present, as well as indication of by how many the comparisons per representation can be reduced.

Until more evidence is gathered on these and possibly other pathways to increase the efficiency of CJ while maintaining the advantage of higher reliabilities, it is recommended for practitioners to use CJ with randomly generated pairs and report the *SSR*. Additionally, studies tracking the efficiency-reliability trade-off for CJ and preferably also making the comparison with marking using rubrics are warmly welcomed to further evidence the CJ claims of reliability as well as efficiency.

SOLUTIONS AND RECOMMENDATIONS

The previous sections showed that CJ can be a promising alternative for the assessment of competences. This chapter lists cases when CJ is of additional value and in which cases it may not be. CJ can help to tackle problems when teachers want to score performance assessments and high reliabilities need to be achieved. Firstly, CJ shows to be very promising since standardisation of tasks and rubrics does not impair validity. Thereby, validity is enhanced by the more natural judgement assessors undertake. Also, because scores of single representations are defined by comparisons with several other representations and by several assessors, the final scale represents a shared consensus of what quality comprises. Secondly, the CJ method has clear benefits in light of quality measures. Though more studies are required that use CJ twice on the same set of representations and examine how the results correlate, in general, by cancelling out the assessor effects that are detrimental in rubric settings, high reliabilities (above .80) in terms of the *SSR* have been reported. Next to reliability, assessor *Infit* and representation *Infit* can be calculated. The former indicates how far an assessor deviates from the group consensus while the latter denotes how much doubt there is on a representation in a group of assessors. Discussion about the conceptualisation, used in scoring, of this assessor or this representation is fruitful in building a shared understanding about what quality is and comprises, which enables discussion in schools, departments and even among students. Third, CJ is hopeful regarding its efficiency, particularly in cases wherein the development of rubrics and training of assessors is time-consuming.

However, this chapter also showed that in order to execute a CJ assessment, there are some prerequisites. Firstly, more than one assessor needs to be available. That means CJ is less applicable for classroom assessments where only one teacher or assessor needs to assess all students' tasks. It is, however, very useful in cases where larger groups of students need to be assessed (Newhouse, 2013). Secondly, in cases wherein the formative side of the assessment is more prominent that the summative side, CJ is less suitable. The generation of qualitative and personal feedback is less inherent to the CJ judgement process. Although some tools generate personall feedback, it is unclear if and to what extent the comparative approach increases competention among students and enhances learning. Thirdly, CJ is less able to communicate to the students the dimensions whereon the competence is judged, especially in comparison with rubrics.

Also, some strengths of CJ can be applied in other assessment methods, e.g. rubrics. For example the strength of shared consensus can be implemented by the development of the rubrics, or when the rubrics are filled in. This way, final scores reflect the shared consensus more closely. Thus, adding more assessors to the assessment team adds reliability in rubrics as well, although in current practices double marking is not often applied.

FUTURE RESEARCH DIRECTIONS

Because CJ has only recently been introduced, there are many research directions to explore. Regarding the validity of the method, most research has focused on the comparability of the scores to other scoring methods (Attali, 2014; Jones et al., 2014). Additionally, a few studies revealed that standardisation of tasks impairs validity (Jones & Inglis, 2015), and the construct validity (Whitehouse, 2012). However, more research is needed to investigate when and how assessors can make valid decisions. Bramley (2007) points out that assessors need to apprehend enough relevant features of both representations. This may imply that CJ is too cognitively demanding for assessors when the representations get too complex. Therefore, more knowledge is necessary on how to select and train assessors. The tension between the necessity of a shared consensus and the aim to do justice to the incongruity of quality should be better understood. Further research can provide these insights by recruiting different types of assessors, by comparing the work of novices with the experts or by taking a more qualitative approach towards how conceptualisation leads to assessors' decision-making.

Concerning CJ's efficiency, many research questions are important to address. Though the method is believed to be profitable, conclusive evidence on this is lacking. The efficiency of the CJ method is most often improved by using an adaptive version. However, recent evidence shows that such adaptive procedures are likely to inflate reliability. Fortunately, a number of other pathways to increase the method's efficiency can be investigated, such as developing a calibration set or using a scale with benchmarks to swiftly categorise representations. In addition to pathways to increase efficiency, further research is clearly warranted that compares rubrics and CJ with regards to the time investment needed to achieve a desired reliability level. Additionally, more research should address questions elaborating the impact, causes and solutions to deal with *Infit* assessors and representations.

The last aspect that demands further research is the students' experience with this method and the possibilities of this method to enhance learning. Seery et al. (2012) and Jones and Alcock (2013) have focused on how this method enhances learning when used for peer assessment. However, more research is needed regarding in which cases CJ is helpful. As argued by Sadler (2009b, 2010), students need to gain understanding on what quality comprises by making more holistic judgements. CJ can help with this and immediately provide input for discussion. The same is true for training applications when making comparisons. Also, to our knowledge, no research has been conducted on how this method provides feedback for students that enhances their learning. Although several tools provide different types of feedback, no study has focussed on the learning effects on the long run.

CONCLUSION

This chapter introduces CJ as an alternative approach for the large-scale assessments of competences. The chapter developed a wide-ranging argument with regard to the advantages of this method. However, many aspects of this method are still under-researched and CJ seems not to be the best scoring alternative for all cases. Nevertheless, it needs to be emphasized that traditional marking methods are characterised by several disadvantages which can be overcome with CJ. The innovative character of the method and the associated good practices shown in this chapter are promising in order to improve current large-scale, summative assessments practices in higher education.

NOTE

Marije Lesterhuis and San Verhavert contributed equally to this book chapter as first authors.

REFERENCES

Albanese, M. (2000). Challenges in using rater judgements in medical education. *Journal of Evaluation in Clinical Practice*, 6(3), 305–319. doi:10.1046/j.1365-2753.2000.00253.x PMID:11083041

Andrich, D. (1978). Relationships between the Thurstone and Rasch approaches to item Scaling. *Applied Psychological Measurement*, 2(3), 449–460. doi:10.1177/014662167800200319

Andrich, D. (1982). An index of person separation in latent trait theory, the traditional KR-20 index, and the Guttman scale response pattern. *Education Research and Perspectives*, 9(1), 95–104.

Anshel, M. H., Kang, M., & Jubenville, C. (2013). Sources of acute sport stress scale for sports officials: Rasch calibration. *Psychology of Sport and Exercise*, 14(3), 362–370. doi:10.1016/j.psychsport.2012.12.003

Attali, Y. (2014). A ranking method for evaluating constructed responses. *Educational and Psychological Measurement*, 74(5), 795–808. doi:10.1177/0013164414527450

Azarfam, A. Y. (2012). Basic considerations in writing instruction & assessment. *Advances in Asian Social Science*, 1(1), 139–150.

Baartman, L. (2008). *Assessing the assessment. Development and use of quality criteria for Competence Assessment Programmes*. (Dissertation), Universiteit Utrecht, Utrecht.

Baker, E. L., O'Neil, H. F., & Linn, R. L. (1993). Policy and validity prospects for performance-based assessment. *The American Psychologist*, 48(12), 1210–1218. doi:10.1037/0003-066X.48.12.1210

Bejar, I. I. (2012). Rater cognition: Implications for validity. *Educational Measurement: Issues and Practice*, 31(3), 2–9. doi:10.1111/j.1745-3992.2012.00238.x

Black, B. (2008). Using an adapted rank-ordering method to investigate January versus June awarding standards. *Paper presented at theFourth Biennial EARLI/Nortumbria Assessment Conference*, Berlin, Germany.

Bloxham, S., & Price, M. (2015). External examining: Fit for purpose? *Studies in Higher Education*, 40(2), 195–211. doi:10.1080/03075079.2013.823931

Bradley, R. A., & Terry, M. E. (1952). Rank analysis of incomplete block designs. The method of paired comparisons. *Biometrika*, 39(3-4), 324–345. doi:10.1093/biomet/39.3-4.324

Bramley, T. (2005). A rank-ordering method for equating tests by expert judgment. *Journal of Applied Measurement*, 6(2), 202–223. PMID:15795487

Bramley, T. (2007). Paired comparison methods. In J. B. P. Newton, H. Goldstein, H. Patrick, & P. Tymms (Eds.), *Techniques for monitoring the comparability of examination standards* (pp. 246–294). London: QCA.

Bramley, T. (Ed.). (2015). *Investigating the reliability of Adaptive Comparative Judgment*. Cambridge, UK: Cambridge Assessment.

Bramley, T., Bell, J. F., & Pollitt, A. (1998). Assessing changes in standards over time using Thurstone paired comparisons. *Education Research and Perspectives*, 25, 1–24.

Bramley, T., & Black, B. (2008). Maintaining performance standards: aligning raw score scales on different tests via a latent trait created by rank-ordering examinees' work. *Paper presented at theThird International Rasch Measurement conference*, University of Western Australia, Perth.

Bramley, T., & Gill, T. (2010). Evaluating the rank-ordering method for standard maintaining. *Research Papers in Education*, *25*(3), 293–317. doi:10.1080/02671522.2010.498147

Brooks, V. (2012). Marking as judgment. *Research Papers in Education*, *27*(1), 63–80. doi:10.1080/02671520903331008

Crisp, V. (2013). Criteria, comparison and past experiences: How do teachers make judgements when marking coursework? *Assessment in Education: Principles, Policy & Practice*, *20*(1), 127–144. doi:10.1080/0969594X.2012.741059

Darling-Hammond, L., & Snyder, J. (2000). Authentic assessment of teaching in context. *Teaching and Teacher Education*, *16*(5), 523–545. doi:10.1016/S0742-051X(00)00015-9

Derrick, K. (2012). Developing the e-scape software system. *International Journal of Technology and Design Education*, *22*(2), 171–185. doi:10.1007/s10798-011-9193-1

Greatorex, J. (2007). Contemporary GCSE and A-level Awarding: A psychological perspective on the decision-making process used to judge the quality of candidates' work. *Paper presented at theBritish Educational Research Association conference*, London.

Heldsinger, S., & Humphry, S. (2010). Using the method of pairwise comparison to obtain reliable teacher assessments. *Australian Educational Researcher*, *37*(2), 1–19. doi:10.1007/BF03216919

Heldsinger, S., & Humphry, S. (2013). Using calibrated exemplars in the teacher-assessment of writing: An empirical study. *Educational Research*, *55*(3), 219–235. doi:10.1080/00131881.2013.825159

Jones, I., & Alcock, L. (2012). Using Adaptive Comparative Judgement to assess mathematics. *The De Morgan Forum*. Retrieved from http://education.lms.ac.uk/2012/06/using-adaptive-comparative-judgement-to-assess-mathematics/

Jones, I., & Alcock, L. (2013). Peer assessment without assessment criteria. *Studies in Higher Education*, *39*(10), 1774–1787. doi:10.1080/03075079.2013.821974

Jones, I., & Inglis, M. (2015). The problem of assessing problem solving: Can comparative judgement help? *Educational Studies in Mathematics*, 2015, 1–19.

Jones, I., Swan, M., & Pollitt, A. (2014). Assessing mathematical problem solving using comparative judgement. *International Journal of Science and Mathematics Education*, *13*(1), 151–177. doi:10.1007/s10763-013-9497-6

Jonsson, A., & Svingby, G. (2007). The use of scoring rubrics: Reliability, validity and educational consequences. *Educational Research Review*, *2*(2), 130–144. doi:10.1016/j.edurev.2007.05.002

Kane, M., Crooks, T., & Cohen, A. (1999). Validating measures of performance. *Educational Measurement: Issues and Practice*, *18*(2), 5–17. doi:10.1111/j.1745-3992.1999.tb00010.x

Kendall, M. G. (1955). Further contributions to the theory of paired comparisons. *Biometrics*, *11*(1), 43–62. doi:10.2307/3001479

Kimbell, R. (2007). Project e-scape: A Web-based Approach to Design and Technology Learning and assessment.

Kimbell, R., Wheeler, A., Miller, S., & Pollitt, A. (2007). *E-scape Portfolio Assessment-a research and development project for the Department of Education and Skills (DfES) and the Qualifications Curriculum Authority (QCA). Phase 2 report*. London: Goldsmiths, University of Londen.

Kimbell, R., Wheeler, T., Stables, K., Shepard, T., Martin, F., Davies, D., et al. (2009). e-Scape portfolio assessment: A research & development project for the Department of Children, Families and Schools, phase 3 report. London: Goldsmiths, University of London.

Laming, D. (2003). *Human judgment: the eye of the beholder*. Andover: Cengage Learning EMEA.

Linacre, J. M., & Wright, B. D. (1994). Dichotomous Infit and Outfit mean-square fit statistics. *Rasch Measurement Transactions*, *8*(2), 360.

Luce, R. D. (1959). On the possible psychophysical laws. *Psychological Review*, *66*(2), 81–95. doi:10.1037/h0043178 PMID:13645853

Lumley, T. (2002). Assessment criteria in a large-scale writing test: What do they really mean to the raters? *Language Testing*, *19*(3), 246–276. doi:10.1191/0265532202lt230oa

Mack, M. G., & Ragan, B. G. (2008). Development of the mental, emotional, and bodily toughness inventory in collegiate athletes and nonathletes. *Journal of Athletic Training*, *43*(2), 125–132. doi:10.4085/1062-6050-43.2.125 PMID:18345336

Martin, S. (1997). Two models of educational assessment: a response from initial teacher education: if the cap fits.... *Assessment & Evaluation in Higher Education*, *22*(3), 337–343. doi:10.1080/0260293970220307

McMahon, S., & Jones, I. (2014). A comparative judgement approach to teacher assessment. *Assessment in Education: Principles, Policy & Practice*, *22*(3), 1–22.

Moss, P. A. (1994). Validity in high stakes writing assessment: Problems and possibilities. *Assessing Writing*, *1*(1), 109–128. doi:10.1016/1075-2935(94)90007-8

Newhouse, C. P. (2013). Computer-based practical exams in an applied Information Technology course. *Journal of Research on Technology in Education*, *45*(3), 263–286. doi:10.1080/15391523.2013.10782606

Newhouse, C. P., & Cooper, M. (2013). Computer-based oral exams in Italian language studies. *ReCALL*, *25*(03), 321–339. doi:10.1017/S0958344013000141

Pollitt, A. (2004). Let's stop marking exams. *Paper presented at the IAEA Conference*, Philadelphia.

Pollitt, A. (2012a). Comparative judgement for assessment. *International Journal of Technology and Design Education*, *22*(2), 157–170. doi:10.1007/s10798-011-9189-x

Pollitt, A. (2012b). The method of adaptive comparative judgement. *Assessment in Education: Principles, Policy & Practice*, *19*(3), 281–300. doi:10.1080/0969594X.2012.665354

Pollitt, A., & Crisp, V. (2004). Could comparative judgements of script quality replace traditional marking and improve the validity of exam questions? *Paper presented at the Paper presented at theBritish Educational Research Association Annual Conference*, Manchester.

Pollitt, A., & Elliott, G. (2003). Finding a proper role for human judgement in the examination system. *Paper presented at the QCA 'Comparability and Standards' seminar*, Newport Pagnell. Retrieved from http://www.cambridgeassessment.org.uk/research/confproceedings

Raikes, N., Scorey, S., & Shiell, H. (2008). Grading examinations using expert judgements from a diverse pool of judges. *Paper presented at the34th annual conference of the International Association for Educational Assessment*, Cambridge, UK.

Rasch, G. (1960). *Probabilistic Models for Some Intelligence and Achievement Tests, Expanded Edition (1980) With Foreword and Afterword by BD Wright. Copenhagen*, Denmark: Danish Institute for Educational Research.

Sadler, D. R. (1989). Formative assessment and the design of instructional systems. *Instructional Science*, *18*(2), 119–144. doi:10.1007/BF00117714

Sadler, D. R. (2009a). Indeterminacy in the use of preset criteria for assessment and grading. *Assessment & Evaluation in Higher Education*, *34*(2), 159–179. doi:10.1080/02602930801956059

Sadler, D. R. (2009b). Transforming holistic assessment and grading into a vehicle for complex learning. In G. J. (ed.) (Ed.), Assessment, learning and judgement in higher education (pp. 1-19). Nathan: Griffith Institute for Higher Education. doi:doi:10.1007/978-1-4020-8905-3_4doi:10.1007/978-1-4020-8905-3_4

Sadler, D. R. (2010). Beyond feedback: Developing student capability in complex appraisal. *Assessment & Evaluation in Higher Education*, *35*(5), 535–550. doi:10.1080/02602930903541015

Seery, N., Canty, D., & Phelan, P. (2012). The validity and value of peer assessment using adaptive comparative judgement in design driven practical education. *International Journal of Technology and Design Education*, *22*(2), 205–226. doi:10.1007/s10798-011-9194-0

Shay, S. (2005). The assessment of complex tasks: A double reading. *Studies in Higher Education*, *30*(6), 663–679. doi:10.1080/03075070500339988

Thurstone, L. L. (1925). A method of scaling psychological and educational tests. *Journal of Educational Psychology*, *16*(7), 433–451. doi:10.1037/h0073357

Thurstone, L. L. (1927). A law of comparative judgment. *Psychological Review*, *34*(4), 273–286. doi:10.1037/h0070288

Van Weijen, D. (2007). *Writing processes, text quality, and task effects. Empirical studies in first and second language writing*. Utrecht: Netherlands Graduate School of Linguistics.

Verhavert, S. (2015). Construction of a benchmark categorization algorithm for Comparative Judgement: a simulation study. *Paper presented at theAEA-Europe 16th Annual Conference*, Glasgow, UK.

Whitehouse, C. (2012). *Testing the validity of judgements about geography essays using the Adaptive Comparative Judgement method*. Manchester: AQA Centre for Education Research and Policy.

Whitehouse, C., & Pollitt, A. (2012). *Using adaptive comparative judgement to obtain a highly reliable rank order in summative assessment*. Manchester: AQA Centre for Education Research and Policy.

Wright, B. D., & Linacre, J. M. (1994). Reasonable mean-square fit values. *Rasch Measurement Transactions*, 8(3), 370.

KEY TERMS AND DEFINITIONS

Adaptive Comparative Judgement: A not at random mode to pair representations taking into account the already known information about their quality in order to improve the efficiency of Comparative Judgement.

Comparative Judgement: A method to scale performances of students using comparisons.

Competence: The integrated whole of knowledge, attitudes and skills which enables people to successfully solve (complex) problems.

High-Stakes Assessment: Assessments with important consequences for students.

Performance Assessment: An assessment wherein the intended measured competence is directly measured in an authentic or simulated context.

Quality Measures: Measures and modes to assess the quality of the assessment.

Reliability: The degree to which scores are not due to error.

Summative Assessment: Assessments with the purpose of making statements on the ability of students, for example for certification or entrance.

Validity: The degree to which a measured competence and its interpretation and use corresponds with the intended measured competence.

ENDNOTE

[1.] Note that Pollitt (2012a) refers to Rasch alpha as Cronbach's alpha and interprets it in terms of internal consistency. However, Rasch alpha and Cronbach's alpha are not entirely the same. It was pointed out that, although the formula of Rasch alpha is equivalent to the formula of the KR-20, which is a specific case of Cronbach's alpha, the values of Rasch alpha and the KR-20 are not the same for the same data. This is because calculations of the former are based on a non-linear transformation of the raw scores whereas calculations of the latter are based on the raw scores themselves (Andrich, 1982).

Section 2
Research– Based Evidences on Assessment

Chapter 8
Students' Conceptions of Understanding and Its Assessment

Rebecca Hamer
International Baccalaureate, The Netherlands

Erik Jan van Rossum
University of Twente, The Netherlands

ABSTRACT

Understanding means different things to different people, influencing what and how students learn and teachers teach. Mainstream understanding of understanding has not progressed beyond the first level of constructivist learning and thinking, ie academic understanding. This study, based on 167 student narratives, presents two hitherto unknown conceptions of understanding matching more complex ways of knowing, understanding-in-relativism and understanding-in-supercomplexity requiring the development of more complex versions of constructive alignment. Students comment that multiple choice testing encourages learning focused on recall and recognition, while academic understanding is not assessed often and more complex forms of understanding are hardly assessed at all in higher education. However, if study success depends on assessments-of-learning that credit them for meaning oriented learning and deeper understanding, students will put in effort to succeed.

INTRODUCTION

"At the heart of teaching for understanding lies a very basic question: What is understanding? Ponder this query for a moment and you will realize that good answers are not obvious." David Perkins wrote this in 1993, shortly after Entwistle and Entwistle had observed that within research on students' deep level learning and the search for personal understanding, the concept of understanding itself had been "rather taken for granted" (1992, p. 3; 1997). Both quotes indicate that many – educational researchers and lay people alike – use the word 'understanding' often without checking whether their own interpretation, the meaning they themselves put into the concept, is shared by others. Indeed as of 2015, a

DOI: 10.4018/978-1-5225-0531-0.ch008

simple search in the literature on the keyword *understanding* will confirm what Newton, Newton and Oberski observed in 1998, namely that many sources on designing teaching for high quality learning, deep learning or understanding, still "assume that what students believe counts as understanding in a subject is the same as what their teacher believes" (p. 45) or that teachers themselves at least agree on what constitutes understanding. This chapter will demonstrate that both assumptions are untrue. On a daily basis, teachers are "faced with a diverse collection of conceptions on what is relevant to understanding" in their classroom (Newton & Newton, 1998, p. 351) affecting the outcome of their teaching because their students´ views on understanding are "likely to shape how and what they learn" (p. 341) determining the quality of the learning outcome (van Rossum & Schenk, 1984). At the same time, teachers' views on what constitutes good or deep learning and understanding influence what and how they teach, how they use teaching materials to shape the learning environment (van Rossum & Hamer, 2010) and how they assess and award student exam performance (Samuelowicz & Bain, 2002). In the end, the lack of understanding students' and teachers' conceptions of understanding and the possible clashes between them may well result in ineffective learning and/or teaching, compromising the benefit of education to graduates and society (Khiat, 2010).

The focus of learners in formal education on study success and passing exams makes assessment a powerful tool to influence student learning (Gibbs, 1999). Unfortunately it has proven more common that assessment shifts learners towards learning focusing on recall and reproduction than towards higher quality learning (e.g. Newble & Clarke, 1986). It remains difficult to design valid and reliable assessments fostering deep learning and understanding unless they are designed so that "students can show [deep understanding] and *gain credit for it*" (Newton & Newton, 1998, p. 356, emphasis added). In this chapter the views of students are presented on what constitutes understanding and what they feel is an appropriate assessment model that would credit them for *learning for understanding*.

Evidently, in order to credit students for understanding, assessment tasks need to be designed that enable students to demonstrate the different levels of understanding, whilst corresponding rubrics, criteria and mark schemes would need be written that clearly describe the desired levels of deep understanding indicating what credit is to be awarded for the different levels of understanding shown. This chapter provides empirical evidence of a range of qualitatively different perceptions of deep understanding in cognitive learning that exist in the minds of learners and teachers. These perceptions or conceptions of understanding form a hierarchical taxonomy with at least two conceptions of understanding beyond what is currently assumed (e.g. Bloom's taxonomy and improvements thereon). The presented taxonomy of understanding will support the formulation of a hierarchy of desired (or expected) learning outcomes within criteria or mark schemes that potentially better reflect the full range student performances possible. The creation of such hierarchies of expected learning outcomes forms the heart of the curriculum and assessment design principle of constructive alignment (Biggs, 2003). In constructive alignment, the levels in the hierarchy of desired or expected outcomes are interpreted as different learning outcomes. Using the distinct levels of learning outcome in the hierarchy, teaching, learning and assessment activities can be chosen that align with each level. If implemented successfully, constructive alignment can be used to shape learning, teaching and indeed assessment activities, both formative as well as summative, aimed at the different levels of understanding and so create a learning path towards the more complex forms of deep understanding.

BACKGROUND

Conceptions of Understanding: A Short History

Understanding is associated with higher quality learning, in-depth or deep learning. Examining views on deep learning then could shed light on the meaning of understanding. In studying the characteristics of surface and deep learning, Entwistle and Ramsden (1983) described six approaches to learning. Three approaches described aspects of surface learning, where learning is primarily a memorisation and retrieval task (S2, S3) usually separate and unconnected to other learning tasks (S1). However, only D3 refers to meaning oriented learning, which meets the current view on deep learning. Deep learning then would seem to be defined as the process through which one reaches understanding, but the nature of understanding itself was still not much clearer (see Table 1).

Table 1. Linking learning and teaching conceptions to conceptions of understanding

	Säljö (1979)	Van Rossum & Hamer (2010)		Entwistle & Ramsden (1983)	Entwistle & Entwistle (1992; 1997)	Newton, Newton & Oberski (1998)	Khiat (2010)	Irving & Sayre (2012)
	Learning Conception	Learning-Teaching Conception	Conception of Understanding*	Deep and Surface Learning	Conception of Understanding	Learning by Memorisation or Understanding	Conception of Understanding (of mathematics)	Conception of Understanding
1	Learning as the increase of knowledge	Increasing knowledge - Imparting clear/well structured knowledge	Understanding every word, every sentence	S1. Unrelated knowledge and tasks	A. Reproduction content without clear structure from lecture notes	-	-	-
2	Learning as memorising	Memorising - Transmitting structured knowledge (acknowledging receiver)	Answering exam questions by reproduction	S2. Memorisation S3. Unreflective retrieval	B. Reproduction content and logical structure from lecture notes	-	Functional Understanding	A. To use and apply C. Teach someone else
3	Learning as the acquisition of facts, procedures etcetera, which can be retained and/or utilised in practice	Reproductive understanding/ application or Application foreseen – Interacting and Shaping	Reproducing the main points (using selectivity); using or discussing what is learned	D1. Linking to personal experiences D2. Linking to prior or familiar knowledge	C. Using own structure, mainly from lecture notes D. Adjusting structures from reading to meet exam requirements	Understanding as a capability in application	Procedural Understanding	B. Use and apply in different contexts D. Explain in more than one way, using analogies
4	Learning as the abstraction of meaning	Understanding subject matter - Challenging to think for yourself / developing a way of thinking	Making connections between sources, constructing the author's intention	D3. Reflection on underlying structure or intention of task	E. Developing an individual conception of the discipline	Understanding as having a mental structure	Conceptual Understanding	E. Apply model, consolidate knowledge
5	Learning as an interpretative process aimed at the understanding of reality	Widening horizons - Dialogue teaching	Formulating arguments for or against, and using what is learned in your own argumentations	-	-	-	-	-
6	-	Growing self awareness - Mutual trust and authentic relationships: Caring	-	-	-	-	-	-

* Van Rossum, Deijkers & Hamer, 1985; Van Rossum, 1988; Van Rossum & Hamer, 2010

In 1985, van Rossum, Deijkers and Hamer examined students' interpretations of a number of concepts commonly used in educational settings, including insight, application, views on learning, good teaching and understanding. They found five qualitatively different conceptions of understanding. This study suggested that these conceptions or views were logically linked in the sense that sets of interpretations (or conceptions) formed profiles of meaning making. Students expressing a particular view on learning, would hold to a specific set of meanings for all the other concepts included in the study. This meant that particular learning conceptions were linked to particular interpretations of understanding, and to particular qualitatively different learning outcomes (van Rossum, 1988; van Rossum & Schenk, 1984). In 1992, using interviews with students regarding revision strategies, Entwistle & Entwistle formulated five 'forms of understanding': a set of students' approaches to demonstrating conceptual understanding that points towards the dominant, often destructive role assessment plays in deep learning and the search for personal understanding:

1. Reproducing content from lecture notes without a clear structure;
2. Reproducing content and logical framework from lecture notes;
3. Using own structure for individual topics, mainly from lecture notes;
4. Adjusting structures from strategic reading to meet exam requirements;
5. Developing an individual conception of the discipline from wide reading.

In 1997, Entwistle & Entwistle formulated these five forms of understanding in a slightly different way, emphasising even more the critical influence of assessment on constructing personal meaning. As Biggs (1996) commented, the first four of the forms of understanding do not in any way match the interpretation of understanding from an academic perspective. In fact A and B sound suspiciously like learning conceptions 1 and 2 (van Rossum et al., 1985, van Rossum & Hamer 2010, see Table 1). While in C and D at least some attempts are made to adjust the provided structure to a more personalised utility, the focus on exam relevancy also brings learning conception 2 to mind (van Rossum & Hamer, 2010, p. 25). All in all, the authors agree with Biggs (1996) that of the five 'forms of understanding' only E has relevance for deep learning, although perhaps the assessment dominated nature of the majority of the forms of understanding found here can be traced to the exam oriented context in which the data were collected. Around the same time, Newton and colleagues published a set of studies examining conceptions of understanding, comparing those of university lecturers, new graduates and sixth form students (Newton et al., 1998; Newton & Newton, 1998), focusing on understanding in history and science. Newton et al. describe two conceptions of understanding that lecturers and new graduates share:

*   Understanding as a capability of application, where knowledge of laws, regularity and patterns is applied in problem solving (science) / creating a plausible narrative and to explain events (history); and
*   Understanding as having a mental structure, where a mental structure/picture is constructed to explain laws, regularity and patterns, placing them in a broader context, with an ability to apply attached (science and history).

The supports expected to achieve each of these types of understanding contain clues to how they differ. Understanding as a capability of application is associated with knowledge seen as tools in a toolbox to apply, a preference for the use of concrete examples, preferred teaching activities such as organising information, providing instruction and modelling processes as well as a focus on problem solving and task performance as indicators of understanding. This mostly points towards a reproduction orientation, linking this conception of understanding to learning-teaching conception 3, Reproductive application (Van Rossum & Hamer, 2010). The focus on creating a mental structure links the second conception of understanding firmly to learning-teaching conception 4.

In 2010, Khiat examined students' conceptions of understanding of mathematics in engineering and found three hierarchical conceptions of understanding (p. 1475-1476):

- Functional Understanding capturing the understanding of how and when to use various formulae and procedures and being able to describe what happens when using them, linking this conception of understanding to learning-teaching conception 2;
- Procedural Understanding which is the ability to model the steps in solving problems which seems to refer to reproductive application or learning-teaching conception 3 level thinking; and
- Conceptual Understanding referring to the ability to understand how the formulae are derived, which seems to encapsulate the type of understanding based on constructing mental models or structures of a discipline or topic which is characteristic for learning conception 4.

Khiat also differentiated Disciplinary Understanding which refers to essential disciplinary knowledge and Associational Understanding, referring to the ability to recognise which disciplinary knowledge and procedures or solution strategies are relevant and can be applied within the problem posed. Both Disciplinary and Associational Understanding are necessary to function regardless of hierarchical sophistication of understanding, they refer to the 'stuff' to use and 'knowing when' to use it respectively.

Irving and Sayre (2013) examined conceptions of understanding of upper-level physics students and describe five qualitatively different categories that seem to represent three levels of thinking, recognising finer distinctions within views on understanding as application and understanding in explanation where only (E) 'Understand when can apply mathematical description, consolidate knowledge' refers to a mental model and connecting and consolidating knowledge, both hallmarks of the first level of constructivist learning, level 4. This would suggest that the other four conceptions (A) through (D) reflect learning-teaching conception 2 and 3 thinking.

In Table 1, various sources regarding conceptions of understanding are linked to learning conceptions (Säljö, 1979) and epistemic development (van Rossum & Hamer, 2010) and so to levels of sophistication in thinking and meaning making. The learning-teaching conception model includes the rare sixth learning conception (van Rossum & Taylor, 1987) which existence was corroborated by Marton, Dall'Alba & Beatty (1993) and is further elaborated in van Rossum & Hamer (2010). Linking these conceptions of understanding back to the definition used within the *Teaching for Understanding* approach comprising a range of performances of understanding, suggests that understanding defined as flexible performance is describing a level of thinking similar to learning-teaching conception 4, or the first level of constructivist learning:

…understanding a topic of study is a matter of being able to perform in a variety of thought-demanding ways with the topic, for instance to: explain, muster evidence, find examples, generalize, apply concepts, analogize, represent in a new way, and so on. (Perkins, 1993)

Whilst this short overview already demonstrates that there are clearly multiple qualitatively different interpretations of understanding, refuting the common assumption described in the introduction, it also points towards a major gap in the knowledge base. It seems mainstream understanding of understanding has not progressed beyond the first level of constructivist learning and thinking. At least two additional complex conceptions of understanding can be postulated (van Rossum and Hamer, 2010) and need to be described in more detail in order to design assessments aimed at crediting these hitherto undescribed types of deep understanding.

The approach taken by many of the researchers mentioned above has limited understanding and deep learning to the academic perspective (discipline bound level-4-thinking) while insights from epistemology point towards higher levels of complexity in understanding and deep learning. In order to prepare students for the 21st century, it is crucial to examine more closely the more complex levels of understanding and deep level learning. Descriptions of these levels of understanding are certainly to be found in literature (e.g. Cook-Greuter, 1999/2005; Csikszentmihalyi, 1993; Kegan, 1994; Labouvie-Vief, 1990; Palmer, 1998). This study aims to examine whether these complex conceptions truly exist 'in the wild' and are not thought constructs of researchers and philosophers. Considering that there are at least three constructivist conceptions of learning and knowledge, by association there must be at least three qualitatively different interpretations of understanding that are connected to three qualitatively different approaches to deep learning.

Dimensions of Development in Understanding

However, in this chapter the literature is explored further to see if there are dimensions along which developments of understanding or epistemology seem to progress, and that therefore can serve as cues to guide our search. In 1992, Entwistle and Entwistle identified a number of characteristics related to the nature of understanding, the process of developing understanding and dimensions of understanding. In Table 2, these characteristics are regrouped to examine possible relationships between them.

Table 2. Aspects of the experience of understanding (Entwistle & Entwistle, 1992; 1997)

The nature of understanding	Developing understanding	Dimensions of individual understanding
Feelings of satisfaction Confidence about explaining	Active engagement with the task	
Meaning and significance	Relating previous knowledge and experience in ways which transform the information and create personal meaning	Breath of understanding (quantity of relations to other knowledge and materials)
Coherence and connectedness		Depth or level of understanding (Quality of knowledge network)
Flexibility in adapting and applying	Using or developing structure	Source of and nature of structure. Sources ranging from external authority (teachers, lecture notes, books and exams) to transformative personal construction
Relative irreversibility 'provisional wholeness'		

Examining this table, four groupings of characteristics can be distinguished. In the upper left hand cells of Table 2 the emotional aspect of understanding are grouped together, including satisfaction and increased confidence. Positive emotions, such as feelings of increase confidence and control, are indeed a hitherto somewhat underexposed element in the examination of understanding, whilst they are connected to learning that requires active cognitive or intellectual engagement (Morgan & Beaty, 1997). The opposite is also true, where students are confronted with distressingly low levels of challenge and intellectual engagement, they become disillusioned and occasionally rebellious (Disenchantment in van Rossum & Hamer, 2010, p. 412; Lindblom-Ylänne & Lonka, 1999).

In linking 'making connections with previous knowledge and experience' to the 'breath of understanding' as well as 'meaning and significance', the process, thoroughness and result of increased connectedness are themselves connected. Evidently, the quality of understanding, or depth, is directly related to the experience of coherence or connectedness of knowledge. Connectedness and coherence is an aspect of understanding that was very dominant as well in the conceptions of understanding found in Van Rossum et al. (1985).

Developing a structure, by various means, is essential to flexible performance, the ability to adapt and apply knowledge in new ways (Entwistle & Entwistle, 1997) and in solving ill-structured problems. In the right hand column, Entwistle and Entwistle distinguish qualitatively different sources for constructing a structure. Although commonly mentioned by students, especially the external authority based sources of structure seem less appropriate to deep learning.

Clustering the aspects of 'provisional wholeness' and 'relative irreversibility' together highlights the somewhat paradoxical nature of understanding. The paradoxical nature of these aspects can be better understood when considering that these aspects could reflect qualitatively different conceptions of deep learning and understanding. Kegan (1994) poses that when moving from reproductive to constructivist ways of knowing, the new understanding leads to feelings of provisional wholeness, but that once entering relativist thinking one realises that wholeness is inherently unattainable. The resulting feeling of 'unanchoredness' can only be resolved by moving to an even more sophisticated *sixth order of consciousness* which Kegan describes in discussing reconstructive postmodernism. Palmer states that thinking and understanding includes the ability to "embrace a view of the world in which opposites are joined" (Palmer, 1998, p. 66), in short the ability to think-the-world-together, confirming the role of paradoxical thinking in the more complex ways of knowing.

Turning to epistemology for additional insights, Entwistle and Peterson (2004) present a more complex theoretical background for embedding deep learning – and the search for personal meanings. Van Rossum and Hamer (2010) travelled a similar path and discussed epistemological aspects of deep learning and understanding in much greater detail, integrating the idea of profiles of meaning making into the broader concepts common in epistemological research, *ways of knowing* (Baxter Magolda, 2001; Belenky et al., 1986/1997) and *orders of consciousness* (Kegan, 1994). Both approaches have integrated the idea of 'expanding awareness' as a significant characteristic of the development of conceptions with the notion of sets of conceptions being hierarchically inclusive – meaning that less complex conceptions are integrated in broader, more complex conceptions of a particular phenomenon. Through this, expanding awareness becomes an integral part of development.

The dimensions of individual understanding presented in Table 2 seem to capture some metacognitive characteristics of deep learning: "organised studying, time management, *effort* and concentration, involving both self-regulation and an awareness of learning in context" (Entwistle & Peterson, 2004, p. 416, emphasis added; Vermunt, 1996, 1998) as well as a personal, intrinsic orientation (Entwistle & Peterson, 2004).

Perry (1970) was the first to report that learners do not all develop in the same way, nor at the same speed. Some students seem to consciously turn away from development, as is found in van Rossum and Hamer as well (Nostalgia in van Rossum & Hamer, 2010, p. 412), while other students grab the opportunity to develop with gusto. McCune and Entwistle propose an interesting aspect that might help to explain these differences, *alertness* or open-mindedness (2011, p. 304). Alertness, and open-mindedness may prove essential for the development towards deep level learning and personal understanding.

In the longitudinal study of Baxter Magolda (e.g. 1992, 2001, 2009) the developmental perspective is elaborated in three dimensions: the cognitive or epistemological dimension, the interpersonal or relational dimension and the intrapersonal or identity dimension. Regarding increasing complexity in thinking, the identity development is the most noteworthy. In reconstructive postmodernism (Kegan, 1994) the self expresses itself in making decisions and commitments that outline and define it, linking it to the issue of identity development. Hamer and van Rossum (2010) coined the label *self-defining self* for this sixth way of knowing and understanding.

The recognition of the issue of identity development implies that the development of ways of meaning making and understanding, especially beyond learning conception 4, become increasingly personalised. This suggests that in the more complex and constructivist levels of thinking and understanding, the language will become less technical and rational, and more personal and organismic (Labouvie-Vief, 1990). Indeed it was the unique flavour of the language providing the crucial tip-off in differentiating the sixth learning conception (van Rossum & Taylor, 1987; van Rossum & Hamer, 2010). The unique language typical for level-6-thinkers *and* level-6-teachers can also be found in *The Courage to Teach* (Palmer, 1998) and is elaborated in van Rossum and Hamer (2010).

Kegan (1994) proposed a dynamic for development – stepping out of embeddedness – where one moves from being subject, "those elements of our knowing … that we are identified with, tied to, fused with, or *embedded in*" to object, where "those elements of our knowing … that we can reflect on, handle, look at, be responsible for, relate to each other, take control of, internalize, assimilate, or otherwise *operate upon*… We *have* object; we *are* subject" (Kegan, 1994, p. 32). Translating this dynamic to understanding means that students embedded in learning conception 3 *are* able to criticise the conception of understanding at level 2: reproduction on a test. However, these level 3 students as yet cannot see the limits of their own conception of understanding, reproductive application – they are reproductive appliers. And what they certainly cannot yet understand is the essential nature of level four thinking, the academic or scientific way of knowing. The dynamic of 'stepping out of embeddedness' may prove useful to identify new views on learning, knowing and understanding.

Where Kegan (1994) proposed self-authorship or level-4-thinking as crucial to function in a modern democratic society, Barnett (2004) proposed that the current reality is far more complex than this modern world. In this supercomplex world, there are two sources of uncertainty that affect learning and understanding. Firstly there is the commonly discussed quantitatively defined uncertainty: the inability to assimilate all that is known. Supercomplexity however, refers to a more fundamental uncertainty following the realisation that each way of constructing the world is inescapably flawed, incomplete and unwhole, and that many such flawed, incomplete and unwhole perceptions of reality exist side by side. The uncertainty in supercomplexity refers to the quality of what is knowable. A supercomplex world is consistent with the relativist worldview of level-5-thinkers. Barnett proposes that higher education should prepare students for this experience of extreme uncertainty to prevent a destabilisation of the self. Such destabilisation of the self underlies Perry's cynical approach to knowledge expressed in gamesmanship, where one dismisses all theory and knowledge as equally flawed and thus unworthy of commitment (Perry, 1970) and Kegan's (1994) negative version of level-5-thinking, deconstructive postmodernism. The way out of destabilisation lies in the move to level-6-thinking, by making commitments (Perry, 1970), by taking a personal stand grounded in internal foundation (Baxter Magolda, 2001) or by moving to reconstructive postmodernism, where the process of learning and knowing is seen as an end in itself (Kegan, 1994). A pedagogy for supercomplexity then should foster the move toward a way of being, resulting in students developing courage and "a willingness to go on by themselves" (Barnett, 2004, p. 254).

Considering the process of achieving understanding and various models of thinking, the following twelve cues may signal a shift in focus characteristic of a more complex conception of understanding,

1. Emotion connected to (deep) learning and understanding
2. Experience of connection and coherence
3. Adaptation and flexible application to unknown situations and issues
4. Paradoxical thinking
5. Expanding awareness
6. Metacognition and self-regulation
7. Personal, intrinsic orientation
8. Alertness and open-mindedness
9. Identity development
10. Language
11. Stepping out of embeddedness
12. Willingness to go on by themselves

METHOD

The *research questions* central to this study are

- Whether more sophisticated conceptions of understanding can be found in a sufficiently large sample,
- Whether these conceptions of understanding contain elements suggested to be central to epistemological development, and
- What type of assessment students feel would be appropriate to measure their understanding of the subject or discipline.

Participants were 167 second year psychology students at the University of Twente in the Netherlands close to the German border. The majority were Dutch, with 32 per cent Dutch speaking German students, 69 per cent was female.

The *data* consisted of written essays: a student course assignment to write down their own interpretation of 'understanding' and to indicate what type of assessment they thought would be appropriate to assess this type of understanding. The task was a 'homework assignment' in a second year course on qualitative research and was not graded. It was presented as practice in order to get a feel for qualitative analysis of narratives. Participants submitted their essay electronically and gave informed consent for use for research purposes.

These narratives were *analysed* using the phenomenographic method described in Marton (1986) and in more detail in van Rossum and Hamer (2010).

To enable *reporting* to the international research community, quotes were translated from the original Dutch by the authors, one of whom is a native speaking bilingual English-Dutch. Translations stay close to the original for authenticity and may therefore contain translated expressions and sometimes sound slightly stilted.

RESULTS: STUDENTS' CONCEPTIONS OF UNDERSTANDING

Returning briefly to the query posed by David Perkins in the introduction, researchers are not the only ones to realise, perhaps belatedly, that the word 'understanding' is anything but simple. Students in this study quickly came to the same conclusion,

In this assignment we're supposed to explain what understanding means to you. At first glance this seems easy. Understanding is a word I use often and I should be able to write an essay about it. Piece of cake! But the longer I think about it, the more difficult it becomes. I realise that I do not have a good definition of the concept and that the word is far more complex than you would think at first. (Annabel)

Annabel is one of the second year psychology students asked to write down their own interpretation of 'understanding' and, as a learning task, to attempt to analyse their own description. To illustrate how students themselves distinguish between levels of deep learning and understanding, sometimes dismissing 'simple' ways as 'not really understanding', a number of prototypical student responses are quoted below. The quotes published here for the first time have been used before in presentations at conferences (Van Rossum & Hamer, 2011, 2013).

Reproduction Oriented Conceptions of Understanding

The three least complex views on understanding are characterised by an essentially reproduction orientation. As with the first learning conception, the most simple conception of understanding found in this sample is indeed atomistic and quantitative, echoing the unreflectiveness of S1 (Entwistle & Ramsden, 1983).

To me, understanding is when you experience something new, for instance reading an article with new information. You may have previous knowledge when reading this article, and then you try to code the familiar with the new information, or better, you add the new. (…) The connection between my story about understanding and my story about appropriate assessment is that there must be knowledge, if there is no knowledge one cannot answer any exam questions, however ideal these are. (Clara, level-1-thinker)

Clara's lack of reflection on the nature of learning is reflected in the broad strokes description of her preferred assessment model: focused on answering questions assessing knowledge. At the next level, Agnes also expresses a conception of understanding that is aimed at memorisation, however the response contains signs of reflection on the breath of understanding, its characteristics, depth and role in learning,

When do you understand something? (…) Do you understand a sentence when you understand each word? But when do you understand each word? Is that when you know the meaning of each word? And if you do know the meaning of each individual word, do you understand the whole? And is the literal meaning of each word automatically the meaning of the whole? Is it necessary to know the meaning of each word? (…) And how can we link the concept 'understanding' to texts you not only need to read, but need to learn also. Is understanding something the same as learning it? Or is it only necessary to understand something in order to be able to learn something? And is it possible to learn something without understanding it? (...) Intuitively I would say that you need to understand texts before you can learn them. But then, looking back at learning languages, you memorised lists of words, you didn't have to understand. (…) what if that is the only possible way of learning for someone, where would this bring you? I think it will carry you pretty far. (Agnes, level-2-thinker)

After observing that learning without understanding might carry you very far in education, Agnes consciously chooses an assessment model that credits surface learning, recall and recognition. In doing this she confirms the experience that if learning for understanding or meaning is *not* credited, students will knowingly (and purposefully, although perhaps not always willingly) turn away from meaning oriented learning in search of study success (e.g. Newble & Clarke, 1986; Lindblom-Ylänne & Lonka, 1999).

Looking at my own way of learning, understanding the subject matter is not always really necessary. I need to understand what is said in the text, usually this means knowing concepts and not understanding. This goal is to know the author and the content of a theory. I do not so much learn in order to be able to apply it. So I think that for me multiple choice tests are ideal. Then I only need to recognise the concepts. (Agnes, level-2-thinker)

Although Agnes seems to realise that there may be more to understanding, to her learning is mostly a task of retrieval and recognition without intellectual engagement, calling to mind S2 and S3 (Entwistle & Ramsden, 1983), going to the length of actively dismissing application. In contrast Lilly, in describing her conception of understanding, emphasises the need for application to achieve understanding. Deeper understanding then is not a question of knowing more, but knowing differently, namely through memorisation *and* application: when and how to use knowledge, supporting Khiat's (2010) finding that Disciplinary and Associational Understanding are already linked to reproduction or Functional Understanding and not themselves part of the hierarchy of conceptions of understanding.

A word in itself has a meaning, but a word within a larger context can have a completely different meaning than the one you gave it initially. Now the question is not what it means to understand language, but also what it means to understand when you are learning for something. When do you get the subject matter treated in a book and do you get its meaning? Do you understand a particular subject when you pass an exam by memorising a summary the night before and getting a good grade? Or do you understand it better when you try to apply the subject matter in small tests and assignments with the intention to know it better? (…) That is why I feel that you know and understand it better when you regularly do assignments or practicals and apply the subject matter, opposed to only learning facts and forgetting them a week later. (Lilly, level-3-thinker)

Lilly not only prefers types of assessment that are active, she also prefers a high frequency and collaborative learning as these increase active engagement. It is clear why this approach to learning and understanding is often called active learning. However, nowhere in this type of narrative is there an indication that what is learned is changed, adapted or tailored to different contexts, making the approach primarily reproduction oriented.

For me, weekly group activities, practicals and assignments are ideal. This way I keep working with the subject matter and keep involved. I value the communication with my fellow students, by learning in small groups I stay concentrated because you want to contribute to the group. The big advantage of practicals and assignments is that you are actively engaged with the subject matter and so, will understand it better. I understand more quickly if I can apply it. (Lilly, level-3-thinker)

Lilly's story displays many aspects of learning conception 3, as defined by Säljö (learning as the acquisition of facts, procedures etcetera, which can be retained and/or utilised in practice) and is also recognisable in Vermunt's application directed learning style (1996, 1998). As such, contrary to Entwistle and Peterson's statement (2004, p. 417), this learning style can hardly be seen as adding new features to the study of learning and understanding. It may be clear that these three interpretations of understanding do not fit the disposition to understand for oneself (McCune & Entwistle, 2011).

Meaning Oriented Conceptions of Understanding

Olivia represents rational level-4-thinking, the students viewing learning and understanding from an analytical and systemic perspective. She also makes the distinction between surface understanding and deep understanding, equating the latter to academic understanding. Her story covers a range, but not all of the twelve cues listed above. Central in the narrative is the experience of connection and coherence that understanding brings, while it ends with the adaptation and application to unknown situations. There are references to personal and intrinsic motivation as well as self-regulation of learning.

In superficial information processing you are focused on memorising as many facts or details as possible. It is a passive approach to understanding. Separate facts are not assembled into a structure, so that they remain incoherent. In deep information processing you focus on discovering meanings: "what is really meant by this?" In this way you engage actively with the subject matter in four related ways. Firstly, by reading critically, posing questions and remembering important points. Secondly, by seeking connections between what you want to understand and what you already know about the subject. Thirdly, by imposing structure on what you want to understand by making comparisons and drawing conclusions. And fourthly, by reflecting. In deep information processing you also make use of elaboration; paraphrasing the content, looking for analogies, making notes, referring to other sources on the same content, explaining to others and posing questions. Then you also try to reorganise the information for yourself by creating a scheme clarifying the relationships between concepts. (...) When you are intrinsically motivated, you are prepared to put in more effort and time to understand something. (...) Understanding refers to describing reality, how this fits together and how various systems, e.g. eco systems, work. (...) when you really understand something you are able to apply the meaning of a concept or system (...) to your daily activities. (Olivia, level-4-thinker)

Olivia's story includes many of the understanding performances (Perkins, 1993): "… explain, muster evidence, find examples, generalize, apply concepts, analogize, represent in a new way, and so on". However, all these thought demanding activities are contained: they are always framed within a particular disciplinary way of thinking and the critical appraisal is not extended to include the system itself. The latter is the distinguishing feature of the fifth order of consciousness (Kegan, 1994) the example below is the first of the more complex conceptions of deep understanding that are discussed above. Kate extends the analytical approach of level-4-thinking to include the need to look at things from different perspectives, relativity in level-5-thinking.

To understand a concept, an idea or person means to be able to feel what is meant. More and more I'm becoming convinced that no single idea, no single event and no single person can be interpreted from only one perspective. I feel, the overarching (meta) level required to be able to take different perspectives is conditional in order to say that something or someone is understood. The moment you can debate pro as well as against a proposition, underpinning your arguments, then you have understood a subject well. In that case the subject has become three dimensional. In addition to debating you can show your understanding of an issue by explaining it to someone unfamiliar with it. Although, I feel that this form of understanding may be more superficial than debating (…) understanding means that you can look at an issue from a distance and you can follow different interpretations and build an argument for each of them. (Kate, level-5-thinker)

At this level emotion is reintroduced in the experience of understanding, as well as an open-mindedness to other perspectives, exemplifying expanding awareness. By introducing the metaphor of three dimensions and later discussing observing an issue from a distance, she describes stepping out of embeddedness as a central part of understanding.

Writing an essay leaves the assessed free to interpret … The disadvantage of this form of assessment is that it only calls for only one interpretation. … I feel using a debate or discussion is better. … In that way participants are actively and flexibly engaged with the issue at hand, and need to react quickly to changes in perspective. (Kate, level-5-thinker)

The need to recognise different perspectives leads these students to doubt the appropriateness of an essay as an assessment tool for 'understanding-in-relativity.' Assessment would seem to require more interaction in order to provide the flexibility to manipulate the issue to discuss or analyse, leading them to propose more debate like or oral assessment approaches.

The stories of the final group of students presented here are characterised by a distinctive use of language. These students talk about identity, the meaning of life, wellbeing, wisdom, caring, mutual respect, existential and irresolvable issues: as Barnett (2004) proposed, the narratives take an ontological turn.

People do not like uncertainty. They try to avoid uncertainty by surrounding themselves with stuff and people or by following a religion that answers their questions. (…) By keeping busy living, you can temporarily delay the confrontation with all that is uncertain and especially with death: the ultimate uncertainty. However, delaying is not escaping. (…) Understanding things is another formula for certainty: not understanding something you want to understand leads to uncertainty and frustration makes you keep on looking. Understanding something is a base to build on further and can give relief. You can place what you understand in context and link it to other pieces of the world you have understood. This way you expand your world view with more schemata, concepts, et cetera. By understanding more and more, your life becomes coherent and you can make choices, pursue goals, et cetera. Imagine that you wouldn't understand anything. Your life would have no direction at all. By understanding something, the understood is nearer to yourself. It becomes something you know, or even a part of who you are (...) understanding something new gives a feeling of development. You feel progress is made, you learned something. So, there is less stagnation than without understanding. It would be wonderful if you could live within uncertainty, and still be able to make a good life of it. So that you could die without it being a complete surprise, because you have learned to understand (on a deeper level than rationally) that you will need to let everything go and that you have already practiced a bit with letting go. But that is quite a task ... and extraordinarily remarkable if you succeed. (Sophia, level-6-thinker)

In this response the paradox of 'provisional wholeness' and continuing uncertainty are manifest and linked to identity development. At the same time the response contains reference to the need to develop personal courage and a willingness to go on. In Sophia's story all these issues can be recognised, and she has an interesting suggestion for assessment of understanding with unusual topics or criteria.

To assess understanding a qualitative interview would seem appropriate. Topics for this interview could include certainty, closeness to self, context, direction, development and change, and feelings of relief. (Sophia, level-6-thinker)

Addressing the Research Questions

As is demonstrated above, a larger sample can indeed contain narratives describing new, more complex and epistemologically sophisticated conceptions of understanding than found previously (van Rossum & Hamer, 2011, 2013). The analysis also confirmed the existence of three essentially reproduction orientations, see Table 3.

Students with less sophisticated conceptions of understanding suggested various ways of assessing knowledge. In particular multiple choice questions (MC) assessing (factual) knowledge were linked to the two least sophisticated views on understanding and learning. Students linked these methods to learning for recognition without deep understanding, sometimes explicating that this did not require 'real understanding' but was sufficient to get a pass. More application oriented views on understanding would ideally be assessed through practicals and cases.

The study further presents a set of three descriptions of understanding that are more consistent with constructivist or deep learning. In these narratives students differentiate between surface understanding and deep understanding, equating the latter to academic understanding, and interpreting 'application' to mean proficiency in systemic thinking and reasoning including many of the understanding performances (Perkins, 1993). However, at level 4 all these performances are always framed *within* a particular disciplinary way of thinking. At level 5 understanding is achieved only after observing and analysing an issue from different (disciplinary) perspectives. At level 6 the performances are framed within the full complexity of life.

So how does this translate to the everyday classroom? Imagine a teacher teaching an undergraduate course explaining e.g. aggression from different disciplines. At the end the teacher asks the students in general whether they have understood it all and if anyone has questions. Typically, no-one has questions,

Table 3. Students' conceptions of understanding and assessment of 'real understanding' (Van Rossum & Hamer, 2013)

	Conception of Understanding	Conception of Assessing Understanding
1	Understanding every word, every sentence	Knowledge questions
2	Answering exam questions, reproduction of (certain) knowledge	Multiple choice for assessing recognition Open questions for assessing reproduction
3	Applying knowledge to practical situations (simple)	Frequent testing (sequential parts of total) Open questions for assessing reproduction Practical assignments and cases for assessing practical application and own ideas
4	Reorganising knowledge into your own systemic structure.	Open questions for assessing independent thinking, analytical skills and making connections Cases and assignments for assessing application in new/unfamiliar situations Questions and cases need to be interesting and motivating
5	Formulating arguments for or against, and using what is learned in your own argumentations, multiple perspectives	Assignments for assessing taking different/other perspective(s) Oral / interview / debate
6	A basis to build your life around, a temporary relief from uncertainty, less stagnation in living; getting closer to the self	Life for assessing self-knowledge and the development of self-awareness: 'making your own way'

and most of them nod or murmur "yes". What does this tell the teacher really? Based on many hundreds of narratives (e.g. van Rossum & Hamer, 2010; N = 1208 to date) three out of four students will nod and think to themselves one of the following three responses:

Level 1: Yes, you said it, you're the expert. So why should I question anything you said;
Level 2: Yes, you told us, explained it and answered our questions. I can reproduce this when asked; or
Level 3: Yes, I now know when and how to use this information and can apply it correctly in practical/ professional situations.

This may seem disappointing for academic knowing and understanding. But in an average size lecture hall there will certainly be a few students, about one in five or so, who will think,

Level 4: Yes, I understand the thinking, the reasoning, the logical structure for myself. I can connect it to other knowledge I have. It has made me see the issue in its full complexity.

And occasionally there may be a student or two, perhaps one in twenty, who nod and think,

Level 5: Ah (pensive) yes, I see it differently now than before. You can look at it from different perspectives, possibly leading to a different conclusion.

On occasion, a teacher may recognise a student who is an outlier, doesn't really fit and sometimes asks weird questions or requests individual assignments because he/she is fed up with working with others. The teacher might find this student difficult and critical. Good chance that this student, when nodding, means to say,

Level 6: Yes, I feel this may be significant to *me*. I can take a reasoned stand towards it and if it feels essential to *my being* I will make it my own. This helps me understand life a little better, feel better, but only temporarily because there is always more to question, to know and to understand.

For now this study provides the content for the missing cell in Table 1: the sixth conception of understanding (see Table 3). However, true to the fundamental insight of level-6-thinking, this is probably not the final, most complex conception of understanding to be found (e.g. Cook-Greuter, 1999/2005).

How do conceptions of understanding affect preferences for assessment methods? The reactions of the participants are clear, in general very few students feel that academic understanding is assessed very often in higher education, and more sophisticated forms of understanding are usually not assessed at all. These students are particularly outspoken about the irrelevance of multiple choice testing (MC) for assessing any type of understanding. Students almost never feel intellectually challenged by MC-exams and admit that this type of assessment in particular makes them intellectually lazy, pointing them towards surface level learning as the most strategic approach to study success. Interestingly, this study suggests students with more sophisticated conceptions of understanding would welcome 'good assessment' of real understanding, suggesting assessment methods that credit formulating multiple perspectives and arguments for instance in qualitative interviews (orals) or interactive debates.

The point made by students seems clear: if study success depends on assessments of learning that are designed to credit deeper learning and learning for meaning, students are willing to put in the effort to succeed. This means that to create effective and appropriately aligned pedagogies (or learning environments) aimed at the intellectual richness of learning-for-understanding will require more study into the creation of valid and reliable types of assessments-of-learning (summative assessment) supporting higher levels of understanding.

CONCLUSION

The need to understand 'understanding' is not academic, at its heart lies the wish to discover how to design education and assessment that would more effectively foster the development of deep learning and conceptual understanding – in short to uncover the contours of a higher education version of *teaching for understanding* as well as a framework for *assessing for understanding*.

This study demonstrates that when a sufficient number of responses are collected six qualitatively different views on understanding can be identified. Each of these six conceptions of understanding is characterised by a specific set of themes regarding the purpose of learning and the nature of understanding. It may be clear that the first three, least sophisticated interpretations of understanding focusing on reproduction are not really appropriate to academic learning. This study further suggests that there are indeed at least three interpretations of understanding that would be appropriate to teaching and learning in higher education, two of which are described for the first time here:

- Reasoned, analytical academic understanding: understanding systems;
- Understanding-in-relativism: understanding disciplinary limits and uncertainty; and
- Understanding-in-supercomplexity: understanding in and with uncertainty.

Not only can 'stepping out of embeddedness' prove useful to identify new views on learning, knowing and understanding, it might imply that designing *higher education teaching for understanding* according to the principles of constructive alignment (Biggs, 2003) may require further detailing depending on the level of understanding that is aspired. If the current version of constructive alignment aims at academic, evidence based reasoning, thinking and understanding (level 4). Higher education proposing to aim for more complex forms of understanding and thinking, will need to implement one or more versions of constructive alignment aimed at these more sophisticated forms of understanding. Using the current terminology the authors suggest to develop *relativist alignment* for level-5 understanding and *inner alignment* for level-6 understanding leading to a set of three versions of alignment in pedagogy:

- Constructive alignment leading to academic analytical understanding
- Relativist alignment leading to understanding-in-relativism, and
- Inner alignment leading to understanding-in-supercomplexity.

Considering the literature on the predominantly surface learning oriented ways of knowing of first year students in higher education, a constructivist developmental pedagogy in higher education would require a succession of these three forms of educational alignment. However, one must remember that the development towards higher levels of understanding is only possible through increasing tolerance of uncertainty and usually involves a "disturbance of the self" (Kegan, 1994). So only when students are supported sufficiently, will they take on the challenges presented to them with a willingness-to-go-on by themselves (Barnett, 2004). So within each pedagogy, the construction of *holding environments* (Kegan, 1994) will prove essential for epistemological development.

DISCUSSION

Based on the reactions of students, this chapter demonstrates that students in general are not of the opinion that academic understanding is assessed very often in higher education. They are particularly outspoken about the irrelevance of multiple choice testing (MC) for assessing any type of understanding. Contrary to what various test developers may think, students almost never feel intellectually challenged by MC-exams and admit that this type of assessment in particular makes them intellectually lazy, pointing them towards surface level learning as the most strategic approach to study success (e.g. van Rossum & Hamer, 2010, 2013). The suggestion to assess understanding with open question or essay exams would not seem to be the whole solution (Entwistle & Entwistle, 1997). Elton and Laurillard stated in 1979, "The quickest way to change student learning is to change the assessment system" (quoted in Biggs, 1996, p. 5). A conclusion that is supported time and time again by research (e.g. Gibbs, 1999). Taken together, this means that to create effective and appropriately aligned pedagogies (or learning environments) aimed at higher levels of understanding will require more study into the nature of the types of assessment fitted to particular ways of understanding. Interestingly, students could prove a fruitful source for suggestions on 'good assessment' (see Table 3).

The current study supports the design of different assessment practices aimed at rewarding different types of understanding, in particular when designing assessments for understanding that go beyond recall, reproduction and reproductive application of fixed strategies and approaches. In addition, it shows that where recall and reproduction can be assessed with high levels of reliability using MC, short and middle length answer items, using less reliably graded assessment types, e.g. case studies or problem based learning in itself may still only assess understanding aimed at reproduction. In the experience of students, deeper levels of understanding, that lead to changes in the self, in the relationship between the self and others or the world one lives in, require a different assessment format, including at the very least long essay responses detailing and evaluating different perspectives, case study or problem solving in unfamiliar situations, and oral assessments including debates. These formats are all associated with lower levels of inter-judge reliability, indicating that the trade-off between reliability and validity may need to shift towards validity and accepting lower than ideal levels of inter-judge reliability (Bloxham, den-Outer, Hudson & Price, 2016) if education is serious about assessing complex ways of understanding.

What is not discussed in this chapter is the role of the teacher in fostering deeper forms of learning and understanding. This issue is treated in extensive detail in van Rossum and Hamer (2010), and gives rise to a number of caveats concerning all too enthusiastic expectations of educational innovations based predominantly on constructivist materials or new technologies.

What would a pedagogy for supercomplexity mean for higher education? Barnett feels there are two distinct challenges universities face: "first, bringing students to a sense that all descriptions of the world are contestable [relativism or level-5-thinking], and, then, second, to a position of being able to prosper in such a world in which our categories even for understanding the situations in which we are placed, including understanding ourselves, are themselves contested" (2004, p 252-253). From the epistemological perspective this suggests that the duty of the university is to teach for self-awareness and responsibility. Barnett suggests a university *teaching for wisdom*, with wisdom far surpassing the more common interpretations of analytic understanding and deep level learning. The issue of teaching for wisdom is discussed at length in van Rossum and Hamer (2010, chapter 10). Barnett (2004) expects that this pedagogy will be characterised by a very different use of language. A language "caught in terms such as self-belief, self-confidence and self-motivation ... But even a language of that kind does not quite do justice to the pedagogical accomplishments in question. For these accomplishments point us, surely, to a language of self, of being, and of such terms as energy, authenticity and will" (Barnett, 2004, p. 254). Such a pedagogy for uncertainty, and wisdom, requires "open relationships between teacher and taught. ...The pedagogical frames, therefore, are bound to be open, as each party in the pedagogical transaction discloses her/himself to the other. ... The openness of the pedagogical frames is not just epistemological but it is ontological in nature. *The students come to know each other as persons; and to a degree, too, they come to know their teachers as persons."* (Barnett, 2004, p. 258, emphasis added). Indeed, in this pedagogy "We teach who we are" (Palmer, 1998, p. 1) and learn who we are (van Rossum & Hamer, 2010). The aim of *teaching for wisdom* then would be instilling dispositions – enduring habits of feeling, thinking and acting – so that one can thrive in a supercomplex world: what Barnett calls a *being-for-uncertainty*.

Being-for-uncertainty ... is characterized ... by certain kinds of disposition. Among such dispositions are carefulness, thoughtfulness, humility, criticality, receptiveness, resilience, courage and stillness. (Barnett, 2004, p. 258)

It is interesting to note the overlap between the dispositions listed in this study and above, and the International Baccalaureate's (IB) Learner Profile which is aimed not at young adults in higher education, but much younger age groups. The IB Learner Profile (IBLP) describes the desired learning outcome of an IB education, focusing on ten learner characteristics and dispositions. IB graduates are to be inquirers, critical thinkers, communicators, who are knowledgeable, reflective, open-minded, caring, principled, courageous and balanced. The IBLP Was adopted across all four international education programmes offered to over 1 million children from 3 to 18 in148 countries in the world. In adopting this ambitious goal for these age groups and providing increasing guidance on the pedagogy to support the Learner Profile, as well as investing in assessment research to support appropriate examination models, it would seem the IB is feeling its way towards preparing its graduates for the 21st century and supercomplexity at a much younger age than is usually proposed.

REFERENCES

Barnett, R. (2004). Learning for an unknown future. *Higher Education Research & Development*, *23*(3), 247–260. doi:10.1080/0729436042000235382

Baxter Magolda, M. B. (1992). *Knowing and Reasoning in College*. San Francisco: Jossey-Bass.

Baxter Magolda, M. B. (2001). *Making Their Own Way*. Sterling, Virginia: Stylus Publishing.

Baxter Magolda, M. B. (2009). *Authoring your Life*. Sterling, Virginia: Stylus Publishing.

Belenky, M. F., Clinchy, B. M., Goldberger, N. R., & Tarule, J. M. (1986/1997). *Women's ways of knowing: The development of self, voice and mind*. New York: Basic Books.

Biggs, J. B. (1996). Assessing Learning Quality: Reconciling institutional, staff and educational demands. *Assessment & Evaluation in Higher Education*, *21*(1), 5–15. doi:10.1080/0260293960210101

Biggs, J. B. (2003). *Teaching for quality learning at university: what the student does* (2nd ed.). Berkshire: SRHE and Open University Press.

Bloxham, S., den-Outer, B., Hudson, J. and Price, M. (2016). Let's stop the pretence of consistent marking: exploring the multiple limitations of assessment criteria. *Assessment and Evaluation in Higher Education*. doi:10.1080/02602938.2015.1024607.

Cook-Greuter, S. R. (1999/2005). Postautonomous Ego Development [Doctoral Dissertation]. Harvard University Graduate School of Education.

Csikszentmihalyi, M. (1993). *The Evolving Self – a psychology for the third millennium*. New York: HarperCollins Publishers.

Entwistle, A. C., & Entwistle, N. J. (1992). Experiences of understanding in revising for degree examinations. *Learning and Instruction*, *2*(1), 1–22. doi:10.1016/0959-4752(92)90002-4

Entwistle, N. J., & Entwistle, A. C. (1997). Revision and the Experience of Understanding. In F. Marton, D. Hounsell, & N. J. Entwistle (Eds.), *The Experience of Learning* (2nd ed., pp. 145–155). Edinburgh: Scottish Academic Press.

Entwistle, N. J., & Peterson, E. R. (2004). Conceptions of learning and knowledge in higher education: Relationships with study behaviour and influences of learning environments. *International Journal of Educational Research*, *41*(6), 407–428. doi:10.1016/j.ijer.2005.08.009

Entwistle, N. J., & Ramsden, P. (1983). *Understanding Student Learning*. New York: Nichols.

Gibbs, G. (1999). Using Assessment Strategically to Change the Way Students Learn. In: Brown, S. & Glaser, A. (Eds.) Assessment Matters in Higher Education. (pp. 41-53). Buckingham: Open University Press.

Irving, P. W., & Sayre, E. C. (2013). Upper-level Physics Students' Conceptions of Understanding. Paper presented at 2012 Physics Education Research Conference. *ProceedingsAIP Conference* (*Vol. 1513*, pp. 98-201). doi:doi:10.1063/1.4789686

Kegan, R. (1994). *In over our Heads. – The mental demands of modern life*. Cambridge, Mass: Harvard University Press.

Khiat, H. (2010). A Grounded Theory Approach: Conceptions of Understanding in Engineering Mathematics Learning. *Qualitative Report*, *15*(6), 1459–1488.

Labouvie-Vief, G. (1990). Wisdom as integrated thought: historical and developmental perspectives. In R. J. Sternberg (Ed.), *Wisdom, its nature, origins and developments* (pp. 52–83). Cambridge, UK: Cambridge University Press. doi:10.1017/CBO9781139173704.005

Lindblom-Ylänne, S., & Lonka, K. (1999). Individual ways of interacting with the learning environment – are they related to study success? *Learning and Instruction*, *9*(1), 1–18. doi:10.1016/S0959-4752(98)00025-5

Marton, F. (1986). Phenomenography: A research approach to investigating different understandings of reality. *Journal of Thought*, *21*(3), 28–49.

Marton, F., Dall'Alba, G., & Beaty, E. (1993). Conceptions of learning. *International Journal of Educational Research*, *19*(3), 277–300.

McCune, V., & Entwistle, N. J. (2011). Cultivating the disposition to understand in 21st century university education. *Learning and Individual Differences*, *21*(3), 303–310. doi:10.1016/j.lindif.2010.11.017

Morgan, A., & Beatty, L. (1997). The world of the learner. In F. Marton, D. Hounsell, & N. Entwistle (Eds.), *The Experience of Learning* (2nd ed., pp. 217–237). Edinburgh: Scottish Academic Press.

Newble, D. I., & Clarke, R. M. (1986). The approaches to learning of students in a traditional and an innovative problem-based medical school. *Medical Education*, *20*(4), 267–273. doi:10.1111/j.1365-2923.1986.tb01365.x PMID:3747871

Newton, D. P., & Newton, L. D. (1998). Enculturation and Understanding: Some differences between sixth formers' and graduates' conceptions of understanding in History and Science. *Teaching in Higher Education*, *3*(3), 339–363. doi:10.1080/1356215980030305

Newton, D. P., Newton, L. D., & Oberski, I. (1998). Learning and conceptions of understanding in history and science: Lecturers and new graduates compared. *Studies in Higher Education*, *23*(1), 43–58. doi:10.1080/03075079812331380482

Palmer, P. J. (1998). *The Courage to Teach*. San Francisco: Jossey-Bass.

Perkins, D. (1993). Teaching for Understanding. *American Educator: The Professional Journal of the American Federation of Teachers*, 17(3), 28-35. Retrieved from http://www.exploratorium.edu/IFI/resources/workshops/teachingforunderstanding.html

Perry, W. G. (1970). *Forms of intellectual and ethical development in the college years: A scheme*. New York: Holt, Rinehart & Winston.

Pratt, D. D. (1992). Conceptions of Teaching. *Adult Education Quarterly*, 42(4), 203–220.

Säljö, R. (1979). Learning in the learner's perspective. I: Some common sense conceptions. University of Göteborg, Mölndal.

Samuelowicz, K., & Bain, J. D. (2002). Identifying academics' orientations to assessment practice. *Higher Education*, 43(2), 173–201. doi:10.1023/A:1013796916022

Van Rossum, E. J. (1988). Insight into Understanding. In R. Säljö (Ed.), *The Written World* (pp. 195–208). Berlin, Heidelberg: Springer-Verlag. doi:10.1007/978-3-642-72877-8_13

Van Rossum, E. J., Deijkers, R., & Hamer, R. (1985). Students' learning conceptions and their interpretation of significant educational concepts. *Higher Education*, 14(6), 617–641. doi:10.1007/BF00136501

Van Rossum, E. J., & Hamer, R. (2010). *The Meaning of Learning and Knowing*. Rotterdam: Sense Publishers.

Van Rossum, E. J., & Hamer, R. (2011, September). Analysing deep learning and understanding: getting the meanings clear first. *Paper presented at EARLI*, Exeter, UK.

Van Rossum, E. J., & Hamer, R. (2013, April). Students' Conceptions of Understanding and Assessment of 'Real Understanding'. Poster presentation at 13th AERA, San Francisco, USA.

Van Rossum, E. J., & Schenk, S. M. (1984). The relationship between learning conception, study strategy and learning outcome. *The British Journal of Educational Psychology*, 54(1), 73–83. doi:10.1111/j.2044-8279.1984.tb00846.x

Van Rossum, E. J., & Taylor, I. P. (1987, April). The relationship between conceptions of learning and good teaching: A scheme of cognitive development. *Paper presented at theAnnual Meeting of the American Educational Research Association*, Washington DC, U.S.A.

Vermunt, J. D. (1996). Metacognitive, cognitive and affective aspects of learning styles and strategies: A phenomenographic analysis. *Higher Education*, 31(1), 25–50. doi:10.1007/BF00129106

Vermunt, J. D. (1998). The regulation of constructive learning processes. *The British Journal of Educational Psychology*, 68(2), 149–171. doi:10.1111/j.2044-8279.1998.tb01281.x

KEY TERMS AND DEFINITIONS

Assessment Model: The collection of principles and practices assessing the quality of learning (learning outcome), such as type of question items, number of exam components, marking procedures e.g. the use of mark schemes, rubrics or criteria, and so on.

Assessment-for-Learning: Formative and classroom assessment practices aimed at diagnosing gaps and misconceptions in knowledge and understanding with the aim to provide feedback to the learner and to improve learning.

Assessment-of-Learning: Summative assessment, externally marked examinations, with the aim to assess the quality of the learning outcome.

Constructive Alignment: A principle of backward engineering teaching and learning activities, and assessment tasks, to ensure construct validity regarding the desired learning outcome. Starting from the highest quality learning outcome and an underlying hierarchy of intermediate learning outcomes, choosing and shaping the learning, teaching and assessment activities so they are all aimed at creating a clear learning path enabling learners to achieve and demonstrate the various quality levels of learning expected (Biggs, 2003).

Deep Learning: Learning focused on critically examining new facts, procedures and ideas, connecting these to prior knowledge and personal cognitive structures aimed at meaning making.

Epistemology: The theory of knowledge, especially with regard to its methods, validity, and scope, and the distinction between justified belief and opinion.

Learning Conception: A description of how a group of learners interpret the meaning of learning.

Phenomenography: A method for describing qualitatively different ways in which people understand of conceptualize an aspect of their world …, focusing on the point of view of the respondent (Pratt, 1992).

Surface Learning: Learning focused on memorising facts, procedures and ideas, storing these as isolated, unconnected items without critical appraisal aimed at reproduction.

Chapter 9
Teacher Self–Assessment of Feedback Practices in an EFL Academic Writing Class – A Reflective Case Study

Eddy White
University of Arizona, USA

ABSTRACT

Unlike studies of teacher feedback on student writing, research into teacher self-assessment of their own feedback practices is quite rare in the assessment literature. In this reflective case study, the researcher/ teacher systematically analyzed feedback practices to clearly determine the form and kind of formative feedback being provided on student essays, and also to compare these feedback practices to recommended practice from the feedback literature. The research took place in an academic English writing course for third-year students at a Japanese university. A close examination of the teacher feedback on the first draft of 21 student essays was undertaken, and more than 800 feedback interventions were identified and coded. Results of this investigation show a number of patterns of practice in giving feedback, including; extensive use of questions in teacher commentary, very limited use of praise comments, and varying amounts of feedback provided on individual essays. Results also show that the feedback practices discovered through this investigation align well with recommended best practice. The case study positions the teacher as 'learner' in this feedback process, and calls for similar published research describing in detail what teachers do when providing feedback to students on their work.

DOI: 10.4018/978-1-5225-0531-0.ch009

For many years I taught in universities... I marked thousands of scripts without examining what the scripts could teach me about my capacity as a teacher and examiner. (Ashby, 1984, p. v)

The teacher... is continually exerting influence on the students and the learning situation. By studying his own behavior in some systematic, objective manner, the teacher may gain further insights into his own pattern of influence. (Amidon & Flanders, 1967, p. 72)

I. INTRODUCTION

With classroom-based assessment, in all its variety and complexity, the teacher engages in a process of collecting information about what a student understands, knows and can do. Giving feedback to students on how we view that information, with the aim of helping improve their understanding, knowledge and abilities, is a fundamental part of the teaching process. This report is an account of teacher self-assessment (TSA), an examination of written feedback provided on student essays to gain insight into my role and performance as teacher and feedback provider. It is an exercise in critical appraisal; an analysis of one facet of pedagogic practice.

Teacher's feedback can have a significant impact on improving student's writing. However, "this role is complex and requires careful reflection to be used effectively" (Hyland, 2003, p. 192). A careful, systematic self-assessment of the written feedback produced and provided to students in an EFL academic writing course at a university in Japan is the focus of this investigation. In the context of that third-year academic writing course, written feedback on 21 first drafts of student essays will be described in a systematic manner. The investigation is guided by the following two research questions:

1. What is the nature and form of the feedback I give to students on the first drafts of their academic essays?
2. How do my feedback practices compare with recommended practice in the feedback literature?

The first question above may be answered by closely analyzing and classifying written feedback provided on one representative set of essay first drafts. The second question will be answered by using an external, outside lens to view the feedback practices identified in responding to question 1. As will be seen, one seminal feedback article in particular (Gibbs & Simpson, 2004-2005) will provide the external measuring stick that comprises the second element of this two-track investigation.

It should be noted that how students engaged with this feedback, and how they felt about the process, are outside the scope of this particular report and intended for alternative publication.

Case Study Research

According to Yin (2009), "A case study is an empirical inquiry that investigates a contemporary phenomenon in depth and within its real-life context." (p. 18). The real-life context described here is an in-depth report into the contemporary phenomenon of an EFL writing teacher providing formative feedback to students on their work. The set of 21 student essay first-drafts, and the feedback I provided on them, is the 'case' examined and described here. According to Burns (2000, pp. 460-479) case studies have the following characteristics:

- A case study must be a bounded system – an entity in itself.
- A case study must involve the collection of very extensive data to produce understanding of the entity being studied.
- The main techniques used in case studies are observation, interviewing, and document analysis.
- Sampling is usually non-probability, with the case chosen on the basis of some relevant criterion.
- In *purposive, purposeful, or criterion-based sampling,* a case is selected because it serves the real purpose and objectives of the researcher of discovering, gaining insight and understanding into a particularly chosen phenomenon (original emphasis, p. 465).
- Data analysis involves the devising of a coding system that permits higher order categories and conceptual analysis to develop.

As the reader will note, all of the case study characteristics listed above are evident in this report, and this investigation may be classified as a reflective case study

The principle objective of case study research is the deep understanding of a specific process, and the actors and interactions involved, by focusing on the process itself rather than on the results, on discovering rather than confirming (Burns 2000, Woodside 2010). Reaching an in-depth understanding of my formative feedback on a set of student compositions is the principle objective of this reflective case study.

Reflective Practice

It is widely recognized that a central tenet of the teaching-learning process is reflective practice (Harford & MacRuairc, 2008), and there are numerous references to this reflective teaching concept in the language teaching education literature (Akbari, 2007). Lucas (1991) defines the term 'reflection' as systematic inquiry into one's own practice in order to improve that practice and form a deeper understanding of it. Similarly, Richards and Lockhart (1994) write that reflective teaching is an approach in which teachers "collect data about teaching, examine their attitudes, beliefs, assumptions, and teaching practices, and use the information obtained as a basis for critical reflection" (p. 1). This description is a close approximation of the processes described in this investigation. Teacher feedback data was collected, examined and used as a basis of critical reflection on formative feedback practice. Reflection-on-action (Schon, 1983, 1987), a hind-sighted, rearview look, is the type of practice engaged in here as the critical analysis of student essays and written feedback on them began approximately three months after this particular writing class had finished.

Feedback: Definition and Importance

There are a number of definitions of feedback in the assessment literature (see, for example, Ramaprasad 1983; Nicol & Macfarlane-Dick, 2006; Hattie & Timperley, 2007) which are similar to the definition by Wiggins (1993) used in this study: "Feedback is information that provides the performer with direct, usable insights into current performance, based on tangible differences between current performance and hoped for performance" (p. 182.). A primary purpose for such formative feedback is in closing the gap between initial and subsequent student task performance (Sadler, 1989). Rather than focusing on summative feedback (the end-point feedback which includes a final assessment of student performance), this report deals with providing students with user-friendly, formative feedback; the type which is intended to feed forward into better student performance of the task at hand. In their review of the feedback literature, Hattie and Timperly (2007) noted:

Feedback is one of the most powerful influences on learning and achievement, but this impact can be either positive or negative. Its power is frequently mentioned in articles about learning and teaching, but surprisingly few recent studies have systematically investigated its meaning. (p. 81)

The case study reported on here is one such example of a systematic feedback investigation.

Feedback in Assessment for Learning (AfL)

This feedback investigation was embedded in a larger doctoral research project into applying assessment for learning (Afl) principles and practices to a higher education EFL context. Stiggins (2007) provides the following succinct description of AfL, "Assessment *for* learning: the use of the formative assessment process and its results as an instructional intervention designed to increase - not merely to monitor and grade - pupil learning." (p. 17). In their comprehensive review of formative assessment, Black and Wiliam (1998) emphasized the large and consistent positive effects that quality feedback has on student learning, compared with other aspects of the teaching process.

According to Black et al. (2003), feedback to the learner is an essential part of formative assessment for two reasons: it assesses their current level of achievement; and indicates what the next steps should be to improve. The authors provide a warning call to teachers against providing solely summative feedback in the form of marks or grades, and promote the need for more formative-style 'feedback for learning'. The following excerpt from Black et al. (2003) explains the point as follows:

Feedback which focuses on what needs to be done can encourage all to believe that they can improve. Such feedback can enhance learning, both directly through the effort that can ensue and indirectly by supporting the motivation to invest such effort. (p. 46)

Feedback provided with the expectation that all students can improve on their initial performance was a key element in the teacher response to student essays in this report.

Teacher Self-Assessment (TSA) of Feedback

As will be seen, the TSA described here is unusual in the literature on writing feedback. Most self-assessment research in writing has centered on student self-assessment of their writing, rather than teachers' self-assessment of their own written feedback. Little is known about teacher self-assessment of the written feedback they provide, especially for second language writing instructors (Montgomery & Baker, 2007). On the other hand, the issue of teachers' reflective practices has been the subject of an extensive body of writing.

Teacher self-assessment is also referred to as 'teacher self-evaluation', and Airasian and Gullickson (1997) offer a good description of what that term entails:

Teacher self-evaluation is a process in which teachers make judgments about the adequacy and effectiveness of their own knowledge, performance, beliefs, or effects for the purpose of self-improvement. In self-evaluation, the teacher becomes responsible for examining and improving his or her own practice.

It is the teacher who collects, interprets, and judges information bearing on personal practice. It is the teacher who frames criteria and standards to judge the adequacy of his or her beliefs, knowledge, skills and effectiveness. Teacher self-evaluation is evaluation of the teacher by the teacher and for the teacher (p.3).

This explanation is also a good description of the process engaged in for this report into the nature of my feedback practices. It may be added that TSA can also be considered 'for the students' as well as for the teacher, as they may also benefit from such reflective actions and any resulting refinement of pedagogic knowledge or practice.

Teacher Feedback on Student Writing

Teacher feedback on student writing has been an area of extensive research, exploring the following issues in particular: the effectiveness of grammar correction; different points of feedback focus-error, content, organization; the use of coding schemes; student correction behaviors; teacher correction behaviors; negative versus positive feedback; students' views on types of feedback and the clarity of teacher feedback (O'Brian, 2004).

Due in part to the plethora of research and publications about teacher feedback on student writing (see, for example, recent reviews in Hyland, 2006; Hyland & Hyland, 2006; Stern & Solomon, 2006; Hattie & Timperley, 2007; and Shute 2008), the importance of effective feedback has become more widely recognized in both mainstream education and second language writing. Across the education spectrum of courses and contexts, effective feedback is viewed as critical for both encouraging and consolidating student learning (Hyland & Hyland, 2006).

The scarcity of research and writing on teacher self-assessment of the feedback they provide to students lies in stark contrast to the extensive body of teacher feedback research. Despite the increasing number of studies looking at teacher feedback on student writing in recent years, very few of them focus on teacher self-assessment of their own feedback practices. Almost all of the literature on teacher feedback discusses what other teachers or research subjects do when giving feedback, and very few writers examine their own practices (in print at least). Brown and Glover (2006) sum up the state-of-play in this area as follows:

Given the high value that students place on individualized written feedback, the role that good-quality feedback may play in aiding student learning . . . and the significant time costs to teachers in its delivery, it is surprising that few attempts have been made to classify systematically the different types of teacher comments that constitute feedback so that the quality of feedback can be analyzed. (p. 82)

Surprising indeed. Only a few reports in the related literature pay attention to TSA of their written feedback, and these are from L1 writing contexts. Most L2 writing research has focused on student perceptions rather than the teachers' perspectives of their practice. Self-assessment studies have focused on student self-assessment to improve their writing performance, rather than on teacher self-assessment to improve their feedback performance (Montgomery & Baker, 2007).

One of the few accounts of a teacher evaluating and critiquing their own written feedback practices is a case study into teacher response by Straub (2000). In a freshman writing class at an American college, Straub investigated his written comments on the writings of one student. This occurred over a period of time, and he provided a detailed contextual examination of his feedback response practices. Straub found that his responses to student writing were shaped by such factors as: the sequence of assignments and classroom instruction, his teaching style, and the work and needs of individual students. Straub frames his TSA in light of ten practical strategies for responding to student writing that he identified in the responding-to- writing literature. He compares his feedback practices to those recommended practices, which are listed in Table 1.

Straub (2000) was convinced that for students to develop as writers they needed not only a lot of writing practice, but also "a lot of response from readers about how that writing is working for them" (p. 27).

In a study at an American university, Montgomery and Baker (2007) obtained data from 15 teachers and 98 students in an intensive ESL program. Their investigation had three foci: how much local and global written feedback teachers give; how TSA and student perceptions coordinated; and how well teachers' self-assessments matched their performances. Among other things, they found that the coordination between TSA and actual performance was not strong, showing that teachers may not be fully aware of the amount and type of feedback they were providing. Montgomery and Baker (2007) also found that teachers did not provide the same amount of feedback to each student and that in general the 15 teachers gave substantial amounts of local feedback, but little of the global variety (i.e. related to content, organization). These results were not reflected in the TSA's the teachers provided, pointing out the discrepancy between perceived and actual feedback practice. Montgomery and Baker (2007) called for further TSA research in L2 writing to encourage teachers to become more aware of their feedback practices, and help improve its effectiveness as a result.

These two articles, Straub (2000) and Montgomery and Baker (2007), were the only ones identified in a feedback literature review that directly deal with published accounts regarding TSA of feedback research. Thus, this case study is one of the few existing accounts of a teacher's systematic classification and examination of their own formative feedback practices detailing the amount and type of responses provided to students on their writing.

Feedback: Best Practices (Gibbs and Simpson, 2004-2005)

In order to self-assess my feedback practices, as well as having a set of student scripts that include my feedback to analyze and scrutinize, a criterion-based framework of recommended practices is required

Table 1. Practical strategies for written feedback practices (Straub, 2000)

1. Turn your comments into a conversation.
2. Create a dialogue with students on the page.
3. Do not take control over the text: instead of projecting your agenda on student writing and being directive, be facilitative and help students realize their own purposes.
4. Limit the scope of your comments.
5. Limit the number of comments you present.
6. Give priority to global concerns of content, context, and organization before getting overly involved with style and correctness.
7. Focus your comments according to the stage of drafting and the relative maturity of the text.
8. Gear your comments to the individual student behind the text.
9. Make frequent use of praise.
10. Tie your responses to the larger classroom conversation.

to compare them with. One article in particular, Gibbs & Simpson (2004-05) contains a number of recommended feedback conditions and principles, providing a set of criteria for an assessment instrument.

In their paper (entitled, *Conditions under which assessment supports students learning*), Gibbs & Simpson (2004-05) argue that student learning is best supported by assessment when a series of conditions are met. After examining a wide range of case studies, these authors identified 11 conditions for assessment to support learning. Seven of these assessment conditions are specifically related to the quantity, timing, and quality of teacher feedback and how students respond to it (the other four important conditions relate to assessments' influence on the volume, focus and quality of student studying). Gibbs and Simpson write that these conditions are concerned with "how the provision of feedback affects students learning behavior-with how feedback results in students taking action that involves, or does not involve, further learning" (p. 17). Table 2 lists these seven feedback conditions intended to promote student learning.

These seven conditions will form one strand of the Seven/Seven framework used here to self-assess my written feedback practices. Gibbs and Simpson (2004-05) make reference to theory, empirical evidence and their own practical experience to justify the list of conditions they have set. In describing how these ideas may be used, they write, "These conditions are offered as a framework for teachers to review the effectiveness of their own assessment practice" (p.3).

The investigation reported here takes up this offer. The Discussion section below will revisit these recommended best practices as a basis for assessing my feedback practices in the context of this academic writing course at a Japanese university. It should be noted that I was not aware of and had not read this source prior to starting data collection for this research project, so it did not influence my feedback practices in any way.

Next we move on to describe how this investigation was carried out.

II. METHODOLOGY

Context and Course Overview

Tokyo Woman's Christian University is a liberal arts institution in Japan, and a graduation requirement for students in the Department of English is to complete a 20-25 page final thesis in English. The third year writing course, *Junior Composition* (JC), is a crucial preliminary course in teaching students the

Table 2. Seven feedback conditions influencing learning (Gibbs & Simpson, 2004-05)

1. Sufficient feedback is provided, both often enough and in enough detail
2. The feedback focuses on students' performance, on their learning and on actions under the students' control, rather than on the students themselves and on their characteristics
3. The feedback is timely in that it is received by students while it still matters to them and in time for them to pay attention to further learning or receive further assistance
4. Feedback is appropriate to the purpose of the assignment and to its criteria for success
5. Feedback is appropriate, in relation to students' understanding of what they are supposed to be doing
6. Feedback is received and attended to
7. Feedback is acted upon by the student

fundamentals of the academic writing and research they will need to complete the senior year graduation thesis. JC classes have from 20-25 students, and the yearlong program is divided into two parts: JC 1 (April – July), and JC 2 in the second semester (Sept.- Jan.). There are approximately 15 weekly classes during the semester, each for 90 minutes. In general, the overall goals for this academic writing course are similar to those reflected in such writing courses in any number of higher education settings; "to both produce texts that are regarded as competent and successful by their intended audiences and to become self-sufficient in constructing acceptably accurate prose" (Hyland, 2003, p. 184). Developing competent, self-sufficient writers of academic research papers in English is the key task for teachers of the JC course.

Typical of JC classes, the students in the particular class involved in this case study were all Japanese women in the 20 to 21-year-old age range. The class had 23 students. As for English writing ability, it is very difficult to generalize as to proficiency-levels. The only pre-requisite for entering this third-year course simply required passing (obtaining a 50% grade) a sophomore English writing course. The range and amount of feedback provided on individual essays is an indication of the mixed levels of English writing proficiency for this group of Japanese students.

Despite the high stakes nature of the course (passing JC is a requirement for advancing to the senior year), the curriculum is loosely structured and it is up to individual teachers to choose course content (of either a literature, or linguistics nature as stipulated by Dept. of English guidelines), and the writing activities that will develop student skills. Teachers are also left to make their own decisions regarding assessment of student's work, and the provision of feedback to them.

Essays and Assessment

In my particular JC class, students were required to write three essays in the first semester and two in the second. For all essays, students were required to submit both a first and a final draft. Formative, written feedback was provided to students on their first drafts. These drafts were returned, and students had one week to edit and revise before submitting the final version. This version was then summatively assessed and given a final grade. In the weekly 90-minute classes, students were provided with instruction, and carried out tasks related to both the particular topic being focused on in the essay task, and to academic research and writing itself (e.g. writing effective thesis statements, paraphrasing sources). Table 3 shows the seven steps in a typical cycle of essay writing and feedback/assessment in the JC course.

Table 3. Steps in the JC essay writing and assessment process

1. Instruction, students become familiar with content & source materials (3-4 classes)
2. Essay topics provided considered, decided **(Week 1)**
3. Students submit first draft of essay **(Week 2)**
4. Teacher first draft feedback (formative assessment)
5. Students begins editing and revising **(Week 3)**
6. Students submit final draft of essay **(Week 4)**
7. Teacher final draft feedback/essay graded (summative assessment)

All JC essays followed the same seven-step pattern, before proceeding to the next essay topic. Brown and Glover (2006) refer to such a writing-feedback cycle as 'the performance-feedback-reflection-performance-feedback loop' (p. 43). Step 4 in this cycle, related to teachers' written feedback on student first drafts, is the particular area of interest for this feedback self-assessment case study. It should be noted that opportunities for self - and peer - assessment were included during this essay-writing process. This report deals with the second half of the writing course, JC 2, and, as a representative sample, one particular essay students wrote (on the linguistic topic of 'slang') and my feedback on it.

Student essays were assessed in the first semester (JC 1) using a three-criteria scoring rubric comprised of content, organization and language use. In the second semester, the same assessment rubric was used with the addition of a new criterion 'use of source material.' New for JC 2, particular focus was placed on students' use of MLA style documentation of sources, especially the use of parenthetical citations and a Works Cited list at the end of the essay. Appendices A and B show the summative assessment rubric used for final essay drafts.

Essay Task

This TSA report discusses the feedback provided for the first essay of JC 2, on the linguistic topic of 'slang'. Three short source readings (2-4 pages in length) were provided to students related to this topic. Students were also required to find two of their own additional sources, from the Internet or campus library, for possible use in the essay. A minimum of three sources was required in writing the paper. After three or four classes focused on the topic of slang - familiarizing students with the sources provided, and essay construction (particularly MLA documentation of sources) - students were required to bring the sources they had found to class. These were then evaluated together as a class for reliability and usefulness, and students were presented with the slang essay questions. The essay topics were related to: the main characteristics of slang, why a negative impression of slang exists, or why slang is so popular and commonplace. Students were required to submit a five-paragraph essay; approximately 700-800 words in length (2 ½-3 pages), with MLA formatted documentation of sources. As usual in the JC writing cycle, after receiving the essay questions they were given one week to produce the first draft of the essay.

First Draft Feedback

Teacher feedback on the slang essay first drafts came in three forms:

1. Use of indirect correction code symbols;
2. Direct marginal teacher comments; and,
3. An overall feedback report attached to the back of the essay.

In the JC course, I decided to follow the now common practice of using a correction code indicating the location and type of errors or other problems with the writing. Research suggests that the use of such a correction code is effective in stimulating student response and developing self-editing strategies (Hyland, 2003). Student first drafts were marked using the following codes shown here in Table 4.

It should be remembered that by the time of this slang-topic essay, in JC 1, students had already written three essays in which this coding scheme was used on first drafts and were quite familiar with the coding symbols. These particular symbols arose from those most commonly used in the JC course

Table 4. Correction symbols used on essay first drafts

R = rewrite (awkward, unclear English)	**0** = missing word
? = meaning not understood	**pl** = plural
g = grammar problem	**cap** = capitalization
ww = wrong word	**sp** = spelling
wf = wrong word form	**=** - join together (sentences)

writing reference book, (*The Pocket Wadsworth Handbook, 3rd Edition,* Kirszner & Mandell, 2006); they were shortened and simplified so as not to overwhelm students with excess correction coding on their first drafts.

The second form of teacher feedback was handwritten commentary on the essays. These comments are related to content or presentation of ideas in the text (for example, 'citation needed'), and are instances of the teacher as reader responding to texts 'on the fly' (Hyland, 2003).

The final type of written feedback was the completion of a feedback report, an overall indicator of essay strengths and weaknesses, attached to the end of the first draft. This feedback report used the same criteria as would be used in the final (summative) assessment. The feedback report consisted of a set of four criteria (content, organization, language use, and use of source material) which were assessed on a weak to strong continuum, and brief handwritten commentary was provided informing students how they had performed in relation to each one. Table 5 shows the feedback report attached to the end of each first draft.

Providing written feedback is a time-consuming business, and the amount of time involved in checking these slang essays should be briefly noted here. On average, responding with feedback to each first draft took anywhere from 15-to 25 minutes. This time varied depending on the content of the essay, and the English writing proficiency exhibited by the student (i.e. more proficient writers had fewer problems in their essays, requiring less time for feedback provision).

Table 5. First draft feedback report (adapted from McCormack and Slaght, 2005)

Junior Composition   **First Draft Feedback**
Student: _____

1. **Content**: Clearly focused content, relevant to the essay topic. Length, scope and level of detail are appropriate/relevant. Ideas are well presented and developed, with supporting evidence from a variety of sources. It is evident that the writer knows the topic well.
(**strong** < - - - - - - - - - - - - * - - - - - - - - - - - > **weak**)

2. **Organization:** Overall structure and main ideas are clearly organized and easy to follow. Introduction has general comments about the topic, followed by a well-written thesis statement. In the body of the essay, supporting ideas are effectively linked together and 'flow' coherently, making it easy for the reader to follow. Conclusion summarizes main points and effectively brings the essay to a finish.
(**strong** < - - - - - - - - - - - - - * - - - - - - - - - - - - > **weak**)

3. **Language use:** Ideas are clearly expressed, with wide, accurate usage of *vocabulary* and *grammar*; any errors do not interfere with communication. Formal academic style is used (e.g. formal expressions, longer sentences, impersonal tone, etc.). Use of a range of linking words and phrases to join ideas at paragraph and sentence level.
(**strong** < - - - - - - - - - - - - - * - - - - - - - - - - - > **weak**)

4. **Use of source material**: Effective use of a range of sources. These are appropriately incorporated into the body of the essay through *paraphrase*, *summary*, and *quotation*. Shows ability to synthesize well from several sources to support ideas. Works Cited page and in-text referencing follow MLA format. No obvious or conscious plagiarism.
(**strong** < - - - - - - - - - - - - - * - - - - - - - - - - - > **weak**)

Overall:

Data Collection

At the end of the writing cycle for the slang-topic essay, after summative assessments of final drafts were completed and as we began the final essay topic for JC 2, I asked students if I could use their slang-topic essays for research purposes. Specifically, I asked them to return to me the final draft of their essay (with my attached summative assessment) to be photocopied, as well as the first draft of the essay. Students agreed, and, thus, I was able to collect 21 essay pairs, including a first draft containing my feedback, and the edited and revised final version of the same essay. As the first drafts contained the feedback I had provided, those 21 versions became of particular interest and formed the main data set for this case study. Two of the 23 students in the class did not return the first drafts of their essay.

It should be noted that my decision to focus on feedback in doing research about teaching writing was made months after provision of feedback on the particular essays used here. At the time of requesting and collecting essays from this JC class, I had a general idea to do some research on student writing, without a specific research focus. As such, the amount and type of feedback provided on the first draft of these slang-topic essays was in no way affected by the research process itself.

Data Analysis

Each of the first drafts was closely examined and the numbers and types of feedback interventions were coded. A 'feedback intervention' (FI), according to Kluger and DeNisi (1996), is defined as "actions taken by an external agent to provide information regarding some aspects of one's task performance" (p. 255). In this context, such interventions will refer to the corrective symbols and comments I provided on each essay. The correction code FI's were categorized into the symbol types listed in Table 3 (e.g. wrong word, spelling, grammar).

Coding and Types of Feedback Interventions

Approximately three months after the completion of this particular JC 2 class, analysis of the feedback provided on the set of 21 essays was begun. This involved the counting and coding of each feedback intervention (FI) on essay first drafts. These FI's were separated into the following three categories:

1. **Correction Code Symbols:** a range of ten different symbols were used to direct students in editing and revising first drafts (seen in Table 3);
2. **Comments:** these included marginal comments (single words, phrases, sentences), and those comments written directly above or below sentences;
3. **Other FI's:** these included: (**1**) crossing things out (words, sentences), (**2**) making corrections (fixing, adding, re-writing), (**3**) indicating that words or phrases be moved, through using arrows, lines, or circles, etc. (**4**) a number providing an evaluation of the essays' thesis statement as follow: 1= 'good'; 2= 'OK, but rewrite to make clearer, smoother'; or 3 = 'major changes needed, completely rewrite'. These numbers (a 1, 2, or 3) were written next to the thesis statement, at the end of the introductory paragraph, for each essay.

As for teacher commentary, typically in the form of marginal notes, a system for categorizing types of written feedback established by Haines (2004) was used. The seven feedback categories developed by

Haines, and used here, are: regulatory instructions, advisory comments, descriptive observation, rhetorical questions, direct criticism, praise, and correctness. It should be noted that this coding of written commentary does *not* include the commentary provided on the feedback report attached to each first draft.

The type and style of my FI responses to student writing can be seen in Table 6, which shows the first page of a student first draft. The feedback interventions shown in Table 6 are typical of those that can be seen on the total set of 21 first drafts, and representative of the type of feedback students were provided with in this writing course.

The counting and coding of symbols and written commentary, as well as a consideration of responses provided on the feedback reports attached to each draft, provided a clear, yet complex, picture of what exactly I was doing when providing first draft feedback on student compositions in this Junior Composition class.

Table 6. Student essay extract (page 1) with teacher feedback

Blue = Teacher Feedback	2= Thesis OK, but Rewrite	Red = Student Revisions

III. RESULTS

For the set of 21 first drafts, a total of *828 feedback interventions* were identified and recorded. Table 7 is a record of the FI breakdown per student for each of the three classification categories described earlier (correction code symbols, other FI's, and comments). At the bottom of the table, a percentile breakdown of the total number of FI's for all essays is also provided for each of the three categories.

As can been seen from the table, the number of FI's per essay ranged from a low of 20 (Asako) to a high of 58 (Aya). The mean average for all 828 responses was approximately *39 FI's per essay*. More than half of the FI total (51%) was comprised of correction code symbols.

Teacher written commentary comprised 34% of the FI's provided on this set of essays, with 283 examples identified and recorded. The seven category coding system for teacher comments developed by Haines (2004) is shown in Table 8, with examples from the JC student's slang-topic essays.

Table 7. Feedback Intervention (FI) record on essay first drafts (N=21 essays)

Essay Writer	Correction Code Symbols	Other FI's	Comments	FI Total per Essay
1. Natsumi	15	8	7	30
2. Chisako	12	10	9	31
3. Chihiro	24	6	10	40
4. Yukako	26	2	7	35
5. Kano	17	9	6	32
6. Mariko	33	10	13	56
7. Kurumi	30	6	14	50
8. Sachiko	12	5	11	28
9. Asami	22	4	25	51
10. Mio	19	3	17	39
11. Aki	24	7	13	44
12. Akiko	21	9	10	40
13. Shoko	28	3	17	48
14. Aya	34	4	20	58
15. Yumiko	28	6	19	53
16. Keiko	5	5	18	28
17. Misaki	19	6	15	40
18. Akiko	15	5	20	40
19. Yumiko	19	6	8	33
20. Asako	11	3	6	20
21. Saki	8	6	18	32
Totals	**422**	**123**	**283**	**828**
% of FI total	*51%*	*15%*	*34%*	

Table 8. Types of written comments (Haines, 2004), with slang-topic essay examples

Written Comment Types	Feedback Examples
1. Regulatory instructions	*No first names for in-text citations*
2. Advisory comments	*Use an example from English, not Japanese*
3. Descriptive observation	*Almost the entire paragraph is a Wikipedia quote*
4. Rhetorical questions	*People use slang for this reason?*
5. Direct criticism	*Difficult to read and understand*
6. Praise	*Very good paragraph*
7. Correctness	*Not all slang disappears*

The category of 'correctness' here does not refer to language use errors, but to any content (ideas or information) in the essay that may be mistaken or erroneous. The first type, 'regulatory instructions', in Haines's (2004) categorization system refers to feedback on adhering to prescribed rules or instructions for the writing task. In the case of this JC essay, using proper MLA format and documentation of sources was particularly important.

From the 21 first drafts, each of my FI comments, in the form of a word, phrase, or sentence were counted, and these *283 written comments* were catalogued according to Haines's (2004) categorization. Table 9 shows the numbers for the written feedback commentary I provided to students on their first drafts. A percentage of the total is also provided for each category.

Table 9 shows that the main type of commentary provided were rhetorical questions, comprising more than half the total (55%). The 'praise' category contained the fewest comments, just 2% of the total number.

As noted in Table 4, 15% of all interventions were categorized as 'Other FI's' (i.e. crossing things out, making corrections, instructions to move words, and numerically evaluating thesis statements). These FI' were not individually numbered and categorized due to the difficulty of doing so.

However, the correction code symbols used for feedback, 51% of all FI's, were counted and categorized. A breakdown of the *422 correction code symbols* provided on the 21 essays is shown in Table 10, including a percentage breakdown.

Table 9. Record of first-draft feedback written commentary (N=21 essays)

Type of Written Feedback	Number	%
1. Regulatory instructions	28	10%
2. Advisory comments	34	12%
3. Descriptive observation	11	4%
4. Rhetorical questions	156	55%
5. Direct criticism	25	9%
6. Praise	5	2%
7. Correctness	24	8%
Total ⇒	**283**	

Table 10. Correction code symbol record for individual essays (N = 422 symbols)

Essay writer	R	?	g	ww	wf	0	pl	cap	sp	=	Total
1. Natsumi	6		1	5	3						15
2. Chisako	5	3	1	1		2					12
3. Chihiro	16	3	3				1			1	24
4. Yukako	16	3	5	1			1				26
5. Kano	10	2	3	1		1					17
6. Mariko	10	16	4		1		1		1		33
7. Kurumi	15	13	1						1		30
8. Sachiko	9	3									12
9. Asami	7	8		1	2	1		2		1	22
10. Mio	10	4	1	1	1		1		1		19
11. Aki	11	3	5	3	1	1					24
12. Akiko	5	8	7	1							21
13. Shoko	13	11	3		1						28
14. Aya	16	14	1	2					1		34
15. Yumiko	12	10	3	1	1			1			28
16. Keiko	3	2									5
17. Misaki	12	6	1								19
18. Akiko	1	10	1	2					1		15
19. Yumiko	11	4	1	2	1						19
20. Asako	7	3	1								11
21. Saki	4	3		1							8
Symbol Totals	**199**	**129**	**42**	**22**	**11**	**5**	**4**	**3**	**5**	**2**	**422**
Percentages	*47%*	*31%*	*10%*	*5%*	*2.6%*	*1.1%*	*.9%*	*.7%*	*1.1%*	*0.4%*	

R = rewrite (awkward, unclear English) **0** = missing word

? = meaning not understood **pl** = plural

g = grammar problem **cap** = capitalization

ww = wrong word **sp** = spelling

wf = wrong word form **=** - join together (sentences)

The most common symbols used ('R' and '?') comprised a total of 78% of the correction code FI's. The next highest number of symbols used were the grammar symbol (10%), followed by the vocabulary symbols ('ww,' 'wf') making up approximately 8% of FI's used. Together, these five most common symbols made up approximately 95% of correction code feedback provided on these essay first drafts. The number of symbols per essay ranged from a low of 5 (Keiko), to a high of 34 (Aya). The mean average of 422 correction code symbols provided as feedback was approximately 20 symbols per essay.

The overview in Table 11 provides a simple, descriptive statistical analysis of numeric data examined, counted and coded in this case study. High and low scores show the largest and smallest number of feedback interventions on an essay for each grouping. A wide range in number of responses per individual essay, and in standard deviation scores, is evident here.

Table 11. Statistical overview of FI data (N = 21 essays)

FI Data Group	Total	Mean (per essay)	SD	High	Low
Correction code symbols	422	20.1	8.0	34	5
Other FI's	123	5. 8	2.3	10	2
Comments	283	13.4	5.4	25	6
All FI's	**828**	**39.4**	**10.3**	**58**	**20**

As noted earlier, an important part of teacher feedback provided to JC students was the feedback report sheet attached to the back of each first draft. Feedback was given on the four key areas of content, organization, language use and use of source material. Table 12, showing feedback given to three students, will give the reader a feel for the type of commentary provided on these reports.

IV. DISCUSSION

Case studies, as Burns (2000) reminds us, "are based on the premise that a case can be located that is typical of many other cases. Once such a case is studied it can provide insights into the class of events from which the case has been drawn" (p. 461). As noted, the teacher feedback provided on this set of

Table 12. Feedback provided on first draft reports for three students

Feedback Criterion	1. Natsumi	2. Chisako	3. Mariko
1. Content	Focused and relevant content. Essay shows you know the topic well. The BBC section doesn't fit well with the essay so you need to think about that part.	Content is focused on one main point, but the essay is too short. Ideas need to be developed into longer, stronger paragraphs. Some information is unnecessary.	The content is focused, but some ideas need to be better presented and developed. Some parts are difficult to read and understand.
2. Organization	Good organization. Structure is easy to follow. Intro and conclusion work well also. Again, the BBC section interrupts the flow of the essay.	Structure of the essay is organized but this also needs to be improved. A more clearly written thesis statement and concluding paragraph are essential.	Structure and main ideas need to be better organized. The thesis statement should be clearer. Summarizing main points in the conclusion is also important.
3. Language Use	Some problems here, but the essay is mostly easy to read and understand.	Expression of ideas is sometimes unclear. Better grammar/vocabulary will make the essay stronger.	Some serious problems with language use, communication often breaks down. You need to express your ideas more clearly.
4. Use of source material	Sources are effectively used and cited. Page numbers are needed with some in-text citations.	Sources are used and cited, too much perhaps at times (ex. final paragraph). More of your own analysis, commentary is needed.	While you do use source material effectively at times, your Works Cited page and in-text citations need to follow MLA format.
Overall	A good first draft Natsumi. Editing and revising should make it even stronger.	This is a rough draft, Chisako. It is focused and organized, but serious editing and revising are needed to make the essay longer and stronger.	Lots of work needed to turn this into an effective essay, Mariko. Do a good job on editing and revising for a better final draft.

essays may be considered typical of the style and amount of feedback I provide on essays for this JC course. As such, with regard to *this* teachers' formative feedback on student essays ('the class of events from which the case has been drawn'), the case study can provide insights regarding patterns of practice. However, noting a key limitation of case study research, Burns (2000) also warns that drawing any general conclusions from a case is 'rather hazardous'. Heeding this warning, any conclusions arising from this case study that may be more widely applicable to other teachers and contexts in general will be avoided.

Through the process of a self-assessment of written feedback practice in an academic writing course, this case study reports one teachers' reflective attempt to focus a spotlight on my written feedback practices and form a deeper understanding of what it is I do when responding to student writing. The set of 21 essay first drafts used as data sources, and the more than 800 feedback interventions they contain, provided a basis for critical reflection (Richards & Lockhart, 1994) and examination of my formative responses to student essays.

The results section above provides a detailed response to the primary focus of this reflective case study; examining the nature, form, and amount of feedback I provided to students on their essay first drafts. The close examination and description of the results described enabled me to find out what exactly I do when giving feedback on the set of essays comprising the 'complex bounded system' in this case study. Discovering and tabulating 828 feedback interventions on 21 essays, and the detailed classification of the types provided to students, has answered the initial research question posed and helped solve this particular 'puzzle of practice'. As the results section contains the answer to the research question posed, this discussion section will be limited to a short commentary of the more salient points evident from the data set, and patterns of my feedback responses uncovered in this reflective process.

First of all the sheer number of feedback interventions is quite surprising, with an average of 39 per essay. I had no idea that I was providing so much feedback on individual essays. The range of feedback for this class is also surprising; from 28 feedback interventions (Sachiko) to 58 FI's included in another paper (Aya), and the varying numbers of FI's in between for the other student writers. I consider the key reasons for this wide range to be related to both the English language proficiency and writing competency of individual students. Some students are simply more proficient English writers than others, and the amount and type of feedback provided to individuals on their essays is reflection of this fact.

A further surprise for me in counting and coding the feedback interventions comprising the data set for this investigation was the types of written feedback revealed by using Haines (2004) categorization system. The teacher commentary provided on first drafts was intended to promote student reflection about the slang topic and what they had written about it. As indicated in the results section, more than half (55%) of the feedback comments provided on the body of student essays were rhetorical questions. Here are a few such feedback examples from the essays:

- Do you 'think carefully' about when to use slang?
- If this negative image is the main feature of slang, why is it so popular and widely used?
- Is it illegal to use slang?
- In what way? The connection is not clear.

According to Black and Jones (2006), questions are useful ways of framing feedback comments because they initiate thinking, and their questioning nature encourages students to start improving on the work in question. As this investigation was a reflective exercise, I was not aware of this Black and James (2006) rationale for framing feedback in question format until much later than when the feedback was provided. Indeed, there was no plan to make use of a questioning format in the feedback, and I was quite surprised to see how extensively it was used across the entire set of 21 first drafts. I cannot identify why I adopted such a questioning form of commentary at the time of giving feedback, nor did I consciously intend to do so. Much later refection and speculation on a rationale (unconsciously held, perhaps) for this dominant pattern of feedback responses would be that it was hoped that such question-form commentary would serve as prompts for students' critical reflection on the current state of their essays (i.e. on what they had written, how the reader might interpret it, and whether intended meaning was effectively communicated or not).

It was also revealing to me to discover that of the 283 written comments I provided on the 21 essays, only 5 (2%) we identified and coded as praise commentary. One of the practical strategies recommended in the writing response literature summarized by Straub (2000), and delineated in Table 2 at the beginning of this report, was to 'make frequent use of praise'. The fact that I made very limited use of praise, in fact, raises another 'puzzle of practice' arising from this case study. It should be noted, however, that praise comments may be more common on the attached feedback reports that provide an overall formative assessment rather than feedback written on the essays themselves. Whether this is a fact was not investigated in the data analysis, but is indicated as a possibility in, for example, the overall comments provided to one student (Natsumi) recorded in Table 12 (i.e. e. "A good first draft Natsumi.").

After examining the results of my feedback practice for these 21 essays, I am also now in a position to respond to the second key question in the introduction: How do my feedback practices compare with those recommended in the feedback literature? I can now engage in a self-assessment of these practices, using best practices recommended by Gibbs and Simpson (2004-05). Those seven feedback conditions influencing learning listed in Table 2 of the Introduction section, are formatted as questions here for the purposes of reflecting on my feedback practices from a different perspective.

1. **Is Sufficient Feedback Provided, Both Often Enough and in Enough Detail?** Yes, students are provided with sufficient feedback, in terms of frequency and specificity. With respect to timing, one week after the first draft is submitted students receive feedback on it in the following class. Timing is crucial issue for feedback, the faster the better. Ideally, students would be able to receive teacher feedback within a few days of producing the first draft. This is not practically possible in such an academic writing setting as this, and dealing with more than 20, five-paragraph essays. Students receiving essay feedback one week later, is considered to be timely in this case. According to Gibbs and Simpson (2004-05), in order for feedback to be useful, it has to be quite specific. The writers of these 21 essays received a lot of detailed feedback through correction code symbols, teacher on-essay commentary, and the attached end sheet providing an overall formative evaluation of each script. The feedback is also specifically connected to the assessment criterion for the essay.

2. **Does the Feedback Focus on Students' Performance, on Their Learning and Actions Under Their Control (Rather Than on Students Themselves and Their Characteristics)?** The feedback provided does focus on the essay produced. The feedback, guided by the assessment criteria, is focused on the skills and knowledge that students need to develop (e.g. MLA documentation). The essay editing and revising process is under the students' control, and the final version produced is directly related to how much effort students put into this process of making the final draft of the essay stronger. Through the feedback provided, students are informed "where they have gone wrong and what they can do about it" (Gibbs & Simpson, 2004-05, p. 18). Gibbs and Simpson also note

the fact that when personal characteristics are tied with critical feedback it can have a negative effect on students' sense of competence, or self-efficacy. For this JC slang essay, data analysis shows that feedback is not directed toward students themselves; it is task-focused, rather than ego-focused. One minor exception is the use of student names in the overall comment at the bottom of the end sheet, which may serve to create the impression of 'a conversation' with each student about their work. In any case, the feedback provided is performance-focused, not student-focused

3. **Is the Feedback Timely, Received by the Students While It Still Matters to Them?** Yes, students receive a host of feedback about their performance, while that performance is still going on. The feedback is directly of import to the final draft of the essay they must produce one week after the formative feedback has been received. The teacher feedback provided on the essay first draft can be used to improve the 'work-in-progress'. In his seminal article about formative assessment, Sadler (1989) wrote that an essential condition for improvement is that the student "is able to monitor continuously the quality of what is being produced *during the act of production itself*"(p. 121, emphasis in original). Gibbs and Simpson also note that feedback must be relevant to ongoing work for it to be most meaningful.

4. **Is the Feedback Appropriate to the Purpose of the Assignment and to Its Criteria for Success?** In this particular case, the focus of the essay was to produce a good five-paragraph research essay based on at least three sources. Particular focus was paid to use of source material and MLA documentation. The feedback provided was appropriate to these assignment purposes, and was directly related to them. The feedback end sheet, in particular, emphasized the key criterion (content, organization, language use, use of source material) and teacher comments included here informed students clearly of essay expectations (e.g. 'Works Cited page and in-text referencing do not follow MLA format.'). In order to orient themselves effectively to the assignment task, student understanding of success criteria is important (Gibbs & Simpson, 2005-05). Sadler (1989) also deemed it essential "that the student comes to hold a concept of quality roughly similar to that held by the teacher" (p.21). First draft feedback provided on the slang essay was directly related to assignment purposes and success criterion.

5. **Is Feedback Appropriate, In Relation, to Students' Understanding of What They Are Supposed to Be Doing?** Gibbs and Simpson (2004-05) tell us that "Feedback needs to be sensitive to what kind of writing is expected and what students are likely to understand about it" (p23). The task presented to students for this slang-topic essay, including the choice of essay questions and teacher expectation of student knowledge and usage of the related slang source material, is clearly laid out for students. The feedback provided is also appropriate to their understanding of the slang topic and ability to write a clear research essay focused on the question they had selected. It should be remembered that this was the fourth essay students had written (and received feedback on) in this JC course; students were quite clear as to 'what they were supposed to be doing' and the feedback provided was appropriately focused.

6. **Is Feedback Received and Attended To?** A number of studies have described students paying little or no attention to (summative) feedback provided by teachers, a point of much frustration and irritation for the feedback provider. Gibbs and Simpson (2004-05) identify a number of steps that can be taken to engage students with feedback, including "using two-stage assignments with feedback on the first stage, intended to enable the student to improve that quality of work for a second stage submission, which is only graded" (p. 24). According to Cooper (2000), such an assessment system, synergizing formative and summative elements, can improve the performance

of almost all students, especially the weaker ones. This slang essay (as with all JC papers) was a two-stage assignment, and as such feedback was received by students and attended to in the editing and revising process.

7. **Is Feedback Acted Upon by Students?** Yes. As noted, students are given feedback in sufficient time and quantity to edit and revise their first draft. The class in which first drafts are returned is always designated as an 'editing/revising workshop' in the essay production cycle. This is the beginning of the re-writing process, and over the coming days students work on improving their essay prior to submission of the final draft in the following weeks' class. James (2006) writes: "Only learners can do the learning, so they need to act upon information and feedback if their learning is to improve" (p. 8). JC students did engage with the feedback provided, often making extensive revisions (and improvements) between first and final drafts.

According to Gibbs and Simpson (2004-05), feedback works best to support learning when these seven conditions are adhered to. My written feedback practice in this JC course meets all seven of these standards, and, as such, is supportive of student learning and their efforts to be better academic essay writers.

With regard to judging the effectiveness of formative assessment, Yorke (2003, p. 483-484) poses the following question: "Is what the assessor has done regarding feedback the best that could have been done (or-more weakly-reasonable in the circumstances)?"

While perhaps there is room for improvement with regard to my feedback practices (e. g. an improved correction code, more praise comments for effective writing), considering the context of this third-year writing class at a Japanese university, and the numbers of students and amount of writing to respond to, I am satisfied that the feedback provided was at least 'reasonable in the circumstances'.

This case study has been an example of reflective practice, but such a process is a means rather than an end in itself. Akbari (2007) reminds us that, "From a practical viewpoint, it must be borne in mind that reflection is not an end, but a means to an end; the end sought is better student learning and more efficient teacher performance." (p. 204).

Improved student learning and more effective teaching are indeed worthy goals to pursue, and this investigation reports on one step of this teacher/researcher's journey down that road. As noted in the introduction, this area of teacher self-assessment of feedback practices has been very little explored by researchers or classroom teachers. There is much to be learned from exploring the terrain together, and hearing other voices and experiences from teachers exploring their feedback practices. Perhaps making such individual reflective practice projects as this one become one of various TSA experiences that become published accounts, we can develop into more of a collaborative practice in reflective language teaching. In this way we can learn with and from each other, as well as from the students that we teach.

V. CONCLUSION

Thus, the critical educator will see him/herself as a co-worker with students in pursuit of education rather than a provider of knowledge for passive recipients. (Grundy, 1989, p. 96)

This reflective case study, involving teacher self-assessment of feedback on writing, focused on gaining a clearer picture of the form and nature of the feedback I provided on a set of essays by a group of 21

Japanese writers, and whether my practices aligned with those recommended the feedback literature. The case study forms part of a larger doctoral investigation into putting assessment for learning (AfL) into practice in an EFL context with adult learners. A key element of AfL theory and practice is the idea that the teacher is also a learner in the classroom, and assessment for *teacher* learning is a central theme in this report. This reflective case study documents my attempts to become a more 'critical educator' through the self-assessment of my written feedback practices. Among other things, it has resulted in, and reinforced, my feeling of also being a learner in the courses I teach; 'a co-worker with students in pursuit of education', as Grundy (1989) phrases it.

But such a teacher self-assessment as described here is a not a summative activity, but a formative one (McColskey & Egelson, 1993), in which improvement in pedagogic understanding and practice is seen as an ongoing, continuous process. Just as AfL is firmly grounded in a constructivist theory of learning (see, for example, James et al., 2007), my learning about effective feedback provision, and the realities of my own practice, is knowledge that is being continuously constructed and refined. According to Lambert and Coombs (1998, p. 10):

Learning is a constructive process that occurs best when what is being learned is relevant and meaningful to the learner and when the learner is actively engaged in creating his or her own knowledge and understanding by connecting what is being learned with prior knowledge and experience.

As an ESL/EFL instructor and specialist in classroom-based assessment, I also see myself as being actively engaged in becoming both a more effective teacher and an even more assessment literate professional. As such, my ongoing learning about effective feedback and assessment is indeed 'relevant and meaningful'.

As noted, this case study is one of the few such examples in the feedback literature of a teacher engaging in an examination of feedback practices that is systematic and objective (as far as possible in any such *self* - assessment, which is, by definition, a subjective process). This case study is a reflective assessment of my own behavior as a feedback provider. Perhaps, it may also provide a possible framework or model for other teachers to follow in order to closely examine their own feedback practices, and describe what the observed behaviors and patterns reveal.

As baseball icon, and purveyor of unintended wisdom, Yogi Berra noted, "You can see a lot by watching." As critical educators and language teaching professionals, our understanding of the provision of effective feedback to students on their writing will benefit from other teachers publishing accounts, such as this one, of closely watching their feedback practices and systematically describing what they see and do. By doing so we become learners in our classrooms, working with our students in pursuit of education.

REFERENCES

Airasian, P., & Gullickson, A. (1997). *Teacher Self-Evaluation Tool Kit*. London: Corwin Press, Inc.

Akbari, R. (2007). A critical appraisal of reflective practice in L2 teacher education. *System, 35*, 192–207. doi:10.1016/j.system.2006.12.008

Amidon, E., & Flanders, N. (1967). *The Role of the Teacher in the Classroom: A Manual for Understanding and Improving Teacher Classroom Behavior*. Minneapolis: Association for Productive Teaching.

Ashby, E. (1984). Forward. In *I.M. Brewer, Learning More and Teaching Less*. Guildford: Society for Research into Higher Education.

Black, P., Harrison, C., Lee, C., Marshall, B., & Wiliam, D. (2003). *Assessment for Learning: Putting it Into Practice*. Berkshire, England: Open University Press.

Black, P., & Jones, J. (2006). Formative assessment and the learning and teaching of MFL: Sharing the language learning road map with the learners. *Language Learning Journal*, *34*(1), 4–9. doi:10.1080/09571730685200171

Black, P., & William, D. (1998a). Assessment and classroom learning. *Assessment in Education: Principles, Policy & Practice*, *5*(1), 7–74. doi:10.1080/0969595980050102

Brown, E., & Glover, C. (2006). Evaluating written feedback. In C. Bryan & K. Clegg (Eds.), *Innovative Assessment in Higher Education* (pp. 81–91). New York: Routledge.

Burns, R. (2000). Introducing Research (4th ed.). French's Forest, NSW: Pearson.

Gibbs, G., & Simpson, C. (2004-05). Conditions under which assessment supports learning. *Learning and Teaching in Higher Education*, *1*, 3–29.

Grundy, S. (1989). Beyond Professionalism. In W. Carr (Ed.), Quality in Teaching: Arguments for a Reflective Profession (pp. 79-100). London: Falmer Press.

Haines, C. (2004). *Assessing Students Written Work: Marking Essays and Reports*. London: Routledge-Falmer. doi:10.4324/9780203465110

Harford, J., & MacRuairc, G. (2008). Engaging student teachers in meaningful reflective practice. *Teaching and Teacher Education*, *24*(7), 1884–1892. doi:10.1016/j.tate.2008.02.010

Hattie, J., & Timperly, H. (2007). The power of feedback. *Review of Educational Research*, *77*(1), 81–112. doi:10.3102/003465430298487

Hyland, K. (2003). *Second Language Writing*. Cambridge: Cambridge University Press. doi:10.1017/CBO9780511667251

Hyland, K., & Hyland, F. (2006). Feedback on second language students' writing. *Language Teaching*, *39*(02), 83–101. doi:10.1017/S0261444806003399

Hyland, K., & Hyland, F. (Eds.). (2006). *Feedback in Second Language Writing: Contexts and Issues*. Cambridge: Cambridge University Press. doi:10.1017/CBO9781139524742

Kirszner, L., & Mandell, S. (2006). *The Pocket Wadsworth Handbook* (3rd ed.). Boston: Thomson Wadsworth.

Kluger, A. N., & DeNisi, A. (1996). The effects of feedback interventions on perfor-mance: A historical review, a meta-analysis, and a preliminary feedback intervention theory. *Psychological Bulletin*, *119*(2), 254–284. doi:10.1037/0033-2909.119.2.254

Lambert, N., & Coombs, B. (1998). *How students learn: Reforming Schools through Learner-centered Education*. Washington: American Psychological Association. doi:10.1037/10258-000

Lucas, P. (1991). Reflection, new practices and the need for flexibility in supervising student-teachers. *Journal of Further and Higher Education, 15*(2), 84–93. doi:10.1080/0309877910150209

McColskey, W., & Egelson, P. (1993). *Designing Teacher Evaluation Systems that Support Professional Growth*. Greensboro, N.C: University of North Carolina at Greensboro, South Eastern Regional Vision for Education.

McCormack, J., & Slaght, J. (2005). *Extended Writing and Research Skills, Teachers Book*. Reading, UK: Garnet Publishing Ltd.

Montgomery, J., & Baker, W. (2007). Teacher written feedback: Student perceptions, teacher self-assessment and actual teacher performance. *Journal of Second Language Writing, 16*(2), 82–99. doi:10.1016/j.jslw.2007.04.002

Nicol, D., & Macfarlane-Dick, D. (2006). Formative assessment and self-regulated learning: A model and seven principles of good feedback practice. *Studies in Higher Education, 31*(2), 199–218. doi:10.1080/03075070600572090

O'Brian, T. (2004). Writing in a foreign language: Teaching and learning. *Language Teaching, 37*(1), 1–28. doi:10.1017/S0261444804002113

Ramaprasad, A. (1983). On the definition of feedback. *Behavioral Science, 28*(1), 4–13. doi:10.1002/bs.3830280103

Richards, J., & Lockhart, C. (1994). *Reflective Teaching in Second Language Classrooms*. New York: Cambridge University Press. doi:10.1017/CBO9780511667169

Sadler, R. (1989). Formative Assessment and the Design of Instructional Systems. *Instructional Science, 18*(2), 119–144. doi:10.1007/BF00117714

Schon, D. A. (1983). *The Reflective Practitioner*. New York: Basic Books.

Schon, D. A. (1987). *Educating the Reflective Practitioner*. San Francisco: Jossey-Bass.

Shute, V. (2008). Focus on formative feedback. *Review of Educational Research, 78*(1), 153–189. doi:10.3102/0034654307313795

Stern, L., & Solomon, A. (2006). Effective faculty feedback: The road less traveled. *Assessing Writing, 11*(1), 22–41. doi:10.1016/j.asw.2005.12.001

Stiggins, R. (2007). Conquering the formative assessment frontier. In J. McMillan (Ed.), *Formative Classroom Assessment: Theory into Practice* (pp. 8–27). New York: Teachers College Press, Colombia University.

Straub, R. (2000). The student, the text, and the classroom context: A case study of teacher response. *Academic Writing, 7*, 23–55.

Wiggins, G. (1993). *Assessing Student Performance*. San Francisco: Jossey-Bass.

Woodside, A. (2010). *Case Study Research: Theory, Methods, Practice*. London: Emerald Group Publishing Limited.

Yin, R. (2009). *Case Study Research* (4th ed.). London: SAGE Inc.

Yorke, M. (2003). Formative assessment in higher education: Moves towards theory and enhancement of pedagogic practice. *Higher Education, 45*(4), 477–501. doi:10.1023/A:1023967026413

APPENDIX A

Essay Final Draft Assessment Rubric, Front Page
(Adapted from McCormack & Slaght, 2005)

Table 13. Research paper assessment: Final draft

Student name:														
Letter Grade		E		D			C			B			A	
Mark as (%)	Below 60%	60-62	63-66	67-69	70-72	73-76	77-79	80-82	83-86	87-89	90-92	93-96	97-100	
Performance Level	VERY LIMITED		WEAK			FAIR			GOOD			EXCELLENT		
1. Content														
2. Organization														
3. Language use (vocabulary, grammar)														
4. Use of source material														
Overall grade: _____														
Comments:														

APPENDIX B

Essay Final Draft Assessment Rubric, Back Page
(Adapted from McCormack & Slaght, 2005)

1. Content

Clearly focused content, relevant to the essay topic. Length, scope and level of detail are appropriate/relevant. Arguments are well presented and developed with supporting evidence from a variety of sources. It is evident that the writer knows the topic well.	A
Generally well-focused content. May be lacking in level of detail or development of ideas and/or limited in scope (which may affect length). Much of the content describes rather than critically analyzes. Arguments/main ideas may be inconsistent or insufficiently developed.	B
At times, essay focus may be lost; some content may be irrelevant. Clearly limited in level of detail, superficial treatment of subject with no development of ideas. Shows lack of knowledge of the topic. May be very short. Little or no evidence of evaluation of ideas, mostly at level of describing. No clear argument/thesis evident.	C
No obvious focus; clearly content inadequately researched; unable to deal with topic (probably very short) or widespread plagiarism has made it impossible to assess true level of the essay. Too much personal/anecdotal material.	D / F

2. Organization

Overall structure and main ideas are clearly organized and easy to follow. Introduction has general topical sentences, followed by a well-written thesis statement. In the body of the essay, supporting ideas are effectively linked together and "flow" coherently making it easy for the reader to follow. Conclusion summarizes main points and effectively brings the essay to a finish.	**A**
Overall structure and main ideas are generally easy to see. Introduction and conclusion are appropriately linked to the main body. At times there may be a tendency to move from one idea to another with no attempt to link them.	**B**
Difficult for reader to determine overall structure/identify main ideas. May be due to poor language control (i.e. grammar, vocabulary), which also affects cohesion. Introduction/conclusion may be inadequate. Frequent move from one idea to another with no attempt to link them.	**C**
Ineffective attempt to organize the essay. Very difficult for the reader to follow the text. The introduction fails to give the reader an overview/clear idea of what will follow or widespread plagiarism has made it impossible to assess true level of the essay	**D / F**

3. Language Use

Ideas are clearly expressed, with wide, accurate usage of vocabulary and grammar. Any errors do not interfere with communication. Formal academic style used (e.g. formal expressions, longer sentences, impersonal tone, etc.) Use of a range of linking words and phrases to join ideas at paragraph and sentence level.	**A**
Ideas are usually clearly expressed. Linking of ideas within paragraphs generally appropriate, but at times may be lacking between sections. Some vocabulary and/or grammar problems, but generally do not interfere with communication. Spelling and or punctuation errors do not interfere with comprehension.	**B**
Some ideas are simply expressed, but others are not clearly expressed. Linking between and within sentences may be inconsistent. Fairly serious vocabulary and/or grammar problems; can interfere with communication. Spelling and/or punctuation may be seriously flawed.	**C**
The level of vocabulary and grammar is so consistently weak that the end product fails to achieve it's purpose due to ineffective communication (or widespread plagiarism has made it impossible to assess the true level of the essay).	**D / F**

4. Use of Source Material

Effective use of a range of sources. These are appropriately incorporated in the body of the essay through paraphrase/quotation/summary. Shows ability to synthesize well from several sources to support ideas. Works Consulted page and in-text referencing follow MLA conventions and a range of sources are used. No obvious/conscious plagiarism.	**A**
Effective use of sources, mostly when summarizing/paraphrasing ideas clearly. Shows some evidence of synthesis of information. Works Consulted and use of sources show an understanding of the concept of referencing, though this is not always followed (e.g., not in alphabetical order, name of publisher missing, in-text references include first name, etc.). No obvious/ conscious plagiarism.	**B**
Limited sources used, and summary/paraphrase of ideas not always clear. Some attempt at synthesis of ideas. Clearly has problems writing a Works Consulted page and incorporating in-text sources in an appropriate way, although there is some attempt to do this. Poor language control (grammar, vocabulary) may be a factor. Suspicion of plagiarism in some sections.	**C**
Inadequate attempt to use source material, e.g., may only use one source or none. Content based mainly on student's views with little or no evidence to support it. Shows little understanding of the importance of referencing and academic writing conventions. No Works Consulted page, or, where this exists, does not follow appropriate MLA format.	**D / F**

Chapter 10
Feedforward. The Key to Improve Learning in Higher Education

Maite Fernández-Ferrer
University of Barcelona, Spain

Laura Pons-Seguí
University of Barcelona, Spain

ABSTRACT

In higher education context, it is important to stimulate feedback and students' self-regulation. Shute (2007) ensures that giving a formative feedback means to communicate information to the students to change their thinking or behavior in order to improve their learning. This improvement through constant feedback has been the basis of the experience presented below. The work presented here is part of the project "Design, implementation and evaluation of proposals for sustainable feedforward" (reference REDICE2014-966), funded by the Institute of Education Sciences at the University of Barcelona, which aims to design and implement feedforward practices in different degrees at the Spanish universities participating in the project. The analysis of this research highlights what kind of feedback is being implemented in higher education and which the perceptions of students and teachers relating to the implemented practices and the obtained results are.

INTRODUCTION

The Higher Education European framework has placed the student in the center of the learning process. This new approach has defined the teaching process in terms of students' learning outcomes, by looking for the coherence between these learning outcomes, the tasks and the assessment (Biggs, 2003).

In this context, the feedback is a process that enables students to obtain information about their work in order to identify some general guidelines that can be applied in any kind of task or project. Moreover, the feedback makes possible students can recognize the strengths of their task so that they can elaborate

DOI: 10.4018/978-1-5225-0531-0.ch010

a better work (Boud & Molloy, 2013:6). When the students are given the necessary information to correct their errors, teachers are guiding their students so that they can acquire the contents (Shute, 2008).

There are several studies that have proven feedback has a relevant impact on students learning (Black & Wiliam, 1998). Feedback plays a key role to decrease the gap between what the students currently know and their learning goals (Sadler, 1989; Mory, 2003; Poulos & Mahony, 2008). Therefore, the fact that feedback is effective or is significant for the student's learning and performance (Carless, Salter, Yang & Lam, 2011). Moreover, feedback can improve students' confidence and motivation to learn (Yuan & Kim, 2015).

Thereby, feedback is one of the most powerful education strategies that is related to the student's success (Boud, 2000; Nicol, Thomson & Breslin, 2014). Provide feedback to the students can be a key strategy to build their knowledge reflectively (Nicol, 2013) provided that the student knows what to do with this feedback, as well as, he internalizes professors' messages so that he can self-assess his work. Hence, provide feedback is one of the educative strategies that can have a major impact on student's success and in his learning improvement. Feedback can be provided by the professor or the students. However, previous research has proven that professors' feedback tends to be more accurate and provides more information (Luo & Gao, 2012).

In this context, a lot of research has been conducted to improve learning and teaching process through feedback. However, it is necessary to take into account that exist some important characteristics that determinate if a feedback is effective or not (Yuan & Kim, 2015). The first element is *the content of the feedback*. Feedback is effective when the content provided is specific (Mory, 2003; Hattie & Timperley, 2007) and it should inform students about their learning goals and how to improve their work (Yuan & Kim, 2015). A second element is the *timing of the feedback*. When the feedback is not provided regularly enough, the students tend to lose interest in it and focus their attention on something new (Gibbs & Simpson, 2003). A third aspect is *the dialogue through feedback*. The students must understand the feedback in order to use it (Price, 2005), even though, in many cases, it is too difficult for the students to understand it. Fourthly, the *source of feedback* is also important. In general, feedback is more effective when it comes from different sources and not just from a single one (Brinko, 1993). Finally, it is important the student *follow-up with feedback*. That is, for an effective feedback, the students need to act towards it, although feedback is not well-used or not used in some occasions (Bloxham & Campbell, 2010). To motivate students to use the feedback, students could ask their students to revise their work based on the feedback received to rewrite the work and send it again to the teacher (Covic & Jones, 2008).

According to Hounsell, McCune, Litjens and Hounsell (2008) a good feedback must have the following four characteristics:

1. Involve the students to define what a high-quality result is.
2. Motivate the students to develop self-assessment and self-regulation skills.
3. Enable students to set their goals and plan their learning process.
4. Promote assessment tasks that increase students' agreement and dedication.

As Boud and Molloy (2013) have highlighted, feedback is key nowadays due to students' diversity and professional profiles but, above all, due to the continuous learning framework. Feedback is really important not only for those who receive the feedback, but also for those who provide it. Feedback specially helps students to develop collaborative competencies because they have to assess their classmates work from a critical perspective (Nicol & MacFarlane, 2005; Boud & Molloy, 2013).

Consequently, one of the main objectives of Higher Education is the development of the capacity to self-assess one's work and detect the areas that need to be improved without being told and assessed by a professor. Nicol (2010) confirms that this capacity of a self-regulated learning is essential for Higher Education students. Nicol (2010) proposes the High-Impact Assessment and Feedback Activities (HIA-FAs), a group of evaluation activities that promote the development of self-regulated learning.

This self-regulation can be defined as a process that helps students to structure their learning tasks through appropriate cognitive, affective and behavior adjustments (Boekaerts, 1999). Moreover, the students that are self-regulating their learning effectively, they also have a better academic performance (Pressley & Ghatala, 1990; Pressley & Harris, 2006; White & Frederiksen, 2005). To emphasize this idea, Boud and Molloy (2013) collected the six elements that improve the efficacy of the feedback focused on self-regulation: capacity to create an inner feedback; the ability to self-assess; the students' availability to invest time and effort to analyze and incorporate the feedback; the level of confidence in the answers; the assignment of success or failure and the capacity to ask for help.

The formative self-evaluation aims to reflect on the own work and know and have a good perception of what is correct and what needs to be improved (Boud, 2000). It is the capacity to criticize how you have done something and detect the errors in order to use the next time more of what worked and less of what did not work previously. It is an evaluation that allows to wonder about what you have done (the process) and how well you have done it (the product). In general, students with higher capacity tend to underestimate their performance, whereas students with a lower capacity overestimate it. Moreover, students with a lower capacity have problems to self-assess their work accurately and correctly taking into account that the main aspect is not that students and professors agree, but the learner knows how to self-evaluate himself appropriately (Weimeer, 2014).

Therefore, there is a new link between feedback and formative assessment. Several studies explain how feedback promotes self-assessment based on defined criteria (Bollag, 2006). Furthermore, Shute, Hansen and Almond (2007) ensures that the formative feedback means communicating information to the student so as to modify their thought or behavior to improve their learning.

A higher stage in the process of formative assessment is the feedforward. Feedforward implies the students use the feedback they have received in future tasks with the aim to promote their learning (Rae & Cochrane, 2008) and improve their work (Boud & Molloy, 2013). Moreover, the feedforward has some advantages in comparison with the traditional feedback. Feedback tends to be one-way, finalist and generic, whereas feedforward is a spiral feedback. Consequently, the feedforward should enable to anticipate the criteria for a future task and the students have an active role in his learning process (Boud & Molloy, 2013):

The goal of the feedforward is to guide the students to use the feedback from a task to the following tasks, therefore, encourage the student learning (Rae & Cochrane, 2008:226)

It's a process through which the students gather information about their work in order to appreciate the similarities and differences between the appropriate criteria and the strengths of the work with the aim to generate a better task (Boud & Molloy, 2013:6)

In short, the work that is presented here is based on what the international bibliography has defined as good practices in the processes of providing feedback to the students (Hounsell et al., 2008; Narciss,

2008; Carless, Salter, Yang & Lam, 2010; Nicol, 2011; Boud & Molloy, 2013). This improvement through continuous feedback has been the base of this experience.

This experience has offered the opportunity to the students to improve their learning through an external feedback, encouraging them to use this feedback about their work to produce another piece of it but with higher standards (Boud, 2000). This experience is based in the value of providing feedback to the students to facilitate the improvement of their learning and qualifications, investigating the extent to which this experience has a positive impact on the future tasks of the students to complete the feedback's wheel (Sadler, 1989) and students and professors' opinions and perceptions.

METHODOLOGY

Context

In the framework of the use of feedback as a strategy to improve the learning, this article presents part of the investigation "Design, implementation and evaluation of sustainable feedforward proposals" funded by the Institute of Education Science from the University of Barcelona and carried out during the years 2014-2015.

It is a biannual Project (2014-2016) coordinated by the university of Barcelona in which other universities participate. These universities are: The Open University of Catalonia (UOC), the University of the Balearic Islands (UIB), the university Rovira i Virgili (URV), the technical university of Catalonia (UPC), the Autonomous university of Barcelona (UAB) and the university of Barcelona (UB) (table 1):

The aim of this Project is to implement and evaluate different feedforward proposals. For this reason, several proposals of continuous assessment with a formative end were designed. It was planned the work evidences that would be collected and the type of feedback that would be provided.

The objectives of this Project are:

Table 1. Universities participanting and a brief summary of the experiences developed

University	Subject	Semestre	Degree	Credits	Number of Students
UB	TFG (final projecte of the degree)	8th	Primary Education	6	15
UB	Organization and Educative institutions management	3r	Pedagogy	6	65
UB	Design and interactive production	2n	Master of teaching and learning environments mediated by ICT	6	20
UIB	TFG (final projecte of the degree)	8è	Kindergarten Education	6	40
UAB	Organization and the groups	1r. i 2n.	Pedagogy and Social Education	12	80
UOC	Practicum I i/o Practicum II	7è	Psicopedagogy	6	15
UPC	Mathematics	1r.	Biosystems engineering	6	160
URV	Cross-curricular Project (2nd year)	3r. i 4t.	Pedagogy and Social Education	4,5	63
URV	Advice and guidance in Education	5è i 6è	Pedagogy	12	25

- To know students' and professors' perceptions about the feedforward practices.
- To contrast the perceptions of the people involved in this experience.
- To analyze if exists a correlation between students' perception and students' academic performance.
- To analyze if there are correlation between the perceptions of the students and the professors with the feedforward typology implemented.

Even though the group of researchers has already worked on different proposals to provide feedback, in this occasion the challenge was to analyze the use the students made of the feedback received and the extent to which it helped them to address the following tasks. For this reason, each university decided the subject in which they would develop the experience and designed the system to provide feedback, as well as, the agents involved in this process (feedback via Moodle, peer-assessment, etc.).

Therefore, the professors of each university have designed, implemented and assess their own feedforward proposals in some of their subjects during the academic year 2014-2015. Each experience developed their own mechanisms to verify the provided feedback had been useful and if it was evident in their production or their future tasks. Hence, all the experiences asked different versions from the same task, aiming to improve the quality of the first version according to the suggestions made by the professor or a classmate.

Method and Instruments

All these variables have been used to analyze the effect of this experience on student's motivation, learning improvement, students' perception of their own learning and performance. This research has used a mix-methods approach using quantitative and qualitative methods to collect the data and analyze it. The strategies and instruments used were:

1. A satisfaction and learning perception of the students' questionnaire.
2. Professors' opinion questionnaire.
3. Documentary analysis of the feedforward evidences.
4. Analysis of the feedforward content.
5. Comparative analysis of the academic results (with other groups or other courses).

Even though each experience was different, all of them used the same questionnaire and rubric to analyze the feedback qualitatively. Both questionnaires (students and professors' questionnaire) assessed the satisfaction relative to this experience. There was a specific section about the feedback and aspects relative to the learning assessment and competencies development. This section used a 6-point Likert scale (1-strongly disagree, 6- extremely agree) so that participants could rate the degree of agreement or disagreement with each statement. The questionnaires also included three open-ended questions so that participants could express their opinion.

On the other hand, there were two versions of the students' questionnaire since there were experiences that used peer-feedback and others who did not. For this reason, the experiences using peer-feedback included a section that intended to analyze the intention of the feedback provided to their peers. This section was added in order to contrast it to the section about the intention of the feedback received that both versions of the questionnaire shared.

Data Analysis

The analysis of the results is focused on the answers obtained in professors' questionnaire (n=14) and students' questionnaire (n=247). Moreover, the results analyzed here are divided in two parts. A general analysis of participants' degree of satisfaction and opinion will be presented in the first part where quantitative and qualitative data analysis is used. In the second part, the students' perceptions about the characteristics of the feedback provided and received are explored using a quantitative analysis.

Non-parametric tests are used to analyze quantitative data in order to explore significant differences between means, main effects of categories, as well as, correlations. On the other hand, qualitative methods have been used to explore the open-ended questions. Participants' answers were coded and categorized into meaning categories. The categories are:

1. Assessment
    a. Feedback
    b. Peer-assessment
    c. Tracking
2. Characteristics of the task
    a. Tool (Twitter, Moodle, Blog…)
    b. Teamwork
3. Regularity
    a. Continuity
4. Self-regulation
    a. Get involved
    b. Reflection
    c. Go further
5. Learning
6. Motivation
7. Amount of work

In short, here we present a general overview of the professors and students' opinion and perception of the feedforward in the students' learning process and performance.

RESULTS

Professors and Students' Perceptions about the Feedforward Experience.

One of the aims of this study was to inquiry the degree to which the formative assessment had a positive effect on the students' learning process and the acquisition of competencies. For this reason, the students and the university professors were asked to answer a questionnaire about the feedforward experience they were involved.

As for the degree of participants' satisfaction, quantitative analysis is based on the data gathered in the closed-ended questions from the questionnaire.

Figure 1. Participants' opinion mean

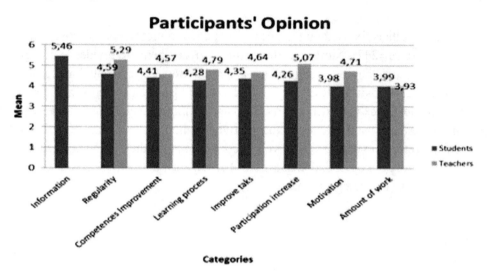

Figure 1 shows students and professors' reported means for each of the categories explored. In general, professors tended to perceive the feedforward experience as more positive than students did. The items that got a higher score on the part of the professors was the regularity between each feedback provided (mean 5.29) followed by the students' increase of participation (5.07). However, the students considered that the most positive aspect of this experience was the information provided about the experience (mean 5.46). Moreover, students' considered that the regularity with which the feedback was provided (mean 4.59) was another of the strengths of this experience.

On the contrary, the categories the professors rated with a lower score were the amount of work (mean 3.93) this experience involved and competencies improvement (mean 4.57). It seems professors consider this formative assessment increased considerably their amount of work. However, this increase of work did not imply students improved their competencies. According to the students, the amount of work the feedforward experience involved was the main weakness of this experience (mean 3.99). In addition, they did not think this formative assessment increased their motivation towards the subject (mean 3.98).

Several Independent Mann-Whitney U tests were run in order to analyze if there was a significance difference between professors and students' means for each category analyzed. The results revealed that there was only a significant difference between professors and students' mean for motivation item (Mean. Professors=4.71 vs. Mean. Students=3.98; $U=1270$, z=-2.834, $p=.005$), but not for the rest of the categories.

Several related Samples Friedman's Two-Way of variance analysis tests were run in order to know if there was a main effect of category for professors' scores. The results showed that there was not a main effect of category ($\chi2(6)=8,665$, $p=.193$). Therefore, there were not significant differences across categories, meaning that professors believed these feedforward experiences allowed students to improve their learning, the task, the competencies, their motivation and their participation up to the same extend. However, the fact that the category amount of work got a similar mean score as the other categories means that, even though these experiences increases professors amount of work, it is not perceived as something negative.

The same procedure was followed to analyze any main effect of category for students' scores. It was found that there was a main effect of category ($\chi2(7)=84,935$, $p<.001$). The all pairwise comparisons with the significant values (p) adjusted to the number of comparisons revealed that there was a significant difference between motivation and learning process ($p=.010$), competencies improvement ($p<.001$), tasks improvement ($p<.001$), participation increase ($p=0.23$), information ($p<.001$) and regularity ($p<.001$) scores. Moreover, there is a significant difference between the amount of work scores and competencies improvement ($p=.002$), task improvement ($p<.001$), information ($p<.001$) and regularity ($p<.001$). Hence, students believed the feedforward experience increased significantly their amount of work, but not their motivation towards de subject. In addition, students considered this experience had enabled them to improve their learning process, tasks, competencies and participation to the same extend.

Moreover, it was also analyzed if there was any significant correlation between the categories regularity of the feedback provided, competencies improvement, learning process and task improvement. Several Spearman's rho tests were run. It was found a significant positive correlation for professors' scores between competencies and task improvement ($r=.527$, $p=.030$) and learning process and task improvement ($r=.620$, $p=.008$). However, there was not a significant correlation between competencies improvement and learning process ($r=.300$; $p=.242$). Consequently, professors believed the feedforward allowed improving the task, but not necessarily the competencies and the learning process at the same time.

On the other hand, students' scores highly correlate for competencies improvement and learning process ($r=.811$, $p<.001$); competencies improvement and task improvement ($r=.739$, $p<.001$) and learning process and task improvement ($r=.702$, $p<.001$). Finally, regularity scores significantly correlate with competencies improvement ($r=.463$, $p<.001$) and task improvement ($r=.426$, $p<.001$). Therefore, students considered the feedforward enable them to improve the task, their learning process and their competencies. However, the more frequent the feedback, the more they perceived they improved their task and competencies.

Several Spearman's rho tests were run with the purpose to explore if there was a relationship between the categories participation, motivation and amount of work. In terms of professors' scores, there was a significant positive correlation between motivation and participation increase ($r=.511$, $p=.036$) but not between the other categories. This means that professors believed the more motivated the students were, the more their participation increased.

As for the students, participation increase scores significantly correlate with motivation ($r=.702$, $p<.001$) and amount of work ($r=.418$, $p<.001$). Likewise, motivation scores significantly correlate with amount of work ($r=.560$, $p<.001$). Students thought the least amount of work, the more motivated they were and the more their participation increase. As in the case of the professors, the more motivated the students were, the more they participated.

The open-ended questions of the questionnaire were analyzed qualitatively. For this reason, different meaning categories were created and validated. The first open-ended question aimed at exploring what positive aspects had the feedforward experience. According to the professors (figure 2), the aspect they considered more positive was the regularity with which the feedback was provided. The professors also considered that one of the strengths of this experience was the feedback provided. Moreover, they reported that the feedforward process allowed the students to go further, get involved and reflect on their own practice:

I think that receiving comments about the aspects that should be improved, as well as, planning specific sessions to give and receive feedback is beneficial for the students (UB_4).

Figure 2. Positive aspects of the feedforward experience according to the professors.

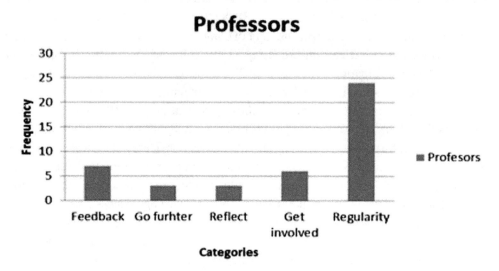

The fact that the students knew their work would be read and assessed by their classmates caused the students' made a bigger effort to do a great job (UAB_2).

The students received feedback regularly after finishing each topic. Moreover, they had the chance to apply it into future tasks (UB_2).

According to the students (figure 3), the feedforward process is one the main strength of this experience, followed by the characteristics of the activity. Furthermore, the students believed the feedforward process increased their motivation towards the subject and the activity. Finally, the students thought this

Figure 3. Positive aspects of the feedforward experience according to the professors.

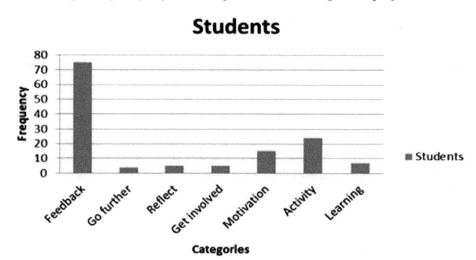

Figure 4. The positivist aspect of the feedforward experience according to the professors.

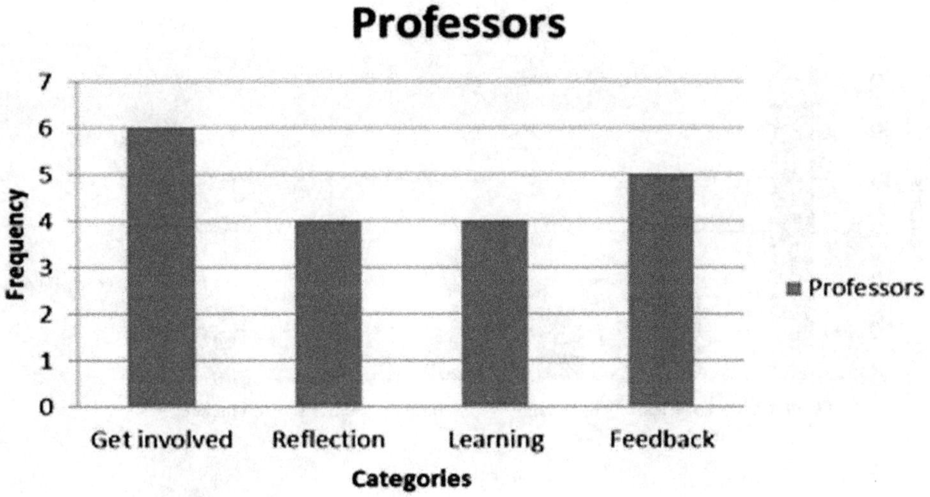

experience help them to improve their learning, as well as, to get involved, to go further and to reflect on their own practice:

To know how your classmates consider you are doing your job (URV_4).

Everyone gets involved and assesses your work what has allowed us to improve our project (UAB_2).

The learning you obtain during and after the feedforward process (UB_5).

When you assess the work of one of your classmates, then you have to revise your own work, just to make sure you have not made the same mistakes (URV_10).

The second open-ended questions aimed to know what the most positive aspect of this experience was. The university professors believed students get more involved while doing the feedforward experience. In addition, the feedback provided was perceived as one of the strengths of the experience, as well as, the students' learning. Finally, the feedforward enhanced students' reflection and self-regulation according to the professors (figure 4).

Pupils realized that correcting classmates' mistakes helped them to identify their own (UB_2).

The feedback enables the students' to readdress their work and learning, to answer some questions, to go further […]. It also helps the students to identify what they are doing well (UOC_1).

As for the students, the feedback provided and received during the experience was the most positive aspect of the feedforward experience. Moreover, they thought it allowed them to improve their learning and their task. Likewise, the feedforward enhanced tracking, looking for more information, as well as, going further (figure 5):

Figure 5. The positivist aspect of the feedforward experience according to the students.

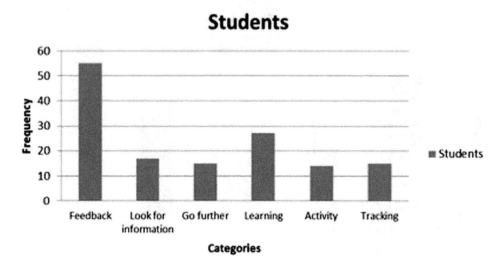

Knowing what other people think about your work (UB_6).

Learning from my own mistakes and my classmates' project (URV_7).

Including knowledge from different subjects and sources to sort out the project (URV_14).

The feedforward encourages looking for more information and learn from the others (UB_70).

The third opened question from the questionnaire intended to know what the weaknesses of the feedforward experience were. Professors namely reported two: the amount of work and students' involvement (figure 6). Professors believed the experience added extra work to them, since they had to the task

Figure 6. Weaknesses of the experience according to the professors.

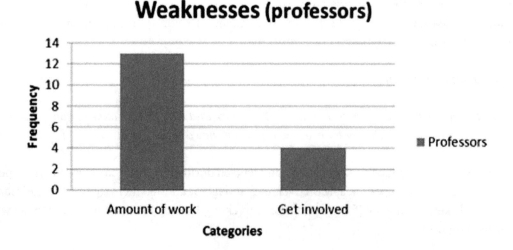

Figure 7. Weaknesses of the experience according to students.

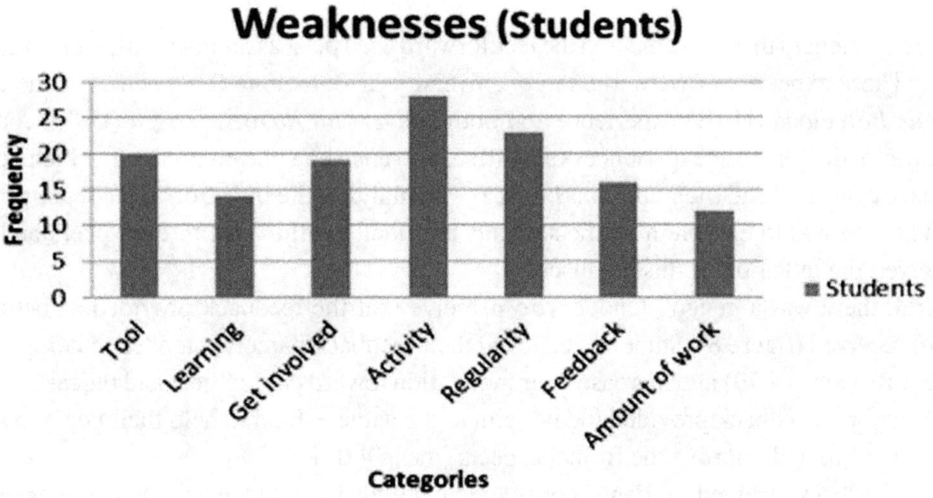

Weaknesses (Students)

several times. In addition, they did not always consider it increased students' involvement in the subject and in their learning process:

This experience has been done with a large amount of students and, therefore, it implies more work than quantitative assessment (UB_4).

You need a lot of time to provide feedback to each student and make sure they use it (UIB_4).

Students believe peer-assessment is not fair since each student's involvement is different (UAB_3).

Students namely identified seven different weaknesses in this experience (figure 7). The characteristic of the activity was the weakness more frequently reported. The activity characteristic is understood as the type of task students had to develop. Moreover, students believed the frequency with which the feedback was provided was not always sufficient enough. The students also complaint about the tool used as a support for the feedforward experience (blog, Moodle, Twitter…). Moreover, they thought the level of implication of each student was different. In addition, the participants believed the learning obtained did not justify the amount of work this experience implied:

Feedback should be provided more often (UB_14).

Too much work (URV_12).

Up to a certain point, you need your classmate feedback to improve the task. However, not all my classmates put the same effort to provide feedback (UAB_2).

Students' Perceptions about the Feedback Provided and Received

Some of the experiences that implemented the feedforward used peer-assessment to develop the formative assessment. These experiences were: the three University of Barcelona (UB) contexts, the *Universitat Autonoma de Barcelona* (UAB) experience and both *Universitat Rovira i Virgili* (URV) contexts. The students participating in those experiences (n=140) had to answer a questionnaire in which not only was the experience evaluated and their opinions but also was analyzed the intention of feedback provided and received. The aim was to explore how the students provided feedforward to their peers and how their peers perceived the intention of this feedback.

In general, there was a general tendency to perceive that the feedback provided as better than the feedforward received (figure 8). Students' believed their feedback namely intended to help their peers to improve the task (mean 4.79) and increase their motivation towards the subject and the task (mean 4.63). On the contrary, the feedback provided did not aim to the same extend to help their peers to acquire the content (mean 3.96) and improve the formal aspects (mean 4.07).

As for the feedback received, students' considered it mainly intended to help them to improve the task (mean 4.62) and their learning process (mean 4.37). However, students did not perceive the feedback received put emphasis on the formal aspects (mean 3.86) and the acquisition of the contents (mean 3.86). Overall, the feedforward provided and received is believed to focus more on the task than on self-regulation.

Several related-samples Wilcoxon Signed Rank Test were run in order to analyze if there were a statistical significant difference between the perception of the feedback provided and the feedback received. It was found that there was a significant difference for the rating scores of the categories improve the task (Mean 4.79 vs. Mean4.56; $T=709, p=.008$), motivation (Mean 4.63 vs. Mean 4.29; $T=561, p<.001$) and formal aspects (Mean 4.07 vs. Mean 3.86; $T=934, p=.002$). However, there was not a statistical significant difference between the feedback provided and received for the categories improve the learning process ($p=.143$), acquire the content ($p=0.67$) and develop the competencies ($p=.365$).

Figure 8. Students' perceptions about the feedforward provided and received

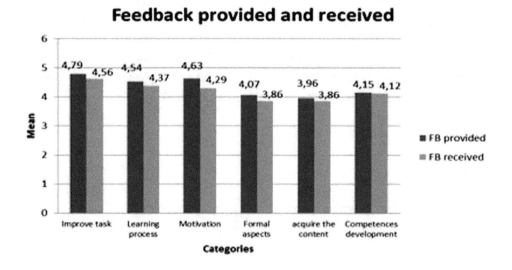

Figure 9. Frequencies across experiences for each category (feedback provided)

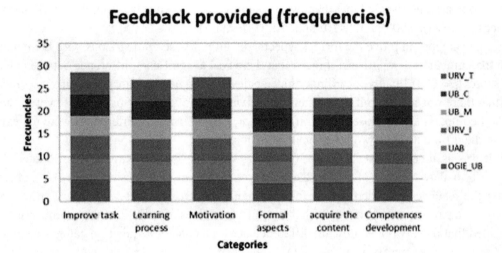

Figure 10. Frequencies across experiences for each category (feedback received)

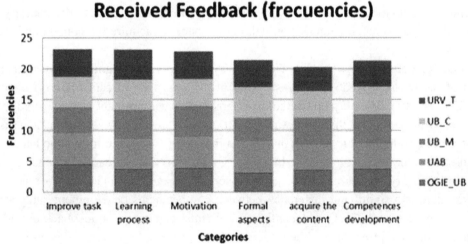

Several Independent Kurskal-Wallis Tests were run in order to explore if the distribution of the provided feedback scores was the same across experiences (figure 9). It was found that the distribution across universities was the same for all the categories: improve task (p=.199), improve the learning process (p=.474), increase the motivation (p=.741), improve the formal aspects (p=.067), acquire the content (p=.517) and develop the competencies (p=.532). Therefore, since the distribution was the same, the different experiences scores could be analyzed as a single one.

The same procedure was followed to analyze the distribution of the received feedback scores (figure 10). The results of the test revealed that the distribution was the same for the categories improve the task (p=.684), increase the motivation (p=.062) and acquire the content (p=.464). However, the distribution was not the same for improve the learning process ($H(5)$=22,275, p<.001), improve the formal aspects ($H(5)$=19,163, p=.002) and develop the competencies ($H(5)$=14,532, p=.013). The all pairwise comparisons for the category improve the learning process with the significant values (*p*) adjusted to the number of comparisons revealed that there was a significant difference between the OGIE and URV_T experiences' scores (*p*=.009) and OGIE and UB_C (*p*=.009).

As for the category improve the formal aspects, the all pairwise comparisons with the *p* values adjusted to the number of comparisons showed that there was a significant difference between OGIE and URV_T scores (*p*=.003). Finally, regarding competencies development category, the pairwise comparisons showed that there was not a significant difference between any of the distributions. However, the OGIE and URV_I comparison was closed to significance (*p*=.087). Since the differences were not extremely important, the different scores would be analyzed altogether.

Once it was assured the distribution of the scores were the same or similar, two Related-Samples Friedman's Two-Way Analysis of Variance were run so as to explore a possible main effect of category. Regarding the feedback provided, it was found a significant main effect of category ($\chi2(5)$=89,892, *p*<.001). The all pairwise comparisons with the significant values (*p*) adjusted to the number of comparisons revealed that there was a significant difference between content acquisition category and learning process (*p*=.025), task improvement (*p*<.001) and motivation increase (*p*<.001). Moreover, there was a significant difference between the distribution of formal aspects' scores and task improvement (*p*<.001) and motivation increase (*p*<.001). Finally, there is a significant difference between competencies development scores and task improvement (*p*=.003) and motivation (*p*=.002). Therefore, the peer-feedback mainly intended to help the peers to improve their task and motivate them. On the contrary, the peer-assessment did not put so much emphasis on helping the peers to acquire the content and improve the formal aspects.

The second Related-Samples Friedman's Two-Way Analysis of variance aimed at analyzing the distribution of the received feedback scores. It was also found a significant main effect of category ($\chi2(5)$=77,258, *p*<.001). The all pairwise comparisons with the significant values (*p*) adjusted to the number of comparisons showed that there was a significant difference between formal aspects category and competencies development (*p*=.026), motivation increase (*p*=.003), improve the learning process (*p*<.001) and task improvement (*p*<.001). In addition, there was a significant difference between content acquisition category and learning process improvement (*p*=.003) and task improvement (*p*<.001). Furthermore, there is a significant difference between competencies development category and task improvement category (*p*=0.22). Consequently, the students' perceived the feedback provided mainly intended to help them improve the task and their learning process. However, the peer-assessment did not aim to improve the formal aspects and acquire the content.

DISCUSSION

This study aimed at analyzing university professors and students perceptions about the feedforward experience they were involved in. They were asked to answer a questionnaire in which there were closed and open-ended questions.

In general, professors perceived these experiences more positively than students did. However, there were not significant differences between professors and students opinions, but for motivation. Professors believed this experience increased students' motivation towards the subject, whereas students did not consider the formative assessment increased their motivation. In line with Hounsell and Litjens (2008), this perceived difference could be explained because the feedback provided did not take into account one of the characteristics of a good feedback: promote assessment tasks that increase students' agreement and dedication.

Interestingly, both professors and students believed the regularity with which the feedback was provided was one of the strengths of the experience. In fact, one of the basic elements feedback should have is the timing because, as Gibbs and Simpson (2004) report, if the feedback is not provided regularly enough students lose interest in it.

Professors also thought that the students' increase of participation was another positive aspect. On the contrary, students considered that another strength of the experience was the information provided about it before starting the experience.

However, above all, professors and students agreed with the fact that the main strength of this experience is the feedback provided and received. In line with Shute, Hansen and Almond (2007), students believed feedback allow them to improve their task thanks to the guidelines provided.

Nevertheless, this formative assessment implies an increase of the amount of work what is reported as the main weakness of the experience.

In addition, professors did not believe the feedback provided was linked with an improvement of the acquisition of the competencies. In fact, professors did not perceive the feedback allowed students to improve their competencies to the same extend they improved the task or their learning process. It is possible that the feedback was focused on the improvement of the task instead of self-regulation and, therefore, it does not guarantee a better acquisition of the competencies. As previous research has pointed out (Boud & Molloy, 2013; Hounsell & Litjens, 2008) the feedback must have some characteristics and provide some guidelines that allow the students to self-regulate their own task. Moreover, it could be the case that, as Nicol (2010) and Price (2005) suggests, students did not improve their competencies because they did not know what to do with this feedback.

However, students believed the feedforward had allowed them to improve up to the same extend the task, their learning process and the acquisition of the competencies. This idea agrees with what previous research has reported about feedforward. As Pressley & Ghatala, 1990; Pressley & Harris, 2006; White & Frederiksen, 2005; Boud & Molloy (2013) and Rae and Cochrane (2008) reported, one of the advantages of the feedforward is that it not only helps improving the task, but the learning and the competencies. Nevertheless, because of the high correlation between learning process and acquisition of competencies categories, it could be the case students did not clearly differentiate the concepts learning process and competencies acquisition.

As in previous research, students believed the feedback they provided was better than the feedback received. Surprisingly, significant differences between the feedback provided and received could not be found for learning process and competencies improvement categories. One possible explanation could be the fact that both the feedback provided and received was reported to be focused on improving the task. Consequently, the feedback did not put emphasis on developing self-regulation strategies that could enhance the acquisition of competencies. On the other hand, in line with previous research (Luo & Gao, 2012), it could be the case that peer-feedback was not as accurate as professors' feedback.

However, students reported they had learnt by providing feedback to their peers, since they had to verify that they had not made the same mistakes as their classmates. Recent research has also highlighted the idea that feedback and peer-assessment help students to develop collaborative competencies and assess the peer's work from a critical perspective (Nicol & MacFarlane, 2006; Boud & Molloy, 2013).

CONCLUSION

This study has allowed to shed some light on formative assessment in higher education. First of all, the feedback provided tends to be focused on the task rather than on self-regulation. Therefore, it is more difficult students can improve their learning process and competencies from this feedback. However, as Nicol (2010) highlights, one of the aims of Higher Education should be to help students to develop their self-assessment and self-regulation capacities.

In line with recent research, the fact that the same task is being reassessed several times is positive and allows students to learn from their mistakes. Unexpectedly, professors did not think these experiences allowed students to develop their competencies. However, students consider the formative feedback helps them to improve the task and their learning.

On the other hand, the feedback received is not always perceived as better than the feedback provided. Nevertheless, students believe peer-assessment allows them to learn from their peers' mistakes and develop their critical capacity.

However, this study presents some limitations that should be improved in future research and need to be considered when interpreting the results of this research. First of all, the heterogeneity of the environments where the feedforward experiences were developed makes it difficult to assess the impact of the feedback on students learning and competencies.

The agent who provided the feedback varied across experiences. Therefore, the nature and intention of the feedforward varied considerably depending on who provided it (a professor or a peer).

On the other hand, the feedforward tended to be focused on the specific task where the feedback was provided. Consequently, it is not clear enough the impact that these formative assessments had on the learning process and the acquisition of the competencies.

Nevertheless, since this study has arisen new questions that are worth analyzing, it would be interesting that future research creates similar environments where it could be analyzed the impact of feedback on students learning process and the acquisition of competences. In addition, it would be necessary that future research could identify the typology of feedback (focused on the content, structure, agents, frequency and tool) that has the most positive impact on students' learning and performance.

Furthermore, it would be also interesting to create experiences where sustainable and efficient feedback could be provided in order to avoid increasing the amount of work at the same time that the key elements of a good feedback are kept.

Finally, one of the current challenges of higher education is to develop students' self-regulation and self-assessment competencies. Therefore, more experiences that intend to develop these abilities need to be conducted.

REFERENCES

Biggs, J. (2003). *Teaching for quality learning at university* (2nd ed.). Buckingham: Open.

Black, P., & Wiliam, D. (1998). Assessment and classroom learning. *Assessment in Education: Principles, Policy & Practice*, 5(1), 7–74. doi:10.1080/0969595980050102

Bloxham, S., & Campbell, L. (2010). Generating dialogue in assessment feedback: Exploring the use of interactive cover sheets. *Assessment & Evaluation in Higher Education*, 35(3), 291–300. doi:10.1080/02602931003650045

Boekaerts, M. (1999). Motivated learning: Studying student situation transactional units. *European Journal of Psychology of Education, 14*(1), 41–55.

Bollag, B. (2006). Making an art form of assessment. *The Chronicle of Higher Education, 56*(10), 8–10.

Boud, D. (2000). Sustainable Assessment: Rethinking assessment for the learning society. *Studies in Continuing Education, 22*(2), 151–167. doi:10.1080/713695728

Boud, D., & Molloy, E. (2013). Rethinking models of feedback for learning: The challenge of design. *Assessment & Evaluation in Higher Education, 38*(6), 698–712. doi:10.1080/02602938.2012.691462

Brinko, K. T. (1993). The practice of giving feedback to improve teaching: What is effective? *The Journal of Higher Education, 64*(5), 574–593. doi:10.2307/2959994

Carless, D., Salter, D., Yang, M., & Lam, J. (2011). Developing sustainable feedback practices. *Studies in Higher Education, 36*(4), 395–407. doi:10.1080/03075071003642449

Covic, T., & Jones, M. K. (2008). Is the essay resubmission option a formative or a summative assessment and does it matter as long as the grades improve? *Assessment & Evaluation in Higher Education, 33*(1), 75–85. doi:10.1080/02602930601122928

Gibbs, G. & Simpson, C. (2003). Does your assessment support your students learning? *Journal of Learning and Teaching in Higher Education,* 1(1), 3-31.

Hattie, J., & Timperley, H. (2007). The power of feedback. *Review of Educational Research, 77*(1), 81–112. doi:10.3102/003465430298487

Hounsell, D., McCune, V., Litjens, J., & Hounsell, J. (2005). *Subject overview report for biosciences. Universities of Edinburgh.* Durham, Coventry: ETL Project.

Luo, T., & Gao, F. (2012). Enhancing classroom learning experience by providing structures to micro-blogging-based activities. *Journal of Information Technology Education, 11,* 199–211.

Mory, E. H. (2003). Feedback research revisited. In D. H. Jonassen (Ed.), *Handbook of research for educational communications and technology* (pp. 745–783). New York: Macmillan.

Narciss, S. (2008). Feedback strategies for interactive learning tasks. In J. M. Spector, M. D. Merrill, J. van Merrienboer, & M. P. Driscoll (Eds.), *Handbook of research on educational communications and technology* (pp. 125–143). New York: Lawrence Erlbaum Associates.

Nicol, D. (2010). From monologue to dialogue: Improving written feedback processes in mass higher education. *Assessment & Evaluation in Higher Education, 35*(5), 501–517. doi:10.1080/02602931003786559

Nicol, D. (2013). Resituating feedback from the reactive to the proactive. In D. Boud & L. Molloy (Eds.), *Feedback in Higher and Professional Education: understanding it and doing it well* (pp. 34–49). Routledge.

Nicol, D., & Macfarlane-Dick, D. (2005). Rethinking formative assessment in higher education: a theoretical model and seven principles of good feedback practice. In Reflections on assessment (Vol. 2, pp. 105-119). Mansfield: Quality Assurance Agency.

Nicol, D., Thomson, A., & Breslin, C. (2014). Rethinking feedback practices in higher education: A peer review perspective. *Assessment & Evaluation in Higher Education, 39*(1), 102–122. doi:10.1080/02602938.2013.795518

Poulos, A., & Mahony, M. J. (2008). Effectiveness of feedback: The students' perspective. *Assessment & Evaluation in Higher Education, 33*(2), 143–154. doi:10.1080/02602930601127869

Pressley, M., & Ghatala, E. S. (1990). Self-regulated learning: Monitoring learning from text. *Educational Psychologist, 25*(1), 19–33. doi:10.1207/s15326985ep2501_3

Pressley, M., & Harris, K. R. (2006). Cognitive strategies instruction: From basic research to classroom instruction. Handbook of Educational Psychology, 2, 265-286.

Price, M. (2005). Assessment standards: The role of communities of practice and the scholarship of assessment. *Assessment & Evaluation in Higher Education, 3*(3), 215–230. doi:10.1080/02602930500063793

Rae, A. M., & Cochrane, D. K. (2008). Listening to students: How to make written assessment feedback useful. *Active Learning in Higher Education, 9*(3), 217–230. doi:10.1177/1469787408095847

Sadler, D. R. (1989). Formative assessment and the design of instructional systems. *Instructional Science, 18*(2), 119–144. doi:10.1007/BF00117714

Shute, V. J. (2008). Focus on formative feedback. *Review of Educational Research, 78*(1), 153–189. doi:10.3102/0034654307313795

Shute, V. J., Hansen, E. G., & Almond, R. G. (2007). *An assessment for learning system called ACED: Designing for learning effectiveness and accessibility.* ETS Research Report No. RR-07-26, Princeton, NJ.

Weimer, M. (2014). Developing Student's Self-Assessment Skills. *Faculty Focus.* Retrieved from http://www.algonquincollege.com/pd/2015/03/30/how-important-is-student-self-assessment/#sthash.uJx2WOwa.dpuf

White, B., & Frederiksen, J. (2005). A theoretical framework and approach for fostering metacognitive development. *Educational Psychologist, 40*(4), 211–223. doi:10.1207/s15326985ep4004_3

Yuan, J., & Kim, C. (2015). Effective Feedback Design Using Free Technologies. *Journal of Educational Computing Research.*

Chapter 11
Teaching for
Epistemological Change:
Self-Direction through Self-Assessment

Gloria Nogueiras
University of Alcalá, Spain

David Herrero
University of Alcalá, Spain

Alejandro Iborra
University of Alcalá, Spain

ABSTRACT

As higher education teachers, the authors are committed to supporting students in their epistemological development, specifically in their transition towards self-direction. In this chapter, they share their experience of using self-assessment in a Teacher Training Degree course as a way to both enhance self-direction and assess its development. A thematic analysis of the self-assessments of a sample of 30 students is carried out, and four themes are identified: 1) the degree of authorship, 2) the degree of elaboration, 3) "taking notice of" subtle levels of analysis, and 4) the identification of temporal milestones throughout the course. These themes enable a different pattern of mental complexity to be identified, a complexity which is understood as evidence of students' different degrees of self-direction. The findings are discussed in the light of developmental constructivist theories. In addition, some implications for education regarding the current debates on self-assessment literature are presented.

DOI: 10.4018/978-1-5225-0531-0.ch011

INTRODUCTION

The deepest order of change that human beings are capable of demonstrating is epistemological change. A change in epistemology means transforming one's way of experiencing the world. (Keeney, 1983, p.7).

Nowadays society requires individuals to have complex personal and interpersonal competences in order to be successful workers, learners, and citizens (Drago-Severson, 2011; Kegan, 1994; King & Siddiqui, 2011). These demands, which involve being adaptable, reflective, autonomous, self-regulated and capable of communicating and co-operating with others (Dochy, Segers, & Buehl, 1999), are underlain by the need for individuals to develop increasingly complex ways of knowing. That is to say, by the need to experience what has been termed as epistemological development (Kegan, 1994; Mezirow, 2000; Taylor & Cranton, 2013).

From an educational perspective, the challenges and supports needed to enhance such epistemological development are not provided by transmission-oriented approaches, which usually put the emphasis on students' reproducing factual knowledge (Gow & Kember, 1990). In this sense, higher education involves new challenges for the students, such as the demand to be more autonomous and active learners (Pérez, Shim, King, & Baxter-Magolda, 2015). Some educational practices that have shown to promote more independent ways of learning are the following: engagement in research, service learning, intergroup dialogue and active pedagogies that include self-assessment procedures (Kuh, Kinzie, Schuh, Whitt, & Associates, 2005).

Self-assessment, widely recognised as a challenge for higher education students, could be a good candidate to foster their epistemological development. As defined by Boud (1995), this kind of formative assessment has become more frequent in the context of higher education. Although self-assessment has been traditionally identified as a practice aimed at improving learners' assessment of their own competence and performance in the process of learning a discipline (Boud, 1995), recent investigations associate self-assessment with the enhancement of students' metacognitive competence (Mok, Lung, Cheng, Cheung, & Ng, 2006). In addition to this, self-assessment has also been related to the promotion of lifelong learning (Boud, 1995) and self-regulation (Pintrich & Zusho, 2002). However, few studies include students' development explicitly within the scope of self-assessment. With the exception of works like Yorke's (2003), self-assessment is still understood as a competence instead of as a qualitative change in the way of making sense of one's experience.

In this regard, we posit that a theory of formative assessment should include knowledge related to learning and assessment, but also to students' development. As Yorke (2003, p. 487) states, "a formal assessment task is constructed by the assessor, bearing in mind the structure and progression of the subject discipline(s) involved, an appreciation of the sequencing of intellectual and moral development progression of students (...), and a *knowledge of the current level of intellectual development of his or her students*" (emphasis ours).

This conception of self-assessment as a developmental resource fits with a constructivist approach to learning. From this perspective, learning involves a change not only in *what* we know, but also in *how* we know. This is the core idea of theories such as Transformative Learning, which depicts learning as a process of examining, questioning, and revising our understandings, assumptions and expectations about the world in the light of new experiences which might challenge our previous assumptions and guide future action (Mezirow, 2000). In this sense, transformative learning involves an epistemological change rather than a mere change in behavioural or competence repertoires, or an increase in the quantity of knowledge (Kegan, 2000).

In a transformative view of learning, assessment cannot be a simple matter of checking the presence of right answers in students' exams, but must be considered as a continuous and formative process which is fundamental for learning (Black & Wiliam, 2009; Margalef, 2014) and also for development (Baxter Magolda, 2009; Landreman, Rasmussen, King, & Jiang, 2007). From this perspective, self-assessment should consist of activities that involve the development of the same competences which the learning context seeks to promote. This is what Biggs (1996) calls "constructive alignment", and it might provide an interesting framework for investigating how higher education teachers can both facilitate students' epistemological change and assess its occurrence. In this connection, Gibbs (1999) points out that innovative assessment practices foster in students qualities that are typical of more sophisticated epistemological levels of thinking.

Considering self-assessment practices from a developmental perspective could provide new contributions to the debates on: 1) when to initiate this kind of formative assessment practice in higher education, and what is the appropriate timing for the teacher to provide feedback (Nulty, 2011); 2) whether self-assessment should be an optional or a mandatory requirement for the students (Leach, 2012); 3) the convergent or divergent nature of the feedback provided by teachers to the student's self-assessment arguments (Yorke, 2003); and 4) the importance of differentiating between self-evaluation, which is related to grades, and self-assessment, which is related to qualitative productions attached to learning processes (Andrade & Valtcheva, 2009).

The Learning Experience to be Self-Assessed

In this chapter we focus on a course on Developmental Psychology addressed to freshmen students of a Teacher Training Degree. A key feature of this course is that at the same time as students are learning about development, they are encouraged to consider their own developmental processes as an object of inquiry and reflection. For us, this is a key element in undergoing epistemological development. More specifically, as higher education teachers, our aim is to enhance the epistemological shift of the students towards self-direction. (see for example, Nogueiras, Iborra, & Herrero, 2016; Nogueiras & Iborra, 2016)

The kind of epistemological change involved in becoming a self-directed learner is well described by Kegan's (1994, 2000) constructive-developmental theory. Kegan describes how throughout development individuals make meaning of themselves as they shift from a simplistic reliance on authority to more complex ways of knowing with the result that they become increasingly aware of their own and others' beliefs, values and interpersonal relationships. It is this emergence of the capacity to intentionally coordinate one's beliefs, values and interpersonal loyalties which marks the transition towards self-direction, a more complex stage in Kegan's developmental theory.

In an attempt to enhance students' self-direction, our course employed a collaborative learning methodology (Anderson, 1997; Iborra, García, Margalef, & Pérez, 2010) and an experiential learning model (McWhirter, 2002). Collaborative learning aims to promote learning by doing, interacting and sharing ideas with peers. In doing so, there is the opportunity to acknowledge others' frames of reference and to stimulate reflection that enables the movement from externally to internally grounded decision making (Baxter Magolda, 2000; King & Siddiqui, 2011). An experiential learning model proposes that the teaching of any topic begins with the students' exploration of their intuitive understandings. Only then are formal theoretical models provided by the teacher for comparison with students' personal and group experiences. In this way, experiential learning is thought to heighten students' awareness of their own epistemological assumptions and how they may be revised.

Furthermore, the progressive development of students' commitment towards their own learning was expected to be facilitated through two main principles that guided our teaching practice: the generation of a context of choice, where students' participation in any learning activity was always voluntary; and not grading students throughout the course, but providing them with qualitative feedback.

According to Nicol and MacFarlane-Dick (2006), good feedback practice in order to support learners' self-regulation requires an initial clarification of what is good performance by exemplifying goals, criteria and possible standards of different levels of learning complexity and, for us, even developmental achievement. In our case, this was accomplished by providing the students with a document that illustrated different grades of complexity in former students' answers provided in a final integrative assignment[1].

In line with Nicol and MacFarlane-Dick (2006), the teacher must also facilitate students' self-assessment and encourage their dialogue about learning with teachers and other peers. In this vein, at the end of the course and within the context of a final integrative assignment, students were asked to produce a self-assessment about their learning process. We chose self-assessment, among other assessment sources, as a way to monitor and supervise how and how far the competence of self-direction had been or was being developed by the students. For the students, self-assessment was a space where they could review their learning processes over time in the light of the theoretical and processual distinctions addressed throughout the course, by taking a reflexive stance towards themselves and having the opportunity to go beyond their current performance. For us, students' self-assessments were sources of evidence of how far they had gone in terms of autonomy, responsibility, creativity, complexity, self-awareness, and ultimately, self-direction.

Purpose of the Present Study

The main goal of this study is to show how self-assessment can function as a lever for the enhancement of students' epistemological development, more specifically of their transition towards self-direction. In particular, we want to explore to what extent self-assessment might enhance students' ability to reflect on their learning processes so that they become aware of any developmental change they may experience during the four months that the course lasted. Also, we aim to explore how our implicit learning and teaching conceptions work in our assessment practices, with a view to increasing our awareness of what we assess and how.

METHOD

Participants and Course Structure

The research context of the present study was a course on Developmental Psychology addressed to freshmen students of a Teacher Training Degree. The course was held at a Spanish university throughout the first semester of academic year 2014/2015. The participants were 149 students (57.72% women, average age 19.98, age range 18-39) distributed in three groups (69, 28 and 52 students respectively) and taught by two of the authors of this chapter. The course took place over 28 sessions (42 hours) in a 15-week period.

Within the course, students were encouraged to explore their implicit conceptions about development and to contrast them with classical theoretical perspectives that were embodied throughout the course, such as the orthogenetic principle[2] and the idea of epigenesis[3] (first module). Examples of how these theoretical perspectives work were provided in relation to the different dimensions of development, such as socio-affective, cognitive and moral (second module). In doing so, some of the activities proposed were the analysis of different cases through readings, videos, experiential exercises or collaborative discussions. At the end of the course, the theoretical content and the competences developed by the students were integrated in the analysis of two complex cases through deep discussion of two films[4] (third module).

Sample

The students forming the sample of this study were selected through a purposive and criterial process (Miles & Huberman, 1994). Our purpose was to count on enough cases, both in number and in variety, for different degrees of complexity to be exhibited in the students' written self-assessments. In order to distinguish and operationalize these different degrees of complexity we referred to students' final grades for the course (Merit with Distinction, Merit, Good, Pass and Fail). Two cases of each of these five different grades were selected from each group of students so that the sample was composed of 30 students (66.66% women, average age 20.27, age range 18-39), 10 from each of the three groups. Students were informed about the conduct of this research and given guarantees as to the confidentiality of the information gathered. In subsequent sections of the chapter, the sample students will be referred to by a randomly assigned number from 1 to 30, by their gender and by the grade they achieved.

Data Collection

The data set consisted of the students' self-assessments written at the end of the course. Students were encouraged to confront the self-assessment as they deemed most appropriate, but some issues for reflection were suggested:

1. *What did you learn? Concepts and ideas related to the content of the course, competences that go beyond the content, questions you would like to ask now, learning about your way of learning or others' way of learning.*
2. *How did you feel about the group activities and the discussions with your peers?*
3. *Regarding what you did and what you did not do throughout the course, how and why did you do it?*

Data Analysis

The students' texts were subjected to a thematic analysis (Braun & Clarke, 2006) carried out with the aid of the software *NVivo* (Richards, 1999). In order to perform the coding process, an inductive approach was adopted. This approach involved being open and sensitive to the meanings expressed by the students instead of looking for specific features linked to existing theoretical models. In this sense, it was important to pay attention not only to the themes found in the texts (*what*), but also to the way in which the themes were addressed (*how*) by the different students. From our point of view, this focus on the *how* is what may furnish an account of the different degrees of complexity in the different ways students make meaning. In order to identify and define the themes, the 399 codes resulting from the first inductive analytical approach to students' texts were examined in relation to their frequency across and within subjects and its theoretical relevance. Thus, the joint consideration of certain codes enabled us to identify several main themes, which were of significance for understanding the cases in greater depth. Subsequently, a deductive approach was adopted: once the preliminary thematic structure had been defined, it was checked by re-examining those codes which appeared in two or more cases (174 codes) in order to identify which of them also fitted the themes in such a way that they could be included in them.

FINDINGS

The analysis of the students' self-assessments enabled us to identify four themes which proved of great value for understanding more deeply the students' learning and developmental experiences throughout the course. The four themes were: 1) the degree of students' authorship, 2) the degree of elaboration, 3) "taking notice of" subtle levels of analysis, and 4) the identification of temporal milestones throughout the course. In what follows, these themes are described and excerpts from students' self-assessments are provided in order to illustrate them and to show subtleties and nuances with regards to *how* the different students are located within each theme.

Theme 1: Degree of Students' Authorship

The first theme refers to the outcome of students' learning processes in terms of authorship. Under this heading, two main traits were identified which provided clues about different degrees of authorship quality. At one end of the spectrum, there was evidence of students "being dependent" on the teacher or on external sources of authority and organization. At the other, there was evidence of students' "self-directing their own learning", which meant they were autonomous in the process of constructing their own learning.

As a consequence of the passive attitude developed in the course of previous experiences in transmissive learning contexts, most students exhibited great dependence on external structure and guidelines, mainly at the beginning of the course. In this sense, the next quote exemplifies the emotions of a student when describing how the features of the course were not matching her expectations:

S19 (Female, Pass): *It would help a lot to know exactly what our mistakes are and how to correct them. But in order to be able to do that, the first thing you need are experts able to identify the qualities and faults in the students in order to show and teach them self-direction. The problem is that this is not easy and many teachers want us to be autonomous and self-capable without teaching us beforehand. This creates frustration in students at not knowing what to do.*

Student dependence is expected in the presence of experts who determine what to do and how. This student is not conscious of the paradox of teaching to be self-directed: if you teach it in a direct way you are preventing self-direction itself; nor is she conscious of the difference between the learning of factual knowledge and a kind of learning that involves a qualitative change in the way we organize our experience. Thus, the emotion of frustration can be taken as evidence of not being able to achieve that kind of qualitative change, which in this case is linked to the learning of complex skills.

We also found students at an intermediate point between the two poles of being dependent and being author of one's own learning. This is exemplified in the next quote:

S7 (Male, Merit): *Nobody has asked us to do anything, any homework. Teachers provided us with all the available information so we could access whenever we wanted. For me this way of teaching is interesting... but managing one's freedom is complex, all the more so when we are so busy during the semester and we just skip what is not mandatory.*

This student is conscious of the paradox related to having freedom of choice. On the one hand, that freedom is appealing; on the other hand, it is still tempting and comfortable to remain dependent on external variables such as the demands from other courses which mean that activities which are not compulsory are pushed to one side.

For her part, the following student manifests that she would have liked to be in a more predictable and less open learning context, which once again shows the students' preference for the security guaranteed by external guidance. From a wider perspective, however, at the end of the course she also notices that the purposes underlying the learning proposal were aimed to promote the students' independence:

S14 (Female, Good): *There are some things that I would have preferred to do differently. In particular, I wish I had known what we were going to do every week, rather than having to wait to be in class in order to find it out. Sometimes we found ourselves lost with regards to some questions and we didn't get an answer, so we felt frustrated. However, now I know that the goal [of the course] was to find the answer for ourselves.*

Finally, the opposite pattern to dependence on the teacher entailed becoming a self-directed learner. This involved leaving behind conceptions of learning based on the passive transmission of knowledge and consolidating a new conception of learning as a process where students construct and use their own understanding willingly. This can be appreciated in the following quote:

S6 (Female, Merit with Distinction): *Learning doesn't mean being a passive subject listening to the talk that any teacher gives or taking a book and notes to memorize them and write them down in an exam whose purpose will be to check what has been memorized. What learning really entails is thinking for oneself, knowing how to resort to the knowledge acquired in order to use it in daily cases... To learn is a verb which requires willingness.*

In addition to the transition towards a new learning conception, this trait of autonomy might be related to the experience of more complex and internal changes regarding one's self-conception, as illustrated in the next quote:

S21 (Male, Merit with Distinction): *I think that in this degree I can build that sort of knowledge that makes me evolve and develop towards a more complex stage and, in this way, learn not only academically, but also personally.*

Interestingly, in expressing his wish "to learn not only academically" but also about himself as a person, this student acknowledges the possibility of undergoing a developmental change towards more complex stages. Thus, for him learning and development seem to go hand in hand.

Theme 2: Degree of Elaboration

The second theme encompasses the degree of elaboration evidenced in the students' written self-assessments. We were able to distinguish between two poles on the scale of elaboration. On the one hand, there was the process which involves "making connections" between concepts proceeding from a varied array of theoretical sources, discussions held in class, other courses, case studies or personal experiences. On the other hand, there is the process we have termed "a lack of elaboration", which is associated with superficial and simplistic analysis of one's learning process based on concrete information.

The following excerpt illustrates the case of a student who is able to consider jointly course content, her personal experiences and her own change over time:

S23 (Female, Merit): *I've carried out a sort of exploration about myself, my mourning process and my affective bonds... My grandfather died in October. I saw him every year but I did not have any great affective bond with him. Then, when he died I did not cry... I could see how everybody was sad at the funeral, but I was not able to shed any tears... All that was quite weird for me... since I've never been able to be so distant from anything... I was not attached to him. When he was alive he usually made me angry, and he treated me and my sister differently... I didn't feel valued or loved by him, and I guess that it is the reason for my reaction... A year before, my great-aunt died. My affective bond with her was special... When I knew that she was quite ill, I asked my mother to go to see her, although we lived far away... What I mean is that given these experiences and after this course, now I'm able to explore and distinguish different types of affective bonds and to realize that they might be related to the different reactions that we have during our periods of mourning.*

In contrast, the next quote is an example of making connections solely with theoretical content which are neither elaborated nor related to personal experience:

S8 (Female, Pass): *At the beginning, I thought of development as the physical evolution of a person... However, throughout the classes I learnt that [development] is not only this, but that we can also consider it as the evolution of a person in terms of salary, imagination, thinking, personality...*

The competence of elaborating knowledge in a personal way, rather than repeating what experts say, is quite difficult to attain since it stems from the possibility of making connections and from the complexity of such connections.

Finally, the next excerpt is a good example of lack of elaboration. The student mentions the course, one possible application of what has been taught, and her own progress over time. However, there is not much detail in what she describes.

S9 (Female, Fail): *I think that with this course we've learned fundamental things in order to make children to learn in the best way. I think that I've progressed from the first day I entered the classroom to today, and I think that it will be quite useful for my professional career.*

The absence of personal connections does not allow the student to understand what she refers to in more complex ways, since her epistemological assumptions and her previous life experiences remain unquestionable, and possibly not even perceived, in the light of the course content.

Theme 3: "Taking Notice of" Subtle Levels of Analysis

The third theme refers to the phenomenon of "taking notice of" or being aware of different and subtle levels of analysis when reflecting on one's learning process. Examples of this are distinguishing between process and content, differentiating previous and current points in time, or paying attention to the teachers' intentions and their organization of the course sessions. In our opinion, taking notice of such subtle levels of analysis is evidence of the occurrence of an epistemological change, that is, a qualitative change in the way in which something is perceived and therefore understood: it is a matter not only of *what* constitutes an object of consideration, but *how* that object is considered. A new content can be "noticed", so to speak, and that is evidence of a new way of "seeing" things.

The following quote is a good example of gaining insight into the process of making sense of the course as a whole:

S17 (Female, Merit): *Even though I knew that this course was going to help us to understand or deal with others, I didn't think that it was going to be like this. Like what? Well, I guess that here comes the tricky part: I think that all the activities and all the concepts that we have learnt don't mean anything by themselves, but they are like a "bridge" that has to be connected to reach the other side, which for me is like a flash of light.*

The following quote shows a student being aware for the first time of the fact that responsibility for her learning lies with her alone:

S6 (Female, Merit with Distinction): *One [question proposed by one of the teachers] that raised my consciousness is the following: "Do you want to learn? It just depends on you". This one made me think more than others because it showed me that the teachers don't have to motivate me, nor the course, nor anybody else. The only person responsible for my engaging with learning is me, and that's something I don't want to forget.*

In the following excerpt, a student acknowledges and identifies three different levels of analysis: the level of the content provided throughout the course (*what* theoretical content was provided during the course), the process followed throughout the course (*how* the course was taught in terms of its methodology) and even the purpose the whole process (*why* some contents were chosen and why they were taught in a specific sequence and using an experiential method, that is, the underlying principles).

S11 (Female, Merit with Distinction): *One thing that I understood is that you [she is addressing the teacher] didn't want us to focus on theory, otherwise you would have given us notes and would have set theoretical exams... Now I understand that you were not asking us to be psychologists. You were asking us to be teachers who understand how their students understand the world, to understand why they are how they are, and to avoid judging them at first sight, to understand that in the classroom there are a lot of developmental processes going on, including our own development.*

The above quotes are evidences of the kind of epistemological change which leads one to a different way of making sense of one's learning experience. In order to find out when this qualitative or epistemological change is more likely to take place, it is worth considering how students refer to temporal phases or key chronological moments of the course.

Theme 4: Identification of Temporal Milestones throughout the Course

Connected as it is to the third theme, the fourth embraces the temporal milestones identified by the students when reflecting on their own learning processes. This involves the comparison of two or more temporal moments during the course: a starting point, an end point, and sometimes also intermediate moments.

As mentioned above, at the beginning of the course most of the students felt disoriented and frustrated because the demands of the classes did not fit their expectations. These quotes are good examples of the general feeling about this period:

S4 (Male, Merit with Distinction): *At the beginning, the course might seem frustrating because we are used to taking notes or to [dealing with] teachers who recite the lesson.*

S30 (Female, Fail): *I hardly understood anything at the beginning of the course and although they [the teachers] explained it again I still did not understand...*

These initial impressions contrast with how students perceived the course at the end, when they elaborated the final integrative assignment and the self-assessment. Then, most students used the metaphor of a "bridge" in order to describe their experience throughout the course. This was influenced by a chapter entitled "Learning: The Teacher Wants Us to Be Self-Directing" (Kegan, 1994), where the author uses the metaphor of a bridge to describe the transition from the third to the fourth order of consciousness. This metaphor fits well with most students' descriptions of their experiences throughout the course. However, there are two main differences in its interpretation. On the one hand, the metaphor of the bridge is understood as a description of learning information and concepts; on the other hand, it is an analogy of a personal development towards more complex ways of meaning making. Thus, it may refer to a learning transition or a developmental transition in accordance with a student's prior interpretation of the metaphor.

The following is a superficial interpretation of the metaphor, in which a student understands the bridge as an analogy of his learning process and views himself as nearing the end:

S2 (Male, Pass): *I have been progressively putting into practice the theoretical concepts in real-life situations and I have been learning concepts that I did not know when the course started. I have almost reached the end of the bridge and, for example, while elaborating this assessment I keep noticing that I have been learning more than I thought and that the uncertainty and fear that I experienced at the beginning have progressively disappeared to the point that I have almost ended the crossing of the bridge.*

It was also common for students to feel they were in the middle of the process, in those cases where they understood learning as a mere process of knowledge acquisition in which they remain the same:

S28 (Female, Pass): *I think that I am halfway or, at least, that I am trying to cross the bridge. I strive to understand and assimilate the new language that is used in this course but I think that there is something that still resists inside me, something that clings onto a traditional way of teaching.*

We also found examples where the meaning of the metaphor is related to personal development and not just to a change in terms of knowledge acquisition. The following excerpt is a case in point:

S21 (Male, Merit with Distinction): *I think that in this course one has started to build, on both sides of the river, the ends of a bridge which symbolizes the individual development towards a higher mental, cognitive and consciousness stage. The foundations have started to be built: the foundations of a bridge that takes us to the shore of mental independence, self-organisation, more analytical and critical thought, and also a fuller acceptance of oneself, more unfettered by the valuations and models coming from the external world.*

Finally, there were occasions when students referred to intermediate moments of the course. One instance of an event that seems to have acted as a trigger of change commenced with a post reflecting on the quality of the students' participation that one of the teachers wrote on his personal blog. Some students felt singled out, and this led to a face-to-face conversation in class between the teacher and the students. This event took on significance for various students, who became more aware and critical of their own attitude, as the next excerpt illustrates:

S25 (Male, Good): *I just took the course seriously when I saw what it meant after talking that day. [...] That moment after the comments in your post [teacher's post] and the subsequent conversation that we had in class was what sparked my interest in the course.*

DISCUSSION

In this study our twofold purpose was to explore the role of self-assessment as a useful resource for collecting evidence of the epistemological development of our students, and to investigate to what extent this kind of assessment resource can promote such development. In this respect, our findings show the value of self-assessment both for gathering information and for influencing its quality. That is to say, the context of a self-assessment enables an epistemological change towards self-direction to be described and also prescribed.

Literature on self-assessment highlights its relevance in the promotion of metacognitive skills (Mok et al., 2006) and, above all, of what are termed "self-regulatory processes" (Butler & Winne, 1995; Nicol & Macfarlane-Dick, 2006; Paris & Paris, 2001; Pintrich & Zusho, 2002) or "self-directed learning" (Long, 1989). Within this literature, self-regulated learning is defined as "an active constructive process whereby learners set goals for their learning and monitor, regulate, and control their cognition, motivation, and behaviour, guided and constrained by their goals and the contextual features of the environment" (Pintrich & Zusho, 2002, p.64). For its part, the definition of self-directed learning is usually very similar as in Mok et al. (2006), where self-directed learners are described as those who are capable of "goal setting, self-monitoring, self-assessment and self-correction" (p. 416).

The epistemological change that we have been referring to so far goes beyond the previous conceptualizations of self-regulation and self-direction; to be more precise, it more closely resembles the transition towards what Kegan conceptualizes and terms "self-direction" (Kegan, 1994). Kegan defines "self-direction" as the developmental stage in which individuals carry out mental tasks based upon internal criteria rather than following external approval. This concept was developed further by Baxter

Magolda (1999), who incorporated it into the framework of a constructive developmental pedagogy, referring to it as self-authorship. For Baxter Magolda, self-authorship is the result of a developmental transition from a reliance on externally to internally driven ways of thinking (Baxter Magolda, 2001).

One reason why the concept of self-authorship is more complex than the notions of self-regulated and self-directed learning commonly used in the literature on self-assessment is that it comprises three dimensions of development. The first epistemological or cognitive dimension has to do with how one makes meaning of knowledge; the second intrapersonal dimension is related to how one views one's identity; and finally, the third interpersonal dimension encompasses how one constructs one's relationships with others. Thus, "individuals who are 'self-authoring' consider multiple perspectives, reflect on their own values and motivations, and utilize goals and perspectives that are internally grounded and evaluated as a foundation for meaning making" (Barber, King, & Baxter Magolda, 2013, p. 870).

The first theme to emerge from our analysis describes the above mentioned transition from relying on external authorities to the creation of an internal capacity to define one's beliefs, values, goals, responsibilities, understandings and even sense of identity. The texts we analyzed gave evidence of variability in where the students situated themselves on a scale from more dependent to more autonomous ways of giving meaning to their experiences. The first theme is also an example of how the complex demands of self-assessment helped students to reflect on their experience throughout the course and therefore to become aware of their own processes of change. The students' texts furnished examples of at least three different positions with respect to students' authorship: dependent, intermediate and autonomous. These meaning-making positions can be found in theoretical models which seek to describe the transition towards self-authorship (Barber et al., 2013; Pérez et al., 2015). These structural models are useful for identifying the different positions that the students may experience at different moments in the course or even in their academic career. However, they do not illustrate what processes are required to move from one position towards the next one, or how the students organize information differently at the distinct stages.

In that respect, both the second theme, "degree of elaboration", and the third theme, "taking notice of subtle levels of analysis", provide useful information about the processes which shape the different epistemological states involved in the acquisition of a particular complex competence, namely, information management. What is at stake here is not *what* information is organized but *how* it is organized. Thus, in order to create a sense of authorship, at least in the cognitive domain, it is necessary to actively connect information from different sources and to fashion it objectively or subjectively depending on whether the information relates to personal experience or not. This cognitive demand challenges the expectations of the students, who are used to more simplistic ways of understanding the learning process. That they were clearly aware of this point when reporting on the initial moments of the course is demonstrated by the fourth theme. In this regard, we can compare those students' texts describing how they felt at the beginning of the course with this excerpt cited by Barber et al. (2013, p. 881) from a freshman student called Jade:

So far the papers I have been writing [are] so much less writing for what the teacher wants, which is what I have really done up until now; it's really writing the argument that you find. I think they [the faculty] really encourage that as they give you lots of different prompts and they are pretty ambiguous and they are hard to start with, but then you really find a point that you actually want to make and it's much more interesting to write about.

Although connecting information is evidence of a new way of organizing information, taking notice of subtle levels of information is the demonstration of to what extent there has been a real appropriation of this new way of processing and understanding. This entails not only that students have learnt theoretical concepts but also that that they have initiated or completed an epistemological change. The sudden realization of the meaning of an activity, or even the reason and purpose of a certain methodology or sequence of exercises, is evidence of a new way of making sense of one's experience. An example of this is being able to distinguish the content of learning (*what* was learnt or taught) from the processes organizing such content (*how* it was learnt or taught), and even from the reasons and purposes of that learning (*why* it was learnt or taught in the first place).

The fourth theme shows how students identified specific moments during the course that acted as points of contrast which enabled them to compare themselves in different moments as an example of reflecting on their learning experience (Cowan, 2006). It is in the process of elaborating their self-assessment that the students can integrate their "reflections in action" performed during the course from a broader perspective. Examining the final moments of the course and comparing them with initial and key intermediate events provide students with an opportunity to "reflect on" their experience and practice in a new and complex way. Carrying out this kind of reflective practice (Schön, 1983) is what will lead the students to be able to "reflect for" learning in future courses and, what is more, in their future professional or personal life.

Educational Implications

The importance of restructuring existing educational practices in order to intentionally promote student's self-authorship is a common concern (Barber et al., 2013; Yorke, 2003). Self-assessment within a formative context is one of the responses to such restructuration. In this line, the experience discussed in this chapter contributes to some of the debates about how to implement self-assessment in the context of higher education.

According to our experience, we agree with Nulty (2011) on the need for introducing self-assessment practices in the first year of higher education programs in order to promote deeper, reflective, critical and sustainable learning through time. As we have seen in the results section, not all the students took advantage of this resource, but at least they had the opportunity to explore their sense of authority and autonomy as creators of their own development. Some of the abilities that higher education students need to develop are: identifying standards and criteria, applying these to one's own and to others' work, and understanding how those standards have been applied by others to one's own work. The self-reflective skills we have referred to are part of a self-authoring way of processing information, and the sooner students begin to experience it the better (Cassidy, 2007).

With regards to the timing, in our view the optimal moment for carrying out a self-assessment which is intended to enhance developmental change in the students is at the end of the learning process. Traditionally, research on assessment practices has revolved around the importance of stating goals and standards so that students can monitor their own progress towards those goals (Schunk & Zimmerman, 1994; Pintrich, 1995). However, from a developmental perspective that follows epigenetic and orthogenetic principles, the issue of how to share and present the learning and developmental goals is not as simple as, for example, their being made explicit by the teacher at the beginning of a course. The epigenetic principle considers that development is created step by step, so that every step generates the conditions for the next one. This suggests that an objective stated at the beginning of a process can probably not be completely understood. For example, if the objective is to transform our students into self-directed learners, they will not understand what this means unless they can actually self-direct their own experience. The epigenetic principle does stress the emergent nature of the comprehension of the objectives, which can be understood and then explicitly set out and shared once students begin to achieve them. Their identification, as we discussed in relation to the third theme of our findings, is evidence of its achievement.

One corollary of this is that our preference for a final self-assessment might be better understood. The use of self-assessment during the learning process is useful for generating feedback for both teacher and students in terms of learning goals accomplishment, as well as for fostering reflection on prior knowledge, self-efficacy and expectations (Mok et al., 2006). However, the potential value of a comprehensive final self-assessment is that students can reflect on their whole learning process from a more evolved perspective than they had at the beginning of the course. In this regard, as we showed in the fourth theme of our results, qualitative change takes time to emerge and reflecting on one's own process is part of that change. Thus, the performance of a self-assessment at the end of the course might help students compare themselves at different moments. The following excerpt illustrates this:

S11 (Female, Merit with Distinction): *I think that the teacher's role in this process was to give us the materials and indirectly and directly the instructions in order to build it [the bridge], but the building itself was in our hands and I think that I didn't understand the instructions until a few days ago. That is to say, even when I could have done more, I had done a lot but I needed the change of perspective to make use of everything I had done.*

On the issue of whether the self-assessment should be optional or compulsory, like Leach (2012) we maintain the importance of presenting it as something negotiable. However, the most important thing for us is to generate a context of optionality during the whole course. Thus, the proposal of a final integrative assignment which includes an open self-assessment and a self-evaluation is negotiated throughout the course. Although students could opt for a more traditional assessment procedure, they were continually encouraged to choose the self-assessment proposal as we explained to them that it was designed to help them to integrate all the work done during the course. In contrast to the results obtained by Leach (2012), 65% of whose students preferred more traditional assessment procedures, almost all of our students chose our self-assessment approach. Once again, what is important for us is to generate contexts that facilitate willingness and active decisions on the part of our students so that they can then reflect on the reasons that justify their actual practice.

DIRECTIONS FOR FUTURE RESEARCH

The present study gives us some clues to help improve our teaching practice. One of them is in the line of performing a more systematic monitoring of the students throughout our courses in order to obtain more detailed evidence about the quality of their learning and developmental processes. Such monitoring could be carried out in two ways: on the one hand, by gathering time-series-data at the end of every class session in order to capture students' experiences regarding criteria such as complexity, usefulness, interest, comfort and fun; on the other hand, by carrying out formative tests at the end of every module in an attempt to check what information is being processed by the students and identify possible gaps.

At the level of general research into innovative assessment practices in higher education, we believe that the future of this field goes hand in hand with the need to understand that educational assessment: 1) is a process; 2) as such, is inherent to and permeates the learning process; 3) must be understood as a path to promoting both learning and development, not only as a means of checking the attainment of learning goals; and 4), must be built around meaningful activities for learners.

CONCLUSION

The learning experience presented here is a good example of how educational contexts can largely enhance students' epistemological development (Baxter Magolda, 2000, 2004; Iborra et al., 2009; Kegan, 1994, 2000; Nogueiras & Iborra, 2016). This study analyzed the self-assessments produced by students participating in a higher education course and aimed at enhancing self-direction, where self-assessment itself was understood as a means to both promoting and evaluating the development of such competence. As such, we believe that our approach might provide food for thought for higher education practitioners seeking to improve both the promotion of competences and the assessment practices used to evaluate them from a formative perspective. Additionally, this research has given us the opportunity to make explicit our implicit conceptions about learning and teaching and to investigate how they work in practice, above all in regard of how they guide our assessment practices.

ACKNOWLEDGMENT

The authors are grateful to the students who participated in the present study. They also would like to thank the anonymous reviewer for his/her useful suggestions on a previous version of this chapter. The first and the second author were generously funded by a grant for the Training of University Teachers from the University of Alcalá (Spain).

REFERENCES

Anderson, H. (1997). *Conversation, language, and possibilities: A postmodern approach to therapy*. New York, NY, US: Basic Books.

Andrade, H., & Valtcheva, A. (2009). Promoting learning and achievement through self-assessment. *Theory into Practice*, *48*(1), 12–19. doi:10.1080/00405840802577544

Barber, J. P., King, P. M., & Baxter Magolda, M. B. (2013). Long strides on the journey toward self-authorship: Substantial developmental shifts in college students' meaning making. *The Journal of Higher Education*, *84*(6), 866–896. doi:10.1353/jhe.2013.0033

Baxter Magolda, M. B. (1999). *Creating contexts for learning and self-authorship: constructive-developmental pedagogy*. Nashville, Tenn.: Vanderbilt University Press.

Baxter Magolda, M. B. (2000). Teaching to Promote Holistic Learning and Development. *New Directions for Teaching and Learning*, *82*(82), 88–98. doi:10.1002/tl.8209

Baxter Magolda, M. B. (2001). *Making their own way: Narratives for transforming higher education to promote self- authorship*. Sterling, VA: Stylus.

Baxter Magolda, M. B. (2004). Evolution of a constructivist conceptualization of epistemological reflection. *Educational Psychologist*, *39*(1), 31–42. doi:10.1207/s15326985ep3901_4

Baxter Magolda, M. B. (2009). *Authoring your life: Developing an internal voice to navigate life's challenges*. Sterling, VA: Stylus.

Biggs, J. B. (1996). Enhancing teaching through constructive alignment. *Higher Education*, *32*(3), 347–364. doi:10.1007/BF00138871

Black, P., & Wiliam, D. (2009). Developing the theory of formative assessment. *Educational Assessment, Evaluation and Accountability*, *21*(1), 5–31. doi:10.1007/s11092-008-9068-5

Boud, D. (1995). *Enhancing learning through self-assessment*. London: Kogan Page.

Braun, V., & Clarke, V. (2006). Using thematic analysis in psychology. *Qualitative Research in Psychology*, *3*(2), 77–101. doi:10.1191/1478088706qp063oa

Butler, D. L., & Winne, P. H. (1995). Feedback and self-regulated learning: A theoretical synthesis. *Review of Educational Research*, *65*(3), 245–281. doi:10.3102/00346543065003245

Cassidy, S. (2007). Assessing 'inexperienced' students' ability to self-assess: Exploring links with learning style and academic personal control. *Assessment & Evaluation in Higher Education*, *32*(3), 313–330. doi:10.1080/02602930600896704

Cowan, J. (2006). *On Becoming an Innovative University Teacher: Reflection in Action*. UK: McGraw-Hill Education.

Dochy, F., Segers, M., & Buehl, M. (1999). The relation between assessment practices and outcomes of studies: The case of research on prior knowledge. *Review of Educational Research*, *69*(2), 145–186. doi:10.3102/00346543069002145

Drago-Severson, E. (2011). A Close-up on Adult Learning and Development Diversity: Adult Growth in Cohorts and Collaborative Groups. In C. Hoare (Ed.), *The Oxford Handbook of Reciprocal Adult Development and Learning* (pp. 461–489). New York: Oxford University Press.

Gibbs, G. (1999). Using assessment strategically to change the way students learn. In S. Brown & A. Glaser (Eds.), *Assessment matters in higher education* (pp. 41–53). Buckingham: Open University Press.

Gow, L., & Kember, D. (1990). Does higher education promote independent learning? *Higher Education*, *19*(3), 307–322. doi:10.1007/BF00133895

Iborra, A., García, L., Margalef, L., & Pérez, V. (2009). Generating Collaborative Contexts to promote learning and development. In E. Luzzatto & G. DiMarco (Eds.), *Collaborative Learning: Methodology, Types of Interactions and Techniques* (pp. 47–80). New York: Nova Science Publishers.

Keeney, B. P. (1983). *Aesthetics of change*. New York: Guilford.

Kegan, R. (1994). *In over our heads: the mental demands of modern life*. Cambridge: Harvard University Press.

Kegan, R. (2000). What 'form' transforms? In J. Mezirow (Ed.), *Learning as transformation* (pp. 35–70). San Francisco: Jossey-Bass.

King, P., & Baxter Magolda, M. B. (1996). A Developmental Perspective on Learning. *Journal of College Student Development, 37*(2), 163–173.

King, P. M., & Siddiqui, R. (2011). Self-Authorship and Metacognition: Related Constructs for Understanding College Student Learning and Development. In C. Hoare (Ed.), *The Oxford Handbook of Reciprocal Adult Development and Learning* (pp. 113–131). New York: Oxford University Press; doi:10.1093/oxfordhb/9780199736300.013.0053

Kuh, G. D., Kinzie, J., Schuh, J. H., & Whitt, E. J. et al. (2005). *Student Success in College: Creating Conditions That Matter*. San Francisco: Jossey-Bass.

Landreman, L. M., Rasmussen, C. A., King, P. M., & Jiang, C. X. (2007). A Phenomenological study of the development of university educators' critical consciousness. *Journal of College Student Development, 48*(3), 275–295. doi:10.1353/csd.2007.0027

Leach, L. (2012). Optional self-assessment: Some tensions and dilemmas. *Assessment & Evaluation in Higher Education, 37*(2), 137–147. doi:10.1080/02602938.2010.515013

Long, H. B. (1989). Self-directed learning: Emerging theory and practice. In H. B. Long (Ed.), *Self-Directed Learning: Emerging Theory and Practice* (pp. 1–12). Norman, OK: Oklahoma Research Center for Continuing Professional and Higher Education of the University of Oklahoma.

Margalef García, L. (2014). Evaluación formativa de los aprendizajes en el contexto universitario: Resistencias y paradojas del profesorado. *Educación XX1, 17*(2), 35-55.doi:10.5944/educxx1.17.2.11478

McWhirter, J. (2002). Re-modelling NLP. Part Fourteen: Re-Modelling Modelling. *Rapport,* 59.

Mezirow, J. (2000). Learning to think like an adult: Core concepts of transformation theory. In J. Mezirow et al. (Eds.), *Learning as transformation: Critical perspectives on a theory in progress* (pp. 3–33). San Francisco: Jossey-Bass.

Miles, M. B., & Huberman, A. M. (1994). *Qualitative Data Analysis: An expanded sourcebook*. London: Sage.

Mok, M., Lung, C. L., Cheng, P. W., Cheung, H. P., & Ng, M. L. (2006). Self-assessment in higher education: Experience in using a metacognitive approach in five case studies. *Assessment & Evaluation in Higher Education, 31*(4), 415–433. doi:10.1080/02602930600679100

Nicol, D., & Macfarlane-Dick, D. (2006). Formative assessment and self-regulated learning: A model and seven principles of good feedback practice. *Studies in Higher Education, 31*(2), 199–218. doi:10.1080/03075070600572090

Nogueiras, G., Iborra, A., & Herrero, D. (2016). Dialogical Podcasts to Promote Reflection and Self-Direction in Higher Education. In *Proceedings of EAPRIL 2015, Issue 2*, (March 2016, pp. 233-245). Retrieved from: https://eaprilconference.files.wordpress.com/2015/11/proceedings-eapril-2015.pdf

Nogueiras, G., & Iborra, A. (2016, forthcoming). *Understanding and promoting self-direction in freshman and master's students: A qualitative approach*. Behavioral Development Bulletin.

Nulty, D. (2011). Peer and self-assessment in the first year of university. *Assessment & Evaluation in Higher Education, 5*(36), 439–507. doi:10.1080/02602930903540983

Paris, S. G., & Paris, A. H. (2001). Classroom applications of research on self-regulated learning. *Educational Psychologist, 36*(2), 89–101. doi:10.1207/S15326985EP3602_4

Pérez, R. J., Shim, W., King, P. M., & Baxter Magolda, M. B. (2015). Refining King and Baxter Magolda's model of intercultural maturity. *Journal of College Student Development, 56*(8), 759–776. doi:10.1353/csd.2015.0085

Pintrich, P. R. (1995). Understanding self-regulated learning. *New Directions for Teaching and Learning, 1995*(63), 3–12. doi:10.1002/tl.37219956304

Pintrich, P. R., & Zusho, A. (2002). The development of academic self-regulation: The role of cognitive and motivational factors. In A. Wigfield & J. S. Eccles (Eds.), *Development of achievement motivation* (pp. 249–284). San Diego, CA: Academic. doi:10.1016/B978-012750053-9/50012-7

Pizzolato, J. E. (2005). Creating Crossroads for Self-Authorship: Investigating the Provocative Moment. *Journal of College Student Development, 46*(6), 624, 641. doi:10.1353/csd.2005.0064

Richards, L. (1999). *Using NVivo in Qualitative Research*. London: Sage.

Schön, D. (1983). *The reflective practitioner*. New York: Basic Books.

Schunk, D. H., & Zimmerman, B. J. (1994). *Self-regulation of learning and performance: Issues and educational applications*. Lawrence Erlbaum Associates, Inc.

Taylor, E. W., & Cranton, P. (2013). A theory in progress? Issues in transformative learning theory. *European Journal for Research on the Education and Learning of Adults, 4*(1), 33–47. doi:10.3384/rela.2000-7426.rela5000

Van Geert, P. (2003). Dynamic systems approaches and modeling of developmental processes. In J. Valsiner & K. J. Conolly (Eds.), *Handbook of developmental psychology* (pp. 640–672). London: Sage.

Werner, H. (1957). The concept of development from a comparative and organismic point of view. In D. Harris (Ed.), *The concept of development*. Minneapolis, MN: University of Minnesota Press.

Winnicott, D. (1962). *The Maturational Processes and Facilitating Environment*. London: Hogarth Press.

Yorke, M. (2003). Formative assessment in higher education: Moves towards theory and the enhancement of pedagogic practice. *Higher Education, 45*(4), 477–501. doi:10.1023/A:1023967026413

KEY TERMS AND DEFINITIONS

Collaborative Learning: learning approach that aims to promote learning by doing, interacting and sharing ideas with peers and teachers while being part of a learning community.

Developmental Bridge: metaphorical description of an epistemological transition. In the context of the present chapter, it is related to the transition from third-order of consciousness (based on a dependent and passive pattern of relationship with others) towards fourth-order of consciousness (based on an independent and active pattern of relationship with others and oneself), according to Robert Kegan's theoretical model of development (1994).

Epistemology: the basic premises that underlie action and cognition and shape how we perceive, think, understand and act.

Epistemological Development: the path through increasingly complex ways of making sense of the world and operating in it.

Experiential Learning from a DBM Approach: Learning methodology that starts with individuals' exploration of their natural experience and intuitive understanding about the topics under study and is then complemented with the introduction of formal theoretical models by the teacher, so that these might be compared with personal and group experience. (McWhirter, 2002)

Formative Assessment: assessment whose main purpose is to provide information to students in order to help them to fill the gap between their current and future states of learning.

Self-Assessment: space for individuals to contemplate their learning processes over time from a reflective stance facilitating criticism and encouraging the introduction of improvements in their performance.

Self-Authorship: being able to utilize goals and perspectives that are internally grounded and evaluated as a foundation for meaning-making.

Self-Direction: complex competence that entails the ability to think critically, show initiative, set and pursue one's own goals and self-evaluate one's own processes.

Transformative Learning Theory: theory according to which learning is considered as a process of examining, questioning and revising one's current understandings and assumptions, thus opening the way to the development of more complex understandings and assumptions.

ENDNOTES

[1]   This is available online in the following address: http://goo.gl/fpvKxH

[2]   "Wherever development occurs it proceeds from a state of relative globality and lack of differentiation to a state of increasing differentiation, articulation and hierarchical integration". (Werner, 1957, p. 126).

[3]   "The form of a structure is literally constructed by the construction process itself, as every step creates the conditions for the next step". (Van Geert, 2003).

[4]   Examples of these films are "Secretos del Corazón" (Montxo Armendáriz, 1997), "Monsieur Lazhar" (Philippe Falardeau, 2011) and "Boyhood" (Richard Linklater, 2014).

Chapter 12
Student Participation in Assessment Processes:
A Way Forward

Victoria Quesada
Univesidad de Cádiz, Spain

Eduardo Garcia-Jimenez
Universidad de Sevilla, Spain

Miguel Angel Gomez-Ruiz
Universidad de Cádiz, Spain

ABSTRACT

The participation of students in higher education assessment processes has been proven to have many benefits. However, there is a diverse range of techniques and options when implementing participative assessment, with each offering new possibilities. This chapter focuses on the topic of student participation in assessment processes, and it explores the main stages when it can be developed: participation in design, during implementation, and in grading. This chapter also considers the different modalities that can be used, especially self-assessment, peer assessment, and co-assessment and the three stages that characterise them. Finally, it analyses three experiences of student participation in higher education assessment, highlighting their strengths and weaknesses. These experiences show how participative assessment can be developed in everyday classes, in groups, or individually and how participative assessment can occur in different class settings. They also demonstrate the importance of design, assessment literacy, and some difficulties that might appear during the process.

INTRODUCTION

Students have been objects of evaluation in traditional assessment approaches; they have been those who have received the actions of others without themselves being considered as active agents in the process. This perspective makes students' continuous learning more difficult because it does not prepare

DOI: 10.4018/978-1-5225-0531-0.ch012

students to make complex judgements and decisions in the uncertain context that they will encounter in the future (Boud & Falchikov, 2006). Indeed, student involvement in assessment-related actions, including designing instruments, deciding on the assessment criteria, assessing tasks, qualifying processes or products, and providing feedback on performance, gives students the opportunity to work on and improve abilities such as reasoned decision-making, creativity, and problem solving (As demonstrated in Gómez, Rodríguez & Ibarra, 2013).

This chapter discusses different approaches, modalities, and experiences that involve university students in the assessment of both their own performance and assignments and those of their peers. The manner in which student participation is implemented has its own benefits and disadvantages, and it should always be kept in mind that greater participation in the decision-making process during assessment facilitates self-regulated learning to a greater extent than low participation (Nicol, 2007; Orsmond et al., 2013).

To this end, when designing their courses, teachers should always take into consideration that 'implementing participative strategies, in which the voices of students are encouraged and considered, requires effort from both lecturers and students. For lecturers, this effort mainly involves planning and design. As far as students are concerned, participative assessment requires a greater amount of time and effort than non-participative assessments' (Quesada, Rodríguez & Ibarra, 2016, p.49).

CONCEPTUAL ANALYSIS

Modalities of Assessment

For a long period of time, assessment at the university level was conceived solely in terms of assessment performed by faculty members. However, involving students in the assessment of their learning is a growing trend. Indeed, promoting student participation in the assessment process is now part of the assessment policy in universities (Rodríguez, Ibarra & García, 2013).

Student participation in the assessment process might be constrained to performing an assigned task. In contrast, it might be assumed to be an extended practice that includes students in the decision-making process with regard to the most important aspects of the assessment process, from the design of assignments to the provision of feedback. A wide range of alternatives can be found between these two positions.

In general, it can be claimed that student involvement can be integrated at any time in the assessment process. Furthermore, this process can be divided conceptually into three distinct stages or steps (Rodríguez, Ibarra & García, 2013):

1. **Involvement in the Assessment Design**: This stage includes negotiating the evaluation approach and the various aspects of planning, including the assessment criteria, the assignments to be completed, the agents responsible for their execution, the instruments to be completed, and the weighting of the grades.
2. **Involvement in the Implementation of the Actual Assessment:** At this stage, depending on who assesses and who is assessed, up to four modalities of assessment can be identified. These modalities are detailed below.
3. **Involvement in the Grading Process**: In this last step, the information provided by those in charge of the assessment is reflected in the final grades obtained in the subject.

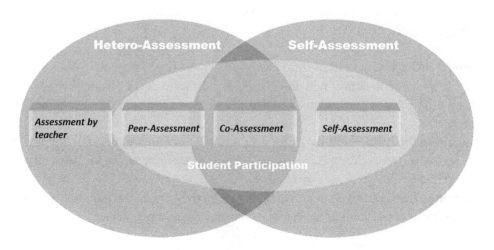

Bearing in mind these three stages and the various elements that compose assessment a great diversity of potential participatory combinations may be available to students. These range from simply negotiating the assessment criteria to being able to decide on any aspect of the design, being responsible for executing the assessment, and having their grades reflected in the final scores. The only logical constraint is students' inability to participate in the grading if they have not previously been involved in the implementation of the actual assessment.

Despite the possible diversity that exists, the most common circumstance found in the literature and in practice is that students participate in the assessment of their own performance or that of their peers through the existing participatory modalities of assessment.

After including students in the evaluative process, three modalities that make students responsible for the implementation of the assessment have been conceptualised, depending on who the assessor is and whose task or performance is being assessed. These are:

1. Self-assessment
2. Peer assessment
3. Co-assessment

Figure 1 allows a better understanding of these modalities of participation, offering the possibility of observing the relationships between the terminological dichotomy of self-assessment (assessing oneself) versus hetero-assessment (assessing someone else) and the four modalities of assessment commonly used. The assessment performed by the teaching staff can be regarded as exclusively hetero-assessment, in contrast to student self-assessment. Between these two extremes lies co-assessment or joint assessment by the teacher and the student. Finally, peer assessment is essentially a form of hetero-assessment. There are two types of assessment in which peer assessment and self-assessment intersect, specifically when a student assesses the product of his or her work team or when the group itself evaluates its performance, because both assessments will take into account the work performed by oneself and by others simultaneously.

Figure 1. Student involvement and the modalities of assessment
(Gómez, Rodríguez and Ibarra, 2011, p.42) Source: Gómez, Rodríguez, and Ibarra, 2011

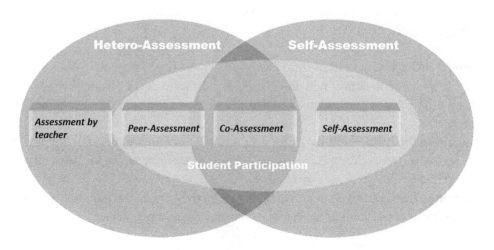

Next, further details regarding the three modalities that allow students' involvement in assessment are presented.

Assessing One's Work: Self-Assessment

Self-assessment is one of the most characteristic forms of student involvement in the assessment process. Boud (1995) defines it as the act of questioning and judging oneself and making decisions on the next steps to be taken. Roberts (2006, p.3) provides a more academic definition, understanding self-assessment as 'the process of having the learners critically reflect upon, record the progress of, and perhaps suggest grades for their own learning'. Similarly, Mok et al. (2006) focus on the learning dimension of self-assessment as a method for increasing knowledge regarding learning itself to improve present and future strategies. In addition, Gómez, Rodríguez, and Ibarra (2011) regard self-assessment as a way of assessing and learning in which students analyse and evaluate their performance.

These definitions focus on two aspects of assessment: reflecting on one's work and learning. Indeed, there are many authors who highlight the advantages of self-assessment and its influence on student learning; it ought to be considered that during the self-assessment process, students are active agents and co-responsible for the assessment process, which increases their engagement in the activities that are undertaken (Nicol and Macfarlane-Dick, 2006); they learn from their own experiences. Assessing their own performances promotes students' critical thinking skills (Hanrahan and Isaacs, 2001) and empowers them (Taylor and Robinson, 2009), which means that it strengthens students' abilities, making them more confident and increasing their autonomy. In line with this, Mok et al. (2006) argue that self-assessment develops students' understanding of their own learning, and therefore, students also develop the ability to regulate their own learning. Self-regulation (Boekaerts, Maes, and Karoly, 2005; Butler and Winne, 1995; Nicol & McFarlane-Dick, 2006; Zimmerman, 2002) refers to the process of students determining which learning strategies work or do not work for them.

Self-assessment is a practice that, even today –according to recent research –, is not typically present in classrooms. A longitudinal study in an American institution confirms that although there has been an increase in the use of self-assessment, its use remains low (Taras, 2014). Another recent study conducted in Spain with a sample of 427 university teachers shows that although the majority of respondents believed that self-assessment was an important modality of assessment, only 9.4% of them used it on a regular basis in their courses (Quesada, Rodríguez & Ibarra, 2016). In this sense, Taras (2015, p.5) reflects on 'why self-assessment is often ignored, despite theories demonstrating that self-assessment is an essential part of self-regulated learning and learners (surely an aim of HE)'.

Assessing Someone Else's Work: Peer Assessment

A common practice regarding student participation includes situations in which the student assesses the work or performance of a single peer, a group of peers, or the entire class, preferably using relevant criteria (Fachikov, 2001). This assessment may entail grading the work performed by peers or providing feedback on their work through comments. When assessment focuses on providing feedback and revision to peers, the term peer review is used. In general terms, peer assessment can be defined as the 'arrangement for learners to consider and specify the level, value, or quality of a product or performance of other equal status learners' (Topping, 2009, p.20).

Figure 2. Methods of peer-assessment
(Translated from and based in Ibarra, Rodríguez & Gómez, 2012 p.213) Source: Ibarra, Rodríguez & Gómez, 2012

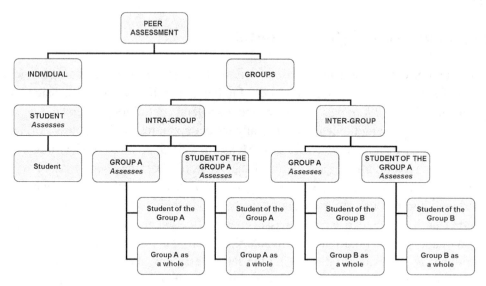

The first definitions of peer assessment always emphasised its group nature (Falchikov, 1986). Indeed, many taxonomies referred to the existence of only two types of peer assessment (Syvan, 2000): intra-group and intergroup. Roberts (2006) proposed using the term "group assessment" to refer to all the existing types of group evaluation in general, especially with the aim of replacing the concept of "intra-group" peer assessment. Subsequently, individual peer assessment, of one student by another, was explicitly included in this classification as a third basic option (Falchikov, 2005; Prins et al., 2005). Thus, there are a total of nine basic methods for performing peer assessment (See Figure 2).Two of them can also be viewed as types of self-assessment, specifically inter-group peer assessment, in which a group assesses an entire group (Rodríguez, Ibarra, and García, 2013:204), and intra-group peer assessment, in which a member assesses his or her entire group.

Specialised studies have identified various benefits from peer assessment (Sambell and McDowell, 1998; Dochy, Segers, and Sluijsmans, 1999; Sivan, 2000; Hanrahan and Isaacs, 2001; Segers and Dochy, 2001; Prins et al., 2005; Nicol and Macfarlane-Dick 2006; Ljungman and Silén, 2008):

1. **The Improvement of Learning Processes and Products:** Peer assessment increases learning while promoting self-regulation and the development of skills and performance; it becomes an incentive to improve individual work and group work and also stimulates deep critical thinking.
2. **The Development of Soft Skills:** Empathy, responsibility, teamwork, negotiation, and cooperation are developed.
3. **The Ability to Make Sensible Judgements and to Evaluate Is Improved:** Peer assessment contributes to making students' assessments more accurate.
4. **Its Importance in Developing a Professional Career:** Involvement in peer assessment activities has been considered a key element in the working world.

Assessing One's Work in Collaboration with the Teacher: Co-Assessment

Co-assessment or collaborative assessment was defined by Falchikov (1986) as the type of assessment in which students and teachers negotiate and discuss the assessment criteria and the final grade. Dochy et al. (1999) conceive of it as a joint effort to achieve a "shared goal". Gómez, Rodríguez, and Ibarra (2011; 2012) understand co-assessment to be the joint assessment by faculty and students of the learning demonstrated by the latter. Therefore, it can be deduced that co-assessment is a type of consensual and participatory assessment in which faculty and students negotiate and conduct a joint revision and evaluation of the task completed by the students, which might include grading the task. Nonetheless, as Bovill and Bulley (2011) suggest, there may be a great variety in the quality and quantity of this collaboration.

In order to avoid errors in the use of co-assessment it should be specified that co-assessment is not implemented when professors assess a piece of work, and students assess the same piece of work through self-assessment with no joint reflection or discussion, for co-assessment is more than merely two actors assessing the same assignment, it implies that teachers and students negotiate, discuss and agree on the evaluation of what is assessed.

Collaborative assessment has significant benefits because it brings into play not only the strategies and benefits of self-assessment but also the contrast between one's assessment and the assessments of faculty members. Co-assessment promotes deep learning (Knight & Yorke, 2003) because it improves students' understanding of their performance (Deeley, 2014) and increases students' confidence (Boud & Falchikov, 2007; Knight & Yorke, 2003) effort and motivation (Dochy et al. 1999). It might be expected that co-assessment also enhances empowerment and self-regulation. Similarly, since reflection and discussion are prominent in this type of assessment co-assessment heightens skills related to communication, negotiation, and argumentation.

A study (Quesada, Gómez, Cubero, 2015) developed with three lecturers implementing co-assessment with first-year students consistently throughout one of their courses showed that lecturers found it to be highly beneficial, they felt that co-assessment had developed students responsibility and self-regulation, transparency of the process, a better classroom climate and trust among teachers and students.

Despite its significant benefits, of the three types of participatory evaluation, co-assessment is the least frequently used (Quesada, Rodríguez and Ibarra, 2016; Rodríguez et al., 2012), the least well-known, and the modality that causes the most uncertainty among university teaching staff (Quesada et al., 2016) because teachers must sit down with students and discuss the outcome of the assessment. A principal drawback that teachers might consider when deciding whether to implement co-assessment is the amount of time they need to develop such practices (Quesada, Gómez, Cubero 2015), which might be a problem in very large groups of students. Another drawback is that teachers must be confident in their expertise and flexible and open to students' suggestions and opinions; it is possible that a teacher is not up to the task and implements a 'false co-assessment' in which the he or she does not actually negotiate because he or she has a previous grade in mind that is not discussed, changed or threatened regardless of the co-assessment. In addition, teachers must expect the unexpected; assessment is a deeply emotional process, and many situations may arise from this situation. However, some solutions that minimise these drawbacks can be considered; teachers could implement co-assessment in group activities, which would decrease the amount of time needed; in addition, a research study (Rodríguez, Quesada & Ibarra, 2016) has shown that when lecturers receive training, they consider themselves more likely to implement participative practices (and co-assessment) in their courses.

Participative Assessment in Practice: Experiences

This section presents three experiences of student participation in assessment processes that were developed for undergraduate courses. The context, development, and research findings achieved in each experience are presented. Finally, the strengths and weaknesses are analysed.

Experience 1: Group Self-Assessment and Peer Review

The first experience illustrates an approach to student participation in assessment through group self-assessment and peer review.

This experience was implemented in the first-year Systematic Observation and Context Analysis course that is part of the degree in Early Childhood Education at the Universidad de Cádiz. The sessions of the course were divided into two types: large-group sessions of all 67 students that consisted of lectures and theory-related activities and small-group sessions for groups of 34 and 32 students that involved putting theory into practice and developing a group assessment task.

Assessment in the course entailed two tasks: an individual task, in which each student wrote an essay on the topic, and a group task, which was developed progressively throughout the course. The group task ended with the writing of a report on a topic of the students' own choosing. Student motivation in the task was very high, apparently because they could make use of the strategies in authentic situations.

In this task, students had to complete multiple activities.

- **Activity 1**: Planning an observation design: First, students had to choose a Pre-School and define its main features. Once the school was chosen and they had access to the centre, students performed multiple non-systematic observations to decide on the topic of observation. Afterwards, students started their observation design in which they established the observation object, i.e., what to observe; the objectives; the temporalisation; and the role of the observer.
- **Activity 2**: Observation methods: Students chose the observation methods that they were going to use to gather information and designed them.
- **Activity 3**: In-context observations and data analysis: Students had to go to the school and implement the observations that they had designed; they had to record the data using the methods planned. Additionally, during observations, students were asked to write their thoughts and reflections in a journal during the process as a preliminary analysis of the data. During and after the observations, students also categorised the data and analysed them to draw some conclusions.
- **Activity 4**: Writing the observation report: The observation report included all the information needed to understand the process and the results. It had an introduction, brief framework, context, objectives, methods, results, conclusions, bibliography and reflection on the topic. This task comprised all the aforementioned activities and was the task that was officially submitted and graded at the end of the course.

During the entire process, the teacher provided feedback on the activities that were developed: While performing each activity, oral and informal feedback was provided during the small-group sessions, if requested; after completing the activities, formal written feedback was provided by the professor.

The four activities culminated in the report. Before its submission to be graded, students had to deliver a draft version of the report for on-line peer review; additionally, each group was asked to specify three aspects on which they would like to receive feedback. No formal training on how to perform assessment was offered; however, the assessment criteria were explained so that students could better understand them. On this occasion, peer review was not anonymous; because grades were not provided, the lecturer considered knowing who provided the feedback and whose task students were reviewing to be an advantage.

Each group of students reviewed the reports of two different groups of peers using EVALcomix, an on-line system for facilitating the process. While reviewing the report, students had to address, if possible, the three questions posed by the reviewed group and also offer other comments on the formal aspects of the report (structure, format, coherence) and its content (clarity, depth of the ideas, and results). The following intentions guided this work: 1) Students could review the work of their peers and provide feedback on how to improve it; 2) students learned from the reviewing process and therefore could implement improvements in their own report by determining good and bad performances based on the work of their peers; and 3) students would benefit from the reviews of their peers and improve their work before the final submission.

After receiving the reviewed report, students had time to consider the reviews provided by their peers and modify and improve the assignment before the final submission. To further promote student reflections on their work, students were asked to write a qualitative self-assessment and attach it in the final submission. The teacher believed that in doing so, they would conduct a final review of their work and improve it.

After the experience, a questionnaire was administered to analyse student satisfaction and perceptions; 49 of the 67 students participated. Overall, most of the students were very satisfied with the experience: 77.6% of the students believed that the experience was positive, whereas 20.4% felt otherwise. Self-assessment was valued higher than peer review: 75.5% of the students expressed that they very much liked having the opportunity to self-assess their own work, whereas only 55.1% held the same view with regard to reviewing the work of their peers (34.7% indicated that they liked it some and 10.2% not at all).

Students considered that self-assessment and peer review benefited their learning in the following aspects (from the most frequently noted to the least):

- Developing an open attitude (n=15): accepting mistakes, criticism, different perspectives, and critical thinking.
- Improving performance and future tasks (n=15): improving performance, learning from mistakes and correcting them, organising one's own learning, and deepening the understanding of contents.
- Learn to assess (n=14): reflect on one's own work, do constructive reviews, review and correct mistakes.
- Learning from the performance of their peers (n=11): work, organisation, and mistakes.
- Learning from the reviews received (n=7).
- Very little (n=5).

Similarly, most of the students (n=15) noted as a positive aspect the fact that they were able to improve their own performance after peer review, seeing the work of their peers or through self-assessment, and, having the opportunity to know whether they were on the right path. Other aspects that were noted as very positive were to having the opportunity to know their peer's opinions on their work (14 students), followed by having the chance to see the work of their peers (9 students). In that regard, many students considered it very enriching to see different approaches to the same task; one student stated that "We can see how each group worked, and we can evaluate our own task".

Five students reasoned that the opportunity to assess had been very positive. Finally, another aspect that was advanced was the use of the virtual on-line system for peer review and self-assessment (n=4); two students believed that it had been very useful, and two other students appreciated its speed for peer review.

The limitations or drawbacks revealed were mainly technical issues (16 students): technical glitches in the on-line system used for peer review, difficulties using the virtual campus, and complications with the internet connection while reviewing the work of others.

Another drawback found was the concern over plagiarism; many students (10) expressed their concern, by stating that other students could copy ideas from the work they had submitted.

This fear might be due to the competitive nature of some students, and it is very controversial in relation to the peer review process, which, indeed, entails the ability to review good and bad performances so that students can learn and improve their own work.

Other limitations or concerns that were identified by some of the students were the reliability of the reviews and suggestions (n=4); the lack of ability to answer some of the questions posed by their peers (n=2); a lack of time or an excessive workload (n=1); the fear of hurting their peers' feelings; the difficulty of being objective; and the fact that some peers did not complete the peer review or did not take it seriously. Four students stated that they did not find any limitations.

Experience 2: Self and Peer Assessment as Grading

This experience provides an example of students participating in the grading process. It was developed over three years (from 2010 to 2013) for an elective course for the Bachelor's Degree in Educational Psychology from the University of Cádiz (Spain). Specifically, a total of 56 students participated, distributed across the three academic years: 12 in 2010-2011, 20 in 2011-2012, and 24 in 2012-2013.

The course, always taught by the same teacher, was titled Qualitative Research Methods. It lasted four months, and its main objective was designing and developing a full research study, taking a qualitative approach. To achieve this objective, the methodology focused on students' completion of a guided project over the entire term, which implied performing the key steps in a research study, from the design of the project to the drafting of the final report, including the design of the instruments, the collection of the data, and an oral presentation on the findings. The project was done individually or in pairs, and accounted for 80% of the final grade in the course, with the latter being supplemented by individual theoretical work that consisted of answering on-line questionnaires and open-ended questions.

The course was offered during the final year of the degree programme; thus, the participants already had academic experience at the university level. It is important to emphasise that this experience was performed in a blended learning degree, limiting personal interactions to approximately seven or eight sessions per course. Thus, the learning management system used (Moodle) for communication and reviewing assignments was of particular importance in the learning process, in addition to the teaching website, designed specifically to guide students in their projects (Gómez-Ruiz, Rodríguez-Gómez, Ibarra-Sáiz & Gallego-Noche, 2013).

The task details and the general dynamics of the course were explained on the first day, in addition to the assessment design proposed by the teacher, which implied student participation in the assessment and grading process. The proposal was accepted by the students in the three classes; in some cases, students were surprised by this original approach.

Research began during the second week, when the object of study was defined and a first draft of a research project that included planning the next steps to be taken began to be drawn. After submitting the first projects, the teacher revised them and offered feedback, without grades, to each student through Moodle assignments. After receiving this information, students had to redo their work and deliver their final draft.

The second stage involved the design of instruments and the subsequent collection of data. Once again, the students virtually proposed a set of instruments that were assessed by the teacher, and offered written feedback. Subsequently, students had to submit improved version of the product. Finally, students analysed the data and prepared the final report and oral presentation for the class. Feedback for these last few steps was provided in addition to the final grade.

Once the process was complete, the research work was assessed and graded using the following modalities and weightings:

1. **Teacher assessment:** 50% of the grade
2. **Self-assessment:** 25% of the grade
3. **Peer assessment:** 25% of the grade

It is important to note that one of the sessions in the course was specifically devoted to training students so they could conduct this assessment. During this training session, all of the details on the process were explained in depth, doubts were resolved, and an assessment was conducted using the same instrument that would be used later.

A fundamental feature of this experience was the assessment instrument used. A detailed e rubric with two versions was designed to address the various modalities of assessment: one version for teacher assessment and self-assessment regarding the entire process and another version for peer assessment evaluating the final report and oral presentation. Each student had to complete two rubrics: one for self-assessment and another for peer assessment of a project assigned at random. EvalCOMIX, a web service for e-Assessment was used.

The scale used for assessing each attribute on the rubric was divided into four levels: Poor (values from 5 to 25), Acceptable (30 to 50), Outstanding (55 to 75), and Excellent (80 to 100). Each level had a full corresponding descriptor to facilitate grading. Finally, for comments, the rubric had an open mandatory field in which students had to justify their assessment in writing, highlighting positive and negative aspects of the project assessed.

To understand student perceptions on self- and peer assessment when their grading was reflected, two discussion groups were created. The attending students were questioned about their opinions and judgements on the experience, among other issues. Several positive aspects and difficulties can be extracted.

The students considered their participation in the assessment process to be something positive with regard to their professional training and the responsibility it entailed, as reflected in the final grade. They believed it was a fair and democratic form of grading, not only because the entire process was taken into account but also because students' own assessments of their performance were considered.

I was able to assess all my work, not only the final result, but the time, interest, and concern related to the class... These are things that do not have to do with the final product and that are not usually taken into account, but I really value them. S10-3

Similarly, students considered that the feedback from the rubric given by their peers and the teacher, in addition to comparing one's project with that of others, provides valuable lessons that would improve their future work.

It also helps you to compare the work done by your classmates with yours, and that's when you start to really evaluate your own work. You get ideas and see ways to improve what you've done. S10-4

Finally, as highlights, they also noted the coherence between the assessment system and the learning methodology as one of the strengths of the experience, in addition to the usefulness of conducting formal evaluations that included grading.

However, as anticipated, the difficulties encountered when facing the assessing assignment were considerable. The comments repeatedly noted that this was an unusual practice and as such it was a complex task; the students were not used to it. They perceived that it entailed several ethical dilemmas, and they doubted their own ability to provide accurate assessments, demanding more training in this regard during the entire educational system, not only at the university level.

We are not used to assessing others, especially at that level... I find it really interesting, but it is something we don't work on specifically in primary education and very little in secondary school, so when you arrive and they tell you that you give two points and other two are given by your classmates, you say, Huh!... S11-1

However, one of the greatest concerns of the students was being fair in their grading, either with themselves or with their classmates. They noted that when assessing their peers, being critical is a difficult task, given that they empathise with the other students, as they are in the same situation and know the effort required to pass a university course. With regard to self-assessment, they thought that they would have a tendency to overestimate their work due to sheer self-interest or on the grounds that those projects represent their best effort.

When you are assessing a project, you need to have a criterion, and even though you gave us the guidelines, you are affected by your role as a student ... I will always benefit my classmates; I won't harm them. S11-6

As to the accuracy of the ratings given by students, the scores provided by the students who participated in the self-assessments and peer assessments were analysed and compared with each other and with teacher assessment. As expected, the modality of assessment with the highest scores was self-assessment, with a mean of 8.53 on a scale from 0 to 10 (standard deviation (SD) 0.77). Peer assessments averaged 7.80 (SD 0.95). Finally, the mean for the teacher assessments was 7.01 (SD 0.48).

The Spearman coefficient was calculated (Table 1) to determine whether there was some type of correlation between the three modalities of assessment

Table 1. Correlations between self-assessments, peer assessments, and teacher assessments

		Self-Assessment	Peer As.	Teacher As.
Self-assessments	**Correlation Coefficient**	1.000	-0,284(*)	-0.058
	Sig. (bilateral)		0.034	0.673
Peer As.	**Correlation Coefficient**		1.000	0,293(*)
	Sig. (bilateral)			0.028
Teacher As.	**Correlation Coefficient**			1.000
	Sig. (bilateral)			

* Correlation is significant at the 0.05 level (bilateral).

The data in Table 1 show that there was a significant negative correlation between self-assessment and peer assessment and a significant positive correlation between peer and teacher assessment. There was a weak, non-significant negative correlation between self-assessment and teacher assessment. In other words, the students seemed to assess other students' projects in a manner that was consistent with that of the professor; however, self-assessment seemed to be affected by other elements. Indeed, it is possible that peer and teacher assessments compensated for the high scores in self-assessment to the point of creating a negative correlation.

To conclude, an odd event that occurred during the experience is worth noting since it can help the reader think about roles during assessment and how the weight of the final grade can affect an adjusted assessment process. During the first year, after receiving his final grade, a student complained because he thought he deserved a higher grade. The teacher was surprised to see that his grade was exactly the same as that provided by the student in the self-assessment. The obvious question was, 'Why did the student not rate him more generously?' The response was that he thought that by being very critical, the teacher would "reward" him by giving him a higher grade. In the end, the student's grade did not change, but this event showed that all things being equal, students felt that the teacher still held power over the entire assessment process.

Experience 3: Group Peer Review

This experience occurred at the University of Seville in the four-years-Degree in Early Childhood Education. A total of 180 first-year students organised into three groups of 60 students in the theory classes and six groups of 30 students in the practical classes were enrolled in this degree. They all attended the "Diagnosis in Education: Observation and interview in early childhood education" course.

The students did not have prior training on learning assessment, and their only practical experience in this field was what they had acquired as pupils throughout their schooling. Approximately 75% of the students came to the University from secondary schools and were approximately 18 years of age. The remaining 25% were approximately 22 years of age, had completed professional training related to early childhood education, and had practical experience, especially in educational institutions that teach children ages 0 to 3 years.

In the "Diagnosis in Education: Observation and interview in early childhood education" course, students learn to observe, record, and assess the behaviour of children from 0 to 6 years of age and to interview their families. To do so, they rely on video and audio recordings, images, writing, drawings, etc. that were previously created in the classroom or during breaks. Similarly, students also have access to recorded interviews of families conducted by teachers. In the first course, given that students do not have contact with children 3, 4, and 5 years of age, the audio-visual recordings, images, and written documents help them approximate an actual class. Students learn how to complete rating scales, check lists, rubrics, critical incident reports, and teacher journals. To interview families, they learn to design questionnaires and interviews. Finally, students learn how to complete assessment reports in accordance with the protocols established by school administrators and to inform families about the results of teaching and assessment of children.

This experience has been implemented since the 2011-2012 academic year. The three teachers of the course, who share the same syllabus and assessment procedure, participated in it. Its origin lies in the need for students not only to learn the fundamentals of learning assessment but also to acquire the skills that will enable them to assess their own students when they become teachers in a few years. In this sense, the goals set by allowing student participation in the assessment of learning are the following:

- To involve the students in the practice of evaluation in authentic assessment that is not simulated or mediated (via audio and/or video recording).
- To facilitate the practice of assessment for students through the development of assessment criteria and standards, the design and implementation of assessment tools, grading, and the provision of feedback.
- To help students transfer the knowledge and skills acquired in the 'Diagnosis in Education: Observation and interview in early childhood education' course that are related to the procedures of observation, recording, and learning assessment of children between 0 and 6 years of age (checklists, estimate scales, rubrics, etc.) to assess the learning of peers who are enrolled in the course. This transfer will help students learn to assess children from 0 to 6 years of age once they become teachers.
- To put students in situations that allow them to reflect on the fundamentals, scope, and consequences of learning assessment and also to discuss controversial issues regarding learning assessment, including the power associated with grading and the implications of assessment in people's present and future lives.

The students who participated in this experience performed, in pairs, a peer review of the work done by their peers in the 'Diagnosis in Education: Observation and interview in early childhood education' course. Before starting the peer review process, the students did not receive any specific training except for the following instructions:

1. Review and assess the work performed by your classmates in practical activity X.
2. Once the assignment review has been completed and drafted, give the assignment a score from 0 to 10 and send your assessment to the teacher through the Blackboard platform.

The decision to offer only brief instructions to the students prior to revising their peers' work is based on the conviction that according to the teachers own experience, students are naturally equipped to assess others in certain situations (e.g., eating, anticipating a potential danger, buying a product, etc.) as members of the human race. They know how to gather information, assess its significance according to certain criteria, compare the current situation with previous situations, weigh the different existing alternatives, and make decisions. Consequently, all that one must do is create the situations that allow students to realise what they already know and apply their assessment-related skills. Once they achieve this task, it is necessary to train them to help them systematise and formalise their learning. In short, the teachers believed that their students are adults and should learn as adults, that is, by learning from experience and reflecting on said experience (Kolb, 1984).

Peer review was performed during the practical sessions and in small groups of 3 to 4 members, who could remain unchanged or vary with each new review. Each small group assessed a total of 6 assignments performed in an academic period between February and June, with a focus on oral language, writing, reading, numbering, personal autonomy, etc. Each review was performed by a different group of peers; thus, for example, group 1 never assessed the assignments performed by group 2 more than once.

Teachers considered both the assignments themselves and the reviews performed by peers. To that end, teachers used rubrics developed *ad hoc* for each assignment. The rubrics, scores, and feedback obtained by the groups were transmitted to the students through the Blackboard platform.

Once assessed by the teacher, the students had access to their peers' reviews for both their group and the other groups. This exchange of reviews and assessments occurred throughout the different assignments performed throughout the course. Thus, students could learn to improve their reviews by analysing the reviews of other students who were positively assessed by the teachers and could compare those with their own or by asking other groups for guidance or requiring explanations that justify the scores and comments made by their peers.

The ongoing analysis of this experience during the four academic courses, and based on the outcomes achieved by the students and their own assessments collected in questionnaires with open-ended questions and classroom discussions, allowed us to create the following strengths, weaknesses, opportunities, and threats (SWOT) analysis.

Among the strengths of peer review obtained from this analysis, the following should be noted:

1. Peer review brings students closer to the knowledge and skills related to the learning assessment used by an early childhood education teacher.
2. It puts into practice both the "innate" knowledge and skills related to assessment and the knowledge and skills acquired in students' childhood and uses them in the context of formal education (university and preschool).
3. Individually and in groups, peer review facilitates students' analysis of and reflection on basic assessment-related issues, including design, development, outcomes, and implications. It makes them reflect on the importance of assessment criteria, the use of instruments for systematic assessment, the importance of feedback or the consequences of assessment, and how to transmit their feedback to others, all in a context in which one must assess and be assessed by others.

Among the weaknesses of peer review detected in our experience, the following are noteworthy:

•   Peer review was performed in groups, not individually. Up to a point, this feature alienated students from their future practice as teachers, given that in most cases they will have to assess children without their peers' help. However, what was learned in this peer review will help these future teachers to discuss assessment criteria, feedback, etc. with others.
•   The students who participated in this experience learned to be thorough and precise in the review of their peers' work and to give accurate feedback, but they had difficulties when grading the as-

signments completed by their peers. Grading skills did not improve as much as the other assessment skills did.
- The experiment conducted in this module was unique. The remaining courses in the curriculum did not use peer review, or at least not in the terms presented here.

The opportunities offered to students through this experience can be summarised as follows:

- Students participated in an assessment process and made decisions on basic features as though they were actually teachers: they defined the criteria, chose the assessment procedures, assessed the work of others, provided feedback, graded, and informed others of their assessment.
- Students learned to make assessments that they could apply as teachers in early childhood education or in any other professional activity. They learned the theory and practice that could be applied to knowledge acquired in their professional field.
- Participating in this experience helped students regulate their learning to the extent that it allowed them to identify their learning goals and analyse and assess their progress according to these goals.

The threats posed to this peer review experience could be:

- The increased number of students enrolled or the assignment of professors to the "Diagnosis in Education: Observation and interview in early childhood education" course. In some academic courses, some professors have taught up to 120 students.
- Changing the professors who teach the course, given that the allocation of professors changes for every academic course and there is the possibility that new professors disapprove of the peer review approach.
- The pressure exercised by those who are against peer review. In a context in which this methodology is a minority, it is difficult to maintain it without the support of students.

JOINT ANALYSIS OF THE EXPERIENCES

The analysis of the three experiences was conducted using a technique developed by Miles and Huberman (1994) that uses a display matrix for a cross-site evaluation. Table 2 shows a matrix in which the columns refer to the three experiences and the rows to a series of questions that allow for comparison and joint review.

The matrix displays the similarities and differences observed between the experiences. One major finding obtained is that student participation in assessment can be integrated into day-to-day classroom life. Student involvement in assessment can be integrated into different types of education contexts, such as face to face or blended learning, with a diverse number of students enrolled in a course, and it can occur over several academic years.

A second finding is that students can participate in the assessment, individually or in groups, using different methods such as self-assessment, peer review, and peer assessment. Similarly, students are offered the possibility of grading their peers' work, or simply reviewing and giving feedback to their peers. Finally, students can participate in all or some of the activities related to assessment. Thus, the students can define the assessment criteria and standards, design assessment tools and apply them, provide feed-

Table 2. Matrix of the experiences presented

	Experience 1	**Experience 2**	**Experience 3**
Teaching	Face to face	Blended learning	Face to face
Sample	67 first-year students; half of the group in practice sessions	56 senior students, approximately 20 students per academic year	180 first-year students. 30 per classroom in practice sessions
Time frame	1 academic year	3 academic years	4 academic years
Academic tasks	One individual task and one group (4-5 students) task developed throughout the course (4 activities)	Only one individual task developed over three and a half months	6 small groups (3-4 students) tasks, 2-3 weeks each one
Assessment training	No	Yes	No
Student participation	Group self-assessment and peer assessment as peer review	Self-assessment and peer assessment	Group peer assessment as peer review
Assessment process participation	Implementation	Implementation, grading	Design, implementation
Marks by students	No	Yes	No
Type of participation in the assessment process	Application of toolkits developed by teacher and feedback	Application of toolkits developed by teacher, feedback, marks	Criteria and definition of standards, toolkits design, and feedback
Achievement and student satisfaction	Students' perceptions were positive about their participation in the assessment process. Most of them believed that self-assessment and peer assessment helped them improve their learning.	A statistically significant positive correlation was found between peer assessment and teacher assessment, and a negative correlation was found between self-assessment and peer assessment. Students believed that their participation led to assessment that was fairer and more democratic.	Most of the students improved their assessment skills and were able to transfer their theoretical knowledge and previous experiences about assessment to assessment practices as prospective teachers.
Concerns related to assessment	Plagiarism by peers; The reliability and validity of peer review; the fear of hurting their peer's feelings	Empathy with peers could interfere with a fair assessment	Scoring tasks completed by peers; they would be able to improve their skills related to the score
What issues about student participation in assessment could be improved	Excessive workload because students had to devote extra time to assessment. Some students felt that they did not have enough experience and confidence to assess	Students tended to overvalue their performance in the self-assessment process.	Student participation in assessment is an unusual experience in their courses.

back to their peers, and grade their work. Although it did not occur in any experience, they could also suggest assessment assignments. In conclusion, students participation in assessment is a social control tool so that 'the introduction of peer assessment should assure that specific valuable learning activities take place, even if the teacher cannot control everything (…) and may be an external motivator to work harder and perform better' (Gielen, Dochy, Onghena, Struyven & Smeets, 2011, p.721-722)., A third and motivating finding shows that student's learning augments when they are involved in the assessment. students increase their understanding of the nature of assessment and their ability to evaluate the work of others. In addition, students improve their understanding of the topics and subjects that they are studying due to the feedback provided on the quality of their work. Sometimes they become aware of key issues related to their participation in the assessment, including the possibility of being fair and democratic. In other cases, they can transfer learning to their future professional practice. In general, the students are satisfied with the opportunity provided by their participation in a learning assessment process, whether assessing their own work or that of their peers. These results are quite consistent with several of the potential benefits of student participation in the assessment process cited by Ozogul, Olina & Sullivan (2008, p.199), which include 'improved student performance, a more active role in their own learning, a greater awareness of the evaluation process and scoring criteria, and an increased understanding of the instructional content'.

Finally, a fourth issue refers to some of the most significant concerns that students had when they participated in the assessment. Students aspire to be fair and to give consistent and unbiased assessment because they empathised with their peers when they made mistakes or their assignments were not completed. Nonetheless, they also show their concerns regarding the plagiarism of their work or fear that low ratings could hurt the feelings of their peers. Similarly, students worry because they could not improve their assessment skills, especially those related to grading their peers' work.

FUTURE RESEARCH DIRECTIONS

An interesting aspect in which the three experiences show inconclusive data relates to student training in giving assessment. In experience 1, it was not considered necessary to provide training to the students. In experience 3, the teachers deliberately decided not to offer prior training on assessment to students so that initially, they would be able to use their "innate" assessment skills and subsequently incorporate the knowledge and skills that the students themselves identified as necessary to their assessment of the learning of their peers. In experience 2, however, students were deliberately trained, which was deemed necessary to address their own and their peers' learning assessment.

The analysis of these experiences evidences the dilemma of whether prior training is needed to involve students in an assessment process, and if so, what content should be included. It seems that no consensus has been reached on this topic. Nonetheless, some universities have included this training in their policies, creating materials to promote them.

In Anglo-Saxon universities, especially in Australia and the United Kingdom, student involvement in assessment enjoys a certain tradition and institutional recognition. In this sense, the policies on learning assessment defined by these universities often explicitly recognise the role of students in assessment and the need to involve them in it. In some universities, students have access to materials aimed at providing the information and training required to fulfil the assignments associated with their involvement in assessment. Thus, for example, in Australia, materials aimed at facilitating student involvement in self-assessment and peer assessment processes can be found at the University of Technology Sydney (http://www.uts. edu.au/research-and-teaching/teaching-and-learning/assessment/involving-students/peer-assessment). At the University of Queensland, there are explicit references regarding the manner in which students can participate in learning assessment (http://www.tedi.uq.edu.au/peer-assessment-tools. And at Griffith University, a guide that addresses peer assessment process is at the disposal of the students in https://www. griffith.edu.au/__data/assets/pdf_file/0016/142108/GuidePeerSelfAssessment-Long.pdf. In the United Kingdom, the University of Reading has published materials in the form of advice, guidance, and tools to facilitate peer assessment (https://www.reading.ac.uk/engageinassessment/peer-and-self-assessment/ peer-assessment/eia-peer-assessment.aspx), also, Newcastle University has developed different documents that explain the importance and significance of peer assessment, its implementation, etc. (http://www. ncl.ac.uk/quilt/resources/assessment/resources/peer.htm). In Ireland, the University College of Dublin analyses when student participation in assessment is appropriated and provides some resources to carry it out (http://www.ucd.ie/teaching/resources/assessment/whoassesseslearning/).

Similarly, some research projects conducted by Spanish universities have focused on training university students in assessment, among which the 'Development of professional competencies through participatory evaluation and simulation using web tools' (DevalSimWeb[1]) project and the 'Development of Sustainable e-Assessment -improving assessment skills in university students through virtual simulations' (DEVALS) project are noteworthy. Both projects, led by the University of Cádiz with the participation of European and Latin American universities, have designed and developed training programmes on assessment for learning for university students from different subject areas. The proposals contained in these training programmes promote student involvement in the assessment process in different modalities. The results obtained in both projects seem to highlight the importance of receiving training before participating in the assessment processes and acquiring the soft skills related to assessment that are developed based on this training (decision-making, team work, problem solving, etc.) and the satisfaction that comes with it, as perceived by the students themselves.

One future line of work relates to studying the objectives, the content of student training in the assessment process, and the working methodologies best suited to such training.

CONCLUSION

As the three experiences presented here show, the scope of effective student participation in assessment should be expanded, and research should be conducted to help determine which types of participation ought to be promoted and which aspects ought to be emphasised (design, implementation, or rating). Such studies should be tailored to the courses or semesters and take into account students' prior experience. It should also be determined whether they should be implemented in the classroom, in blended-learning, or on-line.

Through these three experiences some areas for improvement related to student involvement in assessment can be identified. A general and much-needed enhancement is that teachers promote situations where students have more opportunities to participate in the assessment process, in different courses and throughout their studies, such that they acquire the knowledge, skills, and experience necessary to fully address the issues posed by assessment of and for learning and the confidence to put them to good use. Without these opportunities, student involvement in the assessment process can become little more than an anecdote from their academic life, with little influence on their learning and future professional life.

Another important consideration is that students should be consulted before being involved in the assessment process. Institutions of higher education and teachers should provide information to students regarding the strengths and weaknesses of their involvement in assessment and what this involvement really entails.

Similarly, for this practices to be possible both teachers and students need progressive training on assessment (Quesada et al., 2016; Rodríguez et al. 2016). As Price et al. (2012, p.10-11) state, 'assessment literacy should include an appreciation of assessment's relationship to learning, a conceptual understanding of assessment, an understanding of criteria, the skills of self-assessment and peer assessment, knowledge of technical approaches to learning, and possession of the ability to select and apply the appropriate approaches and techniques to the task at hand'. In addition, such participation and training should be planned carefully to avoid overloading students by merely adding this task to an already heavy workload.

Another aspect to consider is the stability of the activities and the assignments performed. For these participatory experiences to be successful, it is necessary for them to be implemented progressively and continuously, adapting them to the students and polishing those aspects that do not work to improve the assessment process from one year to the next.

ACKNOWLEDGMENT

DevalS research project. Reference numberEDU2012-31804. Financed by Ministerio de Economía y Competitividad. Dirección General de Investigación científica y técnica

REFERENCES

Boekaerts, M., Maes, S., & Karoly, P. (2005). Self-regulation across domains of applied psychology: Is there an emerging consensus? *Applied Psychology*, *54*(2), 149–154. doi:10.1111/j.1464-0597.2005.00201.x

Boud, D. (1995). *Enhancing Learning through Self-Assessment*. London: Routledge.

Boud, D., & Falchikov, N. (2006). Aligning assessment with long-term learning. *Assessment & Evaluation in Higher Education*, *31*(4), 399–413. doi:10.1080/02602930600679050

Boud, D., & Falchikov, N. (2007). Aligning assessment with long-term learning. *Assessment & Evaluation in Higher Education*, *31*(4), 399–413. doi:10.1080/02602930600679050

Bovill, C., & Bulley, C. J. (2011). A model of active student participation in curriculum design: Exploring desirability and possibility. In C. Rust (Ed.), *Improving Student Learning Global Theories and Local Practices: Institutional, Disciplinary and Cultural Variations* (pp. 176–188). Oxford: The Oxford Centre for Staff and Educational Development.

Butler, D., & Winne, P. H. (1995). Feedback as self-regulated learning: A theoretical synthesis. *Review of Educational Research*, *65*(3), 245–281. doi:10.3102/00346543065003245

Deeley, S. (2014). Summative co-assessment: A deep learning approach to enhancing employability skills and attributes. *Active Learning in Higher Education*, *15*(1), 39–51. doi:10.1177/1469787413514649

Dochy, F., Segers, M., & Sluijsmans, D. (1999). The Use of Self-, Peer and Co-assessment in Higher Education: A review. *Studies in Higher Education*, *24*(3), 331–350. doi:10.1080/03075079912331379935

Falchikov, N. (1986). Product comparisons and process benefits of collaborative peer group and self-assessments. *Assessment & Evaluation in Higher Education*, *11*(2), 144–166. doi:10.1080/0260293860110206

Falchikov, N. (2001). *Learning together: peer tutoring in higher education*. London: Routledge Falmer. doi:10.4324/9780203451496

Falchikov, N. (2005). *Improving Assessment Through Student Involvement. Practical solutions for aiding learning in higher and further education*. London: Routledge-Falmer.

Gielen, S., Dochy, F., Onghena, P., Struyven, K., & Smeets, S. (2011). Goals of peer assessment and their associated quality concepts. *Studies in Higher Education, 36*(6), 719–735. doi:10.1080/03075071003759037

Gómez-Ruiz, M. A., Rodríguez-Gómez, G., & Ibarra-Sáiz, M. S. M.S. (2011). Caracterización de la e-evaluación orientada al e-aprendizaje. In G. Rodríguez & M.S. Ibarra (Eds.), e-Evaluación Orientada al e-aprendizaje estratégico en Educación Superior (pp. 33-56). Madrid: Narcea

Gómez Ruiz, M. A., Rodríguez Gómez, G., & Ibarra Sáiz, M. S. (2013). Development of Basic Competencies of Students in Higher Education through Learning Oriented e-Assessment. *RELIEVE: Revista Electrónica de Investigación y Evaluación Educativa, 19*(1). doi:10.7203/relieve.19.1.2609

Gómez-Ruiz, M. A., Rodríguez-Gómez, G., Ibarra-Sáiz, M. S., & Gallego-Noche, B. (2013). Aprendiendo a investigar con una Web docente: Una experiencia de realización de trabajos de investigación en el ámbito universitario mediante un sistema de gestión de contenidos. *Proceedings of XVI Congreso Nacional-II Internacional de Modelos de Investigación Educativa* (pp. 725-733). Alicante: AIDIPE.

Hanrahan, S., & Isaacs, G. (2001). Assessing self- and peer assessment: The students' views. *Higher Education Research & Development, 20*(1), 53–70. doi:10.1080/07294360123776

Ibarra Sáiz, M. S., Rodríguez Gómez, G., & Gómez Ruiz, M. A. (2012). La evaluación entre iguales: Beneficios y estrategias para su práctica en la universidad. *Revista de Educación, 359*, 206–231.

Knight, P.T. & Yorke, M. (2003). *Assessment, Learning and Employability*. Maidenhead: SRHE/Open university Press/McGraw-Hill Education.

Kolb, D. A. (1984). *Experiential learning. Experience as the source of learning and development.* Englewood Cliffs, New Jersey: Prentice Hall.

Ljungman, A. G., & Silén, C. (2008). Examination involving students as peer-examiners. *Assessment & Evaluation in Higher Education, 33*(3), 289–300. doi:10.1080/02602930701293306

Mok, M. M. C., Lung, C. L., Cheng, D. P. W., Cheung, R. H. P., & Ng, M. L. (2006). Self-assessment in higher education: Experience in using a metacognitive approach in five case studies. *Assessment & Evaluation in Higher Education, 31*(4), 415–433. doi:10.1080/02602930600679100

Nicol, D. (2007, May 29-31). Principles of good assessment and feedback: Theory and practice. REAP International Online Conference on Assessment Design for Learner Responsibility. Retrieved from http://www.reap.ac.uk/reap07/Portals/2/CSL/keynotes/david%20nicol/Principles_of_good_assessment_and_feedback.pdf

Nicol, D., & Macfarlane-Dick, D. (2006). Formative assessment and self-regulated learning: A model and seven principles of good feedback practice. *Studies in Higher Education, 31*(2), 199–218. doi:10.1080/03075070600572090

Orsmond, P., Merry, S., & Reiling, K. (2002). The use of exemplars and formative feedback when using student derived marking criteria in peer and self-assessment. *Assessment & Evaluation in Higher Education, 27*(4), 309–323. doi:10.1080/0260293022000001337

Ozogul, O., Olina, Z., & Sullivan, H. (2008). Teacher, self and peer evaluation of lesson plans written by preservice teachers. *Educational Technology Research and Development*, *56*(2), 181–201. doi:10.1007/s11423-006-9012-7

Prins, F. J., Sluijsmans, M. A., Kirschenerand, P. A., & Strijbos, J. W. (2005). Formative peer assessment in a CSCL environment: A case study. *Assessment & Evaluation in Higher Education*, *30*(4), 417–444. doi:10.1080/02602930500099219

Quesada Serra, V., Gómez Ruiz, M. A., & Cubero Ibáñez, J. (2015). La evaluación colaborativa en educación superior: descripción de una experiencia con alumnos de primer curso [co-assessment in Higher Education: an experience with first-year students]. *Proceedings of V International Conference, the challenge of improving assessment (pp.562-566). Girona, Spain: Universitat de Girona.*

Quesada-Serra, V., Rodríguez-Gómez, G., & Ibarra-Sáiz, M. S. (2016). What are we missing? Spanish lecturers' perceptions of their assessment practices. *Innovations in Education and Teaching International*, *53*(1), 48–59. doi:10.1080/14703297.2014.930353

Roberts, T. S. (2006). *Self, Peer and Group Assesment in E-Learning*. Hershey, PA, USA: IGI Global. doi:10.4018/978-1-59140-965-6

Rodríguez-Gómez, G., Ibarra-Sáiz, M. S., Gallego-Noche, B., Gómez-Ruiz, M. A., & Quesada-Serra, V. (2012). The student's voice in assessment: A pathway not yet developed at university. *RELIEVE*, *18*(2), 1–21. doi:10.7203/relieve.18.2.1991

Rodríguez Gómez, G., Ibarra Sáiz, M. S., & García Jiménez, E. (2013). Autoevaluación, evaluación entre iguales y coevaluación: Conceptualización y práctica en las universidades españolas[Self-assessment, peer-assessment and co-assessment: conceptualisation and practice in Spanish Universities]. *Revista de Investigación en Educación*, *11*(2), 198–210.

Rodríguez-Gómez, G., Quesada Serra, V., & Ibarra-Sáiz, M. S. (2016). Learning-oriented e-assessment; the effects of a training and guidance programme on lecturers' perceptions. *Assessment & Evaluation in Higher Education*, *41*(1), 35–52. doi:10.1080/02602938.2014.979132

Sambell, K., & McDowell, L. (1998). The construction of the hidden curriculum: Messages and meanings in the assessment of student learning. *Assessment & Evaluation in Higher Education*, *23*(4), 391–402. doi:10.1080/0260293980230406

Segers, M., & Dochy, F. (2001). New assessment forms in problem-based learning: The value-added of the students' perspective. *Studies in Higher Education*, *26*(3), 327–343. doi:10.1080/03075070120076291

Sivan, A. (2000). The implementation of peer assessment: An action research approach. *Assessment in Education: Principles, Policy & Practice*, *7*(2), 193–213. doi:10.1080/713613328

Taras, M. (2015). Student-centred learning and assessment: fact or fiction.

Taras, M. (2015). Studen Self-Assessment: What have we learned and what are the challenges? *RELIEVE*, *21*(1). doi:10.7203/relieve.21.1.6394

Taylor, C., & Robinson, C. (2009). Student voice: Theorising power and participation. *Pedagogy, Culture & Society*, *17*(2), 161–175. doi:10.1080/14681360902934392

Topping, K. J. (2009). Peer assessment. *Theory Into Practice*, *48*, 20–27.

Zimmerman, B. J. (2002). Becoming a self–regulated learner: An overview. *Theory into Practice*, *41*(2), 64–70. doi:10.1207/s15430421tip4102_2

KEY TERMS AND DEFINITIONS

Assessment Literacy: The understanding of the assessment process and all its components (criteria, tools, modalities, etc.), the comprehension of how assessment relates to the learning process and the ability to use this knowledge to implement in-context assessment practices for any specific goal.

Co-Assessment: Also termed collaborative assessment, it is a consensual and participatory type of assessment in which teachers and students negotiate and perform a joint revision and evaluation of a task completed by the students, which may include grading the task.

Empowerment: This term originally comes from the concept of giving power to students. In this paper, it is understood as the process by which students gain a principal role in the teaching and learning process, and in the assessment process, by strengthening their abilities and participation and making them more confident, which increases their autonomy and self-sufficiency.

Feedback: Information provided to the student after assessment to help reduce the gap between the level of performance achieved and the level that is expected.

Peer Assessment: A participative assessment modality in which a student or group of students reflect on, give comments about, or evaluate the performance or task of a peers or group of peers. Peer assessment might also include the grading of the task.

Peer Review: A participative assessment practice, included within peer assessment strategies, in which a student or group reviews the task or performance of a peer or group of peers. The focus of the revision is to analyse the task and provide constructive feedback.

Rubric: An assessment matrix where the assessment criteria and levels of quality are specified. Typically used to assess student performance, rubrics provide descriptions of each level and might also include grades. They facilitate the transparency of what is expected and provide feedback on the task. Rubrics are very helpful when students participate in the assessment process, mainly for self-, peer, and co-assessment.

Self-Assessment: A participative assessment modality in which students reflect on and value their own performances individually or in a group.

Self-Regulation: The process by which students decide on what they want to learn and to what depth. Once they do so, they attempt to follow up on what they have learned, controlling and modifying their learning strategies as necessary.

ENDNOTE

[1]   Information available at http://avanza.uca.es/devalsimweb/

Chapter 13
Peer assessment in an Online Context:
What Do Students Say?

Alda Pereira
Universidade Aberta, Portugal

Luis Tinoca
University of Lisbon, Portugal

Isolina Oliveira
Universidade Aberta, Portugal

ABSTRACT

In this work, making use of Tinoca, Oliveira and Pereira (2013) framework for assessment quality in digital contexts, we discuss the students' perspective about self and peer assessment practices in online environments. This research is based in the analysis of the students' perceptions in a fully online master's course being offered in a distance education university since 2007. We discuss the students' representations since that date until the present, reflecting on their roles as assessors, the challenges they faced, and the strategies they developed to overcome them. The results illustrate the participants' perceptions of self and peer assessment as innovative practices. There is a strong tendency throughout this period towards greater confidence with these practices, and increased trust in their peers' feedback and competence to share the assessment responsibility. Moreover, the transparency promoted by the sharing during the process and of the final products is recognized as crucial to support the participants' reflection process and competence development.

1. INTRODUCTION

In this chapter we discuss assessment issues in online Higher Education contexts. The most recent technological developments present in these contexts, have greatly influenced not only instructional methods and learning models, but have also had a very specific impact on assessment design.

DOI: 10.4018/978-1-5225-0531-0.ch013

Within this framework, we have witnessed the emergence of philosophy of assessment as a catalyst for student regulated learning. This is in direct opposition with traditional, outdated perspectives that focus mainly on the measurement and ranking characteristics of assessment. In fact, there have been several recent studies emphasizing the benefits of an assessment *for* learning perspective (Brown, 2006; Dierick & Dochy, 2001; JISC, 2010; Nicol, 2007; Sadler & Good, 2006; Sainsbury & Walker, 2007). In this context, the authors developed a conceptual framework, integrating these different perspectives on an edumetric approach of assessment for learning, to support the development of competence assessment strategies in technologically enhanced contexts (Tinoca, Oliveira & Pereira, 2013).

This research is based on a longitudinal study undertaken at Universidade Aberta (Open University) in Portugal, on a course called *"Using ICT for Learning and Teaching"* from the Master's program on *"Educational Communication and Multimedia"* between the years 2007 and 2015. During this time there were a total of 5 editions of the program that were used for this research. Within this course, we specifically researched the digital assessment strategies being used, and for this chapter we particularly focused on competence assessment using self and peer-assessment strategies during group projects.

Also, this research has been supported by the assess.he project (Pereira et al., 2015, Tinoca, Oliveira & Pereira, 2013; Pereira, Oliveira & Tinoca, 2010), where different types of collaborative assessment practices in online courses have been studied. With this goal, we have gathered data from students' online interactions on discussion forums, the work produced by the students (both individually and in small groups), self- and peer-assessment results attained by the students, and answers to questionnaires applied during the different stages of the investigation.

In this particular case we are interested in exploring questions related to self- and peer-assessment strategies during group work in online Open and Distance Learning (ODL). Two main research questions were asked: How do Higher Education students perceive self and peer-assessment practices within an assessment for learning framework? How can self and peer-assessment practices contribute to the quality of competence assessment in Higher Education online environments?

In this chapter, we start by tackling the new challenges for e-assessment in general, and for self- and peer-assessment in digital contexts in particular to introduce the theoretical underpinning for our work. After, we present the methodology used for the study, followed by the analysis and discussion of the attained results. We finish with a discussion of the main conclusions arising from the study.

2. NEW CHALLENGES FOR E-ASSESSMENT

The current widespread of technological devices available to educational institutions, particularly for communicating and interacting, has fueled the growing use of elearning models, both in blended formats and completely online. In this context, it is ever more pressing to rethink current assessment models, in order to (re)design them, taking full advantage of these environments features. This shift has been labelled as electronic assessment (e-assessment) or digital assessment (JISC, 2010).

At the same time, we have witnessed the recognition of the inadequacies of traditional assessment strategies to foster student learning, as a consequence of their excessive focus on ranking and classification. As a response to this problem, we have seen a large growth over the last three decades of alternative assessment strategies. Dierick and Dochy (2001) call this new culture an *assessment culture*, opposed to the traditional *testing culture*. Brown, Bull and Pendlebury (1997) illustrate this change in the assessment paradigm as a shift from final written exams to continuous assessment, from teacher centered teaching to student centered learning, from implicit to explicit criteria, from products to processes, from contents and learning goals to competences. As Sainsbury and Walker (2007) emphasize, it is necessary to rethink assessment from a collaborative perspective, making better use of the feedback timeliness it can foster, so as to promote and motivate learning through the assessment process.

Even more, the complexity of our current world require from educational institutions, in particular Universities, new demands, expecting them to contribute to the development of autonomous and creative professionals and citizens, capable of innovating in problematic and uncertain contexts. Therefore, it is ever more crucial to develop competences for problem solving, planning, team work, intervention in ill-defined and problematic situations, and reflect about their actions demonstrating the ability for metacognition in uncertain contexts.

As a consequence, one of the biggest challenges facing universities today is the need to radically change their curriculum development from a traditional content based approach to a competence based curriculum. This shift, consequently requires another challenge, moving away from content centered assessment towards competence assessment. Giving meaningfulness to content through the process how the competences to be developed are defined, and the contexts where they will be used.

This conjugation of factors hints the need to change Higher Education traditional educational paradigm. In fact, we are testifying the emergence of a new paradigm in teaching and learning in HE: i) the transformation of old lecture based methods, led by the instructor more or less eloquently, towards new modes that privilege student's active participation; ii) from a characterization of learning based only on the student's attentive presence, towards student's problem and research based engagement; iii) from unidirectional communication on a traditional classroom to diversified modes of dialogue and interaction made possible by new media; iv) from the establishment of curricular goals centered on contents to the definition of competences to be developed; and v) from traditional exam based psychometric approach to assessment, to a new *assessment culture* emphasizing both product and processes where the student is engaged as an actor on its own, and his colleagues, assessment.

This new paradigm stresses the importance of developing competences such as identifying, selecting, arguing, information management, critical thinking, developing sustained judgments, innovating and communicating (both written and orally). Even though the concept of competence is still subject to different interpretations, Gijbels (2011) points out that it can be interpreted from a broad perspective. According to this author, competence refers to "knowledge, attitudes, social skills and motivational aspects in authentic, work-related contexts" (p. 382). According to Blanco (2009), competences are activated through performances that are the expression of the resources that an individual mobilizes in order to carry out a certain activity or task. These resources include knowledge, skills, abilities, attitudes and values constituting the prerequisites that an individual has to solve a certain problem on a specific context (Bolivar, 2010).

New constructivist theories and practices go together with a shift from a "testing" culture to an "assessment" culture (Struyven et al, 2003, p. 190). This approach as lead to the emergence of several complementary forms of assessment such as portfolios, performance tasks, and learning journals (Birenbaum, 2003). Maclellan (2004) stresses that these new forms of assessment help students develop the conceptual and analytical skills, needed to prepare them for future vocational success.

In these new learning technology embedded scenarios, learners must develop their ability to use ICT tools to promote their learning, using and adapting them to their personal learning needs. Moreover, within a lifelong learning framework, learners are expected to be able to reflect about their learning process mediated by new ICT technologies.

In this landscape, the use of ICT to assess competences is a new challenge for formal Higher Education. To clarify these issues, it's fundamental to be more precise when we talk about assessing competences using ICT. For this reason, it is important to define a concept of e-assessment that includes tasks specifically designed for competence assessment with the support of digital technologies. In this way, we propose the concept of alternative digital assessment strategy that refers to all technology-enabled assessment tasks where the design, performance, and feedback must be mediated by technologies (Pereira et al., 2013). Moreover, in order to assure quality assessment in Higher Education, we developed a theoretical framework supported by four dimensions – authenticity, consistency, transparency and practicability – each composed by a set of parameters, aimed at promoting the quality of the assessment strategies being used (Tinoca, Oliveira & Pereira, 2013).

3. SELF AND PEER-ASSESSMENT

Self and peer-assessment are not new to education (Topping, 2003), however there are not many studies dealing with the online environment, in spite of the fact that both self- and peer-assessment are commonplace in professional practice.

Faced with the fast societal changes in today's world, and with the growing volatility in professional contexts, one of the main factors for higher education students' is their ability to acquire and develop self-regulation competences in order to become successful lifelong learners. For that, self- and peer-assessment competences, and the ability to critically analyze one's assessment are key skills, requiring assessment practices in Higher Education to become ever more sustainable (Fastréa, Klinka, Sluijsmans & Merriënboera, 2012).

3.1. Self-Assessment

Topping (2003) introduces self-assessment as an arrangement for learners and or workers to consider and specify the level, value or quality of their own products or performances. He refers its applicability to "several products or performances … such as writing, portfolios, oral and or visual presentations, test performances, other skilled behaviors, or a combination of these" (Topping, 2003, p.58).

Self-assessment actively involves participants in their own learning and their reflection about their own learning processes and results. It takes into account the long term investment required from the learner throughout his learning or work process (Topping, 2003, p.58). However, several questions remain, including: What do self and peer-assessment require from students in terms of cognitive, meta-cognitive and social-affective demands? Through what processes might these benefit students? Under what conditions can these processes be optimized?

Even though self-assessment may be seen as a lonely activity, if the students are required to justify their assessment to the instructor, or to their peers, this may lead to very productive interactions. Self-assessment can result in gains in learner management of learning self-efficacy, and deep rather than superficial learning. Topping (2003) refers that "effects have been found to be at least as good as those from instructor assessment and often better" (p.65). However, the reliability and validity of self-assessment tends to be a little lower and more variable than the reliability and validity of instructor assessment. The reliability and validity of self-assessment tends to be higher in relation to the ability of the learner, the amount of scaffolding, practice and feedback, and the degree of advancement in the course. Other variables, such as: the nature of the subject area, the nature of the product or performance assessed, the nature and clarity of the assessment criteria, the nature of assessment instrumentation, and cultural and gender differences, may also influence the quality of self-assessment.

Osmond and Mary (1997) refer that self-assessment makes students more critical about their work leading them to think more and feeling that they learn more. Contributing for a more structured type of reasoning, self-assessment is seen has challenging but helpful and beneficial.

3.2. Peer-Assessment

A major advantage of peer learning is that it encourages students to take responsibility for their own learning by communicating with other students, providing feedback to other students and receiving feedback from them within the group setting. This lifelong skill is essential in all future work settings. The absence of the instructor as an integral member of the group may also provide them more practice in adopting the reciprocal role. Students gain more practice in communicating in the subject area than is typically the case in learning activities when staff are present. If we value peer learning, group work and collaboration in our teaching and learning, we need to include peer-assessment within the formal assessment for the course. We advocate peer-assessment to be formally assessed and suggest that it should be weighted accordingly in the course assessment design. Unless a group project has a reasonable weighting for the course, i.e. it is a major aspect of assessment, students will not take it seriously. Peer learning and peer-assessment are about students providing feedback to each other for the benefit of the collective effort (Keppell, Au, Ma & Chan, 2006).

For Topping (2003) peer-assessment is an arrangement for learners, and or workers, to consider and specify the level, value or quality of other equal-status learner and or workers. He refers to it use in situations as diverse as writing, portfolios, oral and or visual presentations, test performances, other skilled behaviors, or a combination of these (p.58)

Peer-assessment can be one-way, reciprocal or mutual. In our case, we had mutual group peer-assessment with cognitive, meta-cognitive and socio-affective objectives, in accordance with the competencies being developed. Peer-assessment can create cognitive gains in a set of variables, including levels of time on task, engagement and practice, as well as a greater sense of accountability and responsibility. It enables the identification of knowledge gaps, engineering their closure through explaining, simplification, clarification, summarizing, and cognitive restructuring.

Group work is susceptible to negative social processes such as dilution of responsibility, interaction disabilities and loafing. Social processes might influence and contaminate the reliability and validity of peer-assessment. In a study done by Falchikov (2001) he explored questions related to role ambiguity, relational conflict and status issues and attribution theory. Peer-assessment might be influenced by a variety of aspects including, friendship/enmity, power processes, popularity issues among the group members, perception of criticism as uncomfortable or socially rejecting and inviting reciprocation. Magin (2001) pointed "reciprocity effects" in peer-assessment as responsible for the contamination of results.

Riley (1995) refers that peer-assessment demands social and communication skills, negotiation and diplomacy and can develop teamwork skills. Moreover, we believe, as Marcoulis and Simkin (1991), that peer-assessment may develop competencies such as giving and accepting criticism, argue one's own position and reject others suggestions when justifiable, that represent useful transferable social and assertion competencies. Furthermore, peer-assessment can contribute to promote motivation and personal responsibility, especially if positive feedback is presented first to reduce anxiety, and prepare to accept the ensuing negative/corrective feedback. In the same way, self-confidence, activity and empathy with their peers may increase as a consequence of peer-assessment.

Topping (2003) refers several systemic benefits of peer-assessment. One first clear advantage is that it allows triangulation, contributing to the improvement of the overall reliability and validity. Another advantage is that it empowers students with a greater insight of the institutional assessment process; and also that it can be less time consuming for the instructor. Finally, even though peer-assessment requires an initial time investment to establish, train and organize a successful structure, in the end it leads to cognitive benefits for both students and instructors. Topping (2003) also points out that even though the "reliability and validity of assessment by professional teachers is often low ... the reliability and validity of self-assessment tends to be a little lower and more variable, while the reliability and validity of peer-assessment tends to be as high or higher" (p. 37). This is in agreement with Segers and Dochy (2001) research project on new assessment forms in problem based learning, when they pointed out that Pearson correlation values of peer and tutor scores are significantly interrelated.

Lladó et al (2014), in a study about the use of peer-assessment in several scientific areas in Higher Education concluded that students positively viewed peer-assessment, recognizing its potential to motivate and facilitate learning, prompting and supporting their reflection throughout the learning process. Nevertheless, they also recognize that this process can generate students' anxiety and discomfort about the fact that they are being assessed by their peers. However, there also seem to be qualitative developments on the nature of the provided feedback as the students develop their experience in this process. Cheng and Hou (2015) have pointed out that while initially there is a predominance of an affective dimension on the provided feedback, this diminishes through time, in favor of the development of cognitive and metacognitive dimensions.

4. STUDENTS AND ASSESSMENT IN E-LEARNING CONTEXTS

The active participation of students in assessment practices depends greatly on the strategies used by the instructor. If we take into account the four dimensions and fifteen criteria for quality assessment in technologically enriched contexts (Figure 1), two dimensions seem to be particularly relevant for this case: transparency and consistency.

In fact, the *consistency* dimension emerges as an answer to the traditional demands for validity and reliability, associated with psychometric indicators. It takes into account that the assessment of competences requires the implication of a variety of assessment methods, in diverse contexts, by different assessors, as well as the adequacy of the employed strategies (Dierick & Dochy, 2001). This dimension is comprised by four criteria:

1. Instruction-assessment alignment;
2. Multiplicity of indicators;
3. Relevant criteria; and
4. Competences-assessment alignment. Considering the focus of this particular study, the multiplicity of indicators criteria becomes particularly relevant through the participants' active engagement in self and peer-assessment practices.

Figure 1. Dimensions and criteria for digital assessment quality (Tinoca, Oliveira & Pereira, 2013)

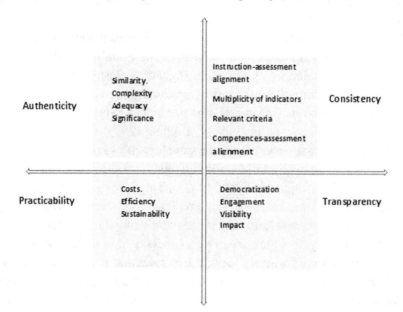

The Multiplicity of Indicators criterion is related to the need of employing a variety of e-assessment methods, contexts, moments, and assessors (Dierick & Dochy, 2001; Herrington & Herrington, 1998). This way, the usage of self-assessment, peer-assessment, besides instructor lead assessment, as well as a diversity of methods and tasks, should be supported in a variety of moments during the learning process. This approach further contributes to the competence assessment program equity by allowing for diverse means of participation.

In this context, self and peer-assessment promote the participants as actors alongside instructors. In a recent study (Pereira et al., 2015) looking into digital assessment practices in Higher Education, it was found that even though instructors value their students self-assessment practices, they do not give it enough credit in order to consider it as part of their formal assessment and classification procedures. In fact, it is not common to ask the students to practice their self-assessment, and in the few instances that this is done it only has formative effects. (Pereira et al., 2015).

This same study revealed the instructors' reticence to integrate peer-assessment practices, given their distrust on the students' ability to be "objective" on their assessment. They consider that students do not have enough knowledge to assess their peers, what is closely related to their incoherent view on the concept of competence, tending to value only content knowledge and not its mobilization in real or future contexts (Pereira et al., 2015).

It should also be noticed that these dimensions and criteria are interdependent, allowing for varying degrees of implementation, conditional to the instructional and assessment strategies being used. Therefore, it is hard to consider the students as assessors without at the same time allowing them to have a full knowledge of the curriculum design and assessment criteria, including even the possibility to propose new curricular goals and participate on the discussion of the competences to be developed and the criteria to assess them. Therefore, the transparency and consistency dimensions are closely related, in particular when we take into account the democratization and engagement criteria.

The *transparency* dimension intends to make the entire assessment program visible and comprehensible for all participants. For this reason, it is important that the students are able to understand the fairness of their assessment, as precisely as their instructors, requiring them to have a complete knowledge of all assessment criteria and their relative weights. According to Dierick and Dochy (2001) and McDowell (1995), the clarification of the assessment criteria coupled with the fact that the students have prior knowledge of the competence assessment program has a positive impact on their learning. This dimension is operationalized with four criteria:

- **Democratization**: Refers to the availability and possible participation in the definition of the assessment criteria (Dierick & Dochy, 2001). The students should know, from the onset, what the assessment goals are and who their assessors are going to be. This way, they know immediately what is expected from them, and can adjust their learning processes accordingly (McConnell, 2006).
- **Engagement**: Related to the availability and possible participation in the definition of the learning goals (Maclellan, 2004a) and performance conditions for the proposed tasks, such as the structure, format, and media (Pereira, Tinoca & Oliveira, 2010). It allows students/learners to participate in the definition of their learning environment, further contributing to their active participation, commitment and responsibility (Oliveira, Tinoca & Pereira, 2011).
- **Visibility**: Refers to the possibility of presenting/sharing their learning processes and/or products with others (peers, assessors, instructors, community, etc.) (Gulikers, Bastiaens & Kirchner, 2004). This criteria, by means of making processes and product visible to other students allows for a greater confidence on the assessment process being used, minimizing any feelings of discomfort.
- **Impact:** Related to the effects that the e-assessment strategies have in the learning process and in the design of the educational program (Baartman, Bastiaens, Kirschner & Vleuten, 2007). According to Brinke (2008) the assessment design must have a positive impact in the learning process.

In a study by Pereira et al. (2015), it was possible to verify that in most cases instructors are careful to inform the students about the assessment tasks and criteria. Nevertheless, this process is not usually subject to discussion, being also absent the students' participation on the definition of the learning goals or competences to be developed. On the engagement criteria, even though the discussion is minimal, it is sometimes observed that students are allowed to select the technological devices to be used. This fact is even more pressing when they are asked to developed a technologically based product.

5. CONTEXT OF THE STUDY

The design used for this course was structured around completely asynchronous complementary instructional strategies. Firstly, it was based on the participants' independent study and reflections of the presented documents requiring them to read critically, to identify the main thesis defended by the authors, and elaborate their opinions. Secondly, it required that participants to work collaboratively with their peers, participating in online forums where they debated and collectively (re)constructed their learning. Thirdly, participants were expected to choose a theme, from within a set given by the instructors, and work in small groups to find the best solutions for the problems and cases that they were confronted with (4 weeks to develop the group project, and 2 weeks to discuss it). And finally, to develop an individual final paper based on a literature review or on the report of a pedagogical experience. The role of the online instructor varied throughout the course, according to each phase objectives. During a first phase, when the participants were engaged in big group discussions, the instructor worked as a facilitator and a critical observer; during the group work stage the responsibility for the discussion leadership was entirely the responsibility of the participants, with the instructor being only a critical observer and interacting only when requested.

The group project was developed during the fourth stage of this Curricular Unit. The activity for this task required the participants to design and present a learning trajectory supported by a technological tool, for an educational context of their choice. Throughout the 5 studied courses, there has been an increase on the widespread of technological tools being used to carry out this group work projects (blogs, wikis, videos, digital storytelling, games, etc.). The groups were composed by students interested in using the same technological tool, and have to answer the challenge: How can the chosen technology be used to support a successful learning trajectory?

As a group they develop a proposed learning task making use of the chosen technological tool that must describe the way it will support a learning trajectory theoretically grounded on the readings done throughout the semester (and others that they are encouraged to autonomously pursue).

The assessment of the group project was divided in two parts: 1) the process of elaboration of the project (1/2 of the grade); and 2) the final project product (1/2 of the grade). Since the Instructors responsible for this Curricular Unit recognized from their previous experience that in this type of activity the participants often develop a large majority of their work outside of the Virtual Classroom Software (VCS) and use other tools (such as Skype, Facebook, Google Talk), it was decided to attribute the responsibility of assessing this component to the participants. The Instructors, however, developed a set of criteria that the participants should use to guide their self and peer-assessment. These criteria included:

- Commitment to the group project.
- Relevance/pertinence of the research made.
- Presentation of innovative elements to the project.
- Contribution to the group dynamic.

These criteria were proposed by the instructors to the students in the beginning of the semester as part of the Learning Contract (Pereira, Tinoca & Oliveira, 2010) and open to discussion/negotiation in an online forum specifically tasked with this objective.

Once the group project had ended each group was responsible for sending the instructors a small document with the classification attributed to each participant accompanied by a written justification. This document must be previously negotiated and agreed upon by all group members, and include everyone's self- and peer-assessment. Also, each group must make their final product available to everyone in an online forum to be analyzed by all other colleagues. After this, the participants are required to individually give critical feedback to the different projects, as well as react to the comments that their group project received.

The total group project is worth 6 points (out of 20 for the entire course) and is assessed by both instructors and students. The final product is assessed by the instructors (3 points) and the process of developing the group project is assessed by the students (3 points).

6. DATA COLLECTION AND ANALYSIS

The participants from the five studied courses represent a relatively homogenous group in terms of nationality (Portuguese), professional identity and culture (teachers and professional instructors), forming a gender balanced group with ages mostly between 30 and 55 years old. Nevertheless, there has also been a tendency for the recent emergence of a more international student population that is starting to slightly change this distribution. In fact, in the two latest course editions, we have started to enroll students from different countries and professions. In particular, we are witnessing the reduction of teachers enrolling on the program and the emergence of a more diversified set of professionals.

The gathered data has originated from three different sources: questionnaires used during the 2007 and 2015 editions; the Learning Contract online discussion forums where both student and instructors participated from all 5 editions; and the self- and peer-assessment reports submitted by all groups.

Data analysis involved iterative analysis and revision of the coding scheme (Miles & Hubberman, 1994). Two of the researchers derived the initial coding key from the ideas embedded in the data gathered from the questionnaires (Q1, n=23; Q2, n=7), and from the online discussion forums used during the Learning contract discussion, and from the group project self and peer-assessment produced by the participants.

During the analysis the initial coding key was revised to account for emergent sub-codes and all of the data was recoded using the final coding scheme. Some of the codes were quantified in order to foster a more meaningful comparison of the data by allowing patterns to be identified and further explored (Chi, 1997). We then identified emerging themes in the coded data, and generated preliminary assertions for each research question based on the data. The third researcher tested the viability of the generated assertions by seeking both confirming and disconfirming evidence from the available data sources. The data was processed using the NVIVO10® qualitative data treatment software.

The theoretical interpretation of the data emerged from its systematical analysis, implying a very close relationship between them (Strauss & Corbin, 1998). It is important to clarify that this interpretation of the theory is sustained by a set of well-defined categories (concepts or themes) that are systematically interrelated through statements of relationship originating a theoretical framework that explains the situation being studied.

This analysis was also guided by the previous results from project @ssess.he (Pereira et al., 2015) that illustrated the fragility of the transparency dimension as the least implemented. This led the researchers to revisit their data looking for clues of its presence during the proposed activities.

Table 1. Main categories

Categories	Description
It's perfect on paper	Illustrates the participants' agreement with the suggested assessment process, including self and peer-assessment, but with difficulties in operationalizing it.
Responsibility	Explores the participants' awareness that competence and responsibility are cornerstone to this assessment practices
Reflective practices	Presents the participants reflections on the benefits that they have identified for their practice, improving their reflective practices and critical thinking.
Lack of trust in their peers	Includes reasons that make the participants refrain from trusting their peers' ability to perform an impartial assessment.

7. RESULTS

From the produced analysis, four main categories emerged that we now present from the most represented to the least: it's perfect on paper; lack of thrust in their peers; reflective practices; and responsibility (Table 1).

It's Perfect on Paper

This theme illustrates the participants' agreement with the suggested assessment process but difficulties in operationalizing it. They agree with the proposal that the elaboration of the project is assessed by the participants, based on criteria previously defined, while the instructor becomes responsible only for the final group product, also with previously defined criteria. What is more, the participants agreed with the suggested methodology were they had to participate individually in discussion forums, complete a group project and present a final paper.

In all program editions the Learning Contract, with the proposed assessment criteria was open to discussion with the students. However, after some initial clarifications required by the students and some punctual clarifications, what is more notorious is the overwhelming agreement with the proposed assessment strategy. This posture seems to be indicative of the students' recognition that assessment shouldn't be the sole responsibility of the instructor, but must also value the students' contributions through self and peer-assessment.

This can be clearly seen on the comments posted online in the Learning contract discussion Forum where Manuela (teacher) says *"I agree with both the Contract and the assessment strategy!"*

When asked if they endorse the proposed assessment process, almost all the participants agreed with it "I agree with the proposed separation of final product assessment from the process of participation in the development of the project... It's perfect on paper." (Amalia), leaving the final product assessment as the instructor's responsibility, while the assessment of the group work project elaboration stayed in the hands of the participants "The proposed process seems appropriate to this situation." (Fatima).

In the first two editions the Learning Contract discussion forum the participants showed some discomfort towards peer-assessment arguing that it was not part of their professional culture, representing a new practice. Particularly with the public discussion of their projects and with the impact of the self and peer-assessment processes on their final grade. Ana, a 2009 student said "I share with my colleagues the discomfort in assessing my "peers" because, has we know, this will require not only a quantification but also a justification where it will be clear the degree of participation of the other colleagues on the group activities, their attitudes and abilities".

Nevertheless, also in these first editions there were some students who recognized peer-assessment as a positive way to receive feedback to improve their professional practices. This was the case with Paulo, a 2009 teacher who said that:

Has a teacher I am used to open my classroom doors to be voluntarily observed by other colleagues, not for ranking my practice but to receive feedback to improve it. For some time now I also observe my colleagues... I accept that my colleagues assess me, for my contribution to the group project, recognizing that I will give my best to productively complete all tasks.

Figure 2. It's perfect on paper category (2015)

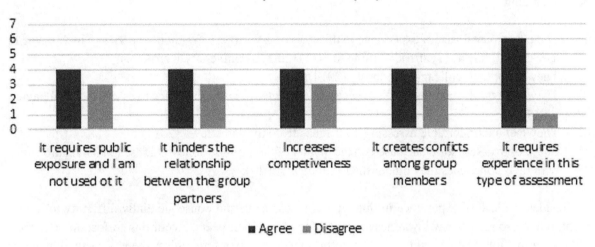

However, it can also be noticed that by the end of the semester, for some of the participating students, peer-assessment created some divergences with their initial opinions. In spite of the overall agreement with the proposed assessment process, some participants pointed out barriers to the implementation of this type of assessment. Firstly, they consider it dangerous to the social interaction between the group participants, in the words Rute (Professional Development (PD) trainer) "It's always a very delicate question that may raise relationship problems between the group participants, compromising the group work." Also Lucas, teacher and trainer says "(the assessment) may be inflated or distorted by personal or relational reasons consequence of an insufficient knowledge about their peers."

Often, they point out their colleagues' lack of courage and lack of justice to successfully perform their peers' assessment "…as long as the participants had the courage and the sense of justice that we often lack". (Amalia). Finally, even though the participants agree with the proposed assessment process their previous experiences, in other settings, makes them feel more comfortable transferring to the instructor the responsibility for identifying and penalizing the participants that do not fully contribute to the group work process "The instructor … should question the group and assess the participants' individual contributions to the group work." (Carla, teacher), "The instructor should be informed whenever one of the participants is not contributing" (Rute, PD trainer)

This ambiguity has been present through the last edition (2014) when in the last questionnaire we can observe that when faced with the statements "it makes assessment more fair than if it was done by the instructor only" almost all participants (6 out of 7, 86%, 2014) agree. However, they also reveal different opinions when confronted with statements regarding their peer-assessment experiences (see figure 2).

Lack of Thrust in Their Peers

In this theme are included some of the reasons that make the participants refrain from trusting their peers ability to perform an impartial assessment.

Thus, the second most emerging theme was the lack of confidence that the participants demonstrated on their peers' ability to perform the self and peer-assessments. Several reasons emerged for this situation including:

1. The participants' lack of experience in this type of assessment "Without experience in this type of assessment, it is a very difficult thing to do." (Ricardo, University Instructor);
2. They doubt their colleagues' honesty (2014);
3. They don't think that they have the necessary knowledge and experience to assess their colleagues (2014);
4. They feel uncomfortable assessing colleagues from the same level (2014);
5. It is hard to assess someone based on the quality of their online contributions, and the relationships with their colleagues may hinder their judgment (2014).

Besides the lack of experience in this type of assessment, and consequentially difficulty to implement, other also refer the awkwardness of having to assess their peers. According to Joaquim (teacher) "It's not something that the students feel comfortable doing, therefore, unless there is a situation where someone is clearly not participating the tendency is to return to the instructors the same classification for all group members…"

While others reinforce the idea that this is not a competitive setting "as we are not here to compete, and usually empathize with our colleagues the most common result is to only say good things about them, except in very flagrant situations." (Victor, teacher).

More recently, Lídia (teacher trainer) recognized that "it is hard to assess the colleagues, I am afraid to hurt others' feelings, I don't want to fuel an unhealthy competition, I may be unfair when I don't know the real causes behind some colleague's slack of participation".

Others show a more emotional response showing a complete distrust for their peers reasons for the classifications that they have attributed "I do not believe in my colleagues peer-assessment results" (Matilde, teacher), "Some colleagues do not fully participate in the group work process and are not able to be objective on their assessment, shifting the group participants' classifications." (Carolina, teacher, 2009).

All these reasons are usually accompanied by a preference for shifting this responsibility to the instructor "The solution may be to warrant that all of the group work is done in such a way that is visible and can be monitored by the instructor. This way the assessment would be fairer." (Marta, teacher), "It would be better if each group always worked in a visible space where they were forced to present all the work process, so that the instructors could accompany the group progress." (Catarina, teacher).

Furthermore, between 2010 and 2015 the implementation of self-assessment practices was ever more accepted by the participants, and implemented without resistances or conflicts. This is also confirmed by the quality and fairness of their self and peer-assessment reports and by the consensus portrayed by the participants during the discussion and negotiation of the Learning Contract.

In table 2 we can observe the way one particular group (X) was able to distribute the classifications resulting from their self and peer-assessment process according to the negotiated criteria and considering each student's contribution to the project. In this case, we can observe how the maximum points were only given to two group members on the first criteria. The presented classifications where the result of negotiation and justified by the group members in a variety of ways. Even though different students started by presenting different classifications they were able to come to an agreement about the final scores for each.

Table 2. Group X self- and peer-assessment (2012)

Points on a 1 to 3 scale				
	Me (Luisa)	**Carla**	**Ana**	**Cláudia**
1. Analysis of the chosen topic	2	2	3	3
2. Critical reflection	1	1	1	1
3. Focus on the main issues	2	2	2	2
4. Originality of the project's presentation	2	2	2	2

Figure 3. Lack of trust category (2015)

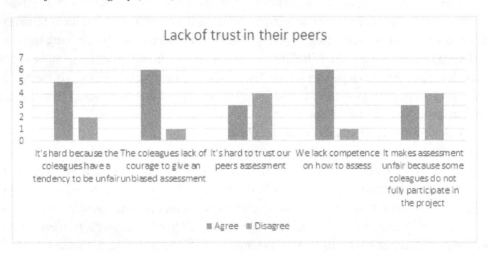

When we questioned the 2014 participants'' we could also realize that some of these issues continue to be present (see Figure 3).

Reflective Practices

Here we present the participants reflection on the benefits that they have identified for their practice, improving their reflective practices and critical thinking.

In the first two editions, almost half of the participants (43) have recognized the benefit of this assessment process to their reflective practices. This category is reinforced during the next editions, in particular when we evaluate the students' self and peer-assessment reports.

Considering the learning, our activity was very enriching and required us to conduct research. Our learning perspective using the video as a resource is something concrete, real, accessible and not has hard as it seems. I reflected about it and concluded that with a little effort, research and planning, by the educator, we can promote a significant leaning trajectory (Fátima, teacher)

For Iolanda (designer) "the group dynamic worked very well, as well as the development of the project, thanks to the positive commitment of all group members.

The results seem to indicate that the participants' reflective practices about the work that they have performed and their own process of learning constitute a fundamental piece of online learning and assessment settings. The fact that they have to write about a certain theme and answer questions posed by their peers makes them ponder and reassess their initial positions before posting their own answers. This is illustrated when Maria José (teacher) says: "It allows us to ponder on what we did, on what we didn't do, and on what we could have done."

They distinguish this assessment process as responsible for provoking them to reflect about their own participation in the group work as well as that of their peers "I consider this type of assessment very important as it prompts us into reflecting about our own performance and that of our colleagues." (Catarina, teacher or when Carolina (teacher) says: "it makes be more conscientious about our learning process."

Related to the emphasis given by the participants to their reflective practices and self-assessment procedures emerges a related dimension associated with the development of a critical thinking attitude about their own work and participation, as well as that of their peers, while allowing them to rethink their way of engaging in group work. "It allows us to develop a critical thinking perspective about our work" (Pedro, teacher), or when Rafael, a teacher that also has executive functions in his schools reflects: "I consider it very important as it forces us to be reflective about our own work, stimulates a critical attitude that surpasses the natural complicity between colleagues."

Another student, Luísa (ICT trainer) considers that:

We could have done a better job with this, particularly with our critical reflection. I consider that the critical reflection was the most important part in this task, and should be more explicitly presented on the report that we shared with the group. Even so, our proposal was very descriptive and detailed trying to portray our mental image of the game to our colleagues. We tried to focus their attention on how the game could be used in a classroom to foster learning.

However, there are aspects valued by the participants' comments in this dimension, in particular the contribution to social interaction and relationships. They recognize an advantage in this practice for their social interaction with their colleagues, as Pedro (teacher) says, "it favors our inter-personal relationships." Establishing good working social interactions/relationships may benefit collaborative learning, or in other words, when they exist, participants may feel more willing and confident to contribute and

Figure 4. Reflective practices category (2015)

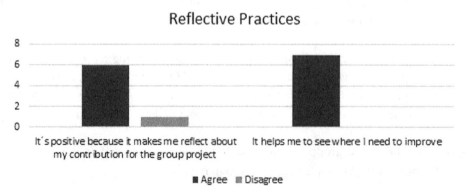

support each other. Finally, it is something that they consider important to translate into their professional setting, "If I don't accept to be assessed how can I assess my own students?" (Marta, teacher).

In spite of all the identified positive aspects, the results also indicate that this is a task that the participants consider difficult to implement, but to which they recognize merit, as Marta (teacher) puts it "it is a difficult thing to do, however, the contribution of my peers can help me introduce corrections in my way of working," or in the words of Carolina (teacher) "When we are asked to complete our self and peer-assessments in a group work, it is not an easy task to achieve, but it carries positive effects".

On the 2014 edition, this practice seems reinforced by the participants' answers to the questionnaire, as illustrated in figure 4.

These comments show how much metacognitive and reflective practices can be important for learning and assessment in online settings. Moreover, they alert us to the difficulties associated with their implementation, in particular in the cases of peer-assessment. The aptitude to communicate and share knowledge (emotional, theoretical or procedural) requires a considerable effort and reflective ability.

Responsibility

In this theme we explore the participants' awareness that competence and responsibility are cornerstone to this assessment practices. The theme responsibility emerged on 35% of the participants that seem to accept self- and peer-assessment so long as the participants assume responsibility for their learning

The participants aren't children, they're adults and responsible persons, and as such, they are self-conscious of the work that they have done and should be able to self-assess themselves and their colleagues. (Carla, teacher)

However, they recognize that it is not a common practice in their culture to make public this type of assessment. It is a judgment that they are used to make informally, but not publicly, as Susana, PD trainer says:

What was asked isn't new. We always perform that "judgment" after a group work, we just aren't used to having to verbalize it and take on responsibility for it. In this type of learning process it is important that we start taking on that responsibility maturely.

The participants also consider this an important process to make accountable for their lack of participation those colleagues that did not contribute to the group work, and the instructor is not aware of it, as Sandra (teacher) puts it, "It's important, as sometimes the final product is hurt as a consequence of the lack of cooperation of some colleagues, and consequently if just the product is assessed that assessment is often unfair."

In most cases this reflection was quite clear, has when Iolanda (designer) said "in my opinion the three group members contributed equally with their knowledge in order to collaboratively construct a good project. We all gave our best and are satisfied with the final product". Or when Fialho (teacher) said "we kept to our plan, and completed all the different stages. I dare to state that we both have a clear conscious, the development of the video was a very demanding task, but we were always in contact, discussing ideas, testing the prototypes and debating the definition of our concept.

Figure 5. Responsibility category (2015)

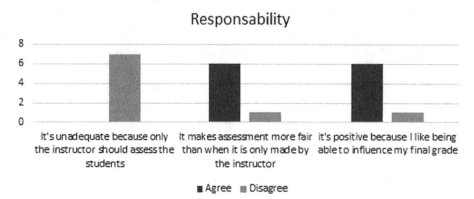

This awareness that competence and responsibility are cornerstone is also transparent in the 2015 students questionnaire responses – see figure 5, where they clearly assume that they should be actively engaged to make assessment more fair and consider positive to influence their final grade.

The final group work product is seen by most of the participants as their main task. Their contribution is usually enthusiastic and dynamic, implying the assumption of responsibility to complete their part in the project. They also contribute to the analysis and assessment of the required data and resources necessary for the project development. Likewise, they are receptive to their peers' comments about their work, and also to participate in the assessment of the work done by them. All this implies that they must be ready to take risks and assume responsibility for their work. However, the results show us that some of the participants in this study still need to develop their practices in this area.

8. DISCUSSION

This longitudinal study was centered on the assessment design for a master's degree course. In this section we present and discuss, in particular, how self- and peer-assessment was used, grounded in the dimensions of consistency and transparency proposed on the theoretical framework for the quality of competence based digital assessment (Tinoca, Oliveira & Pereira, 2013). We analyzed the participants' answers to questionnaires, their online interactions in forums where they had a chance to discuss the Learning Contract (Oliveira, Pereira & Tinoca, 2009) as well as their self- and peer-assessment reports.

The relationship between the main themes identified in this research is illustrated in Figure 6. Clearly the most prevalent conclusion must be the participants support for this assessment strategy, clearly translated on theme "It's Perfect on Paper". Furthermore, they identify as benefits its promotion of reflective practices and of the participants' responsibility. Nevertheless, they recognize difficulty in the operationalization of this process in the theme "Lack of trust in their peers".

Remembering our initial research questions, we wanted to know: How do Higher Education students perceive self and peer-assessment practices within an assessment for learning framework? How can self and peer-assessment practices contribute to the quality of competence assessment in Higher Education online environments?

Figure 6. It's Perfect on Paper

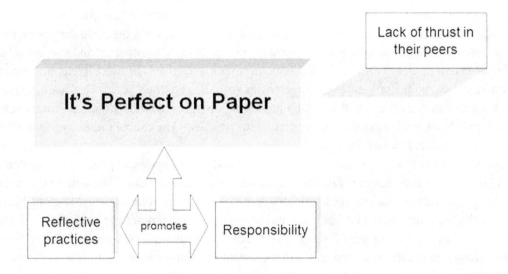

Let us start by addressing the first research question. In general we have observed that the large majority of the participants agreed with the suggested process for assessing the group project. The instructors are responsible for the assessment of the final product that accounts for 1/2 of the final project grade, while the participants are responsible for the assessment of the group work process that accounts for another 1/2 of the project grade. This is clearly visible in the description of the finding entitled "It's Perfect on Paper". The participants are able to identify the advantages of this practice for their own assessment and for their professional life, in areas that go from the development of social and relational competencies to the improvement of their argumentative skills. In fact, "students should develop sustainable assessment skills that enable them to assess their performance and to keep learning throughout life" (Boud, 2000).

However, it is precisely on this identified benefit to their social competences that they start raising some issues concerning the operationalization of this process. The participants seem to consider that because they have to play the role of evaluators and assess their group peers contribution to the project, this will hinder their social interaction. Moreover, they do not recognize on their colleagues the necessary sense of justice and courage to make a fair and unbiased judgment of themselves and their peers. Also, their lack of previous experience with this type of assessment increases their distrust about the validity of the judgments produced by their peers. According to Fastré et al (2012) "at the start of an educational program, students are often unable to take full responsibility for assessing their own learning and development because of their lack of expertise in the domain" (p.2).

This is probably a reflection of these participants past unidirectional educational and professional experience, where there is *one* clear responsible for the evaluation and classification process. Only recently have we started to notice the appearance of assessment processes where the participant's contribution is expected and valued. We make the argument here for the importance of collaboration in online ODL and assessment processes to go with it, as "what is assessed in a Course or a program is what is valued" (Swan et al., 2006, p.45).

In the described context, it is understandable why the finding about the lack of trust on their peers is so prevalent. The participants have little or no experience in this type of assessment, they do not feel comfortable in the role of evaluator, and consequentially, distrust their peers to attain that role too. It is still very hard for these participants to accept an instructor that positions himself in a more horizontal role with respect to them, and they demand from him to position himself more vertically as an arbiter of knowledge (McConnell, 2006). To obviate this problem, it is very important to clearly explicit and discuss the assessment criteria to be used, to make the process as fair, transparent and less biased as possible. The chance to participate and collaborate in group projects gives the participants the opportunity to confront their own points of view and competencies with those of their peers. This learning is crucial if we consider that in daily life situations, namely in professional contexts, individuals are continuously confronted with their peers' judgments, being crucial to critically reflect about the discrepancies between their self-assessment and that of their peers.

To answer our other research question: How can self and peer-assessment practices contribute to the quality of competence assessment in Higher Education online environments? We will now comment on the remaining two themes that emerged from our research: reflective practices and responsibility. The results from this research show that both self and peer-assessment require the participants to exercise responsibility for their own learning. This agrees with the previous work of Vonderwell et al. (2007). In fact, these authors emphasize that "student self-determination and responsibility influenced the degree that the students took advantage of the asynchronous nature of online discussions" (p. 320). However, this is not something that the participants are used to be responsible for, even though they recognize that it is something that they usually do informally, but with no consequences.

The participants recognize the importance of group work but are concerned about the damaged provoked by those who do not cooperate and contribute to the final product, hurting its success. For this reason, this type of assessment process allows them to re-establishes some measure of justice distinguishing the contributions of each of their peers for the final product. Moreover, the results also indicate that participants recognize in this way of assessing group work the advantage of re-establishing justice on the process for all those situations where the instructor is not able to supervise the contributions of each participant. These results also reinforce the importance of using a multiplicity of assessors, strengthening the assessment's consistency through triangulation of sources. Furthermore, it strongly supports the participants' empowerment and ownership for their learning (Topping, 2003).

In this research, all the participants have pointed out the importance of this assessment process to promote their own reflective practices about their work and that of their peers. The awareness of what they have learned, and how they learned it, as well as the monitorization and self-assessment are also present in others research (Nicol & MacFarlane-Dick, 2006; Sluijmans, Prins & Martens, 2006; Vonderwell et al., 2007). Furthermore, some of the participants go one step further and recognize the relevance of this process and its influence on the development of a critical thinking attitude towards their participations and the work that they have done. Some participants will only post their responses after carefully analyzing those of their peers, in order to compare and contrast their points of view and their competences, identifying strengths and weaknesses in their learning process.

The relationship between these assessment practices and their professional practice is also highlighted by several participants as significant, for allowing them to develop assessment competencies that they recognize as important and valuable for their own practice. In fact, McConnell (2006) emphasizes that self and peer-assessment processes allow participants to assess "their own work in ways that are applicable to their future professions .... (and) help students develop enterprising competences" (p.91).

However, given the great diversity of professional and cultural backgrounds amongst the participants and their very different professional responsibilities, it is clear that there are differences on the perceptions and operationalization of these assessment practices. Previous academic experiences centered on the instructor and rooted on the excessive focus on summative assessment, condition the way these new assessment practices are perceived. Another explanation may also be the participants' backgrounds where performance assessment may not be yet a common practice.

Even so, the results indicate that students value self- and peer-assessment, recognizing that it not only increases the assessment's credibility, but also makes it fairer by including other assessors beyond the instructor. Individually, it also has the benefit of impacting their own perception of the frailties of their work and about how to improve it. This is particularly aligned with the consistency and transparency dimensions discussed within the theoretical framework for the quality of competence based digital assessment (Tinoca, Oliveira & Pereira, 2013)

9. CONCLUSION

In this study we discussed a longitudinal project centered on self and peer-assessment practices on the context of an online group project. Even though there have been some minor constraints, the overall balance is clearly positive. However, these assessment strategies should not be considered in isolation, as simple tools to promote the participants' motivation, or to reduce the instructor's workload. In fact, the lack of trust on the peers can undermine these assessment processes, hindering the participants' commitment and consequently the assessment's validity and reliability. Also the participants' diverse backgrounds, academically and professionally, must be carefully considered.

In the context of online competence assessment, it is crucial to have a clear conceptual framework allowing us to evaluate the quality of the proposed assessment practices within an overall coherent assessment design. Within this context, both self- and peer-assessment constitute forms of assessment that should be implemented, and therefore require appropriate types of activities to do so. The significance that the participants attribute to these activities will be reflected on the way that they participate, conceptualize and discuss the questions that will be raised. This process contributes to the participants' inner dialogue and self-reflection, and also to the dialogue with their peers in the community, in every learning environment.

To design online competence assessment programs, where formative and summative assessment practices are present, requires the clear definition and discussion of the assessment criteria, to promote the participant's appropriation of the competence development program that we want them to learn. In this context, metacognition processes are essential as "student awareness of these metacognitive processes can enhance assessment practices" (Vonderwell & Alderman, 2007, p. 324). Furthermore, it is important to make the assessment design open to discussion and negotiation involving the participating students, including the proposed assessment criteria. This democratization process is essential to warrant the quality of the proposed assessment tasks. In fact, if we want to promote the participant's motivation and engagement, it is desirable to make use of a range of methods and assessment strategies. Therefore, the defined assessment criteria should reflect the desired forms of participation, helping the participants to identify and understand what is valued.

In this research, the participants have initiated a learning process, engaged in discussions centered on selected themes, and completed individual and group activities, related to their professional practices, framed by a set of assessment criteria for each particular activity. This research leads us to believe that the participants benefit when the instructor shares with them a set of "exemplary practices" about working in small groups, with the goal of facilitating their acquisition of metacognitive and self-regulatory competencies, to go in hand with a more regulatory stance from the instructor.

It is necessary to develop a sense of thrust between the instructor and the participants, and between the participants themselves, otherwise there will always be a subconscious climate of distrust with inevitable consequences in the assessment process. For the participants to engage and trust on the proposed assessment procedures by their peers, it is fundamental for them to believe that they are working with a common goal and that the assessment is taken seriously by all. Given the participants very diverse personal, cultural and professional backgrounds it is quite important to promote the discussion and clarification of the proposed assessment criteria, and even prolong the time frame for this discussion if necessary. Throughout this process, besides being necessary to develop and maintain a shared authorship relationship between instructor and participants, it is necessary to support the creation of settings and activities that will in turn promote the development of the participants' self-assessment criteria.

REFERENCES

Boud, D. (2000). Sustainable assessment: Rethinking assessment for the learning society. *Studies in Continuing Education*, 22(2), 151–167. doi:10.1080/713695728

Boud, D., & Falchikov, N. (2006). Aligning assessment with long-term learning. *Assessment & Evaluation in Higher Education*, 31(4), 399–413. doi:10.1080/02602930600679050

Brown, S. (2004). Assessment for learning. *Learning and Teaching in Higher Education*, 1, 81–89.

Cheng, K.-H., & Hou, H.-T. (2015). Exploring students' behavioural patterns during online peer-assessment from the affective, cognitive, and metacognitive perspectives: A progressive sequential analysis. *Technology, Pedagogy and Education*, 24(2), 171–188. doi:10.1080/1475939X.2013.822416

Chi, M. (1997). Quantifying qualitative analysis of verbal data: A practical guide. *Journal of the Learning Sciences*, 6(3), 271–315. doi:10.1207/s15327809jls0603_1

Comeaux, P. (2005). Assessment and learning. In P. Comeaux (Ed.), *Assessing Online Learning* (pp. xix–xxvii). Bolton, MA: Anker Publishing Company, Inc.

Dierick, S., & Dochy, F. J. R. C. (2001). New lines in edumetrics: New forms of assessment lead to new assessment criteria. *Studies in Educational Evaluation*, 27(4), 307–329. doi:10.1016/S0191-491X(01)00032-3

Dillenbourg, P. (1999). What do you mean by "collaborative learning"? In P. Dillenbourg (Ed.), *Collaborative learning: Cognitive and Computational approaches* (pp. 1–19). Oxford: Elsevier.

Fastréa, G. M., van der Klinka, M. R., Sluijsmansa, D., & van Merriënboera, J. (2012). Towards an integrated model for developing sustainable assessment skills. *Assessment & Evaluation in Higher Education*, 2012, 1–20.

Garrison, R & Anderson, T. (2003). *E-Learning in the 21st Century: A framework for research and practice*. Routledge.

Joint Information Systems Committee. (2010). *Effective Assessment in a Digital Age*. Retrieved from http://www.jisc.ac.uk/media/documents/programmes/elearning/digiassass_eada.pdf

Lladó, A. P. et al.. (2014). Student perceptions of peer-assessment: An interdisciplinary study. *Assessment & Evaluation in Higher Education*, *39*(5), 592–610. doi:10.1080/02602938.2013.860077

McConnell, D. (2006). *E-Learning Groups and Communities*. Berkshire: Open University Press.

Miles, M., & Hubberman, A. M. (1994). *Qualitative data analysis*. Thousand Oaks, CA: Sage.

Nicol, D. (2007). Principles of good assessment and feedback: Theory and practice. From the *REAP International Online Conference on Assessment Design for Learner Responsibility*, 29th-31st May, 2007. Available at http://ewds.strath.ac.uk/REAP07

Nicol, D. J., & MacFarlane-Dick, D. (2006). Formative assessment and self-regulated learning: A model and seven principles of good feedback practice. *Studies in Higher Education*, *31*(2), 199–218. doi:10.1080/03075070600572090

Oliveira, I., Pereira, A., & Tinoca, L. (2009). The contribution of the Learning Contract for authentic assessment in online environments. *Proceedings of the European Association for Research on Learning and Instruction 13th Biennial Conference*, Amsterdam, Netherlands.

Pereira, A., Mendes, A. Q., Morgado, L., Amante, L., & Bidarra, A. (2007). *Modelo Pedagógico Virtual da Universidade Aberta*. Lisboa: Universidade Aberta.

Pereira, A.; Mendes, A. Q.; Mota, J. C.; Morgado, L. & Aires, L.L. (2003). *Discursos, Série. Perspectivas em Educação*, 1, 39-53.

Pereira, A., Oliveira, I., Amante, L., & Pinto, M. C. (2013). How can we use ICT to assess competences in higher education: The case of authenticity? *Proceedings of 5th International Conference on Education and New Learning Technologies EDULEARN '13*, Barcelona.

Pereira, A., Oliveira, I., & Tinoca, L. (2010). A Cultura de Avaliação: que dimensões? In F. Costa, G. Miranda, M. I. C. João, & E. Cruz (Eds.), *Actas do I Encontro Internacional TIC e Educação: TICeduca 2010*. Lisboa.

Pereira, A., Oliveira, I., Tinoca, L., Pinto, M. C., Amante, L., & Pereira, A. et al.. (2015). *Desafios da Avaliação Digital no Ensino Superior*. Lisboa: Universidade Aberta.

Perret-Clermont, A.-N., Perret, J.-F., & Bell, N. (1991). The social construction of meaning and cognitive activity in elementary school children. In L. Resnick, J. M. Levine, & S. D. Teasley (Eds.), *Perspectives on socially shared cognition* (pp. 41–62). Washington, DC: American Psychological Association. doi:10.1037/10096-002

Rovai, A. P. (2004). A constructivist approach to online college learning. *The Internet and Higher Education*, *7*(2), 79–93. doi:10.1016/j.iheduc.2003.10.002

Sadler, P. M., & Good, E. (2006). The Impact of Self- and Peer-Grading on Student Learning. *Educational Assessment*, *11*(1), 1–31. doi:10.1207/s15326977ea1101_1

Sainsbury, E. J., & Walker, R. A. (2007). Assessment as a vehicle for learning: Extending collaboration into testing. *Assessment & Evaluation in Higher Education, 33*(2), 103–117. doi:10.1080/02602930601127844

Sluijsmans, D. M. A., Prins, F., & Martens, R. (2006). A framework for integrated performance assessment in E-Learning. *Learning Environments Research, 9*(1), 45–66. doi:10.1007/s10984-005-9003-3

Swan, K., Shen, J., Fredericksen, E., Pickett, A., Pelz, W., & Maher, G. (2000). Building knowledge building communities: Consistency, contact and communication in the virtual classroom. *Journal of Educational Computing Research, 23*(4), 389–413.

Swan, K., Shen, J., & Hiltz, S. R. (2006). Assessment and Collaboration in Online Learning. *Journal of Asynchronous Learning Networks, 10*(1), 45–62.

Tinoca, L., Oliveira, I., & Pereira, A. (2013). A conceptual framework for e-assessment in Higher Education – authenticity, consistency, transparency and practicability. In S. Mukerji & P. Tripathi (Eds.), Handbook of Research on Transnational Higher Education Management. Hershey, PA, USA: IGI Global.

Vonderwell, S., Liang, X., & Alderman, K. (2007). Asynchronous Discussions and Assessment in Online Learning. *Journal of Research on Technology in Education, 39*(3), 309–328. doi:10.1080/15391523.2007.10782485

Chapter 14
Serious Games for Students' E-Assessment Literacy in Higher Education

María Soledad Ibarra-Sáiz
Universidad de Cádiz, Spain

Gregorio Rodriguez-Gomez
Universidad de Cadiz, Spain

ABSTRACT

In this chapter it will present partial results from the DevalS Project (Developing Sustainable Assessment – Improving Student's Assessment Competence through Virtual Simulations), financed by the Spanish Ministry of Economy and Competitiveness (Ref. EDU2012-31804). The results will be focused on the use and usefulness of serious games for e-assessment literacy from a students' point of view. Firstly, it will introduce the project. Secondly, it will review the serious games that have been developed and implemented in different undergraduate courses. Finally, it will present the results and conclusions of surveys undertaken by students.

ORGANIZATION BACKGROUND

The DevalS project was developed and carried out by the EVALfor Research Group (Assessment within Training Contexts) Ref. SEJ509, with funding obtained from the Andalusian Research, Development and Innovation Plan of the Junta de Andalucía, Spain. This research group comprises of teachers in the area of Research Methods and Assessment in Education (MIDE) of the University of Cadiz, established in 1995 to institutionalize the research being carried out in the area.

Both groups are involved in similar areas of work focusing on research methodology, assessment, training and consulting within organizations as well as research and innovation using new technologies. These themes have been developed through a large number of research, development and innovation (R + D + i) projects led by members of the MIDE team and financed through various national and interna-

DOI: 10.4018/978-1-5225-0531-0.ch014

tional public tenders and which involved researchers from different branches of knowledge, universities and countries.

Over the past decade many researchers from different universities have worked in this area with the research group and this collaboration has resulted in the official incorporation within the EVALfor Research Group of several Doctors from the University of Seville, primarily in the area of Educational Research Methods. Currently, EVALfor is a competitive and inter-university research team, consisting of research Doctors, university lecturers, doctoral fellows in training, professionals and technicians. EVALfor Research Group collaborates closely with Educational Evaluation and Guidance (GE2O) and InterAction and eLearning (GRIAL) research groups, both from the University of Salamanca, Spain.

The previous experience of the EVALfor Group in recent years in relation to the subject of this chapter is focused on the implementation and the results of the following research projects:

- **DevalS Project:** The *Development of Sustainable e-Assessment – Improving students' assessment skills using virtual simulations*. National Programme of Fundamental Research Projects. Ministry of Finance and Competition. Ref. EDU2012-31804.
- **DevalSimWeb Project:** The development of skills through participation in assessment and simulation using web tools. ALFA European Commission. Contract No. DCI-ALA / 19.09.01 / 11/21526 / 264-773 / ALFAIII (2011) -10.
- **PROALeval Project:** From grading to e-feedforward. Innovative strategies and tools for assessment/feedforward and the development of skills in university students. Ref. EA2011-0057. Ministry of Education. Order EDU / 3537/2011 of 12 December, by which subsidies are granted for the implementation of actions under the Program of Studies and Analysis aimed at improving the quality of Higher Education and university teaching. (BOE. 312 of 28 December 2011).
- **INevalCO Project:** Innovation in skills assessment: Design and development of procedures and tools for assessing skills in mixed/virtual environments with the participation of undergraduate students. Ref. EA2010-052. Ministry of Education. Order EDU / 2680/2010 of 14 October, by which subsidies are granted for the implementation of actions under the Program of Studies and Analysis, aimed at improving the quality of Higher Education and university teaching. (BOE 251, of 16 October 2010)
- **Re-Evalua Project:** Reengineering of e-assessment, technologies and skills development for teachers and university students. Ref. P08-SEJ-03502. Call: Incentives for research excellence projects. Junta de Andalucía, Ministry of Innovation, Science and Enterprise. (BOJA No. 7 of 13 January 2009).
- **EvalHIDA Project:** Assessment of skills using asynchronous tools for dialogic interaction (forums, blogs and wikis). Ref. EA2008-0237. Ministry of Education. Resolution of 14 July 2008 (BOE 194 of 12 August 2008).

SETTING THE STAGE

The DevalS project *The Sustainable development of e-assessment – Improving the assessment skills of university students using virtual simulations*, was developed under the VI National Plan for Scientific Research, Technological Development and Innovation 2008-2011 and researchers from 8 Spanish[1] and 2 Australian[2] universities collaborated, together with several interested observers from Spain and other

Figure 1. Challenges and principles of assessment as learning and empowerment
(Rodríguez-Gómez and Ibarra-Sáiz, 2015: 3)

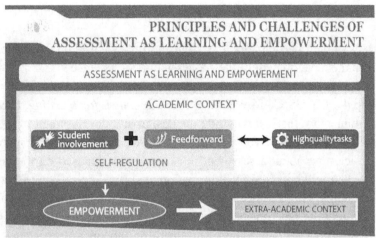

countries. This project is the continuation of previous work undertaken by the EVALfor Research Group focused on electronic assessment.

The framework on which the proposal is based focuses firstly on assessment as learning and empowerment, a conceptual approach currently being developed by some members of the EVALfor Research with its initial foundations in sustainable and learning-oriented assessment (Boud, 2000; Boud & Soler, 2015; Carles, Joughin & Liu, 2006) and, secondly, on the increasing incorporation of ICT into Higher Education.

The assessment as learning and empowerment approach, illustrated in Figure 1, is based on three key challenges: 1) the participation of students in the assessment of their own learning in a way that is transparent and promotes dialogue; 2) feedforward, focused on encouraging strategies that provide proactive information on the results of assessment; 3) both participation and feedforward must be considered during the planning of the assessment tasks, which are characterized by being challenging and meaningful and promoting reflective, analytical and critical thinking, i.e. realistic and high quality tasks. The implementation of innovation around these three challenges within the academic context promotes self-regulation of their own learning among students. Furthermore, it will also enhance their empowerment within extra-academic, personal and professional contexts, which means the development of transversal competences such as data analysis, application of knowledge, reasoning, communication, problem solving, ethical awareness, decision making, teamwork, creativity and independent learning (Rodríguez-Gómez and Ibarra-Sáiz, 2015: 2).

To meet the first challenge, the DevalS project responds to the importance, as demonstrated by several other studies (Falchikov, 2005; Strijbos & Sluijsmans, 2010; Taras, 2015), of achieving the active participation of university students in the assessment of their own learning as a means to develop their ability to learn throughout life. One general objective of this research was to verify empirically the results and impact obtained from the use of a training course (DevalS Course: *How to use assessment for learning*) based on simulations in a virtual learning environment, on the development of university students' assessment competence, defined in terms of *data analysis, application of knowledge, independent learning and reasoning*. The research attempts to answer three main questions:

- Can be promote the development of assessment competence among university students through simulations using virtual learning environments?
- To what degree are training activities based on simulations in virtual environments effective and efficient?
- What impact does student participation in training activities based on simulations in virtual environments have on the development of their assessment competence?

In order to develop the DevalS Course: *How to use assessment for learning*, it was necessary first to define the logical framework that would guide the design and development of the course. Figure 2 illustrates this logical framework. The DevalS course is based on student participation in the process of assessment and on learning about assessment in a way that is focused on the development of the required competencies that will be assessed (information analysis, application of knowledge, independent learning and reasoning). These competencies are divided among the three modules into which the DevalS course is structured, the final one being of an applied nature covering five different specialties. The development is carried out following the ERCA learning sequence (Experience, Reflection, Conceptualization and Action), based on the model proposed by Kolb (1984) and Kolb & Kolb (2005), by which the course is structured into events, sequences and episodes in which a variety of resources are used, such as frameworks, guidelines, microvideos and texts as well as technological resources ranging from virtual courses to tools which help with the design of assessment processes, the management and creation of assessment instruments and serious games.

Figure 2. Logical framework of DevalS courses How to use assessment for learning

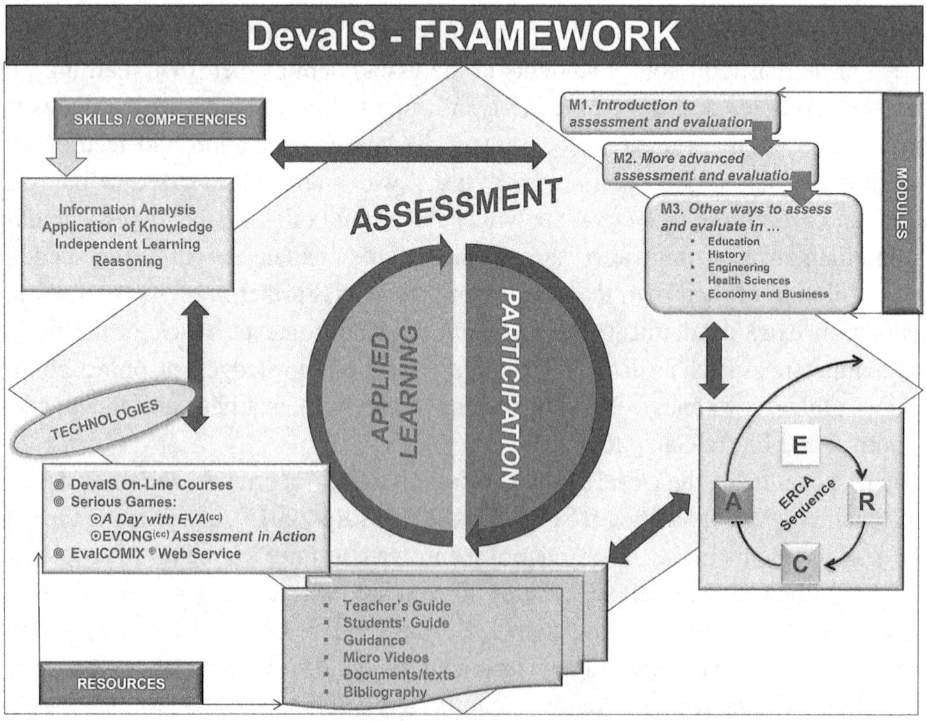

CASE DESCRIPTION

From a global perspective Brown (2015) highlights the need to consider "the specific capabilities that many believe are necessary 'literacies' for effective tertiary studies in the 21st century. These include academic literacy, information literacy, assessment literacy, digital literacy, social and interpersonal literacy" (p. 88). The aim of presenting this case study is to respond to the following question: to what extent do university students consider that the use of serious games improves their understanding of key aspects of the assessment of learning? Consequently, the case is primarily framed within the context which Brown (2015) refers to assessment literacy and, secondly as digital literacy. The concept of e-assessment literacy is used in response to the need to improve students' literacy in the area of assessment but specifically within a technologised or digital context.

Several authors have demonstrated the need to design and implement ways to improve assessment literacy. Boud and associates (2010) argue that "Students need confidence and competence in making informed judgements about what they produce. They need to develop the ability to evaluate the quality, completeness and/or accuracy of work with respect to appropriate standards, and have the confidence to express their judgements with conviction. This requires deliberately managed assessment processes and practice that relates to judgements required in professional practice and mature community engagement" (p.2). Similarly, Price, Carroll, O'Donovan & Rust (2011) maintain that learning is more effective when students understand the assessment process. "In fact, it has been shown that students' assessment performance can easily be improved by supporting their understanding of assessment tasks and criteria" (p. 485).

Price et al. (2012: 10-11) believe that:

assessment literacy encompasses:

- *An appreciation of assessment's relationship to learning;*
- *A conceptual understanding of assessment (i.e. understanding of the basic principles of valid assessment and feedback practice, including the terminology used);*
- *Understanding of the nature, meaning and level of assessment criteria and standards;*
- *Skills in self- and peer assessment;*
- *Familiarity with technical approaches to assessment (i.e. familiarity with pertinent assessment and feedback skills, techniques, and methods, including their purpose and efficacy); and*
- *Possession of the intellectual ability to select and apply appropriate approaches and techniques to assessed tasks (not only does one have the requisite skills, but one is also able to judge which skill to use when, and for which task).*

Ultimately, it is a matter of helping students to understand how assessment works within a Higher Education context. The case presented here is therefore focused on how simulation games can play an important role in students' formative development and in enhancing their literacy about these issues.

The DevalS course How to use assessment for learning was designed and delivered in various Spanish universities with the aim of being able to respond to the question raised earlier concerning the extent to which university students believe that using serious games improves their learning about key aspects of assessment. The course consists of two common modules and one specific module for Arts and Humanities, Health Sciences, Education, Business and Engineering and Architecture. The students' perceptions on the issues were identified by using survey techniques through different questionnaires as they worked through the course. This chapter presents partial results from two specific questionnaires with Likert type questions on a scale of 1-6, which were designed to collect information on general aspects, the usability and the effectiveness of the serious games used in the DevalS Course.

Technology Concerns

Assessment appears to exist within the educational scenario as something that is not susceptible to changes, modifications or innovations, as other elements of the teaching-learning processes are, such as teaching methods, spaces or educational resources. But a significant shift is now taking place such as never before in the field of assessment of learning. We are witnessing a time when change is taking place, both at the level of policy and practice. This is evident from the contributions of Gibbs and Simpson (2004-05), as well as Boud and Falchikov (2006), Bloxham and Boyd (2007), Carless, Joughin and Liu (2006), Nicol, Thompson & Breslin (2014), Sambell, Mcdowell and Montgomery (2013) or Brown (2015).

For some time, university lecturers have used different platforms (known as "virtual campuses") developed by universities to encourage the incorporation of ICT into the teaching-learning process. The use of these resources ranges from treating the platform as a simple repository of materials, through to exploiting it for the delivery of blended training courses and to the design and delivery of entire formal qualifications, based on the use of platforms like Moodle or WebCT, among others. The traditional image of a university lecturer teaching from a lectern is being replaced by teacher-student interaction mediated by the use of ICT, moving the reality of the teaching-learning from the classrooms into virtual spaces.

The use of ICT in university teaching and learning can be seen as a positive development. In the case of assessment in particular, Barberá (2006) highlights three changes technology has brought: 1) automatic assessment in the sense that the technology has databases that relate to each other so that answers and immediate corrections can be delivered to students; 2) encyclopaedic assessment, referring to the wealth of content handled in a more or less complex source or from different sources; and 3) collaborative assessment that enables the visualization of collaborative processes such as debates, forums or group working.

However, Gibbs (2006), in analyzing computer-assisted assessment, especially in regard to the use of multiple choice tests, shows that although there is evidence of a quantitative increase in student learning when this type of assessment is used, there is little evidence concerning the benefits to the quality of learning.

Boud (2006) suggests four major areas for innovation in Higher Education:

- Generate alternatives to traditional practices which are dominated by exams in which content is merely regurgitated and standardized tests.
- Involve students more actively, not only in the processes and activities of teaching and learning, but in the assessment processes themselves.
- Generate new ways of presenting outputs, performances and results.
- Recognize the power of self-assessment on learning and how changes introduced in assessment have much a greater influence on student learning than changes made in any other area of the process.

New contributions are emerging based on the use of technology, such as e-portfolios, but it is necessary and urgent to rethink the status of e-assessment so that education and technology become more aligned. Thus, the use of ICT adds another element of complexity to the assessment function, such as introducing a new means of interaction between teachers and students that makes the assessment process more difficult and intricate. Thus, the four areas of innovation suggested by Boud (2006), if considered from the perspective of the use and implementation of technologies, represent significant challenges for the development of assessment in the immediate future.

Although the idea of using simulations as part of the learning process is not new and had its beginnings in the 1980s, more and more authors and research support the idea of increased student motivation and the use of simulations generates additional educational experiences such as problem solving and the development of interpersonal skills.

The combination of a powerful tool that delivers learning activities with a simple method for designing e-assessment activities and the potential of simulations can be an ideal starting point for the implementation of complex e-assessment strategies endorsed by the new approaches and concepts of assessment and an excellent way to start the process towards assessment literacy.

Technology Components

The EVALfor Research Group is involved in developing different technological tools to facilitate both assessment and assessment literacy. Among them are the DINNO®[3] desktop tools, which enable design innovations in Higher Education assessment and DIPeval_PRO®[4], which facilitates the design of assessment procedures, together with the EvalCOMIX®[5] web service, which supports the management and construction of assessment instruments.

The web service EvalCOMIX® together with two serious games were incorporated within the DevalS Course *How to use assessment for learning,* which itself was designed and delivered using a virtual campus, based on a Moodle platform, for use by students.

The key technological elements are outlined below together with the virtual campus, the EvalCOMIX® web service and the serious games.

Virtual Campus

The DevalS course virtual campus was developed using a Moodle platform and produced by the University Institute of Educationsl Sciences (IUCE) at the University of Salamanca. The author of each module was responsible for designing them for delivery via the virtual campus.

The initial interface screen of the DevalS course is reproduced at Figure 3, and shows how the EvalCOMIX® icon is incorporated so that students and teachers can access the resource directly.

A range of multimedia resources and activities was designed for each of the three modules that formed the DevalS course. There was a Student Handbook for each module to help them complete each task and undertake the assessment. Every module also contained specific articles, reviews, LAMS (Learning Activity Management System) based learning sequences, short videos, etc. Figure 4 illustrates the activities and resources used within Task 2 of Module 2 *More advanced assessment.*

Figure 3. DevalS course interface

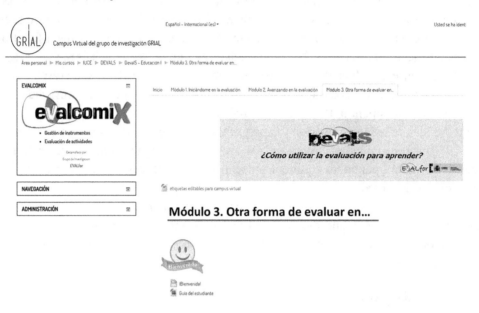

Figure 4. Indicative list of resources and activities on the virtual campus

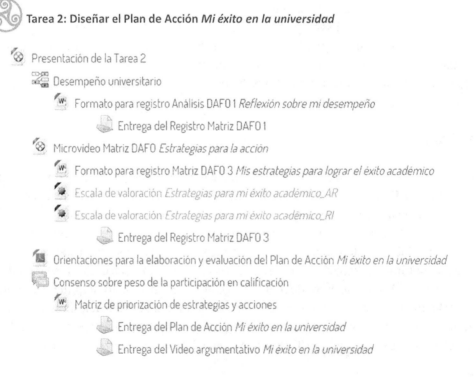

Figure 5. Examples of the instruments used with the EvalCOMIX® web service

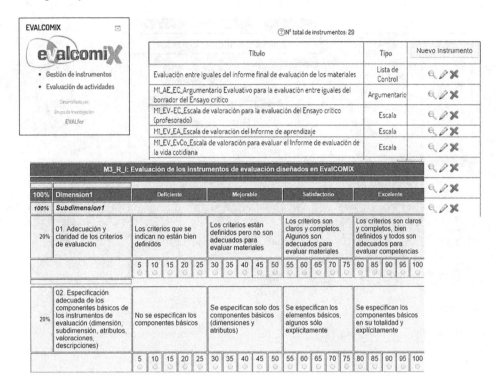

The EvalCOMIX® Web Service

By using the EvalCOMIX® web service tutors can design a variety of assessment instruments such as checklists, rating scales, marking schemes, assessment discourses and semantic differentials. A total of 29 different instruments were designed for the DevalS course. Figure 5 presents an illustrative list of these instruments and part of one of the rubrics used in the course.

All of these assessment instruments had been previously introduced to the students so that they could guide their learning. Students were also able to participate in the assessment processes in terms of assessment methods, self-assessment and peer assessment using the EvalCOMIX® web service incorporated into the Moodle based virtual campus.

Serious Games

In the DevalS Course *How to use assessment for learning*, two serious games are used. The first game, (*A day with Eva*[(cc)]) initially developed within the context of the DevalSimWeb[6] Project, was designed in order to introduce students to the concept of assessment and develop skills such as decision making, analytical judgment, critical thinking and problem solving. A second game (EVONG [(cc)] -*Assessment in Action*) aims to extend the use of assessment into professional contexts. Both games are described below.

Figure 6. Summary of the structure of A day with Eva [(cc)]

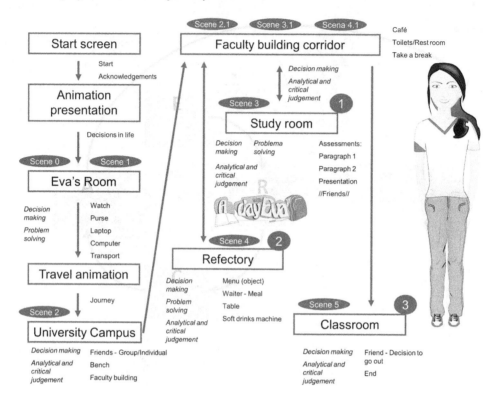

A Day with Eva [(cc)] Game

The serious game *A day with Eva* [(cc)] (Figure 6) is a graphic interactive "Point and Click" adventure game structured around different scenarios (student bedroom, university campus, faculty building, study room, dining room and classroom). In playing the game the student must take a number of everyday decisions that will help them reflect on the key issues and use assessment within a familiar everyday context.

EVONG [(cc)]: Assessment in Action

The serious game *EVONG* [(cc)]: *Assessment in Action* (Figure 7) is based around the creation and management of the NGO (Non-Governmental Organization) called "Cooperation, Education and Development". The game is designed so that students will:

- Apply knowledge they gain about assessment, establish criteria and make appropriate judgements leading to formal assessment.
- Make decisions in a reasoned and coherent way, recognise the options available to them and the goals to achieve and to propose strategies aimed at achieving them.

Unlike *A day with Eva* [(cc)], *EVONG* [(cc)]: *Assessment in Action* has three profiles from which each player can choose which one(s) they want to play as. These profiles are:

Figure 7. Partial scenario of the serious game EVONG [(cc)]: Assessment in Action

- Project Coordinator (responsible for project management.
- Finance and Quality Coordinator (responsible for quality and finance).
- Institutional Relations Coordinator (responsible for social responsibility, communication and relations with other organizations).

Management and Organizational Concerns

As mentioned above, the DevalS Course *How to use assessment for learning* is designed with the aim of developing and improving the assessment competence of university students, from the first year of their degree, encouraging their active participation in the process of assessing their own learning as a means to develop their learning ability throughout life. This objective is to be achieved through:

- The deployment of four transversal skills.
- The implementation of the principles of sustainable assessment and assessment as learning.
- The contextualization and design of modules for each of the degree courses within the selected subject areas.
- The development and integration of serious games.
- The development and integration of services and open source tools.

Table 1. Skills developed by the DevalS Course

Information Analysis	Application of Knowledge
Select, review and organise available information to identify and extract from it the most relevant and pertinent ideas.	Use and apply the knowledge acquired (concepts, principles, procedures, attitudes) to the development of academic and professional outputs.
Independent Learning	**Reasoning**
Acknowledge and assess your own learning needs, set your learning objectives, and plan, manage and implement learning strategies to help you achieve them.	Develop, put forward and defend ideas, opinions or theories in a clear and coherent way in order to articulate and share viewpoints that are reasoned, convincing and constructive.

Table 2. Duration and characteristics of the DevalS course How to use assessment for learning

Module		Duration and Format		
		Virtual	Attendance	Total
M1	Introduction to assessment	12 h.	3 h.	15 h.
M2	More advanced assessment	12 h.	3 h.	15 h.
M3	Other forms of assessment: (5 modules)	16 h.	4 h.	20 h.
Duration and format of DevalS Course		40 h.	10 h.	50 h.

The transversal skills considered relevant to assessment and around which the course is designed and which are developed and evaluated during its implementation, relate to: information analysis, application of knowledge, independent learning and reasoning. Table 1 presents definitions of these skills.

Organization and Structure of the DevalS Course How to Use Assessment for Learning

The DevalS Course is structured into three modules and takes 50 hours (2 ECTS credits) and is mostly virtual; 40 virtual classroom hours and 10 hours of class attendance (Table 2).

The first module introduces students to the basic concepts of assessment and the first serious game is introduced (*A day with Eva* ⁽ᶜᶜ⁾). In the second unit the students consider assessment in more depth and play the second serious game titled *EVONG* ⁽ᶜᶜ⁾: *Assessment in Action*. Finally, in the third module the students use the concepts they have been introduced to within specific contexts: such as Education, Economics, Engineering, Health or Humanities (Figure 8).

Figure 8. Structure of DevalS Course How to use assessment for learning

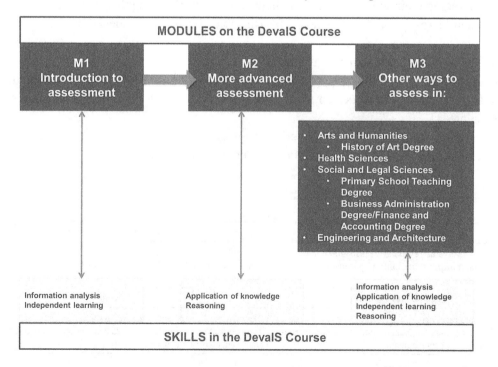

Table 3. Materials and resources available in the DevalS Course How to use assessment for learning

Students	Lecturers
DevalS Virtual Course.	DevalS Virtual Course.
DevalS Course Student Handbook • Guide to learning and assessment tasks. • Assessment processes. • Assessment instruments.	DevalS Course Lecturers' Handbook.
• Microvideo presentations. • Microvideos on assessment.	Microvideos on assessment[7].
• Scientific articles. • Reviews and texts for reading and analysis.	Articles and scientific texts.
Forums, wikis.	Forums.
EvalCOMIX® integrated within the DevalS virtual course. • Review and assessment.	EvalCOMIX® integrated within the DevalS virtual course. • Instrument design. • Organisation of instruments and and assessment modes. • Effective feedback, and feedforward.
Serious game *A day with Eva* [(cc)]	DINNO®. Design framework for de innovation in Higher Education.
Serious game *EVONG*[(cc)] *– Assessment in Action*.	DIPeval_PRO®. Design of assessment processes.

Course Methodology and Resources of the DevalS Course *How to Use Assessment for Learning*

The DevalS Course methodology is characterized by being active and participatory. Workshops and collaborative activities take place in the classroom-based sessions. During the virtual sessions the activities focus on reading texts, performing individual tasks, watching short videos, playing serious games, participating in forums and wikis, reviewing and assessing their own and their peers' outputs and activities.

Figure 9. Example of a leaflet

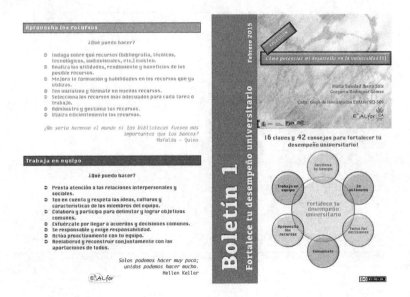

Figure 10. Microvideo on SWOT

Figure 11. Microvideo on self-regulation

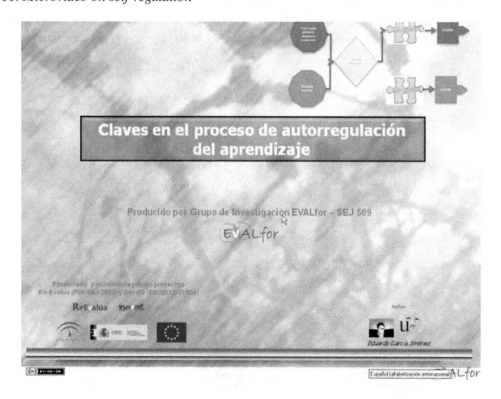

Table 4. Sample distribution by serious game, gender, university and subjects

	EVA		EVONG	
	n	**%**	**n**	**%**
Gender				
Male	24	18.0	12	21.4
Female	109	82.0	44	78.6
University				
Rovira i Virgili	36	27.1	25	44.6
Seville	25	18.8	7	12.5
Salamanca	72	54.1	24	42.9
Subjects				
Art History	12	9.0	10	17.9
Childhood Education	46	34.6	31	55.4
Labour Relations	24	18.0	15	26.8
Pedagogy	46	34.6	-	-

The monitoring, guidance and supervision by the university lecturers is focused on providing effective feedback or feedforward to students so they can improve their results, outputs or performances during the process. It is done through features within the virtual campus (forums, email, EvalCOMIX®, etc.) and in face-to-face individual or small group tutorials.

Various materials are produced during the course using resources that make up the DevalS Course. They are outlined in Table 3 and categorised as either resources for lecturers or resources for students.

Figures 9-11 illustrate some of the resources designed for use on the DevalS Course.

Results

The results obtained in terms of the perception that students expressed about the use of serious games integrated within the DevalS Course are given below.

Table 4 shows the distribution of the questionnaires completed by students after playing each of the games. For the game A *day with Eva* [cc], included in Module 1, a total of 133 students responded and in the case of *EVONG* [cc]: *Assessment in Action*, incorporated in Module 2, 56 students responded, with the majority of responses from females in both cases.

In the game A *day with Eva* [cc], students were asked about their level of knowledge about assessment before and after playing the game. Specifically, students were asked their opinions about their knowledge of the following:

1. Assessment in general.
2. Assessment criteria.
3. Peer assessment.
4. Self-assessment.
5. Assessment instruments.

Figure 12. Level of knowledge expressed by students before and after completing the game A day with Eva [cc]

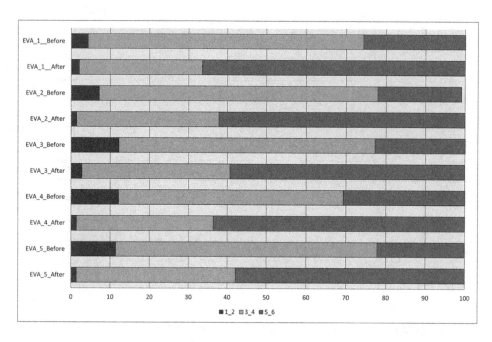

Figure 13. Average scores before and after completing the game A day with Eva [cc]

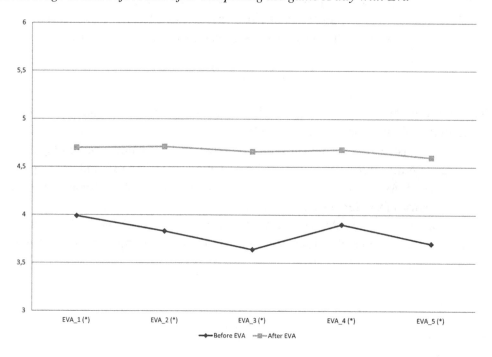

Figure 12 shows the response rates of students, both before and after completing the game, to each of the five elements: Assessment in general (EVA_1), Assessment criteria (EVA_2), Peer assessment (EVA_3), Self-assessment (EVA_4) and Assessment instruments (EVA_5). The scores are classified into three levels: those expressing little knowledge (scores 1-2), an average level of knowledge (3-4) and a high level of knowledge (scores 5-6).

The Figure 12 demonstrates how for all five elements the scores indicating a high level of knowledge (values 5 and 6) increase after completing the game. Overall it is evident that the number of students indicating a high level of knowledge about every element before playing the game is between 20% and 25%. In contrast, after completing the game that figure rises to between 58% and 74%, producing an average increase of slightly more than 35% in terms of the level of understanding that students have of the key elements of assessment.

With regard to a knowledge of assessment in general (EVA_1), prior to playing the game just 25.8% indicated a high level of knowledge whilst, after completing the game, this figure rises to 66.5% of students. In terms of assessment criteria (EVA_2), the initial figure for students stating they had a high level of knowledge was 21.2% with that figure rising to 62.2% after completing the game. With regard to knowledge about peer assessment (EVA_3) a total of 22.9% of students said that before completing the game they had a high level of knowledge but after completing the game this percentage increases to 59.2%. In relation to self-assessment (EVA_4) the percentages confirming a high level of knowledge rises from 30.7% to 63.6% pre and post playing the game. Finally, those claiming a high level of knowledge of assessment instruments (EVA_5) prior to playing the game represent 22.1% whereas the figure rises to 57.9% after completing the game.

Figure 13 shows these differences even more clearly when average scores on each of the five aspects are presented. When performing the Wilcoxon test for repeated measures, in all cases it was found that these differences are statistically significant (p <.05), with the biggest differences found in the scores for assessment criteria (EVA_2), peer assessment (EVA_3) and assessment instruments (EVA_5). The initial average score for assessment criteria (EVA_2) is 3.83 which subsequently rises to 4.71. The initial average score for peer assessment (EVA_3) rises from 3.64 to 4.66 and for assessment instruments the score rises from 3.7 to 4.6. The smallest differences are found in relation to knowledge about assessment in general (EVA_1) where the score rises from 3.99 to 4.7 and for self-assessment (EVA_4), the scores for which rise from 3.9 to 4.68.

Regarding the game *EVONG* [cc] *- Assessment in Action*, students were asked about their level of knowledge about specific aspects of assessment, both before and after completing the game. The questions related to the following nine elements:

1. Assessment in general.
2. Assessment criteria.
3. Peer assessment.
4. Self-assessment.
5. Assessment instruments.
6. Types of assessment (of institutions, programmes, learning).
7. Feedback.
8. Planning assessment actions or activities.
9. Selecting and implementing strategies for achieving goals.

Figure 14. Level of knowledge expressed by students before and after completing the game EVONG (cc)*: Assessment in Action*

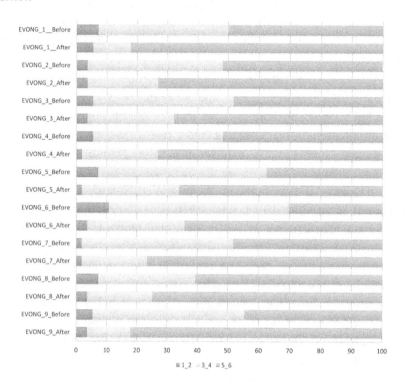

The response rates of students before and after completing the game *EVONG* are presented in Figure 14 in relation to each of the nine elements: Assessment in general (EVONG_1), Assessment criteria (EVONG_2), Peer assessment (EVONG_3), Self-assessment (EVONG_4), Assessment tools (EVONG_5), Types of assessment (EVONG_6), Feedback (EVONG_7) Planning actions or activities (EVONG_8) and Selecting or implementing strategies for achieving goals (EVONG_9). For each of the nine specific elements of assessment (Figure 9), responses indicating a high level of knowledge (values 5 and 6) increase after completion of the game *EVONG* (cc)*: Assessment in Action*.

When analysing the results following completion of this second simulation game it must bear in mind that the students had previously played the *A day with Eva* game and therefore their knowledge about elements of assessment was likely to be greater. It can see, in fact, from the results presented in Figure 14 that the degree of knowledge expressed prior to playing the second game is higher than for the *A day with Eva* game. Between 30.4% in relation to types of assessment (EVONG_6) and 60.7% in relation to planning tasks and activities (EVONG_8) indicate a high level of knowledge. In contrast, initial scores in relation to *A day with Eva* indicating a high level of knowledge were between 20% and 25%.

It is evident that students indicate a higher level of knowledge after completing the second simulation game such that, overall, the improvement in their level of knowledge amounts to an average of 26%. The main increases in percentages occur firstly with selecting and implementing strategies to achieve goals (EVONG_9), for which the proportion of students indicating a high level of knowledge rises from 44.6% to 82.2%. A second large difference is seen in relation to knowledge of different types of assessment (EVONG_6), where scores rise from 30.4% to 64.2%. Finally, a difference in excess of 30% is found in relation to a high level of knowledge about assessment in general, where the scores rise from 50% to 82.1%.

In contrast to this, the smallest differences are registered in the case of planning assessment tasks and activities (EVONG_8) which start at 60.7% and rise to 75%; knowledge of peer assessment (EVONG_3) where the increase is from 48.2% to 67.9% and assessment instruments, the scores for which increase from 37.5% to 66%.

Figure 15 clearly illustrates these differences in the average scores for each of the nine elements. The Wilcoxon test for repeated samples was applied, confirming in all cases that the differences are statistically significant (p <.05). The main differences between the perceptions of students before and after playing the game correspond to the areas relating to assessment instruments (EVONG_5), types of assessment (EVONG-6) and feedback (EVONG_7), whereas the smallest difference occurs in relation to planning of assessment tasks and activities (EVONG_8).

In conclusion, from the results presented here it can be seen that the use of the serious games *A day with Eva* [cc] and *EVONG* [cc]: *Assessment in Action* increases the perception of knowledge among students regarding both the essential and the more specific elements of assessment such as the elements relating to assessment criteria, assessment instruments, assessment methods (self- and peer assessment), feedback, etc.

CURRENT CHALLENGES FACING THE ORGANIZATION

It is intrinsic to the function of universities to deliver continuous improvement in the teaching-learning process and this implies they must incorporate innovations that facilitate and contribute to this process

Figure 15. Average scores before and after completing the game EVONG [cc]: Assessment in Action

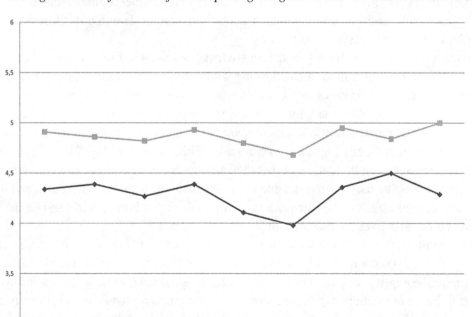

in general, and to assessment processes in particular. They must also tackle the challenges facing Higher Education in responding to emerging needs arising from an ever-changing social context.

There are four key challenges to address as a priority; 1) changing the approach to and practice of the assessment of learning; 2) incorporating enabling technologies into the assessment process; 3) improving assessment literacy and 4) the development of university policies that encourage change and improvements in assessment processes.

Higher Education, by its very nature, functions across multiple contexts that demand a change in perspective and in how assessment is delivered. Assessment as learning, sustainable learning and strategic learning cannot be delivered through traditional and customary assessment practices. It requires an openness of mind and it is necessary to be vigilant and anticipate the changing needs and environment. Assessment should provide students with opportunities to improve, foster their development in extra-academic contexts and enable their personal and professional development. That is to say, it should never limit the personal and professional future of students. In this regard, it is important that all assessment activities carried out in universities are connected with the real world and that they are both challenging and motivating. Furthermore, they must demand of students a high level of applied knowledge, analytical thinking and the use of different intellectual strategies. It is also important to promote participation, accountability and confidence in students in their own processes of assessment. It is also paramount that students receive effective feedback from their teachers, mentors, other students, professionals or employers, allowing them to improve their performance and achieve self-assessment skills that will enable them to develop and grow throughout their lives and in all areas in which they operate.

Work has been ongoing for some time to bring together these premises about assessment through the use of appropriate enabling technologies. Virtual teaching and learning, blended learning, group sizes, etc. all transform both the times and the traditional spaces in which the process of teaching and learning and assessment have taken place. They require the use of technological tools to deliver assessment, but always in tune and aligned with current trends in assessment so that progress made is never lost.

Another challenge, or rather an urgent need, relates to assessment literacy and to developing the skills required to successfully address the implementation of innovations. Training in these areas should be aimed at both students and university lecturers.

In this chapter attention has been focused on students' assessment literacy and it has shown how, through the use of simulation games, it can develop with very positive results. But, not surprisingly, to acquire assessment literacy it is necessary to understand assessment, both theoretically and empirically, which means that university staff, the tutors or other professionals involved in the educational processes of the university should be experts in assessment in order to implement assessment in their modules and promote assessment literacy, all of which demands specific high-level training. This assessment literacy is essential for everyone simply by the fact that they are teachers and in the various modules, subjects and professional areas that they are responsible for, assessment needs to be undertaken and it is simply not acceptable to continue using the same assessment practices that have already shown themselves to be outdated and not to deliver the best student learning outcomes.

If assessment literacy is vital in order to undertake assessment, it is even more important, indeed it is essential, to develop assessment literacy among teachers and students. In acquiring assessment literacy educators need to be experts, they need to have an acknowledged background in innovation and research in assessment. Years of teaching experience alone are not enough to acquire assessment literacy, as it runs the serious risk of delivering educational practice that is unsuitable and detrimental to student learning. Consequently, it must fight against any institutional dilution of education on assessment and assessment literacy. In short, teachers and students alike need to undergo training processes that enable them to effectively address their responsibility as assessors in a way that encourages the self-regulation of student learning and promotes lifelong learning. To achieve the training and literacy levels needed by competent professionals also requires a supportive institutional context.

Progress in assessment must be based on innovation and research and the results of these activities should be reflected in and enhance assessment practice. But it is also vital that university policies both promote and support major changes. Such an important issue as assessment, which leads within universities to professional accreditation, cannot be sustained entirely by the personal motivation or activity of individual teachers or groups of teachers. It is necessary to remember, for example, that in relation to guidance, proposals and perspectives on assessment within the context of Spanish universities, there are only regulations in place covering the grading of students in relation to the formal exams which they are entitled to take. It is essential to have institutional and political commitment at a regional and national level that drives change and the transformation of assessment practice into all university classrooms. Also, it is necessary for universities and all appropriate agencies to promote and support training and assessment literacy, delivered by competent professionals in a way that facilitates change and leads to better assessment practice.

SOLUTIONS AND RECOMMENDATIONS

The EVALfor Research Group has been working in the field of developing the assessment literacy of university teachers and students. The design of the DevalS course focusing on educating university students, or training programs developed in the context of DevalSimWeb Project, one of which is aimed as teachers and two at students, show how this type of training improves the skills of both students and university teachers in this process and how the technologies used are useful for guiding and encouraging this process, although not without some difficulties.

In the near future, therefore, it will be important to review these training courses and the features offered by the technological tools developed in recent years that have been included in training programmes for university teachers and students. Furthermore, it will be necessary to promote the incorporation of the required changes in educational practice, developing new tools to respond to new emerging needs and to consolidate the progress made so far.

The introduction of innovations into assessment processes requires the active participation of teachers and students but also institutional support. In this regard, it has been proved that in the case of the Spanish universities there have been few changes so far incorporated into the rules governing the assessment process (Ibarra-Sáiz and Rodríguez-Gómez, 2010; Rodríguez-Gómez, Ibarra Sáiz and García-Jiménez, 2013) and that it is increasingly important to design and develop assessment policies that focus attention on student learning and not merely on providing marks and certificates.

The dissemination of the work of university teachers, either individually or collectively, through innovation networks, publications, conferences and seminars, constitutes a vital element in constructing the underlying professional knowledge on which university policies can be based. In this regard, the coordination, support and dissemination functions offered now and in the future by associations such as RED-U (Teaching in Higher Education Network) or SEDA (Staff and Educational Development Association) are essential and demand the support not only of professionals that belong to them but also of universities themselves.

Finally, it must be remembered that in a technologised context there remains the risk of merely ticking as innovative assessment practices that, when analyzed from a pedagogical and conceptual dimension, are merely updated methodologies. Universities have the means and resources to enable high quality interconnections, but the challenge is how these technological resources are used and what they are used for. In short, it is vital to integrate technology but its use must be based on well-founded professional knowledge and not on its greater or lesser degree of novelty.

REFERENCES

Barberá, E. (2006). Aportaciones de la tecnología a la e-Evaluación. *RED Revista de Educación a Distancia, Monográfico VI*. Retrieved from http://www.um.es/ead/red/M6/barbera.pdf

Bloxham, S., & Boyd, P. (2007). *Developing Effective Assessment in Higher Education. A Practical Guide*. New York: Open University Press - MCGraw Hill Education.

Boud, D. (2000). Sustainable Assessment: Rethinking assessment for the learning society. *Studies in Continuing Education, 22*(2), 151–167. doi:10.1080/713695728

Boud, D. (2006). Foreword. In C. Bryan & K. Clegg (Eds.), *Innovative Higher Education* (pp. xvii–xix). London: Routledge.

Boud, D. et al. (2010). *Assessment 2020: Seven propositions for assessment reform in higher education*. Sydney: Australian Learning and Teaching Council.

Boud, D., & Falchikov, N. (2006). Aligning assessment with long term learning. *Assessment & Evaluation in Higher Education, 31*(4), 399–413. doi:10.1080/02602930600679050

Boud, D., & Soler, R. (2015). Sustainable assessment revisited. *Assessment & Evaluation in Higher Education, 2015*, 1–14. doi:10.1080/02602938.2015.1018133

Brown, S. (2015a). *Learning, Teaching and Assessment in Higher Education. Global Perspectives*. London: Palgrave Macmillan.

Brown, S. (2015b). International perspectives on assessment practice in Higher Education. *RELIEVE - Revista Electrónica de Investigación Y Evaluación Educativa, 21*(1). doi:10.7203/relieve.21.1.6403

Carless, D., Joughin, G., & Liu, N.-F. (2006). *How Assessment supports learning: learning-oriented assessment in action*. Hong Kong: Hong Kong University Press. doi:10.5790/hongkong/9789622098237.001.0001

Falchikov, N. (2005). *Improving Assessment Through student Involvement. Practical solutions for aiding learning in higher education and further education*. London: RoutledgeFalmer.

Gibbs, G. (2006). How assessment frames student learning. Cordelis Bryan and Karen Clegg. In *Innovative Assessment in higher education* (pp. 23–36). Abingdon: Routledge.

Gibbs, G., & Simpson, C. (2004). Conditions under which Assessment supports Student Learning. *Learning and Teaching in Higher Education, 1*, 3–31.

Ibarra-Sáiz, M. S., & Rodríguez-Gómez, G. (2010). Aproximación al discurso dominante sobre la evaluación del aprendizaje en la universidad. *Revista de Educación*, (351), 385–407.

Kolb, A. Y., & Kolb, D. A. (2005). Learning Styles and Learning Spaces. *Enhancing Experiential Learning in Higher Education*, *4*(2), 193–212.

Kolb, D. A. (1984). *Experiential Learning: Experience as The Source of Learning and Development*. Prentice Hall, Inc. doi:10.1016/B978-0-7506-7223-8.50017-4

Nicol, D., Thomson, A., & Breslin, C. (2014). Rethinking Feedback in Higher Education: A Peer Review Perspective. *Assessment & Evaluation in Higher Education*, *39*(1), 102–122. doi:10.1080/02602938.2013.795518

Price, M., Carroll, J., O'Donovan, B., & Rust, C. (2011). If I was going there I wouldn't start from here: A critical commentary on current assessment practice. *Assessment & Evaluation in Higher Education*, *36*(4), 479–492. doi:10.1080/02602930903512883

Price, M., Rust, C., O'Donovan, B., Handley, K., & Bryant, R. (2012). *Assessment Literacy. The Foundation for Improving Student Learning*. Oxford: Oxford Brookes University.

Rodríguez-Gómez, G., & Ibarra-Sáiz, M. S. (2015). Assessment as Learning and Empowerment: Towards Sustainable Learning in Higher Education. In M. Peris-Ortiz & J. M. Merigó Lindahl (Eds.), *Sustainable Learning in Higher Education. Developing Competencies for the Global Marketplace* (pp. 1–20). Springer International Publishing; doi:10.1007/978-3-319-10804-9_1

Rodríguez-Gómez, G., Ibarra-Sáiz, M. S., & García-Jimenez, E. (2013). Autoevaluación, evaluación entre iguales y coevaluación: Conceptualización y práctica en las universidades españolas. *Revista de Investigacion en Educación*, *11*(2), 198–210.

Sambell, K., McDowell, L., & Montgomery, C. (2013). *Assessment for Learning in Higher Education*. London: Routledge.

Strijbos, J. W., & Sluijsmans, D. (2010). Unravelling peer assessment: Methodological, functional, and conceptual developments. *Learning and Instruction*, *20*(4), 265–269. doi:10.1016/j.learninstruc.2009.08.002

Taras, M. (2015). Student self-assessment: What have learned and what are the challenges? *RELIEVE - Revista Electrónica de Investigación y Evaluación*, *21*(1). doi:10.7203/relieve.21.1.6394

KEY TERMS AND DEFINITION

Assessment as Learning and Empowerment: An assessment that, within an academic context, facilitates the learning of students, giving priority to involving them in the assessment process, promoting strategies that provide proactive information to students on their progress and results and which is delivered through high quality tasks that require intellectual rigor, are relevant, meaningful, authentic, and provide support, guidance and direction to students so as to encourage self-regulation to acquire meaningful learning.

E-Assessment: Assessment mediated by the use of technology resources.

Learning-Oriented Assessment: An assessment where a primary focus is on the potential to develop productive student learning processes.

Serious Games: The serious games are simulations of real-world developed in order to train users.

Student Assessment Literacy: Students' understanding of the purposes of assessment and the processes surrounding assessment.

Student Empowerment: Process through which the student participation in assessment is encouraged in order to facilitate self-regulation.

Sustainable Assessment: An assessment that meets the needs of the present in terms of the demands of formative and summative assessment, but which also prepares students to meet their own future personal and professional learning needs.

ENDNOTES

[1]   University of Cadiz - EVALfor Research Group (Coordinator), University of La Laguna, University of La Rioja, University of Salamanca, University of Seville, University of Valencia, Polytechnic University of Barcelona and Rovira i Virgili University.

[2]   University of Technology, Sidney and Macquarie University.

[3]   http://dinno.evalfor.net/ Developed by the EVALfor Group UCA. http://www.evalfor.net.

[4]   http://dipeval.uca.es/ Developed by the EVALfor Group UCA. http://www.evalfor.net.

[5]   http://evalcomix.uca.es/ Developed by the EVALfor Group. UCA. http://www.evalfor.net.

[6]   DevalSimWeb Project – *Development of professional competencies through participation in assessment and simulations using web tools*. Contract nº DCI-ALA/19.09.01/11/21526/264-773/ALFAIII (2011)-10. ALFA III Program. Financed by the European Commission.

[7]   Available at http://www.youtube.com/user/evalfor.

Section 3
Innovative Practices in Students' Assessment

Chapter 15
Designing Assessment, Assessing Instructional Design:
From Pedagogical Concepts to Practical Applications

Stefanie Panke
University of North Carolina at Chapel Hill, USA

ABSTRACT

Assessment plays a vital role in delivering, evaluating, monitoring, improving and shaping learning experiences on the Web, at the desk and in the classroom. In the process of orchestrating educational technologies instructional designers are often confronted with the challenge of designing or deploying creative and authentic assessment techniques. For an instructional designer, the focus of assessment can be on individual learning, organizational improvement or the evaluation of educational technologies. A common question across these domains is how to translate pedagogical concepts such as authenticity and creativity into concrete practical applications and metrics. Educational technologies can support creative processes and offer connections to authentic contexts, just as well as they can curtail creativity and foster standardized testing routines. The chapter discusses theoretical frameworks and provides examples of the conceptual development and implementation of assessment approaches in three different areas: Needs assessment, impact assessment and classroom assessment.

INTRODUCTION

In the fabric of education assessment is the thread that creates the seams and stitches that define the pattern of learning experiences in today's higher education ecosystem: "Practically everybody in the academic community gets assessed these days, and practically everybody assesses somebody else" (Astin, 2012). Why is assessment such a ubiquitous topic, particularly when it comes to educational technology? At an expert meeting about 'Futures for Technology Enhanced Learning (TEL)' that took place June 2011 in Lisbon, Portugal renowned educational technology specialists, among others David Kennedy, James Morrison and George Siemens were gathered to talk about their vision for technology enhanced

DOI: 10.4018/978-1-5225-0531-0.ch015

learning within the next ten years. From the diverse collection of topics that emerged for further debate, assessment was selected as "the fabric of education of education". An important challenge for designing meaningful assessment touches upon the very nature of learning: the tension between performance and mastery. Learners in various settings for various reasons find themselves in a situation where their attention and focus is directed towards performing, i.e., getting a good grade, passing an exam, completing a certificate. Meaningful transfer learning, however, requires not only the immediate desire to succeed in a test, but also the volition to master a skill or gain a new competence that can impact the learner's trajectory in future settings, As Ambjorn Naeve, moderator of the 2011 TEL expert meeting pointed out: "We need to get past the emulation society, where instead of learning you spend all your energy on convincing others what you know" (TELMAP, 2011).

This chapter discusses the role of assessment in the context of instructional design. It offers guidance in form of an exploratory tour d'horizon of the crossing of design and assessment to instructional design professionals as well as researchers and practitioners engaged in the scholarship of teaching and learning (SoTL).

INSTRUCTIONAL DESIGN

Gustavson and Branch (2002) characterize instructional design as a complex process that is creative, active and iterative. A comprehensive definition stems from Reiser (2001): "The field of instructional design and technology encompasses the analysis of learning and performance problems, and the design, development, implementation, evaluation and management of instructional and noninstructional processes and resources intended to improve learning and performance in a variety of settings, particularly educational institutions and the workplace" (Reiser, 2001, 57).

Instructional designers make use of systematic procedures and employ a variety of instructional media in order to orchestrate teaching and learning experiences that achieve specific goals, such as effectiveness, efficiency, relevance, flow or transfer learning. Instructional design (ID) models (see Figure 1) aggregate theoretical concepts in a process workflow to inform instructional-strategy decisions, among the most referenced are:

- **ADDIE (cf. Molenda, 2003):** Instructional design is conceptualized as an iterative process that comprises of the five distinct steps analysis, design, development, implementation and evaluation.
- **Pepple in the Pond (Merrill, 2002):** This clearly sequenced, task-driven training approach was developed by David Merrill. Starting from a concrete problem scenario prior knowledge is activated, the learners then watch a demonstration of the skills needed to solve the problem, they practice the application of these skills and eventually transfer to a new situation. Many web-based training modules follow this model.
- **Constructivist Learning Environments (Jonassen, 1999):** David Jonassen's model follows the constructivist understanding of learning as a process in which the learner develops and tests hypotheses to generate knowledge through active engagement. The strong emphasis of learner centered activities is reflected in this model. Important steps in this approach are modeling, coaching and scaffolding.

Figure 1. Three instructional design models: An overview

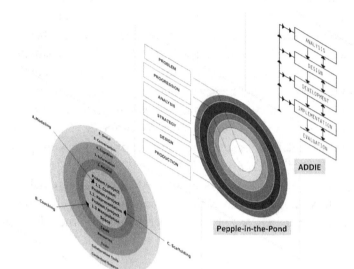

The extent to which theories and models are actually deployed by ID practitioners varies (Christensen & Osguthorpe, 2004). Kenny, Zhang, Schwier and Campbell (2005) point out that while instructional designers make use of ID models, it is clear that they do not spend the majority of their time working with them, nor follow them in a rigid fashion. They also engage in a wide variety of other tasks that are not reflected in ID models. Vice versa, many higher education administrators, teachers, and students perform instructional design tasks without necessarily using the label or being aware of ID models. Despite this variety, typically, the everyday works of instructional designers as well as the majority of instructional design projects entail assessment and evaluation components. The reason is simple: As Angelo and Cross (1993) observe "Teaching without learning is just talking" – without formal or informal assessment instructional designers cannot gauge the effectiveness of their work.

FACETS OF ASSESSMENT

Learning and assessment are two sides of the same coin, and they strongly influence each other (Gulikers, Bastiaens & Kirschner, 2004). But what coin are we looking at? In the field of instructional design, we juggle several, different currencies. Creating assessments that addresses the individual learner is not necessarily the only focus. Instructional designers may be working on organizational development and change management or interested in evaluating educational technologies and techniques. Let me clarify this multifaceted perception of assessment by contrasting it with three different, distinctively singular angles.

1.   The first perspective simply equates assessment with giving feedback to the learner. The idea is that to learn effectively, we need to know how well we are doing and the goal of assessment is to provide information on what we have and haven't learned so far: "Effective learning occurs when

students receive feedbacks, i.e. when they receive information on what they have (and have not) already learned. The process of generating such information is assessment" (Entwistle, 2000).

2. The second perspective sees assessment as a holistic endeavor that goes beyond giving feedback to an individual learner. Instead, the goal of assessment is on organizational development - the functioning of the institution and its people. By gathering information on students, staff and organizational units, assessment seeks to improve the learning organization: "We view assessment as the gathering of information concerning the functioning of students, staff and institutions of higher education. The information may or may not be in numerical form, but the basic motive is to improve the functioning of the institution and its people" (Astin, 2012).

3. The third perspective views assessment as design research – as a way to harvest knowledge about what works and what doesn't in a systematic way. Educational technology is trend-driven – emerging technologies shape instructional design practice. At the same time, we accumulate instructional design expertise through best practices, case studies and empirical data on the design of learning material. Assessment allows us to gather data on how well interventions in a learning setting perform – that is, if they have a positive influence on student learning. "Assessment and evaluation emerge as a crucial topic in advanced educational technology today. As we clear the logistical and technical hurdles for getting reasonable computer applications into the classroom, we must now focus our attention on how well these interventions perform. [...] how do we "define and measure effectiveness" in an environment that increasingly asks for proof of results?" (Carlson, 1998).

Instructional designers deal with all of these three perspectives on assessment – feedback for individual learning, data for organizational improvement and evaluation of educational technologies and techniques. More and more, this task does not equate to creating multiple-choice quizzes, but instead calls for creative and authentic assessment techniques. Critical thinking, communication, problem solving, creative innovation and professionalism are learning objectives that cannot be easily measured through multiple-choice tests.

AUTHENTIC ASSESSMENT

Fostered by the rise of constructivist learning theory, authentic assessment, a.k.a. performance assessment as well as connected approaches and tools –such as rubrics, portfolios and competency-based learning outcomes –have been discussed in educational research since the mid-nineties. This paradigm shifts from 'assessment of learning' towards 'assessment for learning' plays an important role for changing from input to output orientation of teaching and learning and support students' critical thinking abilities (Rennert-Ariev, 2005). Instead of assessing how well students can reproduce knowledge imparted by the instructor (input), the focus shifts to the competencies students can apply (output). Competencies are an integrated, complex construct of knowledge, skills and attitudes that can be used in order to solve arising problems and succeed in handling (new) situations (Baartman et al., 2007).

Since learning and assessment are two sides of the same coin, learning goals and assessment techniques need to be aligned. If we want to change student learning in the direction of competency development, we need to align problem-based, competency-oriented instruction with authentic assessment (Gulikers, Bastiaens & Kirschner, 2004). For instructional designers this means to shift from creating quizzes towards designing activities. This is more time-consuming and difficult and it is less clear what will and will not work. "For learning objectives not easily measured by multiple choice or true/false questions, assessment and evaluation can be time-consuming and difficult" (Anders, 2012).

How can instructional designers create activities that are meaningful, contextualized and connected to real-world problems? Though there is no alchemistic formula, it is important to understand that authenticity is a continuum. Gulikers, Bastiaens & Kirschner (2004) distinguish five dimensions of authentic assessment: (a) the task, (b) the physical context, (c) the social context, (d) the results, and (e) the criteria. Each dimension forms a continuum, which means that authenticity is not an all or nothing trait. Furthermore, authenticity is a subjective measure. The perception of what authenticity is may vary among individuals as a result of educational level, personal interest, or amount of professional experience (Gulikers, Bastiaens & Kirschner, 2004).

Often times, when we talk about 'authentic assessment' in the instructional design process, we really mean creative assessment. We are looking for techniques that are engaging, surprising, puzzling, challenging, unexpected or different. This can happen in many ways – creating a mindmap, producing a comic strip, developing an information graphic, creating a game. It does not necessarily mean to be as close as possible to the 'real world'.

A great way to frame assessment in the disciplines are threshold concepts. The idea of threshold concepts emerged from a UK national research project into the possible characteristics of strong teaching and learning environments in the disciplines for undergraduate education. Meyer and Land (2003, 2005) characterize threshold concepts with the following qualities: transformative (significant shift in the perception of a subject), integrative (exposing the previously hidden interrelatedness of something), oftentimes bounded (demarcating academic territories), probably irreversible (unlikely to be forgotten, or unlearned only through considerable effort) and potentially troublesome (often problematic for learners, because the concept appears counter-intuitive, alien, or incoherent).

Disciplines have 'conceptual gateways' or 'portals' that lead to a previously inaccessible way of thinking in a process of liminal transition - these are 'threshold concepts'. An example from the social sciences is that 'you cannot make causal inferences from correlational data'. Mastering a threshold concept puts learners in a liminal state where they oscillate between old and emergent understandings - just like an ethnographic researcher who not outside, but also not quite inside the group. So one way to think about assessment is to identify the threshold concepts in the domain you are working on and coming up with creative ways to help learners traverse these portals. Threshold concepts allow instructional designers to support assessment for learning. This type of assessment encourages students to question their preconceptions and evaluate their grasp of crucial concepts in their discipline. Within an organization, assessment for learning confronts stakeholders with their preconceived notions of organizational issues or initiatives, and fosters the shared understanding of problem scope as well as crucial components that are difficult to conceptualize.

INSTRUCTIONAL DESIGN CASES STUDIES

The following sections provides examples of the conceptual development and implementation of assessment approaches in three different areas:

1.   **Needs Assessment:** At the outset of an instructional design project, we work with stakeholders to gather data that helps us to reach the audience effectively, design user-friendly interfaces or for-

mulate an organizational strategy. Typical techniques in needs assessment are for instance focus groups, surveys, qualitative interviews, personas and scenarios.

2. **Impact Assessment:** Once the program or project is launched, instructional designers seek to understand how learners access online material or move through the curriculum, which helps us improve their experience. Data sources comprise Web analytics, social media metrics, learning analytics, surveys and interviews.

3. **Classroom Assessment:** In the classroom, instructional designers aim to implement assessment techniques that support students' critical thinking abilities and transfer learning skills. This includes peer-to-peer assessment, rubrics, portfolios and problem-based learning.

Needs Assessment

Rossett (1987) defines needs assessment as the systematic study of problem or innovation, incorporating data and opinions from varied sources, in order to make effective decisions or recommendations about what should happen next. Typically, needs assessment is conducted to identify the gap between an actual product or situation and the perceived optimal solution. However, what is the 'problem' and what is the 'optimal solution', are questions that different stakeholder will answer in different ways. Needs assessment is thus first and foremost a communicative task that benefits greatly from creative techniques.

The example discussed here focuses on needs assessment at the organizational level for the purpose of redesigning a university website through participatory design techniques. Needs assessment for IT products traditionally is conducted in a passive mode in which researchers or developers observe and interview users as they perform instructed tasks or to give their opinions about product concepts generated by others. The concept of participatory design describes the paradigm shift from 'users as subjects' to 'users as partners'. Instead of being a research subject, people are given influence and room for informing, ideating, and conceptualizing activities in the early design phases (Sanders & Stappers, 2008). "Co-creation practiced at the early front end of the design development process can have an impact with positive, long-range consequences" (Sanders & Stappers, 2008, 9).

The UNC School of Government's web presence has evolved considerably over the past several years. Most significantly, its website was transformed from a static site to the content management system Drupal in 2011. Two years later, the School faced the common organizational IT-challenge of updating the website's content management system from Drupal 6 to Drupal 7. Usually, this is a complex, technical web development task that involves little stakeholder participation besides testing. In our case however, we used the opportunity to spark a participatory website redesign process. The website workshop series took place over the course of one year (August 2013- June 2014). The resulting documentation[1] informed follow-up discussions with different division (Marketing and Communication, Publications, Development, Program Support), a three-day retreat of the application development team, the decision-making of the School's management team, as well as the work of the graphical user interface designer.

The workshops series had four parts focusing on audience, content, categories, and navigation (Panke, Allen & McAvinchey, 2014). The workshops followed a logical progression that built on shared concepts and understanding. The series comprised a total of 11 sessions that lasted 90-120 minutes in length. Two groups of 10, respectively 15 faculty members went through the sequence of workshops based on their respective areas of specialization in 'state and local government' or 'courts and judicial administration'. Participation was voluntary and there was no incentive for faculty members apart from the intrinsic motivation to contribute to the website information design process. In addition to faculty, representatives from program support staff and marketing joined the sessions. While the initial introductory discussions involved the full group, attendance in each session varied and yielded typically 8-10 participants. Overall, those involved in the workshops represented approximately 40% of the overall faculty in the School.

- **Workshop 1 'Audience':** Understanding the diversity in audience, the motives for visiting the website, the user's various needs, idiosyncrasies, preferences, concepts and backgrounds is one of the core challenges in design. A clear definition of core audiences was an essential first step towards identifying redesign goals. To this end, we used the 'personas technique' to create and share narratives.
- **Workshop 2 'Content':** During the workshop, the participants systematically described the content faculty and staff members are regularly posting on the School of Government website. We gave participants visual building blocks to piece together a conceptual representation of how different information resources should be represented on the web. The goal was to separate, sort and describe the individual components of different types of web content. To this end, we provided 45 icons that depicted both components and features a given information resource could entail. Features included for instance filters, sorting abilities, previews, navigation menus and purchase options.
- **Workshop 3 'Metadata':** During the third workshop, we discussed website metadata, information about information. The goal was to leverage categories and tags to create dynamic connections between different content items. Achieving this goal required to develop a set of categories that fit both the contents' subject orientation and the target audiences' needs. We 'tagged' web content with luggage labels, used mindmap printouts and stickers to vote on existing informal categorizations, as well as a blank mindmap ('taxonomy-on the-fly') to generate a new, shared taxonomy for the organization.
- **Workshop 4 'Navigation':** In the workshop, we invited participants to think about the website as a museum that exhibits the School's concept, work and content. Analogous to a museum building, the website needs a lobby that welcomes visitors and offers guidance on what to find where. It also needs wings, rooms, stairs, passageways and signage to move around to pursue specific interests. Inspired by examples of applying the Lego Serious Play method in web design, we distributed Lego Duplo building blocks, construction plates as well as additional paper signs and cards.

The School of Government launched a new, mobile friendly website in August 2015. It reflects the content types and taxonomies developed in the faculty workshops. The workshops offered a roadmap throughout the year-long implementation process. Since the launch, the bounce rate for the website decreased by 5% for desktop users 11% for mobile users. The average user visits 5 pages, in comparison to 3 on the old website. Document downloads have increased by 37% and general pageviews by 50%. Possibly even more important, the website keeps being a focus point for continuously refining the knowledge management infrastructure of the organization in an agile development process (Figure 2).

Impact Assessment

In instructional design our involvement usually carries on after the program or project is launched. At this point, we seek to understand its impact and conduct formative evaluation. We want to know how people use the material, move through the curriculum or interact with the learning environment. Ideally,

Figure 2. Content workshop result and related mockups

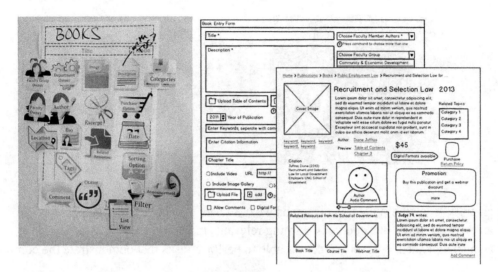

we not only collect this data, but turn it into activities and adjustments that help improve the learners' experience.

Data is the new oil – this saying has gained prominence not only in business and sales, but also in education. Learning Analytics, the use of data to personalize learning, inform mentoring, track outcomes and evaluate program effectiveness, has evolved as a central educational technology trend over the past few years. Usually when you hear learning analytics, you think about dashboards embedded in a learning management system that gives feedback to both learners and teachers based on an abundance of data gathered in a large, undergraduate program or MOOC. However, learning analytics does not necessarily have to look like this.

The example discussed here focuses on competency assessment at a program level. Assessing student learning is a necessary prerequisite for any program that wants to know whether it is achieving its learning objectives. In addition, many accrediting bodies require the assessment of learning objectives. The case study describes how the Carolina MPA program used rubrics in the process of implementing a competency-driven curriculum. In 2013, the Carolina MPA began to monitor program effectiveness with competence assessment rubrics. Prompted by a shift in accreditation standards that call for a competency-focused curriculum, the Carolina MPA has undergone a complete curriculum redesign. The faculty committee developed a set of eight broad competencies with 24 intermediary competencies that together define the learning outcomes the Carolina MPA seeks to impart. Starting in fall 2012, all program requirements and basic course content were built around these competencies and the program leadership wanted to track if the program was achieving its goals.

In close collaboration of instructional designers, program leaders and program faculty, eight analytical rubrics were developed to capture how well students are performing in central competencies. The intermediary competencies served as analytical descriptors for the main learning outcomes. The rubrics articulate fundamental criteria for each intermediary competency (IC), which together form the eight main competencies for The MPA program. Each IC comprises descriptors and indictors for different levels of attainment (cf. Figure 3):

Figure 3. Exhibition map / floor plan and resulting sitemap

 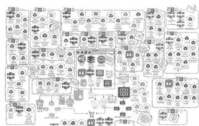

- At an entry level, the student understands what it takes to become competent.
- At an evolving level, the student is learning relevant skills.
- At an accomplished level, the student is able to perform tasks that demonstrate the competency.

Each core curriculum class is tied to 2-3 distinct intermediary competencies. Faculty usually choose a specific assignment that matches the competence they are asked to track. The data is entered and stored using the grade book feature of UNC's learning management system Sakai.

The system is designed to track how well the program is performing over time in meeting the new accreditation standards. In addition, the rubrics help identify and address areas of the curriculum that are not preparing students to the level the program seeks to achieve. The Carolina MPA is conducting a small-scale 'learning analytics'. It is a performance indicator on the program level where this data is a treasure chest for making pedagogical choices that program leadership can combine with background on student characteristics, for instance if they are in the online or residential track, if they have prior work experience, etc. (cf. Figure 4 and Figure 5).

Classroom Assessment

There are many techniques to implement assessments that support students' critical thinking abilities and transfer learning, but among those, portfolios are probably the tool of choice to monitor and demonstrate competence development. Though they originated in art-related programs and in disciplines with significant writing components, portfolios have been adopted in multiple domains since the mid-1990s both in secondary and higher education (Lorenzo & Ittelson, 2005). A well-designed e-portfolio is a systematically curated exhibition of work products. The collection as a whole presents the student's learning goals, learning processes, and learning outcomes. A modern portfolio is usually in a digital format, which makes it easy to create links between artifacts and reflections. Students use portfolios to collect their work, select and highlight examples to showcase, as well as reflect, discuss and advance their learning.

In the Carolina MPA program the student portfolio is a pivotal piece of the redesigned, competence-oriented curriculum. It forms the central graduation milestone before the oral exam. Students use the portfolio to document their level of competence in central learning outcomes of the program. They take a one-hour credit course in their final semester to compile the portfolios. During the course PUBA 746, students prepare their portfolio and work in small groups to give each other feedback. After the course,

Figure 4. Levels of attainment used in Carolina MPA Competence Assessment Rubrics

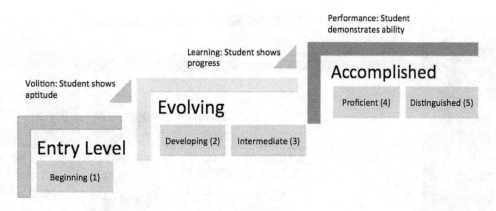

Figure 5. Aggregated performance means for central learning outcomes of different student groups (2012/2013), n=46

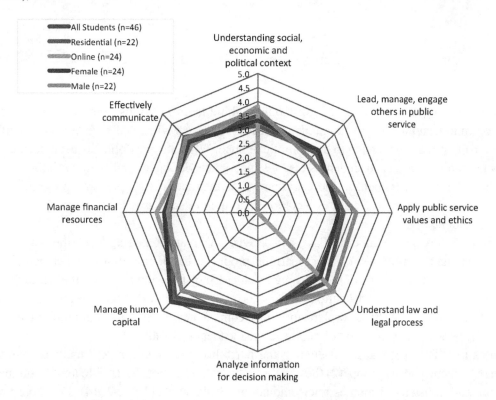

the portfolio is assessed by a three-person faculty committee in a pass or revise mode. In spring 2014, the program completed the portfolio process with the first cohort of 18 students. Challenges and milestones of implementing the portfolio process for the Carolina MPA included finding a suitable technical infrastructure, clarifying the purposes and expectations for student portfolios, scaffolding the portfolio process, fostering peer feedback and improvement, developing strategies and tools for assessing portfolios, and evaluating the effectiveness of the portfolio process (Figure 6).

Figure 6. Portfolio screenshot

After completing the class PUBA 746, students submit their portfolios for review to a three-person faculty committee and it becomes a graduation record. Students who need to revise their portfolio are allowed to resubmit a new version to the committee once. When the portfolio has been deemed to meet the passing requirements, each student is responsible for scheduling an oral exam with the committee.

For the portfolio assessment in the Carolina MPA, instructional support and program leadership together designed a rubric to clarify expectations and quality standards for the faculty committees as well as the students.

The rubric has two basic modes: 'Pass' and 'Revise'. To reach a passing level, the portfolio should express the student's ability to (1) select learning products that demonstrate competence (2) provide accurate analytical descriptions of the learning product (3) display and structure the learning products in a cogent and easy-to-follow structure (4) offer thorough personal reflection upon what it means to be and takes to get competent (5) show plans for future competency development and lifelong learning (6) include a deliberate personal vision of public service leadership (Table 1).

We obtained IRB approval for evaluating the portfolio process in a mixed method approach that included (1) a faculty focus group, (2) the course evaluation results of PUBA 746 and (3) online survey for students, administered 2 months after graduation (Panke & Stephens, 2014). From our participatory experience in conducting the class and supporting the portfolios and data collected in the research, student portfolios need substantial support and commitment throughout the program. Implementing e-portfolios at a program-level is a complex process that includes establishing competence-oriented learning outcomes; choosing a portfolio infrastructure; creating scaffolds for navigation, presentation and content selection; developing assessment rubrics; conducting training sessions for students and faculty; guiding the students through a portfolio course; and fostering peer feedback among students and faculty.

Table 1. Assessment rubric

	Revise Student needs to revise the portfolio and resubmit to the committee		Pass The committee accepts the portfolio. The student may schedule the oral exam.	
	Major Revisions (1)	**Minor Revisions (2)**	**Acceptable (3)**	**Commendable (4)**
Structure	The structure of the portfolio is incomplete, confusing or misleading.	The structure of the portfolio is clear for the most part, but needs improvement in selected areas.	The structure of the portfolio is clear.	The structure of the portfolio effectively guides the audience.
Selection	The selection of learning products does not fit the competencies or fails to address all competencies.	All mandatory and elective competencies are addressed in the selection of learning products but in some cases do not match well.	The selected learning products demonstrate the mandatory and elective competencies effectively.	The selected learning products demonstrate the mandatory and elective competencies and document the student's learning process.
Description	Throughout the portfolio, the descriptions of learning products contain spelling, grammatical and factual errors or incomplete information.	Though most of descriptions of learning products are complete and correct, some contain minor errors.	The descriptions of the learning products are complete and correct.	The descriptions are well written, concise and effectively guide the reception of the learning products.
Reflection	Throughout the portfolio, the student fails to address the competencies meaning, his/her level of competence and competency development.	The student provides incomplete information on his/her level of competence (e.g., assessment lacks reasons/ not all competencies covered). The portfolio includes attempts to reflect upon the learning process, but needs improvement in selected areas.	The student offers reasonable assessment of his/her level of competence. The portfolio thoroughly reflects the learning process.	The student offers a well-founded, comprehensive assessment of his/her level of competence. The portfolio communicates the competencies' meaning and importance in the student's individual context. The portfolio shows how the student's level of competency evolved through the program.
Planning	The portfolio does not include any plans for future competency development.	The portfolio provides insufficient information on future competency development.	The portfolio includes sufficient information on future competency development.	The portfolio reports a thoughtful plan for future competency development and lifelong learning that is connected to the student's self-assessment.
Vision	The vision of public service leadership lacks clarity and depth and fails to reference leadership frameworks as well as personal reflection.	The student's vision of public service leadership contains attempts to incorporate literature references and personal reflection, but lacks clarity.	The portfolio offers a personal, clear vision of the student's public service leadership style that cites academic literature and includes personal reflection.	The portfolio offers a personal vision of the student's public service leadership style that critically discusses various leadership models and frameworks. The vision is connected to the reflection and planning sections of the portfolio.

Both for students and faculty members, assessing portfolios is a crucial and difficult aspect of the portfolio process. The faculty reviewers have to develop a shared approach to qualify an appropriate level of reflection and adequate selection of learning products in the portfolios. Though the portfolio assessment rubric was a useful instrument for assessing the portfolios, it did not prevent both students and faculty from unrealistic expectations about the quality of learning products, the level of reflection and the detail and comprehensiveness of faculty feedback.

To harness portfolios for both learning and as evidence of achievement, we need to understand the tensions that exist between these uses (Trevitt, McDuff & Steed, 2014). On the one hand, we ask students to create personal, reflective narratives, on the other hand the program defines the learning outcomes and assessment criteria. This tension surfaced in our case study: Although we saw indicators of portfolio ownership, i.e., that students introduced non-classroom learning products, few students believed they could repurpose and reuse the portfolio. A related tension is the documentation vs. showcase kinds of portfolios (Hewett, 2004). The UNC MPA portfolio course asks students to be critical of their path toward competence in their profession and identify areas of growth (per documentation), while the faculty assessors are looking for signs of accomplishments of competence (showcase).

CONCLUSION

This chapter described that for an instructional designer the focus of assessment can be on individual learning, organizational improvement or the evaluation of educational technologies and techniques. Authentic and creative assessment is not only a goal for classroom and online learning, but also for these other types of assessment that fall in the domain of instructional design. The reason being that we feel tensions between measure and treasure. What we measure through standardized tests and metrics is not necessarily what we treasure. Vice versa, what we really care about, we oftentimes cannot operationalize. For individual learning, there is a growing dissatisfaction with standardized test scores. On the organizational level, we hear criticism about program rankings and the prevalence of the social science citation index. In educational technology research, we see the limitations of the experimental paradigm.

Educational technologies open up new and different ways of looking at data by taking individual strengths and skills into account instead of filing students – or organizations – through standardized routines. For the organization as well as the individual, the assessment needs to become a part of the learning process, not an end in itself.

This chapter provides theoretical frameworks and practical examples that practitioners can re-use, repurpose and adapt to approach assessment with open, creative minds, instead of a one-size-fits-all approach. Instructional designers and teachers should feel empowered to create their own road to authentic assessment and recognize the multiple ways in which media can be leveraged to support assessment.

REFERENCES

Anders, A. (2012). Creating Custom Learning Assessment and Student Feedback Applications with Google Apps Script. In A. H. Duin, F. Anklesaria, & E. Nater (Eds.), *Cultivating Change in the Academy: 50+ Stories from the Digital Frontlines at the University of Minnesota in 2012.*

Angelo, T. A., & Cross, K. P. (1993). *Classroom Assessment Technologies* (2nd ed.). San Francisco: Jossey-Bass Publishers.

Astin, A. W. (2012). *Assessment for excellence: The philosophy and practice of assessment and evaluation in higher education.* Rowman & Littlefield Publishers.

Baartman, L. K., Bastiaens, T. J., Kirschner, P. A., & Van der Vleuten, C. P. (2006). The wheel of competency assessment: Presenting quality criteria for competency assessment programs. *Studies in Educational Evaluation, 32*(2), 153–170. doi:10.1016/j.stueduc.2006.04.006

Baartman, L. K., Bastiaens, T. J., Kirschner, P. A., & van der Vleuten, C. P. (2007). Evaluating assessment quality in competence-based education: A qualitative comparison of two frameworks. *Educational Research Review, 2*(2), 114–129. doi:10.1016/j.edurev.2007.06.001

Carlson, P. A. (1998). Advanced Educational Technologies - Promise and Puzzlement. *Journal of Universal Computer Science, 4*(3), 210–215.

Christensen, T. K., & Osguthorpe, R. T. (2004). How Do Instructional-Design Practitioners Make Instructional-Strategy Decisions? *Performance Improvement Quarterly, 17*(3), 45–65. doi:10.1111/j.1937-8327.2004.tb00313.x

Entwistle, N. (2000, November). Promoting Deep Learning through Teaching and Assessment Conceptual Frameworks and Educational Contexts. *Proceedings of the TLRP Conference*, Leicester.

Gulikers, J. T., Bastiaens, T. J., & Kirschner, P. A. (2004). A five-dimensional framework for authentic assessment. *Educational Technology Research and Development, 52*(3), 67–86. doi:10.1007/BF02504676

Gustafson, K. L., & Branch, R. M. (2002). What is instructional design. In *Trends and issues in instructional design and technology* (pp. 16-25).

Hewett, S. M. (2004). Electronic portfolios: Improving instructional practices. *TechTrends, 48*(5), 24–28. doi:10.1007/BF02763526

Jonassen, D. H. (1999). Designing constructivist learning environments. *Instructional design theories and models: A new paradigm of instructional theory, 2*, 215-239.

Kenny, R., Zhang, Z., Schwier, R., & Campbell, K. (2005). A review of what instructional designers do: Questions answered and questions not asked. *Canadian Journal of Learning and Technology/La revue canadienne de l'apprentissage et de la technologie, 31*(1).

Lorenzo, G., & Ittelson, J. (2005). An overview of e-portfolios. *Educause learning initiative, 1*, 1-27.

Merrill, M. D. (2002). Pebble-in-the-pond model for instructional development. *Performance Measurement, 41*(7), 41–44.

Meyer, J., & Land, R. (2003). *Threshold concepts and troublesome knowledge: linkages to ways of thinking and practising within the disciplines*. UK: University of Edinburgh.

Meyer, J. H., & Land, R. (2005). Threshold concepts and troublesome knowledge (2): Epistemological considerations and a conceptual framework for teaching and learning. *Higher Education, 49*(3), 373–388. doi:10.1007/s10734-004-6779-5

Molenda, M. (2003). In search of the elusive ADDIE model. *Performance Improvement, 42*(5), 34–37. doi:10.1002/pfi.4930420508

Panke, S., Allen, G., & McAvinchey, D. (2014). Re-Envisioning the University Website: Participatory Design Case Study. *Proceedings of World Conference on E-Learning in Corporate, Government, Healthcare, and Higher Education 2014* (pp. 1540-1549). Chesapeake, VA: AACE.

Panke, S., & Stephens, J. (2014). Demonstrating Competencies with E-Portfolios: The Carolina MPA. *Proceedings of World Conference on E-Learning in Corporate, Government, Healthcare, and Higher Education 2014* (pp. 1511-1529). Chesapeake, VA: AACE.

Reiser, R. A. (2001). A history of instructional design and technology: Part II: A history of instructional design. *Educational Technology Research and Development, 49*(2), 57–67. doi:10.1007/BF02504928

Sanders, E. B. N., & Stappers, P. J. (2008). Co-creation and the new landscapes of design. *CoDesign, 4*(1), 5–18. doi:10.1080/15710880701875068

Shum, B., Simon and Deakin Crick, Ruth (2012, April 29 – May 2). Learning dispositions and transferable competencies: pedagogy, modelling and learning analytics. *Proceedings of the 2nd International Conference on Learning Analytics & Knowledge*, Vancouver, British Columbia, Canada. doi:10.1145/2330601.2330629

TELMAP. (2011). *Report on engagement, dissemination and awareness results.* European Commission Seventh Framework Project. Retrieved from http://www.telmap.org/sites/default/files/D7%202a_v2.pdf

Trevitt, C., Macduff, A., & Steed, A. (2014). [e]portfolios for learning and as evidence of achievement: Scoping the academic practice development agenda ahead. *The Internet and Higher Education, 20*, 69–78. doi:10.1016/j.iheduc.2013.06.001

KEY TERMS AND DEFINITIONS

Authenticity: Paradigm shift from 'assessment of learning' towards 'assessment for learning', offering real-world problems and contexts that are meaningful to the learner.

Classroom Assessment: Measuring Student Learning in a classroom setting, both face-to-face and online.

Impact Assessment: Monitoring product or program, identifying consequences and measuring performance based on pre-defined metrics and aligned with the instructional or organizational goals.

Instructional Design: Based on analysis of problems or needs, the design, development, implementation, evaluation and management of processes and resources that foster learning and knowledge sharing.

Needs Assessment: At the outset of projects, defining problem, solution and scope, based on a systematic analysis, incorporating data and stakeholder feedback.

Rubrics: Qualitative description of metrics to assess learners, in order to improve transparency and fairness of assessment procedures.

Thresholds: Crucial, difficult, complex or counter-intuitive concepts that, once mastered, open up a new understanding of a domain.

ENDNOTE

[1] https://itd.sog.unc.edu/sites/itd.sog.unc.edu/files/Notebook-Website-Workshops.pdf

Chapter 16
As Life Itself:
Authentic Teaching and Evaluation of Professional Consulting Competencies in a Psychology Course

Esperanza Mejías
Universitat Autònoma de Barcelona, Spain

Carles Monereo
Universitat Autònoma de Barcelona, Spain

ABSTRACT

The authors present an innovative practice of authentic evaluation of competences carried out in the "teaching and learning strategies" course of the psychology degree. The evaluation proposal central to this course is based on a real, relevant and socializing practice context in which students have to act as counsellors to respond to a high-school teacher's request: to improve a teaching sequence or unit. In order for this authentic project to work and generate a gradual construction of learning, course teachers used a series of evaluation strategies directed at the assessment of both the result and the learning process and aimed at facilitating students' learning self-regulation and teachers' provision of educational help. Results show that students value the processes of formative assessment because they allow them to act in an authentic context. In turn, teachers are highly satisfied with the involvement and quality of the projects.

CONTEXTUALIZATION OF THE PROPOSAL

The teaching and evaluation system we present in this chapter was specifically designed for a particular elective course, "Learning strategies", framed within the Psychology degree and, more precisely, within the Psychology of Education specialization (Faculty of Psychology at the Universitat Autònoma de Barcelona). This elective course takes place in the first semester of the fourth and final year, and has 60 hours of on-site lessons. It is based on a firm belief that learning should be functional and motivating in order for it to be significant. The bases of the proposal are articulated through three basic areas:

DOI: 10.4018/978-1-5225-0531-0.ch016

promotion of the professional counselling competencies, learning-service focused on the student and authenticity of the designed teaching and assessment activities.

The main goal of the course – as well as of all the subjects in the Psychology of Education specialization – is to train competent counsellors in solving the prototypical and emerging problems students will find in their professional future professional. Working in a cooperative group structure, students should counsel a teacher about the design of a teaching unit. This unit should be adapted to the characteristics of his group-class and integrate teaching of learning strategies.

The following sections describe the innovation carried out on the course, detailing how the organization of the learning-service was, and the support provided to students to achieve such participation. We will focus on showing the formative evaluation processes, noting those activities and resources that, from our point of view, enable students to self-regulate their learning. Also, we will analyse the results obtained by students and the possible impact on their professional community. Finally, we will discuss advantages and limitations of some of the activities planned and provide some future-oriented indications for improvement.

AUTHENTIC TEACHING AND EVALUATION PROCESSES IN HIGHER EDUCATION

Before proceeding to describe the educational experience, it is necessary to know the theoretical assumptions that have guided our practice. First, we must define what we mean by learning-service project, since it is the backbone of the course. According to Puig (2007), *"learning-service is an educational approach that combines learning and community service processes into a well-articulated project in which participants are trained by working on real needs of their surrounding environment with the aim of improving it"*. Thanks to this exchange – the collaboration between current and future professionals – students learn first-hand what it means to participate in the professional community. This means that learners will have to go beyond acquiring knowledge to practice their interaction, problem-solving, organizational and management, and communication abilities. In other words, they will have to learn how to act strategically if they want to be competent in facing professional problems.

The benefits of this methodology, learning while a service is performed – in this case counselling teachers——, have been widely demonstrated in recent studies, mostly focused on the university level and in different disciplines (Martin & Puig, 2014; Mayor & Rodríguez, 2015, Ramón, Juárez, Martínez & Martin, 2015). Research results indicate an increase of knowledge, higher appreciation of community's beliefs and values, increased interest due to a better understanding of both theoretical and practical aspects, and high involvement in the project's development process and its subsequent implementation.

In the experience we present, we wanted to adopt this methodology, not only for its effectiveness on students' learning processes, but also for the needs of teachers. Teachers require in-service training in acquiring new resources and strategies, requests that are often constrained because of the lack of time to engage in transforming and optimizing their class sessions. The fact that a group of students counsels them on their daily practice and develop some materials that they can use immediately, allows them to participate in the project without having to spend a lot of extra time on it. In this way, we can intervene in a double line: students' learning and improvement of the practice of other education professionals. Also, it is worth noting that this exchange has been highly valued, especially with regard to the update of ideas involving the participation of passionate students and the transference from theory to real life.

Within this general context, the planning of specific activities is based on two key points: the development of professional competencies and authentic and formative evaluation. Development of competencies refers to students' ability to participate in tasks of their future professional community and to cope with the real problems of that community. That is, it is a pedagogy focused on the acquisition and practice of the abilities and strategies required to build up a professional role, in this case, in the field of Psychology of Education. Based on this, we define a competent performance as the effective resolution of complex problems in a situated way, through the selection and application of knowledge and strategies (Castelló, Monereo & Gómez, 2009). This definition emphasizes the need to recognize and recreate in our own lessons those contexts and practices of the professional field, as well as challenges and tasks that could cause a problematic situation. In turn, it indicates that activities should include tasks of information management, adjustment to the conditions, activation of social skills, etc., which are cross-cutting to most professional activities and not usually taught due to their unspecificity. Therefore, lessons planning go beyond the transmission of knowledge and involve students on case resolution in a practical and emotional way.

On the other hand, authenticity is the keyword of functional and meaningful learning. It helps students be motivated enough to become actively involved in the tasks and connect them with the world outside the classroom. By authentic teaching and evaluation practices we mean those where the purpose and resolution conditions as well as the demand are accurate, that is, are very similar to those found in real contexts of action (Castelló, 2009; Monereo, 2009).

Talking about authenticity in current educational context and, especially, in the university sector, is important for two educational reasons: the increase in motivation achieved in relation to the internalization of knowledge and the opportunity to connect knowledge with a real professional practice. This idea point is a discourse that we keep on hearing from students year after year, and it relates to the construction of university courses aimed at, not only research but also professionalization – formerly called apprenticeship———. Thus, using practices focused on real problems also responds to students' claim for more practical lessons (in the sense of discovering the usefulness and applying what has been learnt).

Therefore, if we combine both concepts, we find that the connection with reality, the recreation of situations where students can apply the acquired knowledge and assess their own performance is, without doubt, the key to higher education based on the development of professional and personal roles. It is necessary to identify the prototypical and emerging problems one will have to face in the professional context, in order to recreate them at the university and assess students' performance and results achieved during that process.

The Authentic and Formative Assessment at University

We mentioned above that in order to prepare a course, it is essential, almost in the first place, to determine what we want to assess. Teachers' assessment of students' learning is often conditioned by what teachers want to measure (the amount of knowledge acquired, its quality, progression, the support they need, etc.) and from what context they should assess it (the institutional culture, the intention and the recipient...). The aim of the assessment can be set towards social – proving learning, holding the institution accountable – or educational purposes – analysing the support offered, collecting the students' progress – . Assessment methods are chosen on the basis of the balance between the two purposes (Remesal, 2011). Some studies highlight the importance of educational policies and the education system, since they determine, or often even impose, assessment tools developed by external agents (Brown, Hui, Yu & Kennedy, 2011; Brown & Michaelides, 2011).

All these factors determine not only conceptions but also the way we assess and therefore, the planning of learning goals. In fact, assessment severely influences what is taught and especially, what is learnt. The first day of class, it is common to hear students asking about the evidences to be submitted for grading, and even during the course, they ask if that topic or another will appear in the exam. The retroactive effects assessment on learning and teaching clearly indicate that, if we want to improve our educational practices, we must begin to question assessment.

Therefore, we start from the conviction that the purposes of assessment, aimed at regulating processes and analysing and communicating results, have to be reflected in teachers' practices. For that reason, we have to plan evaluation activities tailored to the different objectives, defining who, how, when and why activities need to be evaluated. The realization of these dimensions allows students and teachers to develop a high-quality educational process.

In choosing assessment methods, if we focus on when and for which purpose we want to evaluate, in the literature approaches mainly oriented to account for students' learning are frequent. They differ from one another according to what is evaluated: a single result at the end of a process (summative evaluation); a regulation process to promote students' decision making (formative evaluation) or teachers' adjustment of support (educational evaluation); and according to the way evidences are collected and what they are used for (classroom assessment for an "in-situ" adjustment) (Sanmartí, 2008). What we want to emphasize is that there is a wide range of alternatives aimed at impacting the learning process, which promotes a change in regular teaching activities, especially in the university context.

This new assessment path coincides with the new competency-based teaching approach which, as previously mentioned, promotes more complex teaching and learning processes because it goes beyond knowledge to focus on how each student, based on his learner's profile, is able to apply knowledge in solving a problem. Under this new approach, assessment is required to be based on competencies. It also has to focus on analysing resolution processes and do it in an individualized way in order to adjust support. It is, therefore, necessary to do both a formative and educational evaluation. Assessing and teaching become two processes that differ only by their focus (on acquiring or proving), by the limitations imposed on students and by the way students can live the activities in which they participate.

In the experience we present, we found the authentic formative and educational evaluation to be the methods and practices that best suit the assessment and development of professional competencies at university. Within this field of study, the literature describes what characteristics and methods are part of an authentic evaluation (Darling-Hammond & Snyder, 2000; Gulikers, Bastiaens & Kirschner, 2004; Monereo, 2009), the effects this type of assessment has on learning (Kearney, 2012; Meyers & Nulty, 2009) and how its purposes are influenced by the use of authenticity-based methods (Monereo, Castelló, Duran & Gómez, 2009).

According to Monereo (2009; p.23), authentic evaluation "aims at specifically assessing the decision-making process needed to solve a complex problem in which different knowledge and competencies have to be activated and applied through coordination. Learners have to demonstrate the crucial strategic capacity to regulate their own behaviour and to adjust to unexpected changes, thereby justifying the actions taken". The similarity between what is assessed and the real situations that students might face is an element that has been identified as essential in different studies (Guliker, Kester, Kirschner & Bastiaens, 2008; Monereo, 2009; Meyers & Nulty, 2009). We start from the premise that these practices keep a high resemblance with the context and with the problem situations that are specific to a particular professional field. This relationship is present in the performance conditions and in the cognitive demands, and it can happen in different levels, depending on the required tasks.

Before further discussing these methods further, it should be clarified that authenticity is not necessarily reality. This dimension refers to the degree to which tasks are realistic, that is: they are similar to their counterparts in real life; are relevant, as there is an explicit utility in contexts close to the student; and are socializing, since they involve a position in a specific role in the community in which the practice is located (Gulikers et al., 2008). These three aspects must, of course, keep a clear correspondence with the problem that arises and should be adapted to the level at which teaching takes place, adjusting the physical and social conditions, the applicability and the prior knowledge needed to solve the problems.

Research on authentic evaluation is still emerging, since there are more practical initiatives than research studies attempting to examine its theoretical relevance and its distinction with similar notions. In fact, although there are some common references that agree in highlighting the mentioned key features (realism, relevance and socialization), many works give preponderance to one of these dimensions to the detriment of the others. This indicates that authenticity can be understood as a continuum in which the aforementioned components are integrated in different doses.

In the field of higher education, students have to master the knowledge of their discipline and use it strategically to respond to specific issues. This imperative is linked to the very nature of the studies: training professionals to act competently in their respective areas. Therefore, many authors have found in authentic evaluation the appropriate method to certify the acquisition of competencies and to promote in-depth learning in different disciplines of higher education (e.g., Carter, 2013; Love, McKean & Gathercoal, 2009; Raymond, Homer, Smith & Gray, 2013).

Authentic evaluation models that have been put into practice show both the level of learning achieved (summative aspect) and the process carried out (formative aspect), in relation to what and how students learnt during the assessment (educational aspect), which already provides this model with much diversity since it integrates previous approaches. In addition, this learning is usually situated and cannot be materialized in pre-determined products or fixed processes, but may differ from one student to another. All these aspects must match the degree of realism, relevance and socialization of the competency that is developed and evaluated.

This conceptualization of teaching and evaluation takes us away from the so-called 'test culture' (Clark & Rust, 2006), with multiple-choice tests and a closed-ended questions, which has been widespread, always under the objectivity motto, because it is easy to apply and mark. We believe that these techniques can be useful at times in order to obtain quick information on what students can say about a topic. However, there is no evidence to ensure that questions allow them to show everything they have learnt. This method, widely used in higher education (also due to its usefulness, as the number of students is very high), should be eliminated if we want to certify that future professionals are competent and to help them to be. In turn, this will also retroactively improve our teaching.

Finally, as we noted above, the relevance of designing experiential learning activities is perfectly akin to educational counsellors' need of knowing their professional reality, because planning the support and counselling without knowing the object/subject would be meaningless. On the other hand, we must also remember that if acting competently means adjusting decision-making to the context, it is important for students to learn how to self-regulate. The assessment methods will help them acquire this learning.

The Development of Professional Competencies through the Participation in an Authentic Context

The teaching and authentic evaluation system we have presented was planned for the *Learning strategies* course, an elective course in the fourth year of the Psychology degree at the *Universitat Autònoma de Barcelona* (UAB), with a teaching load of 6 credits. Since we started this new system of education 15 years ago, it has had an average of 45 students, quite a high number if we consider that this is an elective course in an area of intervention – education – that is not the most popular in Psychology.

Before delving into this, it is worth highlighting that a previous study was carried out regarding the project. This research, showed that an education based on authenticity promotes the development of professional competencies and increases motivation of all participants, including the advised teachers who, in turn, learn from students' work (Monereo Sanchez & Suñé, 2012). In this particular study, we began to implement practices aimed at implementing a formative evaluation, such as the modification of the assessment conditions (where students could have access to previous working notes), and a real assessment, like the development of a final test involving a real case resolution. Based on these positive results and following these lines, the experience we present goes beyond that to develop a system to acquire competencies through learning-service and authentic formative evaluation.

The purpose of this course is to help students design a competency-based teaching unit for a real classroom group, responding to a demand of counsel of a teacher of preschool, primary, secondary education and even university, in some of the schools with whom we have a collaboration agreement. Thus, lessons revolve around the project, so that students have the opportunity to apply the knowledge they acquire in the lessons to a real context. This links directly to the idea of giving relevance to the curriculum content of the course, as the objectives coincide with the ones a professional of Psychology of Education should have.

The course is taught during the first semester (September-February) and has two sessions per week of two hours each (a total of 60 hours). From the beginning, we share with students the objectives, content and syllabus of each session, which gives detail about methodology. They also have a *Moodle* platform where all the resources and basic information to follow the lessons are available.

There are two types of lessons, one per week: theoretical-practical and practical-experimental lessons. The former is designed to work on the contents and basic strategies of the course through participatory and reflective activities. The latter, is devoted to the participation in the real project of the learning-service, and to the development of the teaching competency unit, applying the knowledge and competencies acquired in previous sessions. With two weekly lessons, students find a balance between acquiring knowledge and applying it in a constant cycle that provides space and time to revise knowledge, redefine it in case of misunderstanding and re-elaborate it in order to be used with a real purpose.

The theoretical and practical lessons begin with feedback on the follow-up questionnaire (see Appendix 3) about how the previous lessons were valued (activity explained in the next section). There is also a reflection on some of the key concepts of the course from three sources: a) the most frequent concerns expressed by students in the follow-up questionnaire; b) an activity that includes those concepts; c) or a dramatization in which teacher and students, or only students, take on certain roles, assigned during the last lesson, in order to pose a problematic or incidental situation that is then analysed and discussed with all the group (for example, a parent complains about the low level of conceptual content of a given school; or teachers of the same department, with very different conceptions on evaluation, discuss about choosing an assessment method). Afterwards, according to the lesson plan, the contents are introduced with different examples. The lessons finish an activity that integrates the points raised during the lesson.

As the course belongs to the educational area, most of the content refers to how teachers can do a strategic teaching through which students can progressively become more autonomous at regulating their learning. Therefore, many of the methods used in lessons are the same as the ones taught as content. The method becomes part of the same message, by practising what we preach. This feature also links with the concept of authenticity.

In the practical lessons, students experience some of the most time-consuming teaching methods and the autonomous and guided work on the development of the final product. As we have indicated, that product is the design of a competency-based Teaching Unit in which content, objectives, activities, assessment and adjustment to students' diversity are planned in relation to a theme and contents requested by a real teacher.

This document is the basis of the project "Reciprocal Learning of Professional Competencies" (AR-CPRO, 2009), which constitutes the community in which students participate during the learning-service. The ARCPRO project was created from two basic premises:

1. The fundamental objective of a university course, in line with the European Convergence for Higher Education (Bologna Plan), is to promote the professional competencies needed to deal with typical and emerging problems of the future profession of our students (psycho-educational consultants).
2. In order to achieve this, it is essential to confront students with real teaching situations, where contexts and problems keep a high resemblance with the ones students will find later on during his professional practice.

In order for learning-service to be effective, apart from facilitating the interaction between university students and school teachers, the collaboration is structured according to the following objectives:

- To promote reciprocal training and learning between UAB Psychology students and school teachers.
- To promote the acquisition of autonomous learning strategies of from preschool, primary, secondary and university students who participate in the project.
- To produce educational materials (text, audiovisual and multimedia) on teaching learning strategies, good educational practices, etc.

Three mechanisms guide the process of constant interaction and collaboration between school teachers and university students around the Teaching Unit: data collection about students, the classroom, the context/institution and the teacher; short in-service teachers training sessions in their schools about a certain teaching method or material; and previous presentation of the teaching unit to the course teachers, when students receive feedback that allows them to improve the unit. This final product, the Teaching Unit, is given to the school teachers so they can use it in their practice, and it is included in the project database.

As a result of the continuing implementation of the project, the platform http://www.sinte.es/arc_pro/ was created, in order to gather the best Teaching Units developed since the first edition of the project. This page is a database of good practices useful for teachers looking to innovate in their daily practice. Materials can be searched by level of education, courses, teaching strategies being developed or strategic knowledge that is applied[1].

To materialise the participation in this project, in the practical lessons there is time to apply the contents, solve questions, and receive feedback on products and on the resolution process. Some sessions consist of autonomous work, where students should collect data from other students and from the school (by interviewing teachers, applying questionnaires to students at school, etc.) and analyse them in order to pinpoint the objectives and design the activities they will present as a final product.

At the organizational level, at the beginning of the course we contact several preschools, primary and secondary schools, and more recently, also some university departments that are part of the project. Each year, some teachers of these schools decide to take part voluntarily in the project – most of them repeat the experience – and share with students of our course their own knowledge, objectives and also students. In turn, teachers provide guidance on some of the methods and strategies that should be used to deal with the content they want to teach. This information exchange will be consistent throughout the course, both in person or on-line.

Finally, it should be noted that the development of the teaching unit is done in teams as occurs in the workplace where collaboration between professionals is necessary to achieve an objective. Teams are composed of up to five students and have a cooperative structure. This teaching methodology is one of the best in promoting the acquisition of the social skills needed to develop competencies. At the same time, it facilitates experimentation of strategies, since they can practise in a real and safe context (peer group) by applying the knowledge during the interactions by practising.

The distribution of roles is the best characteristic to a cooperative structure in which every student is actively involved (Topping, 2005). In our case, the roles are: a curriculum content specialist, a teaching methodology specialist, a learning method specialist and a coordinator. The coordinator is chosen on the basis of the initial assessment (those who obtained higher scores) and the others are chosen by consensus based on knowledge and personal motivations. Apart from structuring interaction, we as course teachers mediate to make interaction effective by solving the problems reported through the follow-up tools we apply (questionnaires, minutes of meetings...).

Once the general information on the course is detailed, as well as its structure and methodology, we will now explain the assessment, focusing on those activities and instruments that allow us to collect data to adjust educational support, facilitate students' self-regulation and prove they have developed the professional competencies of a psycho-educational consultant.

The Authentic and Formative Assessment in the Development of Professional Competencies

We will now examine in-depth the assessment activities aimed at meeting the four purposes we mentioned earlier, that is, accreditation of the progress, assessment of the results, learning and teaching regulation. The emphasis is on analysing the learning and teaching regulation processes, but maintaining our goal of accrediting and judging the degree of acquisition of competencies. In *Table 1* we summarize the basic characteristics of each assessment activity we carry out, explained below.

First, we will refer to the assessment activities focused on adjusting the teaching processes that are planned and implemented. This type of evaluation, performed by teachers on their own practice, largely determines the effectiveness of course program and the efficiency of the support provided to students. The aim is, on the one hand, to collect indicators to optimize time, resources and teaching support and, on the other, to be transparent about what we will do and what we expect our students to do.

Table 1. Implemented assessment activities and their characteristics

	Purpose of the Assessment	**Person Who Assesses**	**Time of Application**	**Instrument**	**Indicators**
Assessment Activity	Why do we assess?	Who assesses?	When do we assess?	How do we assess?	What do we assess?
Prior knowledge initial test	Formative	Teacher	Prior to the course	Exam	Background information
Online follow-up questionnaire	Formative Educational	Teacher Students	Throughout the course	Open questionnaire	Lessons Teamwork process
Team contract: roles, organization and rules	Educational	Students	Throughout the course	Commitment document	Teamwork process
Shared quality indicators	Educational	Students	Throughout the course	Scoreboard	Result/Product
Teaching Unit preparation guide	Educational	Students	Throughout the course	Preparation guide	Resolution process
Working minutes on team meetings	Formative Educational	Teacher Students	Throughout the course	Template	Teamwork process
Feedback on the Teaching Unit	Formative Result	Teacher	In the middle of the process	Document with corrections	Result/Product
Presentation of the Didactic Unit	Result/Product	Teacher Teachers	End of the course	Assessment rubric	Result/Product Acquired competencies
Case resolution test	Result/Product	Teacher	End of the course	Exam	Acquired competencies
Questionnaire on the course	Formative	Teacher	End of the course	Open questionnaire	Course

At the beginning of the course, a prior knowledge assessment is carried out in order to adjust the level of deepening of the contents and to know students' profiles so we can build heterogeneous teams in which peer support is effective. In this initial evaluation, they must analyse a case in which three teachers of the same course – social sciences – teach the same content – meteorology concepts – to a group of high-school students. They use different teaching methods and express different views about the sense of learning their course. On the other hand, students have to indicate their motivation towards the course and their professional interests, whether linked to Education or to other branches of Psychology. The correction of this test and the information obtained on students' interests allows us to form heterogeneous groups, in terms of knowledge (high, medium and low), level of motivation and interest in the course and, as far as possible, we try to distribute male students, always a minority, among teams.

Once lessons start and teams are organized, it is important to collect information on how objectives are being achieved. We employ a follow-up questionnaire (see Appendix3) after each lessons to assess what students value regarding: the clarity, interest and utility of the session, the support and motivation students claim to have had, unsolved questions, recommendations for the teacher to improve the course and issues they would like to address.

This questionnaire, designed in an online format (Google Form) and with a response time lower than 5 minutes, is a formative assessment activity aimed at promoting reflection about learning and assessment conceptions. The simple fact of asking students how they "experience" the lessons at a curriculum and emotional level increases their engagement, as they feel they are part of a community built around a shared project. At the same time, having to assess the course activity helps students see they can also assess themselves and others. The fact that the course teacher is the first one to be assessed boosts this idea and a positive view of the assessment.

The questionnaire is also an instrument that influences the quality of education, because it provides data on how students learn, thus allowing us to redirect the activities planned, solve doubts and clarify content so that students achieve the learning goals. In an evaluation system based on a final exam, this information is not revealed until the end of the course, when there is no time to redirect the process. But above all, the questionnaire serves to adjust expectations and discuss about the topics and content that we should cover in order to move closer to the shared objective of counselling real teachers and thus, learn how to learn.

Finally, to collect general data about the organization and satisfaction with the course, we apply a final questionnaire to assess the course development and implement changes in the following years. These changes are shared with the new students in order to show the functionality of these processes and then value them again.

Next, we are going to describe the formative evaluation activities aimed at collecting indicators about the process and facilitating students' self-regulation. In this case, the instruments used have the ability to serve teacher and students in two ways: to show the learning indicators achieved by students and guide students on the process they should follow and on its quality levels.

On the one hand, we plan assessment activities directed by the teacher that are aimed at the self-regulation of learning. The first block of activities involves the delivery of qualitative feedback on the product under construction (the Teaching Unit). Feedback analyses the work done so far by commenting on the positive advances and the contents that should be revised in order to improve the product. Thus, this evaluation ensures that students stay involved in their work while reducing their anxiety, since they know what they need to improve and have the time to do it.

The second block of activities aims at evaluating teamwork. As we mentioned above, in order for learning to be truly cooperative, we need to structure and regulate interaction among students. To do so, we collect and assess each meeting minutes. Moreover, in the weekly follow-up questionnaire we include a section about the level of compliance of the objectives during that week, the involvement of team members, the task performed by the coordinator and the aspects they think they should improve on their performance.

Furthermore, we offer students tools designed to be used during the whole process to self-regulate the learnings, having access to them whenever they consider it necessary. We are not talking about resources such as consulting previous works, books and online information, or tutoring sessions with teachers, but about documents explicitly developed to judge the process and the outcome. As for the resolution process of the authentic problem, which is the development of the Teaching Unit, students have a guide to create it and quality indicators on the characteristics and content of the unit. The instrument also includes the quantitative criteria for corrections, so that students know what to do, how to do it and how their work will be assessed according to those levels of quality. Regarding groups, at the beginning of the course each one of them is told to write down a team contract (see Appendix 1) in which they describe the distribution of roles and the overall planning and they agree on certain labour standards so that they can predict potential incidents and anticipate solutions as would be the case in a real context.

Thirdly, as we explained when defining assessment purposes, it is necessary to certify students' learning, a crucial fact in university studies in which obtaining a degree leads to the accreditation to work as a professional in a real context. Therefore, it is of the utmost importance to ensure and account for the acquisition of students' competencies.

At this point, we have a great deal of information on the actions and progress achieved by each group and we know quite precisely their progression. However, this is not enough to give an accreditation because, at the end, what really determines professionals' competency in real life is whether they response and solve the problem or a task at hand. For that reason, we assess the product by recreating an authentic situation: the presentation of the Teaching Unit to the teachers who requested our help. These teachers come to the university to judge the work of the prospective consultants, providing their views and assessing, with a maximum of two points out of ten, the designed project. This final activity of authentic evaluation allows students to show *in site* the competencies developed and course teachers to evaluate them in a real practice context.

Also, considering there are a wide variety of problems to face as future educational consultants, we apply an individual assessment test involving the resolution of a plausible case. To solve this test, students have free internet access, notes and materials previously designed for the occasion, and the possibility of using their mobile phones or to pose a question to the teacher. As a result, conditions closely resemble a situation in which, working on their own as consultants, they face a new problem where the knowledge and strategies developed during the creation of the Teaching Unit could be transferred. Thus, the course teacher ensures not only that the knowledge and strategies planned have been achieved, but also that promoted and experienced professional competencies have been developed.

Finally, students' level of acquisition of the objectives must be accounted for. For this reason, the instruments used to assess the product and the case resolution (guide for the preparation of the product, presentation and final exam) have rubrics with qualitative and quantitative criteria. In this way, we can put a final grade that will be part of the student record.

In short, in higher education we can lose the fear to innovate thanks to the activity of sharing assessment criteria through documents and instruments such as the orientation basis, the tables of indicators or the assessment rubrics (see Appendix 2). Excuses such as that assessing the complexity of learning is detrimental to objective or fair assessment would not be valid, since when sharing product and process criteria allows for judging and assessing the acquisition of competencies.

Moreover, by referring to authenticity, we must remember that in real life processes differ according to people, context and time, even if knowledge and strategies are similar. Therefore, by properly structuring the evaluation system with agreed objectives, clear criteria for correction, shared quality indicators and process analysis, we can estimate quite objectively the whole range of evidences and results and have solid arguments to determine whether students have been able to solve the problem.

RESULTS

We conducted a study aimed at analysing the effects of the formative and authentic assessment on students' learning. We focused on the final assessment, the case resolution activity. Our hypothesis was that grades would be higher because students could use class notes during the final assessment test.

To confirm our hypothesis we confronted two groups of students in two assessment situations: one group had access to the materials (notes and other information) during the test, and the other did not. The case activity was the same for both groups. After doing the activity, we marked all the answers and compared the results.

Table 2. Grades in the final assessment for both

Groups		Final Assessment
Group without notes (n=38)	Average	6.08
	Minimum	3.67
	Maximum	8.33
	SD	1.18
Group with notes (n=27)		6.73
	Average	4.67
	Minimum	8.67
	Maximum	1.17

If we analyse the results of each group (see Table 2), we observe that the group that had access to the information during the test obtained a higher grade than the other group, showing that letting students use their notes in a final test improves their performance.

However, although significative, the difference between groups is quite small; a positive result if we take into consideration that an authentic case resolution situation like the one we used does not require extra information. Moreover, the small difference also supports the idea that both group developed professional competences in the process of an authentic learning combined with a formative assessment, and thus they were able to solve the case.

On the other hand, in order to see whether participants valued this type of authentic teaching, students were asked to answer the final survey on satisfaction (described above along with the other instruments used in the course). School teachers also responded to a questionnaire about their satisfaction with the collaboration.

Both students and teachers valued the counselling process. Students mentioned that the possibility to act in a real school context promoted their motivation and gave functionality to the contents learnt in class. They also mentioned problems related with the lack of time to do the final Project and some difficulties in the group coordination. In turn, teachers manifested their intention to continue their collaboration in the following years. They valued the teaching unit as a resource they would put into practice.

LIGHTS AND SHADOWS IN EDUCATIONAL INNOVATION BASED ON AUTHENTICITY

Teaching Innovation processes usually demand great knowledge of the subject matter as well as teaching strategies based on a sound psycho-educational theoretical framework to justify their selection. At university level, teacher training is commonly aimed at increasing disciplinary knowledge, and, to a lesser extent, methodological knowledge. However, following our experience and some studies on professional identity (Freese, 2006; Kreber, 2010, Lamote & Engels, 2010; Monereo, Weise & Alvarez, 2013), we can assert that what really ensures that innovation occurs and is sustained is the knowledge about competencies (conceptions, strategies and feelings), the class group and the context in which the teaching-learning processes (resources, regulations, traditions...) will occur. From the data collected in the real context, teachers can focus on acquiring strategies to address the most common incidents and consider this practice as an opportunity to increase his teaching competency and build a more conscious and satisfying identity.

Conducting activities to know how students learn, live and conceptualize their learning, their new concerns and arising issues greatly facilitates the introduction of appropriate changes in the university courses. This two-way communication allows us to do something that appears to be prohibited in higher education: to connect with students, encouraging them to actively participate in their own learning, to accompany and teach them how to self-regulate (instead of believing they know how to do it or think they should know it).

Another benefit of the innovation is related to the ultimate aim of the course: students' development of the professional competencies of a psycho-educational consultant. We can say that all students who were involved in the learning process acquired the knowledge and strategies needed to ensure their application in the real demand and defend them in front of teachers, each student at a different level of achievement (as they also had different previous competencies and knowledge).

The results support that, by performing authentic activities, learning is more functional, motivating and effective for students, arousing positive attitudes toward teamwork and the profession. And all this despite the fact that this type of approach requires more time and more tasks than a simple dossier or a single exam at the end of the course.

The participation in real consulting situations acts in two ways: first, it assigns students responsibility and commitment, since the successful performance of a situation or task depends partially on them; and second, it maintains a certain tension and dedication given that dynamic situations require a rather continuous attention, a genuine immersion in the professional community and the use of multiple resources and supports. To quote the title of this chapter, "as the life [of a consultant] itself".

The limitations of this evaluation system are more related to the lack of resources than to the method itself. We are still far from actually using the full potential of current information networks and technologies. We are not referring to the provision of resources in different formats (our follow-up questionnaires are *online*, mail communications, contents on a Moodle platform, etc.) but to the effective management of the data we may dynamically and quickly collect, analyse and return.

NEW PURPOSES FOR THE AUTHENTIC EVALUATION AND LEARNING

With regard to the lack of resources, we think that if we have these measuring tools at our disposal, we can cover more information about the learning process (how students think, the quality of their group interactions, the way they analyse the information, what representation systems are more effective for them, etc.) and thus, qualitatively improve the teaching support and extend it to a larger number of students per classroom in an individualized way.

As for the second limitation, we would need technical and functional instruments, which contain and are built from the analysed routes of resolution with an in-depth data collection, and which specify a greater number of variables for each assessment indicator. It must be considered that, at the same time, these instruments should have a practical and especially feasible use, this is, that temporary and human resources (in terms of teachers' ideas, emotions, etc.) allow it.

In short, we strongly defend and recommend the use of a methodology based on authenticity and formative evaluation, as it greatly improves the development of professional competencies, with special emphasis on students' self-regulation of learning and on the construction of their professional role. It must be stressed that these changes require a strict organization of time and resources, as well as instruments adapted to the context in a way that all activities are meaningful and functional. We must highlight that these changes require a strict organization of time and resources, as well as a set of instruments adjusted to the context, in order for activities to be meaningful and functional and authentic evaluation to promote the development of professional competencies.

REFERENCES

ARCPRO (Aprendizaje Recíproco de Competencias Profesionales). (2009). Retrieved from http://www.sinte.es/arc_pro/

Brown, G. T. L., Hui, S. K. F., Yu, F. W. M., & Kennedy, K. J. (2011). Teachers' conceptions of assessment in Chinese contexts: A tripartite model of accountability, improvement, and irrelevance. *International Journal of Educational Research, 50*(5-6), 307–320. doi:10.1016/j.ijer.2011.10.003

Brown, G. T. L., & Michaelides, M. P. (2011). Ecological rationality in teachers' conceptions of assessment across samples from Cyprus and New Zealand. *European Journal of Psychology of Education, 26*(3), 319–337. doi:10.1007/s10212-010-0052-3

Carter, T. M. (2013). Use what you have: Authentic assessment of in-class activities. *RSR. Reference Services Review, 41*(1), 49–61. doi:10.1108/00907321311300875

Castelló, M. (2009). *La evaluación auténtica en secundaria y universidad*. Barcelona: Edebé.

Darling-hammond, L., & Snyder, J. (2000). Authentic assessment of teaching in context. *Teaching and Teacher Education, 16*(5-6), 523–545. doi:10.1016/S0742-051X(00)00015-9

Freese, A. R. (2006). Reframing one's teaching: Discovering our teacher selvesthrough reflection and inquiry. *Teaching and Teacher Education, 22*(1), 100–111. doi:10.1016/j.tate.2005.07.003

Gulikers, J. T. M., Bastiaens, T. J., & Kirschner, P. A. (2004). A Five-Dimensional Framework for Authentic Assessment. *Educational Technology Research and Development, 52*(3), 67–86. doi:10.1007/BF02504676

Gulikers, J. T. M., Kester, L., Kirschner, P. A., & Bastiaens, T. J. (2008). The effect of practical experience on perceptions of assessment authenticity, study approach, and learning outcomes. *Learning and Instruction, 18*(2), 172–186. doi:10.1016/j.learninstruc.2007.02.012

Kearney, S. (2012). Assessment & Evaluation in Higher Education Improving engagement: The use of "Authentic self-and peer-assessment for learning" to enhance the student learning experience. *Assessment & Evaluation in Higher Education, 38*(7), 875–891. doi:10.1080/02602938.2012.751963

Kreber, C. (2010). Academics' teacher identities, authenticity and pedagogy. *Studies in Higher Education, 35*(2), 171–194. doi:10.1080/03075070902953048

Lamote, C., & Engels, N. (2010). The development of student teachers: Professional identity. *European Journal of Teacher Education, 33*(1), 3–18. doi:10.1080/02619760903457735

Love, D., McKean, G., & Gathercoal, P. (2009). Student webfolios and authentic assessment in information systems.*Proceedings of the 2009 International SIGED: IAIM Conference*.

Martín, X., & Puig, J. M. (2014). Trabajo por proyectos y servicio a la comunidad. Aprendizaje servicio en la asignatura de educación en valores. Revista CIDUI. Retrieved from http://www.cidui.org/revistacidui/index.php/cidui/article/view/719/690

Mayor, D., & Rodríguez, M. D. (2015). Aprendizaje-servicio: construyendo espacios de intersección entre la escuela-comunidad-universidad. *Revista Profesorado*, 19(1), 262-279. Retrieved from http://www.ugr.es/~recfpro/rev191ART11.pdf

Meyers, N. M., & Nulty, D. D. (2009). How to use (five) curriculum design principles to align authentic learning environments, assessment, students' approaches to thinking and learning outcomes. *Assessment & Evaluation in Higher Education*, 34(5), 565–577. doi:10.1080/02602930802226502

Monereo, C. (2009). *Pisa como excusa. Repensar la evaluación para cambiar la enseñanza*. Barcelona: Graó.

Monereo, C., Castelló, M., Durán, D., & Gómez, I. (2009). Las bases psicoeducativas del proyecto PISA como guía para el cambio en las concepciones y prácticas del profesorado de secundaria. *Infancia y Aprendizaje*, 32(3), 421–447. doi:10.1174/021037009788964105

Monereo, C., Sànchez, S., & Suñé, S. (2012). La enseñanza auténtica de competencias profesionales. Un proyecto de aprendizaje recíproco instituto-universidad. *Revista Profesorado,* 16(1), 79-101. Retrieved from http://www.ugr.es/~recfpro/rev161ART6.pdf

Monereo, C., Weise, C., & Álvarez, I. M. (2013). Cambiar la identidad docente en la Universidad. Formación basada en incidentes dramatizados. *Infancia y Aprendizaje*, 36(3), 323–340. doi:10.1174/021037013807533043

Puig, J. M., Batlle, R., Bosch, C., & Palos, J. (2007). *Aprendizaje servicio. Educar para la ciudadanía*. Barcelona: Ministerio de Educación y Ciencia y Octaedro.

Ramón, E., Juárez, R., Martínez, B., & Martín, S. (2015). Impacto de un proyecto de aprendizaje-servicio con estudiantes de enfermería. *Metas de Enfermería*, 18(2), Retrieved from http://www.enfermeria21.com/revistas/metas/articulo/80711/

Raymond, J. E., Homer, C. S. E., Smith, R., & Gray, J. E. (2013). Nurse Education in Practice Learning through authentic assessment: An evaluation of a new development in the undergraduate midwifery curriculum. *Nurse Education in Practice*, 13(5), 471–476. doi:10.1016/j.nepr.2012.10.006 PMID:23140801

Remesal, A. (2011). Primary and secondary teachers' conceptions of assessment: A qualitative study. *Teaching and Teacher Education*, 27(2), 472–482. doi:10.1016/j.tate.2010.09.017

Sanmartí, N. (2008). *10 ideas clave: evaluar para aprender*. Barcelona: Graó.

Topping, K. (2005). Trends in Peer Learning. *Educational Psychology*, 25(6), 634–645. doi:10.1080/01443410500345172

KEY TERMS AND DEFINITIONS

Authentic Evaluation: Set of evaluation methods that are characterized by a high degree of realism (similar to a real situation), relevance (connection with the near context) and socialization (participation in a community).

Cooperative Learning: Learning based on peer support in order to make it more effective. Cooperative learning methods are characterized by the structuring of the task and the distribution of responsibilities among team members. The conditions for cooperative learning to be effective are: positive interdependence, individual accountability, positive interactions, development of social skills and self-reflection of the team.

Formative Assessment: Type of evaluation whose objective is to collect indicators about how students learn to give them feedback that allows them improve.

Learning Strategies: All strategic actions are characterized by the use of knowledge (concepts, procedures and values) and skills to achieve a goal. Strategies are composed of three key moments: planning, self-regulation and self-evaluation.

Professional Competencies: Activation of knowledge and strategies for the effective and efficient resolution of a Real problem that occurs in a certain context. The professional competencies are activated in a situation where a person has to act in accordance to the expectations of a professional community; in our case, in accordance to the role of educational counsellors.

Service-Learning: Learning that occurs when learners participate in a community and work to a real need of this community. For that, the process of collaboration is structured by combining activities of reflection about the practice and new intervention processes.

Teaching Strategies: Set of methods that teach students to think, guiding them in the process of appropriation of the contents through a cession of control (raising students' autonomy).

ENDNOTE

[1]   This project has been recognized by the Department of Education of the local regional government, Generalitat de Catalunya, and its use is recommended for all teachers in the public school system.

APPENDIX 1: TEAM CONTRACT

Table 3. Name of the team

Role	Name	Phone Number	E-Mail
Coordinator			
Responsible for Content			
Responsible for Learning Strategies			
Responsible for Teaching Strategies			

Table 4. Minutes of the meetings

Responsible for minute-writing	
Responsible for sending questions	

Table 5. Internal regulations (faults and consequences)

Rules	Consequences
Everyone will have to attend team meetings in which it is agreed that all members must be present.	*1. In the event of missing a meeting, the person will have to justify his absence and find ways to compensate it (to send the task in advance, to expand a section, to perform that task assigned to him by the team...)* *2. In the event of missing more than two sessions without just cause, the remaining members will ask him to change his attitude and if he does not, they will vote for or against his tenure in the team.*

Table 6. Signatures

Coordinator	Resp. Content	Resp. Learning Strategies	Resp. Teaching Strategies

APPENDIX 2: INDICATORS AND QUANTIFICATION FOR THE ASSESSMENT OF THE TEACHING GUIDE

Table 7. Team

Presentation/ Title (2%)	Context/ Problems/ Contents (10%)	Assessment (4%)	Documentation (2%)	Diversity (10%)	Sessions Development (13%)	Critical Incident (7%)	Annexes (1%)	Others (1%)	Grade
Suggestive title: 1% Presentation: clear and motivating 1%	- Clear and complete context 1% - Authentic problems and complexity level 6% - Consistent contents 3%	- Formative and summative evaluation: 2% - Consistent weighting: 2%	- Varied (paper and digital): 1% - Updated and relevant: 1%	- Students data: 1% - Charts and interpretation: - 3% Complete and relevant guidelines: 5% - Others: 1%	- Complete and coherent sequence: 2% - Relevant contents: 3% - Appropriate teaching methods: 3% - Appropriate learning strategies: 3% - Star interest activity: 1% - Others: 1%	- Background and description (1%) - Actors (2%) - Intervention: what to intervene on (2%), how to intervene (1%) and indicators of change (1%)	- Materials - Self-assessment	- Journal, summaries, tools, artwork, etc.	

APPENDIX 3: CLASSSES AND TEAMWORK FOLLOW-UP QUESTIONNAIRE

This follow-up questionnaire of the Course "Teaching and Learning Strategies" (year 2014-2015) aims to collect information to help adjust educational assistance and improve learning. It's anonymous, so please respond sincerely. Thank you very much!

Table 8. Questionnaire. You can only answer once, after each lesson and when the teacher instructs you to. Estimated time: 5 minutes.

Name of the team_number of student *

Session date *

Regarding the session...

Rate clarity *

	1	2	3	4	5	6	7	8	9	10	
Little	○	○	○	○	○	○	○	○	○	○	Much

Rate interest and usefulness *

	1	2	3	4	5	6	7	8	9	10	
Little	○	○	○	○	○	○	○	○	○	○	Much

Rate your level of attention/motivation *

	1	2	3	4	5	6	7	8	9	10	
Little	○	○	○	○	○	○	○	○	○	○	Much

Indicate the questions you still have so that we can discuss them in the next lesson and complement the explanation with additional information.

Is there any issue you would like us to introduce? Tell us which one.

Finally, any suggestions for improving classes (regarding contents, methods, activities, etc.) will be helpful.

Table 8. Continued

Regarding teamwork...

Rate the compliance with the objectives during this week *

	1	2	3	4	5	6	7	8	9	10	
Little	○	○	○	○	○	○	○	○	○	○	Much

Rate the involvement of the rest of members during this week *

	1	2	3	4	5	6	7	8	9	10	
Little	○	○	○	○	○	○	○	○	○	○	Much

Rate the work performed by the coordinator during this week *

	1	2	3	4	5	6	7	8	9	10	
Little	○	○	○	○	○	○	○	○	○	○	Much

Finally, please indicate the aspects to improve in the performance of your team

*Mandatory

APPENDIX 4: ORIENTATION FOR OBTAINING INFORMATION

1. About the school, the course and classroom students, the TU content, the teacher:
   a. Contents to be developed in the Teaching Unit:
      i. Programming (objectives, contents, procedures, activities…).
      ii. Materials (textbooks, sheets, etc.).
      iii. Difficulties and typical mistakes.
      iv. Test, assessment.
      v. Etc.
   b. Students from the class:
      i. Number.
      ii. Gender.
      iii. Level of performance.
      iv. Level of motivation.
      v. **Preferences:** Input-output, grouping (habit of teamwork), persistence, rate of learning, work habits-autonomy, discipline, interaction with others, affective climate, etc.
      vi. Students with specific characteristics or difficulties: language, sensory disabilities, behavioural problems, excessive shyness, bands, couples, special gifts, leadership, delinquency, drugs, etc.
      vii. Etc.
   c. Teaching characteristics and preferences:
      i. Ideal class.
      ii. Presentation of the educational programme of previous years.
      iii. Conceptions, beliefs.
      iv. Representation of students of this class.
      v. Expectations, motivations, interests.
      vi. Preferences as a teacher.
      vii. Etc….
   d. Classroom characteristics, spaces, time and available resources:
      i. Sketch.
      ii. Furniture, spaces.
      iii. Times, schedules...
      iv. Resources: blackboard, video, audio, PowerPoint, computers-Internet (Wi-Fi), library, others...
      v. Etc...
2. About the procedure – strategy:
   a. **To Obtain Information:**
      i. Note-taking (literal, graphic, structural, procedural, pattern model …).
      ii. Internet search (search engines, directories, webs, meta-search engines…).
   b. **To Interpret Information:** Representation of a particular idea in different languages (verbal, mathematical, graphic, symbolic…).
   c. **To Analyse or Interpret Information:** Data analysis (underlining, synoptic tables, statistical charts, data tables…).

    d.   **To Understand and Order Information:**
- i.   Interrogation patterns.
- ii.   Concept maps.
- iii.   Mind maps.
- iv.   Heuristic UVE (or Gowin's V).
- v.   Flow charts.
- vi.   Timelines.
- vii.   Schemata.
- viii.   Double-entry tables.

    e.   **To Communicate Information:**
- i.   Scripts.
- ii.   Revision of drafts.
- iii.   Collaborative writing.

3.   About teaching methods:

    a.   Strategy presentation:
- i.   Modelling.
- ii.   Case analysis and discussion.
- iii.   Role-plays.
- iv.   Interviews with experts.
- v.   Thinking cases.

    b.   Guided practice:
- i.   Self-interrogative patterns.
- ii.   Interrogative guides.
- iii.   **Methods with Cooperative Groups:** Reciprocal teaching, jigsaw or star, roleplaying.
- iv.   **Methods with Collaborative Groups:** Peer tutoring, roleplaying.

    c.   Autonomous practice and assessment:
- i.   Progressive dossier of notes.
- ii.   Problems.
- iii.   Portfolios.
- iv.   Retrospective reports.
- v.   Cognitive analysis of tasks.
- vi.   Incidents or simulations.
- vii.   Projects.

5.   **About the Critical Incident:** Information on a particularly shocking situation that has distressed and unsettled the teacher.

Chapter 17
Demonstrating Positive, Learner–Centred Assessment Practice in Professional Development Programmes

Patrick Baughan
City University London, UK

ABSTRACT

The purpose of this chapter is to examine the role that professional development programmes for higher education lecturers and teachers can play in promoting positive, learner-centred assessment practice. Whilst they vary in their coverage, these programmes address a broad range of teaching, learning and other pedagogical issues, and almost all include assessment and good assessment practice as a key component of their curriculum. Therefore, this chapter is used to explain and argue that professional development programmes can and should have a key and distinctive role in developing and sharing innovative assessment practice. The argument is supported by drawing on series of seven principles and ideas, as well as a single-institution case study. Points and arguments are also supported with a range of theory, literature and examples, as well as the experience of the author in working on one programme of this type.

INTRODUCTION AND BACKGROUND TO PROFESSIONAL DEVELOPMENT PROGRAMMES

This chapter examines the role that professional development programmes for higher education lecturers and teachers can play in promoting and sharing positive, learner-centred assessment practice. Significant attention has been given to the importance of assessment as a key issue in the student learning process (Bloxham & Boyd, 2007; The Higher Education Academy, 2012; Sambell, McDowell & Montgomery, 2013) and it is in this capacity that these programmes can play a major role. They also provide an excellent opportunity to distil the considerable and bewildering literature and advice on good assessment

DOI: 10.4018/978-1-5225-0531-0.ch017

practice to lecturers and teachers who may themselves be early in their careers and lack experience of what good assessment 'is' or who devise assessments on the basis of their earlier experiences of *being* assessed. By introducing participants to assessment issues in professional development programmes, they are more likely to take greater account of them in undertaking their own teaching, assessment and course design, and therefore, devise better assessment tasks for their own learners.

In this chapter, the author will present a number of guiding principles about learner-centred assessment practice for inclusion in professional development programmes, followed by a single-institution case study. The chapter will draw on a mixture of theory, literature and case study examples, will offer guidelines to a range of practitioners, and will show how the use of good assessment procedures and methods can make genuine and deep contributions to the student learning process. The central discussion will be supported through a 'multi-tier' approach: first, by way of a discussion of selected literature about assessment and assessment practice; second, through an examination of a number of key assessment principles which, it is argued, could form a valuable part of teaching *about* assessment; and, third, by reference to the author's experience of teaching and facilitating discussion and innovation about assessment issues as part of one professional development programme. It should be pointed out that although the author works in a UK university, the themes and arguments in this piece are aimed towards an international audience.

First, however, some more detailed background about professional development programmes will be offered.

In general, these are postgraduate programmes provided primarily for higher education staff in lecturing or teaching roles, or who are about to begin work in such a role; put more simply, they are programmes for staff involved in the teaching or facilitation of other students. They attract participants from many different backgrounds (Butcher & Stoncel, 2012) and are focused on teaching and good academic practice in higher education, sometimes addressing more general issues about the study of higher education. Although their curricula vary, they tend to encompass a broad range of teaching, learning and other pedagogical issues such as curriculum design, assessment and feedback, student support and technology enhanced learning. Some include research-based content, enabling learners to undertake small-scale academic practice or higher education research themselves; some introduce newer or more 'niche' areas such as sustainability in the curriculum. Programmes are normally module based and undertaken part-time, and comprise coursework or other assessments leading to a qualification similar to 'conventional' or student-based programmes of study. Conventionally, participants may choose one from a number of qualifications depending on the modules and credits they undertake. For example, qualifications may be awarded at the levels of postgraduate certificate, postgraduate diploma and, at some institutions (such as the author's home institution), at MA level. In recent years, programmes of this type have become more popular around the world (Trigwell, Rodriguez and Han 2012) and are a feature of many, though not all, higher education systems.

Professional development programmes are often managed and run by educational development staff. Educational development (sometimes referred to as academic development or faculty development in different contexts) '...focuses on enhancing teaching and learning, promoting high quality teaching through academic programmes and seminars, and supporting staff in areas of pedagogy' (Baughan, 2015, p. 3). However, in some institutions they maybe coordinated through different departments or sections, or other members of faculty might also be involved in programme management or teaching. For instance, teaching may be undertaken by lecturers based in other organisations or departments (Cilliers and Herman 2010; Bamber, 2008; Donnelly, 2008). In some countries, such programmes are accredited; for example, in the United Kingdom most are accredited by The Higher Education Academy (HEA).

The author has been working and teaching on one such programme for more than ten years (the MA Academic Practice Programme, at City University London) and has therefore written this chapter to draw attention to the valuable role that programmes of this type can play in promoting, innovating and sharing positive, learner-centred assessment practice.

The next section develops the discussion by presenting a number of enhancement ideas for programme designers, academic leaders, and facilitators and students of these programmes. Whilst it is hoped that many of these points will already be addressed in different ways in professional development programmes, some should provide new ideas for inclusion and be of value to both teachers and learners. The ideas are intended to demonstrate the unique role that professional development programmes can play in promoting positive, learner-centred assessment practice. The points are not intended to form a complete list, as individual programmes will offer different and additional strategies and ideas for good assessment practice.

PROFESSIONAL DEVELOPMENT PROGRAMMES AND ASSESSMENT PRACTICE: ENHANCEMENT IDEAS

In the preceding paragraphs, it has been suggested that professional development programmes can play an important role in educating and innovating about assessment. But how? And why? This section seeks to address these questions and discusses seven ideas which collectively illustrate the unique role that such programmes have in teaching, promoting and innovating in the enhancement of assessment practice. Consequently, this section provides a 'case' in favour of such programmes, but more importantly, argues that they can act as a 'bedrock' for the promotion of effective and learner-centred assessment by adopting the enhancement ideas discussed below. The ideas raised have different origins, ranging from models and theories on the one hand, to discussion points based on research and the experience of the author, on the other. Further, the material is intended to be of value to any higher education colleagues involved in teaching and assessment who want or need to develop their capabilities in assessment practice. However, even in the context of discussing professional development programmes themselves, a prescriptive or 'one size fits all' guide is not being advocated. Clearly, programmes are distinctive from one another and there are different disciplines, issues and priorities to be considered in individual learning and teaching contexts. Advice and guidance on assessment needs to take account of 'meso' factors, such as those of the organisation and the discipline or field of study. So, it is recognised that the ideas raised below will have different levels of relevance or urgency in different places.

Assessment Models and Principles

There are now many assessment models, frameworks and guides, accessible and potentially useful to anyone involved in assessment as a teacher or learner. Broadly speaking, these models have been developed to help course designers, teachers and other parties develop good assessment techniques. They provide guidelines about important areas of the assessment process, such as design, methods, criteria and assessment for learning. Consequently, they have clear relevance in professional development programmes where there is an opportunity to explore and apply them to the teaching contexts which participants are themselves working within. Professional development programmes provide fertile grounds for exploring and discussing assessment models, as well as considering them in different disciplinary contexts. It will be useful, therefore, to identify selected models and principles to enable readers to see some examples of them and follow up on some of them for their own work. A number of models are now identified on the basis of being previously used by educational developers or referred to in other published studies. However, effort has also been made to include models from different origins and with varying emphases. The intention is not to provide a comprehensive list and explanation of each model (this would necessitate a very long book chapter!), but reveal the range and diversity of them and provide a 'flavour' of what is going on.

With its forward-looking title and aspirational basis, a good starting point is 'Assessment 2020' (Boud & associates, 2010) which comprises seven propositions for assessment reform in higher education, including '...students and teachers become responsible partners in learning and assessment' and '...students are inducted into the assessment practices and cultures of higher education'. Each of the propositions is then elucidated on. Some institutions have put into practice a number of the ideas promulgated in this model. Carless (2009) focuses on a framework for learning oriented assessment for encouraging 'productive student learning', and Lea (2012) offers seven 'basic principles of assessment' as part of some 77 recommendations for practice in teaching and learning in higher education. The assessment advice includes the principles that 'assessment should be aligned with learning outcomes and learning and teaching strategies' (a point which will be revisited below in discussions about constructive alignment) and 'assessment should be balanced between the formative and the summative' (this too being a key good practice principle which will be considered in this chapter). The UK Higher Education Academy (HEA) and the Assessment Standards Knowledge Exchange (ASKe) developed an assessment based 'manifesto for change' which makes a case for 'transforming' assessment in higher education and includes an 'assessment review tool' for practitioners. It presents six tenets which are: assessment for learning; ensuring assessment is fit for purpose; recognising that assessment lacks precision; constructing standards in communities; integrating assessment literacy into course design; ensuring professional judgements are reliable (HEA, 2012). Elsewhere, Gibbs and Simpson (2004-5) focus on the evaluation of assessment arrangements and propose a set of 'conditions under which assessment supports learning', presenting arguments about using assessment as a means to 'support worthwhile learning' (p. 3). Their discussion, like those of many other authors, also refers to the importance of good feedback practices.

In addition, there exist an increasing number of 'bespoke' models, often focusing on specific aspects of the assessment process. For example, Fastre, van der Klink, Sluijsmans and van Merrienboer (2013) proposed an integrated model for developing sustainable assessment skills, enabling students to assess their learning and performance throughout life. Kearney (2012) proposed two models on authentic learning and authentic assessment through self and peer assessment, these being AASL (authentic assessment for sustainable learning) and ASPAL (authentic self- and peer-assessment for learning.

Most assessment models tend to be generic as opposed to being linked to a specific discipline, but their inclusion in professional development programmes is valuable in the sense that it allows participants to consider their value in the contexts of their *own* disciplines, bearing in mind the likelihood that participants will have different disciplinary backgrounds and homes. Note that a minority of models do account for the disciplinary level, such as work on peer assessment (Llado, Soley, Sansbello, Pujolras, Planella, Roura-Pascual, Martinez and Moreno, 2014). It is not suggested here that those teaching on professional development programmes should introduce all such models, but it is being suggested that they provide a valuable enhancement opportunity, that assessment advice and practice is supported with reference to some of them and that learners are signposted to others, as collectively they provide a range of useful tools for the assessment designer to draw upon. This should not be difficult to achieve as there is some commonality amongst many of the models anyway. However, there are areas of difference too, since, for example, some seek to improve practice and others link more closely to institutional policy about learning, teaching and assessment.

In sum, there is value in lecturers, teachers and assessment designers having an awareness and understanding of different assessment models and principles, so that they are able to make more informed decisions about applying one or more of these to their own working contexts. This is not to suggest that staff need a complete knowledge. Indeed, the range of available assessment frameworks, principles and guidelines could cause confusion, as users may need to identify which to use to guide their work, and this in turn may be influenced by factors such as experience and the disciplinary home of the practitioner. Nevertheless, it *is* being advocated that professional development programmes might usefully draw upon some of them. Facilitators of professional development programmes maybe able to advise on which models lends themselves well to different contexts. In the future, there is a need for further comparison and synthesis of these models to extrapolate more general good practice guidelines from them and test them at the disciplinary level (Baughan & Morris, 2014).

Assessment *for* Learning (AfL)

No account of assessment models would be complete without some reference to the Assessment *for* Learning (AfL) model, which has also been widely discussed in other literature such as Sambell et al (2013). Its value makes it worth singling out for consideration here and in professional development programmes. Indeed, anyone involved in assessment or assessment design should find it a good and usable informant to their practice. Correspondingly, coverage of this model in a professional development programme should provide genuine insight to learners about how to devise learning-based assessment tasks for their own students. There are several reasons for the particular value of this model, one of these being that it encapsulates much of what this chapter argues for anyway: that is, it promotes a learner-centred approach to assessment. AfL offers a holistic approach to the assessment process, a key contribution being that it represents a shift away from assessment merely as testing or evaluation *of* learning. It is guided by the key principle that '*all* assessment… should contribute to helping students to learn and to succeed' (p. 3). It draws on theory but can be applied to most assessment contexts relatively easily. Sambell et al (2013) discuss the holistic nature of the model through six principles which are based around authentic assessment; balancing formative and summative assessment; creating opportunities for practice; designing formal feedback to aid learning; providing informal feedback; developing students as self-assessors and lifelong learners. Clearly, it offers relevance within the framework of a professional development programme in its emphasis on authentic, original and meaningful assessment tasks. Nevertheless, some authors have gone further and questioned whether the distinction between assessment *of* and assessment *for* learning is enough: Crisp (2012) argues that assessment may serve a wider range of purposes, which should be articulated to learners before individual assessment tasks take place. Professional development programmes can offer a good forum to consider contemporary questions of this type.

Constructive Alignment

The theory of constructive alignment is attributable to the work of Biggs (2003) (see also Biggs & Tang, 2011) and probably represents a fundamental term to those already working in educational development and staff who manage and teach on professional development programmes. However, it is likely to be less familiar to many staff working in specific disciplines who are nevertheless tasked with designing, teaching, and assessing modules or other student learning. For this reason, and also because it is relatively straightforward to apply in different disciplinary contexts, professional development programmes provide a sensible opportunity to introduce this theory and encourage its application. Constructive alignment involves considering the entire spectrum of teaching activities in an integrated way, and ensuring that the various constituent elements are planned and implemented in close association with one another. To take an example of this, a lecturer who has overall responsibility for a particular module will need to undertake a series of activities. These might include (and the following is not necessarily a complete list): writing or updating learning outcomes; undertaking curriculum design or review; planning and timetabling lectures and tutorials; lesson planning; devising student-based activities; developing appropriate assessment tasks; providing feedback to students. There are dangers that these activities may not always be undertaken in conjunction with one another; a busy teacher may quickly devise or refresh an assessment task without reminding themselves of the learning outcomes; rushed feedback to students may not address assessment criteria or be adequately linked to the intended outcomes of the programme. If this occurs, and students (explicitly or implicitly) become aware of it, they may reduce attendance at lectures or become less involved in teaching, because they come to view assessment as 'something to be done' as opposed to seeing it as something that follows on, links to, and develops from the earlier learning process. Students will learn more effectively if assessment tasks are clearly aligned to earlier learning and teaching, and if feedback is also clearly aligned to the assessment task, and past and future learning. Constructive alignment is about integration of all aspects of the learning and teaching process to promote deeper and more meaningful learning, and a key part of this is assessment. Constructive alignment can be introduced at an early stage in professional development programmes as it relates to all aspects of the teaching and learning process but it is suggested here that it provides a good 'integrating concept' relevant to *any* academic practice or learning and teaching based programme.

Deploying a Range of Assessment Methods

Many degree programmes at universities around the world are conservative in their use of assessment methods, with all the disadvantages that are associated with this. For example, an anecdotal look around social science degree programmes reveals that many rely largely on 'traditional' teaching methods (lectures and tutorials) and 'traditional' assessment methods – most likely to be a series of essays, followed by a dissertation or project. There is nothing wrong with these assessment methods, but what can become problematic is the repeated use of the same assessment method again and again. For many, this is likely to become boring; students may become less motivated by 'yet another essay'. It also advantages some students (those that enjoy or are good at responding to particular assessment methods) and disadvantages others (those that are less good at adopting a particular assessment method, or find it challenging). There are further disadvantages associated with using a limited range of assessment methods too. Different assessment methods enable students to practise and develop different skills, so a limited use of assessment methods means that student learning becomes restricted. In addition, evidence shows that the repeated use of certain assessment methods maybe more likely to lead to plagiarism or other forms of academic misconduct (Carroll, 2007): the extraordinary growth in professional 'essay writing services' provides ample evidence of this problem. It is far better, therefore, to incorporate a range of assessment methods in any given programme of study in situations in which this is possible (which it should be for most programmes). There are numerous assessment methods which might involve students undertaking any number of different activities, and 'doing' rather than just 'writing'. Students are likely to remain more motivated and develop a broader suite of skills which, potentially, can arm them better for the workplace. Yet many teaching staff seemingly remain unaware of the constraints posed by adopting a very limited repertoire of assessment methods. Surely then, professional development programmes provide an ideal forum for introducing and explaining the case for assessment diversification and offering examples of different assessment methods *in situ*. Further, with their inter-disciplinary composition of learners, such programmes enable learners from different disciplinary backgrounds to share ideas about assessment methods that they might already have experienced. Finally, it should be acknowledged that there are, at times, disadvantages associated with particular assessment methods – some require more resourcing than others – but the author would argue here that these are much outweighed by the benefits. Lecturers and teachers are likely to enjoy the use of a diverse suite of assessment methods, as, by definition, this adds variety to resultant marking and feedback processes.

The Value of Formative Assessment

It is helpful to draw a distinction between summative and formative types of assessment. Summative assessment refers to assessment *of* learning, usually against a set of criteria, and usually for measurement or certification. It is also normally an 'end product' by which a judgment is made about how the learner has 'performed'. Educational developers and staff teaching on professional development programmes are invariably keen, however, to draw a distinction between the aforementioned (summative) assessment, and formative assessment. The latter is best understood as referring to assessments that do not contribute towards a final qualification or score, and are therefore used for practice and for learning. Formative assessment can be used to increase or develop student understanding of an issue or area, or as a 'practice run' for a later summative assessment. In other words, this is assessment for learning as opposed to assessment of learning. There are various advantages associated with formative learning, such that students can become more involved in their own learning process, being able to focus on learning as opposed to certification or testing. This distinction and arguments for using more formative assessment should be explored in the curricula of any professional development programme for new teachers or lecturers. Again, these programmes provide an excellent opportunity to introduce the different functions of formative and summative assessment, encourage participants to try them out as part of their own learning, and subsequently, adopt them when devising assessments in programmes which they are involved in.

Assessment Design and Plagiarism Prevention

There are additional benefits associated with utilising a range of assessment methods in a given programme of study. First, the use of a number of methods provides the opportunity to be more innovative in assessment by trying new ideas and, for example, providing learners with the chance to be more fully involved in their own assessment (and therefore their own learning process). Second, research on assessment is fairly consistent in suggesting that the selection of an appropriate range of assessment methods within a programme can reduce the opportunities for, and desire to undertake plagiarism (Carroll, 2007). Where assessments simply ask students to regurgitate or write about something (such as in the conventional essay), plagiarism might be more likely, and this is especially the case where an assessment of this type is used repeatedly. The use of more innovative assessment methods in which students are involved in the assessment process or asked to *do* something (for example, relating what they have learned to their own experience) is likely to make it more difficult and less attractive for students to plagiarise. Similarly, more innovative and learning-based assessments methods should engage students and dissuade them form looking for short-cuts for completion of their work. Thus, the use of innovative, learner-centered assessments may encourage good academic practice as well, although students should also always be introduced to academic practice and academic conduct issues in any programme of study. Professional development programmes provide an excellent forum by which to introduce learners to plagiarism prevention in general (Baughan, 2013) and to how explaining and promoting the use of good assessment practice can itself act as a deterrent to plagiarism. For this author, it remains a concern that not all professional development programmes do address plagiarism prevention and the relationship between assessment design and plagiarism prevention, for if they did, participants would be able to design more 'plagiarism-resistant assessments' in their own work. This has to be beneficial to everyone: for universities, departments, and teachers (who do not wish to be involved in recording plagiarism statistics nor dealing with the consequences of plagiarism) and for students (for whom plagiarism activity is always going to be negative as it dilutes learning and usually bears other consequences).

The Disciplinary Opportunity Provided by Professional Development Programmes

This chapter has already referred to the disciplinary component in professional development programmes. Learners on such programmes normally comprise a mixture of new and more experienced teachers and lecturers who are seeking to develop their skills and expertise in teaching. Programmes tend to attract learners who are themselves from different disciplines and backgrounds, reflecting the disciplinary make-up of the individual institution. This disciplinary heterogeneity provides rich grounds for discussing, applying and testing assessment principles, ideas and arguments, such as those that have been raised above. In a way then, such programmes afford a unique opportunity to discuss, use and evaluate different assessment approaches and methods, and involve the learners in the assessment process. Indeed, disciplinary contexts could be better accounted for in all aspects of teaching, learning and assessment (Neumann, Parry & Becher, 2002) so that we should be able to offer assessment advice to practitioners at both generic and disciplinary levels. Professional development programmes may be able to help address some of these gaps.

To close this section, the enhancement ideas discussed above form 'bedrocks' of good assessment practice, and have been discussed in this section on the basis that professional development programmes are good places in which to share and discuss them – and possibly develop new ideas and new areas for research. Learners undertaking such programmes can then apply these principles and innovations to their own teaching and learning contexts.

Having examined these ideas, consideration will now be given to how they have already been applied in the context of a specific higher education institution.

A CASE STUDY EXAMPLE

This section illustrates the enhancement ideas raised above by way of a case study example, that being the MA Academic Practice programme at City University London. It does this by discussing a variety of mandatory and elective modules and assessments that it includes and how the enhancement ideas raised in the previous section have been applied to these modules and assessments. The author of this chapter has a long term involvement in this programme and was its Programme Director for several years.

The MA Academic Practice programme is well established at City University London, although it has also been reviewed and updated on several occasions to ensure that its content continues to meet the needs of its participants and more general developments in teaching, learning, and higher education policy. Each year, approximately 100 participants undertake the opening *Learning, Teaching and Assessment* module and a substantial proportion of them continue and complete additional year 1 modules. Following this, smaller numbers move on to subsequent (year 2 and year 3) modules, depending on their own professional circumstances, aspirations and interests. As most participants also work full- or part-time, the programme itself is organised on a part-time basis and is intended to be as flexible as possible. The full MA is designed such that it can be completed in 3 years on this basis, but many participants 'step off' after completing a smaller number of modules, which enables them to achieve an alternative qualification (see below). Later modules, including the research module that leads to the award of MA, are aimed primarily at those with more specialist interests in pedagogical issues and research in higher education. However, credit is awarded for all modules that are completed and passed, whilst, under certain circumstances, a participant can take some time out of the programme and rejoin later if their work circumstances necessitate this.

The programme promotes and encourages learner-centred assessment in two ways: first, through teaching *about* assessment in its opening (foundation) module entitled *Learning, Teaching and Assessment*, and second, by *modelling* good assessment practice through all of its constituent modules. The programme is flexible in design to enable learners to undertake individual modules for professional development or study for a qualification (postgraduate certificate; postgraduate diploma; MA). It also includes modules on curriculum design and evaluation, student support and personal tutoring, personal development planning, academic leadership, technology enhanced learning (2), and various research-based modules.

The rest of this section will take these two areas in turn: first, how assessment is taught in the opening module as a foundation part of the programme, and then how innovative and learner-centred assessment is modelled through all the modules.

Teaching about Assessment

The opening module addresses learning, teaching, assessment and feedback with smaller sections given over to other, related topics. Assessment theory and practice forms a central part of the module, with learners also participating in a variety of activities based on their own professional practice. Areas covered include: purposes of assessment, formative and summative assessment; assessment in relation to the broader teaching and learning process (constructive alignment); assessment methods (in which learners are directed to resources offering ideas for different use of assessment methods); assessment criteria; validity and authenticity in assessment; and writing assessment plans. The sessions and activities are related particularly closely to good feedback practice (including, for example 'feed forward') so that it can be understood that assessment and feedback should both be used in a way which contributes to student learning. Participants undertake a number of activities with each other, including exchanging experiences of using different assessment methods and redesigning an existing assessment. Indeed, whilst key assessment topics are addressed, much emphasis is placed on encouraging learners to work together to exchange experiences and good practices, such that their own learning is collaborative and meaningful. By introducing assessment issues using a variety of teaching and facilitation strategies, it is hoped that learners will be able to apply key assessment principles and ideas to their own teaching, thus enriching their own students' learning experiences. Following completion of the module for each cohort, learners are asked to evaluate how useful they found it to be and whether they expect to be able to implement the enhancement ideas that it has introduced to their own professional contexts. The module consistently attracts very positive evaluation results.

In addition, plagiarism issues are introduced as a sub-topic during the subsequent *Student Support and Personal Tutoring* module. This addresses definitions and types of plagiarism and related activities, student perspectives on plagiarism, plagiarism prevention, and, importantly, the relationship between assessment design and plagiarism prevention. Feedback for this module suggests that learners have found it useful to have been introduced to the link between assessment design and plagiarism prevention and, again, have been able to apply the advice and activities to their own working contexts.

Modelling Positive Assessment Practice

A key tenet of the programme is to 'practise what we teach': that is, the programme philosophy is that it should model the academic practices that it promotes (see Baughan, 2013). For example, the curriculum emphasises the importance of learning-based assessment, so it is imperative that it models good assessment throughout its own curriculum. It does this in various ways, also adopting each of the seven enhancement ideas introduced in the last section. Crucially, learners are not simply assessed through tests of what they have undertaken (assessment of learning), but they undertake a variety of different types of assessments, and are active agents in designing components of the assessment process, drawing on principles of assessment *for* learning (Sambell et al., 2013). The author now provides some actual examples of assessment methods used on the programme, detailing how these have led to deeper learning and better pedagogic practice amongst its participants.

First, a range of assessment methods have been used, so that learners are able to experience the learning benefits of being assessed in different ways for different skills. In this sense, it draws on the benefits of student centered assessment, discussed by authors such as Falchikov (2004) and Pickford and Brown (2006). Examples of assessment methods used in individual modules include: a lesson or assessment plan, self, peer and lecturer assessed presentations, a written self-assessment, a reflective blog, a social bookmarking activity, and an educational research project yielding a dissertation, learning artifact, or conference paper and article for submission to a journal. Participants have responded positively to being assessed with these different methods, this proving beneficial for providing ideas for designing their own programmes and workshops. They are also encouraged to submit a formative (draft) work for almost all written assessments that they undertake.

The assessment methods used on three of the modules will now be elaborated on to show how assessment can be used innovatively and as a genuine tool for learning. For the aforementioned *Learning, Teaching and Assessment* module, participants are asked to write a teaching plan or an assessment plan for a teaching activity that they are involved in; this provides the opportunity for them to draw on theory and principles discussed in the module and apply these to a real working situation. In addition, for the same module, they are invited to self-assess their plan using the same pro-forma and criteria that the lecturers subsequently use; this provides them with the opportunity to practise writing feedback, drawing on advice raised during teaching of the module.

For the *Curriculum design and evaluation* module, participants each undertake a presentation for a curriculum review project they would like to undertake in their own professional context. For this assessment, however, they (as a group) are asked to set *their own assessment criteria* by which their presentations will be assessed, this providing them with additional involvement in the assessment process and practice in writing assessment criteria. Over the course of a day, each participant provides a 15-minute presentation, and all are assessed using the pre-set criteria by themselves, by their peers (other learners in the class) and by the lecturer, and an overall mark and grade is finalised on the basis of working out an average of the various marks awarded. Overall, participants have a deep involvement in the assessment of this module. As an approach, it offers a good application of several of the assessment ideas discussed in the previous section.

Finally, the *Research Project and Publication* module is the closing module for those participants who want to undertake an educational research project and obtain an MA qualification. Learners attend small group sessions and undertake a piece of higher education based research under the guidance of a supervisor. However, assessment of the project is made as flexible as possible to enable participants to 'use' their research following completion of the course if they wish to. Thus, they can elect to write up their work under one of four formats: a 'traditional' dissertation format, for the reporting of empirical research; a literature based dissertation format; or a 'publication route' in which they choose a conference they would like to present their work at and a journal they would like to submit it to - in this case, they submit their conference presentation, their submitted article, and a number of shorter overview documents in a portfolio style work. There is a fourth option for those who prefer to 'make' a learning artifact, such as a physical object or learning technology, in which the 'product' is submitted in whatever format it has been created in, along with a shorter report. The overall intention of these assessment options is to provide learner choice and enable participants to undertake a higher education project which they can take away and use in their own working lives.

This section has examined good assessment principles and innovations in the context of a case study example, focused around a single professional development programme. It is hoped that the real-world examples documented above demonstrate that assessment can be creative, learner-focused and fun, rather than merely a mundane 'means to an end' and device for certification.

Evaluations and Lessons Learnt

In its earlier years of operation (up until 2005) the MA Academic Practice programme featured a restricted range of assessment methods. Almost all modules were assessed using 3,000 word essays, except for one or two which required participants to undertake presentations or projects. Although the programme was popular and received some positive feedback, other feedback from participants undertaking it at the time indicated that it featured too many essays and that this was repetitive. When the programme was reviewed by the University (in 2005), similar comments were made, and the course team was asked to diversify the range of assessment methods used. This was timely because, at the same time, various academic articles and books were being published about enhancing assessment in higher education, and there was a clear call for both assessment and feedback processes to be improved in the higher education sector.

Lessons were learned from these evaluations and experiences, and changes were made. The programme now features a much wider range of assessment methods, which provide learners with more variety and more involvement in the assessment process, and, consequently, in their own learning. Participants are encouraged to provide written evaluations for each module they undertake, answering questions about its curriculum, teaching quality, and assessment and feedback processes, through the use of a standard (university-wide) feedback form. These collated evaluations are discussed at programme management committee meetings and where necessary, refinements to any of these areas (teaching, curriculum, assessment, feedback processes) can be made. Indeed, students are advised of how the programme management committee have acted upon their feedback to ensure transparency of process.

In general, the close contact between the programme team and participants mean that evaluation results are excellent. To take the curriculum design and evaluation module as an example, overall feedback scores are in the domain of 4.5 out of 5 (between 80% - 90% each year). Some recent feedback comments on this module include:

- 'Assessment is very good and different from other modules'.
- 'I felt that writing a presentation for an assessment was a real challenge, but I enjoyed the challenge'.
- 'Innovative marking model'.
- 'The assessment really pushes you to achieve'.

There have, of course, been occasions in which participants have raised concerns about a particular assessment, though not about an assessment method. These concerns tend to be over the timing of an assessment deadline or the wording of an assessment task, but when such issues arise they are dealt with as quickly as possible, and, where necessary, discussed amongst the course team. It is unlikely that any set of assessments can be perfect for every learner, but assessments can follow good practice guidelines, and a final 'lesson learnt' that is worth sharing with readers of this chapter is that where students do raise concerns about an assessment task, it is helpful to have guidelines and processes in place to deal with these and make an amendment as quickly as possible if this is needed. The establishment of sound procedures for managing and developing good assessment is, then, the last key ingredient to be emphasised in this chapter to ensure positive, learner-centred assessment practice in professional development programmes.

CLOSING POINTS

This chapter has examined the role of professional development programmes for higher education lecturers and teachers for developing and sharing innovative, learner-centred assessment practice. After offering some background about such programmes, seven enhancement ideas (in the form of guiding principles) were introduced and discussed, and it was argued that professional development programmes can play a distinctive and valuable role in promoting and disseminating these. Following this, a single-institution case study was used to illustrate how these enhancement ideas have been applied in one such programme. It has been suggested that professional development programmes can provide an ideal mechanism and space to model innovative assessment practice, but the ideas presented here should also provide a useful interpretation and synthesis of key issues in assessment design and be of wider value to academic leaders, course designers, lecturers, educational developers and students.

Whilst they vary in their coverage, professional development programmes provide an excellent environment for promoting good assessment practice amongst a multi-disciplinary community of learners. In conclusion, staff who feel that their knowledge and application of assessment might benefit from refreshing, as well as any other staff with an interest in assessment, might do well to get involved in a professional development programme.

REFERENCES

Bamber, V. (2008). Evaluating Lecturer Development Programmes: Received Wisdom or Self-Knowledge? *The International Journal for Academic Development, 13*(2), 107–116. doi:10.1080/13601440802076541

Baughan, P. (2013). Practising what we teach: Addressing plagiarism prevention issues on professional development programmes for higher education teachers. *The International Journal of Learning in Higher Education, 19*(3), 157–165.

Baughan, P. (2015). Sustainability policy and sustainability in higher education curricula: The educational developer perspective. *The International Journal for Academic Development, 20*(4), 319–332. doi:10.1080/1360144X.2015.1070351

Baughan, P., & Morris, E. (2014, September). Synthesising and applying assessment models to higher education practice: the disciplinary and the generic. *Paper presented at The European Conference of Educational Research (ECER)*, Porto, Portugal.

Biggs, J. (2003). *Teaching for Quality Learning at University* (2nd ed.). Buckingham: Society for Research into Higher Education / Open University Press.

Biggs, J., & Tang, C. (2011). *Teaching for Quality Learning at University* (4th ed.). Maidenhead: Society for Research into Higher Education / Open University Press.

Bloxham, S., & Boyd, P. (2007). *Developing Effective Assessment in Higher Education: a practical guide*. Maidenhead: McGraw Hill / Open University Press.

Boud, D. et al. (2010). *Assessment 2020: Seven propositions for assessment reform in higher education*. Sydney: Australian Learning and Teaching Council.

Butcher, J., & Stoncel, D. (2012). The Impact of a Postgraduate Certificate in Teaching in Higher Education on University Lecturers Appointed for Their Professional Expertise at the Teaching-Led University: "It's Made Me Braver. *The International Journal for Academic Development, 17*(2), 149–162. doi:10.1080/1360144X.2011.620107

Carless, D. (2009). Learning-oriented assessment: Principles, practice and a project. In L. H. Meyer, S. Davidson, H. Anderson, R. Fletcher, P. M. Johnston, & M. Ress (Eds.), *Tertiary Assessment & Higher Education Student Outcomes: Policy, Practice & Research* (pp. 79–90). Wellington, New Zealand: Ako Aotearoa.

Carroll, J. (2007). *A Handbook for Deterring Plagiarism in Higher Education* (2nd ed.). Oxford: The Oxford Centre for Staff and Learning Development.

Cilliers, F. J., & Herman, N. (2010). Impact of an Educational Development Programme on Teaching Practice of Academics at a Research-Intensive University. *The International Journal for Academic Development, 15*(3), 253–267. doi:10.1080/1360144X.2010.497698

Crisp, G. (2012). Integrative assessment: Reframing assessment practice for current and future learning. *Assessment & Evaluation in Higher Education, 37*(1), 33–43. doi:10.1080/02602938.2010.494234

Donnelly, R. (2008). Lecturers' Self-Perception of Change in Their Teaching Approaches: Reflections on a Qualitative Study. *Educational Research, 50*(3), 207–222. doi:10.1080/00131880802309317

Falchikov, N. (2004). *Improving Assessment Through Student Involvement*. London: RoutledgeFalmer.

Fastre, G. M. J., van der Klink, M. R., Sluijsmans, D., & van Merrienboer, J. G. (2013). Towards an integrated model for developing sustainable assessment skills. *Assessment & Evaluation in Higher Education, 38*(5), 611–630. doi:10.1080/02602938.2012.674484

Gibbs, G. & Simpson, C. (2004-5). Conditions under which assessment supports students' learning. *Learning and Teaching in Higher Education*, 1, 3-29.

Kearney, S. (2012). Improving engagement: The use of 'Authentic self- and peer- assessment for learning' to enhance the student learning experience. *Assessment & Evaluation in Higher Education*. doi:10.1080/02602938.2012.751963

Lea, J. (2012). 77 things to think about… teaching and learning in higher education. Canterbury Christ Church University. Retrieved from http://www.celt.mmu.ac.uk/policy/ltmmu/docs/77%20Things%20to%20 Think%20About%20in%20Learning%20and%20Teaching%20in%20HE.pdf

Llado, A. P., Soley, L. F., Sansbello, R. M. F., Pujolras, G. A., Planella, J. P., Roura-Pascual, N., & Moreno, L. M. et al. (2014). Student perceptions of peer assessment: An interdisciplinary study. *Assessment & Evaluation in Higher Education, 39*(5), 592–610. doi:10.1080/02602938.2013.860077

Neumann, R., Parry, S., & Becher, T. (2002). Teaching and Learning in their Disciplinary Contexts: A conceptual analysis. *Studies in Higher Education, 27*(4), 405–417. doi:10.1080/0307507022000011525

Pickford, R. & Brown, S. (2006). *Assessing Skills and Practice*. London: Routledge.

Sambell, K., McDowell, L., & Montgomery, C. (2013). *Assessment for Learning in Higher Education*. Abingdon, Oxon: Routledge.

The Higher Education Academy. (2012). *A Marked Improvement: Transforming assessment in higher education*. Retrieved from http://www.heacademy.ac.uk/assessment

Trigwell, K., Rodriguez, K. C., & Han, F. (2012). Assessing the Impact of a University Teaching Development Programme. *Assessment & Evaluation in Higher Education, 37*(4), 499–511. doi:10.1080/02602938.2010.547929

KEY TERMS AND DEFINITIONS

Assessment for Learning: Refers to the development of assessment which contributes to the learning process. It can be distinguished from assessment of learning, which is about testing and suggests completion of a module or programme.

Assessment Principles (and Assessment Models): Tools for the assessment practitioner or course designer, and are intended to help in the development of good quality, learning based assessment. There exist a wide range of principles frameworks and ideas, some of which are also theoretically informed, and which each offer advice and ideas about good assessment practice. Many assessment principles have overlaps with one another, but there are also differences and some are, for example, broad ranging, whilst others focus on specific aspects of assessment.

Constructive Alignment: A model which purports that the various different elements of the teaching and learning process, such as curriculum design, teaching planning, assessment design, and provision of feedback, should all be considered in conjunction (in alignment) with one another, as opposed to in an isolated manner. The model is normally attributed to the work of Biggs (2003).

Higher Education Teachers and Lecturers: Encapsulates a broad category of staff but, for purposes of this chapter, refers to anyone involved in teaching or tutoring students in a higher education setting.

Innovative Assessment: Refers to the use of newer techniques in any area of assessment, and especially in the use of assessment methods. For example, innovative use of assessment in the context of a particular programme could refer substituting a 'traditional' assessment method such as an essay, for one in which the learners used a novel technology or draw upon their own experience in order to complete an assessment task.

Learner-Centred Assessment Practice: Refers to assessment which is not focused purely on testing or certification but accounts for learner needs and promotes learning as part of the assessment process. Learner-centred assessment is that which supports and develops the learner, may account for previous learner feedback, and contributes to the learning process. Learner-centred assessment may also involve a deeper role for the student in the assessment process; for example, in having a role in determining what the assessment is or what assessment criteria may be used.

Positive Assessment Practice: Refers to assessment which is not just for testing or evaluation but is intended to engage the learner, usually by making an active contribution to their own learning process. Positive assessment is also that which is engaging or even enjoyable for the learner.

Professional Development Programmes: Normally postgraduate level programmes for higher education staff that have a lecturing, teaching, or other role in the student learning process. They are intended to enable learners to improve and develop their work in teaching, learning and other areas of pedagogy.

Chapter 18
Assessing the Non-Cognitive Domains:
Measuring What Matters Well

James G. M. Crossley
University of Sheffield, UK

ABSTRACT

Good assessment assures attainment and drives learning. In vocational and practical programmes, the important learning outcomes are non-cognitive skills and attitudes - for example, dexterity, situational awareness, professionalism, compassion, or resilience. Unfortunately, these domains are much more difficult to assess. There are three main reasons. First, the constructs themselves are tacit - making them difficult to define. Second, performance is highly variable and situation-specific. Third, significant assessor judgement is required to differentiate between good and poor performance, and this brings subjectivity. The chapter reviews seven existing strategies for addressing these problems: delineating the constructs, using cognitive assessments as a proxy, making the subjective objective, sampling across performances and opinions, using outcome measures as a proxy, using meta-cognition as a proxy, and abandoning the existing measurement paradigm. Given the limitations of these strategies, the author finishes by offering three promising ways forward.

INTRODUCTION

Some rise by sin, and some by virtue fall. (Measure for measure, Shakespeare & Lever, 1997)

Good assessment can serve many purposes that might broadly be defined as summative (for example assessing for licensure, regulation, selection or ranking), formative (through transparent performance targets, developmental feedback, and self-monitoring as part of self-regulation), and evaluative (faculty or institutional quality assurance). It is precisely because assessment is so purposeful and powerful that this book matters.

DOI: 10.4018/978-1-5225-0531-0.ch018

Figure 1. A visual illustration of reliability and validity (Gareis & Grant, 2008)

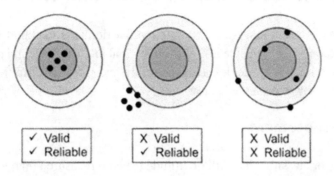

Definitions of assessment vary widely in emphasis. In every case however, assessment claims to be something more than unstructured consideration or appraisal; it claims to make measurements with reasonable measurement characteristics that can be trusted. When assessment fails to tell the truth, there are negative consequences. The educational assessment community has developed a technical language to describe the many ways in which assessments can fail. Assessment results can be *unreliable* – prone to error so that they yield different outcomes when repeated. They can be *invalid* – in that they estimate or reflect some characteristic that is not what was intended. They may have an adverse *educational impact* – driving learning away from its intended outcomes. It is also possible for assessment to have favourable measurement characteristics, but to be unaffordable, unacceptable or unfeasible to implement. Figure 1 illustrates the measurement concepts of reliability and validity.

Bloom, and many subsequent educators, have broadly categorised learning as cognitive (knowledge), psychomotor (skills), and affective (attitudes) (Bloom, 1971). Assessing the cognitive domains has been the primary business of higher education institutions for most of their history. However, the competency movement, and the expanding scope of higher education programmes, bring the new and particular challenge of teaching and assessing the non-cognitive domains (skills and attitudes). The non-cognitive domains are central to good performance in many vocational courses (e.g. medicine, dentistry, law) and many practical courses (e.g. the building and mechanical trades). A failure to design good assessments to cover these domains is as serious as a failure to design domain-appropriate teaching and learning activities. It will render the assessment programmes invalid as a reflection of the intended learning, and it will undermine the impact of the taught curriculum.

Furthermore, authentic practice in each of the vocational and practical fields above doesn't draw on the cognitive, psychomotor and affective domains one at a time; it draws on them simultaneously and in an integrated way. Epstein, for example, defines competence in the profession of medicine as:

...the habitual and judicious use of communication, knowledge, technical skills, clinical reasoning, emotions, values, and reflection in daily practice for the benefit of the individuals and communities being served. (Epstein & Hundert, 2002)

It is therefore likely that authentic assessment will need to reflect this integration; it may not be sufficient to design psychomotor and affective measures to apply in parallel with knowledge measures.

This chapter will address the particular challenges of assessing the non-cognitive domains. Most of the examples and evidence will be drawn from the field of medicine because this is the literature with which the author is most familiar. However, the principles apply similarly across all the disciplines.

THE CHALLENGES OF ASSESSING THE NON-COGNITIVE DOMAINS

At their simplest, the challenges of assessing the non-cognitive domains are threefold. First, the objects of assessment are tacit; second, performance is highly contextual and variable; and third assessment relies on subjective judgement. Each of these threatens reliability and validity – and thus the trustworthiness of assessment. Each problem is expanded below:

Tacit Objects of Assessment

It is far harder to define or classify what skill or attitude is being measured than what domain of knowledge is being measured. Consider the following non-cognitive aspects of performance:

- Dexterity
- Situational awareness
- Professionalism
- Compassion
- Integrity
- Team working
- Resilience

Educators in vocational fields tend to agree about the importance of these qualities, but assessment requires a clear definition of each – and this is a much more difficult task. Key educational leaders & investigators still espouse profoundly different views about the definition, nature and stability of these constructs. Without agreement on such fundamental groundwork it's hard even to get started with designing and evaluating assessments.

Take professionalism as an example. Surveying healthcare professionals from a range of disciplines in the UK, Bryan Burford and colleagues report that:

Participants' interpretation of 'professionalism' encompassed many and varied aspects of behaviour, communication and appearance (including, but not limited to, uniform), as well as being perceived as a holistic concept encompassing all aspects of practice. (Burford, Morrow, Rothwell, Carter, & Illing, 2014)

Similarly, Richard and Sylvia Cruess, the most widely-published authors on professionalism in medical education write:

There are several challenges in teaching professionalism. The first challenge is to agree on the definition to be used in imparting knowledge of the subject to students and faculty. (Cruess & Cruess, 2012)

So the first challenge is this: even the professional and educational communities most closely involved may disagree over how to describe what is being assessed. It is even possible that these tacit constructs or 'traits' don't actually exist in any stable or measurable sense – as we shall see below. Unless the object of assessment is stable and agreed upon it is very difficult to proceed with assessment at all.

Variable Performance

Knowledge recall has self-evident reliability. A student who responds correctly to a particular question is likely, within the short term, to respond correctly to the same question if repeated. Furthermore, because the stimulus–response cycle is brief in recall tests, a large number of items can be sampled in a short space of time. This allows the domain to be sampled widely.

However, when higher levels of cognition are tested than recall, this observation breaks down completely. Empirical studies in elementary education illustrate this phenomenon very clearly. In 1993 in the context of elementary science and mathematics, Richard Shavelson and colleagues subjected some carefully designed assessment outcomes to a variance component analysis (G-study in generalisability theory) (Shavelson, Baxter, & Gao, 1993). The assessments had been designed to reflect higher-order thinking in each discipline using carefully designed problems to test large numbers of students from a sample of schools mainly in the US state of California. However the students' performance was highly task-specific. Performance on one task failed to predict performance on another task in the same discipline.

Much earlier attempts in postgraduate education to design problems to reflect the hypothetical trait of 'medical problem solving' had drawn identical conclusions. In a seminal essay, reflecting on their milestone work 'Medical problem-solving: an anlysis of clinical reasoning' (Elstein, Shulman, & Srafka, 1978), Arthur Elstein and colleagues wrote:

The research team that assembled for the Medical Inquiry Project believed it could contribute … by identifying the strategies and intellectual operations – not contents – that separated expert from less expert physicians … The finding of case specificity clearly challenged both assumptions. Clinicians who employed a perfectly successful strategy in one case often had difficulty in the next. (Elstein, Shulman, & Sprafka, 1990)

Figure 2. A model of cognitive and non-cognitive levels of learning

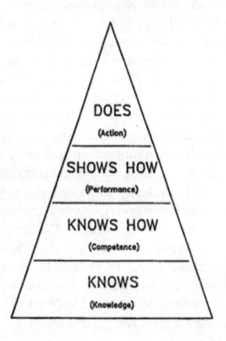

It may be helpful at this stage to introduce Miller's triangle to inform the discussion of cognitive and non-cognitive performance (Figure 2) (Miller, 1990). George Miller used this framework to describe the task before the assessment community in medical education in 1990, and the practical simplicity of the model means that it is still useful today. In his triangle, Miller distinguishes between two cognitive levels ('knows' and 'knows how') and two behavioural levels ('shows how' and 'does').

The two studies cited above, by Shavelson and Elstein, evaluate assessments aimed at Miller's level of 'knows how'. They are treating scientific and mathematical aptitude, and medical problem solving as spheres of competence or traits. Their results show highly variable performances – sometimes called context or case specificity. This suggests one of two possible conclusions. Either stable traits do not exist, or stable traits do exist but they are typically expressed (and therefore measured) in a highly variable fashion.

The first explanation is now probably the prevailing view. For example, Cees van der Vleuten and colleagues, summarising the current theoretical position in competence assessment, write:

Personality traits are unobservable, 'inferred', stable traits, distinct from other traits and characterised by monotonous linear growth. A typical example of a trait is intelligence ... The trait approach was a logical extension of psychometric theory, which had its origins in personality research. However, empirical research in education contradicted the tenets of the personality trait approach, revealing that the expected stability across content / tasks / items was very low at best. (van der Vleuten, Schuwirth, Scheele, Driessen, & Hodges, 2010)

Since the late 1960s the discipline of cognitive psychology has studied experimentally human reasoning and, in particular, human memory. Glenn Regehr and Geoff Norman have reviewed the key findings of that literature and written about its relevance to educators (Regehr & Norman, 1996). The striking theme of the cognitive literature is that almost no learning mechanisms operate in a content-free manner. The semantic networks through which long-term memory operates, the prototypes and examples through which categorisation occurs, and the analogy-based transfer that connects a known problem solving strategy to a new problem are all content-rich. This may well be what drives the observed performance variation. It seems that learners do not learn scientific skills or mathematical problem solving; rather they learn lots of science and lots of mathematics. Their mechanisms for storing, organising and cross-retrieving that learning so that it can be applied to a different task are based on idiosyncratic and content-based similarities and not on discipline boundaries or on traits.

It is important to acknowledge, however, that this doesn't disprove the existence of skills and attitudes as traits. The fact that they are not usually clearly reflected in routine assessment data – or even research data – may still be an example of type II error resulting from inadequate measurement methods. A number of authors remain committed to the identification of skills and attitudes as traits – either by careful revision of taxonomy (in search of a 'true' psychological taxonomy), or by developing better measures, or by more careful analysis of existing data. One good example of the latter is the application of structural equations to assessment data by investigators such as Paul Wimmers (Wimmers & Fung, 2008). Such analyses raise the possibility that skill traits are operating but that their expression is highly contextual.

As we move up the triangle, content specificity persists and deepens. Variable performance thus affects some of cognitive assessment and all of non-cognitive assessment with increasing complexity.

The classic example from medicine in Miller's 'shows how' domain is Harden and Gleeson's Objective Structured Clinical Examination (OSCE) (Harden & Gleeson, 1979). This is an assessment of perfor-

Figure 3. The relationship between competence and performance (or performance and action) (Rethans et al., 2002)

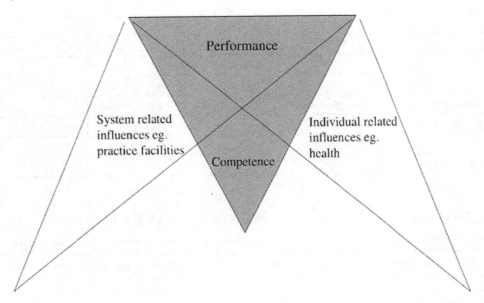

mance under controlled conditions in which the learner is presented with several assessment stations. Each station provides a stimulus requiring a verbal or behavioural response that reflects some aspect of the work of a doctor – for example undertaking a clinical examination; or a technical procedure (like taking a blood sample); making a diagnosis; or explaining a problem to a patient or family member. In every published and routine evaluation the learners' performance is highly dependent on the content of the station. There is no consistent evidence that learners who perform well on a station representing one clinical discipline (for example neurology) are more likely to perform well on another station in the same discipline. Similarly, there is no consistent evidence that learners who perform well on a station representing one skill (for example communication) are more likely to perform will on another station representing the same skill.

Moving up to Miller's action domain, uncontrolled situational and individual factors come into play. It might seem reasonable to expect a candidate to perform at their best in a controlled assessment like an OSCE, but the day-to-day actions of a professional are inevitably impacted by the demands of the workplace (such time pressure, equipment availability and other members of the team etc.) and by personal fluctuations (such as tiredness and stress). This additional level of complexity is summarised in the Cambridge Model in Figure 3 (Rethans et al., 2002). Box 1 gives an illustration of performance variability from medical practice.

In short then, both higher-level cognition and non-cognitive performance are highly variable. This variability is a profound barrier to valid and reliable assessment. But there is yet one more problem: non-cognitive assessment also depends on judgement.

Table 1. Variance component table for the matrix in Figure 4 – showing both absolute variance components and the proportions of all variance (as %)

Effect	Variance	%
Judge (Var j)	1.7	24.5
Candidate (Var p)	2.6	37.9
Brief (Var i)	0.2	3.5
Judges' candidate-related subjectivity (Var j*p)	0.6	8.4
Judges' item-related subjectivity (Var j*i)	0.0	0.0
Candidates' item-related aptitude (Var p*i)	0.4	6.0
Residual variance (Var p*i*j)	1.3	19.6

Box 1. Dr Brown – an illustration of performance variation in medical practice

Doctor Brown undertakes dozens of interpersonal consultations every single day. Sometimes she spends the majority of the time listening and facilitating her patients in reaching their own solutions. On other occasions she negotiates a joint plan with her patients. On still other occasions she seems to take complete control and sets out a point-by-point plan in detail merely looking for the patient's assent.

It may be that Dr Brown has very unstable collaborative skills. Perhaps her behaviour is coloured by content and reflects her command of the medical aspects of the consultation (confident in some areas and less in others). Perhaps her consultation style varies according to how much time she has before the next patient is due, or whether or not she has a headache.

However, it may be that Dr Brown has stable, highly intuitive interpersonal skills and recognises in some patients the desire and ability to manage their own problems, and, in others, a total collapse of morale and a desire to be led through the maze until they can begin to cope again.

Subjective Interpretation

Even when assessors agree on what is being assessed, and when they observe the same performance, they must exert some judgement to decide what is good and what is not. This subjectivity also threatens reliability.

Many routine assessments in the non-cognitive domain depend on an assessor's judgement of a learner's performance. The data from these assessments don't allow the learners' performance variability to be separated from the assessors' subjectivity. However, data from blinded dual-assessor programmes or from assessment experiments (where multiple judges observe a specimen performance such as a video) can be used to quantify and compartmentalise the various sources of variation. Data like these demonstrate strikingly predictable patterns. Consider the scores shown in Figure 4. These are marks that three judges have awarded to three candidates for three assignments in the performing arts – where each candidate has provided a response to three briefs and all three judges have scored all nine performances.

The judge means in column 10 demonstrate that the three judges differ in their stringency or leniency. For example, even though they have marked the same nine performances judge 2's mean score is more stringent than judge 3's. For shorthand, we will call this source of variance Var_j (for judge).

The candidate means in row d demonstrate that the candidates vary in their ability on this set of briefs. For example, even though they have responded to the same three briefs, and been marked by the same three judges, candidate 2 has a lower score than candidate 1. For shorthand, we will call this source of variance Var_p (for person).

Figure 4. A score matrix containing 3 judges' marks for 3 performances by 3 candidates

Column 1-10 →

	Candidate 1			Candidate 2			Candidate 3			Judge means
	Q 1	Q 2	Q 3	Q 1	Q 2	Q 3	Q 1	Q 2	Q 3	
Judge 1	10	8	9	6	5	6	8	7	3	6.9
Judge 2	9	8	8	3	5	4	7	3	4	5.7
Judge 3	10	8	10	7	6	7	10	9	9	8.4
Candidate means	8.9			5.4			6.7			

Row a-d ↓

The mean scores for briefs one, two and three are not shown, but they are also different – 7.8, 6.6, and 6.7 respectively. This shows that brief 2, for example, was more difficult than brief one for this group of candidates. For shorthand, we will call this source of variance Var_i (for item).

If judge stringency, candidate ability and assignment difficulty were the only three sources of variation, then it would be possible to predict all the scores in the matrix based on the candidate, the brief and the judge. However, the actual scores are not predictable in this way. To give an obvious example, cell c1 contains a score of 10 where the most able candidate has performed the easiest brief and been marked by the most lenient judge. However, there are several other cells with scores of 10 (e.g. c7).

Close inspection reveals that this 'unexpected' variation is itself not random. Columns 4 and 6 contain candidate 2's marks for assignments one and three. In the view of all three judges, this candidate performed as well on brief 3 as on brief 1 or better. This is in contrast to the overall difficulty of brief 3 compared with brief 1 and suggests that candidate 2 has more aptitude for brief three than brief one. Perhaps he or she understood the challenge of brief 3 particularly well. For shorthand, we will call this source of variance Var_{p*i} – or, in plain English, the candidates' item-specific aptitude.

Now examine cells a1-3 and cells a7-9. This shows that judge 1 prefers candidate one's performances to candidate three's performances on all briefs (which is typical). However, comparing cells c1-3 with cells c7-9 demonstrates that judge 3 is equally happy with the performances of candidates 1 and 3 (which is atypical). Perhaps there is something in the style or content of candidate three's performances that judge three favours. They may share a particular approach to movement or interpretation. For shorthand, we will call this source of variance Var_{p*j} – or, in plain English, that part of judge subjectivity that is attributable to the candidate or person.

Sometimes a part of judge subjectivity is also attributable to the item (Var_{p*j}). For example, a judge may have a particular 'hobby horse' about how things should be done. He or she will then mark assignments

Figure 5. The problem with non-cognitive assessment – a summary

NATURE UNCERTAIN >	EXPRESSION VARIABLE >	PERCEPTION SUBJECTIVE

on that particular item idiosyncratically – usually giving lower marks than other judges and lower than his or her own usual mark (unless, of course, a candidate aligns with that judge's particular hobby horse).

Even bearing all of these 'systematic' factors in mind, some variation is still unexplained. For example, cell a9 contains a score of 3 – jointly the lowest score in the matrix. This is not explained by candidate ability, judge stringency, assignment difficulty, candidate aptitude for brief 3 (compare cell c9), or that part of judge subjectivity attributable to candidate (compare a7&8), or that part of judge subjectivity attributable to assignment (compare a3&6). For shorthand, we will call this source of variance Var_{p*j*i} – or, in plain English, residual error.

There are techniques for decomposing these sources of variance – based on variance component analysis. For interest only, the variation in these scores decomposes as shown in Table 1. This means that when we compare the score given by a single judge to a candidate on a single performance with the score given by a different single judge to a different candidate on a different assignment, only 38% of the difference is due to the candidates. The majority of the difference is due to the variable stringency and taste of the judges and the different difficulty and suitability of the assignments. The data above are only provided as an illustration, but the results of the analysis are fairly typical for any judgement-based assessment. Candidate ability typically accounts for 20-40% of variance. Judge stringency, judge candidate-related subjectivity, candidate item-specific aptitude, and residual variation typically account for 10-25% of variance each.

The point is this: since almost all non-cognitive assessment depends on judgement, all the sources of error listed above impact heavily on the reliability of the assessments.

Summary

In summary then, every layer of the assessment process is unstable in non-cognitive assessment. The nature of the constructs being assessed is uncertain, the way in which those constructs are expressed is highly context specific, and the way in which any given action or performance is perceived is subjective. Figure 5 summarises the problem. Given these huge barriers, the obvious question is: what strategies have been tried to improve non-cognitive assessment, and what do we know about their success?

STRATEGIES FOR ASSESSING THE NON-COGNITIVE DOMAINS

Delineating the Constructs

If you're restoring a house, it's wise to begin with the foundations. Similarly, if we want to progress with non-cognitive assessment, we must work out the nature and classification of the non-cognitive domains. If we don't know what we're assessing, how can we even start? The Dr Brown vignette in Box 2 illustrates the point.

Box 2. Dr Brown – assessment starts with defining the domain or construct of interest

One of Dr Brown's patients has complained that she wasn't given any choices in her blood pressure consultation. She says: "The doctor didn't listen to what I had to say. She just told me that I needed to lose weight and that was the end of the discussion."

The senior partner in Dr Brown's practice wants to assess Dr Brown's performance as part of investigating the complaint. This was a blood pressure consultation. He might choose to assess her knowledge of blood pressure treatment. Perhaps she's not up to date with the treatment options and always recommends weight loss. On the other hand, it may be that she doesn't understand how to run a clinical consultation. In all her consultations she rushes to provide a solution before she's understood the patient's concerns and expectations because she's disorganised in her consultation management. Or maybe she has an attitude problem. Perhaps she has become bored of giving the same advice about blood pressure time after time so she isn't paying full attention. Perhaps she has a personal bias against people who are overweight and it affects the way in which she relates to most or all overweight patients.

Clearly a useful assessment of Dr Brown's performance can only begin once the relevant performance domain has been chosen.

Figure 6. A cartoon representation of non-cognitive constructs as anatomically-based cognitive functions (Yule et al., 2008)

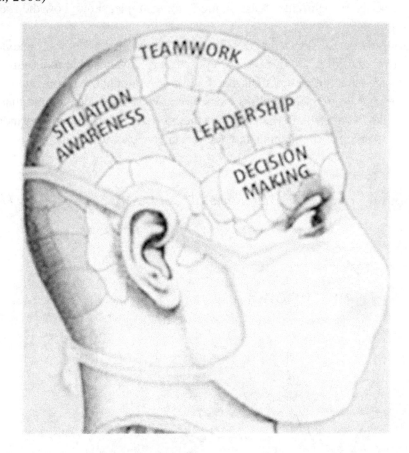

This field, delineating tacit constructs, has probably occupied more of the literature than any other aspect of non-cognitive assessment. Unfortunately, all that published work has not moved the field forward very much. There is a lack of taxonomic rigour and significant confusion over the meaning of some key terms (Figure 6).

The most prevalent literature is filled with consensus statements classifying the non-cognitive domains. Sometimes these are derived systematically using incident data, task analysis (Byrne & Long, 1976), or content analysis of appropriate datasets (Crossley & Davies, 2005; Khera, Stroobant, Primhak, Gupta, & Davies, 2001). More often they are derived by more or less systematic consensus methods. Most major western health economies have derived descriptions of the non-cognitive domains that underpin the performance of doctors in practice. For example, the General Medical Council, UK articulates that the doctor must function as 'scholar & scientist', 'practitioner' & 'professional' (GMC, 2009). The Royal College of Physicians and Surgeons of Canada describe the CanMEDS doctor as 'medical expert', 'communicator', 'collaborator', 'manager', 'health advocate', 'scholar', and 'professional' (Frank & Danoff, 2007). The Association of American Medical Colleges define the doctor as 'knowledgeable', 'skillful', 'altruistic', and 'dutiful' (Medical School Objectives Writing Group, 1999). There are some encouraging aspects to these classifications. The same constructs emerge in many different contexts, and they usually describe recognisable ideas. Figure 7, for example, shows how the frameworks above might be mapped together.

However, a brief inspection shows that they are often not explicit about their taxonomic stance. In the illustration above, 'dutiful' and 'altruistic' are posed as relatively stable traits. In contrast, 'Health advocate' and 'manager' are roles or functions that draw on several spheres of competence. 'Practitioner', 'scholar' and 'professional' are identity terms – describing what someone is rather than just what they do or what they're like. As a result, frameworks like these often cross taxonomic boundaries within the same classification to produce overlapping and non-exhaustive classifications.

Figure 7. Consensus frameworks: The GMC, CanMEDS and AAMC domains mapped together

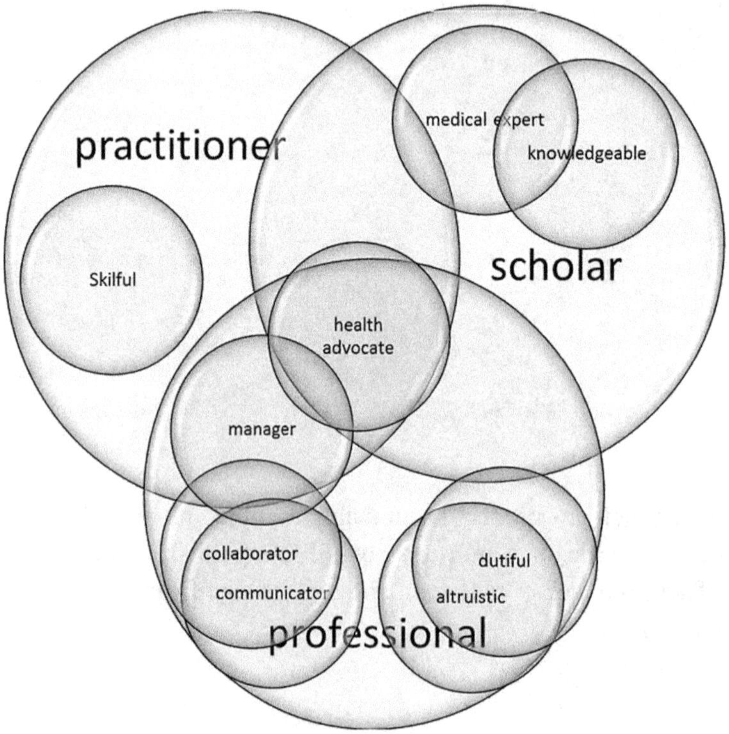

Consensus statements certainly have their uses. They assist in planning and blueprinting assessments, and they help to organise and communicate the assessment outputs. But, in the end, there is little evidence that the constructs they define function as stable traits (van der Vleuten et al., 2010).

There are taxonomy frameworks that can help in deriving robust mutually exclusive and exhaustive classifications. At the simplest level, much confusion could be avoided if a framework consistently adhered to one of Donabedian's three domains (structure – what a person *is* or *is like*, process – what a person *does*, or outcome – what *results* from what a person does) (Donabedian, 1980). Similarly, any classification should be explicit about which of Miller's performance levels is intended (see Figure 2) (Miller, 1990). Even then however, published literature is littered with conflicting interpretations of key terms and this creates significant confusion. For example, the term competence is being used by Miller to indicate a deep understanding, but is more often used in the literature to mean either performance under observation, or a minimum level of ability in practice. The term competency is sometimes used as a synonym for competence and sometimes used to reflect the thinking of the competency movement (Mc-Clelland, 1973), and the outcomes-based education movement (Spady, 1994). These movements argued that all educational activities should be built around a clear view of what the graduate should be able to *do*. Even in this context however it is sometimes used to describe traits (like dutiful) and sometimes used to describe tasks or roles (like health advocate/advocacy). This has become such a problem that there is now a whole new literature re-claiming the tasks and roles ground once occupied by competencies and calling them Entrustable Professional Activites (EPAs) (Ten Cate et al., 2015).

Finally, there are authors who are attempting to delineate non-cognitive constructs by empirical means. However, since the constructs are invisible and tacit, they have to be inferred from indirect measurement data. This is a laborious process since there is no solid ground. If you don't know what you're looking for, *and* you don't know how reliable or valid your measurements are it's extremely hard to interpret any given observation. The lack of solid evidence for the stability of non-cognitive constructs has led many to conclude that they do not exist. However, this is not the only valid conclusion. We still need to be able to explain why, using simple, well-understood terms, we can frequently agree about whether a person is conscientious or haphazard, gentle or brash. We also need to explain why characteristics that were observed in student doctors before qualification strongly predict the likelihood that they will commit serious professional indiscretions (Papadakis et al., 2005). Outside of measurement and assessment research, there is a lot of indirect evidence that non-cognitive performance is, in part, underpinned by relatively stable and commonly recognised traits.

In summary, existing classifications serve an essential role in assessment logistics, but we have made very little progress in delineating a 'true' non-cognitive classification. For those who believe in relatively stable traits, there is much work to be done.

Using Cognitive Assessments as a Proxy

Performance variation becomes a bigger and bigger problem at the higher, non-cognitive, levels of Miller's triangle (see section on variable performance). Therefore, it seems rational to investigate the use of the lower, cognitive levels as proxy indicators of performance and action. Box 3 gives a description of how this would work in the Dr Brown illustration.

Miller himself anticipated that attainment at the lower levels of the triangle would be necessary, but not sufficient for attainment at the higher levels:

Box 3. Dr Brown – assessing action using knowledge and performance

The senior partner in Dr Brown's practice has thought about the nature of the patient complaint (see box 2) and decided to investigate her relational performance because he thinks that this may underpin the problem. He's aware that her practice will vary from patient to patient and observer opinion will also vary.

Therefore, he decides to send her to an assessment centre where she will be tested on her knowledge of communication skills using written short answer questions and role play scenarios.

The critical question is this: if she knows about relating, and is capable of relating well under assessment conditions, does that mean that she normally relates well in her everyday practice?

... while it may be reasonable to assume that either action or performance implies achievement of the more basic elements of the triangle, measurement of the infrastructure (i.e., knowledge and competence) cannot be assumed to predict fully and with confidence the achievement of the more complex goals. (Miller, 1990)

A number of published studies address this strategy directly. Their findings confirm Miller's position. In a carefully planned experiment in the Netherlands, Jan-Joost Rethans and colleagues arranged for four covert standardised patients to visit each of 36 general practitioners during normal surgery hours (Rethans, Sturmans, Drop, van der Vleuten, & Hobus, 1991). The actors depicted four representative clinical problems and were trained to assess the performance of the doctors they saw. The doctors were then taken to an assessment centre for a controlled assessment where they saw exactly the same four clinical problems represented and assessed in exactly the same way – but not during their normal working day. The doctors performed much better in the controlled assessment. More importantly, their 'shows how' performance in the assessment centre was completely uncorrelated with their day-to-day 'does' practice in normal surgery hours (Pearson co-efficient -0.04). Clearly, actual practice (action) depends on more than just competence. Most follow-up studies have, in fact, shown very low positive correlations between 'shows how' and 'does' performance inviting similar conclusions. Interestingly however, when cognitive tests and performance tests have been compared, even basic cognitive tests do no worse in predicting action than highly sophisticated performance assessments (Ram et al., 1999).

In summary, Miller was right: cognitive attainment goes some way in predicting the non-cognitive levels of attainment (performance and action) but so many other factors also influence performance and action that cognitive assessment alone will not do.

Making the Subjective, Objective

If different observers have any consensus about what is 'a good performance' and what is 'a bad performance' even when they are using subjective judgement (and they do), then their opinions must be based on what they observe. Perhaps then, by drawing their attention to directly observable behaviours that did or did not take place, it is possible to achieve a greater degree of consensus. Perhaps 'a good performance' can be broken down into its separate parts and, by giving each part a mark it's possible to create an objective checklist that virtually guarantees agreement. The Dr Brown illustration given in Box 4 shows how this might work.

This strategy was, and still is, widespread in non-cognitive assessment. The most widespread 'shows how' assessment in medical education is the OSCE described in section on variable performance. One key element of the design of the OSCE is the 'objective' checklist. A relatively complex behaviour such

Box 4. Dr Brown – assessing relational performance by making the subjective, objective

---

The senior partner in Dr Brown's practice wants to assess her relational performance as part of investigating a patient complaint (see box 2). He is planning to observe her, but he's aware that his opinion of her performance may not be the same as another observer, because relating is a very subjective and tacit aspect of performance. She performs well in a controlled assessment centre, but he's worried that this doesn't reflect her usual practice.

Therefore, he decides to use a validated tool for assessing relational performance in real clinical encounters. The tool breaks down relational performance into a checklist of twenty directly observable behaviours that either did or did not take place. After the encounter, the quality of relating is indicated by the sum of those twenty items. They include such questions as:

a) The doctor introduced himself/herself – Yes/No

b) The doctor made eye contact – Yes/No

c) The doctor shook the patient by the hand – Yes/No

---

as safe and effective resuscitation is broken down into its separate parts. Assessors record what they observe and didn't observe, and the resulting total checklist score is intended to reflect the quality of the performance. Similar strategies have been used for 'shows how' and 'does' assessments of relational performance, surgical technique, record keeping, practical procedures, written correspondence etc.

However, investigators studying the impact of objective checklists on assessor subjectivity in 1998 made an intriguing and counter-intuitive discovery. Glenn Regehr and colleagues analysed the results of an OSCE-style examination using three assessor response formats in parallel – a checklist, a checklist accompanied by an overall subjective judgement, and an overall subjective judgement alone without reference to any checklist (Regehr, MacRae, Reznick, & Szalay, 1998). Using the simple subjective judgement, the assessors made wider discriminations between candidates (Var_p from section on subjective judgement) and agreed more closely with one-another (Var_j and Var_{j*p}), than when they recorded their objective observations on a checklist. From a psychometric perspective, wider discrimination and closer agreement adds up to better reliability.

This turns out to be generally true of judgement-based assessment. Almost every analysis of assessments where a subjective judgement is compared with an 'objectified' representation of performance reaches the same conclusion. Judgement is more reliable than objectification. Clearly, this begs the question: why? The most likely answer is that the whole is more than the sum of the parts. A good performance is much more than a series of steps or behaviours. It is the way in which those behaviours are timed, used, weighted and balanced to the particulars of the individual situation that separates a good performance from a poor one. Consider again Box 2 above. If Dr Brown introduces herself, makes eye contact and shakes hands with a patient with whom she has built up a close and informal relationship over years, it is likely to convey coldness rather than warmth. It may be similarly inappropriate in certain cultural scenarios, or, if the patient is expecting serious test results, these formalities might indicate that the news is going to be bad. The same is true for almost every aspect of her interpersonal behaviour; it needs to be adapted to the particular situation. It seems that, given the freedom to judge, appropriately experienced assessors are more likely to agree about when they see a good performance in its context and when they see a poor performance in its context then when they are constrained to checklists.

Of course, there are some advantages to checklists. When a new driver is learning the basics of car control, is may well be helpful to learn and to be assessed on the basic elements of a 'standard' performance – 'mirror, signal, manoeuvre' for example. But later, the 'standard' performance should be varied according to the circumstances. Checklists may be helpful to guide the beginning learner, but, in relation to judgement, they intensify rather than solve the problem of subjectivity.

Sampling across Performances and Opinions

The judgements that assessors make include a shared perspective that moves them towards consensus about a learner's ability (Var_p), but also the individual standards (Var_j) and unique perspectives (Var_{p*j}) that reflect their own expertise, experience and judgement. Perhaps then, rather than trying to conform them to a single 'idealised' view, it is more fitting to seek a view that better represents the combined view of all suitable assessors. If one assessor's view doesn't reflect the universe of all suitable assessors sufficiently well, then perhaps we should bring together enough views to adequately reflect that universe.

Similarly, if one performance reflects, in part, the ability of a learner (Var_p), but also the difficulty of the case or challenge (Var_i) and the aptitude of the learning for that particular challenge (Var_{i*p}), then perhaps we should sample sufficient performances to reflect the learner's ability with the universe of possible challenges.

This, in essence, is the strategy of sampling opinions and performances. We take it for granted in most assessment situations. We ask fifty multiple-choice questions because we know that a learner's response to one question partially reflects their knowledge of the domain, but doesn't predict their knowledge of another part of the domain with sufficient accuracy. But their performance on a larger number of appropriately sampled questions provides a much better indicator of their knowledge of the domain. The Dr Brown illustration given in Box 5 shows how this might work. Figure 8 illustrates the principle of sampling.

The breadth of sampling required to achieve a reasonable representation of a learner's performance with any similar sample of challenges and in the view of any similar sample of assessors can be estimated from the kind of analysis in Figure 4. Those who are interested in psychometrics might like to read Cronbach's seminal book on the dependability of behaviour measurements (Cronbach, Gleser, Nanda, & Rajaratnam, 1972), or the easier texts written by Streiner and Norman (Streiner & Norman, 1995) or

Figure 8. Sampling to obtain a reasonable representation of all possible views and performances. Reproduced with the kind permission of Cees Van der Vleuten.

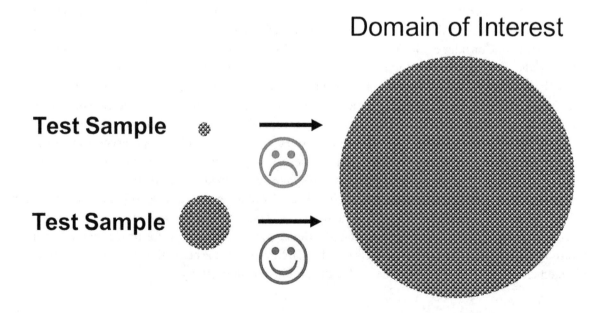

362

Box 5. Dr Brown – assessing relational performance by sampling

> The senior partner in Dr Brown's practice is investigating her relational performance (see Box 2). He is aware that her performance will vary, and that observer opinion will vary. He feels that relational behaviour is too complex and sophisticated for checklist-based objective observation.
>
> He decides to gather a wide and, hopefully, representative sample of her practice and a similarly wide and representative sample of appropriate opinions.
>
> He searches for an appropriate method and decides that he will combine a user survey with a peer survey. Many user surveys are vague in their focus, but he finds one that specifically asks about the relational aspects of performance including items on whether the doctor was successful in listening to and understanding the patient's concerns. Validation studies show that 25 respondents are required before their combined views adequately predict the views of any 25 respondents. He finds a similarly appropriate and validated multi-source feedback instrument for use by the full range of professional colleagues in the practice that requires 15 responses to reach reliability.

by Crossley and colleagues (Crossley, Davies, Humphris, & Jolly, 2002). In essence, where a judgement is highly dependent on the stringency or subjectivity of the assessor then a large number of judgements need to be sampled, and when performance is highly dependent on the particular challenge, then a large number of challenges need to be sampled.

Understanding where the unwanted variation comes from can inform other strategies in addition to sampling. In some situations judges vary widely in their stringency (some using the top end of the scale and others the bottom end – Var_j), but they don't vary widely their taste (i.e. their scores correlate – Var_{p*j}). If so, then it's possible to make the assessment more reliable by ensuring that the same judge(s) assess all learners. This means that the stringency or leniency affects everyone equally. Clearly that's not possible for a large scale assessment – though splitting up the assessment work can go a long way. In a traditional OSCE, for example, learners rotate around 20 or more assessors. Alternatively, it may be appropriate to 'correct' the candidate's scores according to whether they saw a stringent or lenient (set of) judge(s). This kind of correction can be applied manually, but in Item-Response Theory (IRT) it is built into the logit transformation that all scores undergo. The logit score may then provide a 'truer' comparison between candidates than the actual raw score. Those interested in IRT might like to read the excellent and accessible book by Trevor Bond and Christine Fox (Bond & Fox, 2007).

Sampling has been the mainstream strategy for achieving reliable assessments of action (workplace-based assessment) for some years now. A wide range of instruments exists in medicine and commercial settings that draw on evidence from peer opinions, user opinions, peer or supervisor observations in real time or from audio or video records, routine documentation or correspondence review, and case discussions. The main limitation to this strategy is that the wide sampling required poses a significant demand on a large number of busy colleagues. Respondents are also typically unwilling to rate their colleagues poorly even when their performance is poor, and this makes discrimination difficult. In addition, professionals being directly observed are likely to demonstrate their 'best' performance rather than performance in action. As we have already seen, controlled performance doesn't adequately predict usual performance.

Using Outcome Measures as a Proxy

Most professions in which non-cognitive assessment matters are also highly regulated. As a result, large amounts of outcome data are collected routinely as quality indicators. In the field of medicine these include data such as complaint rates, incident reports, satisfaction ratings, clinic non-attendances, ward lengths of stay, unplanned readmissions to hospital, surgical operation times, blood loss estimates,

Box 6. Dr Brown – assessing action using outcome measures

The senior partner in Dr Brown's practice is investigating her relational performance following a patient complaint (see Box 2). He is aware of the limitations of cognitive tests and controlled assessments, and the burdensomeness of direct observation.

He decides to use existing data that may serve as an indicator of the full spectrum of Dr Brown's normal, day-to-day, relational performance as interpreted by a very wide range of clients. He therefore asks the practice manager to create a log of the complaints made against Dr. Brown over her 10 years at the practice, and her scores on the quarterly patient satisfaction survey. As a benchmark, he asks for the comparative figures for the other six general practitioners at the practice.

She has a higher than reference complaint rate, but she points out that most of the complaints cite long waiting times for her clinic rather than her personal practice. She argues that this is because she provides the blood pressure service where capacity is not sufficient to meet existing demand.

---

complication rates, mortality rates etc. The obvious question arises: can data like these be used as indicators of a single professional's performance? Box 6 gives a description of how this would work in the Dr Brown illustration.

Such data are routinely used to appraise the performance of doctors in practice. However, there is remarkably little serious evaluation of this data for assessment. There are some obvious barriers: for example, most important outcomes are not the product of one individual professional's practice, but rather the product of a whole 'system' that includes many members of a multi-professional clinical & support team working in a particular environment of facilities and services. Also, different practitioners typically see clients or patients who are neither matched nor randomly selected. Patients and clients with different problems or with problems of differing severity are likely to have different outcomes. Finally, the clearest and most objective outcome data (such as mortality or complication rates) are extremely rare. Consequently the difference between a practitioner with one adverse outcome in a year and a practitioner with two is highly likely to have occurred by chance.

Across the professions, there are strategies to address each of these difficulties. For example, root-cause analysis helps to discern whether an adverse outcome was caused by the practice of one professional, a whole team, or the system within which they operate. In teaching, exit attainment is corrected for entry attainment to estimate the 'added value'. Similarly in medicine, tools for assessing a patient's pre-treatment condition help to correct for case mix variation so that one practice can be more easily be compared with another. Rare events can be interpreted better using rolling data over several years to reduce the effects of chance. Nevertheless, it remains very unusual for routinely-generated outcome data to be used for assessment purposes on its own.

Using Meta-Cognition as a Proxy

If cognitive measures are a weak proxy for non-cognitive performance and action, what about meta-cognitive measures? The attraction here is two-fold. First, a practitioner's own reflections are a free and readily available window onto a practitioner's performance and action. Like a continuous video recording these recollections offer a way to access and assess what has happened without needing a third party observer. Second, and more significantly, meta-cognitive processes may provide a window onto how a practitioner interprets and manages his or her actions. Thus it may provide information that generalises beyond the specific and predicts responses and actions more generally. This distinctive function is described as part of a much wider analysis of self-assessment by Kevin Eva and Glenn Regehr (Eva & Regehr, 2005). This is the idea: the practitioner who can commentate wisely on what they were doing and why in one instance of their practice is more likely to perform well on a future, different, occasion

Box 7. Dr Brown – assessing action using meta-cognition

The senior partner in Dr Brown's practice is investigating her relational performance following a patient complaint (see box 2). He is aware that her performance will be different from patient to patient. He also knows that relational problems in encounters frequently arise when one party misreads the needs and expectations of the other party.   Therefore he decides to discuss the problem encounter with Dr Brown as a way to assess her capacity to choose the right relational approach. He is interested in whether and how she evaluates the patient's preferences, and how she adapts her communication accordingly. If she attends to the right cues and has the capacity to adapt her communication, then he will feel reassured about her performance with other patients – even if she misjudged with this particular patient.

than a practitioner who just 'got it right this time'. Box 7 gives a description of how this would work in the Dr Brown illustration.

A number of professions use this approach. There are some clear findings. First, self-assessment (where the practitioner is using their own meta-cognitive processes to perform assessment on themselves) does not produce a reliable reflection of their actual practice compared with others (Ward, Gruppen, & Regehr, 2002). In other words, using self-assessment as a free window onto actual practice broadly doesn't work. Second, meta-cognitive capacity is not, in itself, a stable trait. It is highly dependent on content (Eva & Regehr, 2005). However, there is some evidence that self-monitoring of the kind described in the Dr Brown example – moment-by-moment awareness of actions, options and limitation – may, in fact, be a relatively good predictor of performance (Eva & Regehr, 2011). To date, this has only been demonstrated well in cognitive tests. However, it seems an extremely rich area for investigation in the non-cognitive domain.

Changing or Abandoning the Measurement Paradigm

The disappointing characteristics of the measurement paradigm in non-cognitive assessment has driven a recent call for entirely new approaches. Lambert Schuwirth and Cees van der Vleuten, both highly experienced practitioners of the psychometric paradigm, began to write in 2006 about the search for an entirely new approach (Schuwirth & van der Vleuten, 2006). The authors write:

The central assumption in the current model is that medical competence can be subdivided into separate measurable stable and generic traits ... it requires a numerical and reductionist approach ... aspects such as fairness, defensibility and credibility are by necessity mainly translated into reliability and construct validity. These approaches are more and more difficult to align with modern assessment approaches ...

They highlighted a probabilistic approach or the application of Bayes theorem as promising new directions. The obvious attraction is that each measurement doesn't begin 'from scratch'; rather existing intelligence about a learner helps to inform the depth and interpretation of subsequent assessments. This goes a substantial way to overcoming the sampling burden required for reliable 'biopsy' assessments.

More recently, Marjan Govaerts and others have begun to advocate entirely non-metric approaches to assessment (Govaerts & van der Vleuten, 2013). Drawing a clear and reasonable parallel between qualitative research and qualitative assessment, she writes:

Basic principles of rigour specific to qualitative research have been established, and they can and should be used to determine validity in interpretivist assessment approaches. If used properly, these strategies

Box 8. Dr Brown – assessing action using qualitative methods

The senior partner in Dr Brown's practice is investigating her relational performance following a patient complaint (see box 2). He is aware of the limitations of existing assessment methods. In particular he has a conviction that most of Dr Brown's patients and colleagues would be able to describe her strengths and weakness, but that these do not emerge in measurement-based assessments. Therefore he decides to systematically collect narrative descriptions of Dr Brown's performance. He has to decide whether to use observation frameworks or pure, unguided, narrative. He also has to decide how to identify important themes, consonance, dissonance and trustworthiness from all the data.

generate trustworthy evidence that is needed to develop the validity argument ... allowing for in-depth and meaningful information about professional competence.

Box 8 gives a description of how this might work in the Dr Brown illustration.

These movements highlight the very significant crisis point in the development of non-cognitive assessment methods. They are testament to the readiness of experienced investigators to completely re-consider the field. However, at present, these suggested ways forward have not substantially replaced the metric paradigm.

PROMISING DIRECTIONS FOR THE FUTURE

The preceding sections show that it is not easy to assess the non-cognitive domains in a trustworthy manner.

Certainly, one approach will not suit all purposes. The design of any assessment must be driven by its intended purpose (Crossley, Humphris, & Jolly, 2002). For example, objectified checklists may well be a suitable approach for assessing performance in controlled situations for beginners. The clear performance criteria provide a transparent set of objectives for the learner and a common language to help with feedback credibility. These help to achieve a predominantly formative purpose and, perhaps, to document the attainment of a basic minimum standard before progressing to further experience. Similarly, qualitative assessment may be well suited to assessing experts at the highest level of performance or to diagnosing a performance problem. The rich narrative content can describe contextualised performance in action and lends itself to exploring cause and effect or performance options.

However, the majority of non-cognitive assessments are likely to have to serve a partly summative purpose demanding some basic parameters of dependability, and they typically have to be administered on a large scale that is less well suited to time-consuming or individualised formats. This is the type of assessment activity that is looking for a way forward. The author offers some suggestions in this closing section. These suggestions are reasoned and informed, but they are only personal opinions.

The Search for Constructs Needs to Mature and Abandon Merit

Up to the present, the search for non-cognitive constructs has pursued a largely unidimensional approach. Like the cartoon representation in Figure 6, we have been searching for a set of largely non-overlapping building blocks that make up the person – rather like a 'Lego' model. This view is probably an extension of the success of the IQ construct in the cognitive domain, and it has dominated the personality literature until very recently. It means that, largely, our frame of reference has been one of merit – how good or bad is this person's situational awareness for example. However, it seems much more likely that a person is a meld of much more heterogeneous parts – more like a living culture than a 'Lego' model.

Some characteristics are likely to be relatively stable. To take an extreme example, there is good evidence for the clinical stability of certain problem characteristics such as social communication disorders, attention deficit disorders and, perhaps, personality disorders. These have a profound effect on non-cognitive performance. Certain types of assessment, for example assessment for selection, should almost certainly focus on identifying stable problem characteristics like these (Powis, 2015). These assessments probably can and should adopt an unapologetic measurement paradigm – but this is not measurement of merit.

The same is probably true for certain distinctive areas of aptitude. Some practitioners have an idiosyncratic and relatively stable facility for certain domains of performance – for example reading and assimilating large quantities of data. These aptitudes probably also invite a measurement approach – but they are best represented as distinctive aptitudes and not as degrees or merit on a continuous scale.

Indeed, it is probably the insistence on merit as the primary frame of reference that feeds widespread 'failure to fail' in assessors and 'fear of failing' in learners. Who wants to be called, or to call anyone else, anything less than good or, preferably, excellent?

Many other characteristics are best seen through a developmental frame of reference. Emerging mastery and self-regulation depend on what challenge is facing a learner in relation to their zone of proximal development (ZPD) (Smith, Dockrell, & Tomlinson, 1997). As every parent knows, when faced with a challenge that is far beyond their ZPD, a learner is likely to display very limited self-regulation. Thus the expression of any aspect of performance that depends on self-regulation is highly contextual. For such characteristics it doesn't make sense to adopt the stable trait model. A developmental model may be more appropriate describing what the student has mastered thus far as their ZPD progresses. This is not about merit; it's about milestones of progress. A good example is learning to drive. It makes very little sense to describe an early learner as a more or less excellent driver. Either they have mastered a few of the basic skills or they have mastered many. This perspective should profoundly affect the language and focus of most non-cognitive assessment up to the level of expert.

Just as difficulties are mirrored by aptitudes, so also development is mirrored by deterioration. In the latter part of their professional lives, doctors and other professionals experience a deterioration in their performance. This is reflected in higher error rates in medicine. It doesn't make sense to assess for deterioration through a trait or development frame of reference. Almost certainly this is a function of the labour-intensive meta-cognitive work required to toggle between intuitive (type 1) reasoning and analytical (type 2) reasoning. As a practitioner begins to routinely function well within their ZPD with increasing age and experience it is probably more difficult to switch from type 1 to type 2 reasoning when the situation demands. If so, it seems likely that assessment aimed at metacognition is most appropriate. Those professionals who, despite experience, are still able to articulate an analytical reasoning process, and to highlight the circumstances requiring a move from intuitive to analytical reasoning, may be less likely to commit this kind of error.

In summary, it's time to move beyond a 'building block' view of non-cognitive performance constructs, but it may not be necessary or appropriate to abandon hope of defining any measurement constructs. Rather we need multiple frames of reference to assess the several different kinds of factors that influence performance and action. These probably include, at least, stable problems, stable aptitudes, zones of development and meta-cognitive functions.

Rather Than Trying to Control Judgement, Exploit the Power of Judgement

Much of the work in non-cognitive assessment has focused on controlling and limiting judgement to reduce subjectivity. The alternative approach of sampling to obtain a good representation of the universe of subjective opinion has been somewhat disappointing in that very large numbers of judgements are required – suggesting that even appropriate assessors have very limited correspondence in their opinions. However there is a promising new direction here too. Traditionally assessors are asked to express their judgements in terms of merit (poor, satisfactory, good etc.) or in terms of expectation (below/at/above expectation for a newly qualified doctor etc.). However, if the response options are deliberately aligned with the cognitive frameworks that judges naturally use, then their judgements become much more reliable. This has been shown across a large range assessments including surgical skills (Crossley & Jolly, 2012), clinical encounters, directly observed procedures & clinical handovers (Crossley, Johnson, Booth, & Wade, 2011), and anaesthetic skills (Weller et al., 2014). Where traditional and construct-aligned scales have been evaluated in parallel the improvement in reliability is very substantial indeed – typically reducing the number of observations required to one third or one fifth of the traditional number.

This finding is clearly important on a practical level. It makes assessment in the workplace much more feasible. But it also important at a theoretical level. It confirms the conviction that appropriate judges do indeed share a highly consistent view of what good performance is and of when they see it and when they don't. The inconsistency of judges' opinions when they are using traditional response formats must, in retrospect, have been due to their interpretation and use of the format and not their views of the performance. We have been taking good judgements and making them opaque.

There is much work still to be done elucidating the cognitive frameworks that judges use. In medicine, one very important construct is readiness for independent practice or entrustability. Clinician judges seem able to synthesise substantial amounts of information into a single entrustability decision with a high level of agreement. Perhaps this is not surprising, since they are required to make this judgement every day in their normal practice. Second, think aloud methods have highlighted disregard for error as an especially adverse behaviour in any judgement decision and fluidity as an especially positive behaviour (Hyde, Lefroy, Gay, Yardley, & McKinley, 2014). The most compelling option of all however, would be a response format that makes explicit the tacit developmental stages that judges use in reaching a judgement where this is appropriate. A number of explicit developmental frameworks exist – including the RIME framework in undergraduate medicine (DeWitt, Carline, Paauw, & Pangaro, 2008), the KSF framework in UK nursing, and the research skills development (RSD) framework for academic researchers (Willison & O'Regan, 2007). These are all attempts to describe developmental milestones in terms that are authentic to practitioners and meaningful to learners. They have not all yet been tested as assessment response formats, but if they enhance judgements as effectively as readiness for independence, then they will be a substantial step forward in judgement-based assessment. In many ways they will bridge the gap between the metric and qualitative paradigms. They carry the promise of powerful educational impact by setting out for the learner a clear map of progression and by providing a common language for credible feedback (Crossley, 2014).

Purposefully Investigate the Assessment of Meta-Cognitive Processes

Finally, the work on assessment aimed at self-monitoring seems full of promise. Since self-monitoring has the potential to predict other performances beyond the one under observation, it has always held the potential for highly efficient assessment. The recent demonstration that markers of self-monitoring (such as delay or deferral in answering a question) predict performance raises significant hope in this field (Eva & Regehr, 2011). It's also likely that judges' paying attention to fluidity or disregard for error, (Hyde, Lefroy, Gay, Yardley, & McKinley, 2014) and judges' recognising a whole that is more than the sum of its parts, (Regehr, MacRae, Reznick, & Szalay, 1998) are really making inferences about meta-cognitive performance.

REFERENCES

Bloom, B. (1971). *Taxonomy of educational objectives: the classification of educational goals - Handbook 1: Cognitive domain*. New York: David Mackay Company.

Bond, T. G., & Fox, C. M. (2007). *Applying the Rasch model: fundamental measurement in the human sciences* (2nd ed.). Mahwah, N.J.: Lawrence Erlbaum Associates Publishers.

Burford, B., Morrow, G., Rothwell, C., Carter, M., & Illing, J. (2014). Professionalism education should reflect reality: Findings from three health professions. *Medical Education*, *48*(4), 361–374. doi:10.1111/medu.12368

Byrne, P., & Long, B. (1976). *Doctors Talking to Patients*. London: HMSO.

Cronbach, L., Gleser, G., Nanda, H., & Rajaratnam, N. (1972). *The dependability of behavioural measurements: theory of generalizability for scores and profiles*. New York: Wiley.

Crossley, J. (2014). Addressing learner disorientation: Give them a roadmap. *Medical Teacher*, *36*(8), 685–691. doi:10.3109/0142159X.2014.889813

Crossley, J., & Davies, H. (2005). Doctors' consultations with children and their parents: A model of competencies, outcomes, and confounding influences. *Medical Education*, *39*(8), 807–819. doi:10.1111/j.1365-2929.2005.02231.x

Crossley, J., Davies, H., Humphris, G., & Jolly, B. (2002). Generalisability: A key to unlock professional assessment. *Medical Education*, *36*(10), 972–978. doi:10.1046/j.1365-2923.2002.01320.x

Crossley, J., Humphris, G., & Jolly, B. (2002). Assessing health professionals. *Medical Education*, *36*(9), 800–804. doi:10.1046/j.1365-2923.2002.01294.x

Crossley, J., Johnson, G., Booth, J., & Wade, W. (2011). Good questions, good answers: Construct alignment improves the performance of workplace-based assessment scales. *Medical Education*, *45*(6), 560–569. doi:10.1111/j.1365-2923.2010.03913.x

Crossley, J., & Jolly, B. (2012). Making sense of work-based assessment: Ask the right questions, in the right way, about the right things, of the right people. *Medical Education*, *46*(1), 28–37. doi:10.1111/j.1365-2923.2011.04166.x

Cruess, S. R., & Cruess, R. L. (2012). Teaching professionalism - Why, What and How. *Facts Views Vis Obgyn*, *4*(4), 259–265.

DeWitt, D., Carline, J., Paauw, D., & Pangaro, L. (2008). Pilot study of a 'RIME'-based tool for giving feedback in a multi-specialty longitudinal clerkship. *Medical Education, 42*(12), 1205–1209. doi:10.1111/j.1365-2923.2008.03229.x

Donabedian, A. (1980). Explorations in quality assessment and monitoring: Vol. 1. *The definition of quality and approaches to its assessment.* Ann Arbor, MI: Health Administration Press.

Elstein, A., Shulman, L., & Sprafka, S. (1990). Medical Problem-Solving - a 10-Year Retrospective. *Evaluation & the Health Professions, 13*(1), 5–36. doi:10.1177/016327879001300102

Elstein, A., Shulman, L., & Srafka, S. (1978). *Medical problem-solving: an anlysis of clinical reasoning.* Cambridge, MA: Harvard University Press. doi:10.4159/harvard.9780674189089

Epstein, R. M., & Hundert, E. M. (2002). Defining and assessing professional competence. *Journal of the American Medical Association, 287*(2), 226–235. doi:10.1001/jama.287.2.226

Eva, K. W., & Regehr, G. (2005). Self-assessment in the health professions: A reformulation and research agenda. *Academic Medicine, 80*(10 Suppl.), S46–S54. doi:10.1097/00001888-200510001-00015

Eva, K. W., & Regehr, G. (2011). Exploring the divergence between self-assessment and self-monitoring. *Advances in Health Sciences Education: Theory and Practice, 16*(3), 311–329. doi:10.1007/s10459-010-9263-2

Frank, J. R., & Danoff, D. (2007). The CanMEDS initiative: Implementing an outcomes-based framework of physician competencies. *Medical Teacher, 29*(7), 642–647. doi:10.1080/01421590701746983

Gareis, C. R., & Grant, L. W. (2008). *Teacher-made assessments: how to connect curriculum, instruction, and student learning.* Larchmont, NY: Eye On Education.

GMC. (2009). Tomorrow's Doctors: outcomes and standards for undergraduate medical education. (1st ed., pp. 55). Manchester, UK: General Medical Council.

Govaerts, M., & van der Vleuten, C. P. (2013). Validity in work-based assessment: Expanding our horizons. *Medical Education, 47*(12), 1164–1174. doi:10.1111/medu.12289

Harden, R. M., & Gleeson, F. A. (1979). Assessment of clinical competence using an objective structured clinical examination (OSCE). *Medical Education, 13*(1), 41–54. doi:10.1111/j.1365-2923.1979.tb00918.x

Hyde, C., Lefroy, J., Gay, S., Yardley, S., & McKinley, R. (2014). A clarification study of internal scales clinicians use to assess undergraduate medical students. *Paper presented at theOttawa Conference on Medical Education*, Ottawa Canada.

Khera, N., Stroobant, J., Primhak, R. A., Gupta, R., & Davies, H. (2001). Training the ideal hospital doctor: The specialist registrars' perspective. *Medical Education, 35*(10), 957–966.

McClelland, D. C. (1973). Testing for competence rather than for "intelligence". *The American Psychologist, 28*(1), 1–14. doi:10.1037/h0034092

Medical School Objectives Writing Group. (1999). Learning objectives for medical student education--guidelines for medical schools: Report I of the Medical School Objectives Project. *Academic Medicine, 74*(1), 13–18. doi:10.1097/00001888-199901000-00010

Miller, G. E. (1990). The assessment of clinical skills/competence/performance. *Academic Medicine*, *65*(9Suppl), S63–S67. doi:10.1097/00001888-199009000-00045

Papadakis, M. A., Teherani, A., Banach, M. A., Knettler, T. R., Rattner, S. L., Stern, D. T., & Hodgson, C. S. et al. (2005). Disciplinary action by medical boards and prior behavior in medical school. *The New England Journal of Medicine*, *353*(25), 2673–2682. doi:10.1056/NEJMsa052596

Powis, D. (2015). Selecting medical students: An unresolved challenge. *Medical Teacher*, *37*(3), 252–260. doi:10.3109/0142159X.2014.993600

Ram, P., van der Vleuten, C., Rethans, J. J., Schouten, B., Hobma, S., & Grol, R. (1999). Assessment in general practice: The predictive value of written-knowledge tests and a multiple-station examination for actual medical performance in daily practice. *Medical Education*, *33*(3), 197–203. doi:10.1046/j.1365-2923.1999.00280.x

Regehr, G., MacRae, H., Reznick, R., & Szalay, D. (1998). Comparing the psychometric properties of checklists and global rating scales for assessing performance on an OSCE-format examination. *Academic Medicine*, *73*(9), 993–997. doi:10.1097/00001888-199809000-00020

Regehr, G., & Norman, G. (1996). Issues in cognitive psychology: Implications for professional education. *Academic Medicine*, *71*(9), 988–1001. doi:10.1097/00001888-199609000-00015

Rethans, J., Norcini, J., Baron-Maldonado, M., Blackmore, D., Jolly, B., LaDuca, T., & Southgate, L. et al. (2002). The relationship between competence and performance: Implications for assessing practice performance. *Medical Education*, *36*(10), 901–909. doi:10.1046/j.1365-2923.2002.01316.x

Rethans, J., Sturmans, F., Drop, R., van der Vleuten, C., & Hobus, P. (1991). Does competence of general practitioners predict their performance? Comparison between examination setting and actual practice. *British Medical Journal*, *303*(6814), 1377–1380. doi:10.1136/bmj.303.6814.1377

Schuwirth, L. W., & van der Vleuten, C. P. (2006). A plea for new psychometric models in educational assessment. *Medical Education*, *40*(4), 296–300. doi:10.1111/j.1365-2929.2006.02405.x

Shakespeare, W., & Lever, J. W. (1997). *Measure for measure*. Walton-on-Thames: Thomas Nelson & Sons.

Shavelson, R. J., Baxter, G. P., & Gao, X. H. (1993). Sampling Variability of Performance Assessments. *Journal of Educational Measurement*, *30*(3), 215–232. doi:10.1111/j.1745-3984.1993.tb00424.x

Smith, L., Dockrell, J., & Tomlinson, P. (1997). *Piaget, Vygotsky and beyond: future issues for developmental psychology and education*. London, New York: Routledge.

Spady, W. G. (1994). Choosing Outcomes of Significance. *Educational Leadership*, *51*(6), 18–22.

Streiner, D., & Norman, G. (1995). *Health Measurement Scales: A Practical Guide to their Development and Use* (2nd ed.). New York: Oxford University Press.

Ten Cate, O., Chen, H. C., Hoff, R. G., Peters, H., Bok, H., & van der Schaaf, M. (2015). Curriculum development for the workplace using Entrustable Professional Activities (EPAs): AMEE Guide No. 99. *Medical Teacher*, 2015, 1–20. doi:10.3109/0142159X.2015.1060308 van der Vleuten, C. P., Schuwirth, L. W., Scheele, F., Driessen, E. W., & Hodges, B. (2010). The assessment of professional competence: Building blocks for theory development. *Best Practice & Research. Clinical Obstetrics & Gynaecology, 24*(6), 703–719. doi:10.1016/j.bpobgyn.2010.04.001

Ward, M., Gruppen, L., & Regehr, G. (2002). Measuring self-assessment: Current state of the art. *Advances in Health Sciences Education: Theory and Practice, 7*(1), 63–80. doi:10.1023/A:1014585522084

Weller, J. M., Misur, M., Nicolson, S., Morris, J., Ure, S., Crossley, J., & Jolly, B. (2014). Can I leave the theatre? A key to more reliable workplace-based assessment. *British Journal of Anaesthesia, 112*(6), 1083–1091. doi:10.1093/bja/aeu052

Willison, J., & O'Regan, K. (2007). Commonly known, commonly not known, totally unknown: A framework for students becoming researchers. *Higher Education Research & Development, 26*(4), 393–409. doi:10.1080/07294360701658609

Wimmers, P. F., & Fung, C. C. (2008). The impact of case specificity and generalisable skills on clinical performance: A correlated traits-correlated methods approach. *Medical Education, 42*(6), 580–588. doi:10.1111/j.1365-2923.2008.03089.x

Yule, S., Flin, R., Maran, N., Rowley, D., Youngson, G., & Paterson-Brown, S. (2008). Surgeons' non-technical skills in the operating room: Reliability testing of the NOTSS behavior rating system. *World Journal of Surgery, 32*(4), 548–556. doi:10.1007/s00268-007-9320-z

KEY TERMS AND DEFINITIONS

Cognitive: Related to conscious mental processes.

Competence: Unless otherwise stated in the text, this term will be used to mean the ability to display behaviours reaching a required standard under controlled conditions.

Construct: An unobservable entity assumed to have explanatory power and stability.

Meta-Cognition: Higher-order thinking which functions to monitor and regulate operational cognitive and non-cognitive processes.

Non-Cognitive: Related to behaviour or values; underpinned by, but less consciously connected to thinking.

Performance: Unless otherwise stated in the text, this term will be used to mean the behaviours displayed under normal working conditions.

Professionalism: The set of values and behaviours associated with a respected and trusted position in society.

Reliability: The property of a measurement, combining discrimination and precision, indicating the likelihood that a repeat measurement would make the same distinctions.

Subjectivity: The property of judgement, combining stringency variation and taste variation, that results in differences of opinion.

Trait: An inferred stable characteristic underpinning performance.

Validity: The property of a measurement indicating that it reflects the intended construct or dimension.

Chapter 19
Authentic Assessment:
An Inquiry into the Assessment Process at Master's Degree Level

Simona Iftimescu
University of Bucharest, Romania

Romiță Iucu
University of Bucharest, Romania

Elena Marin
University of Bucharest, Romania

Mihaela Monica Stîngu
University of Bucharest, Romania

ABSTRACT

The purpose of this chapter is to analyze and discuss the concept of authentic assessment at Master's degree level. Firstly, this chapter attempts to provide a better understanding of the Master's program within the context of the Bologna system by providing a short historical perspective on the evolution of the Bologna process, as well as trying to identify the true beneficiaries. The chapter also addresses some of the challenges of the assessment process with two main themes: types and aim of the assessment process. Furthermore, the authors focus on the role of the authentic assessment, at a Master's degree level – as reflected by students' perception and correlated with its intended purpose. Drawing on the findings, the authors attempt to shape a description of what authentic assessment is and what it should be at Master's degree level.

INTRODUCTION

The Higher Education reform process is an ongoing process, linked to the development of an international education system within a competitive global society. The aim of the Bologna Process is not to harmonize national educational systems, it is about providing tools to connect them. The main goal is

DOI: 10.4018/978-1-5225-0531-0.ch019

to allow the diversity of national systems to be maintained, while the European Higher Education Area (EHEA) improves transparency between higher education systems, as well as implements tools to facilitate recognition of degrees and academic qualifications, mobility, and exchanges between institutions.

In order to meet the EHEA goals, the universities' mission is to support individuals, by providing them with high quality learning experiences that will enable them to be capable of performing meaningful tasks in the real world. To do so, the university has to be able to evaluate to which extent students acquire a basic level of knowledge and skill in a certain field.

Nevertheless, to keep with the students' centered learning approach, the assessment process has to provide unique experiences that give them the possibility to demonstrate competences. Authentic assessment provides students with the opportunity to perform real-world tasks that demonstrate meaningful application of essential knowledge and skills.

The chapter attempts to provide a better understanding of the Master's program in the Bologna system by providing a short historical perspective on the evolution of the Bologna process, as well as trying to identify the true beneficiaries of a Master's program taking into account that the development of the Bologna process serves the purpose of diversification of higher education. The diversification of higher education is necessary in order to meet the European labor market needs and to heterogeneously increase student population.

Furthermore, we focus on the role of the authentic assessment, at a Master's degree level – as reflected by students' perception and correlated with its intended purpose. By developing this 'meta-assessment', we aim to reveal how relevant the Master's program is for the students and to make inferences on whether the modernization of Higher Education should be reflected in further restructuring of the master's program, in a manner which would better answer the Master's students' needs.

BACKGROUND

A Historical Perspective on the Bologna Process

The Bologna Process is meant to provide a new model of international governance and policy-making in the field of higher education and its main purpose is to engage students, higher education institutions, stakeholders, and public authorities in debate over a common project. This common project aims to the development of new and comprehensive education system that will allow students to choose from a wide and transparent range of high-quality courses and benefit from smooth recognition procedures both within and between national higher education systems.

The transformation of higher education systems and institutions in all developed countries in recent years has been driven by a series of meetings of ministers responsible for higher education at which policy decisions have been made in order to establish a European Higher Education Area (EHEA).

EHEA was launched in March 2010 and among its main objectives was ensuring the development of more comparable, compatible and coherent systems of higher education across Europe. It also targets the concept of teaching methods which focus on the student's learning process and the importance of students' mobility, especially on the subject of increasing mobility and recognition of European university degrees.

In the most recent ministerial meeting, The Yerevan Ministerial Conference, 47 countries with different political, cultural and academic traditions cooperated on the basis of open dialogue, shared goals and common commitments to create a new reform of our higher education systems. According to the

Figure 1. Bologna's Ministerial Conference

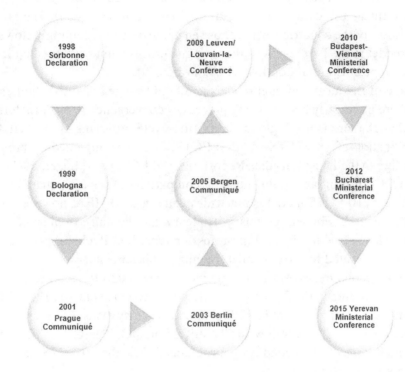

Yerevan Communiqué, the stress was put on enhancing the quality and relevance of learning and teaching, developing more effective policies for the recognition of credits gained abroad, of qualifications for academic and professional purposes, and of prior learning, fostering the employability of graduates throughout their working lives, and making the educational systems more inclusive. But, in order to achieve the goals mentioned above, a series of Ministerial meetings, starting from 1998 till 2015, helped mapping the EHEA as presented in Figure 1.

Since the Berlin Communiqué of 19 September 2003, the Bologna process covers three cycles of studies (Bologna Process, 2003): Bachelor, Master and now PhD cycles. For each cycle, the Bologna process provides the European Higher Education Area descriptors for the level of competences to be reached. For each cycle, there is a corresponding level of competences to be defined as learning outcome. Even though, at present, the Bologna system is considered by most stakeholders as the structural landmark of higher education studies (bachelor, master's and doctorate) […] we cannot ignore the fact that the main goal of the Bologna Process is not the restructuring of studies, but the differentiation among the levels of qualification, in correlation with the levels of complexity of the competences developed (Iucu, 2010).

The Implementation of the Bologna Three-Cycle System

The implementation of the Bologna three-cycle system has been an important goal of the Bologna Process and therefore it has been addressed in all the reports prepared for the Bologna Ministerial summits mentioned above. Since 2012, the data for this indicator are collected by Eurostat and according to the latest released publication that gives a statistical overview on the Bologna process, there are 19 other systems that have progressed in the implementation of the Bologna model, apart from the 11 systems which already had 100% Bologna structure in 2009 (Bulgaria, Cyprus, Denmark, Ireland, Iceland, Lithuania, Latvia, Norway, Turkey, Georgia, Kazakhstan). The greatest progress was registered in some of the countries which chose an unhurried and seemingly slower step-by-step implementation model in the first stages of the Bologna process, but have sped up implementation in recent years (European Commission/EACEA/Eurydice, 2015).

Regarding some of the most common models and credit ranges of ECTS that can be found in the First Cycle, there has clearly been a strong process of convergence in the structure of first cycle programs, even though there is no single model of first-cycle programs in the EHEA. Most countries have a combination of 180 ECTS and 240 ECTS, often accompanied by programs of other durations. According to the latest Eurydice Report, the 180 ECTS workload model is still the most widespread, with 58% of programs following it in comparison to the 37% share of the 240 ECTS workload model. The 210 ECTS model is not widespread in the EHEA, however, it is significant in five countries (Denmark, Finland, Germany, Hungary, and Poland). In most of these countries, the 210 ECTS workload structure is used in professional/applied Bachelor programs where up to 30 ECTS credits are allocated for professional training or placements.

Moreover, in the Second cycle (Master) some models are found to be more popular within the European context. According to the Eurydice report, in the second cycle, the 120 ECTS model is by far the most widespread, being present in 43 higher education systems. On average, in the EHEA, 65% of all second cycle programs follow the 120 ECTS model. The 60-75 ECTS model is used for 16% of programs, 13% of all second cycle programs follow the 90 ECTS model, while 6% of programs have another duration.

The use of ECTS in doctoral studies has also been growing over time. In 2014, 21 systems used ECTS throughout doctoral studies and an additional 14 countries for taught elements only. Twelve countries do not use ECTS in third-cycle programs (European Commission/EACEA/Eurydice, 2015).

In Romania, the most widespread model for Bachelor's level is the 180 ECTS, followed by the 240 ECTS and 210 ECTS, whereas at a Master's level the 120 ECTS is the most widespread, followed by the 90 ECTS model. Neither the 60 -75 ECTS model, nor other models and credit ranges of ECTS are present in the Romanian education system.

In order to support the development of a system of differentiation among the levels of qualification, the role of a Master's program is to provide Master's students with diverse learning opportunities, which allow them to integrate knowledge, handle complexity, formulate judgements and communicate their conclusions to an expert and to a non-expert audience. Moreover, students with a Master's degree will have the learning skills needed to pursue further studies or research in a largely self-directed, autonomous manner (The Bologna Process. Conference on Master-level Degrees, 2003).

Furthermore, as a consequence of trying to develop a general and comprehensive higher education system, the concept of internationalization of Higher Education started to take shape. According to the Organization for Economic Cooperation and Development (OECD), one of the main goals of internationalized higher education is to provide the most relevant education to students, who will be the citizens, entrepreneurs and scientists of tomorrow. Internationalization is not an end in itself, but a driver for change and improvement – it should help generate the skills required in the 21st century, spur on innovation, and create alternatives while, ultimately, fostering job creation (OECD, 2012).

Who Are the True Beneficiaries of a Master's Degree Program?

University plays an important role in preparing truly global citizens who can enter the labor market and contribute to the developing of new and innovative projects that can boost the economy. Regarding the beneficiaries of a Master's program, at the first level we can mention the students as main beneficiaries, and then, as students exit academia, the labor market.

The paradigm stating that students must be seen as main beneficiaries of the education system led to an ongoing process of education reform, that could meet students' needs. Even though it became popular in the 21st century, the concept of *student-centered learning (SCL)* was initially developed during the second half of the twentieth century, when theories of constructivism and constructionism gained popularity, the origins of which lie within the Piagetian theory that stated that:

Individuals' cognitive schemas allow them to establish an orderliness and predictability in their experiential worlds. When experience does not fit with the individual's schemas, a cognitive disequilibrium results, which triggers the learning process. This disequilibrium leads to adaptation. Reflection on successful adoptive operations leads to new or modified concepts, contributing to re-equilibrium. (MacLellan et al, 2004, p. 254)

Having as starting point the Piagetian theory, the concept of student centered learning was seen as one of the possible pedagogical approaches for higher education. According to Collins & O'Brien (2003, cit. in Froyd & Simpson, 2008), *student - centered learning* is an instructional approach in which students influence the content, activities, materials, and pace of learning. This learning model places the student (learner) in the center of the learning process. The instructor provides students with opportunities to learn independently and from one another and coaches them in the skills they need to do so effectively. The SCL approach includes such techniques as substituting active learning experiences for lectures, assigning open-ended problems, and problems requiring critical or creative thinking that cannot be solved by following text examples, involving students in simulations and role plays, and using self-paced and/or cooperative (team-based) learning (Collins &O'Brien, 2003, cit. in Froyd & Simpson, 2008).

At the European level, at The Leuven/Louvain-la-Neuve Ministerial Communiqué, it was attested that the European higher education also faces the major challenge and the ensuing opportunities of globalization and accelerated technological developments with new providers, new learners and new types of learning. Student-centered learning and mobility will help students develop the competences they need in a changing labor market and will empower them to become active and responsible citizens (Bologna Process, 2009).

The philosophy that the student is at the heart of the learning process led to the restructuring of the higher education system, building a more flexible curricula and alternative learning paths in order to satisfy students' educational needs and provide more open access to higher education programs. Master's students will have the opportunity to analyze contemporary issues and practices and will develop a critical understanding of research methods and methodologies.

When dealing with the second cycle of the Bologna process, the internationalization of higher education helped at the implementation of joint Master's programs. This programs, at the European level, should be developed to promote intra-European cooperation and attract talented students and researchers from other continents to study and work in Europe. Particular attention must be paid to solving recognition problems related to joint degrees (The Bologna Process. Conference on Master-level Degrees, 2003).

Also, Master's programs can provide students with a supportive, stimulating environment by connecting them with a strong community than can facilitate their transition from academia to the labor market, where they can apply the gained knowledge and start building a workforce. Furthermore, for HE institutions to provide a supportive and stimulating environment, they need to define or redefine their roles in what teaching, learning and assessment at Master's degree level are concerned and in accordance with its beneficiaries' needs and expectations.

AUTHENTIC ASSESSMENT

The Role of Assessment in a Master's Degree Program

The assessment process - along with teaching and learning, in higher education in general, and at Master's degree level in particular, has changed over the last few years. Therefore, the Bologna Process introduced significant changes with regard to the processes of teaching, learning and also assessment (Pereira et al, 2015), with a more focused approach on student-centered learning.

As more students enter universities than ever before, traditional forms of teaching, learning and assessment are under increasing pressure to change due to a more diverse student profile, globalization, and flexibility in modes of delivery, marketization of higher education, funding and accountability (Gurnam & Chan Yuen, 2013).

Therefore, assessment at Master's degree level is a challenging and complex process both for teachers and students. The complexity of the process is determined by the value attributed to it by different criteria and standards, while the challenges encountered in this process may be determined by different understandings of the purpose and validity of assessment in a Master's degree program by the different actors involved (teachers, students, managers, quality assurance committees, employers etc.).

At European level, in 2008 OECD launched the Assessment of Higher Education Learning Outcomes feasibility study (AHELO), an initiative with the objective to assess whether it is possible to develop international measures of learning outcomes in higher education. The purpose of AHELO was to see whether it is practically and scientifically feasible to assess what students in higher education know and can do upon graduation within and across diverse contexts in a valid and internationally comparable way (Tremblay, Lalancette & Roseveare, 2012). Results suggested that for the generic skills strand, the approach adopted did not involve a consultative process sufficient enough to reach an international agreement on the appropriateness of the instrument content, while for the two discipline-based instruments, agreement was reached by participating stakeholders and experts on frameworks and selected learning outcomes, providing evidence of content validity for each of these two instruments (OECD, 2013). Thus, the contents of a Master's degree program might be multidimensional and complex and, consequently, assessment is also a complex and challenging process.

At national level, students' assessment in higher education is accomplished through periodic examinations organized for each subject in the curricula and it can be performed in the form of oral examination, written papers and/or practical examinations as well as project presentations. In general, there are two regular examination sessions for the students during each academic year. The first examination session is organized at the end of an academic semester, while the second examination session is organized for the students that did not attain or failed one or more subjects' examinations during the regular examination sessions.

Due to the complexity of factors involved, in this part of our chapter we want to particularly focus on the challenges of the assessment process within Master's degree programs with two main themes: types of assessment and the aim of the assessment process. Thus, we will focus on the way the aspects mentioned before are connected and influence each other, as summarized in Figure 3.

For the purpose of this chapter, we will focus our analysis on two main types of assessment: summative and formative. In what the aim of assessment within Master's degree programs is concerned, we will approach assessment from several different perspectives: assessment as a hierarchical tool, assessment as a professional development tool, assessment as a reflective tool, assessment as a motivation tool, and assessment as a feedback tool. Furthermore, the perspective from which we are going to analyze and approach this topic is the one of competency-based assessment. As mentioned at the beginning of our chapter, EHEA proposed the adoption of the ECTS system. Taking this in consideration, the implementation of ECTS determines a shift of paradigm in teaching, learning and assessment in higher education based on competencies, rather than upon subjects and themes of a Master's degree program. Competency-based assessment has not only aims to improve comprehensive or practical learning (Ion & Cano, 2011), but also aims to support professional development of students and give them proper skills they need to adapt in a constantly changing labor market. Considering this, we want to include it in the broader concept of authentic assessment. Authentic assessment is usually discussed in connection to performance measurement which reflects the student's learning, achievement, motivation, and attitudes towards specific learning activities (Callison, 1998). According to Wiggins (1998), authentic assessment is realistic, it requires judgment and innovation, it replicates or simulates real-life contexts, and it allows opportunities to practice and receive feedback in order to refine performances and products. This type of assessment appears to be described through assessment techniques, including portfolios, oral interviews, story or text retelling, writing samples, projects/ exhibitions, experiments/ demonstrations, constructed-response items, teachers' observations (1996, O'Malley and Pierce, cit. in Callison 1998).

As many educationalists have pointed out, the past years have shown a tendency in assessment shifting from summative, product-oriented assessment to formative, process-oriented assessment (Qvortrup and Keiding, 2015). While summative assessment is considered to be a judgement which encapsulates all the evidence up to a given point, for an assessment to be formative, it requires feedback and an indication of how the work can be improved to reach the required standard (Taras, 2005). Without trying to put the label of „good" and „bad" on the types of assessment mentioned before (summative, formative), we will try to analyze the different aims which a specific type of assessment might address.

In what summative assessment is concerned, we can state that one of its main aims is to measures student achievement and to make a hierarchy between students. Therefore, this type of assessment can be linked with the concept of high-stakes assessment where the result of summative assessment can affect the student's future in some way (Trotter, 2006). Elton and Johnson (2002, cit. in Man Sze Lau, 2015) identify that assessment in higher education has been focusing for far too long on summative assessment of students via examinations, essays or reports. Taking this in consideration, we may argue that a summative-only approach to assessment at Master's degree level can lead to some challenges regarding student perception on learning and might determine students to take a more 'surface' approach towards learning. Another challenge this approach might encounter is in what concerns the validity to meet employability agendas (Price et al. 2011, cit. in Flores et al. 2015). Nevertheless, we cannot deny the value added by summative assessment in establishing performance standards in higher education in general and at Master's degree level in particular. In order to overcome some of the challenges mentioned before, we need to focus on the key aspect required for assessment to contribute towards students' learning, namely that summative and formative assessment not only need to be connected with each other, but assessment as a whole need to be connected with the overall learning and teaching.

Ayala et al. (2008) consider that formative assessment leads to increased learning, but the main challenge is how these formative assessments are designed, developed, embedded, and eventually implemented by teachers. Therefore, in order to better understand the value of formative assessment, we need to focus on some of the aims that this approach might follow.

Although formative assessment can be designed in many different ways to accommodate different aims, the main aim is to generate feedback on students' performance in order to improve learning (Falchikov 2005; Sadler 1998, cit. in Weurlander, 2012). The main function of feedback is that it can prompt deeper learning and for that to happen, it is essential to install a feedback process that strengthens the reflective process and indicates things to build on. Sadler (1989) argues that in order to take effective action and to improve, students need to be able to evaluate their own learning and so develop skills in self-assessment.

Taking this into consideration, an adjacent aim of formative assessment can be to make students reflect upon both their learning outcomes and process. Without getting into the theory of reflection as practice in higher education, we need to stress the fact that reflective practice in higher education may tend to be superficial unless it is approached in a consistent and systematic way (Orland-Barak, 2005, cit in Ryan & Ryan, 2013). Therefore, a caution that needs to be taken into consideration is the 'overuse' of reflection. Following similar lines, we can argue that this approach can lead to the situation in which teachers 'pay more attention to the outcomes of reflection rather than to the process itself' (Mena Marcos, Sánchez Miguel & Tillema, 2009, p.13). One way to meet this challenge is by constantly assessing both the needs and the learning styles of the students which may fit this kind of approach. Academic reflection involves a conscious and stated purpose (Moon, 2006) and, as it is generally linked to assessment or professional development, needs to show evidence of learning and developing professional knowledge.

Building on that, next we want to focus on the professional development aim of both summative and formative assessments. Being an experienced and successful practitioner requires both the ability to seek out relevant knowledge and the skills to apply that knowledge in the appropriate way to real situations and, therefore, higher education institutions need to assess not only cognitive knowledge, but also the social and cultural knowledge that is an essential characteristic of a successful practitioner (Harvey & Norman, 2007). As mentioned before, regarding the beneficiaries of a Master's degree program, we can mention both the students and the labor market. For this reason, assessment in Master's degree programs is required to prove to the appropriate external bodies and employers, that the postgraduate students have the necessary competencies for the labor market. Nevertheless, Master's students are evaluated according both to professional competences and their research competences. As a consequence of the paradigm change in higher education through the Bologna process, the significance of research competencies for higher education postgraduates has decreased in favor of professional competencies. This approach might also come as an answer to the many complaints that higher education lacks practical relevance and application orientation. Nevertheless, Zlatkin-Troitschanskaia et al. (2015, p. 400) conclude that

competency assessments in higher education should also take into account interpersonal and professional individual development to gather empirical evidence on the assumed trade-off between general democratic societal and situational - specific requirements.

Therefore, because in a postgraduate program the area of study might be multidimensional and complex, a justifiable approach might be to first narrow down the assessment to key cognitive components of competency, such as job-related skills and knowledge, and only afterwards to assess the more complex components of competency. To summarize, in what professional development as an aim of assessment is concerned, Berlak (1992, p. 25, cit. in Ashford-Rowe, 2014) considers that relevance of assessment in this context is 'the degree to which the assessment is related to what the learner is being prepared to do beyond the particular assessment setting'.

Another aim of both summative and formative assessments is student motivation for learning. For example, as shown in Figure 2, Cauley & McMillan (2010) put student motivation at the core of formative assessment.

In this context, summative assessment can be seen as an extrinsic motivation tool, whilst intrinsic motivation can be a formative assessment tool. Biggs (1999) and Light & Cox (2001) cit. in Trotter (2006) consider that extrinsic motivation might be considered as an unconvincing part of higher education, while intrinsic motivation (love of learning and intellectual development) is generally considered to be more valuable, driving deep learning and the best academic work. Nevertheless, assessment can be used as a motivational tool both for students who are performance-goal oriented and are focused on how teachers judge their performance and for those who are mastery-goal oriented and 'focus on learning and meeting standards' (Cauley & McMillan, 2010, p.3), as opposed to students who focus on comparison among themselves.

Figure 2. Formative assessment cycle (Cauley & McMillan, 2010)

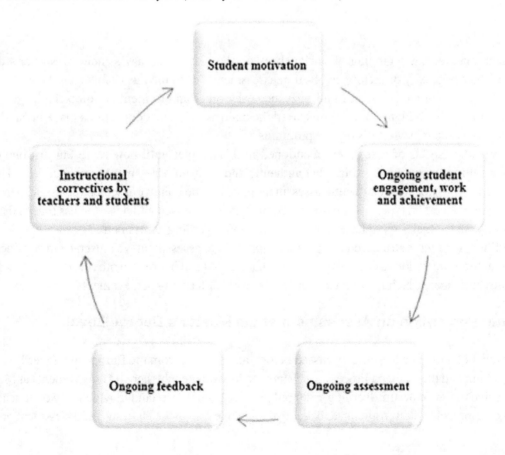

Figure 3. Assessment in Master's Degree programs

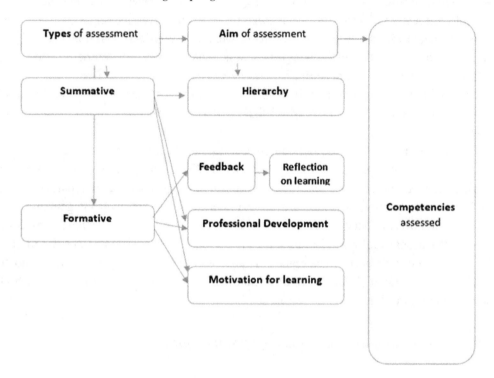

As mentioned at the beginning of our analysis on the role of the assessment in Master's degree programs, the complexity of factors involved in assessment determined us to focus on the way various aspects of assessment are connected and influence each other and to identify some challenges of the different approaches. In Figure 3, we synthesized the main aspects and connections made in our discussion about assessment in Master's degree programs.

However, the aspects of assessment mentioned in this chapter until now represent just one of the many views that can be developed in what authentic and relevant assessment are concerned. The key points in any discussion about authentic assessment must be: the context in which the assessment takes place, the aims of certain types of assessment, competencies assessed and nevertheless the needs of the students assessed, which should be a part of any decision regarding assessment.

In addition, for a more structured and practical approach to assessment we must take in consideration the fact that there are various assessment methods that can be used in order to provide different measures of learning outcomes, which may indicate different levels of learning achievements.

Students Perception on Assessment at the Master's Degree Level

In the context of authentic learning discussed before, and starting from the European Higher Education Area paradigm and the Bologna Process, we wanted to investigate whether and how students at Master's level perceive the shift towards learning-centered practices and understand in which way their academic experience approaches skills training, enhancing their active role in the learning and assessment process.

Therefore, aiming to identify the students' understanding of the purpose and validity of assessment in a Master's degree program, we ran three focus groups for different Master's programs and also used input gathered through an online questionnaire from students (a total of 30 students) in two other programs within the Department of Educational Sciences, Faculty of Psychology and Educational Sciences at the University of Bucharest in Romania. The Department is currently running a number of 12 Masters' programs, comprising a total average of 300 students, whose profiles vary from recent graduates, young professionals, to individuals with 5+ years of professional experience and who are looking for a shift in their careers, or who are compelled to pursue further specialization given the increasing competition on the labor market. The majority of those enrolled in a Master's course also have full-time jobs and attend the Master's classes in the evening.

The evaluation criteria usually comprise different percentages making up for the final grade, and they include attendance (sometimes a minimum percentage is a prerequisite for entering the final exam), active participation in class (which could be considered as part of formative assessment), an individual or group project or research, an oral presentation, a written exam, or a portfolio, which appears to be the main instrument used for assessment. However, the relevance of the portfolio is sometimes debatable, as students argue that the tasks require only research based on few sources and then reproducing the information. In their opinion, there is a lack of innovation in building the assessment tasks and that is why, using Bloom's taxonomy (1956), it appears that the portfolio as an assessment method only manages to develop synthesis competences and not creative ones.

The prerequisites and structure of assessment are usually presented at the beginning of the term by most of the teachers, but the specific criteria and the elements comprised in the evaluation (the specific tasks) are often changed throughout the term. One important aspect is that the course presentation and syllabi are not always shared with students during the first class. It becomes obvious from the answers we gathered that Master's students want to be more involved in decisions regarding the course structure and assessment process, as they demand more predictability in organizing their work-load and setting their own learning objectives. This tendency is reflected across the board, as at Master's level there seems to be a change in the students' perception about assessment and a shift in responsibility. If at Bachelor's level the students act mostly as recipients of information, following the specific guidelines provided by the teachers, at Master's level, students take on more responsibility and tend to use their teachers' recommendations as a starting point in building a more individualized educational path. They appreciate assessment done in an engaging manner and a relaxed atmosphere, allowing for the valorization of each individual, or, how one student summarizes: `letting students know that what they say is not necessarily wrong, but that there is another perspective, another way of thinking; and this gives you courage to think beyond what you thought you knew and accept someone else's opinion'. However, Master's students find it challenging sometimes to reach a balance between the need to express their own opinions, professional expertise and practical experience and some teachers' tendency to constantly return to theoretical aspects, which they tend to prioritize. Students' perception indicates there is an 80%-20% split between theory and practice and, from our conversations, it became obvious that rote learning and an approach based exclusively on the theoretical content do not respond to the learners' needs and expectations.

While looking to understand the criteria, instruments, content, and context of the assessment, we also have to look at a systemic level, in order to understand the premises for a certain approach to the assessment process. First, when discussing public higher education in Romania, it is important to note that the State uses a per capita approach to financing higher education institutions – an aspect which could influence both the admission process and assessment leading to keeping the enrolment from one academic year to the next one, and implicitly the number of places approved on a Master's course for the upcoming academic year. This is also reflected in students' perception about the overall assessment process, as the financing context is believed to have an influence on the assessment's more flexible terms, shaped in such a way that would allow a greater number of students to pass onto the next year and graduate. Second, the premise and structure of the Bologna system itself may call for further reconsideration, as the purpose of the Master's program is yet to be defined in clearer terms and to prove its relevance for the labor market. This is supported by students who say they applied for a Master's program looking for further specialization and who now appear to be rather reticent to some courses which do not respond directly to their interest.

Therefore, when discussing about assessment as a *professional development tool*, or guiding the educational process towards building and validating the academic and professional competences which students and future graduates will use as they enter the labor market, the students' perception is that the Master's certification itself holds little if no value and relevance for the labor market. However, the assessment process is seen as an important component for personal and professional development and, beyond its contribution to cognitive, emotional, affective and attitudinal acquisitions, they believe the main purpose of assessment is to build competencies. Asked whether they believe the competences acquired and assessed throughout a Master's program can actually be translated into their professional activities, the majority agreed that the courses provide them with a new, different perspective and have enabled them to integrate it in their work, leading to an overall improvement. Despite their answer, it may be interesting to note that students encounter difficulties when asked to name specific competencies their work would require, or the ones they expect to acquire at the end of a course, and mostly associate learning with knowing specific content. Nonetheless, the majority did mention general and transferable competences, acquired and developed mostly through the techniques employed in the assessment process, for example multi-tasking, time management, oral presentation, communication, critical thinking, or working in teams. The importance of the assessment process is also underlined in relation to academic development, as the assessment process is believed to contribute to developing competencies for organizing their research, better structuring of the information and knowledge acquired through specific courses and the students consider it helps them better prepare for the final Master's dissertation, also providing the instruments, knowledge and work ethic necessary for taking on a project at a larger scale. One aspect which could further contribute to these would be teacher's feedback as part of the assessment process, provided, unfortunately, less frequently than expected.

The importance of the teacher's role is also reinforced by the Master's students' perception of assessment as a *hierarchical tool*, despite their increased independence in relation to the educational process. Given the less standardized structure and content of the assessment, which they do prefer in lieu of a more standardized type, students made reference to an assessment bias reflected in what they perceive as different assessment standards: 'some pass the exam without having fulfilled the criteria (i.e. attendance prerequisites, active participation in classes etc.), with a lower grade, but pass it, nevertheless'. This perceived bias might have led most students to consider the assessment at Master's level as being `more superficial, not thorough enough`. While the results of the assessment (in terms of grades) are important to some students especially because of the student scholarship for which they could qualify if they are to be in the top percentile of their cohort, for others being proud of the effort put into their work sometimes counts more; however, there is an implied expectation for their work to be rewarded accordingly, assessment also being considered a strong *motivational tool*.

The motivational component of assessment is mentioned not only in relation to the outcome, but also in relation to the process, which facilitates peer-learning and peer-assessment, as Master's students consider both to be very important and relevant for their academic and professional development. Oral presentations and group projects allow students to interact with their peers, who usually work in a similar field, and allow them to learn from each other's experience and also exchange best practices. Thus, the Master's students tend to form a type of academic and professional community, which provides knowledge, information and networking, aiding them further in their professional life. Peer assessment, described by Topping (2009, cit. in Lladó et. al, 2014), as 'an arrangement for learners to consider and specify the level, value, or quality of a product or performance of other equal-status learners', is not mentioned as an institutionalized practice, but rather as an informal process, mainly carried on through feedback and validation of status. Next to teacher and peer assessment, assessment is also seen as a *reflective tool*. Self-assessment becomes a way for the students to reflect on what they have acquired during a course and how they can use it in their personal and professional lives: `it is important to know how much we *really* know`.

Without attempting a generalization based solely on these findings, but reading them through the theoretical lens provided by the first part of the chapter and placing them in context, we tried to identify a potential way to redefine authentic assessment in a way that would be more relevant for both students and teachers, and that would provide a foundation for future research in this field.

SOLUTIONS AND RECOMMENDATIONS

Drawing on the findings and attempting to shape a description of what authentic assessment is, we would first have to start from the relation between the learning content and the assessment process. An authentic and useful assessment depends on the choice of a relevant learning topic and its presentation, and it is important to place it in a real-life context, in which students are encouraged to share their professional experience. Then, the expectations and the assessment criteria should be clearly set and presented at the beginning of the term, after also being discussed with the students. The assessment process should comprise relevant practical applications of the theoretical aspects, built into a comprehensive team project or portfolio that would encompass what was taught and the students' practical experience, shared with peers in an interactive, oral presentation, which would facilitate peer-learning. In what projects and portfolios are concerned, for them to fulfill their purpose, and for feedback to be useful and relevant for students, it needs to go alongside with the entire process of developing these types of products. Therefore, a better and more profound understanding of the defining traits of these types of methods (e.g. projects, portfolios) needs to be taken in consideration when developing authentic assessment processes. Finally, the authentic assessment's defining trait and the key to an authentic assessment process, appears to be the teacher's feedback, ultimately contributing to the students' self-assessment and to reshaping their individual learning objectives. The context leading to an authentic assessment is described in Figure 4.

Thus, the authentic assessment at Master's level cannot be solely regarded as collecting information on student learning and performance based on different sources of evidence (Callison, 1998), but rather as a collaborative process between the teacher and the student, providing the context for sharing experience and peer learning and offering feedback as to enhance the formative purpose of assessment. On the other hand, even though students require feedback and acknowledge its importance, they do not always see it as an opportunity to identify areas of improvement, but rather a way to predict or justify the final

Figure 4. A context for authentic assessment

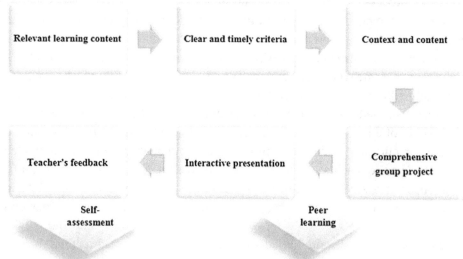

grade they receive. Our investigation indicates there is no clear differentiation between formative and summative assessment in students' perception, the majority associating assessment with activities which are specifically evaluated and graded. Therefore, the assessment would also have to be better described to students, as to help them benefit more of the process itself. Also, as a result of the ECTS system's implementation, the competencies expected to be attained and/or developed throughout a course should be communicated, agreed upon, defined in detail for students to understand their real purpose and connected to competencies required on the labor market, in order to offer students specific guidelines and more clarity on the overall process.

Consequently, in order to enhance authentic assessment, teachers should also focus on the whole educational experience that also includes teaching and learning. In order to have a relevant and useful assessment for their students, teachers need to firstly develop contexts in which competencies are formed and developed and that allow students to practice and receive feedback in order to refine their performances and/or products. Therefore, for an assessment to be authentic it needs not only to be coherent within itself (types, aims, competencies), but also with the overall teaching and learning approaches, which also need to be developed through a competency-based approach.

FUTURE RESEARCH

It appears these initial findings could only scratch the surface of the very complex field of assessment, even more so when we look at it from an integrated perspective, as a triad - together with teaching and learning. Future research could focus on expanding the subject base, first to a greater number of the student population at departmental level, but also looking at Science departments, for example, in order to allow for comparisons and more relevant generalizations. Another perspective which would offer interesting grounds for comparison would be expanding research to similar Master's programs in other European countries, better understanding the interaction and reciprocal influence between assessment, teaching and learning and how, in turn, these influence students and future graduates at their entry on the labor market. Also, connecting research on assessment to data on the labor market could provide a better image on the higher education system's efficiency and effectiveness and allow for input from other relevant stakeholders.

Carrying research on this topic also has a potential to draw attention on the wider system, beyond specific departments or even specific national higher education systems. It brings into debate the role of the Master's cycle itself within the Bologna Process, as well as the need to redefine the balance between nowadays' dominantly academic and research-oriented structure of the Master's program and its professional relevance. Finally, all these could provide grounds to call for a deeper analysis and understanding of the current European higher education overall structure and context, and, potentially, for further restructuring in an attempt to better answer the students' and the labor market's needs.

CONCLUSION

Starting from an overview of the evolution of the Bologna Process and the implementation of the Bologna three-cycle system, we looked into a question which still remains open-ended: who are the true beneficiaries of a Master's degree program? Our option for analyzing this cycle of study was influenced by our concern as practitioners in the field of higher education that the Master's cycle is perceived as falling short of its promise within the Bologna system. We looked into the types and aims of the assessment process, as well as into its role in a Master's degree program, and aimed at starting a conversation about authentic assessment with its direct beneficiaries, the students, deriving from a framework shaped by student-centered learning and competency-based assessment. We did so by running several focus-groups within the Department of Educational Sciences at the Faculty of Psychology and Educational Sciences within the University of Bucharest, investigating how assessment is carried out and what is the students' perception on the process.

Our investigation offered a perspective on assessment practices and techniques at Master's level, and provided us with a better understanding of the different roles assessment can take as a hierarchical, motivational, reflective, or professional development tool. While Master's students appear more independent in shaping their own educational objectives, they still put a great emphasis on traditional grading and there is an unclear understanding of the forms and role of summative and formative assessments. Students found the assessment process to be motivational, especially when it came to recognition from peers and validation of status, and put emphasis on its reflective role, illustrated through self-assessment. While they agree to an extent with the assessment's role in their professional development, Master's students seem to be unsure of which specific competences are developed through a course or a Master's program, focusing more on general, transferable competences, mostly enhanced by the type of assessment technique employed throughout a course.

Students' responses offered us some guidelines on how to further investigate these aspects and helped us shape a wider context for authentic assessment, which appears to be based on several very important pillars: the choice of relevant learning content, communication and collaboration between teacher and students in setting the assessment criteria, practical applications of theoretical aspects, using a comprehensive team project or portfolio presented in front of their colleagues, which would facilitate peer-learning. A very important aspect in the process is the teacher's feedback, which, even though is still mostly seen as an indication on their final grade and less as an input in their learning process, contributes significantly to the students' self-assessment.

These findings underlined the importance of regarding the authentic assessment not as an isolated process, but rather as an essential part of a triad, together with teaching and learning. Also, they brought to question the need to start from a competency-based approach in teaching and learning, which will later also be reflected in assessment, ensuring more coherence to the overall process.

Thus, we can argue that there are some key aspects that academics should take into consideration in what authentic assessment is concerned: shifting from a 'learning outcomes' approach to competency based assessment; developing key competencies in an integrated manner, rather than in decontextualized, standalone courses, and approach assessment in a more flexible and integrated way together with teaching and learning. Also, authentic assessment redefines the role of the teacher, who should no longer be regarded as solely an external assessor of the final product delivered by the students, but an active participant in the process, encouraging a collaborative approach. All these bring about a change in the teaching process, as a `one-size-fits-all` approach is replaced by a more individualized one, where the content becomes relevant to the context and to the personal experience of the learner, where flexibility and adaptability become key words, and where the process of authentic assessment offers the teachers themselves feedback and valuable information, allowing them to constantly improve.

Therefore, authentic assessment triggers an array of changes in all areas of the teaching, learning and assessment processes. The students become more involved in their learning process and gain more awareness on its outcomes, the teachers become partners in this process and use the feedback to improve on their teaching, the different courses offered within a program of study become more coherent as a whole, the system becomes more easily adaptable to the current context, and the Master program in itself becomes more relevant for all the actors involved.

Finally, while the findings discussed in the chapter cannot call for generalizations, they open the way and provide guidelines to further research into authentic assessment, regarded in a more integrated way, alongside teaching and learning. Besides all these, however, the overarching challenge remains that at looking into the Master's degree role within the Bologna system, in an attempt to answer yet another open-ended question: is the Master's degree delivering on its promise?

REFERENCES

Ayala, C. C., Shavelson, R. J., Ruiz-Primo, M. A., Brandon, P. R., Yin, Y., Furtak, E. M., & Tomita, M. K. et al. (2008). From Formal Embedded Assessments to Reflective Lessons: The Development of Formative Assessment Studies. *Applied Measurement in Education, 21*(4), 315–334. doi:10.1080/08957340802347787

Ashford-Rowe, K., Herrington, J., & Brown, C. (2014). Establishing the critical elements that determine authentic assessment. *Assessment & Evaluation in Higher Education, 39*(2), 205–222. doi:10.1080/02602938.2013.819566

Callison, D. (1998). Authentic Assessment. *School Library Media Activities Monthly, 14*(5), 42–50.

Cauley, K. M., & McMillan, G. H. (2010). Formative Assessment Techniques to Support Student Motivation and Achievement. *The Clearing House: A Journal of Educational Strategies, Issues and Ideas, 83*(1), 1–6. doi:10.1080/00098650903267784

European Commission/EACEA/Eurydice. (2015). The European Higher Education[*Bologna Process Implementation Report*. Luxembourg: Publications Office of the European Union.]. *Area*, 2015.

European Commission/EACEA/Eurydice. (2014). *Modernization of Higher Education in Europe: Access, Retention and Employability*. Luxembourg: Publications Office of the European Union.

European Commission/EACEA/Eurydice. (2013). *European Commission Report to the European Commission on improving the quality of teaching and learning in Europe's higher education institutions.* Luxembourg: Publications Office of the European Union.

European Commission. (2009, April 28-29). *Communiqué of the Conference of European Ministers Responsible for Higher Education, Leuvenand Louvain-la-Neuve.* Retrieved from http://www.ehea.info/Uploads/Declarations/Leuven_Louvain-la Neuve_Communiqu%C3%A9_April_2009.pdf

Flores, M. A., Veiga Simão, A. M., Barros, A., & Pereira, D. (2015). Perceptions of effectiveness, fairness and feedback of assessment methods: A study in higher education. *Studies in Higher Education, 40*(9), 1523–1534. doi:10.1080/03075079.2014.881348

Fook, C. Y., & Sidhu, G. K. (2013). Assessment practices in higher education in United States. *Procedia: Social and Behavioral Sciences, 123*, 299–306. doi:10.1016/j.sbspro.2014.01.1427

Froyd, J., & Simpson, N. (2008). Student-centered learning addressing faculty questions about student centered learning. Proceedings of the Course, Curriculum, Labor, and Improvement Conference, 30(11).

Harvey, M., & Norman, L. (2007). Beyond competencies: What higher education assessment could offer the workplace and the practitioner-researcher? *Research in Post-Compulsory Education, 12*(3), 331–342. doi:10.1080/13596740701559779

Ion, G., & Cano, E. (2011). Assessment practices at Spanish universities: From a learning to a competencies approach. *Evaluation and Research in Education, 24*(3), 167–181. doi:10.1080/09500790.2011.610503

Iucu, R. (2010). Ten Years after Bologna: Towards a European Teacher Education Area. In O. Gassner, L. Kerger & M. Schratz (Ed.), Entep - The First Ten Years after Bologna (pp. 53-95). Bucharest, RO: EdituraUniversităţii din Bucureşti.

Man Sze Lau, A. (2015). 'Formative good, summative bad?' – A review of the dichotomy in assessment literature. *Journal of Further and Higher Education*. doi:10.1080/0309877X.2014.984600

Maclellan, E., & Soden, R. (2004). The Importance of Epistemic Cognition in Student-Centred Learning. *Instructional Science, 32*(3), 253–268. doi:10.1023/B:TRUC.0000024213.03972.ce

Marcos, J. J., M., , Sánchez Miguel, E., & Tillema, H. (2009). Teacher reflection on action: What is said (in research) and what is done (in teaching). *Reflective Practice, 10*(2), 191–204. doi:10.1080/14623940902786206

Moon, J. (2006). *Learning journals: A handbook for reflective practice and professional development.* London, UK: Routledge.

OECD. (2013). Assessment of Higher Education Learning Outcomes. Retrieved from www.oecd.org/edu/skills-beyond-school/AHELOFSReportVolume2.pdf

OECD. (2008). *Tertiary Education for the Knowledge Society.* OECD Publishing. doi:10.1787/9789264046535-en

Pereira, D., Flores, M. A., & Niklasson, L. (2015). Assessment revisited: A review of research in Assessment and Evaluation in Higher Education. *Assessment & Evaluation in Higher Education*, 1–25. doi:10.1080/02602938.2015.1055233

Planas Lladó, A., Soley, L. F., Fraguell Sansbelló, R. M., Pujolras, G. A., Planella, J. P., Roura-Pascual, N., & Moreno, L. M. et al. (2014). Student perceptions of peer assessment: An interdisciplinary study. *Assessment & Evaluation in Higher Education*, *39*(5), 592–610. doi:10.1080/02602938.2013.860077

Qvortrup, A., & Bering Keiding, T. (2015). Portfolio assessment: Production and reduction of complexity. *Assessment & Evaluation in Higher Education*, *40*(3), 407–419. doi:10.1080/02602938.2014.918087

Ryan, M., & Ryan, M. (2013). Theorising a model for teaching and assessing reflective learning in higher education. *Higher Education Research & Development*, *32*(2), 244–257. doi:10.1080/07294360.2012.661704

Sadler, D. R. (1989). Formative assessment and the design of instructional systems. *Instructional Science*, *18*(2), 119–144. doi:10.1007/BF00117714

Taras, M. (2005). Assessment – summative and formative – some theoretical reflections. *British Journal of Educational Studies*, *53*(4), 466–478. doi:10.1111/j.1467-8527.2005.00307.x

Tremblay, K., Lalancette, D., & Roseveare, D. (2012). Assessment of Higher Education Learning Outcomes. OECD. Retrieved from www.oecd.org/edu/skills-beyond-school/AHELOFSReportVolume1.pdf

Trotter, E. (2006). Student Perceptions of Continuous Summative Assessment. *Assessment & Evaluation in Higher Education*, *31*(5), 505–521. doi:10.1080/02602930600679506

Weurlander, M., Söderberg, M., Scheja, M., Hult, H., & Wernerson, A. (2012). Exploring Formative Assessment as a Tool for Learning: Students' Experiences of Different Methods of Formative Assessment. *Assessment & Evaluation in Higher Education*, *37*(6), 747–760. doi:10.1080/02602938.2011.572153

Wiggins, G. (1998). *Educative Assessment: Designing Assessments to Inform and Improve Student Performance.* San Francisco, CA: Jossey-Bass.

Zlatkin-Troitschanskaia, O., Shavelson, R.J., & Kuhn, C. (2015). The international state of research on measurement of competency in higher education. *Studies in Higher Education*, *40*(3), 393–411. doi:10.1080/03075079.2015.1004241

KEY TERMS AND DEFINITIONS

Authentic Assessment: An evaluation process that involves multiple types of performance measurement reflecting the student's learning, achievement, motivation, and attitudes.

Bologna Process: A European reform process aimed at creating the European Higher Education Area.

Competency-Based Assessment: Type of evaluation that is organized and developed around competencies, rather than topics or subjects.

ECTS (European Credit Transfer System): A credit system designed to make it easier for students to move between different countries.

Formative Assessment: A type of ongoing assessment that has the purpose to give feedback to students in order to improve their performance.

Ministerial Conference: Regular meetings of ministers from 47 member countries of the European Higher Education Arena (EHEA).

Summative Assessment: Type of assessment that focuses on *student learning* at the end of an instructional unit or course.

Transferable Competences: The knowledge, skills and attitudes that someone developed in various situations that can be used in many other situations.

Chapter 20
Beyond the Walls:
Project-Based Learning and Assessment in Higher Education

Catalina Ulrich
University of Bucharest, Romania

Lucian Ciolan
University of Bucharest, Romania

ABSTRACT

Main goal of the chapter is to focus on project based learning (PjBL) as an effective learning and assessment method effectively used in higher education. Chapter provides an understanding of Romanian higher education contextual challenges, current pedagogy trends and specific examples to support the idea that PjBL leads to the type of authentic learning needed for nowadays students. Theoretical framework and examples are enriched by reflections on undergraduate and master degree students' perceptions on learning process and learning outcomes.

INTRODUCTION

Traditionally, teaching and learning in higher education is dominantly focused on content, on the process of making an informed selection of most relevant and updated information, in the attempt to satisfy both epistemological routes of the disciplines and recent research advancement in the field. A new conditionality was brought into the scene by the needs of the qualifications from the perspective of job-related skills. A consistent movement in designing learning in higher education can be identified under the generic name of outcome-based education, changing somehow the focus from contents to learning achievements. A whole range of learning outcomes started to be defined and set as ground for higher education program design and delivery: standards, competences, qualifications etc. The "new managerialism" made its impact in conceiving the university degrees in terms of content, outcomes and assessment. One of the challenges of these two "waves" or perspectives in thinking higher education teaching and learning is the fact that pedagogy is somehow left behind, meaning that learning process through meaningful interaction among key actors was somehow taken for granted as happening if good quality structural conditions are in place (i.e. relevant content and well-defined outcomes).

DOI: 10.4018/978-1-5225-0531-0.ch020

TEACHING AND LEARNING IN HIGHER EDUCATION. CHANGES AND PARADOXES ANALYZED IN THE ROMANIAN CONTEXT

The need for more focus on learning experiences from the perspective of the new type of learners became more acute in the last years. Even when taking about more generic trends of higher education, such as internationalization, the Executive Agency for Higher Education, Research, Development and Innovation Funding in Romania highlights in a recent report (UEFISCDI, 2013) the specific aspects of teaching as pedagogy, learning environment and learning resources. According to the report, the above mentioned aspects are connected to knowledge-society requirements and scientific evidence. "Curriculum review and course content updating have to be accompanied by an extensive reconsideration of the pedagogy applied in the teaching and learning process. In the era of global communication and unlimited access to knowledge in the virtual space, the traditional instruction paradigm (transfer of knowledge) is more and more replaced by a new model: the learning paradigm based on a holistic approach of all the elements and drivers which contribute to the construction of knowledge and skills through a student centered process (Barr &Tagg, 1995). Universities create a favorable learning environment with wide access to the newest learning resources and to the cutting-edge knowledge and with a more or less individual guidance of the students in their effort to achieve best learning outcomes". (2013, p. 70).

Not only students are changing, as the new generations of digital natives are coming into higher education, but academic staff is changing as well, both in terms of professional identity (see, for instance, Kember & Kwan, 2000; Henard & Leprince-Ringuet, 2011), and in terms of the pedagogy they employ for creating authentic learning experiences (Jenkins et. al. 2003; Hannon, 2009; Herrington & Oliver, 2000; Herrington, 2006).

Quality teaching became an issue of significant importance as the landscape of higher education has been facing continuous changes. The student body has considerably expanded and diversified, both socially and geographically. New students call for new teaching methods. Modern technologies have entered the classroom, this modifying the nature of interaction between students and professors. (Henard & Leprince-Ringuet, 2011, p. 3).

But how are the teaching and learning practices changing in higher education in Romania under all these new and challenging local and international circumstances? How is students' participation seen and encouraged in the daily life of the organization and how they take ownership of their own learning?

Although the system-level and institutional changes are numerous and significant in nature, there are many learning paradoxes, situating higher education reforms in Romania on the edge between solid achievements and (temporary) failures: impact of quality assurance mechanisms on quality of learning and research, the correlation between qualifications framework and level of employment etc.

Some of the key challenges of teaching and learning today in our higher education institutions are briefly described below. Although they are very much visible in Romania, there is no doubt they apply, maybe in different ways and magnitudes, everywhere.

Given the purpose of this chapter, four challenges are selected: one referring mainly to students, one coming from academic staff, one from the learning context and one from learning process itself.

1. Taking Responsibility and Ownership on Students' Own Learning

This first challenge refers to our students, as their independence in learning process is higher now than ever before, due to ubiquitous distribution of knowledge and instant access mechanisms to knowledge.

But this "gift" of accessibility and availability comes with a strong need for meta-reflective skills and capacities for self-regulation during the learning process. Taking responsibility of own learning comes not only from social distribution of knowledge, but also from the diversification of learning opportunities and pathways in higher education. As a student, you need to understand the qualification(s) you would like to achieve, the building blocks in terms of knowledge and skills, and also, your active role as learner in the construction of your own learning experiences. Generalization of lateral learning opportunities, expansion of communities of practice, peer learning in a diverse student environment are now the new frames pushing students to re-define their learning processes and take more and more ownership on them. That requires more than participation and being active; is about co-creation of learning experiences in interaction with academics and new learning contexts. Quite often students are coming into higher education not necessarily ready and prepared for this important task, and this is our leading idea that project-based teaching and learning can make a contribution in this direction.

As stated by Henard & Leprince-Ringuet (2011, p. 28) "Promoting students engagement and learning communities is also likely to enhance the quality of student learning. Universities or teachers that give students incentives to study in groups will improve learning outcomes (Thomas 2002). (…) Institutions can also raise the quality of the learning of their students by underlying the importance students should give to their education."

Looking to our context, a paradox is visible: the need for more ownership and responsibility on students own learning is facing the alarming high rate of drop-outs from universities, and disengagement of students due to various reasons. Many of them need to work in parallel with their studies to be able to pay the costs. Some of the academics provide a low level of methodological innovation in teaching and learning. Also a key factor here is the poor quality and availability of learning support services (i.e. counseling and guidance, mentoring etc.) correlated with the discouraging signs coming from the labor market in economically turbulent times.

Findings of research indicate that different non-traditional student-centered learning environments may support learning outcomes related to self-regulated learning (Blumenfeld et al., 2006, Ratelle et al., 2007; Taylor & Ntoumanis, 2007). Students working in project-based environments reported higher levels of elaboration, critical thinking and metacognition (Stefanou et al., 2013).

2. Challenging Identity Processes of Academic Staff: The Good Researcher - Good Professor Tension

The myth of direct correlation between quality of research and quality of teaching is not necessarily new, since authors like Gibbs (1995) wrote one of the strongest critiques of the idea: "The notion that teaching excellence flows directly from research excellence is absurd: they are in direct conflict, compete for academics attention and only one of them is rewarded" (in Henard & Leprince-Ringuet, p. 18).

But this tension became higher and higher in Romanian universities in the last years, as the evaluation systems both at individual level (academic staff evaluation) and institutional level (study programs and institutions assessment and rakings) clearly inclined the balance in favor of research. As showed in a recent paper (Ciolan, 2013, p. 67): "the political decision to prioritize research has not only systemic and institutional consequences, but is also producing immediate effects on professional identity processes of academic staff in higher education… These explicit tendencies … brought with them an extraordinary pressure and a significant re-positioning from two perspectives: the way university professors do research and (especially) the way they choose to disseminate it in the global scientific community, but also the invested time, effort and attention in publishing research, compared with what they deploy for designing and leading significant learning experiences".

Together with the new generations of students, coming with such a wide range of challenges for higher education institutions, a new generation of professors /academics started to articulate, with a clear focus on scientific competitiveness and advanced research and less consideration for pedagogy, quality of learning and student's needs. The paradox here is that a much higher mass of students attending now higher education and coming with more complicated and sophisticated learning needs are rather being neglected or not sufficiently addressed as the "system" is not valuing this in a formal and structured way. University professors are caught somewhere in between, trying to accommodate transforming students learning needs and characteristics, employers / labor market pressures to provide "new skills for new jobs" and the regulatory mechanisms of their own working places, prioritizing the research dimension.

A possible support in this endeavor could come from research itself. But not from just doing and publishing research for academic reputation and promotion, but from research-based teaching. One perspective come from using research methodologies and perspectives in order to create significant learning framed in inquiry-based project work. The second perspective is related to transferring (own) research results in teaching and learning to advance disciplinary knowledge and critical reflection of students on their own identity construction as professionals.

3. Expertise in Pedagogy: Learning Scenarios Design and Pedagogical Imagination

Whether some like it or not, university is first of all about students and society, and, as stated also in a EC recent paper (2012, p. 11), "Both research and teaching should be supported by sound professional development provision. Yet it is teaching that primarily influences student outcomes, enhances graduate employability and raises the profile of European higher education institutions worldwide. Currently, only a few countries have strategies to promote quality in higher education teaching, including the training of teaching staff in pedagogical skills".

A reconciliation of knowing *how* to teach with knowing *what* to teach is needed. The requirement for expertise in pedagogy comes from the very stringent need to provide authentic learning experiences that would keep the students engaged in a meaningful way with their own learning. Pedagogical imagination is seriously challenged by the generalized presence of new technologies in education and by the simultaneous presence in the same classroom, of digital natives generation with their new learning habits together with mature students who decided to come (back) to university for improving their professional skills.

Research shows that more interaction between students and professors clearly contributes to better learning, but the type of interaction valued by students and enhancing learning comes now together with the need for methodological innovation and creative learning design. Basically, expertise in pedagogy prevents from a de-contextualization of teaching and learning, from creating two parallel worlds of students and teachers.

As underlined by Hannon (2009), "the skills set of professional teachers should shift from subject knowledge towards expertise in pedagogy in order to effectively foster creative learning and innovation attitudes in learners." (in Bocconi et al., 2012, p. 11). The new paradox here is that, while higher education is demanded to ask for new roles of professors, such as mentors, facilitators, coach, scenarists and advisors, to create contexts in which students learn in authentic ways and take ownership not only of their own learning, but of their roles and responsibilities in the learning of others as well (contributors, team members, critical friends, evaluators etc.), in practice can be seen a much slower movement. Although university pedagogy was penetrated seriously by PjBL, by interactive and collaborative methodologies, by research-based education etc., it is still highly anchored in "good old practices": fragmentation instead modularization, rigid frames instead flexibility and personalization, evaluation of static knowledge instead of assessing progress in key competence development etc.

Pedagogical skills and pedagogical imagination are also very much needed, in continuation of the above idea, for creating authentic assessment that enable students and their learning process facilitators to get significant insights not just on quantity and quality of their learning, but also on the way they learn best: experiences, practices, conditions, dispositions, etc. Assessment is a key part of learning and a direct contributor to the way learning takes place.

4. Learning Time and Learning Spaces

What is / is there a good time for learning? How learning time is organized by institutions and individuals? Where do learning take place, under which conditions and contexts?

There are no simple answers to these questions, but apparently learning takes place everywhere, anytime in contemporary world. Disposition for learning and making from learning a state of mind (having your mind alert to learning) seem to be the directions that are challenging, once more, our traditional views on time and space for learning. PjBL, exemplified below both as learning method and evaluation method is clearly bringing students and professors in the situation to differently manage their learning time, according to tasks and communities of practice' dynamic, and not so much according to classical academic schedules. New places and spaces for learning are also somehow intrinsic to project work, which normally goes beyond the walls of university amphitheaters, laboratories or working rooms, to get closer to real world issues and lively communities.

The new opportunities "out there" are still paradoxically challenged by the behavioral patterns both of academic staff and students, feeling more comfortable and safe in their own environment. There is also a reluctance of many stakeholders external to higher education institution to take on board their new roles in facilitating learning.

The reform of organizational dimensions (implementation of Bologna three-cycle system) raised challenges within the higher education systems. Amongst these challenges Szolar identified systemic and programmatic challenges, vocationalization of the academic curriculum, shift from accent on horizontal to vertical differences (stratified and hierarchical national systems based on reputation) and shift from input to output oriented highereducation. Such challenges require not only structural, but also procedural changes, namely new modes and arrangements of teaching, learning and assessment. (Szolar, 2011, p. 1) The UEFISCDI report on Internationalization of Higher Education in Romania in 2013 highlights pedagogy, learning environment and learning resources as key aspects of higher education institutions. Universities are expected to create a favorable learning environment "with wide access to the newest learning resources and to the cutting-edge knowledge and with a more or less individual guidance of the students in their effort to achieve best learning outcomes". (2013, p. 70)

THE NEED FOR PJBL AND ASSESSMENT IN HIGHER EDUCATION

Bringing in higher education the new working methodologies and new interactional strategies with students is a key condition for creating authentic learning experiences. Alexander and Wade (2000) demonstrated that an effective learning environment requires relevant and meaningful tasks and instructors' support that encourages the use of effective learning strategies, and present realistic challenges. Blumenfeld (et al., 2006) showed that the student ownership in learning is proportional to their engagement; therefore, the more engagement in learning has as an effect the deeper learning. The importance of student engagement is widely accepted and researchers found data that support the effectiveness of student engagement on a broad range of learning outcomes (Prince 2004; Hake, 1998; Laws, Sokoloff & Thornton, 1999). In general, higher education student teams either chose a project to work on or work on a project that was commissioned by a client (as in the senior design course or technical institutions); each team acquired different technical content depending on their project topics. Student teams design experiments to test their ideas, identify information resources and establish their own goals, timelines and strategies specific to projects they selected. Engaging students in decision-making process and supporting them develop self-regulation and self-monitoring skills also promote engagement and persistence at learning (Ratelle et al., 2007; Taylor & Ntoumanis, 2007). Students' ownership on learning and engagement rely on various individual, social and environmental factors, such as interest in the task, the value a student places on the task, how competent students feel, instructor's feedback on task performance or the way the learning environment is structured (Stefanou et al. 2013, p.112). Gibbes and Carson (2013) found out that university students experience ownership on learning process when they use PjBL in learning languages. Although many evaluations were mostly positive, detailed analysis revealed contradictions in the activity system, including inequitable divisions of labor, perceived lack of time due to community obligations, or opposition to the rules governing the activity.

Fried-Booth (1982) found that learners using PjBL were motivated by the tangible end products and energized by fieldwork. The experiment conducted in 2010 by Li with 183 second year university students showed that project-led courses' students reported self-improvement, effectiveness of combining communication with other skills and practical applications. Articulating the classroom conditions related to different student self-regulated behaviors, dispositions and attitudes can help deepen our understanding of the ways in which the learning environment might influence students' learning choices. Both autonomy and deep-level engagement have been associated with adaptive motivational orientations and efficacy. The use of problem-driven contexts, authentic contexts, team-based work scenarios and the provision of multiple opportunities for collaboration with ample time to complete assignments are elements that theory suggests should encourage students to exercise independence in problem solving (e.g. Paris & Paris, 2001; Prince & Felder, 2006, 2007). Blackmore & Cousin (2003), earlier Baxter & Magolda (1999) found evidence that students involved in research-based inquiry projects develop more sophisticated levels of intellectual development, while Healey (2005) recommended that designing curricula which develop the teaching–research nexus requires a shift from teacher focused to students as participants in the research process.

PjBL "Then" and "Now": A Brief Historical Overview

From all over the world, for more than one century, teachers advocate and use projects, embodied in experimental laboratory investigations, field trips, creative design artworks or various interdisciplinary activities that enrich and extend the curriculum. Advocating for such an approach needs to clarify what PjBL is and which are main tendencies during its long history, including the 21st century.

The history of the project approach reflects a pendulum movement in regard to educational trends. It shows backs and forth within the European and Nord-American milieus. Michael Knoll (1997) provides comprehensive data about project work, connected to late Renaissance in Italian architecture schools. Later, according to Pannabecker (1995) it incorporated more scientific knowledge and became prominent as part of the syllabus of engineering schools in the United States (1765–1880). The longitudinal analysis of Fallik et al. (2008), from 1880 to 1915 shows that projects were integrated into public schools in America as part of the vocational education movement. Projects were also part of the curriculum of the University of Chicago Laboratory School, although the practice was not clearly referred to as the Project Approach at that time. 1913 Dewey's work Interest and Effort and his idea of "constructive occupations" focus on how students could engage in purposeful activity at the intellectual, physical, and affective levels. The inclusion of projects matched the child-centered approach advocated by Progressive educators at this time. John Dewey and his group promoted projects as means of "learning by doing" based on student self-interest and a constructivist approach. His theoretical analysis of progressive education suggests that subject matter' content, processes, and products are all vital to intelligent activity. Dewey emphasized that the authoritarian knowledge approach of modern traditional education was too concerned with delivering knowledge, and not enough with understanding students' actual experiences. In 1918, Dewey's student William Kilpatrick formalized "The Project Method": education must be experience based, centering on ideals such as open-mindedness and discipline in aim-based activity. Since then, project approach immersed into the Progressive Education movement while "doing projects" became a long-standing tradition in American education (Markham et al. 2003, p. 3). In the United Kingdom, projects became an important characteristic of the curriculum for infant schools (children 5 to 7) in the 20's, according to Susan Isaac (1960) and can be recognized in the curriculum model developed over many years at the Bank Street College of Education in New York City (Zimilies, 1997). The Encyclopedia of Educational Research's editions published in the 40's and 50's have mentions of project method. Due to the focus on improving school outcomes and fostering accountability in the 60's and 70's, the project approach' popularity decreased in the United States (Blumenfeld et al. 1991; Marx et al. 1997; Thomas 2000). Hedge concludes that in the mid 70's PjBL developed as a response to pedagogical theories of" learner-centered teaching, learner autonomy, the negotiated syllabus, collaborative learning, and learning through tasks" (1993, 276). Since 80's the approach has gained popularity, especially in US districts with more autonomy, which are not under strong pressure of high stake standardized testing. At the same time, the use of projects in education blossomed in Europe (especially UK, Germany and Scandinavian countries) and Russia. Nowadays PjBL is much connected to using new learning environment, technological tools and social networking.

Project-Based Work in The 21st Century's Higher Education

Thom Markham (2011, p. 38) advocates for PjBL as valuable experience and promising alternative for the future: students are required to possess both content knowledge and the 21st century learning and dispositions demanded by employers today: critical thinking, collaborating, communicating and creative problem solving, life and career skills, such as leadership and responsibility, self-direction, and social and emotional awareness, and the ability to use them across disciplines.

Frank and Barzilai (2006) documented that PjBL generates an environment promoting technological literacy, where students take advantage of digital tools to produce collaborative products; Frank (2002) demonstrated that students are engaged in active learning and gain multidisciplinary knowledge while working in real world context. The book 21st century skills. Rethinking how students learn (Bellanca and Brandt eds.) analyses skills needed for the future and educational institutions' approaches to include these skills in their repertoire. Microsoft partners in learning (2012) mention collaboration, knowledge construction, self-regulation, real-world problem-solving and innovation, the use of ICT for learning and skilled communication as key skills needed nowadays. Such skills are congruent PjBL which, as a consequence, has more advocates and more visibility on the educationalists' agenda. Influential international organizations highlight the match between the 21st century skills and expected outcomes of effective PjBL (Project Management Institute Educational Foundation, BIE, OECD, Microsoft).

PjBL as Process and Assessment Activity

The National Academy Foundation includes PjBL in curricula for career academies because it motivates students, improves learning and retention, leads to in-depth understanding, provides opportunities to use appropriate technology, and connects school/university to the workplace and the larger world (2013, p. 24). In which ways can PjBL bring such an impact? Which is the potential of PjBL for higher education institutions present and future, taking into account expected learning outcomes, connection to real world and academics' responsibilities? How to organize PjBL activities in higher education in order to balance between individuals and team, learning and assessment? How to use project work with students in order to better balance researching and teaching responsibilities of academics?

PjBL as a Process

Beckett defines PjBL as "long-term activity that involves a variety of individual and cooperative tasks involving planning, research and reporting" (2002, p. 54), while Fried-Booth (2002, p. 6) focuses on student-centeredness "driven by the need to create an end-product." Blumenfeld highlights PjBL "a comprehensive perspective focused on teaching by engaging students in investigation", underlying that projects require a question or problem to organize or drive activities which result in artifacts or products, that culminate in a final product that addresses the driving question. (Blumenfeld et al, 1991, p. 37). Moulton and Holmes (2000) focus on research and collaborative work skills, while Hutchinson (1991, p. 14) stresses on promoting "independent investigation, research skills and cross curricular studies, where learners get the ability to apply their knowledge from other subject areas. Katz, Chard & Kogan argue that project work in curriculum "promotes learners' intellectual development by engaging their minds in observation, raising questions and predicting the answers, and conducting investigations and many other intellectual processes as they study selected aspects of their own environments and experiences in depth." (2014, p. 3) The Gold Standard PjBL developed by the Buck Institute for Education promotes the idea that PjBL is a "teaching method in which students gain knowledge and skills by working for an extended period of time to investigate and respond to a complex question, problem, or challenge using project management techniques" (2013, p. 18) and has eight essential elements: significant content, compelling "need to know", a driving question, student voice and choice, opportunities to build 21st century competencies (collaboration, critical thinking, communication, and creativity), in-depth inquiry

Table 1. Seven principles of project work, by Markham (2012)

1	Identify the challenge: projects start with a big idea, an authentic issue or a vital concept
2	Craft the driving questions: what is the deep understanding that teachers want students to demonstrate at the end of the project?
3	Build the assessment: students always produce a result at the end of the project. The results are assessed according to an assessment plan agreed at the beginning of the project, which covers skills, content and personal strengths or habits of mind
4	Plan backwards: the teacher conceives the PjBL as extended learning experience focusing both on the process and the products, therefore teachers play coaching roles for collaboration or empathic attitudes toward team members
5	Enroll and engage: incorporating from the project start the students voice and choice, using benchmarks and clear schedules
6	Facilitate the teams: like in real working environments, PjBL requires commitment, purpose and results specific to high performing teams
7	Keep the end in mind: non-linear problem solving process, PjBL has high risk of becoming chaotic if not well organized; project should also stimulate reflection and further developments inspired by the project process and results.

(finding answers leads to more questions), critique and revision and public audience for reporting outcomes (idem, p. 54).

The following working definition merges various definitions and foci:

Based on constructivist background, project-based learning (PjBL) is a complex student-centered pedagogy consisting in individually, small or larger groups in-depth extended investigation of a topic or problem, worthy of the student's interests, energy and time, which involves assessment of both process and outcomes.

How to design quality PjBL? Markham (2012, p. 54) answers in the table below providing a methodological framework to be used for designing project-based work and assessment (table 1).

PjBL in Assessment

PjBL embodies teaching, learning and assessment in various proportions; the focus on teaching, individual or group and assessment represents teacher's decision, according to students' profiles and expected learning outcomes. Even if students' empowerment in planning and managing their learning projects is expected, the professor remains central player in students' learning. University faculty plays crucial role in preparing learning environment and challenges, facilitating students' clarification and narrowing an issue or challenge to be investigated, giving support during investigation and final presentations or development of products. Learning is intrinsic and genuinely connected to assessment. In a suggestive way, John Mergendoller considers teachers in PjBL environment "part jazz orchestra conductor, part batting coach, and part jazz composer. The goal is to perform the score (project), but there is room for improvisation by the orchestra members (students) as well as by the conductor." (Mergendoller, 2014, p. 1). Well implemented PjBL requires carefully planned assessment that incorporates formative feedback and multiple evaluations of process and product, content and skills. Markham highlights that PjBL "develops skills necessary in life, workplace, and in any environment requiring self-starting, self-managing, and skillful individuals ... PjBL refocuses education on the student, not the curriculum – a shift mandated by the global world, which rewards intangible assets such as drive, passion, creativity, empathy and resiliency. These cannot be taught out of the textbook, but must be activated through experience". (idem, 39).

Project work requires assessing student performance, including self-assessment methodologies. Some activities embedded in the complex process of PjBL need to have clear marking criteria which should be communicated to students. Moore and Williamson (2005) demonstrated how such criteria enable students to show achievements and outcomes.

FROM THEORETICAL AND METHODOLOGICAL FRAMEWORK TO PRACTICAL EXAMPLES

This section provides a framework to analyze PjBL in higher education and examples collected during last 4 years with University of Bucharest' students enrolled in bachelor and master degree programs of the Faculty of Psychology Education Sciences. Findings are convergent with the literature review: PjBL connects university environment and real world, making possible various collaborative working experiences between students, professionals or community members. The two authors coordinated individual projects, team projects or whole class projects prepared and delivered as assignments for different courses, as following (table 2):

Each type of project will be connected to various impacts on learners' skills taking into account data collected by the authors through observation, questionnaires filled by students in different stages of the project development, individual or team reflective diaries, interviews with faculty and students, content analysis on students' project documents (including personal narratives, posts on blogs or social media) and results of final assessment.

Example 1: Community Intervention

The Theory and practice of civic education course is part of pre-service teacher training module. Starting from 2008, undergraduate students experience authentic learning inspired by Project Citizen (a middle school curricular program implemented in Romania since 2004). Working in small groups for 4 weeks, students carry on the following steps:

Table 2. Types of projects and corresponding study programs

Nr.	Course	Type of Project	Study Program	Study Year
1	Theory and Practice of Civic Education	community intervention projects	BA: Education sciences	first
2	Sociology of Education and Citizenship	community analysis projects research projects	BA: Double Degree UB VIA	second
3	Educational Research	research projects	BA: Education sciences, MA: Educational management and evaluation	second
4	Sociology of Education	research projects	BA: Education sciences	second
5	Educational And Social Policy	policy advocacy projects	BA: Education sciences	third
6	Team Building and Team Leading	case study research projects training/ facilitation projects	MA: Training of trainers	second

1. Identify an important problem in the community and determine which level of government is most directly responsible for dealing with the problem;
2. Gather information (using a variety of methods and tools like observation, photo and video recording, interviews, questionnaires) and evaluate information about the problem from a variety of sources (local inhabitants, stakeholders, children, public authorities etc.);
3. Examine solutions taking into account public policies that now are being used at the community level and also analyze policies being suggested by other people;
4. Develop a public policy in order to address the problem and improve the community life;
5. Develop an action plan and present it to a larger audience to reflect on how it could influence public authorities to adopt your proposed public policy.

Assessment was intrinsic part of the learning process, both formative and summative. During the four weeks of field project work, students received support from tutor. In the end students had poster presentations and oral presentations and the course instructor organized a project case, where students presented their projects, evaluated projects and gave feed-back. Students chose specific problems of the community (e.g. organize a safe crossing zebra in a busy traffic area close to the University building, set up a shelter for street dogs, reorganize a playground, built bike rakes, clean a park, set up a special place for graffiti), but also major problems at a wider level (e.g. recycling, nature protection, eco-friendly urban space, build bicycle lanes, children rights and human rights, anti-discrimination activities, supporting Roma children, prevent school drop-out or child abuse, etc.).

Evaluation of students' projects included the followings, 20 points allocated for each:

1. Relevance of the problem (how serious the problem is in the community/ country, conflicts related to the issue, stakeholders, groups or persons involved and their point of view);
2. Clarity of the project (well organized, easy to understand, correctly written);
3. Information (clear, appropriate, important);
4. Graphic (connected to content, appropriate, generating information, facilitating understanding);
5. Connection to National Curriculum.

Based on these criteria students used rubrics for peer evaluation. Students reported the unique balance between searching for challenging issues (which are relevant from a personal point of view) with a researcher and social activist approach. Such a PjBL example shows developing teaching skills (curriculum design, classroom management, pedagogy) and practicing education for democracy. By designing policy interventions in real community, student teachers learn how to participate competently in a democratic society. Students showed enthusiasm and work persistency for a refreshing experience and had a comprehensive follow up on public policy in Education and Social policy class. They reported as difficult problem clarification and team work: planning, time management, conflict resolution and social loafing.

Example 2: My School's Community

Since 2012, the Sociology of Education and Citizenship class offered to Danish and international students attending the Double Degree program in Bucharest involved both in and out of class activities. First two assignments (Current Events Project in March) and My life in school: a critical reflection (in

April) facilitated students' accommodation to new academic context and theoretical and methodological background. Third assignment *My schools' community* explicitly used PjBL. The underlying principle is that inquiry and educating skills require from future teachers or other professionals to know as much as possible about communities which your organizations or schools serve and to which your clients or students belong. Crosscutting issues were prominent both for preparatory lectures and projects. Students had guiding questions like: What is a community? How will social justice issues in the community inform your planning, teaching and participation in the school community? How will you use of community resources in your activity?

For three weeks, students worked in self-elected groups of three in order to:

- "Map" the school's community profile. Such "first hand" data collected through community inquiry can inform educational and support activity. It primarily aimed at providing international students with the opportunity to think in new ways about the communities in which students or clients live and learn (in Romania and their home country);
- Experience methods of social inquiry: students designed and used specific instrument for data collection and field research;
- Process collected data, analyze the findings and formulate conclusions translated into educational practice;
- Formulate and present the findings (using a variety of media and ICT tools) including recommendations.

Learning and assessment were embedded, students being informed from the very beginning about the performative assessment activity in the final session. Evaluation criteria focused on identifying the community profile highlighting the assets (15%), understanding needs within school/community (15%), multiple perspectives, equity and social justice issues addressed within the school community (15%), use of data collected from inquiry (15%), integration of what students have learned with recommendations for the educational / teaching / support practice (20%) and quality of final oral presentation (20%).

Students reported positive effects of the project work, mainly related to field work and analyzing from a comparative perspective similar institutions and services in their home country and host country for mobility program. The international students (Erasmus or those enrolled in Double Degree program) faced difficulties related to language and identification of relevant issues, but they proved to be more experienced than Romanian students in working together and finalizing the project. All students reported high motivation for the assignment. One third of the projects resulted in complex documentary movies presenting both the process and products; can be assumed that exceeding the assignment's requirements shows high level of engagement.

Example 3: Educational Research Projects

The applied learning in Educational Research (for BA) / Advanced Educational Research (for MA) course takes place through designing, implementing and reporting on a research project. The project approach is generally similar for the two levels, but using a higher level of sophistication in terms of methods and data analysis at master's level, with more focus on qualitative research.

The key stages of the journey are briefly presented below:

- Selection and definition of research problem; articulation of research teams,
- Designing and testing data collection methods and instruments,
- Selection of subjects and data collection,
- Data collection and team processing of obtained data; data analysis and interpretation,
- Presentation of research reports, comparison among teams and merging of research results (scaling up).

Basically, a traditional model of a research project is followed, but with some specific aspects added to emphasize the process of learning. For instance, each student (and implicitly team member) is asked to keep a field journal about how they experienced the role of a researcher when going in the field and working in a research team. Based on these journals, they are engaged in meta-reflection exercises on: interaction with subjects and communities, interaction and cooperation within research team, communication and presentation of research results to an informed audience.

Main satisfaction of the students and most mentioned struggles are very much common: doing field work and getting in contact with real subjects, organizing work and balancing contributions in a diverse research team and making the most of your data in relevant presentation in front of an interested knowledgeable audience. Evaluation based on research projects follows basically both individual and team contribution to quality of the process, final product (research report) and the way it was presented to others, according to assessment matrix used simultaneously for evaluation by two academics (professor and teaching assistant) and by each team to assess others' work (peer assessment). This type of PJBL and assessment contributes to developing the meta-reflective capacities of students, better understating the stages and the meaning of doing educational research and the team work skills. The evaluation process is based on quality of data collection and processing (30%), quality of research report (50%) and capacity to present findings to an informed audience (20%).

Example 4: Sociology of Education

The *Sociology of Education* course aims at developing sociological understanding of education and awareness on specific issues in contemporary world. Undergraduate students are involved in activities like analyzing educational processes and practices through a mixed approach (positivist and interpretative). Course focuses on relationship between school and society (schooling in contemporary world: outcomes from national and international perspective), schools as social systems, schools and social mobility in Europe and worldwide, diversity and equality of educational opportunities, stratification processes within /between schools, authority and identity (interactions, expectations, labeling, school climate and social networks).

Working in teacher-assigned groups, students carried out a research project, enhanced by the overall challenging question "Is there equity in education?". Based on the same logic as in previous example (research project), students used theoretical framework strengthened over the first six weeks and have developed seven projects over four weeks (e.g. gender, ethnicity, residential area and equal educational opportunities; classroom interactions, labeling, expectations, hidden curriculum, ICT and interaction dynamics). Students benefited of continuous support from one (2010, 2011, 2012, 2013) or two professors (2014-2015) who have assisted them in project design and data interpretation.

Project's assessment grounded on:

- **Quality of the Project:** a) formulating research question: theoretical framework, relevance and connection to educational reality (nationally/ internationally), b) research design, c) research methodology, d) fieldwork and data collection, e) findings: analysis and interpretations (55%);
- **Quality of Group Presentation** (25%);
- **Quality of Materials Made Available to Colleagues** (20%).

The process raised for supervisors' issues related to intellectual property and plagiarism. Under supervision students posted materials on the electronic group and presented their findings in front of the class (one-hour presentation and half an hour feedback). As in other research projects type, assessment reflected results of the group work and all materials produced in teams have been made available as learning resources for all students (part of final examination). Peer review was organized after each project presentation. Students had possibility to revise and improve their projects after receiving instructors' feed-back and comments from their classmates.

Final assessment took into consideration points obtained by each group for the project work, individual participation in the class and final examination. All criteria have been presented from the beginning.

The course covered concepts and relevant studies related to sociological analysis of education in connection to democratic life and fostering citizenship in various contexts, relationship between theories of power, poverty, class, gender, ethnicity and broader theories of schooling and development. Instructor made clear connection to previous class on T*heory and practice of civic education and Educational Research*. Students practiced skills in describing, analyzing and assessing policies, programs and activities aiming at fulfilling the equality of educational opportunity principle in democratic societies and also to interpret school-level outcomes, civic participation, solidarity and individual responsibility and recently occurring issues like ubiquity learning or social justice. Through project work students reported that they have gained better understanding of the relationship between social and cultural conditions, education, schooling and democracy (focused on Roma population, SEN students, vulnerable groups, urban and rural discrepancies), and had possibility to express insights about importance of equity in institutions and educational processes.

Students also reported project work as challenging and complex; main benefits relates to whole cycle work (from problem to field work and presenting possible solutions), connection to reality (analysis of data) and opportunity to transfer skills previously gained from other subjects. Difficulties are generated by poor team work experience, time management, lack of appropriate space for group work, difficulties in making transparent individual contribution for the team work, traditional focus on the product, not on the process.

Example 5: Policy Advocacy Projects

During their degree studies, students are dominantly involved in classic academic writing tasks. In the MA on Educational Management and Evaluation, while taking the Educational Policy Analysis module, students are involved in drafting and defending a policy brief. Policy briefs are a particular genre of policy papers, used mainly to persuade target audiences to move to action on a specific policy problem and they are advocating for a specific type of intervention, as results of analyzing available evidences and contextual factors of the policy process.

The key stages of the project are:

- Identify and conceptualize a specific current policy issue in education (evidences that the problem exists, information about the magnitude and consequences of the problem, identification of stakeholders etc.);
- Review and analyze how the issue / problem is approached in own context and in other contexts (map out how the responsible decision makers approached or ignored the issue, analyze policy transfer / learning opportunities from other contexts);
- Design a specific solution or intervention to contribute to solving of the current issue and support the proposed solution with evidences (primary or secondary data, case analysis, etc.); make recommendations for de decision-makers on how to implement the proposed solution;
- Defend the policy brief in front of the audience in a persuasive manner;
- Peer assessment / inter-pares evaluation.

The key idea of these projects is that they invite and motivate students to find and select issues / problems of interest for them, define and analyze them from a policy perspective and try to convince decision-makers to act upon them. Among benefits and in the same time challenges of these projects, students mentioned: drafting an audience-driven instead of content-driven paper, constructing persuasive messages for a target audience, making a brief presentation in a convincing way to move people to action, using a written paper as a communication and advocacy tool.

In specific cases, students assisted by the academic mentors took forward the initiative and really started a broader campaign on their issue and made it on the decision makers' attention and agendas.

The evaluation process is mainly focused on the technical quality of the final product (policy brief), which is assessed by the professor, but also through peer assessment based on eight criteria (focused, evidence-based, limited / problem based, brief, easy to understand, accessible, promotional, practical & feasible). The criteria-based assessment is weighting 80% from the final score, and 20% is for the presentation / quality of communication in front of colleagues.

PjBL and assessment was strategically introduced through a continuum of horizontal initiatives (i.e. research projects in different subjects / courses at the same degree level, namely Bachelor) or vertical ones (i.e. community intervention/ policy advocacy projects at Bachelor and then MA levels). The aim is to contribute not only to a better dynamic of the learning process, but to bring into focus some very important skills for graduates such as transversal soft skills and learning management skills. The way we conceptualize and focus the work with projects in BA and MA educational degrees is described in the correspondence matrix presented in Annex 1, where five categories of projects we use with students are correlated with skills category they contribute the most. This correspondence table is a framework for the way we work with our students, not aiming to be explanatory or valid for all domains. Nevertheless, we it can be useful for reflection and adaptation in each academic domain / degree interested in using PjBL in a meaningful way.

Example 6: Case Studies Projects

Students attending Building and Leading Teams course of Train the Trainers master degree program have been exposed to relevant theories on team work and team development and used different cases in class. Students also became familiar with Robert Stake's case study methodology. For three weeks, learning and assessment engaged students in following activities:

- Identify a team (in a company, institution or organization), negotiate and set up a plan to develop field research;
- Carry on research (following the same stages as presented in example 3): design the case study, prepare data collection tools and methods, collect data, interpret data, write the report;
- Present to the whole class the case study and design training interventions for the teams investigated.

Evaluation of case studies included:

- **Structure:** 10 points.
- **Background of the Case:** 10.
- **Clarity of the Case:** 10.
- **Methodology (Methods, Instruments, Data Collection and Interpretation):** 25.
- **Style:** 10.
- **Interpretation and Conclusions:** 25.

Based on these 6 criteria students performed peer review for each team, using rubrics. Besides that, students critically analyzed their own team's dynamics (using team reflective diaries, individual logs, blogs developed by students) and have developed monitoring, evaluation and insight instruments to reflect on issues, processes and critical elements of teams' effectiveness.

Grounded on case studies, students' teams designed and delivered training sessions in order to improve the teams they studied (as cases) or to replicate positive experiences investigated. This example involves also team teaching experience (Ulrich & Nedelcu 2013), as long as designing the training program was connected to Training Practice workshops taking place during the same semester. Real training sessions (videotaped) made possible for students to put into practice the training programs, which they peer-assessed and commented under supervision.

Master degree students provided rich data about this integrated experience. Students reported that investigations in real contexts enhanced researching skills and their employability, given their immersion in real work environment that provided networking opportunities and genuine professional experiences. They also identified difficulties like working in heterogeneous groups of learners (multi-aged, different ability level or cultural background), time-management stress and interpersonal conflicts. Reflecting on project work, both instructors and students had to address issues like integrity, deontology, access to companies and confidential information.

A REFLECTIVE ANALYSIS OF THE FOUR PJBL CHALLENGES

An academic debate on PjBL in higher education starting from initial four challenges needs a circular loop from project-based learning and assessment. PjBL and assessment address each challenge and, on turn, generate new ones. The authors selected few recommendations from their own experience perspective, illustrated by examples described above.

Responsibility and Ownership on Learning

· "Knowledge is not the only outcome" commented students belonging to projects teams. Students' opinions show that projects are suitable for building sense of control and ownership in learning, positive motivation and enthusiasm for activities (especially community investigations, research in companies, performing training sessions, conducting interviews with experts and professionals, presenting policy briefs, etc.).

· Students reported as beneficial the focus on an issue, the use of various resources and technological tools to communicate, collaborate, conduct research, analyze, create, and share their own work for different audiences. Group presentations many times used sophisticated IT/ media skills and encouraged less extrovert students to talk about process and outcomes, more than in more traditional learning and assessment contexts.

· Metacognitive skills are highlighted, as students felt stimulated to think about what to learn and how to learn, about creativity and critical thinking.

· Experience gained through PjBL had a long-term impact on students' motivation and engagement with an issue. For example, 25-30% of the Training of Trainers master degree students used the case study methodology for final dissertations, 25% of the undergraduate students followed up topics launched by the Sociology of Education course and Social and Educational Policy and obviously used research skills practiced for Educational Research class. Another master student, as result of her research and policy brief on the impact of School after school program on Roma students became member of a Government working group and published her brief "School after school and the perpetuation of inequalities in education."

· Facing difficulties, students became more aware about self-management, time management, regulation and persistence on task and team work. Authors' observations on group work and students learning outcomes are in line with conclusions of the study coordinated by Stefanou (2010), showing that open-ended, project-based courses may not be the best place for students to develop study skills, as these courses do not typically include traditional assessments, such as examinations, that prompt students to set aside time and find good location to study.

Challenging Identity Processes of Academic Staff: The Good Researcher - Good Professor Tension

· Academic staff need to consistently transfer their research skills and outcomes into teaching process.

· PjBL works well in educational institutions where academic staff cooperate to follow students' progress in time, to observe changes in behaviors, attitudes, work habits and different skills.

· Teaching' ethics is challenged by the complexity of learning environments (inside and outside University, face-to-face and virtual, structured or spontaneous) and assessment (performance and outcome-based, individual, group-based).

· Academic communities of practice could model students' integrity, cooperation and networking, both in traditional and virtual learning environments; intellectual property awareness has to be raised not only for research, but also for teaching, community work and other professional activities.

Expertise in Pedagogy: Learning Scenarios Design and Pedagogical Imagination

· Project work' effectiveness is mainly correlated with qualitative factors, like choosing the right issue to be addressed and the capacity of professor/teams of professors to guide, support and provide feedback during the process.

· Academic staff needs competencies in curriculum design: interdisciplinary integrated approach, coherence within curriculum architecture, constructive alignment of assignments with teaching methods and learning outcomes for the module (Biggs 1996, 1999), effective classroom management skills and team teaching activities.

· Even if PjBL involves integrated approach, the course facilitators need to make strategic course design decisions to support the particular outcomes they envisage for students (e.g. particular cognitive or social outcomes they wish to emphasize in their classrooms).

· Implementation of community intervention projects showed that projects can be either designed with a clearly defined outcome or more open-ended with students exploring and "discovering" the desired results. As a consequence, assessment tasks that support learning require re-adjustments and revision of the initial plan while keeping main focus.

· PjBL activities reflects sensitive approach of access and participation from students' diversity perspective (gender, age, ethnicity, SEN, academic level etc.).

· By careful supervision and support provided for PjBL, faculty professors should include skills like risk assessment, risk-taking, creativity, business planning and overcoming fear of failure and also skills to design and develop innovative products.

· Given the genuine connection between ubiquitous learning and PjBL, the project work has strong potential to provide both powerful contextual learning experiences and serendipitous exploration and discovery of the connected nature of information in the real world.

Learning Time and Learning Space

· Project-based work, as long-term approach is time consuming: it requires more class days and up to a couple of weeks. Ongoing unexpected developments can bring either time management problems or missing interest for the topic. Stefanou' team (2010) found out that PjBL design courses have discouraged students' adoption of certain behavioral self-regulatory strategies related to managing study time and environment.

· Both faculty and students need to be aware about benefits and pitfalls of PjBL. Research on learner evaluation provided mixed responses, learners pointing out difficulty of the project work (Moulton & Holmes 2000, Li 2010) and time and effort required to execute project (Beckett 2005).

· Investigations often require field work and meetings with experts or people from community; students practice communication and social skills to get access to relevant informants and also IT to finalize and present the results of their work.

· Conducting studies in organizations, companies or community/ education services providers' students develop social, networking and organizational skills, they understand practitioner's perspective beyond the university, undertaking authentic activities in real context. This is expected to raise students' employability.

CONCLUDING REMARKS

Based on our own observation and discussions with students, but especially on their feedback on project examples described above, PjBL and assessment can be recommended as a strong methodological approach that strengthens the quality of learning process in higher education, both in terms of academic achievement and satisfaction of learners. This approach addresses and directly contributes to a set of skills and values essential for the future professionals, highly neglected in traditional teaching: cooperation, team-work, reflective practice, social responsibility, meta-analysis. All these skills and values are allowing students for better understanding of their own learning process and their future professions. Working in a PjBL and assessment environment brings also significant challenges and risks. From the learning process perspective, one of the most important challenges is how to manage learning and project-work time, especially when trying to integrate it in the classic rigid academic schedules. From the assessment perspective, probably the key challenge is to differentiate for each individual the contribution to project work and to have a consistent and valid evaluation for each student. From a more practical perspective, students reported insufficient development of social skills necessary for team work, time management, conflict management, social loafing, lack of appropriate space for group meetings and strong tradition on valuing the final product much more than the quality of the process.

PjBL requires both structure and flexibility. The project preparation, completion and evaluation bring relevance, transparency and ownership on the assessment process, even if project' trajectory or development can be unexpectedly influenced by ubiquitous milieu. Strengthening the contribution of assessment to the consolidation and sharing of learning achievements makes a consistent case for PjBL. Bringing into focus a diversified typology of projects which can be used both as learning and assessment methods in higher education shows the ways PjBL contribute to authentic experiences for learners, various skills developments and better motivation and results for students and faculty.

REFERENCES

Bocconi, S., Kampylis, P. G., & Punie, Y. (2012). Innovating Learning: Key Elements for Developing Creative Classrooms in Europe. Luxembourg: Publications Office of the European Union (JRC Scientific and Policy Reports).

Ciolan, L. (2013). Învățarea autentică în universitate [Authentic learning in university]. In A. Opre, M. Miclea & R. Iucu (Eds.), Calitate și performanță în activitatea didactică universitară [Quality and Performance in Higher Education Teaching] (pp. 66-86). Cluj_Napoca: Casa Cărții de Știință.

Dewey, J. (1916). *Democracy and education*. New York: Free Press.

Entwistle, N., & Peterson, E. (2004). Conceptions of learning and knowledge in higher education. Relationship with study behavior and influences of learning environments. *International Journal of Educational Research, 41*(6), 407–428. doi:10.1016/j.ijer.2005.08.009

Fallik, O., Bat-Sheva, E., & Rosenfeld, S. (2008). Motivating Teachers to Enact Free- Choice Project-Based Learning in Science and Technology (PBLSAT): Effects of a Professional Development Model. *Journal of Teacher Education, 19*(6), 565–591. doi:10.1007/s10972-008-9113-8

Henard, F. & Leprince-Ringuet, S. (2011). *The path to Quality Teaching in Higher Education. OECD.* Retrieved from www.oecd.org/edu/imhe/44150246.pdf

Katz, L. G., Chard, S. C., & Kogan, Y. (2014). *Engaging children's minds: The project approach* (3rd ed.). Santa Barbara: Praeger.

Kilpatrick, W. H. (1918). The project method. *Teachers College Record, 19,* 319–335.

Knoll, M. (1997). The project method: Its vocational education origin and international development. *Journal of Industrial Teacher Education, 34*(3), 59–80.

Krajcik, J. S., & Blumenfeld, P. C. (2006). Project-based science. In R. K. Sawyer (Ed.), *The Cambridge handbook of the learning sciences. New York* (pp. 317–334). Cambridge.

Markham, T. (2011). Project-based learning: A bridge just far enough. *Teacher Librarian, 39*(2), 39–42.

Mergendoller, J. (2014). *The Importance of Project Based Teaching. Buck Institute for Education.* Retrieved from http://bie.org/%20blog/the_importance_of_%20project_based_teaching

Rethinking Education: Investing in skills for socio-economic outcomes. (2012). COM669, 20.11.2012. Strasbourg: Publications Office of the European Union.

21. st Century Skills Map – Project Management for Learning. (2014). Partnership for 21st Century Learning and Project Management Institute Educational Foundation. Retrieved from http://www.p21. org/storage/documents/Skills%20Map/Project_Management_Skills_Map_Final.pdf

Stefanou, C., Stolk, D. J., Prince, Chen, J. C. & Lord, S. M. (2013). Self-regulation and autonomy in problem- and project-based learning environments. Active Learning in Higher Education, 2013, 94-109.

Thomas, J. W. (2000). A review of research on project-based learning. Retrieved from www.bie.org/research/study/review_of_project_based_learning_2000

Ulrich, C., & Nedelcu, A. (2013). Team-Teaching and Team Work: Perceptions Amongst Students and Staff (A Case Study). *Procedia: Social and Behavioral Sciences, 76,* 853–857. doi:10.1016/j.sbspro.2013.04.219

KEY TERMS AND DEFINITIONS

Authentic Learning: A learning experience / process that engage the learner from a multiplicity of perspectives: cognitive, social, emotional and actional, creating curiosity and disposition for critical inquiry in real life situations and leading to meaningful knowledge and skills.

Case-Study Project: Qualitative research project where students investigate in-depth a case (a team) within real context (private company, institution or organization) and reflect on the quality of its functioning.

Community Intervention Project: Community inquiry project in which students are guided to identify a problem from citizenship perspective, collect data from community members, formulate and advocate for a solution.

Inquiry-Based Learning: Activities for students that promote inquiry rather than absorption of teacher-provided knowledge.

Policy Advocacy Project: Based on real world / social problems or issues under debate, students perform policy analysis tasks, identify a suitable range of options for solving the problem and use evidences to support the chosen solution; they use professional policy communication tools, such as policy briefs to synthesize their proposed intervention and try to influence decision-makers.

Problem-Based Learning (PBL): Pedagogical approach introduced in the 1960s, much used in medicine. Curriculum design involves a large amount of small group teaching and claims greater alignment with educational principles.

Project-Based Learning (PjBL): Based on the constructivist background, PjBL represents a complex student-centered pedagogy consisting in individually, small or larger groups in-depth extended investigation of a topic or problem, worthy of the student's interests, energy and time which involves assessment of both process and outcomes. Students focus on a problem or challenge, work in teams to find a solution to a problem, and often exhibit their work to an adult audience at the end of the project.

Research Project: Inquiry learning project in which students are invited to formulate research questions, choose research methods, design data collections instruments, collect, process and interpret data, document conclusions and communicate results.

Training / Learning Facilitation Project: Students identify learning needs of different groups and design learning programs for fulfilling those needs, piloting eventually the delivery of the program and / or students do pedagogical projects to be piloted in school, under supervision, as part of their training as future teachers/ or trainers/ adult educators.

APPENDIX

Correspondence Matrix: Types of Projects Used in Educational Sciences and the Related Skills Domains to Which They Contribute the Most

The matrix below reflects the categories of skills critical for being enhanced and strengthened in our students. These broad categories were identified through long and consistent professional debates, using research literature, analyzing students' feedback, formal requirements of educational qualifications, employers' requests and policy papers profiling future citizens and professionals. Authors identified five types of projects with different foci appropriate for educational science areas; skill sets and project types are briefly described below.

Table 3. Brief description of the types of projects used in the academic studies of Education sciences students

Contribution to Learning/ Type of Projects	Transversal Soft Skills	Applied Professional Skills	Reflective and Meta-Cognitive Skills	Learning / Self-Management Skills	Research and Knowledge Management Skills
Research Projects				X	X
Community Intervention Projects	X		X		
Training / Learning Facilitation Projects		X		X	
Policy Advocacy Projects	X	X			
Case Study Projects			X		X

Brief Description of Skills Developed by PjBL in Education Sciences Study Programs

Transversal soft skills: transferable learning achievements, relevant to a broad range of jobs and qualifications (e.g. negotiate, generate new ideas, cooperation and team work, creativity, initiative, problem-solving, risk assessment, decision-taking, communication, decision-making, etc.), having in general an interdisciplinary nature and a trans-occupational relevance.

Applied professional skills: part of qualification-specific skills and competences within educational sector, context or occupation (e.g. teaching, curriculum design and development, assessment and evaluation, classroom/ learning groups management, monitoring and evaluation of educational policy and programs, professional development, counseling and guidance etc.) being indispensable in daily practice of the related professions.

Reflective and meta-cognitive skills: awareness of own and others' knowledge, understanding cognitive tasks and the nature of what is required to complete them and awareness of thinking strategies; capacity to reflect, guide and evaluate own / others cognitive processes, what learners know and how they manage learning (reflective practice and "thinking about thinking").

Learning / Self-management skills: refers self-management of own learning, but also to the constructive management of feelings, planning working and leisure time, keeping emotional balance and healthy body, self-control and stress resistance, self-confidence, flexibility, creativity, lifelong learning as conditions for one owns well being.

Research & knowledge management skills: capacity to professionally collect, analyze and interpret quantitative and qualitative data, to find and use information and evidences in a responsible and critical way, to ask relevant questions and formulate hypothesis that can be tested and to communicate knowledge for diverse audiences.

Compilation of References

Ahmadi, M., Helms, M., & Raiszadeh, F. (2001). Business students' perceptions of faculty evaluations. *International Journal of Educational Management, 15*(1), 12–22. doi:10.1108/09513540110366097

Airasian, P., & Gullickson, A. (1997). *Teacher Self-Evaluation Tool Kit.* London: Corwin Press, Inc.

Akbari, R. (2007). A critical appraisal of reflective practice in L2 teacher education. *System, 35,* 192–207. doi:10.1016/j.system.2006.12.008

Albanese, M. (2000). Challenges in using rater judgements in medical education. *Journal of Evaluation in Clinical Practice, 6*(3), 305–319. doi:10.1046/j.1365-2753.2000.00253.x PMID:11083041

Albert, D., Hockemeyer, C., Kickmeier-Rust, M. D., Nussbaumer, A., & Steiner, C. M. (2012). E-Learning Based on Metadata, Ontologies and Competence-Based Knowledge Space Theory. In D. Lukose, A. R. Ahmad, & A. Suliman (Eds.), Knowledge Technology (pp. 24–36). Springer Berlin Heidelberg; Retrieved from http://link.springer.com/chapter/10.1007/978-3-642-32826-8_3 doi:doi:10.1007/978-3-642-32826-8_3 doi:10.1007/978-3-642-32826-8_3

Alberta Education, Aboriginal Services Branch. (2005). *Our words, our ways: teaching First Nations, Métis and Inuit learners.* Alberta, Canada: Minister of Education. Retrieved from https://education.alberta.ca/media/307199/words.pdf

Al-Issa, A., & Sulieman, H. (2007). Student evaluations of teaching: Perceptions and biasing factors. *Quality Assurance in Education, 15*(3), 302–317. doi:10.1108/09684880710773183

Amelung, M., Krieger, K., & Rösner, D. (2011). E-assessment as a service. *IEEE Transactions on Learning Technologies, 4*(2), 162–174. doi:10.1109/TLT.2010.24

Amidon, E., & Flanders, N. (1967). *The Role of the Teacher in the Classroom: A Manual for Understanding and Improving Teacher Classroom Behavior.* Minneapolis: Association for Productive Teaching.

Anders, A. (2012). Creating Custom Learning Assessment and Student Feedback Applications with Google Apps Script. In A. H. Duin, F. Anklesaria, & E. Nater (Eds.), *Cultivating Change in the Academy: 50+ Stories from the Digital Frontlines at the University of Minnesota in 2012.*

Anderson, H. (1997). *Conversation, language, and possibilities: A postmodern approach to therapy.* New York, NY, US: Basic Books.

Andrade, H., & Valtcheva, A. (2009). Promoting learning and achievement through self-assessment. *Theory into Practice, 48*(1), 12–19. doi:10.1080/00405840802577544

Andrich, D. (1978). Relationships between the Thurstone and Rasch approaches to item Scaling. *Applied Psychological Measurement, 2*(3), 449–460. doi:10.1177/014662167800200319

Andrich, D. (1982). An index of person separation in latent trait theory, the traditional KR-20 index, and the Guttman scale response pattern. *Education Research and Perspectives, 9*(1), 95–104.

Angelo, T. A., & Cross, K. P. (1993). *Classroom Assessment Technologies* (2nd ed.). San Francisco: Jossey-Bass Publishers.

Anshel, M. H., Kang, M., & Jubenville, C. (2013). Sources of acute sport stress scale for sports officials: Rasch calibration. *Psychology of Sport and Exercise, 14*(3), 362–370. doi:10.1016/j.psychsport.2012.12.003

ARCPRO (Aprendizaje Recíproco de Competencias Profesionales). (2009). Retrieved from http://www.sinte.es/arc_pro/

Arntzen, E., & Hoium, K. (2010). On the effectiveness of interteaching. *Behavior Analyst Today, 11*(3), 155–160. doi:10.1037/h0100698

Ashby, E. (1984). Forward. In *I.M. Brewer, Learning More and Teaching Less.* Guildford: Society for Research into Higher Education.

Ashford-Rowe, K., Herrington, J., & Brown, C. (2013). Establishing the critical elements that determine authentic assessment. *Assessment & Evaluation in Higher Education, 39*(2), 205–222. doi:10.1080/02602938.2013.819566

Askew, S., & Lodge, C. (2000). Gifts, ping-pong and loops – linking feedback and learning. In S. Askew (Ed.), *Feedback for learning* (pp. 1–18). London: Routledge Falmer.

Astin, A. W. (2012). *Assessment for excellence: The philosophy and practice of assessment and evaluation in higher education.* Rowman & Littlefield Publishers.

Attali, Y. (2014). A ranking method for evaluating constructed responses. *Educational and Psychological Measurement, 74*(5), 795–808. doi:10.1177/0013164414527450

Aultman, L. P. (2006). An unexpected benefit of formative student evaluations. *College Teaching, 54*(3), 251–285. doi:10.3200/CTCH.54.3.251-285

Aviram, A. (2000). Beyond constructivism: Autonomy-oriented education. *Studies in Philosophy and Education, 19*(5-6), 465-489. Doi: :100526711174110.1023/A

Ayala, C. C., Shavelson, R. J., Ruiz-Primo, M. A., Brandon, P. R., Yin, Y., Furtak, E. M., & Tomita, M. K. et al. (2008). From Formal Embedded Assessments to Reflective Lessons: The Development of Formative Assessment Studies. *Applied Measurement in Education, 21*(4), 315–334. doi:10.1080/08957340802347787

Azarfam, A. Y. (2012). Basic considerations in writing instruction & assessment. *Advances in Asian Social Science, 1*(1), 139–150.

Baartman, L. (2008). *Assessing the assessment. Development and use of quality criteria for Competence Assessment Programmes.* (Dissertation), Universiteit Utrecht, Utrecht.

Baartman, L. K., Bastiaens, T. J., Kirschner, P. A., & Van der Vleuten, C. P. (2006). The wheel of competency assessment: Presenting quality criteria for competency assessment programs. *Studies in Educational Evaluation, 32*(2), 153–170. doi:10.1016/j.stueduc.2006.04.006

Baartman, L. K., Bastiaens, T. J., Kirschner, P. A., & van der Vleuten, C. P. (2007). Evaluating assessment quality in competence-based education: A qualitative comparison of two frameworks. *Educational Research Review, 2*(2), 114–129. doi:10.1016/j.edurev.2007.06.001

Bachman, L., & Palmer, A. (2010). *Language assessment in practice.* Oxford: Oxford University Press.

Bailey, R., & Garner, M. (2010). Is the feedback in higher education assessment worth the paper it is written on? Teachers' reflections on their practices. *Teaching in Higher Education, 15*(2), 187–198. doi:10.1080/13562511003620019

Baker, E. L., O'Neil, H. F., & Linn, R. L. (1993). Policy and validity prospects for performance-based assessment. *The American Psychologist, 48*(12), 1210–1218. doi:10.1037/0003-066X.48.12.1210

Bamber, V. (2008). Evaluating Lecturer Development Programmes: Received Wisdom or Self-Knowledge? *The International Journal for Academic Development, 13*(2), 107–116. doi:10.1080/13601440802076541

Barberá, E. (2006). Aportaciones de la tecnología a la e-Evaluación. *RED Revista de Educación a Distancia, Monográfico VI*. Retrieved from http://www.um.es/ead/red/M6/barbera.pdf

Barber, J. P., King, P. M., & Baxter Magolda, M. B. (2013). Long strides on the journey toward self-authorship: Substantial developmental shifts in college students' meaning making. *The Journal of Higher Education, 84*(6), 866–896. doi:10.1353/jhe.2013.0033

Barnett, R. (2004). Learning for an unknown future. *Higher Education Research & Development, 23*(3), 247–260. doi:10.1080/0729436042000235382

Baughan, P., & Morris, E. (2014, September). Synthesising and applying assessment models to higher education practice: the disciplinary and the generic. *Paper presented atThe European Conference of Educational Research (ECER)*, Porto, Portugal.

Baughan, P. (2013). Practising what we teach: Addressing plagiarism prevention issues on professional development programmes for higher education teachers. *The International Journal of Learning in Higher Education, 19*(3), 157–165.

Baughan, P. (2015). Sustainability policy and sustainability in higher education curricula: The educational developer perspective. *The International Journal for Academic Development, 20*(4), 319–332. doi:10.1080/1360144X.2015.1070351

Baxter Magolda, M. B. (1992). *Knowing and Reasoning in College*. San Francisco: Jossey-Bass.

Baxter Magolda, M. B. (1999). *Creating contexts for learning and self-authorship: constructive-developmental pedagogy*. Nashville, Tenn.: Vanderbilt University Press.

Baxter Magolda, M. B. (2000). Teaching to Promote Holistic Learning and Development. *New Directions for Teaching and Learning, 82*(82), 88–98. doi:10.1002/tl.8209

Baxter Magolda, M. B. (2001). *Making Their Own Way*. Sterling, Virginia: Stylus Publishing.

Baxter Magolda, M. B. (2001). *Making their own way: Narratives for transforming higher education to promote self-authorship*. Sterling, VA: Stylus.

Baxter Magolda, M. B. (2004). Evolution of a constructivist conceptualization of epistemological reflection. *Educational Psychologist, 39*(1), 31–42. doi:10.1207/s15326985ep3901_4

Baxter Magolda, M. B. (2009). *Authoring your Life*. Sterling, Virginia: Stylus Publishing.

Baxter Magolda, M. B. (2009). *Authoring your life: Developing an internal voice to navigate life's challenges*. Sterling, VA: Stylus.

Becker, H. S., Geer, B. S., & Hughes, E. C. (1968). *Making the grade: The academic side of college life*. New Jersey: Transaction publishers.

Bejar, I. I. (2012). Rater cognition: Implications for validity. *Educational Measurement: Issues and Practice, 31*(3), 2–9. doi:10.1111/j.1745-3992.2012.00238.x

Belenky, M. F., Clinchy, B. M., Goldberger, N. R., & Tarule, J. M. (1986/1997). *Women's ways of knowing: The development of self, voice and mind.* New York: Basic Books.

Bennani, S., Idrissi, M. K., Fadouli, N., Yassine, B. T., & Ouguengay, Y. A. (2012). Online Project based learning driven by competencies: A systematic strategy proposal for assessment. *Proceedings of the 2012 International Conference on Interactive Mobile and Computer Aided Learning (IMCL)* (pp. 92–97). IEEE. Retrieved from http://ieeexplore.ieee.org/xpls/abs_all.jsp?arnumber=6396457

Biggs, J. (2003). *Teaching for quality learning at university* (2nd ed.). Buckingham: Open.

Biggs, J. (2003). *Teaching for Quality Learning at University* (2nd ed.). Buckingham: Society for Research into Higher Education / Open University Press.

Biggs, J. B. (1996). Assessing Learning Quality: Reconciling institutional, staff and educational demands. *Assessment & Evaluation in Higher Education, 21*(1), 5–15. doi:10.1080/0260293960210101

Biggs, J. B. (1996). Enhancing teaching through constructive alignment. *Higher Education, 32*(3), 347–364. doi:10.1007/BF00138871

Biggs, J. B. (2003). *Teaching for quality learning at university: what the student does* (2nd ed.). Berkshire: SRHE and Open University Press.

Biggs, J., & Tang, C. (2011). *Teaching for quality learning at university: What the student does* (4th ed.). Maidenhead: Open University Press.

Bissonnette, S., & Richard, M. (2001). *Comment construire des compétences en classe: Des outils pour la réforme.* Chenelière/McGraw-Hill.

Bitchener, J. (2008). Evidence in support of written corrective feedback. *Journal of Second Language Writing, 17*(2), 69–124. doi:10.1016/j.jslw.2007.11.004

Black, B. (2008). Using an adapted rank-ordering method to investigate January versus June awarding standards. *Paper presented at theFourth Biennial EARLI/Nortumbria Assessment Conference*, Berlin, Germany.

Black, P., Harrison, C., Lee, C., Marshall, B., & Wiliam, D. (2003). *Assessment for Learning: Putting it Into Practice.* Berkshire, England: Open University Press.

Black, P., & Jones, J. (2006). Formative assessment and the learning and teaching of MFL: Sharing the language learning road map with the learners. *Language Learning Journal, 34*(1), 4–9. doi:10.1080/09571730685200171

Black, P., & Wiliam, D. (2009). Developing the theory of formative assessment. *Educational Assessment, Evaluation and Accountability, 21*(1), 5–31. doi:10.1007/s11092-008-9068-5

Black, P., & William, D. (1998). Assessment and classroom learning. *Assessment in Education: Principles, Policy & Practice, 5*(1), 7–74. doi:10.1080/0969595980050102

Bland, M., & Gallagher, P. (2009). The impact of a change to assessment policy on students from a New Zealand School of Nursing. *Nurse Education Today, 29*(7), 722–730. PMID:19327874

Bloom, B. (1971). *Taxonomy of educational objectives: the classification of educational goals - Handbook 1: Cognitive domain.* New York: David Mackay Company.

Bloxham, S., den-Outer, B., Hudson, J. and Price, M. (2015). Let's stop the pretence of consistent marking: exploring the multiple limitations of assessment criteria. *Assessment and Evaluation in Higher Education.* DOI:10.1080/02602938.2015.1024607.

Bloxham, S., & Boyd, P. (2007). *Developing assessment in higher education: A practical guide*. Maidenhead: Open University Press.

Bloxham, S., & Boyd, P. (2007). *Developing Effective Assessment in Higher Education. A Practical Guide*. New York: Open University Press - MCGraw Hill Education.

Bloxham, S., & Boyd, P. (2007). *Developing Effective Assessment in Higher Education: a practical guide*. Maidenhead: McGraw Hill / Open University Press.

Bloxham, S., Boyd, P., & Orr, S. (2011). Mark my words: The role of assessment criteria in UK higher education grading practices. *Studies in Higher Education, 36*(6), 655–670. doi:10.1080/03075071003777716

Bloxham, S., & Campbell, L. (2010). Generating dialogue in assessment feedback: Exploring the use of interactive cover sheets. *Assessment & Evaluation in Higher Education, 35*(3), 291–300. doi:10.1080/02602931003650045

Bloxham, S., & Price, M. (2015). External examining: Fit for purpose? *Studies in Higher Education, 40*(2), 195–211. doi:10.1080/03075079.2013.823931

Bocconi, S., Kampylis, P. G., & Punie, Y. (2012). Innovating Learning: Key Elements for Developing Creative Classrooms in Europe. Luxembourg: Publications Office of the European Union (JRC Scientific and Policy Reports).

Bodman, S. (2007). *The power of feedback in professional learning. (EdD)*. London: University of London.

Boekaerts, M. (1999). Motivated learning: Studying student situation transactional units. *European Journal of Psychology of Education, 14*(1), 41–55.

Boekaerts, M., Maes, S., & Karoly, P. (2005). Self-regulation across domains of applied psychology: Is there an emerging consensus? *Applied Psychology, 54*(2), 149–154. doi:10.1111/j.1464-0597.2005.00201.x

Bollag, B. (2006). Making an art form of assessment. *The Chronicle of Higher Education, 56*(10), 8–10.

Bols, A., & Wicklow, K. (2013). Feedback - what students want. In S. Merry, M. Price, D. Carless, & M. Taras (Eds.), *Reconceptualising Feedback in Higher Education: Developing dialogue with students* (pp. 19–29). London: Routledge.

Bond, T. G., & Fox, C. M. (2007). *Applying the Rasch model: fundamental measurement in the human sciences* (2nd ed.). Mahwah, N.J.: Lawrence Erlbaum Associates Publishers.

Borst, W. N. (1997). *Construction of engineering ontologies for knowledge sharing and reuse*. Universiteit Twente. Retrieved from http://doc.utwente.nl/17864

Boud, D. (1995). *Enhancing learning through self-assessment*. London: Kogan Page.

Boud, D. (1995). *Enhancing Learning through Self-Assessment*. London: Routledge.

Boud, D. (2000). Sustainable Assessment: Rethinking assessment for the learning society. *Studies in Continuing Education, 22*(2), 151–167. doi:10.1080/713695728

Boud, D. (2006). Foreword. In C. Bryan & K. Clegg (Eds.), *Innovative Higher Education* (pp. xvii–xix). London: Routledge.

Boud, D. (2007). Reframing assessment as if learning were important. In N. Falchikov & D. Boud (Eds.), *Rethinking assessment in higher education: Learning for the longer term* (pp. 14–25). London: Routledge.

Boud, D. et al. (2010). *Assessment 2020: Seven propositions for assessment reform in higher education*. Sydney: Australian Learning and Teaching Council.

Boud, D., & Falchikov, N. (2006). Aligning assessment with long-term learning. *Assessment & Evaluation in Higher Education, 31*(4), 399–413. doi:10.1080/02602930600679050

Boud, D., & Molloy, E. (2013). Rethinking models of feedback for learning: The challenge of design. *Assessment & Evaluation in Higher Education, 38*(6), 698–712. doi:10.1080/02602938.2012.691462

Boud, D., & Soler, R. (2015). Sustainable assessment revisited. *Assessment & Evaluation in Higher Education*, 2015, 1–14. doi:10.1080/02602938.2015.1018133

Bourdieu, P. (1990). *In other words: Essays towards a reflexive sociology*. Stanford, CA: Stanford University Press.

Bovill, C., & Bulley, C. J. (2011). A model of active student participation in curriculum design: Exploring desirability and possibility. In C. Rust (Ed.), *Improving Student Learning Global Theories and Local Practices: Institutional, Disciplinary and Cultural Variations* (pp. 176–188). Oxford: The Oxford Centre for Staff and Educational Development.

Boyatzis, R. E. (1982). *The Competent Manager: A Model for Effective Performance*. John Wiley & Sons.

Boyce, T. E., & Hineline, P. N. (2002). Interteaching: A strategy for enhancing the user-friendliness of behavioral arrangements in the college classroom. *The Behavior Analyst, 25*(2), 215–225. PMID:22478388

Boyle, A., & Hutchison, D. (2009). Sophisticated tasks in e-assessment: What are they and what are their benefits? *Assessment & Evaluation in Higher Education, 34*(3), 305–319. doi:10.1080/02602930801956034

Bradley, R. A., & Terry, M. E. (1952). Rank analysis of incomplete block designs. The method of paired comparisons. *Biometrika, 39*(3-4), 324–345. doi:10.1093/biomet/39.3-4.324

Bramley, T., & Black, B. (2008). Maintaining performance standards: aligning raw score scales on different tests via a latent trait created by rank-ordering examinees' work. *Paper presented at theThird International Rasch Measurement conference*, University of Western Australia, Perth.

Bramley, T. (2005). A rank-ordering method for equating tests by expert judgment. *Journal of Applied Measurement, 6*(2), 202–223. PMID:15795487

Bramley, T. (2007). Paired comparison methods. In J. B. P. Newton, H. Goldstein, H. Patrick, & P. Tymms (Eds.), *Techniques for monitoring the comparability of examination standards* (pp. 246–294). London: QCA.

Bramley, T. (Ed.). (2015). *Investigating the reliability of Adaptive Comparative Judgment*. Cambridge, UK: Cambridge Assessment.

Bramley, T., Bell, J. F., & Pollitt, A. (1998). Assessing changes in standards over time using Thurstone paired comparisons. *Education Research and Perspectives, 25*, 1–24.

Bramley, T., & Gill, T. (2010). Evaluating the rank-ordering method for standard maintaining. *Research Papers in Education, 25*(3), 293–317. doi:10.1080/02671522.2010.498147

Brannon, L., & Knoblauch, C. H. (1982). On students' rights to their own texts: A model of teacher response. *College Composition and Communication, 33*(2), 157–166. doi:10.2307/357623

Braun, V., & Clarke, V. (2006). Using thematic analysis in psychology. *Qualitative Research in Psychology, 3*(2), 77–101. doi:10.1191/1478088706qp063oa

Bremgartner, V., & de Magalhaes Netto, J. F. (2011). An adaptive strategy to help students in e-Learning systems using competency-based ontology and agents. *Proceedings of the 2011 11th International Conference on Intelligent Systems Design and Applications (ISDA)* (pp. 978–983). http://doi.org/ doi:doi:10.1109/ISDA.2011.6121785 doi:10.1109/ISDA.2011.6121785

Brinko, K. T. (1993). The practice of giving feedback to improve teaching: What is effective? *The Journal of Higher Education, 64*(5), 574–593. doi:10.2307/2959994

Brisebois, A., Ruelland, D., Paquette, G., Brisebois, A., Ruelland, D., & Paquette, G. (2005). Supporting self-assessment in a competency approach to learning (Vol. 2005, pp. 2828–2835*). Presented at the E-Learn: World Conference on E-Learning in Corporate, Government, Healthcare, and Higher Education.*

Brookhart, S. M. (2008). *How to give effective feedback to your students.* USA: ASCD publications.

Brooks, V. (2012). Marking as judgment. *Research Papers in Education, 27*(1), 63–80. doi:10.1080/02671520903331008

Brown, S. (2015b). International perspectives on assessment practice in Higher Education. *RELIEVE - Revista Electrónica de Investigación Y Evaluación Educativa, 21*(1). doi:10.7203/relieve.21.1.6403

Brown, E., & Glover, C. (2006). Evaluating written feedback. In C. Bryan & K. Clegg (Eds.), *Innovative Assessment in Higher Education* (pp. 81–91). New York: Routledge.

Brown, G. T. L., Hui, S. K. F., Yu, F. W. M., & Kennedy, K. J. (2011). Teachers' conceptions of assessment in Chinese contexts: A tripartite model of accountability, improvement, and irrelevance. *International Journal of Educational Research, 50*(5-6), 307–320. doi:10.1016/j.ijer.2011.10.003

Brown, G. T. L., & Michaelides, M. P. (2011). Ecological rationality in teachers' conceptions of assessment across samples from Cyprus and New Zealand. *European Journal of Psychology of Education, 26*(3), 319–337. doi:10.1007/s10212-010-0052-3

Brown, G., Bull, J., & Pendlebury, M. (1997). *Assessing students learning in higher education.* New York: Routledge.

Brown, J. S., Collins, A., & Duguid, P. (1989). Situated Cognition and the culture of learning. *Educational Researcher, 18*(1), 32–42. doi:10.3102/0013189X018001032

Brown, M. J. (2008). Student perceptions of teaching evaluations. *Journal of Instructional Psychology, 35*(2), 177–181.

Brown, M. J., Baillie, M., & Fraser, S. (2009). Rating ratemyprofessors.com: A comparison of online and official student evaluations of teaching. *College Teaching, 57*(2), 89–92. doi:10.3200/CTCH.57.2.89-92

Brown, S. (2004). Assessment for learning. *Learning and Teaching in Higher Education, 1*, 81–89.

Brown, S. (2015a). *Learning, Teaching and Assessment in Higher Education. Global Perspectives.* London: Palgrave Macmillan.

Brown, S., & Knight, P. (1994). *Assessing learners in higher education.* London: Kogan.

Bull, J., & McKenna, C. (2003). *Blueprint for computer-assisted assessment.* London: Routledge Falmer.

Bunderson, V. C., Inouye, D. K., & Olsen, J. B. (1989). The four generations of computerized educational measurement. In R. L. Lynn (Ed.), *Educational Measurement* (pp. 367–407). New York: Macmillan.

Burford, B., Morrow, G., Rothwell, C., Carter, M., & Illing, J. (2014). Professionalism education should reflect reality: Findings from three health professions. *Medical Education, 48*(4), 361–374. doi:10.1111/medu.12368

Burns, R. (2000). Introducing Research (4th ed.). French's Forest, NSW: Pearson.

Butcher, J., & Stoncel, D. (2012). The Impact of a Postgraduate Certificate in Teaching in Higher Education on University Lecturers Appointed for Their Professional Expertise at the Teaching-Led University: "It's Made Me Braver. *The International Journal for Academic Development, 17*(2), 149–162. doi:10.1080/1360144X.2011.620107

Butler, D. L., & Winne, P. H. (1995). Feedback and self-regulated learning: A theoretical synthesis. *Review of Educational Research*, *65*(3), 245–281. doi:10.3102/00346543065003245

Butler, R. (1987). Task-involving and ego-involving properties of evaluation: Effects of different feedback conditions on motivational perceptions, interest and performance. *Journal of Educational Psychology*, *78*(4), 210–216.

Byrne, P., & Long, B. (1976). *Doctors Talking to Patients*. London: HMSO.

Caine, R., & Caine, G. (1991). *Making connections: Teaching and the human brain*. Alexandria, Virginia: Association for Supervision and Curriculum Development.

Caine, R., Caine, G., McClintic, C., & Klimek, K. (2005). *12 Brain/Mind Learning Principles in Action: The Field book for Making Connections, Teaching, and the Human Brain*. Thousand Oaks, California: Corwin Press.

Callison, D. (1998). Authentic Assessment. *School Library Media Activities Monthly*, *14*(5), 42–50.

Carless, D. (2006). Differing perceptions in the feedback process. *Studies in Higher Education*, *31*(2), 219–233. doi:10.1080/03075070600572132

Carless, D. (2009). Learning-oriented assessment: Principles, practice and a project. In L. H. Meyer, S. Davidson, H. Anderson, R. Fletcher, P. M. Johnston, & M. Ress (Eds.), *Tertiary Assessment & Higher Education Student Outcomes: Policy, Practice & Research* (pp. 79–90). Wellington, New Zealand: Ako Aotearoa.

Carless, D. (2015). *Excellence in University Assessment: Learning from Award-winning Practice*. London: Routledge.

Carless, D., Joughin, G., & Liu, N.-F. (2006). *How Assessment supports learning: learning-oriented assessment in action*. Hong Kong: Hong Kong University Press. doi:10.5790/hongkong/9789622098237.001.0001

Carless, D., Salter, D., Yang, M., & Lam, J. (2011). Developing sustainable feedback practices. *Studies in Higher Education*, *36*(4), 395–407. doi:10.1080/03075071003642449

Carlson, P. A. (1998). Advanced Educational Technologies - Promise and Puzzlement. *Journal of Universal Computer Science*, *4*(3), 210–215.

Carlton, M., & Levy, Y. (2015). *Expert assessment of the top platform independent cybersecurity skills for non-IT professionals* (pp. 1–6). SoutheastCon; doi:10.1109/SECON.2015.7132932

Carroll, J. (2007). *A Handbook for Deterring Plagiarism in Higher Education* (2nd ed.). Oxford: The Oxford Centre for Staff and Learning Development.

Carter, T. M. (2013). Use what you have: Authentic assessment of in-class activities. *RSR. Reference Services Review*, *41*(1), 49–61. doi:10.1108/00907321311300875

Case, R. (2008). Four principles of authentic assessment. In R. Case & P. Clark (Eds.), *The anthology of social studies: issues and strategies for secondary teachers* (Vol. 2, pp. 359–368). Vancouver, CA: Pacific Educational Press.

Cassidy, S. (2007). Assessing 'inexperienced' students' ability to self-assess: Exploring links with learning style and academic personal control. *Assessment & Evaluation in Higher Education*, *32*(3), 313–330. doi:10.1080/02602930600896704

Castelló, M. (2009). *La evaluación auténtica en secundaria y universidad*. Barcelona: Edebé.

Cauley, K. M., & McMillan, G. H. (2010). Formative Assessment Techniques to Support Student Motivation and Achievement. *The Clearing House: A Journal of Educational Strategies, Issues and Ideas*, *83*(1), 1–6. doi:10.1080/00098650903267784

Cheng, K.-H., & Hou, H.-T. (2015). Exploring students' behavioural patterns during online peer-assessment from the affective, cognitive, and metacognitive perspectives: A progressive sequential analysis. *Technology, Pedagogy and Education*, *24*(2), 171–188. doi:10.1080/1475939X.2013.822416

Chick, N., Karis, T., & Kernahan, C. (2009). Learning from their own learning: How metacognitive and meta-affective reflections enhance learning in race-related courses. *International Journal for the Scholarship of Teaching & Learning*, *3*(1). doi:10.20429/ijsotl.2009.030116

Chi, M. (1997). Quantifying qualitative analysis of verbal data: A practical guide. *Journal of the Learning Sciences*, *6*(3), 271–315. doi:10.1207/s15327809jls0603_1

Christensen, T. K., & Osguthorpe, R. T. (2004). How Do Instructional-Design Practitioners Make Instructional-Strategy Decisions? *Performance Improvement Quarterly*, *17*(3), 45–65. doi:10.1111/j.1937-8327.2004.tb00313.x

Cilliers, F. J., & Herman, N. (2010). Impact of an Educational Development Programme on Teaching Practice of Academics at a Research-Intensive University. *The International Journal for Academic Development*, *15*(3), 253–267. doi:10.1080/1360144X.2010.497698

Clayson, D. E. (2009). Student evaluations of teaching: Are they related to what students learn? *Journal of Marketing Education*, *31*(1), 16–30. doi:10.1177/0273475308324086

Clayson, D. E., & Haley, D. A. (2011). Are students telling us the truth? A critical look at the student evaluation of teaching. *Marketing Education Review*, *21*(2), 101–112. doi:10.2753/MER1052-8008210201

Clements, M. D., & Cord, B. A. (2013). Assessment guiding learning: Developing graduate qualities in an experiential learning programme. *Assessment & Evaluation in Higher Education*, *38*(1), 114–124. doi:10.1080/02602938.2011.609314

Comeaux, P. (2005). Assessment and learning. In P. Comeaux (Ed.), *Assessing Online Learning* (pp. xix–xxvii). Bolton, MA: Anker Publishing Company, Inc.

Comm, C. L., & Manthaisel, D. F. X. (1998). Evaluating teaching effectiveness in America's business schools: Implications for service marketers. *Journal of Professional Services Marketing*, *16*(2), 163–170. doi:10.1300/J090v16n02_09

Considine, J., Botti, M., & Thomas, S. (2005). Design, format, validity and reliability of multiple- choice questions for use in nursing research and education. *Collegian: Journal of the Royal College of Nursing Australia*, *12*(1), 19–24. doi:10.1016/S1322-7696(08)60478-3 PMID:16619900

Cook, D. A., Zendejas, B., Hamstra, S. J., Hatala, R., & Brydges, R. (2013). What counts as validity evidence? Examples and prevalence in a systematic review of simulation-based assessment. *Advances in Health Sciences Education: Theory and Practice*, *19*(2), 233–250. doi:10.1007/s10459-013-9458-4 PMID:23636643

Cook-Greuter, S. R. (1999/2005). Postautonomous Ego Development [Doctoral Dissertation]. Harvard University Graduate School of Education.

Court, K. (2012). Tutor feedback on draft essays: Developing students' academic writing and subject knowledge. *Journal of Further and Higher Education*, *38*(3), 327–345. doi:10.1080/0309877X.2012.706806

Covic, T., & Jones, M. K. (2008). Is the essay resubmission option a formative or a summative assessment and does it matter as long as the grades improve? *Assessment & Evaluation in Higher Education*, *33*(1), 75–85. doi:10.1080/02602930601122928

Cowan, J. (2006). *On Becoming an Innovative University Teacher: Reflection in Action*. UK: McGraw-Hill Education.

Craven, R. G., Marsh, H. W., & Debus, R. L. (1991). Effects of internally focused feedback on the enhancement of academic self-concept. *Journal of Educational Psychology*, *83*(1), 17–27. doi:10.1037/0022-0663.83.1.17

Crisp, G. T. (2010). Interactive e-Assessment – Practical approaches to constructing more sophisticated online tasks. *Journal of Learning Design, 3*(3), 1–10. doi:10.5204/jld.v3i3.57

Crisp, G. T. (2012). Integrative assessment: Reframing assessment practice for current and future learning. *Assessment & Evaluation in Higher Education, 37*(1), 33–43. doi:10.1080/02602938.2010.494234

Crisp, G. T. (2014a). *Designing and using e-Assessments.* Milperra, NSW, Australia: HERDSA Guide, Higher Education Research and Development Society of Australasia.

Crisp, G. T. (2014b). Assessment in Next Generation Learning Spaces. In K. Fraser (Ed.), *The Future of Learning and Teaching in Next Generation Learning Spaces. International Perspectives on Higher Education Research* (Vol. 12, pp. 85–100). Emerald Group Publishing Limited.

Crisp, V. (2013). Criteria, comparison and past experiences: How do teachers make judgements when marking coursework? *Assessment in Education: Principles, Policy & Practice, 20*(1), 127–144. doi:10.1080/0969594X.2012.741059

Cronbach, L., Gleser, G., Nanda, H., & Rajaratnam, N. (1972). *The dependability of behavioural measurements: theory of generalizability for scores and profiles.* New York: Wiley.

Crosier, J. (2011). Please tell me what you are thinking: Workshop in analytical writing for college freshmen. *International Journal of the Humanities, 9*(6), 17–22.

Crossley, J. (2014). Addressing learner disorientation: Give them a roadmap. *Medical Teacher, 36*(8), 685–691. doi:10.3109/0142159X.2014.889813

Crossley, J., & Davies, H. (2005). Doctors' consultations with children and their parents: A model of competencies, outcomes, and confounding influences. *Medical Education, 39*(8), 807–819. doi:10.1111/j.1365-2929.2005.02231.x

Crossley, J., Davies, H., Humphris, G., & Jolly, B. (2002). Generalisability: A key to unlock professional assessment. *Medical Education, 36*(10), 972–978. doi:10.1046/j.1365-2923.2002.01320.x

Crossley, J., Humphris, G., & Jolly, B. (2002). Assessing health professionals. *Medical Education, 36*(9), 800–804. doi:10.1046/j.1365-2923.2002.01294.x

Crossley, J., Johnson, G., Booth, J., & Wade, W. (2011). Good questions, good answers: Construct alignment improves the performance of workplace-based assessment scales. *Medical Education, 45*(6), 560–569. doi:10.1111/j.1365-2923.2010.03913.x

Crossley, J., & Jolly, B. (2012). Making sense of work-based assessment: Ask the right questions, in the right way, about the right things, of the right people. *Medical Education, 46*(1), 28–37. doi:10.1111/j.1365-2923.2011.04166.x

Cruess, S. R., & Cruess, R. L. (2012). Teaching professionalism - Why, What and How. *Facts Views Vis Obgyn, 4*(4), 259–265.

Csikszentmihalyi, M. (1993). *The Evolving Self – a psychology for the third millennium.* New York: HarperCollins Publishers.

Cuenca, L., Fernández-Diego, M., Gordo, M., Ruiz, L., Alemany, M. M. E., & Ortiz, A. (2015). Measuring Competencies in Higher Education. The Case of Innovation Competence. In M. Peris-Ortiz & J. M. M. Lindahl (Eds.), Sustainable Learning in Higher Education (pp. 131–142). Springer International Publishing; Retrieved from http://link.springer.com/chapter/10.1007/978-3-319-10804-9_10 doi:doi:10.1007/978-3-319-10804-9_10 doi:10.1007/978-3-319-10804-9_10

Dahl, S. (2007). The student perspective on using plagiarism detection software. *Active Learning in Higher Education, 8*(2), 173–191. doi:10.1177/1469787407074110

Daly, C., Pachler, N., Mor, Y., & Mellar, H. (2010). Exploring formative e-Assessment using case stories and design patterns. *Assessment & Evaluation in Higher Education, 35*(5), 619–636. doi:10.1080/02602931003650052

Darling-Hammond, L., & Snyder, J. (2000). Authentic assessment of teaching in context. *Teaching and Teacher Education, 16*(5), 523–545. doi:10.1016/S0742-051X(00)00015-9

Darwin, S. (2012). Moving beyond face value: Re-envisioning higher education evaluation as a generator of professional knowledge. *Assessment & Evaluation in Higher Education, 37*(6), 733–745. doi:10.1080/02602938.2011.565114

Davies, A., & Le Mahieu, P. (2003). Assessment for learning: reconsidering portfolios and research evidence. In M. Segers, F. Dochy, & E. Cascallar (Eds.), *Innovation and Change in Professional Education: Optimising New Modes of Assessment: In Search of Qualities and Standards* (pp. 141–169). Dordrecht: Kluwer Academic Publishers. doi:10.1007/0-306-48125-1_7

Dean, C., Hubbell, E., Pitler, H., & Stone, B. (2012). *Classroom instruction that works: Research-based strategies for increasing student achievement* (2nd ed.). Alexandria, VA: ASCD.

Dee, K. C. (2007). Student perceptions of high course workloads are not associated with poor student evaluations of instructor performance. *The Journal of Engineering Education, 96*(1), 69–78. doi:10.1002/j.2168-9830.2007.tb00916.x

Deeley, S. (2014). Summative co-assessment: A deep learning approach to enhancing employability skills and attributes. *Active Learning in Higher Education, 15*(1), 39–51. doi:10.1177/1469787413514649

Dermo, J. (2009). e-Assessment and the student learning experience: A survey of student perceptions of e-assessment. *British Journal of Educational Technology, 40*(2), 203–214. doi:10.1111/j.1467-8535.2008.00915.x

Derrick, K. (2012). Developing the e-scape software system. *International Journal of Technology and Design Education, 22*(2), 171–185. doi:10.1007/s10798-011-9193-1

Dewey, J. (1916). *Democracy and education*. New York: Free Press.

DeWitt, D., Carline, J., Paauw, D., & Pangaro, L. (2008). Pilot study of a 'RIME'-based tool for giving feedback in a multi-specialty longitudinal clerkship. *Medical Education, 42*(12), 1205–1209. doi:10.1111/j.1365-2923.2008.03229.x

Diamond, M. (2004). The usefulness of structured mid-term feedback as a catalyst for change in higher education classes. *Active Learning In Higher Education The Journal Of The Institute For Learning And Teaching, 5*(3), 217–231. doi:10.1177/1469787404046845

Dierick, S., & Dochy, F. J. R. C. (2001). New lines in edumetrics: New forms of assessment lead to new assessment criteria. *Studies in Educational Evaluation, 27*(4), 307–329. doi:10.1016/S0191-491X(01)00032-3

Dikli, S. (2006). An overview of automated scoring essays. *The Journal of Technology, Learning, and Assessment, 5*(1), 4–35.

Dillenbourg, P. (1999). What do you mean by "collaborative learning"? In P. Dillenbourg (Ed.), *Collaborative learning: Cognitive and Computational approaches* (pp. 1–19). Oxford: Elsevier.

Djoub, Z. (2013). Assessment and students' autonomy in language learning. In Z. Arezki, H. Amziane & A. Guendouzi (Eds.), Studies in the teaching and learning of foreign languages in Algeria (pp.197-208). Tizi-Ouzou, Algeria: University of Mouloud Mammeri of Tizi-Ouzou.

Dochy, F., Segers, M., & Buehl, M. (1999). The relation between assessment practices and outcomes of studies: The case of research on prior knowledge. *Review of Educational Research, 69*(2), 145–186. doi:10.3102/00346543069002145

Dochy, F., Segers, M., & Sluijsmans, D. (1999). The Use of Self-, Peer and Co-assessment in Higher Education: A review. *Studies in Higher Education, 24*(3), 331–350. doi:10.1080/03075079912331379935

Donabedian, A. (1980). Explorations in quality assessment and monitoring: Vol. 1. *The definition of quality and approaches to its assessment*. Ann Arbor, MI: Health Administration Press.

Donnelly, R. (2008). Lecturers' Self-Perception of Change in Their Teaching Approaches: Reflections on a Qualitative Study. *Educational Research, 50*(3), 207–222. doi:10.1080/00131880802309317

Downing, K., Kwong, T., Chan, S., Lam, T., & Downing, W. (2009). Problem-based Learning and the development of metacognition. *Higher Education, 57*(5), 609–621. doi:10.1007/s10734-008-9165-x

Drago-Severson, E. (2011). A Close-up on Adult Learning and Development Diversity: Adult Growth in Cohorts and Collaborative Groups. In C. Hoare (Ed.), *The Oxford Handbook of Reciprocal Adult Development and Learning* (pp. 461–489). New York: Oxford University Press.

Draper, S. W. (2009). Catalytic assessment: Understanding how MCQs and EVS can foster deep learning. *British Journal of Educational Technology, 40*(2), 285–293. doi:10.1111/j.1467-8535.2008.00920.x

Duffy, K. (2013). Providing constructive feedback to students during mentoring. *Nursing Standard, 27*(31), 50–56. doi:10.7748/ns2013.04.27.31.50.e7334 PMID:23641638

Duncan, N. (2007). 'Feed-forward': Improving students' use of tutors' comments. *Assessment & Evaluation in Higher Education, 32*(3), 271–283. doi:10.1080/02602930600896498

Dunlap, J. C., & Grabinger, S. (2003). Preparing students for lifelong learning: A review of instructional features and teaching methodologies. *Performance Improvement Quarterly, 1*(2), 6–25.

Dunn, L., Morgan, C., O'Reilly, M., & Parry, S. (2004). *The Student Assessment Handbook. New Directions in Traditional & Online Assessment*. London: RoutledgeFalmer.

Dysthe, O. (2011). 'What is the Purpose of Feedback when Revision is not Expected?' A Case Study of Feedback Quality and Study Design in a First Year Master's Programme. *Journal of Academic Writing, 1*(1), 135–142. doi:10.18552/joaw.v1i1.26

Efklides, A., & Vlachopoulos, S. P. (2012). Measurement of metacognitive knowledge of self, task, and strategies in mathematics. *European Journal of Psychological Assessment, 28*(3), 227–239. doi:10.1027/1015-5759/a000145

El Falaki, B., Idrissi, M. K., Bennani, S., & Associates. (2011). Design an Adaptive Competency-Based Learning Web Service According to IMS-LD Standard. In Innovative Computing Technology (pp. 37–47). Springer; Retrieved from http://link.springer.com/chapter/10.1007/978-3-642-27337-7_5

El-Henawy, W. (2012). *The Effectiveness of a Program Based on Self-Regulated Learning Strategies in Treating Written Expression Difficulties among English Department Students at Faculties of Education* [Doctoral dissertation]. Port-Said University, Egypt.

El-Kechaï, N., Melero, J., & Labat, J.-M. (2015). Quelques enseignements tirés de l'application de la Competence-based Knowledge Space Theory aux Serious Games. *Presented at the IC2015*. Retrieved from https://hal.archives-ouvertes.fr/hal-01170079/document

Elliott, R. J. (2008). Assessment 2.0. *International Journal of Emerging Technologies in Learning, 3*, 66–70.

Elstein, A., Shulman, L., & Sprafka, S. (1990). Medical Problem-Solving - a 10-Year Retrospective. *Evaluation & the Health Professions, 13*(1), 5–36. doi:10.1177/016327879001300102

Elstein, A., Shulman, L., & Srafka, S. (1978). *Medical problem-solving: an anlysis of clinical reasoning.* Cambridge, MA: Harvard University Press. doi:10.4159/harvard.9780674189089

Emery, C. R., Kramer, T. R., & Tian, R. G. (2003). Return to academic standards: A critique of student evaluations of teaching effectiveness. *Quality Assurance in Education, 11*(1), 37–46. doi:10.1108/09684880310462074

Entwistle, N. (2000, November). Promoting Deep Learning through Teaching and Assessment Conceptual Frameworks and Educational Contexts. *Proceedings of theTLRP Conference*, Leicester.

Entwistle, A. C., & Entwistle, N. J. (1992). Experiences of understanding in revising for degree examinations. *Learning and Instruction, 2*(1), 1–22. doi:10.1016/0959-4752(92)90002-4

Entwistle, N. (2000). Approaches to studying and levels of understanding: the influences of teaching and assessment. In J. C. Smart (Ed.), *Higher Education: Handbook of Theory and Research* (Vol. XV, pp. 156–218). New York: Agathon.

Entwistle, N. J., & Entwistle, A. C. (1997). Revision and the Experience of Understanding. In F. Marton, D. Hounsell, & N. J. Entwistle (Eds.), *The Experience of Learning* (2nd ed., pp. 145–155). Edinburgh: Scottish Academic Press.

Entwistle, N. J., & Peterson, E. R. (2004). Conceptions of learning and knowledge in higher education: Relationships with study behaviour and influences of learning environments. *International Journal of Educational Research, 41*(6), 407–428. doi:10.1016/j.ijer.2005.08.009

Entwistle, N. J., & Ramsden, P. (1983). *Understanding Student Learning.* New York: Nichols.

Entwistle, N., Hanley, M., & Hounsell, D. (1979). Identifying distinctive approaches to studying. *Higher Education, 8*(4), 365–380. doi:10.1007/BF01680525

Epstein, R. M., & Hundert, E. M. (2002). Defining and assessing professional competence. *Journal of the American Medical Association, 287*(2), 226–235. doi:10.1001/jama.287.2.226

Erlauer, L. (2003). *The Brain-compatible classroom: Using what we know about learning to improve teaching.* Alexandria, Virginia: Association for Supervision and Curriculum Development.

Eur-Lex (2006). Recommendation of the European Parliament and of the Council of 18 December 2006 on key competences for lifelong learning (2006/962/EC). *Official Journal of the European Union.* Retrieved from http://eur-lex.europa.eu/legal-content/EN/TXT/?uri=celex:32006H0962

European Commission. (2009, April 28-29). *Communiqué of the Conference of European Ministers Responsible for Higher Education, Leuvenand Louvain-la-Neuve.* Retrieved from http://www.ehea.info/Uploads/Declarations/Leuven_Louvain-la Neuve_Communiqu%C3%A9_April_2009.pdf

European Commission. (2012). *Assessment of Key Competences in Initial Education and Training: Policy Guidance.* Commission staff working document. Retrieved from http://eose.org/wp-content/uploads/2014/03/Assessment-of-Key-Competences-in-initial-education-and-training.pdf

European Commission. (2014). *New modes of learning and teaching in higher education.* Retrieved from http://ec.europa.eu/education/library/reports/modernisation-universities_en.pdf

European Commission/EACEA/Eurydice. (2013). *European Commission Report to the European Commission on improving the quality of teaching and learning in Europe's higher education institutions.* Luxembourg: Publications Office of the European Union.

European Commission/EACEA/Eurydice. (2014). *Modernization of Higher Education in Europe: Access, Retention and Employability.* Luxembourg: Publications Office of the European Union.

Eva, K. W., & Regehr, G. (2005). Self-assessment in the health professions: A reformulation and research agenda. *Academic Medicine, 80*(10 Suppl.), S46–S54. doi:10.1097/00001888-200510001-00015

Eva, K. W., & Regehr, G. (2011). Exploring the divergence between self-assessment and self-monitoring. *Advances in Health Sciences Education: Theory and Practice, 16*(3), 311–329. doi:10.1007/s10459-010-9263-2

Evans, C., & Sabry, K. (2003). Evaluation of the interactivity of web-based learning systems: Principles and process. *Innovations in Education and Teaching International, 40*(1), 89–99. doi:10.1080/1355800032000038787

Falchikov, N. (1986). Product comparisons and process benefits of collaborative peer group and self-assessments. *Assessment & Evaluation in Higher Education, 11*(2), 144–166. doi:10.1080/0260293860110206

Falchikov, N. (1995). Improving feedback to and from students. In P. Knight (Ed.), *Assessment for learning in higher education. Staff and Educational Development Series* (pp. 157–166). London: Kogan Page.

Falchikov, N. (2001). *Learning together: peer tutoring in higher education.* London: Routledge Falmer. doi:10.4324/9780203451496

Falchikov, N. (2004). *Improving Assessment Through Student Involvement.* London: RoutledgeFalmer.

Falchikov, N. (2005). *Improving Assessment Through Student Involvement. Practical solutions for aiding learning in higher and further education.* London: Routledge-Falmer.

Falchikov, N. (2005). *Improving Assessment Through student Involvement. Practical solutions for aiding learning in higher education and further education.* London: RoutledgeFalmer.

Falchikov, N., & Boud, D. (2007). *Rethinking assessment in higher education: learning for the longer term.* London: Routledge.

Fallik, O., Bat-Sheva, E., & Rosenfeld, S. (2008). Motivating Teachers to Enact Free- Choice Project-Based Learning in Science and Technology (PBLSAT): Effects of a Professional Development Model. *Journal of Teacher Education, 19*(6), 565–591. doi:10.1007/s10972-008-9113-8

Fastréa, G. M., van der Klinka, M. R., Sluijsmansa, D., & van Merriënboera, J. (2012). Towards an integrated model for developing sustainable assessment skills. *Assessment & Evaluation in Higher Education, 2012*, 1–20.

Finelli, C. J., Wright, M. C., & Pinder-Grover, T. (2010). Consulting the delphi: A new idea for collecting student feedback through the two survey method (TSM). *Journal of Faculty Development, 24*(2), 25–33. Retrieved from http://search.proquest.com/ docview/868918564? accountid=38769

Flores, K. L., Matkin, G. S., Burbach, M. E., Quinn, C. E., & Harding, H. (2012). Deficient critical thinking skills among college graduates: Implications for leadership. *Educational Philosophy and Theory, 44*(2), 212–230. doi:10.1111/j.1469-5812.2010.00672.x

Flores, M. A., Veiga Simão, A. M., Barros, A., & Pereira, D. (2015). Perceptions of effectiveness, fairness and feedback of assessment methods: A study in higher education. *Studies in Higher Education, 40*(9), 1523–1534. doi:10.1080/03075079.2014.881348

Floud, R. (2002). Policy implications of student non-completion: government, funding councils and universities. In M. Peelo & T. Wareham (Eds.), *Failing students in higher education* (pp. 56–69). Buckingham: Open University Press.

Fook, C. Y., & Sidhu, G. K. (2013). Assessment practices in higher education in United States. *Procedia: Social and Behavioral Sciences, 123*, 299–306. doi:10.1016/j.sbspro.2014.01.1427

Frank, J. R., & Danoff, D. (2007). The CanMEDS initiative: Implementing an outcomes-based framework of physician competencies. *Medical Teacher, 29*(7), 642–647. doi:10.1080/01421590701746983

Fraser, S. P., & Bosanquet, A. M. (2006). The curriculum? That's just a unit outline, isn't it? *Studies in Higher Education, 31*(3), 269–284. doi:10.1080/03075070600680521

Freese, A. R. (2006). Reframing one's teaching: Discovering our teacher selvesthrough reflection and inquiry. *Teaching and Teacher Education, 22*(1), 100–111. doi:10.1016/j.tate.2005.07.003

Frey, B. (2014). *Modern Classroom Assessment*. California: Sage Publications.

Frick, T. W., Chadha, R., Watson, C., Wang, Y., & Green, P. (2009). College student perceptions of teaching and learning quality. *Educational Technology Research and Development, 57*(5), 705–720. doi:10.1007/s11423-007-9079-9

Froyd, J., & Simpson, N. (2008). Student-centered learning addressing faculty questions about student centered learning. Proceedings of the Course, Curriculum, Labor, and Improvement Conference, 30(11).

Gareis, C. R., & Grant, L. W. (2008). *Teacher-made assessments: how to connect curriculum, instruction, and student learning*. Larchmont, NY: Eye On Education.

Garrett, N., Thoms, B., Alrushiedat, N., & Ryan, T. (2009). Social ePortfolios as the new course management system. *On the Horizon, 17*(3), 197–207. doi:10.1108/10748120910993222

Garrison, R & Anderson, T. (2003). *E-Learning in the 21st Century: A framework for research and practice*. Routledge.

Gehringer, E. F. (2010). *Daily course evaluation with Google forms*. Paper presented at the American Society for Engineering Educational Annual Conference, Louisville, KY. Retrieved from http://search.asee.org/search/fetch;jsessionid=23t2t08kfrlin?url=file://localhost/E:/search/conference/32/AC%25202010Full1151.pdf&index=conference_papers&space=12974679720360579171667617 8&type=application/pdf&charset

Gibbs, G. & Simpson, C. (2003). Does your assessment support your students learning? *Journal of Learning and Teaching in Higher Education*, 1(1), 3-31.

Gibbs, G. & Simpson, C. (2004-5). Conditions under which assessment supports students' learning. *Learning and Teaching in Higher Education*, 1, 3-29.

Gibbs, G. (1999). Using Assessment Strategically to Change the Way Students Learn. In: Brown, S. & Glaser, A. (Eds.) Assessment Matters in Higher Education. (pp. 41-53). Buckingham: Open University Press.

Gibbs, G., & Simpson, C. (2004). Conditions under which assessment supports students' learning. *Learning and teaching in higher education,* 1(1), 3-31.

Gibbs, G. (1999). Using assessment strategically to change the way students learn. In S. Brown & A. Glaser (Eds.), *Assessment matters in higher education* (pp. 41–53). Buckingham: Open University Press.

Gibbs, G. (2006). How assessment frames student learning. Cordelis Bryan and Karen Clegg. In *Innovative Assessment in higher education* (pp. 23–36). Abingdon: Routledge.

Gibbs, G. (2006). How assessment frames student learning. In C. Bryan & K. Clegg (Eds.), *Innovative assessment in higher education* (pp. 23–36). New York: Routledge.

Gibbs, G., & Simpson, C. (2004). Conditions under which Assessment supports Student Learning. *Learning and Teaching in Higher Education, 1*, 3–31.

Gibbs, G., & Simpson, C. (2004-05). Conditions under which assessment supports learning. *Learning and Teaching in Higher Education,1*,3–29.

Gielen, S., Dochy, F., & Dierick, S. (2003). Evaluating the consequential validity of new modes of assessment: The influence of assessment on learning. In M. Segers, F. Dochy, & E. Cascallar (Eds.), *Optimising new modes of assessment: In search of quality and standards* (pp. 37–54). Dordrecht, The Netherlands: Kluwer Academic Publishers. doi:10.1007/0-306-48125-1_3

Gielen, S., Dochy, F., Onghena, P., Struyven, K., & Smeets, S. (2011). Goals of peer assessment and their associated quality concepts. *Studies in Higher Education, 36*(6), 719–735. doi:10.1080/03075071003759037

Gipps, C. (1994). *Beyond testing*. Washington, DC: Falmer Press.

GMC. (2009). Tomorrow's Doctors: outcomes and standards for undergraduate medical education. (1st ed., pp. 55). Manchester, UK: General Medical Council.

Gokhale, A. (1995). Collaborative learning enhances critical thinking. *Journal of Technology Education, 7*(1), 22–30.

Gómez Ruiz, M. A., Rodríguez Gómez, G., & Ibarra Sáiz, M. S. (2013). Development of Basic Competencies of Students in Higher Education through Learning Oriented e-Assessment. *RELIEVE: Revista Electrónica de Investigación y Evaluación Educativa, 19*(1). doi:10.7203/relieve.19.1.2609

Gómez-Ruiz, M. A., Rodríguez-Gómez, G., & Ibarra-Sáiz, M. S. M.S. (2011). Caracterización de la e-evaluación orientada al e-aprendizaje. In G. Rodríguez & M.S. Ibarra (Eds.), e-Evaluación Orientada al e-aprendizaje estratégico en Educación Superior (pp. 33-56). Madrid: Narcea

Gómez-Ruiz, M. A., Rodríguez-Gómez, G., Ibarra-Sáiz, M. S., & Gallego-Noche, B. (2013). Aprendiendo a investigar con una Web docente: Una experiencia de realización de trabajos de investigación en el ámbito universitario mediante un sistema de gestión de contenidos. *Proceedings of XVI Congreso Nacional-II Internacional de Modelos de Investigación Educativa* (pp. 725-733). Alicante: AIDIPE.

Govaerts, M., & van der Vleuten, C. P. (2013). Validity in work-based assessment: Expanding our horizons. *Medical Education, 47*(12), 1164–1174. doi:10.1111/medu.12289

Gow, L., & Kember, D. (1990). Does higher education promote independent learning? *Higher Education, 19*(3), 307–322. doi:10.1007/BF00133895

Gravett, S., & Petersen, N. (2002). Structuring dialogue with students via learning tasks. *Innovative Higher Education, 26*(4), 281–291. doi:10.1023/A:1015833114292

Greatorex, J. (2007). Contemporary GCSE and A-level Awarding: A psychological perspective on the decision-making process used to judge the quality of candidates' work. *Paper presented at theBritish Educational Research Association conference*, London.

Grice, H. (1975). In P. Cole & J. Morgan (Eds.), *Logic and Conversation* (Vol. 3, pp. 41–58). Syntax and semanticsNew York: Academic Press.

Gruber, T. (2009). Ontology. Encyclopedia of Database Systems, 1963–1965.

Gruber, T. R. (1993). A translation approach to portable ontology specifications. *Knowledge Acquisition, 5*(2), 199–220. doi:10.1006/knac.1993.1008

Grundy, S. (1989). Beyond Professionalism. In W. Carr (Ed.), Quality in Teaching: Arguments for a Reflective Profession (pp. 79-100). London: Falmer Press.

Guàrdia, L., Maina, M., & Sangrà, A. (2013) MOOC Design Principles. A Pedagogical Approach from the Learner's Perspective. *eLearning Papers, 33*. Retrieved from http://www.openeducationeuropa.eu/en/article/MOOC-Design-Principles.-A-Pedagogical-Approach-from-the-Learner%E2%80%99s-Perspective

Guàrdia, L., Maina, M., Barberà, L., & Alsina, I. (2014, November 13). Open resources for implementing ePortfolios in Higher Education. *Paper presented at the1st International Workshop on Technology-Enhanced Assessment, Analytics and Feedback (TEAAF2014),* Barcelona.

Guàrdia, L., Maina, M., Barberà, L., & Alsina, I. (2015, July 2-4). Matriz conceptual sobre usos y propósitos de los eportfolios. *Procedia - Social and Behavioral Sciences, 196,* 106 – 112.

Gulikers, J. (2006). Authenticity is in the eye of the beholder. Beliefs and perceptions of authentic assessment and the influence on student learning [Doctoral dissertation]. Open University of the Netherlands, The Netherlands.

Gulikers, J. T. M., Kester, L., Kirschner, P. A., & Bastiaens, T. J. (2008). The effect of practical experience on perceptions of assessment authenticity, study approach, and learning outcomes. *Learning and Instruction, 18*(2), 172–186. doi:10.1016/j.learninstruc.2007.02.012

Gulikers, J., Bastiaens, T., & Kirschner, P. (2004). A Five-Dimensional Framework for Authentic Assessment. *ETR&D, 52*(3), 67–86. doi:10.1007/BF02504676

Gustafson, K. L., & Branch, R. M. (2002). What is instructional design. In *Trends and issues in instructional design and technology* (pp. 16-25).

Gutiérrez, E., Trenas, M. A., Ramos, J., Corbera, F., & Romero, S. (2010). A new Moodle module supporting automatic verification of VHDL-based assignments. *Computers & Education, 54*(2), 562–577. doi:10.1016/j.compedu.2009.09.006

Haan, P., Britt, M., McClellan, S., & Parks, T. H. (2010). Business students' perceptions of course evaluations. *College Student Journal, 44*(4), 878–887.

Haines, C. (2004). *Assessing Students Written Work: Marking Essays and Reports.* London: RoutledgeFalmer. doi:10.4324/9780203465110

Halpern, D. F. (1999). Teaching for critical thinking: Helping college students develop the skills and dispositions of a critical thinker. *New Directions for Teaching and Learning, 80*(80), 69–74. doi:10.1002/tl.8005

Hamayan, E. (1995). Approaches to alternative assessment. *Annual Review of Applied Linguistics, 15,* 212–226. doi:10.1017/S0267190500002695

Handley, K., & Williams, L. (2011). From copying to learning: Using exemplars to engage students with assessment criteria and feedback. *Assessment & Evaluation in Higher Education, 36*(1), 95–108. doi:10.1080/02602930903201669

Hanrahan, S., & Isaacs, G. (2001). Assessing self- and peer assessment: The students' views. *Higher Education Research & Development, 20*(1), 53–70. doi:10.1080/07294360123776

Harden, R. M., & Gleeson, F. A. (1979). Assessment of clinical competence using an objective structured clinical examination (OSCE). *Medical Education, 13*(1), 41–54. doi:10.1111/j.1365-2923.1979.tb00918.x

Hardiman, M. (2001). Connecting brain research with dimensions of learning. *Educational Leadership, 59*(3), 52–55.

Harford, J., & MacRuairc, G. (2008). Engaging student teachers in meaningful reflective practice. *Teaching and Teacher Education, 24*(7), 1884–1892. doi:10.1016/j.tate.2008.02.010

Harlen, W., & Deakin Crick, R. (2003). *A systematic review of the impact on students and teachers of the use of ICT for assessment of creative and critical thinking skills.* Retrieved from http://eppi.ioe.ac.uk/cms/Default.aspx?tabid=109

Harvey, M., & Norman, L. (2007). Beyond competencies: What higher education assessment could offer the workplace and the practitioner-researcher? *Research in Post-Compulsory Education, 12*(3), 331–342. doi:10.1080/13596740701559779

Haskell, R. E. (1997). Academic freedom, tenure, and student evaluation of faculty: Galloping polls in the 21st century. *Education Policy Analysis Archives, 5*(6), 2.

Hassan, W. (2013). Brain-compatible classroom: An investigation into Malaysia's secondary school science teachers' pedagogical beliefs and practices [Doctoral dissertation]. La Trobe University: Australia.

Hattie, J., & Timperley, H. (2007). The power of feedback. *Review of Educational Research, 77*(1), 181–112. doi:10.3102/003465430298487

Hawksey, M. (2015). *Association for Learning Technology Annual Survey 2014 Data and Report.* Retrieved from http://repository.alt.ac.uk/2358/

Heine, P., & Maddox, N. (2009). Student perceptions of the faculty course evaluation process: An exploratory study of gender and class differences. *Research in Higher Education Journal, 3*, 1–10.

Heldsinger, S., & Humphry, S. (2010). Using the method of pairwise comparison to obtain reliable teacher assessments. *Australian Educational Researcher, 37*(2), 1–19. doi:10.1007/BF03216919

Heldsinger, S., & Humphry, S. (2013). Using calibrated exemplars in the teacher-assessment of writing: An empirical study. *Educational Research, 55*(3), 219–235. doi:10.1080/00131881.2013.825159

Heller, J., Mayer, B., Hockemeyer, C., & Albert, D. (2006). Competence–based knowledge structures for personalised learning. *International Journal on E-Learning, 5*, 75–88.

Heller, J., Stefanutti, L., Anselmi, P., & Robusto, E. (2015). On the Link between Cognitive Diagnostic Models and Knowledge Space Theory. *Psychometrika, 2015*, 1–25. doi:10.1007/s11336-015-9457-x PMID:25838246

Henard, F. & Leprince-Ringuet, S. (2011). *The path to Quality Teaching in Higher Education. OECD.* Retrieved from www.oecd.org/edu/imhe/44150246.pdf

Hepplestone, S., Holden, G., Irwin, B., Parkin, H. J., & Thorpe, L. (2011). Using technology to encourage student engagement with feedback: A literature review. *Research in Learning Technology, 19*(2), 117–127. doi:10.1080/21567069.2011.586677

Herman, J., Aschbacher, P., & Winters, L. (1992). *A Practical Guide to Alternative Assessment.* Alexandria, VA: Association for Supervision and Curriculum Development.

Hettiarachchi, E., Huertas, M. A., & Mor, E. (2013). Skill and Knowledge E-Assessment: A Review of the State of the Art. *IN3 Working Paper Series.* Retrieved from http://journals.uoc.edu/index.php/in3-working-paper-series/article/view/n13-hettiarachchi-huertas-mor/n13-hettiarachchi-huertas-mor-en

Hewett, S. M. (2004). Electronic portfolios: Improving instructional practices. *TechTrends, 48*(5), 24–28. doi:10.1007/BF02763526

He, Y., Hui, S. C., & Quan, T. T. (2009). Automatic summary assessment for intelligent tutoring systems. *Computers & Education, 53*(3), 890–899. doi:10.1016/j.compedu.2009.05.008

Higgins, R. (2000, September 7-10). Be More Critical!: Rethinking assessment feedback. *Paper presented at the British Educational Research Association Conference,* Cardiff University.

Hill, J., & Hawk, K. (2000, November). Four Conceptual Clues to Motivating Students: learning from the practice of effective teachers in low-decile, multi-cultural schools. *Paper presented to the NZARE Conference,* Waikato.

Hnida, M., Idrissi, M. K., & Bennani, S. (2014). Towards an adaptive e-learning system based on individualized paths in a competency-based approach. *Recent advances in educational technologies and education*, 73.

Hnida, M., Idrissi, M.K., & Bennani, S. (2014). A formalism of the competency-based approach in adaptive learning systems. *WSEAS Transactions on Information Science and Applications*, 11, 83–93.

Hodges, L. C., & Stanton, K. (2007). Translating comments on student evaluations into the language of learning. *Innovative Higher Education*, *31*(5), 279–286. doi:10.1007/s10755-006-9027-3

Hoefer, P., Yurkiewicz, J., & Byrne, J. C. (2012). The association between students' evaluation of teaching and grades. *Decision Sciences Journal of Innovative Education*, *10*(3), 447–459. doi:10.1111/j.1540-4609.2012.00345.x

Horowitz, H. (1988). Campus life: Understanding cultural from the end of the eighteenth century to the present (2dfdc ed.). Chicago: University of Chicago Press.

Hounsel, D. (2009). Evaluating courses and teaching. In H. Fry, S. Ketteridge, & S. Marshall (Eds.), *A Handbook for teaching and learning in Higher Education. Enhancing academic practice* (pp. 198–231). New York, London: Routledge.

Hounsell, D., McCune, V., Litjens, J., & Hounsell, J. (2005). *Subject overview report for biosciences. Universities of Edinburgh*. Durham, Coventry: ETL Project.

HR Open Standards Consortium, Inc. (n. d.). Retrieved from http://www.hropenstandards.org/?

Hudesman, J., & Crosby, S., Flugman, b., Issac, S., Everson, H., & Clay, D. B. (2013). Using formative assessment and metacognition to improve student achievement. *Journal of Developmental Education*, *37*(1), 2–13.

Hyde, C., Lefroy, J., Gay, S., Yardley, S., & McKinley, R. (2014). A clarification study of internal scales clinicians use to assess undergraduate medical students. *Paper presented at theOttawa Conference on Medical Education*, Ottawa Canada.

Hyland, K. (2003). *Second Language Writing*. Cambridge: Cambridge University Press. doi:10.1017/CBO9780511667251

Hyland, K., & Hyland, F. (2006). Feedback on second language students' writing. *Language Teaching*, *39*(02), 83–101. doi:10.1017/S0261444806003399

Hyland, K., & Hyland, F. (Eds.). (2006). *Feedback in Second Language Writing: Contexts and Issues*. Cambridge: Cambridge University Press. doi:10.1017/CBO9781139524742

Ibarra Sáiz, M. S., Rodríguez Gómez, G., & Gómez Ruiz, M. A. (2012). La evaluación entre iguales: Beneficios y estrategias para su práctica en la universidad. *Revista de Educación*, *359*, 206–231.

Ibarra-Sáiz, M. S., & Rodríguez-Gómez, G. (2010). Aproximación al discurso dominante sobre la evaluación del aprendizaje en la universidad. *Revista de Educación*, (351), 385–407.

Iborra, A., García, L., Margalef, L., & Pérez, V. (2009). Generating Collaborative Contexts to promote learning and development. In E. Luzzatto & G. DiMarco (Eds.), *Collaborative Learning: Methodology, Types of Interactions and Techniques* (pp. 47–80). New York: Nova Science Publishers.

Idrissi, M. K., Bennani, S., & Hachmoud, A. (2009). An ontology for the formalization of the competences-based approach. *Proceedings of theV International conference on multimedia and ICT in Education (m-ICTE2009), Lisbon (Portugal)* (pp. 22–24).

IMS GLC. RDCEO Specification. (n. d.). Retrieved from http://www.imsglobal.org/competencies/

Ion, G., & Cano, E. (2011). Assessment practices at Spanish universities: From a learning to a competencies approach. *Evaluation and Research in Education*, *24*(3), 167–181. doi:10.1080/09500790.2011.610503

Irons, A. (2010). An Investigation into the Impact of Formative Feedback on the Student Learning Experience [PhD]. Durham: Durham University. Retrieved from http://etheses.dur.ac.uk/890/

Irving, P. W., & Sayre, E. C. (2013). Upper-level Physics Students' Conceptions of Understanding. Paper presented at 2012 Physics Education Research Conference. *ProceedingsAIP Conference* (*Vol. 1513*, pp. 98-201). Doi:10.1063/1.4789686

Iucu, R. (2010). Ten Years after Bologna: Towards a European Teacher Education Area. In O. Gassner, L. Kerger & M. Schratz (Ed.), Entep - The First Ten Years after Bologna (pp. 53-95). Bucharest, RO: EdituraUniversității din București.

Jack, C. (2010). Exploring Brain-Based Instructional Practices in Secondary Education Classes [Doctoral dissertation]. Boise State University.

Jensen, E. (2004). *Brain-compatible strategies* (2nd ed.). California: Crowin Press.

Jensen, E. (2005). *Teaching with the brain in mind* (2nd ed.). Alexandria, VA: Association for Supervision and Curriculum Development.

Jisc. (2007). *Effective practice with e-Assessment. An overview of technologies, policies and practice in further and higher education*. Retrieved from http://www.webarchive.org.uk/wayback/archive/20140615085433/http://www.jisc.ac.uk/media/documents/themes/elearning/effpraceassess.pdf

Jisc. (2009). *Effective Assessment in a Digital Age*. Retrieved from http://www.webarchive.org.uk/wayback/archive/20140614115719/http://www.jisc.ac.uk/media/documents/programmes/elearning/digiassass_eada.pdf

Johnson, L., Smith, R., Willis, H., Levine, A., & Haywood, K. (2011). *The 2011 Horizon Report*. Austin, Texas: The New Media Consortium.

Johnson, M. D., Narayanan, A., & Sawaya, W. J. (2013). Effects of course and instructor characteristics on student evaluation of teaching across a college of engineering. *The Journal of Engineering Education*, *102*(2), 289–318. doi:10.1002/jee.20013

Johnson, V. E. (2003). *Grade inflation: A crisis in college education*. New York: Springer.

Johnstone, A. (2003). *LTSN physical sciences practice guide effective practice in objective assessment: The skills of fixed response testing. LTSN Physical Sciences* Centre. Retrieved from https://www.heacademy.ac.uk/sites/default/files/ps0072_effective_practice_in_objective_assessment_mar_2004.pdf

Johnstone, S. M., & Leasure, D. E. (2015). How Competency-Based Education Can Fulfill the Promise of Educational Technology. In M. Antona & C. Stephanidis (Eds.), Universal Access in Human-Computer Interaction. Access to Learning, Health and Well-Being (pp. 127–136). Springer International Publishing. Retrieved from http://link.springer.com/chapter/10.1007/978-3-319-20684-4_13 doi:doi:10.1007/978-3-319-20684-4_13 doi:10.1007/978-3-319-20684-4_13

Joint Information Systems Committee. (2010). *Effective Assessment in a Digital Age*. Retrieved from http://www.jisc.ac.uk/media/documents/programmes/elearning/digiassass_eada.pdf

Jonassen, D. H. (1999). Designing constructivist learning environments. *Instructional design theories and models: A new paradigm of instructional theory*, 2, 215-239.

Jones, I., & Alcock, L. (2012). Using Adaptive Comparative Judgement to assess mathematics. *The De Morgan Forum*. Retrieved from http://education.lms.ac.uk/2012/06/using-adaptive-comparative-judgement-to-assess-mathematics/

Jones, I., & Alcock, L. (2013). Peer assessment without assessment criteria. *Studies in Higher Education*, *39*(10), 1774–1787. doi:10.1080/03075079.2013.821974

Jones, I., & Inglis, M. (2015). The problem of assessing problem solving: Can comparative judgement help? *Educational Studies in Mathematics*, 2015, 1–19.

Jones, I., Swan, M., & Pollitt, A. (2014). Assessing mathematical problem solving using comparative judgement. *International Journal of Science and Mathematics Education*, *13*(1), 151–177. doi:10.1007/s10763-013-9497-6

Jones, O., & Gorra, A. (2013). Assessment feedback only on demand: Supporting the few not supplying the many. *Active Learning in Higher Education*, *14*(2), 149–161. doi:10.1177/1469787413481131

Jonsson, A., & Svingby, G. (2007). The use of scoring rubrics: Reliability, validity and educational consequences. *Educational Research Review*, *2*(2), 130–144. doi:10.1016/j.edurev.2007.05.002

Jordan, S. (2013, July 9-10). Using e-assessment to learn about learning. *Presented at the2013 International Computer Assisted Assessment Conference*, Southampton.

Jordan, S. (2012). Student engagement with assessment and feedback: Some lessons from short-answer free-text e-assessment questions. *Computers & Education*, *58*(2), 818–834. doi:10.1016/j.compedu.2011.10.007

Kane, M., Crooks, T., & Cohen, A. (1999). Validating measures of performance. *Educational Measurement: Issues and Practice*, *18*(2), 5–17. doi:10.1111/j.1745-3992.1999.tb00010.x

Karpicke, J. D., Butler, A. C., & Roedlger, H. L. (2009). Metacognitive strategies in learning: Do students practice retrieval when they study on their own? *Memory (Hove, England)*, *17*(4), 471–479. doi:10.1080/09658210802647009 PMID:19358016

Katz, L. G., Chard, S. C., & Kogan, Y. (2014). *Engaging children's minds: The project approach* (3rd ed.). Santa Barbara: Praeger.

Kaufeldt, M. (2010). *Begin with the brain: Orchestrating the learner-centered classroom* (2nd ed.). Thousand Oaks, CA: Corwin Press. doi:10.4135/9781483350448

Kay, R. H., & LeSage, A. (2009). A strategic assessment of audience response systems used in higher education. *Australasian Journal of Educational Technology*, *25*(2), 235–249. doi:10.14742/ajet.1152

Kearney, S. (2012). Assessment & Evaluation in Higher Education Improving engagement: The use of "Authentic self-and peer-assessment for learning" to enhance the student learning experience. *Assessment & Evaluation in Higher Education*, *38*(7), 875–891. doi:10.1080/02602938.2012.751963

Keeney, B. P. (1983). *Aesthetics of change*. New York: Guilford.

Kegan, R. (1994). *In over our Heads. – The mental demands of modern life*. Cambridge, Mass: Harvard University Press.

Kegan, R. (1994). *In over our heads: the mental demands of modern life*. Cambridge: Harvard University Press.

Kegan, R. (2000). What 'form' transforms? In J. Mezirow (Ed.), *Learning as transformation* (pp. 35–70). San Francisco: Jossey-Bass.

Kember, D., Leung, D., & Kwan, K. (2002). Does the use of student feedback questionnaires improve the overall quality of teaching? *Assessment & Evaluation in Higher Education*, *27*(5), 411–425. doi:10.1080/0260293022000009294

Kendall, M. G. (1955). Further contributions to the theory of paired comparisons. *Biometrics*, *11*(1), 43–62. doi:10.2307/3001479

Kendle, A., & Northcote, M. (2000). The struggle for balance in the use of quantitative and qualitative online assessment tasks. *Proceedings of ASCILITE 2000*. Retrieved from http://www.ascilite.org/conferences/coffs00/papers/amanda_kendle.pdf

Kenny, R., Zhang, Z., Schwier, R., & Campbell, K. (2005). A review of what instructional designers do: Questions answered and questions not asked. *Canadian Journal of Learning and Technology/La revue canadienne de l'apprentissage et de la technologie, 31*(1).

Khera, N., Stroobant, J., Primhak, R. A., Gupta, R., & Davies, H. (2001). Training the ideal hospital doctor: The specialist registrars' perspective. *Medical Education, 35*(10), 957–966.

Khiat, H. (2010). A Grounded Theory Approach: Conceptions of Understanding in Engineering Mathematics Learning. *Qualitative Report, 15*(6), 1459–1488.

Kienhuis, M., & Chester, A. (2014). Interteaching: A model to enhance student engagement. In M. Gosper, D. Ifenthaler (Eds.), Curriculum models for the 21st century: Using learning technologies in higher education (pp. 135-153). New York, NY, US: Springer Science + Business Media. doi:doi:10.1007/978-1-4614-7366-4_8 doi:10.1007/978-1-4614-7366-4_8

Kilpatrick, W. H. (1918). The project method. *Teachers College Record, 19*, 319–335.

Kimbell, R. (2007). Project e-scape: A Web-based Approach to Design and Technology Learning and assessment.

Kimbell, R., Wheeler, T., Stables, K., Shepard, T., Martin, F., Davies, D., et al. (2009). e-Scape portfolio assessment: A research & development project for the Department of Children, Families and Schools, phase 3 report. London: Goldsmiths, University of London.

Kimbell, R., Wheeler, A., Miller, S., & Pollitt, A. (2007). *E-scape Portfolio Assessment-a research and development project for the Department of Education and Skills (DfES) and the Qualifications Curriculum Authority (QCA). Phase 2 report*. London: Goldsmiths, University of Londen.

Kim, K., Sharma, P., Land, S. M., & Furlong, K. P. (2013). Effects of active learning on enhancing student critical thinking in an undergraduate general science course. *Innovative Higher Education, 38*(3), 223–235. doi:10.1007/s10755-012-9236-x

King, P. M., & Siddiqui, R. (2011). Self-Authorship and Metacognition: Related Constructs for Understanding College Student Learning and Development. In C. Hoare (Ed.), *The Oxford Handbook of Reciprocal Adult Development and Learning* (pp. 113–131). New York: Oxford University Press; doi:10.1093/oxfordhb/9780199736300.013.0053

King, P., & Baxter Magolda, M. B. (1996). A Developmental Perspective on Learning. *Journal of College Student Development, 37*(2), 163–173.

Kirszner, L., & Mandell, S. (2006). *The Pocket Wadsworth Handbook* (3rd ed.). Boston: Thomson Wadsworth.

Kluger, A. N., & DeNisi, A. (1996). The effects of feedback interventions on perfor-mance: A historical review, a meta-analysis, and a preliminary feedback intervention theory. *Psychological Bulletin, 119*(2), 254–284. doi:10.1037/0033-2909.119.2.254

Knight, P.T. & Yorke, M. (2003). *Assessment, Learning and Employability*. Maidenhead: SRHE/Open university Press/ McGraw-Hill Education.

Knight, P., & Yorke, M. (2004). *Learning, curriculum and employability in higher education*. London: Routledge.

Knight, S., Shum, S. B., & Littlejohn, K. (2014). Epistemology, Assessment, Pedagogy: Where Learning Meets Analytics in the Middle Space. *Journal of Learning Analytics, 1*(2), 23–47.

Knoll, M. (1997). The project method: Its vocational education origin and international development. *Journal of Industrial Teacher Education, 34*(3), 59–80.

Kolb, D. A. (1984). *Experiential Learning: Experience as The Source of Learning and Development.* Prentice Hall, Inc. doi:10.1016/B978-0-7506-7223-8.50017-4

Kolb, A. Y., & Kolb, D. A. (2005). Learning Styles and Learning Spaces. *Enhancing Experiential Learning in Higher Education, 4*(2), 193–212.

Kolb, D. A. (1984). *Experiential learning. Experience as the source of learning and development.* Englewood Cliffs, New Jersey: Prentice Hall.

Korkmaz, O. (2012). The impact of critical thinking and logico-mathematical intelligence on algorithmic design skills. *Journal of Educational Computing Research, 46*(2), 173–193. doi:10.2190/EC.46.2.d

Krajcik, J. S., & Blumenfeld, P. C. (2006). Project-based science. In R. K. Sawyer (Ed.), *The Cambridge handbook of the learning sciences. New York* (pp. 317–334). Cambridge.

Kreber, C. (2010). Academics' teacher identities, authenticity and pedagogy. *Studies in Higher Education, 35*(2), 171–194. doi:10.1080/03075070902953048

Kuh, G. D., Jankowski, N., Ikenberry, S. O., & Kinzie, J. (2014). *Knowing What Students Know and Can Do: The Current State of Student Learning Outcomes Assessment in US Colleges and Universities.* Urbana, IL: University of Illinois and Indiana University, National Institute for Learning Outcomes Assessment (NILOA). Retrieved from http://www.learningoutcomesassessment.org/documents/2013%20Survey%20Report%20Final.pdf

Kuh, G. D., Kinzie, J., Schuh, J. H., & Whitt, E. J. et al. (2005). *Student Success in College: Creating Conditions That Matter.* San Francisco: Jossey-Bass.

Kurri Kurri High School. (2009). Authentic Assessment. Retrieved from https://www.det.nsw.edu.au/vetinschools/schooltowork/teachers/kklc/Documents/Authentic%20Assessment%20for%20Toolkit.pdf

Labouvie-Vief, G. (1990). Wisdom as integrated thought: historical and developmental perspectives. In R. J. Sternberg (Ed.), *Wisdom, its nature, origins and developments* (pp. 52–83). Cambridge, UK: Cambridge University Press. doi:10.1017/CBO9781139173704.005

Lambert, N., & Coombs, B. (1998). *How students learn: Reforming Schools through Learner-centered Education.* Washington: American Psychological Association. doi:10.1037/10258-000

Laming, D. (2003). *Human judgment: the eye of the beholder.* Andover: Cengage Learning EMEA.

Lamote, C., & Engels, N. (2010). The development of student teachers: Professional identity. *European Journal of Teacher Education, 33*(1), 3–18. doi:10.1080/02619760903457735

Landreman, L. M., Rasmussen, C. A., King, P. M., & Jiang, C. X. (2007). A Phenomenological study of the development of university educators' critical consciousness. *Journal of College Student Development, 48*(3), 275–295. doi:10.1353/csd.2007.0027

Le Boterf, G. (2015). *Construire les compétences individuelles et collectives: Agir et réussir avec compétence, les réponses à 100 questions.* Editions Eyrolles.

Lea, J. (2012). 77 things to think about… teaching and learning in higher education. Canterbury Christ Church University. Retrieved from http://www.celt.mmu.ac.uk/policy/ltmmu/docs/77%20Things%20to%20Think%20About%20in%20Learning%20and%20Teaching%20in%20HE.pdf

Leach, L. (2012). Optional self-assessment: Some tensions and dilemmas. *Assessment & Evaluation in Higher Education, 37*(2), 137–147. doi:10.1080/02602938.2010.515013

Leki, I. (1991). The preferences of ESL students for error correction in college-level writing classes. *Foreign Language Annals, 24*(3), 203–218. doi:10.1111/j.1944-9720.1991.tb00464.x

Lewis, K. G. (2001). Making sense of student written comments. *New Directions for Teaching and Learning, 87*(87), 25–32. doi:10.1002/tl.25

Lilly, J., Peacock, A., Shoveller, S., & Struthers, D. (2014). Beyond Levels: alternative assessment approaches developed by teaching schools (Research Report). National College for Teaching and Leadership. Retrieved from https://www.gov.uk/government/uploads/system/uploads/attachment_data/file/349266/beyond-levels-alternative-assessment-approaches-developed-by-teaching-schools.pdf

Linacre, J. M., & Wright, B. D. (1994). Dichotomous Infit and Outfit mean-square fit statistics. *Rasch Measurement Transactions, 8*(2), 360.

Lindblom-Ylänne, S., & Lonka, K. (1999). Individual ways of interacting with the learning environment – are they related to study success? *Learning and Instruction, 9*(1), 1–18. doi:10.1016/S0959-4752(98)00025-5

Liu, O. L. (2012). Student evaluation of instruction: In the new paradigm of distance education. *Research in Higher Education, 53*(4), 471–486. doi:10.1007/s11162-011-9236-1

Ljungman, A. G., & Silén, C. (2008). Examination involving students as peer-examiners. *Assessment & Evaluation in Higher Education, 33*(3), 289–300. doi:10.1080/02602930701293306

Lladó, A. P. et al.. (2014). Student perceptions of peer-assessment: An interdisciplinary study. *Assessment & Evaluation in Higher Education, 39*(5), 592–610. doi:10.1080/02602938.2013.860077

Long, H. B. (1989). Self-directed learning: Emerging theory and practice. In H. B. Long (Ed.), *Self-Directed Learning: Emerging Theory and Practice* (pp. 1–12). Norman, OK: Oklahoma Research Center for Continuing Professional and Higher Education of the University of Oklahoma.

Lopes, L. (2015). *Alternative Assessment of Writing in Learning English as a Foreign Language: Analytical Scoring and Self-assessment. Master's Theses.* Bridgewater State University.

Lorenzo, G., & Ittelson, J. (2005). An overview of e-portfolios. *Educause learning initiative, 1*, 1-27.

Lorenzo, G., & Ittleson, J. (2005). *An overview of e-portfolios.*

Love, D., McKean, G., & Gathercoal, P. (2009). Student webfolios and authentic assessment in information systems. *Proceedings of the 2009 International SIGED: IAIM Conference.*

Lucas, P. (1991). Reflection, new practices and the need for flexibility in supervising student-teachers. *Journal of Further and Higher Education, 15*(2), 84–93. doi:10.1080/0309877910150209

Luce, R. D. (1959). On the possible psychophysical laws. *Psychological Review, 66*(2), 81–95. doi:10.1037/h0043178 PMID:13645853

Lumley, T. (2002). Assessment criteria in a large-scale writing test: What do they really mean to the raters? *Language Testing, 19*(3), 246–276. doi:10.1191/0265532202lt230oa

Lund, J. (n. d.). Overview of Authentic Assessment. Retrieved from http://www.pesta.moe.edu.sg/pesta/slot/u3057/PD/Overview%20of%20Authentic%20Assessment%20by%20Dr%20J%20Lund.pdf

Lundqvist, K. Ø., Baker, K., & Williams, S. (2011). Ontology supported competency system. *International Journal of Knowledge and Learning, 7*(3-4), 197–219. doi:10.1504/IJKL.2011.044539

Luo, T., & Gao, F. (2012). Enhancing classroom learning experience by providing structures to microblogging-based activities. *Journal of Information Technology Education, 11*, 199–211.

Macdonald, R. (2006). The use of evaluation to improve practice in learning and teaching. *Innovations in Education and Teaching International, 43*(1), 3–13. doi:10.1080/14703290500472087

Mack, M. G., & Ragan, B. G. (2008). Development of the mental, emotional, and bodily toughness inventory in collegiate athletes and nonathletes. *Journal of Athletic Training, 43*(2), 125–132. doi:10.4085/1062-6050-43.2.125 PMID:18345336

Macknight, C. B. (2000). Teaching critical thinking through online discussions. *EDUCAUSE Quarterly, 23*(4), 38–41.

Maclellan, E., & Soden, R. (2004). The Importance of Epistemic Cognition in Student-Centred Learning. *Instructional Science, 32*(3), 253–268. doi:10.1023/B:TRUC.0000024213.03972.ce

Man Sze Lau, A. (2015). 'Formative good, summative bad?' – A review of the dichotomy in assessment literature. *Journal of Further and Higher Education*. doi:10.1080/0309877X.2014.984600

Marcos, J. J., M., , Sánchez Miguel, E., & Tillema, H. (2009). Teacher reflection on action: What is said (in research) and what is done (in teaching). *Reflective Practice, 10*(2), 191–204. doi:10.1080/14623940902786206

Margalef García, L. (2014). Evaluación formativa de los aprendizajes en el contexto universitario: Resistencias y paradojas del profesorado. *Educación XX1, 17*(2), 35-55.doi:10.5944/educxx1.17.2.11478

Markham, T. (2011). Project-based learning: A bridge just far enough. *Teacher Librarian, 39*(2), 39–42.

Marques, J., Zacarias, M., & Tribolet, J. (2010). A Bottom-Up Competency Modeling Approach. In A. Albani & J. L. G. Dietz (Eds.), Advances in Enterprise Engineering IV (pp. 50–64). Springer Berlin Heidelberg. Retrieved from http://link.springer.com/chapter/10.1007/978-3-642-13048-9_4 doi:doi:10.1007/978-3-642-13048-9_4 doi:10.1007/978-3-642-13048-9_4

Marriott, P. (2009). Students' Evaluation of the use of Online Summative Assessment on an Undergraduate Financial Accounting Module. *British Journal of Educational Technology, 40*(2), 237–254. doi:10.1111/j.1467-8535.2008.00924.x

Martín, X., & Puig, J. M. (2014). Trabajo por proyectos y servicio a la comunidad. Aprendizaje servicio en la asignatura de educación en valores. Revista CIDUI. Retrieved from http://www.cidui.org/revistacidui/index.php/cidui/article/view/719/690

Martin, S. (1997). Two models of educational assessment: a response from initial teacher education: if the cap fits…. *Assessment & Evaluation in Higher Education, 22*(3), 337–343. doi:10.1080/0260293970220307

Marton, F., & Saljo, R. (2005). Approaches to learning. In D. Hounsell (Ed.), The Experience of Learning: Implications for teaching and studying in higher education (3rd ed., pp. 39-58). Edinburgh: University of Edinburgh.

Marton, F., Dall'Alba, G., & Beaty, E. (1993). Conceptions of learning. *International Journal of Educational Research, 19*(3), 277–300.

Marton, F., Hounsell, D., & Entwistle, N. (1984). *The Experience of learning*. Edinburgh: Scottish Academic Press.

Mason, L. L. (2012). Interteaching to increase active student responding and differentiate instruction. *Behavioral Technology Today, 7*, 1–15.

Mauranen, A. (1994). Two discourse worlds: Study genres in Britain and Finland. *FINLANCE. A Finnish Journal of Applied Linguistics*, 13, 1-40.

Mayor, D., & Rodríguez, M. D. (2015). Aprendizaje-servicio: construyendo espacios de intersección entre la escuela-comunidad-universidad. *Revista Profesorado*, 19(1), 262-279. Retrieved from http://www.ugr.es/~recfpro/rev191ART11.pdf

McCarthy, M. A. M. E. Kite (Ed.), *(n. d.) Effective Evaluation of Teaching: A Guide for Faculty and Administration. Using Student Feedback as One Measure of Faculty Teaching Effectiveness* (pp. 30–39).

McClelland, D. C. (1973). Testing for competence rather than for "intelligence". *The American Psychologist*, 28(1), 1–14. doi:10.1037/h0034092 PMID:4684069

McColskey, W., & Egelson, P. (1993). *Designing Teacher Evaluation Systems that Support Professional Growth*. Greensboro, N.C: University of North Carolina at Greensboro, South Eastern Regional Vision for Education.

McConnell, D. (2006). *E-Learning Groups and Communities*. Berkshire: Open University Press.

McCormack, J., & Slaght, J. (2005). *Extended Writing and Research Skills, Teachers Book*. Reading, UK: Garnet Publishing Ltd.

McCune, V., & Entwistle, N. J. (2011). Cultivating the disposition to understand in 21st century university education. *Learning and Individual Differences*, 21(3), 303–310. doi:10.1016/j.lindif.2010.11.017

McGinty, S. (2007). First year Humanities and Social Science students' experiences of engaging with written feedback in a post-1992 university. (PhD). Wolverhampton: University of Wolverhampton. Retrieved from http://wlv.openrepository.com/wlv/bitstream/2436/210189/1/Mcginty%20Phd%20Thesis.docx

McGowan, W. R. (2009). *Faculty and student perceptions of the effects of mid-course evaluations on learning and teaching* [Unpublished doctoral dissertation]. Brigham-Young University, Provo, Utah.

McMahon, S., & Jones, I. (2014). A comparative judgement approach to teacher assessment. *Assessment in Education: Principles, Policy & Practice*, 22(3), 1–22.

McNamee, M. (2011). *The impact of brain-based instruction on reading achievement in a second-grade classroom* [Doctoral dissertation]. Walden University.

McWhirter, J. (2002). Re-modelling NLP. Part Fourteen: Re-Modelling Modelling. *Rapport*, 59.

Medical School Objectives Writing Group. (1999). Learning objectives for medical student education--guidelines for medical schools: Report I of the Medical School Objectives Project. *Academic Medicine*, 74(1), 13–18. doi:10.1097/00001888-199901000-00010

Mergendoller, J. (2014). *The Importance of Project Based Teaching. Buck Institute for Education*. Retrieved from http://bie.org/%20blog/the_importance_of_%20project_based_teaching

Merrill, M. D. (2002). Pebble-in-the-pond model for instructional development. *Performance Measurement*, 41(7), 41–44.

Meyer, J. H., & Land, R. (2005). Threshold concepts and troublesome knowledge (2): Epistemological considerations and a conceptual framework for teaching and learning. *Higher Education*, 49(3), 373–388. doi:10.1007/s10734-004-6779-5

Meyer, J., & Land, R. (2003). *Threshold concepts and troublesome knowledge: linkages to ways of thinking and practising within the disciplines*. UK: University of Edinburgh.

Meyers, N. M., & Nulty, D. D. (2009). How to use (five) curriculum design principles to align authentic learning environments, assessment, students' approaches to thinking and learning outcomes. *Assessment & Evaluation in Higher Education, 34*(5), 565–577. doi:10.1080/02602930802226502

Mezirow, J. (2000). Learning to think like an adult: Core concepts of transformation theory. In J. Mezirow et al. (Eds.), *Learning as transformation: Critical perspectives on a theory in progress* (pp. 3–33). San Francisco: Jossey-Bass.

Miles, M. B., & Huberman, A. M. (1994). *Qualitative Data Analysis: An expanded sourcebook*. London: Sage.

Miles, M., & Hubberman, A. M. (1994). *Qualitative data analysis*. Thousand Oaks, CA: Sage.

Millard, D., Howard, Y., Bailey, C., Davis, H., Gilbert, L., Jeyes, S., et al. (2005). Mapping the e-learning assessment domain: Concept maps for orientation and navigation. *Proceedings of e-Learn 2005*. Retrieved November 20, 2015, from http://eprints.soton.ac.uk/261553/

Miller, G. E. (1990). The assessment of clinical skills/competence/performance. *Academic Medicine, 65*(9Suppl), S63–S67. doi:10.1097/00001888-199009000-00045

Miller, H. G., & Mork, P. (2013). From data to decisions: A value chain for big data. *IT Professional, 15*(1), 57–59. doi:10.1109/MITP.2013.11

Mok, M., Lung, C. L., Cheng, P. W., Cheung, H. P., & Ng, M. L. (2006). Self-assessment in higher education: Experience in using a metacognitive approach in five case studies. *Assessment & Evaluation in Higher Education, 31*(4), 415–433. doi:10.1080/02602930600679100

Molenda, M. (2003). In search of the elusive ADDIE model. *Performance Improvement, 42*(5), 34–37. doi:10.1002/pfi.4930420508

Monereo, C., Sànchez, S., & Suñé, S. (2012). La enseñanza auténtica de competencias profesionales. Un proyecto de aprendizaje recíproco instituto-universidad. *Revista Profesorado, 16*(1), 79-101. Retrieved from http://www.ugr.es/~recfpro/rev161ART6.pdf

Monereo, C. (2009). *Pisa como excusa. Repensar la evaluación para cambiar la enseñanza*. Barcelona: Graó.

Monereo, C., Castelló, M., Durán, D., & Gómez, I. (2009). Las bases psicoeducativas del proyecto PISA como guía para el cambio en las concepciones y prácticas del profesorado de secundaria. *Infancia y Aprendizaje, 32*(3), 421–447. doi:10.1174/021037009788964105

Monereo, C., Weise, C., & Álvarez, I. M. (2013). Cambiar la identidad docente en la Universidad. Formación basada en incidentes dramatizados. *Infancia y Aprendizaje, 36*(3), 323–340. doi:10.1174/021037013807533043

Montgomery, J., & Baker, W. (2007). Teacher written feedback: Student perceptions, teacher self-assessment and actual teacher performance. *Journal of Second Language Writing, 16*(2), 82–99. doi:10.1016/j.jslw.2007.04.002

Moon, J. (2006). *Learning journals: A handbook for reflective practice and professional development*. London, UK: Routledge.

Mora, M. C., Sancho-Bru, J. L., Iserte, J. L., & Sánchez, F. T. (2012). An e-assessment approach for evaluation in engineering overcrowded groups. *Computers & Education, 59*(2), 732–740. doi:10.1016/j.compedu.2012.03.011

Morgan, A., & Beatty, L. (1997). The world of the learner. In F. Marton, D. Hounsell, & N. Entwistle (Eds.), *The Experience of Learning* (2nd ed., pp. 217–237). Edinburgh: Scottish Academic Press.

Morris, L. (2010). *Brain-based learning and classroom practice: A study investigating instructional methodologies of urban school teachers* [Doctoral dissertation]. Arkansas State University.

Mory, E. H. (2003). Feedback research revisited. In D. H. Jonassen (Ed.), *Handbook of research for educational communications and technology* (pp. 745–783). New York: Macmillan.

Moss, P. A. (1994). Validity in high stakes writing assessment: Problems and possibilities. *Assessing Writing*, *1*(1), 109–128. doi:10.1016/1075-2935(94)90007-8

Mueller, J. (2014). *Authentic Assessment Toolbox*. Retrieved from http://jfmueller.faculty.noctrl.edu/toolbox/whatisit.htm#authentic

Narciss, S. (2008). Feedback strategies for interactive learning tasks. In J. M. Spector, M. D. Merrill, J. van Merrienboer, & M. P. Driscoll (Eds.), *Handbook of research on educational communications and technology* (pp. 125–143). New York: Lawrence Erlbaum Associates.

Nasser, F., & Fresko, B. (2002). Faculty views of student evaluation of college teaching. *Assessment & Evaluation in Higher Education*, *2*(2), 187–198. doi:10.1080/02602930220128751

Neumann, R., Parry, S., & Becher, T. (2002). Teaching and Learning in their Disciplinary Contexts: A conceptual analysis. *Studies in Higher Education*, *27*(4), 405–417. doi:10.1080/0307507022000011525

Newble, D. I., & Clarke, R. M. (1986). The approaches to learning of students in a traditional and an innovative problem-based medical school. *Medical Education*, *20*(4), 267–273. doi:10.1111/j.1365-2923.1986.tb01365.x PMID:3747871

Newhouse, C. P. (2013). Computer-based practical exams in an applied Information Technology course. *Journal of Research on Technology in Education*, *45*(3), 263–286. doi:10.1080/15391523.2013.10782606

Newhouse, C. P., & Cooper, M. (2013). Computer-based oral exams in Italian language studies. *ReCALL*, *25*(03), 321–339. doi:10.1017/S0958344013000141

Newton, D. P., & Newton, L. D. (1998). Enculturation and Understanding: Some differences between sixth formers' and graduates' conceptions of understanding in History and Science. *Teaching in Higher Education*, *3*(3), 339–363. doi:10.1080/1356215980030305

Newton, D. P., Newton, L. D., & Oberski, I. (1998). Learning and conceptions of understanding in history and science: Lecturers and new graduates compared. *Studies in Higher Education*, *23*(1), 43–58. doi:10.1080/03075079812331380482

Ng, A., & Hatala, M. (2006). Ontology-based approach to formalization of competencies. Retrieved from http://eprints.iat.sfu.ca/620/

Nicol, D. (2007). Principles of good assessment and feedback: Theory and practice. From the *REAP International Online Conference on Assessment Design for Learner Responsibility*, 29th-31st May, 2007. Available at http://ewds.strath.ac.uk/REAP07

Nicol, D. (2007, May 29-31). Principles of good assessment and feedback: Theory and practice. REAP International Online Conference on Assessment Design for Learner Responsibility. Retrieved from http://www.reap.ac.uk/reap07/Portals/2/CSL/keynotes/david%20nicol/Principles_of_good_assessment_and_feedback.pdf

Nicol, D. J., & Macfarlane-Dick, D. (2004). *Rethinking formative assessment in HE: a theoretical model and seven principles of good feedback practice*. Higher Education Academy. Retrieved from: http://www-new1.heacademy.ac.uk/assets/documents/assessment/web0015_rethinking_formative_assessment_in_he.pdf

Nicol, D., & Macfarlane-Dick, D. (2005). Rethinking formative assessment in higher education: a theoreticalmodel and seven principles of good feedback practice. In Reflections on assessment (Vol. 2, pp. 105-119). Mansfield: Quality Assurance Agency.

Nicol, D. (2010). From monologue to dialogue: Improving written feedback processes in mass higher education. *Assessment & Evaluation in Higher Education, 35*(5), 501–517. doi:10.1080/02602931003786559

Nicol, D. (2013). Resituating feedback from the reactive to the proactive. In D. Boud & E. Molloy (Eds.), *Feedback in higher and professional education: understanding it and doing it well* (pp. 34–49). London: Routledge.

Nicol, D. (2013). Resituating feedback from the reactive to the proactive. In D. Boud & L. Molloy (Eds.), *Feedback in Higher and Professional Education: understanding it and doing it well* (pp. 34–49). Routledge.

Nicol, D., & Macfarlane-Dick, D. (2006). Formative assessment and self-regulated learning: A model and seven principles of good feedback practice. *Studies in Higher Education, 31*(2), 199–218. doi:10.1080/03075070600572090

Nicol, D., & Milligan, C. (2006). Rethinking technology-supported assessment practices in relation to the seven principles of good feedback practice. In C. Bryan & K. Clegg (Eds.), *Innovative assessment in higher education* (pp. 64–77). New York: Routledge.

Nicol, D., Thomson, A., & Breslin, C. (2014). Rethinking feedback practices in higher education: A peer review perspective. *Assessment & Evaluation in Higher Education, 39*(1), 102–122. doi:10.1080/02602938.2013.795518

Nitchot, A., Gilbert, L., & Wills, G. B. (2010). Towards a Competence Based System for Recommending Study Materials (CBSR). *Proceedings of the 2010 IEEE 10th International Conference on Advanced Learning Technologies (ICALT)* (pp. 629–631). Doi:10.1109/ICALT.2010.179

Nogueiras, G., Iborra, A., & Herrero, D. (2016). Dialogical Podcasts to Promote Reflection and Self-Direction in Higher Education. In *Proceedings of EAPRIL 2015, Issue 2*, (March 2016, pp. 233-245). Retrieved from: https://eaprilconference.files.wordpress.com/2015/11/proceedings-eapril-2015.pdf

Nogueiras, G., & Iborra, A. (2016, forthcoming). *Understanding and promoting self-direction in freshman and master's students: A qualitative approach*. Behavioral Development Bulletin.

Noorbehbahani, F., & Kardan, A. A. (2011). The automatic assessment of free text answers using a modified BLEU algorithm. *Computers & Education, 56*(2), 337–345. doi:10.1016/j.compedu.2010.07.013

North Carolina State Department of Public Instruction. (1999). Assessment, articulation, and accountability: a foreign language project. Retrieved from http://files.eric.ed.gov/fulltext/ED436978.pdf

Nulty, D. (2011). Peer and self-assessment in the first year of university. *Assessment & Evaluation in Higher Education, 5*(36), 439–507. doi:10.1080/02602930903540983

O'Brian, T. (2004). Writing in a foreign language: Teaching and learning. *Language Teaching, 37*(1), 1–28. doi:10.1017/S0261444804002113

O'Malley, J., & Pierce, L. (1996). *Authentic Assessment for English Language Learning: Practical Approaches for Teachers*. New York: Addison-Wesley Publishing.

OECD. (2008). *Tertiary Education for the Knowledge Society*. OECD Publishing. doi:10.1787/9789264046535-en

OECD. (2010) *The Nature of Learning: using research to inspire practice*. Retrieved from http://www.oecd.org/edu/ceri/thenatureoflearningusingresearchtoinspirepractice.htm

OECD. (2013). Assessment of Higher Education Learning Outcomes. Retrieved from www.oecd.org/edu/skills-beyond-school/AHELOFSReportVolume2.pdf

Oliveira, I., Pereira, A., & Tinoca, L. (2009). The contribution of the Learning Contract for authentic assessment in online environments. *Proceedings of the European Association for Research on Learning and Instruction 13th Biennial Conference*, Amsterdam, Netherlands.

Olofsson, A. D., Lindberg, J. O., & Stödberg, U. (2011). Shared video media and blogging online. Educational technologies for enhancing formative e-assessment? *Campus-Wide Information Systems, 28*(1), 41–55. doi:10.1108/10650741111097287

Onwuegbuzie, A. J., Daniel, L. G., & Collins, K. T. (2009). A meta-validation model for assessing the score-validity of student teaching evaluations. *Quality & Quantity: International Journal Of Methodology, 43*(2), 197–209. doi:10.1007/s11135-007-9112-4

Orsmond, P., Merry, S., & Reiling, K. (2002). The use of formative feedback when using student derived marking criteria in peer and self-assessment. *Assessment & Evaluation in Higher Education, 27*(4), 309–323. doi:10.1080/0260293022000001337

Ortigosa, A., Paredes, P., & Rodriguez, P. (2010). AH-questionnaire: An adaptive hierarchical questionnaire for learning styles. *Computers & Education, 54*(4), 999–1005. doi:10.1016/j.compedu.2009.10.003

Ory, J. C., & Ryan, K. (2001). How do student ratings measure up to a new validity framework? In M. Theall, P.C. Abrami, & L.A. Mets (Eds.), The student ratings debate: Are they valid? How can we best use them? New Directions for Teaching and Learning [Special issue], 87, 3-15. doi:doi:10.1002/ir.2 doi:10.1002/ir.2

Osuji, U. S. A. (2009). The use of e-Assessments in the Nigerian higher education system. *Turkish Online Journal of Distance Education, 13*(4), 140–152.

Ozden, M., & Gultekin, M. (2008). The Effects of Brain-Based Learning on Academic Achievement and Retention of Knowledge in Science Course. *Electronic Journal of Science Education, 12*(1), 1–17.

Ozogul, O., Olina, Z., & Sullivan, H. (2008). Teacher, self and peer evaluation of lesson plans written by preservice teachers. *Educational Technology Research and Development, 56*(2), 181–201. doi:10.1007/s11423-006-9012-7

Pachler, N., Daly, C., Mor, Y., & Mellar, H. (2010). Formative E-Assessment: Practitioner Cases. *Computers & Education, 54*(3), 715–721. doi:10.1016/j.compedu.2009.09.032

Palmer, P. J. (1998). *The Courage to Teach*. San Francisco: Jossey-Bass.

Panke, S., Allen, G., & McAvinchey, D. (2014). Re-Envisioning the University Website: Participatory Design Case Study.*Proceedings of World Conference on E-Learning in Corporate, Government, Healthcare, and Higher Education 2014* (pp. 1540-1549). Chesapeake, VA: AACE.

Panke, S., & Stephens, J. (2014). Demonstrating Competencies with E-Portfolios: The Carolina MPA.*Proceedings of World Conference on E-Learning in Corporate, Government, Healthcare, and Higher Education 2014* (pp. 1511-1529). Chesapeake, VA: AACE.

Papadakis, M. A., Teherani, A., Banach, M. A., Knettler, T. R., Rattner, S. L., Stern, D. T., & Hodgson, C. S. et al. (2005). Disciplinary action by medical boards and prior behavior in medical school. *The New England Journal of Medicine, 353*(25), 2673–2682. doi:10.1056/NEJMsa052596

Paquette, G. (2007). An ontology and a software framework for competency modeling and management. *Journal of Educational Technology & Society, 10*(3), 1–21.

Paquette, G., Mariño, O., Rogozan, D., & Léonard, M. (2015). Competency-based personalization for massive online learning. *Smart Learning Environments, 2*(1), 1–19. doi:10.1186/s40561-015-0013-z

Paris, S. G., & Paris, A. H. (2001). Classroom applications of research on self-regulated learning. *Educational Psychologist, 36*(2), 89–101. doi:10.1207/S15326985EP3602_4

Partnership for 21st Century Skills. (2009). Assessment: A 21st Century Skills Implementation Guide. Retrieved from http://www.p21.org/storage/documents/p21-stateimp_assessment.pdf

Pellegrino, J. W. (2010). Technology and Formative Assessment. In P. Peterson, E. Baker, & B. McGaw (Eds.), *International Encyclopaedia of Education* (3rd ed., Vol. 8, pp. 42–47). Oxford: Elsevier. doi:10.1016/B978-0-08-044894-7.00700-4

Pennequin, V., Sorel, O., Nanty, I., & Fontaine, R. (2010). Metacognition and low achievement in mathematics: The effect of training in the use of metacognitive skills to solve mathematical word problems. *Thinking & Reasoning, 16*(3), 198–220. doi:10.1080/13546783.2010.509052

Pereira, A.; Mendes, A. Q.; Mota, J. C.; Morgado, L. & Aires, L.L. (2003). *Discursos, Série. Perspectivas em Educação*, 1, 39-53.

Pereira, A., Mendes, A. Q., Morgado, L., Amante, L., & Bidarra, A. (2007). *Modelo Pedagógico Virtual da Universidade Aberta*. Lisboa: Universidade Aberta.

Pereira, A., Oliveira, I., Amante, L., & Pinto, M. C. (2013). How can we use ICT to assess competences in higher education: The case of authenticity?*Proceedings of 5th International Conference on Education and New Learning Technologies EDULEARN '13*, Barcelona.

Pereira, A., Oliveira, I., & Tinoca, L. (2010). A Cultura de Avaliação: que dimensões? In F. Costa, G. Miranda, M. I. C. João, & E. Cruz (Eds.), *Actas do I Encontro Internacional TIC e Educação: TICeduca 2010*. Lisboa.

Pereira, A., Oliveira, I., Tinoca, L., Pinto, M. C., Amante, L., & Pereira, A. et al.. (2015). *Desafios da Avaliação Digital no Ensino Superior*. Lisboa: Universidade Aberta.

Pereira, D., Flores, M. A., & Niklasson, L. (2015). Assessment revisited: A review of research in Assessment and Evaluation in Higher Education. *Assessment & Evaluation in Higher Education*, 1–25. doi:10.1080/02602938.2015.1055233

Pérez, R. J., Shim, W., King, P. M., & Baxter Magolda, M. B. (2015). Refining King and Baxter Magolda's model of intercultural maturity. *Journal of College Student Development, 56*(8), 759–776. doi:10.1353/csd.2015.0085

Perkins, D. (1993). Teaching for Understanding. *American Educator: The Professional Journal of the American Federation of Teachers, 17*(3), 28-35. Retrieved from http://www.exploratorium.edu/IFI/resources/workshops/teachingforunderstanding.html

Perret-Clermont, A.-N., Perret, J.-F., & Bell, N. (1991). The social construction of meaning and cognitive activity in elementary school children. In L. Resnick, J. M. Levine, & S. D. Teasley (Eds.), *Perspectives on socially shared cognition* (pp. 41–62). Washington, DC: American Psychological Association. doi:10.1037/10096-002

Perry, W. G. (1970). *Forms of intellectual and ethical development in the college years: A scheme*. New York: Holt, Rinehart & Winston.

Persky, A. M., Alford, E. L., & Kyle, J. (2013). Not all hard work leads to learning. *American Journal of Pharmaceutical Education, 77*(5), 89. doi:10.5688/ajpe77589 PMID:23788801

Philpott, J. (2009). *Captivating your class: Effective Teaching skills*. UK: Antony Rowe.

Pickford, R. & Brown, S. (2006). *Assessing Skills and Practice*. London: Routledge.

PingSoft. (2007). *HyperAuthor e-Examination System*. Retrieved from http://www.pingsoft.net/english/product/haes.asp

Pinkney, J., & Shaughnessy, M. F. (2013). Teaching critical thinking skills: A modern mandate. *International Journal of Academic Research, 5*(3), 346–352. doi:10.7813/2075-4124.2013/5-3/B.52

Pintrich, P. R. (1995). Understanding self-regulated learning. *New Directions for Teaching and Learning, 1995*(63), 3–12. doi:10.1002/tl.37219956304

Pintrich, P. R., & Zusho, A. (2002). The development of academic self-regulation: The role of cognitive and motivational factors. In A. Wigfield & J. S. Eccles (Eds.), *Development of achievement motivation* (pp. 249–284). San Diego, CA: Academic. doi:10.1016/B978-012750053-9/50012-7

Pizzolato, J. E. (2005). Creating Crossroads for Self-Authorship: Investigating the Provocative Moment. *Journal of College Student Development, 46*(6), 624, 641. doi:10.1353/csd.2005.0064

Põldoja, H., Väljataga, T., Laanpere, M., & Tammets, K. (2012). Web-based self- and peer-assessment of teachers' digital competencies. *World Wide Web (Bussum), 17*(2), 255–269. doi:10.1007/s11280-012-0176-2

Politano, C., & Paquin, J. (2000). *Brain-based Learning with Class.* Winnipeg, Manitoba: Portage and Main Press.

Pollitt, A. (2004). Let's stop marking exams. *Paper presented at theIAEA Conference*, Philadelphia.

Pollitt, A., & Crisp, V. (2004). Could comparative judgements of script quality replace traditional marking and improve the validity of exam questions? *Paper presented at the Paper presented at theBritish Educational Research Association Annual Conference*, Manchester.

Pollitt, A., & Elliott, G. (2003). Finding a proper role for human judgement in the examination system. *Paper presented at the QCA 'Comparability and Standards' seminar*, Newport Pagnell. Retrieved from http://www.cambridgeassessment. org.uk/research/confproceedings

Pollitt, A. (2012a). Comparative judgement for assessment. *International Journal of Technology and Design Education, 22*(2), 157–170. doi:10.1007/s10798-011-9189-x

Pollitt, A. (2012b). The method of adaptive comparative judgement. *Assessment in Education: Principles, Policy & Practice, 19*(3), 281–300. doi:10.1080/0969594X.2012.665354

Poulos, A., & Mahony, M. J. (2008). Effectiveness of feedback: The students' perspective. *Assessment & Evaluation in Higher Education, 33*(2), 143–154. doi:10.1080/02602930601127869

Powis, D. (2015). Selecting medical students: An unresolved challenge. *Medical Teacher, 37*(3), 252–260. doi:10.310 9/0142159X.2014.993600

Pratt, D. D. (1992). Conceptions of Teaching. *Adult Education Quarterly, 42*(4), 203–220.

Pressley, M., & Harris, K. R. (2006). Cognitive strategies instruction: From basic research to classroom instruction. Handbook of Educational Psychology, 2, 265-286.

Pressley, M., & Ghatala, E. S. (1990). Self-regulated learning: Monitoring learning from text. *Educational Psychologist, 25*(1), 19–33. doi:10.1207/s15326985ep2501_3

Price, M. (2005). Assessment standards: The role of communities of practice and the scholarship of assessment. *Assessment & Evaluation in Higher Education, 3*(3), 215–230. doi:10.1080/02602930500063793

Price, M. (2013). Student views on assessment: critical friend commentary. In L. Clouder, C. Broughan, S. Jewell, & G. Steventon (Eds.), *Improving Student Engagement and Development through Assessment: Theory and practice in higher education* (pp. 16–18). London: Routledge.

Price, M., Carroll, J., O'Donovan, B., & Rust, C. (2011). If I was going there I wouldn't start from here: A critical commentary on current assessment practice. *Assessment & Evaluation in Higher Education, 36*(4), 479–492. doi:10.1080/02602930903512883

Price, M., Handley, K., Millar, J., & O'Donovan, B. (2010). Feedback: All that effort, but what is the effect? *Assessment & Evaluation in Higher Education, 35*(3), 277–289. doi:10.1080/02602930903541007

Price, M., Rust, C., O'Donovan, B., Handley, K., & Bryant, R. (2012). *Assessment Literacy. The Foundation for Improving Student Learning.* Oxford: Oxford Brookes University.

Prins, F. J., Sluijsmans, M. A., Kirschenerand, P. A., & Strijbos, J. W. (2005). Formative peer assessment in a CSCL environment: A case study. *Assessment & Evaluation in Higher Education, 30*(4), 417–444. doi:10.1080/02602930500099219

Puig, J. M., Batlle, R., Bosch, C., & Palos, J. (2007). *Aprendizaje servicio. Educar para la ciudadanía.* Barcelona: Ministerio de Educación y Ciencia y Octaedro.

Quality Assurance Agency for Higher Education. (2010). *Code of practice for the assurance of academic quality and standards in higher education.* Retrieved from https://www.brookes.ac.uk/Documents/Students/QAACode/

Quesada Serra, V., Gómez Ruiz, M. A., & Cubero Ibáñez, J. (2015). La evaluación colaborativa en educación superior: descripción de una experiencia con alumnos de primer curso [co-assessment in Higher Education: an experience with first-year students]. *Proceedings of V International Conference, the challenge of improving assessment (pp.562-566). Girona, Spain: Universitat de Girona.*

Quesada-Serra, V., Rodríguez-Gómez, G., & Ibarra-Sáiz, M. S. (2014). What are we missing? Spanish lecturers' perceptions of their assessment practices. *Innovations in Education and Teaching International.* doi:10.1080/14703297.2014.930353

Quirk, R., & Smith, A. (1959). *The teaching of English.* London: Martin Secker & Warburg Ltd.

Qvortrup, A., & Bering Keiding, T. (2015). Portfolio assessment: Production and reduction of complexity. *Assessment & Evaluation in Higher Education, 40*(3), 407–419. doi:10.1080/02602938.2014.918087

Rae, A. M., & Cochrane, D. K. (2008). Listening to students: How to make written assessment feedback useful. *Active Learning in Higher Education, 9*(3), 217–230. doi:10.1177/1469787408095847

Raikes, N., Scorey, S., & Shiell, H. (2008). Grading examinations using expert judgements from a diverse pool of judges. *Paper presented at the 34th annual conference of the International Association for Educational Assessment,* Cambridge, UK.

Ramaprasad, A. (1983). On the definition of feedback. *Behavioral Science, 28*(1), 4–13. doi:10.1002/bs.3830280103

Ramón, E., Juárez, R., Martínez, B., & Martín, S. (2015). Impacto de un proyecto de aprendizaje-servicio con estudiantes de enfermería. *Metas de Enfermería,* 18(2), Retrieved from http://www.enfermeria21.com/revistas/metas/articulo/80711/

Ram, P., van der Vleuten, C., Rethans, J. J., Schouten, B., Hobma, S., & Grol, R. (1999). Assessment in general practice: The predictive value of written-knowledge tests and a multiple-station examination for actual medical performance in daily practice. *Medical Education, 33*(3), 197–203. doi:10.1046/j.1365-2923.1999.00280.x

Ramsden, P. (1992). *Learning to teach in higher education.* London: Routledge. doi:10.4324/9780203413937

Rasch, G. (1960). *Probabilistic Models for Some Intelligence and Achievement Tests, Expanded Edition (1980) With Foreword and Afterword by BD Wright. Copenhagen,* Denmark: Danish Institute for Educational Research.

Raymond, J. E., Homer, C. S. E., Smith, R., & Gray, J. E. (2013). Nurse Education in Practice Learning through authentic assessment: An evaluation of a new development in the undergraduate midwifery curriculum. *Nurse Education in Practice, 13*(5), 471–476. doi:10.1016/j.nepr.2012.10.006 PMID:23140801

Redecker, C. (2013). *The use of ICT for the assessment of key competences* (JRC scientific and policy reports). European Commission, Joint Research Centre. Institute for prospective Technological Studies. Retrieved from http://ftp.jrc.es/EURdoc/JRC76971.pdf

Redecker, C., & Johannessen, Ø. (2013). Changing Assessment — Towards a New Assessment Paradigm Using ICT. *European Journal of Education, 48*(1), 79–96. doi:10.1111/ejed.12018

Regehr, G., MacRae, H., Reznick, R., & Szalay, D. (1998). Comparing the psychometric properties of checklists and global rating scales for assessing performance on an OSCE-format examination. *Academic Medicine, 73*(9), 993–997. doi:10.1097/00001888-199809000-00020

Regehr, G., & Norman, G. (1996). Issues in cognitive psychology: Implications for professional education. *Academic Medicine, 71*(9), 988–1001. doi:10.1097/00001888-199609000-00015

Reid, J. R., & Andesron, P. R. (2012). Critical thinking in the business classroom. *Journal of Education for Business, 87*(1), 52–59. doi:10.1080/08832323.2011.557103

Reiser, R. A. (2001). A history of instructional design and technology: Part II: A history of instructional design. *Educational Technology Research and Development, 49*(2), 57–67. doi:10.1007/BF02504928

Remesal, A. (2011). Primary and secondary teachers' conceptions of assessment: A qualitative study. *Teaching and Teacher Education, 27*(2), 472–482. doi:10.1016/j.tate.2010.09.017

Rethans, J., Norcini, J., Baron-Maldonado, M., Blackmore, D., Jolly, B., LaDuca, T., & Southgate, L. et al. (2002). The relationship between competence and performance: Implications for assessing practice performance. *Medical Education, 36*(10), 901–909. doi:10.1046/j.1365-2923.2002.01316.x

Rethans, J., Sturmans, F., Drop, R., van der Vleuten, C., & Hobus, P. (1991). Does competence of general practitioners predict their performance? Comparison between examination setting and actual practice. *British Medical Journal, 303*(6814), 1377–1380. doi:10.1136/bmj.303.6814.1377

Rethinking Education: Investing in skills for socio-economic outcomes. (2012). COM669, 20.11.2012. Strasbourg: Publications Office of the European Union.

Rezaee, M., Farahian, M., & Morad Ahmadi, A. (2012). Critical thinking in higher education: Unfulfilled expectations. *BRAIN: Broad Research in Artificial Intelligence & Neuroscience, 3*(2), 64–73.

Rhodes, T. L. (2011). Making Learning Visible and Meaningful through Electronic Portfolios. *Change: The Magazine of Higher Learning, 43*(1), 6–13. doi:10.1080/00091383.2011.538636

Richards, J., & Lockhart, C. (1994). *Reflective Teaching in Second Language Classrooms.* New York: Cambridge University Press. doi:10.1017/CBO9780511667169

Richards, L. (1999). *Using NVivo in Qualitative Research.* London: Sage.

Roberts, T. S. (2006). *Self, Peer and Group Assesment in E-Learning.* Hershey, PA, USA: IGI Global. doi:10.4018/978-1-59140-965-6

Rodríguez Gómez, G., Ibarra Sáiz, M. S., & García Jiménez, E. (2013). Autoevaluación, evaluación entre iguales y coevaluación: Conceptualización y práctica en las universidades españolas[Self-assessment, peer-assessment and co-assessment: conceptualisation and practice in Spanish Universities]. *Revista de Investigación en Educación, 11*(2), 198–210.

Rodríguez-Gómez, G., & Ibarra-Sáiz, M. S. (2015). Assessment as Learning and Empowerment: Towards Sustainable Learning in Higher Education. In M. Peris-Ortiz & J. M. Merigó Lindahl (Eds.), *Sustainable Learning in Higher Education. Developing Competencies for the Global Marketplace* (pp. 1–20). Springer International Publishing; doi:10.1007/978-3-319-10804-9_1

Rodríguez-Gómez, G., Ibarra-Sáiz, M. S., Gallego-Noche, B., Gómez-Ruiz, M. A., & Quesada-Serra, V. (2012). The student's voice in assessment: A pathway not yet developed at university. *RELIEVE, 18*(2), 1–21. doi:10.7203/relieve.18.2.1991

Rodríguez-Gómez, G., Ibarra-Sáiz, M. S., & García-Jimenez, E. (2013). Autoevaluación, evaluación entre iguales y coevaluación: Conceptualización y práctica en las universidades españolas. *Revista de Investigacion en Educación, 11*(2), 198–210.

Ronis, D. (2007a). *Brain-Compatible Assessments* (2nd ed.). California: Sage Publications.

Ronis, D. (2007b). *Brain-compatible mathematics*. Thousand Oaks, Calif: Corwin Press.

Rovai, A. P. (2004). A constructivist approach to online college learning. *The Internet and Higher Education, 7*(2), 79–93. doi:10.1016/j.iheduc.2003.10.002

Ryan, M., & Ryan, M. (2013). Theorising a model for teaching and assessing reflective learning in higher education. *Higher Education Research & Development, 32*(2), 244–257. doi:10.1080/07294360.2012.661704

Sadler, D. R. (2009b). Transforming holistic assessment and grading into a vehicle for complex learning. In G. J. (ed.) (Ed.), Assessment, learning and judgement in higher education (pp. 1-19). Nathan: Griffith Institute for Higher Education. doi:doi:10.1007/978-1-4020-8905-3_4 doi:10.1007/978-1-4020-8905-3_4

Sadler, D. R. (1989). Formative assessment and the design of instructional systems. *Instructional Science, 18*(2), 119–144. doi:10.1007/BF00117714

Sadler, D. R. (1998). Formative assessment: Revisiting the territory. *Assessment in Education: Principles, Policy & Practice, 5*(1), 77–84. doi:10.1080/0969595980050104

Sadler, D. R. (2009a). Indeterminacy in the use of preset criteria for assessment and grading. *Assessment & Evaluation in Higher Education, 34*(2), 159–179. doi:10.1080/02602930801956059

Sadler, D. R. (2010). Beyond feedback: Developing student capability in complex appraisal. *Assessment & Evaluation in Higher Education, 35*(5), 535–550. doi:10.1080/02602930903541015

Sadler, P. M., & Good, E. (2006). The Impact of Self- and Peer-Grading on Student Learning. *Educational Assessment, 11*(1), 1–31. doi:10.1207/s15326977ea1101_1

Sainsbury, E. J., & Walker, R. A. (2007). Assessment as a vehicle for learning: Extending collaboration into testing. *Assessment & Evaluation in Higher Education, 33*(2), 103–117. doi:10.1080/02602930601127844

Säljö, R. (1979). Learning in the learner's perspective. I: Some common sense conceptions. University of Göteborg, Mölndal.

Sambell, K., & McDowell, L. (1998). The construction of the hidden curriculum: Messages and meanings in the assessment of student learning. *Assessment & Evaluation in Higher Education, 23*(4), 391–402. doi:10.1080/0260293980230406

Sambell, K., McDowell, L., & Montgomery, C. (2012). *Assessment for Learning in Higher Education*. London: Routledge.

Samuelowicz, K., & Bain, J. D. (2002). Identifying academics' orientations to assessment practice. *Higher Education, 43*(2), 173–201. doi:10.1023/A:1013796916022

Sanders, E. B. N., & Stappers, P. J. (2008). Co-creation and the new landscapes of design. *CoDesign*, *4*(1), 5–18. doi:10.1080/15710880701875068

Sanghi, S. (2007). *The Handbook of Competency Mapping: Understanding, Designing and Implementing Competency Models in Organizations*. SAGE Publications India.

Sanmartí, N. (2008). *10 ideas clave: evaluar para aprender*. Barcelona: Graó.

Saville, B. K., & Zinn, T. E. (2011). Interteaching. *New Directions For Teaching & Learning, 2011*(128), 53-61. doi:10.1002/tl.468

Saville, B. K., Cox, T., O'Brien, S., & Vanderveldt, A. (2011). Interteaching: The impact of lectures on student performance. *Journal of Applied Behavior Analysis*, *44*(4), 937–941. doi:10.1901/jaba.2011.44-937 PMID:22219544

Saville, B. K., Lambert, T., & Robertson, S. (2011). Interteaching: Bringing behavioral education into the 21st century. *The Psychological Record*, *61*(1), 153–165.

Saville, B. K., Zinn, T. E., & Elliot, M. P. (2005). Interteaching versus traditional methods of instruction: A preliminary analysis. *Teaching of Psychology*, *32*(3), 161–163. doi:10.1207/s15328023top3203_6

Schiekirka, S., Reinhardt, D., Heim, S., Fabry, G., Pukrop, T., Anders, S., & Raupach, T. (2012). Student perceptions of evaluation in undergraduate medical education: A qualitative study from one medical school. *BMC Medical Education*, 12, 45-51.

Schleifer, L. F., & Dull, R. B. (2009). Metacognition and performance in the accounting classroom. *Issues in Accounting Education*, *24*(3), 339–367. doi:10.2308/iace.2009.24.3.339

Schmidt, A., & Kunzmann, C. (2007). Sustainable competency-oriented human resource development with ontology-based competency catalogs. In *eChallenges* (Vol. 2007). Retrieved from http://www.researchgate.net/profile/Andreas_Schmidt6/publication/228616563_Sustainable_competency-oriented_human_resource_development_with_ontology-based_competency_catalogs/links/0912f50a27d0b65d31000000.pdf

Schön, D. (1983). *The reflective practitioner*. New York: Basic Books.

Schon, D. A. (1983). *The Reflective Practitioner*. New York: Basic Books.

Schon, D. A. (1987). *Educating the Reflective Practitioner*. San Francisco: Jossey-Bass.

Schunk, D. H., & Zimmerman, B. J. (1994). *Self-regulation of learning and performance: Issues and educational applications*. Lawrence Erlbaum Associates, Inc.

Schuwirth, L. W., & van der Vleuten, C. P. (2006). A plea for new psychometric models in educational assessment. *Medical Education*, *40*(4), 296–300. doi:10.1111/j.1365-2929.2006.02405.x

Scoboria, A., & Pascual-Leone, A. (2009). An 'interteaching' informed approach to instructing large undergraduate classes. *Journal of the Scholarship of Teaching and Learning.*, *9*, 29–37.

Scott, J. (2000). Authentic Assessment Tools. In Custer, R., Schell J. McAlister, B., Scott, J., Hoepfl, M. (Eds.) *Using Authentic Assessment in Vocational Education* (ERIC Clearinghouse on Adult, Career, and Vocational Education, Information Series No. 381) (pp. 33-48). Retrieved from http://calpro-online.org/eric/docs/custer/custer1.pdf

Scottish Qualifications Authority. (2005). *SQA Guidelines on e-assessment for Schools*. Glasgow: Hanover House. Retrieved from http://www.sqa.org.uk/files_ccc/SQA_Guidelines_on_e-assessment_Schools_June05.pdf

Seery, N., Canty, D., & Phelan, P. (2012). The validity and value of peer assessment using adaptive comparative judgement in design driven practical education. *International Journal of Technology and Design Education, 22*(2), 205–226. doi:10.1007/s10798-011-9194-0

Segers, M., & Dochy, F. (2001). New assessment forms in problem-based learning: The value-added of the students' perspective. *Studies in Higher Education, 26*(3), 327–343. doi:10.1080/03075070120076291

Seligman, M. E., & Maier, S. F. (1967). Failure to escape traumatic shock. *Journal of Experimental Psychology, 74*(1), 1–9. doi:10.1037/h0024514 PMID:6032570

Sellenet, C. (2010). Approche critique de la notion de «compétences parentales». *La Revue Internationale de L'éducation Familiale, 26*(2), 95–116. doi:10.3917/rief.026.0095

Shakespeare, W., & Lever, J. W. (1997). *Measure for measure*. Walton-on-Thames: Thomas Nelson & Sons.

Sharples, M., Adams, A., Ferguson, R., Gaved, M., McAndrew, P., Rienties, B., et al. (2014). Exploring new forms of teaching, learning and assessment, to guide educators and policy makers. Innovating Pedagogy 2014: Open University Innovation Report 3. Milton Keynes: The Open University. Retrieved from http://www.openuniversity.edu/sites/www.openuniversity.edu/files/The_Open_University_Innovating_Pedagogy_2014_0.pdf

Shavelson, R. J., Baxter, G. P., & Gao, X. H. (1993). Sampling Variability of Performance Assessments. *Journal of Educational Measurement, 30*(3), 215–232. doi:10.1111/j.1745-3984.1993.tb00424.x

Shay, S. (2005). The assessment of complex tasks: A double reading. *Studies in Higher Education, 30*(6), 663–679. doi:10.1080/03075070500339988

Shum, B., Simon and Deakin Crick, Ruth (2012, April 29 – May 2). Learning dispositions and transferable competencies: pedagogy, modelling and learning analytics. *Proceedings of the 2nd International Conference on Learning Analytics & Knowledge*, Vancouver, British Columbia, Canada. doi:10.1145/2330601.2330629

Shute, V. J., Hansen, E. G., & Almond, R. G. (2007). *An assessment for learning system called ACED: Designing for learning effectiveness and accessibility*. ETS Research Report No. RR-07-26, Princeton, NJ.

Shut, V. J. (2007). Focus on formative feedback. *Review of Educational Research, 78*(1), 153–189. doi:10.3102/0034654307313795

Simpson, J., & Weiner, E. (Eds.). (1989). *The Oxford English Dictionary* (2nd ed.). Oxford: Clarendon Press.

Sitthisak, O., Gilbert, L., & Albert, D. (2013). Adaptive Learning Using an Integration of Competence Model with Knowledge Space Theory. *Proceedings of the 2013 IIAI International Conference on Advanced Applied Informatics (IIAIAAI)* (pp. 199–202). http://doi.org/ doi:doi:10.1109/IIAI-AAI.2013.15 doi:10.1109/IIAI-AAI.2013.15

Sitthisak, O., Gilbert, L., & Davis, H. C. (2007). Transforming a competency model to assessment items. *Presented at the PROLIX Workshop 2007 in conjunction with EC-TEL07*. Retrieved from http://eprints.soton.ac.uk/264541/

Sivan, A. (2000). The implementation of peer assessment: An action research approach. *Assessment in Education: Principles, Policy & Practice, 7*(2), 193–213. doi:10.1080/713613328

Slavkin, M. (2004). *Authentic learning: how learning about the brain can shape the development of students*. Lanham, Maryland: Scarecrow Education.

Slocombe, T., Miller, D., & Hite, N. (2011). A survey of student perspectives toward faculty evaluations. *American Journal of Business Education, 4*(7), 51–57.

Sluijsmans, D. M. A., Prins, F., & Martens, R. (2006). A framework for integrated performance assessment in E-Learning. *Learning Environments Research, 9*(1), 45–66. doi:10.1007/s10984-005-9003-3

Smith, G. S. (2004). Assessment strategies: What is being measured in student course evaluations? *Accounting Education, 13*(1), 3–28. doi:10.1080/0963928032000168977

Smith, L., Dockrell, J., & Tomlinson, P. (1997). *Piaget, Vygotsky and beyond: future issues for developmental psychology and education*. London, New York: Routledge.

Spady, W. G. (1994). Choosing Outcomes of Significance. *Educational Leadership, 51*(6), 18–22.

Stanley, C. (1999). Learning to think, feel and teach reflectively. In J. Arnold (Ed.), *Affect in language learning* (pp. 109–124). Cambridge: Cambridge University Press.

Stefanou, C., Stolk, D. J., Prince, Chen, J. C. & Lord, S. M. (2013). Self-regulation and autonomy in problem- and project-based learning environments. Active Learning in Higher Education, 2013, 94-109.

Stefanou, C., & Parkes, J. (2003). Effects of classroom assessment on student motivation in fifth-grade science. *The Journal of Educational Research, 96*(3), 152–162. doi:10.1080/00220670309598803

Stern, L., & Solomon, A. (2006). Effective faculty feedback: The road less traveled. *Assessing Writing, 11*(1), 22–41. doi:10.1016/j.asw.2005.12.001

Stevens, D. D., & Levi, A. J. (2011). *Introduction to rubrics: An assessment tool to save grading time, convey effective feedback, and promote student learning*. Sterling, Virginia: Stylus.

Stiggins, R. (2007). Conquering the formative assessment frontier. In J. McMillan (Ed.), *Formative Classroom Assessment: Theory into Practice* (pp. 8–27). New York: Teachers College Press, Colombia University.

Stobart, G. (2008). *Testing times: the uses and abuses of assessment*. London: Routledge.

Stödberg, U. (2012). A research review of e-assessment. *Assessment & Evaluation in Higher Education, 37*(5), 591–604. doi:10.1080/02602938.2011.557496

Straub, R. (2000). The student, the text, and the classroom context: A case study of teacher response. *Academic Writing, 7*, 23–55.

Streiner, D., & Norman, G. (1995). *Health Measurement Scales: A Practical Guide to their Development and Use* (2nd ed.). New York: Oxford University Press.

Strijbos, J. W., & Sluijsmans, D. (2010). Unravelling peer assessment: Methodological, functional, and conceptual developments. *Learning and Instruction, 20*(4), 265–269. doi:10.1016/j.learninstruc.2009.08.002

Stuart, M., Lido, C., & Morgan, J. (2012). Choosing a Student Lifestyle? Questions of Taste, Cultural Capital and Gaining a Graduate Job. In T. Hinton-Smith (Ed.), *Widening participation in higher education: casting the net wide?* (pp. 129–145). Basingstoke: Palgrave Macmillan. doi:10.1057/9781137283412.0015

Suffolk County Council. (2001). *How am I doing? Assessment and feedback to learners*. Ipswich: Suffolk Advisory Service. Retrieved from: http://www.slamnet.org.uk/assessment/edp_booklet.htm

Surratt, C. K. & Desselle, S.P. (2007). Pharmacy students' perceptions of a teaching evaluation process. *American Journal of Pharmaceutical Education, 71*(1), 06.

Svinicki, M. D. (2001). Encouraging your students to give feedback. *New Directions for Teaching and Learning, 87*(87), 17–24. doi:10.1002/tl.24

Swan, K., Shen, J., Fredericksen, E., Pickett, A., Pelz, W., & Maher, G. (2000). Building knowledge building communities: Consistency, contact and communication in the virtual classroom. *Journal of Educational Computing Research*, *23*(4), 389–413.

Swan, K., Shen, J., & Hiltz, S. R. (2006). Assessment and Collaboration in Online Learning. *Journal of Asynchronous Learning Networks*, *10*(1), 45–62.

Taras, M. (2015). Student-centred learning and assessment: fact or fiction.

Taras, M. (2005). Assessment – summative and formative – some theoretical reflections. *British Journal of Educational Studies*, *53*(4), 466–478. doi:10.1111/j.1467-8527.2005.00307.x

Taras, M. (2015). Studen Self-Assessment: What have we learned and what are the challenges? *RELIEVE*, *21*(1). doi:10.7203/relieve.21.1.6394

Taylor, C., & Robinson, C. (2009). Student voice: Theorising power and participation. *Pedagogy, Culture & Society*, *17*(2), 161–175. doi:10.1080/14681360902934392

Taylor, E. W., & Cranton, P. (2013). A theory in progress? Issues in transformative learning theory. *European Journal for Research on the Education and Learning of Adults*, *4*(1), 33–47. doi:10.3384/rela.2000-7426.rela5000

TELMAP. (2011). *Report on engagement, dissemination and awareness results*. European Commission Seventh Framework Project. Retrieved from http://www.telmap.org/sites/default/files/D7%202a_v2.pdf

Ten Cate, O., Chen, H. C., Hoff, R. G., Peters, H., Bok, H., & van der Schaaf, M. (2015). Curriculum development for the workplace using Entrustable Professional Activities (EPAs): AMEE Guide No. 99. *Medical Teacher*, 2015, 1–20. doi:10.3109/0142159X.2015.1060308

The Higher Education Academy. (2012). *A Marked Improvement: Transforming assessment in higher education*. Retrieved from http://www.heacademy.ac.uk/assessment

The University of Edinburgh. (2015). Enhancing feedback. Retrieved from www.tla.ed.ac.uk/feedback/index.html

Theall, M., & Franklin, J. (2001). Looking for bias in all the wrong places: A search for truth or a witch hunt in student ratings of instruction? *New Directions for Institutional Research*, *109*(109), 45–56. doi:10.1002/ir.3

Thomas, J. W. (2000). A review of research on project-based learning. Retrieved from www.bie.org/research/study/review_of_project_based_learning_2000

Thurstone, L. L. (1925). A method of scaling psychological and educational tests. *Journal of Educational Psychology*, *16*(7), 433–451. doi:10.1037/h0073357

Thurstone, L. L. (1927). A law of comparative judgment. *Psychological Review*, *34*(4), 273–286. doi:10.1037/h0070288

Tinoca, L., Oliveira, I., & Pereira, A. (2013). A conceptual framework for e-assessment in Higher Education – authenticity, consistency, transparency and practicability. In S. Mukerji & P. Tripathi (Eds.), Handbook of Research on Transnational Higher Education Management. Hershey, PA, USA: IGI Global.

Tinoca, L., Oliveira, I., & Pereira, A. (2014). A Conceptual Framework for E-Assessment in Higher Education: Authenticity, Consistency, Transparency and Practicability. In S. Mukerji & P. Tripathi (Eds.), Handbook of Research on Transnational Higher Education Management. IGI Global (pp. 652–673). Hershey, PA, USA: IGI Global. doi:doi:10.4018/978-1-4666-4458-8.ch033 doi:10.4018/978-1-4666-4458-8.ch033

Tomas, C., Borg, M., & McNeil, J. (2015). E-assessment: Institutional development strategies and the assessment life cycle. *British Journal of Educational Technology*, *46*(3), 588–596. doi:10.1111/bjet.12153

Topping, K. (2005). Trends in Peer Learning. *Educational Psychology, 25*(6), 634–645. doi:10.1080/01443410500345172

Topping, K. J. (2009). Peer assessment. *Theory Into Practice, 48*, 20–27.

Tremblay, K., Lalancette, D., & Roseveare, D. (2012). Assessment of higher education learning outcomes. *Feasibility Study Report, 1*. Retrieved from http://citeseerx.ist.psu.edu/viewdoc/download?doi=10.1.1.269.7308&rep=rep1&type=pdf

Tremblay, K., Lalancette, D., & Roseveare, D. (2012). Assessment of Higher Education Learning Outcomes. OECD. Retrieved from www.oecd.org/edu/skills-beyond-school/AHELOFSReportVolume1.pdf

Trevitt, C., Macduff, A., & Steed, A. (2014). [e]portfolios for learning and as evidence of achievement: Scoping the academic practice development agenda ahead. *The Internet and Higher Education, 20*, 69–78. doi:10.1016/j.iheduc.2013.06.001

Trigwell, K., Rodriguez, K. C., & Han, F. (2012). Assessing the Impact of a University Teaching Development Programme. *Assessment & Evaluation in Higher Education, 37*(4), 499–511. doi:10.1080/02602938.2010.547929

Trotter, E. (2006). Student Perceptions of Continuous Summative Assessment. *Assessment & Evaluation in Higher Education, 31*(5), 505–521. doi:10.1080/02602930600679506

Tullis, J., Finley, J., & Benjamin, A. (2013). Metacognition of the testing effect: Guiding learners to predict the benefits of retrieval. *Memory & Cognition, 41*(3), 429–442. doi:10.3758/s13421-012-0274-5 PMID:23242770

Ulrich, C., & Nedelcu, A. (2013). Team-Teaching and Team Work: Perceptions Amongst Students and Staff (A Case Study). *Procedia: Social and Behavioral Sciences, 76*, 853–857. doi:10.1016/j.sbspro.2013.04.219

Valencia, S., Hiebert, E., & Afflerbach, P. (2014). *Authentic Reading Assessment: Practices and Possibilities*. California: TextProject, Inc.

van der Vleuten, C. P., Schuwirth, L. W., Scheele, F., Driessen, E. W., & Hodges, B. (2010). The assessment of professional competence: Building blocks for theory development. *Best Practice & Research. Clinical Obstetrics & Gynaecology, 24*(6), 703–719. doi:10.1016/j.bpobgyn.2010.04.001

Van Geert, P. (2003). Dynamic systems approaches and modeling of developmental processes. In J. Valsiner & K. J. Conolly (Eds.), *Handbook of developmental psychology* (pp. 640–672). London: Sage.

Van Rossum, E. J., & Hamer, R. (2011, September). Analysing deep learning and understanding: getting the meanings clear first. *Paper presented at EARLI*, Exeter, UK.

Van Rossum, E. J., & Hamer, R. (2013, April). Students' Conceptions of Understanding and Assessment of 'Real Understanding'. Poster presentation at 13th AERA, San Francisco, USA.

Van Rossum, E. J., & Taylor, I. P. (1987, April). The relationship between conceptions of learning and good teaching: A scheme of cognitive development. *Paper presented at theAnnual Meeting of the American Educational Research Association*, Washington DC, U.S.A.

Van Rossum, E. J. (1988). Insight into Understanding. In R. Säljö (Ed.), *The Written World* (pp. 195–208). Berlin, Heidelberg: Springer-Verlag. doi:10.1007/978-3-642-72877-8_13

Van Rossum, E. J., Deijkers, R., & Hamer, R. (1985). Students' learning conceptions and their interpretation of significant educational concepts. *Higher Education, 14*(6), 617–641. doi:10.1007/BF00136501

Van Rossum, E. J., & Hamer, R. (2010). *The Meaning of Learning and Knowing*. Rotterdam: Sense Publishers.

Van Rossum, E. J., & Schenk, S. M. (1984). The relationship between learning conception, study strategy and learning outcome. *The British Journal of Educational Psychology, 54*(1), 73–83. doi:10.1111/j.2044-8279.1984.tb00846.x

Van Weijen, D. (2007). *Writing processes, text quality, and task effects. Empirical studies in first and second language writing.* Utrecht: Netherlands Graduate School of Linguistics.

Verhavert, S. (2015). Construction of a benchmark categorization algorithm for Comparative Judgement: a simulation study. *Paper presented at theAEA-Europe 16th Annual Conference,* Glasgow, UK.

Vermunt, J. D. (1996). Metacognitive, cognitive and affective aspects of learning styles and strategies: A phenomenographic analysis. *Higher Education, 31*(1), 25–50. doi:10.1007/BF00129106

Vermunt, J. D. (1998). The regulation of constructive learning processes. *The British Journal of Educational Psychology, 68*(2), 149–171. doi:10.1111/j.2044-8279.1998.tb01281.x

Vonderwell, S., Liang, X., & Alderman, K. (2007). Asynchronous Discussions and Assessment in Online Learning. *Journal of Research on Technology in Education, 39*(3), 309–328. doi:10.1080/15391523.2007.10782485

Wang, M., Vogel, D., & Ran, W. (2011). Creating a performance-oriented e-learning environment: A design science approach. *Information & Management, 48*(7), 260–269. doi:10.1016/j.im.2011.06.003

Ward, M., Gruppen, L., & Regehr, G. (2002). Measuring self-assessment: Current state of the art. *Advances in Health Sciences Education: Theory and Practice, 7*(1), 63–80. doi:10.1023/A:1014585522084

Weaver, M. R. (2006). Do students value feedback? Student perceptions of tutors' written responses. *Assessment & Evaluation in Higher Education, 31*(3), 379–394. doi:10.1080/02602930500353061

Weimer, M. (2014). Developing Student's Self-Assessment Skills. *Faculty Focus.* Retrieved from http://www.algonquincollege.com/pd/2015/03/30/how-important-is-student-self-assessment/#sthash.uJx2WOwa.dpuf

Weinberg, B. A., Fleisher, B. M., & Hashimoto, M. (2007). Evaluating Methods for Evaluating Instruction: The Case of Higher Education (NBER Working Paper No. 12844). Retrieved from http://www.nber.org/papers/w12844

Weiner, B. (1990). History of motivational research in education. *Journal of Education & Psychology, 82*(4), 616–622. doi:10.1037/0022-0663.82.4.616

Weller, J. M., Misur, M., Nicolson, S., Morris, J., Ure, S., Crossley, J., & Jolly, B. (2014). Can I leave the theatre? A key to more reliable workplace-based assessment. *British Journal of Anaesthesia, 112*(6), 1083–1091. doi:10.1093/bja/aeu052

Werner, H. (1957). The concept of development from a comparative and organismic point of view. In D. Harris (Ed.), *The concept of development.* Minneapolis, MN: University of Minnesota Press.

Weurlander, M., Söderberg, M., Scheja, M., Hult, H., & Wernerson, A. (2012). Exploring Formative Assessment as a Tool for Learning: Students' Experiences of Different Methods of Formative Assessment. *Assessment & Evaluation in Higher Education, 37*(6), 747–760. doi:10.1080/02602938.2011.572153

White, B., & Frederiksen, J. (2005). A theoretical framework and approach for fostering metacognitive development. *Educational Psychologist, 40*(4), 211–223. doi:10.1207/s15326985ep4004_3

Whitehouse, C. (2012). *Testing the validity of judgements about geography essays using the Adaptive Comparative Judgement method.* Manchester: AQA Centre for Education Research and Policy.

Whitehouse, C., & Pollitt, A. (2012). *Using adaptive comparative judgement to obtain a highly reliable rank order in summative assessment.* Manchester: AQA Centre for Education Research and Policy.

Whitelock, D. (2007). Computer Assisted Formative Assessment: Supporting Students to Become More Reflective Learners. In C.P. Constantinou, Z.C. Zacharia & M. Papaevripidou, (Eds). *Proceedings of 8th International Conference on ComputerBased Learning in Science,* (CBLIS'07) (pp. 492-503).

Whitelock, D. (2010). Activating assessment for learning: Are we on the way with Web 2.0? In M. J. Lee & C. McLoughin (Eds.), Web 2.0-Based-E-Learning: Applying Social Informatics for Tertiary Teaching (pp. 319–342). Hershey, PA, USA: IGI Global. doi:doi:10.4018/978-1-60566-294-7.ch017 doi:10.4018/978-1-60566-294-7.ch017

Whitelock, D. (2014, November 13). Empirical Investigations that supported the development of OpenEssayist: A tool for drafting academic essays. *Paper presented at1st International Workshop on Technology-Enhanced Assessment, Analytics and Feedback (TEAAF2014)*, Barcelona.

Whitelock, D., & Brasher, A. (2006). Developing a Roadmap for E-Assessment: Which Way Now? In M. Danson (ed.). *Proceedings of the 10th CAA International Computer Assisted Assessment Conference* (pp. 487–501). Loughborough, UK: Loughborough University.

Whitelock, D. (2009). Editorial: e-assessment: Developing new dialogues for the digital age. *British Journal of Educational Technology, 40*(2), 199–202. doi:10.1111/j.1467-8535.2008.00932.x

Whitelock, D., & Watt, S. (2008). Reframing E-Assessment: Adopting New Media and Adapting Old Frameworks. *Learning, Media and Technology, 33*(3), 151–154. doi:10.1080/17439880802447391

Wiener, N. (1954). *The human use of human beings: Cybernetics and society*. Boston: Houghton Mifflin.

Wiggins, G. (1989). A true test: Towards more authentic and equitable forms of assessment. *Phi Delta Kappan, 70*(9), 703–713.

Wiggins, G. (1993). *Assessing Student Performance*. San Francisco: Jossey-Bass.

Wiggins, G. (1998). *Educative Assessment: Designing Assessments to Inform and Improve Student Performance*. San Francisco, CA: Jossey-Bass.

Wiggins, G. (2001). *Educative assessment*. San Francisco: Jossey-Bass.

Wiliam, D. (2011). *Embedded formative assessment*. Bloomington, IN: Solution Tree Press.

Williams, P. (2014). Squaring the circle: A new alternative to alternative-assessment. *Teaching in Higher Education, 19*(5), 565–577. doi:10.1080/13562517.2014.882894

Williams, R., & Dunn, E. (2008). *Brain-compatible learning for the block* (2nd ed.). California: Sage Publications.

Willison, J., & O'Regan, K. (2007). Commonly known, commonly not known, totally unknown: A framework for students becoming researchers. *Higher Education Research & Development, 26*(4), 393–409. doi:10.1080/07294360701658609

Wills, G. B., Bailey, C. P., Davis, H. C., Gilbert, L., Howard, Y., & Steve Jeyes, S. et al. (2009). An e-learning framework for assessment (FREMA). *Assessment & Evaluation in Higher Education, 34*(3), 273–292. doi:10.1080/02602930802068839

Wilson, A. (2015). An Exploration of Tutor Feedback on Essays and the Development of a Feedback Guide. *European Journal of Open, Distance and E-Learning*.

Wilson, J. H., & Ryan, R. G. M. E. Kite (Ed.), *(n. d.). Effective Evaluation of Teaching: A Guide for Faculty and Administration. Formative teaching evaluations: Is student input useful?* (pp. 22–29).

Wimmers, P. F., & Fung, C. C. (2008). The impact of case specificity and generalisable skills on clinical performance: A correlated traits-correlated methods approach. *Medical Education, 42*(6), 580–588. doi:10.1111/j.1365-2923.2008.03089.x

Winchester, M. K., & Winchester, T. M. (2012). If you build it will they come? Exploring the student perspective of weekly student evaluations of teaching. *Assessment & Evaluation in Higher Education, 37*(6), 671–682. doi:10.1080/02602938.2011.563278

Winchester, T. M., & Winchester, M. (2011). Exploring the impact of faculty reflection on weekly student evaluations of teaching. *The International Journal for Academic Development, 16*(2), 119–131. doi:10.1080/1360144X.2011.568679

Winchester, T. M., & Winchester, M. K. (2014). A longitudinal investigation of the impact of faculty reflective practices on student evaluations of teaching. *British Journal of Educational Technology, 4*(1), 112–124. doi:10.1111/bjet.12019

Winnicott, D. (1962). *The Maturational Processes and Facilitating Environment.* London: Hogarth Press.

Winograd, P., & Perkins, F. (1995). Authentic assessment in the classroom: Principles and practices. In R. Blum & J. Arter (Eds.), *A handbook for student performance assessment in an era of restructuring* (pp. 1–11). Alexandria, VA: Association for Supervision and Curriculum Development.

Wolfe, P. (2001). *Brain matters: Translating research into classroom practice.* Alexandria, Virginia: Association for Supervision and Curriculum Development.

Wood, E.J. (2003). What are extended matching sets questions? *Bioscience Educational eJournal, 1*(1). DOI:10.3108/beej.2003.01010002

Woodside, A. (2010). *Case Study Research: Theory, Methods, Practice.* London: Emerald Group Publishing Limited.

Working Group on 14–19 Reform. (2004). *14–19 Curriculum and qualifications reform: Final report of the Working Group on 14–19 Reform.* Nottinghamshire: DfES.

Wright, B. D., & Linacre, J. M. (1994). Reasonable mean-square fit values. *Rasch Measurement Transactions, 8*(3), 370.

Wright, S. L., & Jenkins-Guarnieri, M. A. (2012). Student evaluations of teaching: Combining the meta-analyses and demonstrating further evidence for effective use. *Assessment & Evaluation in Higher Education, 37*(6), 683–699. doi: 10.1080/02602938.2011.563279

Xanthou, M. (2013). An Intelligent Personalized e-Assessment Tool Developed and Implemented for a Greek Lyric Poetry Undergraduate Course. *The Electronic Journal of e-Learning, 11*(2), 101-114.

Xplore, I. E. E. E. IEEE Standard for Learning Technology - Data Model for Reusable Competency Definitions. (n. d.). Retrieved from http://ieeexplore.ieee.org/xpl/mostRecentIssue.jsp?punumber=4445690

Yang, M., & Carless, D. (2012). The feedback triangle and the enhancement of dialogic feedback processes. *Teaching in Higher Education, 2012*, 1–13.

Yastibas, A. E., & Yastibas, G. C. (2015). The Use of E-portfolio-based Assessment to Develop Students' Self-regulated Learning in English Language Teaching. *Procedia: Social and Behavioral Sciences, 176*, 3–13. doi:10.1016/j.sbspro.2015.01.437

Yin, R. (2009). *Case Study Research* (4th ed.). London: SAGE Inc.

Yorke, M. (2003). Formative assessment in higher education: Moves towards theory and enhancement of pedagogic practice. *Higher Education, 45*(4), 477–501. doi:10.1023/A:1023967026413

Yorke, M. (2003). Formative assessment in higher education: Moves towards theory and the enhancement of pedagogic practice. *The Journal of Higher Education, 45*(4), 471–501.

Yuan, J., & Kim, C. (2015). Effective Feedback Design Using Free Technologies. *Journal of Educational Computing Research.*

Yule, S., Flin, R., Maran, N., Rowley, D., Youngson, G., & Paterson-Brown, S. (2008). Surgeons' non-technical skills in the operating room: Reliability testing of the NOTSS behavior rating system. *World Journal of Surgery, 32*(4), 548–556. doi:10.1007/s00268-007-9320-z

Zacharis, N. (2010). Innovative Assessment for Learning Enhancement: Issues and Practices. *Contemporary Issues In Education Research*, 3(1), 61-70.

Zhao, Z. (2014). Competence Research. In Z. Zhao & F. Rauner (Eds.), Areas of Vocational Education Research (pp. 167–188). Springer Berlin Heidelberg. Retrieved from http://link.springer.com/chapter/10.1007/978-3-642-54224-4_9 doi:doi:10.1007/978-3-642-54224-4_9 doi:10.1007/978-3-642-54224-4_9

Zimmerman, B. J. (2002). Becoming a self–regulated learner: An overview. *Theory into Practice*, *41*(2), 64–70. doi:10.1207/s15430421tip4102_2

Zlatkin-Troitschanskaia, O., Shavelson, R.J., & Kuhn, C. (2015). The international state of research on measurement of competency in higher education. *Studies in Higher Education*, *40*(3), 393–411. doi:10.1080/03075079.2015.1004241

About the Contributors

Elena Cano is currently associate professor at the Department of Didactics and Educational Organization. She has two Bachelors in Educational Sciences and in Economics and Business Administrationand. PhD in Philosophy and Education. PhD Extraordinary Award of the University of Barcelona 1995-1996. She teaches courses in different bachelos and master studies of Pedagogy and Teacher Training, basically on school organization and educational assessment subjects. She belongs to LMI (research consolidated group with a government's recognition) and she mainly researches on assessment and feedback in higher education. She has coordinated two R & D projects on competencies' assessment. Some publications on this topic are Cano, E. (2015). *Evaluación por competencias en educación superior*. Madrid: La Muralla. Portillo, M.C.; Cano, E. (2015). Regulating the Writing Process in the Teacher Training Practicum Guided by Feedback at the University of Barcelona. *Cambridge Journal of Education* pp. 1-25 | DOI: 10.1080/0305764X.2015.1011083 Cano, E.; Cabrera, N. (2013). La evaluación formativa de competencias a través de blogs. La experiencia de seis universidades catalanas. *Digital Education Review*, 23, pp. 46-58. Ion, G.; Cano, E. (2011). Assessment Practices at Spanish Universities: From a Learning to a Competencies Approach. *Evaluation & Research in Education*. Volume 24, Issue 3, 2011, pp: 167-181.

Georgeta Ion is currently associate professor at the Department of Applied Pedagogy of the Universitat Autònoma de Barcelona. She has a Bachelor in Psychology and Educational Sciences by the University of Bucharest, Master Degree in Management and Evaluation in Education by the University of Bucharest and from 2007 is PhD in Educational Sciences by the University of Barcelona with a thesis entitled: "Organisational culture and leadership. An ethnographic study". Her research topics are related to the study of the higher education especially its organization and research management and the students' assessment in higher education. She also collaborates with Spanish and international research groups in topics related to the research-based education and evidence-based decision making in education. The most recent publications are: Ion, G, Cano, E. & Cabrera, N. Competency Assessment Tool (CAT). The Evaluation of an Innovative Competency-Based Assessment Experience in Higher Education. *Technology, Pedagogy and Education*. DOI: 10.1080/1475939X.2015.1134635. Ion, G & Iucu, R. (2015) Does Research Influence Educational Policy? The Perspective of Researchers and Policy-Makers in Romania. En: Curaj, A., Matei, L., Pricopie, R., Salmi, J. & Scott, P. (eds) *The European Higher Education Area: Between Critical Reflections and Future Policies*. Springer, pp.873-889

***

Ivan Alsina PhD student at Universitat Oberta de Catalunya. His research areas are Virtual and Augmented Reality for mental health and higher education. He is also online tutor at UOC, research assistant and expert in quantitative research methods. For further information see: https://www.linkedin.com/in/alsinajurnet

Patrick Baughan is Senior Lecturer in Educational Development at City University London. His research interests are based around assessment in higher education, educational integrity and plagiarism prevention, sustainability in higher education, and the development of emerging researchers. He is a convener for the European Educational Research Association (EERA), undertakes various roles for the Society for Research into Higher Education (SRHE) and is a Senior Fellow of the Higher Education Academy (HEA). He is an educational developer and leads / teaches on several modules of the MA Academic Practice programme at City.

Samir Bennani, Engineer degree in Computer Science in 1982; PhD in Computer Science in 2005; Deputy Director, Manager of Academic and Students Affairs at the Mohammadia School of Engineers (EMI)- Mohamed V University; Professor at the Computer Science Department-EMI; 29 recent Scopus publications papers between 2010 and 2015; Ongoing research interests: SI, Modeling in Software Engineering, Information System, eLearning content engineering, Pedagogical Engineering, tutoring, assessment and tracking.

Mark Carver, PhD, is a research assistant at Edinburgh Napier University where he looks at assessment and feedback practices from an institutional perspective. He has previously researched feedback in teacher education and was a secondary school English teacher.

Sheridan Chambers received her master's degree in Applied Behavior Analysis from Auburn University and obtained certification as a Board Certified Behavior Analyst in 2015. At present, she serves as the Assistant Director of Practicum Training for the ABA Master's program at Auburn. Her current role is to provide individual and group supervision for graduate students at Auburn pursuing a master's degree in ABA and preparing to sit for the BCBA examination. Currently, she oversees the students' implementation of behavior analytic procedures across residential, clinical, and educational settings.

Lucian Ciolan, PhD, is professor of Educational Policy and Educational Research at Faculty of Psychology and Educational Sciences, University of Bucharest, where he is currently holding the position of dean. As member of Educational Sciences Department, he focused his research and publishing interests mainly on areas like influence of behavioral patterns on policy making process, educational policy instruments, policy learning, as well as research of learning (trasdisciplinarity, authentic learning etc.). He coordinates a master degree on Train the Trainers, trying to bridge academic work with applied development projects, mainly under International Centre for Policy Advocacy - an international network of trainers and consultants on policy advocacy. From 2014 Lucian became a member of the Council of European Educational Research Association.

Geoffrey Crisp Pro Vice Chancellor (Education) at University of New South Wales. Carrick Associate Fellowship. Raising the profile of diagnostic, formative and summative e-assessments. Providing e-assessment design principles and disciplinary examples for higher education academic staff. (ALTC Associate Fellow) HERDSA Fellow. ASCILITE Fellow. For further information see: http://newsroom. unsw.edu.au/news/general/pro-vice-chancellor-education-appointed

James G M Crossley is a consultant paediatrician at Chesterfield Royal Hospital where he also serves as the Director of Teaching. He is also a research Professor of Medical Education at the Medical School, University of Sheffield. He has published widely on psychometrics and assessment in the workplace and advises several of the UK Royal Colleges and similar organisations around the world.

Liesje Coertjens is a researcher at Edubron (Department Training and Education Sciences, Faculty of Social Sciences, University of Antwerp) since 2006. Her PhD, which she defended in 2013, focused on the change in learning strategies during the transition from secondary to higher education and statistical concerns in modelling growth. Since 2013, she works as a postdoctoral researcher at Edubron. Next to taking up the day to day coordination of the D-PAC project (www.d-pac.be), she researches quality concerns with performance assessment. More specifically, she investigates the efficiency and reliability of rubrics rating and comparative judgement. Since 2015, Liesje Coertjens also works as a guest professor on Statistics at the University of Antwerp. Starting September 2016, she is appointed Professor on Assessment for Learning at the Catholic University of Louvain.

Sven De Maeyer is a full Professor at the department Training and Education Sciences at the University of Antwerp. His major research interests are methodological issues and measurement problems in educational sciences. Some key topics are: the concrete development and validation of measuring instruments for specific contexts; research into the merits of alternative methods of measuring skills (or broader competences); research into cognitive processes among assessors during competency measurement; research into the preconditions for the use of measuring instruments with different groups or at different measuring moments (measurement invariance); and research into the validity of conclusions based on self-evaluation instruments.

Zineb Djoub is a PhD student and a lecturer at the Department of English of Abdelhamid Ibn Badis University of Mostaganem. She has participated in several national and international conferences and published articles and book chapters such as:Learning through technology:Researching students'views and attitudes (2014), Mobile technology and learner autonomy in language learning (2015), Portfolio training:Getting learners actively involved (2015).Her current interest includes: Learner autonomy, Assessment, teacher education and training, ICT in language teaching and learning.

Vincent Donche is an Associate Professor of Research Methods in Education at the Faculty of Social Sciences, Department Training and Education Sciences of the University of Antwerp, Belgium. His current research interests include student learning, professional learning, academic integration, assessment and educational measurement.

Walaa M. El-Henawy Ph. D in Education (Curriculum and Methods of Teaching English), Lecturer of Curriculum & Instruction (EFL) Faculty of Education, Port-Said University

Maite Fernández-Ferrer has a degree in Education and a master's degree in International Studies and in Social and Educational Action from the University of Barcelona. I am a member of the research group Interactive Media Lab led by Doctor Antonio Bartolomé. Since 2010 I have been part of various studies about competencies and assessment in higher education, as "The education assessment impact on competencies development in the university. The first graduate perspectives" (reference EDU2012-32766) or the "Iberoamerican netw ork for the development of a technological platform to support the evalua- tion of training processes" (reference 512RT0443). Since 2011 I have participated in several scientific conferences on the subject, both national and international, such as ELSE, ECER or INTED. From all this research experience various publications have arisen, both book chapters (as in "Buenas prácticas en la evaluación de competencias. Cinco casos de Educación Superior" or "Evaluar la formación es posible. Evaluación de la transferencia de la formación de formadores con soporte tecnológico") and journal articles. Among my international research experience there is on one hand my stay at the University of Cape Town (South Africa) for six months in 2012 and, on the other hand, my stay at the Universität zu Köln (Germany) for three months in 2015. Nowadays, and thanks to a pre doctoral fellowship from the Catalan government, I am a research assistant at the Universitat de Barcelona where I am teaching in the degrees of Pedagogy and Primary Education, and I am working on my international doctoral program about the massive open online courses and their assessment.

Eduardo Garcia-Jimenez Full time professor in the Faculty of Education at the University of Seville. His research interests include assessment for learning and academic literacies.

Miguel Angel Gomez-Ruiz Full-time lecturer in the Faculty of Education at the University of Cadiz. His research interests include participative and collaborative assessment in Higher Education and new technologies applied to education.

Lourdes Guardia PhD in Educational Sciences at the University of the Basque Country (UPV/EHU). She is associated professor at the Psychology and Educational Science Department and researcher within the eLearn Center (E-Learning Research, Innovation and Training Centre) at the Open University of Catalonia (UOC). She is currently the academic director of the Master's degree in Education and ICT (e-learning). She is a member of the Edul@b Research Group funded by AGAUR (National Goverment). Her current research interests include Techno-pedagogical design and Learning Design, Educational Technology, eAssessment and Teacher Training. She has participated and coordinated several research and innovation projects both nationally and internationally. She is also a member and researcher of the Europortfolio European Network of Experts and Practitioners (EPNET) and the European Chair of Cur- riculum Development and Course Design Area of expertise led by the European Association of Distance Teaching Universities (EADTU). For further details see more info at: http://edulab.uoc.edu/en/?page_id=7

Rebecca Hamer is an educational researcher with more than 30 years experience in studying student thinking and the effect on the quality of learning. As senior policy analyst she has worked for Hague Consulting Group and RAND Corp. focusing in research in education, transport, governance, informa- tion technology, working in multidisciplinary teams. Between 2007 and 2010 she was Research Director for the Dutch national Platform for Science and Technology. In 2010 she co-authored The Meaning of Learning and Knowing with Erik Jan van Rossum, a doctoral thesis reviewing more than 60 years of research into students' ways of knowing. She is currently working at the International Baccalaureate (IB) as Manager Assessment Research and Design in The Hague, Netherlands. Since 2012, the Assessment Research and Design team advises and supports IB curriculum development on improving assessment at DP and MYP level and undertakes research to ensure that IB assessment is valid, reliable, state of the art and fair.

Frank Hammonds received his Ph.D. in psychology from Auburn University in 2002. He is currently an associate professor at Troy University. He teaches a variety of courses including Experimental Psychology, Psychology of Learning, and Evolutionary Psychology. His primary area of interest is behavior analysis.

David Herrero is a Research Fellow and a PhD candidate at the Department of Educational Sciences at the University of Alcalá (Spain), where he teaches Educational Psychology to Teacher Training students. He has a Bachelor in Educational Psychology and a Master Degree in Communication and Learning (University of Alcalá). He has been a Visiting Scholar at Gothenburg University (Sweden). His dissertation approaches, from an ethnographic methodology, the educational use of commercial video games in formal education with adolescents.

Meriem Hnida Ph.D. Candidate at the Laboratory of Research in Computer Science and Education, Mohammadia School of Engineers, Mohammed V University of Rabat, Morocco. My research project is about the use of educational technology and Competency-based Education to improve Students' Learning. My interests lie in the fields of Competency modeling and assessment techniques, Ontological engineering, Educational engineering.

María Soledad Ibarra-Sáiz is a professor of Educational Assessment at the University of Cadiz, and Director of EVALfor Research Group. Her research interests include e-assessment, self- and peer-assessment in Higher Education.

Alejandro Iborra PhD in Psychology. He is associate professor at the University of Alcalá (Spain) where he is director of the Department of Educational Sciences. He has been Visiting Scholar at Exeter and Liverpool John Moores University (UK), Groningen University (NL) and West Virginia University (USA). His research deals with identity formation processes, transitional processes in learning and development, experiential learning, and facilitation processes to promote innovative groups in higher education.

Mohammed Khalidi Idrissi Doctorate degree in Computer Science in 1986, PhD in Computer Science in 2009; Former Assistant chief of the Computer Science Department at the Mohammadia School of Engineers (EMI); Pedagogical Tutor of the Computer Science areas at the Mohammadia School of Engineers (EMI) Professor at the Computer Science Department-EMI; 14 recent publications papers between 2012 and 2015; Ongoing research interests: Software Engineering, Information System, Modeling, IDM, MDA,ontology, SOA, Web services, eLearning content engineering, tutoring, assessment and tracking.

Simona Iftimescu graduated with a double degree in Psychology and Political Science from the University of Bucharest (2009), a Master's degree in Comparative and International Education from the University of Oxford (2011) and a Master's degree in training (Education) from the University of Bucharest (2012), where she is currently pursuing a PhD in Education, with a particular interest in educational audit and quality assurance.

Romiță Iucu is Professor at the, Faculty of Psychology and Educational Sciences, University of Bucharest since 1996, vice-rector of the University of Bucharest since 2004, coordinator of the Center for Development and Training in Higher Education / Center For Development And Training In Higher Education (CDFIS / CHEDT). He has a degree in Pedagogy, postgraduate, Master and PhD in Educational Sciences obtained from the same university in 1999. Internationally member of The International Hall of Fame of Adult and Continuing Education in 2011. Member of European network ENTEP, European Network on Teacher Education Policies, since 2010 and expert at the European Commission at different levels, Thematic Working Group on the Professional Development of Teachers (2010), member of the Executive Board (2006-2010) - CEI - Central European Initiative member EC (2006-2010) Cluster 'Teachers and Trainers "in 2006 The working group was part of the "Bologna Tree Cycles" and in the period 2005 - 2009 was a member of the Working Group "Indicators for teacher and trainers. Areas of academic interest; Policies in teacher training, higher education pedagogy, Classroom Management

Marije Lesterhuis is a PhD student in Education Sciences at Edubron (Department Training and Education Sciences, Faculty of Social Sciences, University of Antwerp). After receiving her MSc in Education Sciences (University of Antwerp), she started her PhD project in 2014. Her research concerns the validity of Comparative Judgement and takes an assessors' perspective. More specific, she investigates how assessors execute Comparative Judgement in writing assessments. Next to that, she contributes to research and valorisation objectives of the D-PAC project (Digital Platform for the Assessment of Competences, www.d-pac.be).

Gina Mariano is an Associate Professor of Educational Psychology in the Division of Psychology at Troy University. She teaches educational psychology courses for elementary and secondary teachers as well as psychology courses for undergraduate psychology majors. Her research interests include student learning, metacognition, and knowledge transfer in college students. Her research also examines faculty development among university instructors and its relationship to student learning.

Elena Marin Assistant lecturer Elena Marin graduated from the Pedagogical School of Bucharest in 1999, has a bachelor degree both in pedagogy and psychology (from the University of Bucharest, graduated in 2009) and has a MA degree in School Counseling and Career Development (2011). She holds a GCDF Trainer (Consultant careers - Global Career Development Facilitator) certificate. Starting with 2013 she is a teacher at the Faculty of Psychology and Educational Sciences, University of Bucharest, and is in charge with the Theory and Methodology of Instruction seminar, the Classroom Management seminar, and also coordinates students teaching practice. The professional main interest is related to initial teaching training and continuing professional development. Another field of interest is related to inclusive education that can be observed in the doctoral thesis.

Esperanza Mejías Macías studied Teacher Training and Pedagogy at University of Barcelona. She worked in several preschools and as coordinator of projects of non formal education. She studied the Interuniversity Master's in Psychology of Education and became a member of the SINTE research team. She writes and researches about learning evaluation and is a PhD student at Autonomous University of Barcelona. She combines research work with assessment and training to teachers and students in different institutions.

Carles Monereo Professor of Educational Psychology at University.

Gloria Nogueiras is currently a Research Fellow and a PhD candidate at the Department of Educational Sciences at the University of Alcalá (Spain), where she teaches Developmental Psychology to Teacher Training students. She has a Bachelor in Teacher Training, a Bachelor in Educational Psychology, a Master Degree in Communication and Learning (University of Alcalá), and a Master Degree in Psychological Intervention with Developmental Behavioural Modelling (University of Valencia). She has been a Visiting Scholar at Groningen University (Netherlands). Her research topics are related to the exploration of learning and developmental processes from a qualitative and dynamic systems perspective. Specifically, in her dissertation she investigates the experience of students participating in experiential and collaborative learning contexts in higher education, with a special focus on their emotional response to demands of self-direction.

Isolina Oliveira, Ph.D. in Educational Psychology, is an Assistant Professor in the Department of Education and Distance Teaching, at Universidade Aberta, Portugal, with experience in the development of both graduate and undergraduate courses, as well active researcher in the areas of teacher education and reflective practice, competence-based learning assessment and group work collaboration in online environments. During four years, she was a researcher focused on k-12 learning assessment at the Educational Innovation Institute, in Lisbon. She has developed and taught online, graduate and undergraduate, courses, as well as conducted research on online education, particularly on online assessment practices. Isolina is a member of the Universidade Aberta Professional Development in E-learning team that has promoted the development of online distance education learning strategies, especially in the framework of the university's pedagogical model. And she is a member of the Elearning and Distance Education Laboratory (Universidade Aberta).

Stefanie Panke is an Instructional Analyst at the University of North Carolina at Chapel Hill. In her current position she conducts instructional design projects that center on assessment and emerging technologies, in particular online publishing, e-books, conceptual web development, portfolios and rubrics. Prior to her current position she worked as Director of E-Learning at Ulm University, Germany. Stefanie holds a PhD in Applied Linguistics from the University of Bielefeld. In 2009, she completed her thesis on the information design of educational websites. During her PhD, Stefanie was a researcher at the Knowledge Media Research Center in Tübingen, Germany, where her team developed an award-winning portal on e-learning in higher education. Stefanie serves as a member of several program committees (ED-MEDIA, E-LEARN, SITE), as a reviewer for e-journals (i.e. MERLOT Journal of Online Learning and Teaching, International Review of Research in Open and Distance Learning), as Social Media Coordinator for AACE (Association for the Advancement of Computing in Education) and as editor for social software at the Educational Technology and Change Journal. Together with Prof. Curtis Ho, Stefanie chairs the AACE Special Interest Group on Assessing, Designing and Developing E-Learning.

Alda Pereira Associate Professor (retired) of the Department of Education and Distance Teaching at Universidade Aberta (the Open University of Portugal), researcher at Laboratory of Distance Education and eLearning (LE @ D). She was Vice-Rector, Director of the Research Institute and Headmaster of Department of Educational Sciences. She coordinated the Doctoral Program in Education and the Master in Educational Multimedia Communication. She was co-author of the Universidade Aberta's Pedagogical Model. She has been coordinating many research projects in e-learning and participating in several international projects.

Laura Pons-Seguí is a Primary English Teacher with a Master's in Applied Linguistics and Second Language Acquisition. Currently, she is doing her PhF in the field of teacher training and school organization. She is a member of the consolidated research group LMI and has participated in several research projects in the field of assessment and competencies in higher education.

Victoria Quesada Full-time lecturer in the Faculty of Education at theUniversity of Cadiz. Her research interests include assessment in Higher Education, and participative and collaborative assessment.

Gregorio Rodríguez-Gómez is a professor of Educational Research Methods at the University of Cadiz, and Director of DevalS Project. His research interests include innovation in assessment and feedback practices in Higher Education.

Mihaela Monica Stîngu is Assistant Lecturer at at the Faculty of Psychology and Educational Sciences (Department of Educational Sciences), University of Bucharest, and coordinates the seminars of Research Methodology in Educational Sciences, Training Methods and Techniques and also Pedagogy in the Teacher Training Department. The main research interests are focused on induction of newly qualified teachers and teaching and learning higher education.

Luís Tinoca is an Assistant Professor at the Institute of Education, University of Lisbon, with experience in the development of both graduate and undergraduate courses, as well as an active researcher in the areas of teacher education, competence-based learning assessment and group work collaboration in online environments. He is a member of the Education Research and Development Unit, and a collaborator at the Distance Education Laboratory. He earned his Ph.D. in Science Education from the University of Texas at Austin in 2004.

Catalina Ulrich, PhD is Professor at the University of Bucharest, Psychology and Education Sciences Faculty and the Head of the Education Sciences Department. She teaches courses on Sociology of Education, Citizenship Education, Team Dynamics, Socio-educational Interventions for Groups at Risk. She has directed evaluation studies for educational and social services projects in Romania and Bulgaria and coordinated impact evaluation for national programs in the field of education for disadvantaged groups and teacher training, including e-learning and the use of mobile devices. Approaching mainly qualitative methodology, she carried out individual research within international projects regarding educational programs and policy analysis, multiethnic communities, multiple discrimination (SLO, INTRAC, UNICEF, Open Society Institute, WB, IOM, OSF Soros, EFA, Wolfensohn Institute, Bernard Van Leer Foundation, ISSA, UNESCO, CEDEFOP). She received a Fulbright Post Doc Senior Award at the University of Illinois at Urbana-Champaign for Project-based Learning: A Multicase Research

Project with a Focus on Education for Diversity in U.S. Secondary Schools and Teacher-Education Programs (2011-2012). As a result of her research she developed research projects on ubiquotous learning, interdisciplinary problem-based learning and project-based learning.

Erik Jan van Rossum studied Experimental as well as Educational Psychology at Leiden University in the Netherlands. Since 1978 he has worked as university lecturer at Tilburg University and the Hotelschool The Hague. In the earlier 1980s he Erik started his studies into learning and teaching conceptions, introducing these concepts as well as phenomenography to the Netherlands. In 1997, the Hotelschool introduced Enterprising Learning, an activating curriculum aimed at promoting epistemological development. This curriculum was based on the developmental epistemological model central to the current study. Since 2008 he has worked as university lecturer Qualitative Methodology at Twente University in the Netherlands. Since the mid 1980s he has co-authored a number of studies with Rebecca Hamer and in 2010 they co-authored The Meaning of Learning and Knowing (SensePublishers) summarising 30 years of their research into student and teacher thinking about learning and good teaching.

San Verhavert graduated as Master of Science in Psychology, Theory and Research (Experimental Psychology) at the KULeuven, Belgium in 2014. In 2013-14, he did a research internship at the University of Oxford on visual attention and learning in healthy subjects and subject with brain damage. Since November 2014, San is working on the Digital Platform for the Assessment of Competencies project (D-PAC) at the department of Training and Education Sciences of the University of Antwerp (Belgium) and his PhD focuses on adaptive selection algorithms for comparative judgment.

Eddy White, PhD, is the Assessment Coordinator at the University of Arizona's Center for English as a Second Language (CESL), and also Associate Professor in the College of Humanities. He specializes in classroom-based assessment, English proficiency testing, and the promotion of assessment literacy development in the English language teaching profession.

Index

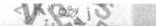

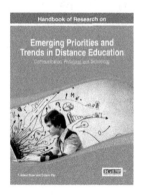
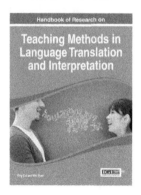
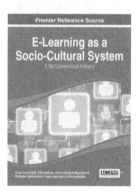